EDWARD
BUSCOMBE

CINEMA
TODAY

PHAIDON
non mini copy

CALLAHAN: I know what you'[re thinking. Did he] fire six shots or only [five? To tell] you the truth, in all [this excitement I've] kinda lost track mys[elf. But being as] this is a .44 Magnum[, the most powerful] handgun in the wor[ld, and it would blow] your head clean off[, you've got to ask] yourself one questi[on: Do I feel lucky?] Well, do ya punk?

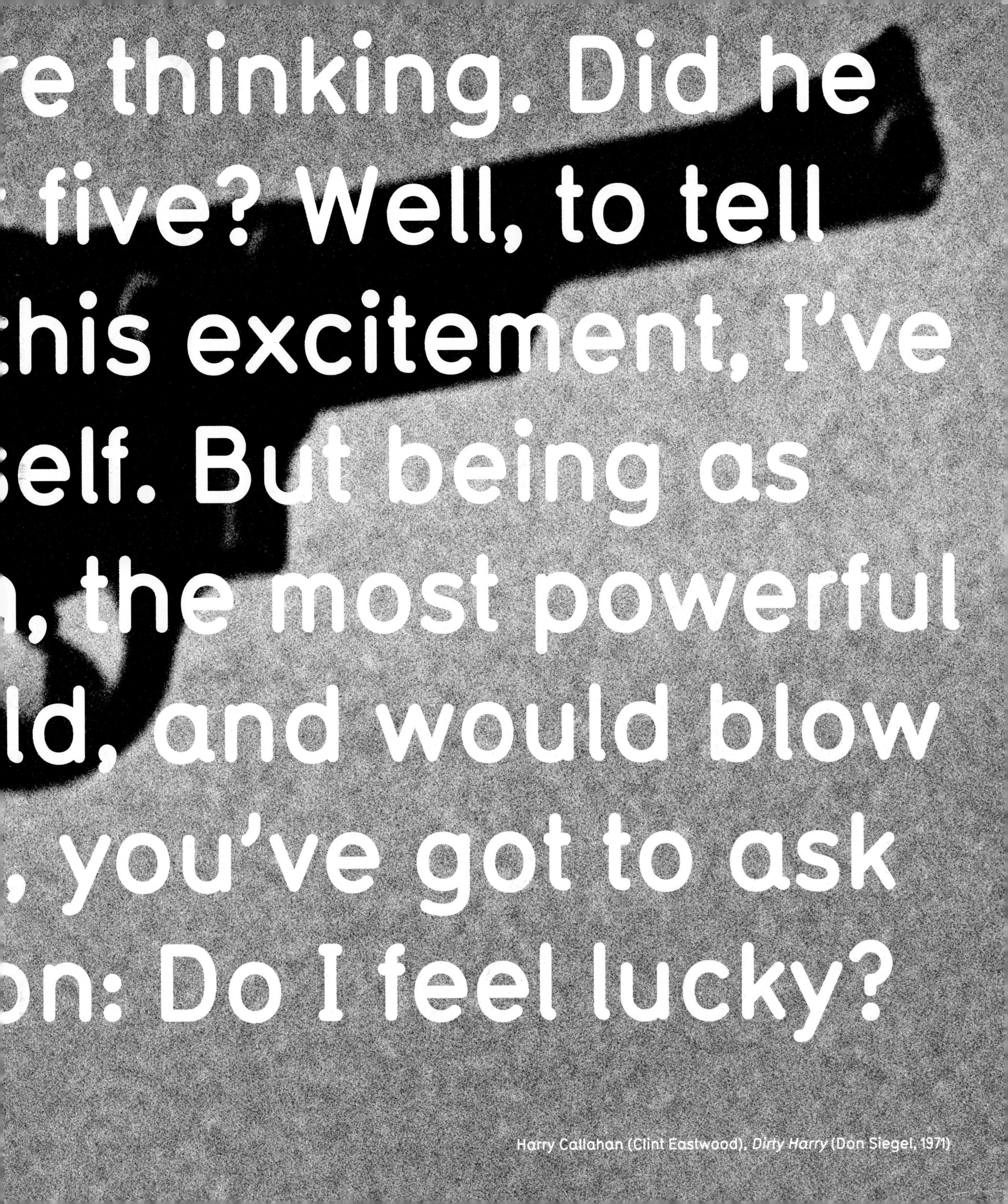

e thinking. Did he
five? Well, to tell
this excitement, I've
self. But being as
, the most powerful
ld, and would blow
, you've got to ask
on: Do I feel lucky?

Harry Callahan (Clint Eastwood), *Dirty Harry* (Don Siegel, 1971)

BILL HARFORD: Well, I suppose th[at] programmed differe[nt]

ALICE HARFORD: Oh, yes, I forgot. M[y] evolution, right? Rig[ht] it in every place they[...] it's just about securit[y] and whatever the fu[...]

BILL HARFORD: A little oversimplif[ied] something like that.

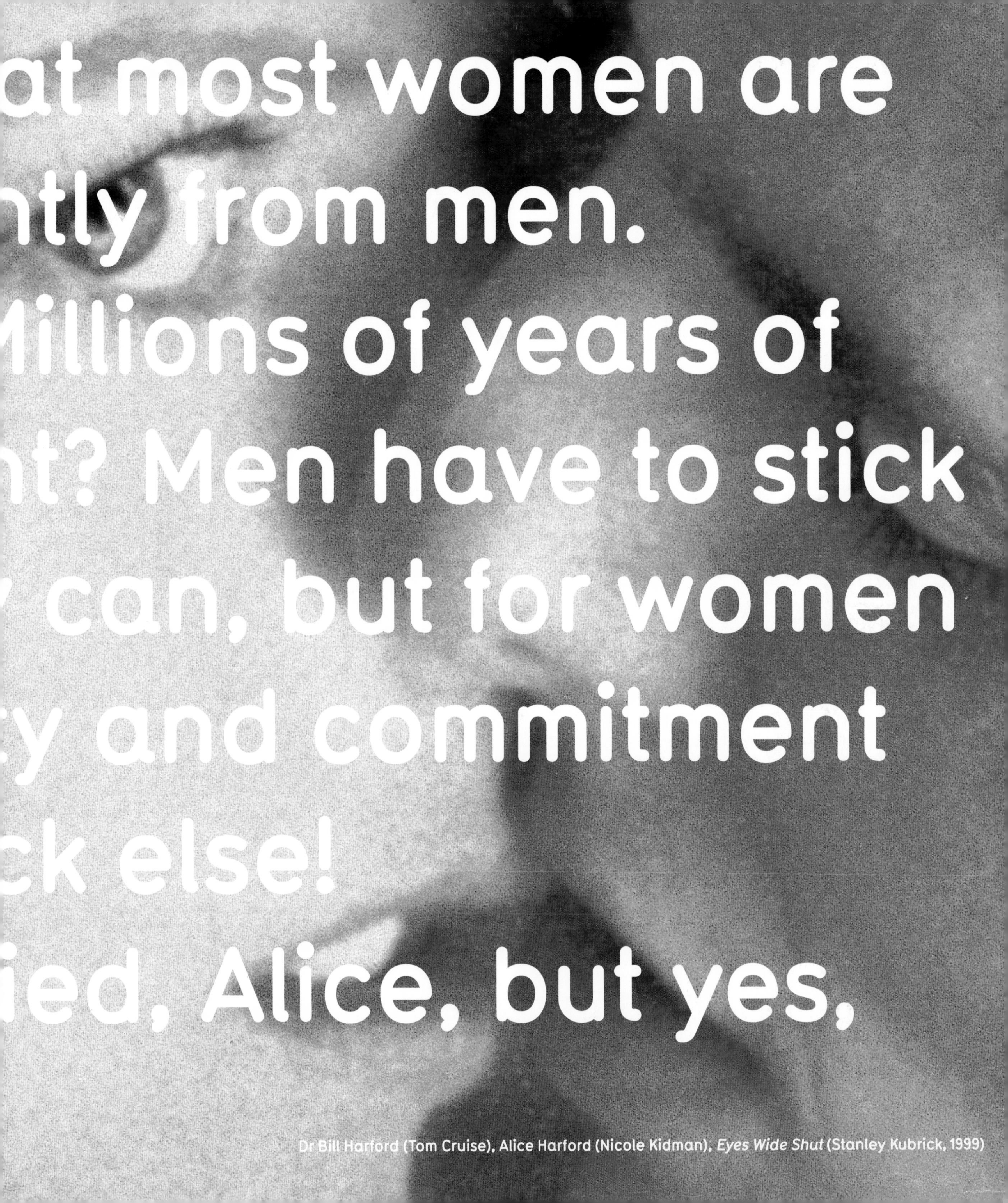

at most women are
ntly from men.
Millions of years of
nt? Men have to stick
y can, but for women
y and commitment
ck else!
ied, Alice, but yes,

Dr Bill Harford (Tom Cruise), Alice Harford (Nicole Kidman), *Eyes Wide Shut* (Stanley Kubrick, 1999)

KRISHNA: "My respected Mo[ther] are well [...] I didn't r[] to the circus but they[] in Chacha's tea shop[] I want to return. As s[] rupees I'll be back [...] about me. When I go[]

LETTERWRITER: That line will cost[]

KRISHNA: Then drop it.

ther I hope you
un away. I returned
y had all left... I work
. I think of home...
oon as I have 500
..] Don't worry
to sleep I miss you."
you 50 paisa extra.

Krishna (Shafiq Sayed), Letterwriter (Anon.), *Salaam Bombay!* (Mira Nair, 1988)

Phaidon Press Limited
Regent's Wharf
All Saints Street
London N1 9PA

Phaidon Press Inc.
180 Varick Street
New York, NY 10014

www.phaidon.com

First published 2003
© 2003 Phaidon Press Limited

ISBN 0 7148 4081 5

Designed by Stephen Coates
Printed in Singapore

Note

When a film is referenced, the accepted English
language title is given followed by the original
title in brackets where appropriate. The film is
subsequently referred to by its English title only.
The director is given in brackets if not cited as
part of the text. The original release date is also
cited in brackets.

Contents

Introduction

Cinema today is a global industry, practised in virtually every country of the world, producing around 4,000 films annually and generating billions of dollars. It can hardly be considered a corpse, as was suggested by a recent book on contemporary American films.[1] Nothing could be more misconceived. Indeed, the fecundity and diversity of world cinema is now greater than it has been since the medium began in the early twentieth century.

That is not to deny that there are difficulties, caused by the severe imbalance in the world market. By the late 1990s American cinema enjoyed overwhelming domination. Though its annual production of just over 700 films a year was matched by Western Europe and exceeded by the Indian subcontinent, the major Hollywood film studios spent more than twice as much on production as the rest of the world combined, and as a result Hollywood film exports earned the United States $6.4 billion in 2000. Only in a few exceptional countries such as India do Hollywood films not have the lion's share of the market. In 2001 all of the top ten films at the world box office were from the United States.[2]

Because of the dominance of Hollywood across the globe, I make no apology for devoting nearly half of this book to US films. These are the films that a world audience goes to see in the millions, not just because of their superior production values but because they tap into the dreams and fantasies of people the world over. In this sense, Hollywood is unlike other cinemas, not so much a national cinema as a supranational one; or perhaps more precisely, a cinema which has internationalized its national preoccupations.

Historically, since the development of the feature-length narrative in the late teens of the last century, Hollywood has also been a genre-driven cinema. Films are conceived and marketed by their type, such as science fiction or horror, each creating a distinct experience for its targeted audience. Even 'independent' cinema may be considered a genre, with its particular subjects and styles. Thus, I deal with US cinema mainly under generic categories.

As for the rest of the world, I have usually discussed the films nation by nation, within broad geographical groupings. Despite coproduction and the ever-strengthening forces of globalization, cinema is still a national affair. It is the individual country that provides the primary market and, usually, offers financial support, partly for economic motives but also because cinema is perceived as fulfilling a vital role in nation-building. Like few other art forms, cinema can present the life of a country to its citizens, can show its particularities and quiddities, and, always an important point, can do so in its own language.

However, as this book shows, there are acute problems in seeking to preserve, or create from scratch, an indigenous cinema culture. Many nations are poor, and cinema has to compete for scarce resources with urgent needs in education or health. Those countries without large populations speaking a world language such as English, Spanish or Chinese face language barriers; many of them have several contending languages within the same nation, adding greatly to the difficulties of a national cinema. Even if films get made and are lucky enough to get exposure on the international film festival circuit, they may never get a release in their home country, where distributors can make bigger profits showing Hollywood films. Government attempts at restricting the distribution of foreign films have frequently met with boycotts from Hollywood, and even modest production subsidies are under attack from the advocates of unrestricted 'free trade'. Each country brings its own national genius to the making of its films, but the dilemmas are usually the same. Is the rationale for a national cinema primarily cultural or economic? Should one try to build a popular cinema which can compete with Hollywood, or go for a minority 'art' cinema which will ensure prestige? One option risks economic disaster, the other the irrelevance of elitism.

Despite the difficulties, each year astonishingly assured and vital films are being made across the globe, in countries as varied as Mexico, Iran, Taiwan and Senegal, as well as in Europe. It used to be thought that the only hope for poor countries was to follow a neo-realist mode of production, using minimal technology, real-life locations and non-professional actors to make low-key stories of everyday life. Today, while neo-realism remains a viable method, it is the extraordinary stylistic variety of world cinema that strikes the viewer. A hundred years after its inception, cinema is in a state of constant renewal.

Above: The Hollywood film studios have been dominant throughout the twentieth century and into the twenty-first century. Only a few countries such as India can claim to produce and exhibit more indigenous films than films produced in Hollywood. The rise of television in particular, along with video, DVD and computer games, has put increasing pressure on Hollywood. But Hollywood has risen to this challenge and become an integral part of this multinational, multimedia industry.

And constant activity. Nearly a dozen films start shooting every day of the year. To view them all would leave no time for sleeping or eating, let alone recording one's impressions. Any survey of world film output must necessarily be a severely restricted sample. In order to ease the burden of selectivity I have narrowed the interpretation of cinema to narrative feature films projected in movie theatres in front of a paying audience, and so, somewhat arbitrarily, I have chosen to omit avant-garde cinema, documentaries, made-for-television films, films released straight to video, and most animated films. Even so, I am all too aware of how much has been left out. I can only hope that the omission of a vast amount of worthwhile material has brought some gains in coherence and understanding.

The first chapter explains why 1970 is a good year in which to start a book on contemporary cinema. The subsequent thirty or so years constitute nearly one third of the entire history of the cinema, and form what we might call its Third Age. During the First Age, up to the beginning of the 1930s, the new-born art evolved its characteristic forms, in particular the feature-length narrative which rapidly became the dominant type of film. Technically, too, the cinema achieved maturity, with the development of colour and sound. In the Second Age, up to the end of the 1960s, with film as the most popular of all art forms, Hollywood consolidated its position as the powerhouse of world cinema. In the Third Age, cinema increasingly found itself in competition with new forms of entertainment, especially television. Its domination challenged also by new kinds of cinema, from other countries and from other viewpoints, Hollywood was forced to reinvent itself. This is where we begin.

1. Hollywood and the Rise of the Blockbuster

CORLEONE: Someday, and that day may never come, I would like to call upon you to do me a service in return.

Don Vito Corleone (Marlon Brando), *The Godfather*
(Francis Ford Coppola, 1972)

Hollywood, like other institutions in the West in the late 1960s, was dominated by a generation that had been in power too long and had lost the habit of learning and adapting. They continued to apply the old formulae, even when it was clear that they were not working any more and that the young no longer wanted what they had to offer. A small number of successful but expensive pictures in the mid-1960s had encouraged Hollywood into a reckless extravagance which produced some of the greatest flops in its history. Twentieth Century Fox alone lost $42 million on three musicals: *Doctor Dolittle* (Richard Fleischer, 1967), *Star!* (Robert Wise, 1968) and *Hello, Dolly!* (Gene Kelly, 1969). Costs had been inflated by the entry of new production companies, just at the time when television networks, which had been enthusiastically buying Hollywood films to fill their schedules, cut back. Overall studio losses in the period 1969–71 – named by film historian Tino Balio 'The Recession of 1969'[1] – were estimated by *Variety* to be a staggering $600 million. The result was a convulsion in the industry, and Warner Bros. and MGM were both taken over.

The transformation involved more than a change of ownership. Since the 1920s, in order to head off official intervention, all studios had agreed to self-regulation, submitting scripts for pre-censorship and conforming to agreed standards of (primarily sexual) morality. In the late 1960s, under pressure from widespread social changes, Hollywood abandoned the Production Code and instituted a ratings system. Instead of all films submitting to the same rules, films were now graded according to the age of the audiences. Once children had been protected in this way, the route was open to more graphic representation of sex, violence and other previously forbidden subjects.

Exhibition patterns were changing too. The growth of new cinemas in shopping malls catered to a younger audience. The lowering of the age of the audience had begun some time before, but accelerated in the 1970s, and by the end of the decade eighty per cent of cinema tickets were bought by the under-thirties.[2] The major studios, run by old men who knew only how to repeat past successes, were slow to recognize the opportunities. In 1969

Left: Initially erected in 1923 by a real-estate company, the famous Hollywood sign on Mt Cahuenga was substantially refurbished in 1978. It continues to be the movie icon of the twenty-first century.

Below: Shooting a street scene in *Hello, Dolly!* (1969) on the Twentieth Century Fox studio lot. One of the last big-budget studio musicals.
Dir: Gene Kelly

Above: Dennis Hopper
as Billy and Peter
Fonda as Wyatt, aka
Captain America,
in *Easy Rider* (1969).
Their names allude to
Western heroes Billy
the Kid and Wyatt
Earp. The freewheeling
story of two drifters
was matched by the
ad hoc style of
production and set
the pattern for the
road movie as an
archetypal genre
of the 1970s.
Dir: Dennis Hopper

came a film which turned upside down all they thought they knew. *Easy Rider*, directed by Dennis Hopper, was about two guys who cruise around America on motorbikes enjoying sex, drugs and rock 'n' roll. The narrative structure was as freewheeling as the protagonists, and it broke one of Hollywood's cardinal rules: there is no happy ending. *Easy Rider* was the joint conception of three men, all of whom had strong connections with traditional Hollywood but who were not in sympathy with what it had become. Peter Fonda was the son of legendary screen star Henry Fonda, the hero of some of John Ford's most noble movies: rejecting this mainstream heritage, he had thrown in his lot with Roger Corman, a producer of cheap but successful 'exploitation' films, those which set out to push back the barriers of what was acceptable on the screen. Dennis Hopper had played many supporting roles, including opposite James Dean in *Rebel without a Cause* (Nicholas Ray, 1955) and *Giant* (George Stevens, 1956), but his refusal to toe the line had led him to be blacklisted by the major studios. Terry Southern was already an icon of the counter-culture scene, the author of a notorious pornographic novel, *Candy*, and a screenwriter whose credits included Stanley Kubrick's satire *Dr. Stangelove or How I Learned to Stop Worrying and Love the Bomb* (1963).

Easy Rider grossed $19 million. It was not the most successful movie of 1969, but it cost a mere $500,000 to make (by contrast, *Hello, Dolly!* had cost $26 million). As a direct result, BBS, a company formed by Bob Rafelson, Steve Blauner and Bert Schneider (the producer of *Easy Rider*), was given a multi-picture contract with Columbia, the studio which, with much trepidation, had released the picture. BBS went on to produce a series of films which were the closest Hollywood ever came to the art cinema of Western Europe. *Five Easy Pieces* (Bob Rafelson, 1970), *Drive, He Said* (Jack Nicholson, 1970), *A Safe Place* (Henry Jaglom, 1971) and *The King of Marvin Gardens* (Bob Rafelson, 1972) all starred Jack Nicholson, whose performance in *Easy Rider* had made him a star. None of these films was a huge hit, but their importance was that, for a time, it seemed as if small-scale, individually tailored films of intelligence and some artistic pretension, aimed at a limited but discerning audience, might

DUKE: I'm Duke and he's Hawkeye.

PAINLESS: Glad to know you. Drop in at my clinic anytime you feel like playing a little poker, or even if a tooth is bothering you.

HAWKEYE: Poker sounds great. When do you play?

MURRHARDT: He said anytime. Day and night, seven days a week. The players change but the game never stops.

Duke Forrest (Tom Skerritt), Captain 'Painless Pole' Waldowski (John Schuck), Hawkeye Pierce (Donald Sutherland), Captain Murrhardt (Danny Goldman), *MASH* (Robert Altman, 1970)

Right: In *Five Easy Pieces* (1970), Jack Nicholson works on an oil rig as an escape from the pressures of middle-class life. After the success of *Easy Rider* (1969) Nicholson was able to appear in films that departed from the well-crafted conventions of Hollywood narrative, and which relied more on character. Dir: Bob Rafelson

Below: Donald Sutherland (facing camera, wearing mask) and Elliott Gould (r) in *MASH* (1970), which eschewed a rigorous structure and depended on the abilities of its actors for much of its impact.

Below right: The poster for *MASH* (1970) neatly brings together the military subject matter, the irreverence and a suggestion of sex. The title stands for 'Mobile Army Surgical Hospital'.

Overleaf: Elliott Gould (with beard, talking) and other members of the medical team chill out in *MASH* (1970). Dir: Robert Altman

get a chance to challenge Hollywood orthodoxy. After all, mused perplexed Hollywood executives, at such low budgets what had they got to lose?

Another film which had succeeded by dispensing with Hollywood's conventional wisdom was *MASH* (Robert Altman, 1970). The film was scripted by Ring Lardner, Jr, who had been blacklisted for years. Set in an army field hospital during the Korean War, the film is a black farce which mingles scenes of gory operations with scabrous comedy. The tone is anarchic and anti-military, and the film scarcely bothers to conceal its obvious reference to the Vietnam War. Like *Easy Rider*, it featured no major stars, and like that film it also challenged orthodox Hollywood film-making technique. Robert Altman had come from television, and although hardly a representative of youth culture (he was forty-five at the time), resisted the conventions of the well-made film. The narrative was fluid and the structure loose, relying on the effect of individual scenes rather than narrative drive. There was much improvisation, and the way in which sound was used became something of an Altman trademark: instead of actors speaking their lines in sequence, much of the dialogue was overlapping, with several conversations being carried on at once.

MASH was the third largest grossing film of 1970 and was also a critical success. Politically it caught the mood of the time, but unlike some of the other radical films which

Hollywood had ventured to make, such as *The Strawberry Statement* (Stuart Hagmann, 1970) or *The Revolutionary* (Paul Williams, 1970), it was immensely enjoyable. For a time it seemed as if the 'New Hollywood' would no longer be a 'dream factory' but would remake itself along the lines of European cinema, with small-scale, almost artisanal companies offering freedom to 'auteurs', individual creators whose films expressed their personality or 'vision' rather than being designed primarily as vehicles for audience enjoyment. Since, in the words of William Goldman's much-quoted phrase, 'nobody knows anything' (that is, Hollywood has never been able to predict accurately what would make a hit), perhaps the best thing would be to throw open the studios to a younger generation.

Thus arose the 'Movie Brats', a new kind of Hollywood film-maker nurtured on a conception of cinema imbibed in the film schools of the East and West Coasts. Martin Scorsese, Francis Ford Coppola, Steven Spielberg, George Lucas, Brian De Palma and Paul Schrader all owed their opportunities in the first half of the 1970s to Hollywood's new-found willingness to give youth its fling. However, the astonishing success of these film-makers in turn changed Hollywood in ways they could not have anticipated, and may not have intended. Coppola had been directing Hollywood features for five years before *The Godfather* (1972), and initially resisted making a film of Mario Puzo's saga of Mafia life, believing that auteurs should originate their own material rather than adapt novels. The film he eventually produced was unconventional in several ways. It was three hours long and the cast were relative unknowns (with the exception of Marlon Brando as Don Vito Corleone; Brando's career, however, was generally considered to have self-destructed at the end of the 1960s). Worst of all for the traditionalists, photographer Gordon Willis had shot the film in a murky half-light – appropriate to its underworld subject but running very much against Hollywood orthodoxy.

The Godfather was an outstanding success, both with audiences and critics. The performances by Brando, Al Pacino and Robert Duvall were brilliant. As often with the ground-breaking films of the early 1970s, the film merged two traditional genres: it cunningly combines family saga – including marriages, christenings and deaths – with the unflinching depiction of organized crime in all its brutality. The Corleone family are monstrous, yet a lengthy sequence in Sicily makes them sympathetic by establishing their roots. Coppola does not wallow in violence, but the scenes where it occurs are memorable – none more so than when a victim discovers the head of a dead horse in his bed. The film also spawned one of the most durable of all Hollywood catchphrases when Duvall explains how he persuaded a reluctant film producer to do their bidding: 'I made him an offer he couldn't refuse.'

Above: Francis Ford Coppola realized that showing the close-knit ties of the family in *The Godfather* (1972) did not make them good people, but it did help the audience identify with them. Marlon Brando (second from l) plays the patriarch Don Corleone, seen here at the wedding of his daughter, together with his three sons (l to r): Sonny (James Caan), Michael (Al Pacino) and Fredo (John Cazale). Right: Violence in *The Godfather* (1972) is sparingly used but often shocking, as when John Marley, who plays Hollywood producer Jack Woltz, is persuaded he has been made an offer he cannot refuse. Dir: Francis Ford Coppola

HOLLYWOOD AND THE RISE OF THE BLOCKBUSTER

The film earned $86 million and helped convince Hollywood that the future of cinema lay in such 'blockbusters' rather than in small-scale pictures, whether routine or experimental. Realizing that only a few productions each year will score well, Hollywood grew to rely on such 'event' movies to assure its viability. Admittedly this tendency had begun earlier, even as far back as the mid-1950s: *The Ten Commandments* (Cecil B DeMille, 1956) was one of the first 'blockbusters', and in the 1960s films such as *The Sound of Music* (Robert Wise, 1965) had similar success. But a list of all-time 'rental champs' produced by *Variety* magazine in 1992 showed that the overwhelming majority were produced after 1970.

This pattern, of huge profits for a small number of films, was continued in 1973. *The Exorcist* (William Friedkin, 1973) was a story of demonic possession filmed with eye-popping special effects including projectile vomiting, rotating heads and levitating bodies. It catapulted the horror film from the most critically despised of genres into mainstream entertainment. Such 'exploitation' films were made viable by the new ratings system and had an immediate appeal to younger audiences, who flocked to see *The Exorcist*. It took as much money as *The Godfather*.

The strategic importance of the blockbuster was to be further consolidated by *Jaws* in 1975. Steven Spielberg's film was based on a novel by Peter Benchley which had already sold several million copies before the film's release, thus providing a launch platform. The story of a man-eating shark ravaging a small New England seaside town had its roots in the horror film, rather like *The Exorcist*. It also owes much to the 'slasher movie' sub-genre, which traces its lineage back to Alfred Hitchcock's *Psycho* (1960) and which was to become a significant part of the production spectrum later in the 1970s. Though well-written and cleverly constructed, the film provides a plentiful helping of grisly moments in a display of half-eaten body parts. As in other slasher films the first victim is a nubile young girl: here she teasingly leads a boy down to the beach, throwing off her clothes as she runs into the sea, only to be 'punished' for her wantonness by being dismembered by the shark. Though hardly radical, the film cunningly places itself on the side of anti-establishment forces. The mayor of the town continually refuses to acknowledge the existence of the shark, thinking only of the town's need for tourist dollars. Eventually the monster is destroyed by three 'outsiders': Quint, a cynical old sea-dog (a scenery-chewing performance by Robert Shaw); Brody (Roy Scheider), the police chief who is a New Yorker; and Richard Dreyfuss as Hooper, a nerdy young oceanographer.

Jaws made $102 million on it first appearance. What makes the film pivotal in the history of New Hollywood is its release strategy. Its producers adopted a policy of saturation booking, placing the film on 464 screens simultaneously. Previously, films were released

Right: Linda Blair as the possessed Regan MacNeil, Kitty Winn as Sharon and Jason Miller as Father Karras experience another demonic visitation in

The Exorcist (1973). Adapted by William Peter Blatty from his bestselling novel, this film still has the power to frighten today. Dir: William Friedkin

The Blockbuster Movie
Jaws (1975)
Dir: Steven Spielberg

Jaws is a well-made film which efficiently manipulates its elements of suspense and horror. As often in horror films, there are those who foolishly or unscrupulously deny the facts (the town council, anxious not to lose tourist dollars if news of shark attacks gets out), those who are sceptical (the police chief), and the experts in arcane knowledge who do battle with the monster; in this case Quint, the salty old sea-dog, and Hooper, the gauche young scientist. The timing of the beast's appearances is cunningly managed: an initial attack against a nude young female swimmer (having something in common with the shower murder in Alfred Hitchcock's 1960 film *Psycho*) is followed by subsequent sightings in which we actually see very little. Finally, there is the climactic battle with the monster, the antithesis of the film's working title *Stillness in the Water*.

However, it is not the inherent qualities of *Jaws* (it won Oscars for Best Film Editing, Best Music, Original Score and Best Sound) which make it a milestone in the development of contemporary Hollywood, but the way it broke the mould of selling a film. The distributors spent $700,000 on television advertising spots, a strategy unheard of at the time, and there was a saturation release pattern, instead of the slow build-up more usual in the 1970s. This was designed to maximize the stimulus of both media advertising and audience word-of-mouth before any negative reviews could kick in. The long-term effect on Hollywood was not only to radically change the ratio of production to promotion costs, but also to imbue producers with a blockbuster mentality. *Jaws* made so much money that henceforth Hollywood wanted every film to be like it, a guaranteed crowd-pleaser. The consequences for originality are with us still.

Country of Origin: USA
Production Company: Universal Pictures/ Zanuck/Brown Productions
Running Time: 124 mins

Producers: David Brown, Richard D Zanuck
Writers: Peter Benchley, Carl Gottlieb
Photography: Bill Butler
Music: John Williams
Editor: Verna Fields
Art Director: Joseph Alves, Jr

Chief Martin Brody: Roy Scheider
Quint: Robert Shaw
Matt Hooper: Richard Dreyfuss
Ellen Brody: Lorraine Gary
Mayor: Murray Hamilton

Above left: Shark attack: the first victim. The Oscar-winning score by John Williams adds to the tension.
Far left: The mechanical monster helps to make this one of the most scary sea movies ever filmed.
Left: Director Steven Spielberg and a real-life Jaws. Spielberg maintains the tension throughout the film.
Above: Richard Dreyfuss, Roy Scheider and Robert Shaw under attack.
Right: The highly effective poster, a single dramatic image conveying the essence of the film.

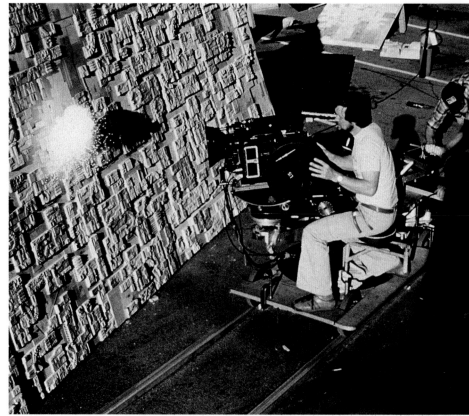

Above: *American Graffiti* (1973) successfully captured the mood of the early 1960s in this classic coming-of-age story. Dir: George Lucas Right: *Star Wars* (1977), later renamed *Star Wars: Episode IV – A New Hope*, was a complete contrast to George Lucas's earlier films, employing state-of-the-art special effects and great attention to visual style. Dir: George Lucas Below: Director George Lucas makes adjustments to a storm trooper's helmet to be worn in *Star Wars* (1977).

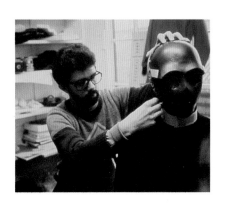

initially to a few first-run theatres, then allowed to build an audience in second- and subsequent-run outlets. The advantage of the new policy was that it maximized the effect of the media blitz for the film, with advertisements on radio and television that took full advantage of the film's menacing and memorable theme music. This was to be the subsequent pattern for all big Hollywood films, where the studios attempted to 'front-load' the audience, maximizing receipts in the first few days to capitalize on the film's event status (and also neutralize any later negative word-of-mouth or hostile reviews).

The success of this strategy meant that the money spent on promoting a film began to rise inexorably. By the late 1990s, it is estimated that advertising expenditure had risen to over $20 million per picture. Costs of production rose rapidly too, partly because of intense competition for bankable stars and because of the huge rewards that accrued to successful pictures. In the fourteen years between 1981 and 1995, according to the Motion Picture Association of America, costs increased from an average of $11.3 million per picture to $36.4 million. This combination of expensive promotion budgets and very high production costs is one of the factors that make it difficult for Hollywood's competitors around the world to challenge its dominance. In a very real sense they constitute an effective barrier to the entry of new producers into the field.

Martin Scorsese's *Taxi Driver*, made in 1976, showed that the artistic, idiosyncratic side of the New Hollywood was still alive, that the new wave was still capable of making brilliant and original pictures. But any thought that the future of Hollywood lay with such productions, however successful, was surely laid to rest the following year, with the extraordinary success of *Star Wars* (George Lucas, 1977). George Lucas had already had a box office hit with *American Graffiti* in 1973, an exercise in small-town nostalgia which derived much of its effectiveness from the use of pop songs from the early 1960s, but no one could have predicted the phenomenon of *Star Wars*. The film is set (unusually for a science fiction film) in the distant past, or as the strapline has it, 'a long time ago in a galaxy far away'. The

hero, Luke Skywalker, must rescue the beautiful Princess Leia from the clutches of the evil
Darth Vader with the aid of a motley collection of friends and helpers – including a couple
of robots, assorted aliens and his mentor Obi-Wan Kenobi. The film constantly plays with
cinematic conventions and iconography. C-3PO, the android, is cousin to the Tin Man in
The Wizard of Oz (Victor Fleming, 1939); Obi-Wan Kenobi, played by the British actor Sir
Alec Guinness, is a cross between Merlin and a Japanese martial arts master; Darth Vader
wears a Nazi-style helmet and raises heavy breathing to a new level. The opening sequence
of warfare in space is like a World War II aerial combat sequence. Later, Luke Skywalker,
having gone on a mission away from his uncle's farm, realizes it has been attacked.
Hurrying back he finds he is too late and the farm is in flames, a scene based on Ethan's
discovery of the burning Edwards farm in John Ford's epic Western *The Searchers* (1956).
Most of the budget went on special effects for the set-piece dog fights in space and the
collection of strange aliens that the hero encounters. The characters are pasteboard, the
dialogue comic-book, but the film has a naive charm, great narrative drive and visual élan.

   Star Wars was a colossal box office hit, but what made it especially significant for the
future of Hollywood was the even bigger amount of money garnered by merchandising.
Exploiting popular films by selling ancillary products was nothing new in Hollywood.
In the 1930s and 1940s cowboy stars such as Tom Mix and Gene Autry had been used to sell
breakfast cereals and children's clothing. But the sheer amount of product sales based on
Star Wars was unprecedented. Clothing, books, toys and games poured out in a torrent. By
the early 1980s it was estimated that its merchandising was raising over $1.5 billion a year.[3]

   Star Wars also confirmed an incipient trend towards the serialization of hit films. *The
Godfather* had a sequel in 1974 and another in 1990. *Jaws 2* (Jeannot Szwarc) was released
in 1978, and a further two sequels were made in 1983 and 1987 respectively. *MASH* had
become a long-running television series in 1972, and *The Exorcist* spawned two sequels.
The first *Star Wars* sequel, *Episode V – The Empire Strikes Back*, directed by Irvin Kershner,

A Box Office Spectacular
Star Wars (1977)
Dir: George Lucas

There is not much science in George Lucas's science fiction spectacular. It is basically an adventure story, replacing six-shooters or swords with laser guns and horses with rockets. The plots turn on the endlessly renewed battle between good and evil, the former represented by the Jedi knights and the mystical Force which they are in touch with, and the latter by the Galactic Empire with its Nazi-like storm-troopers. *Star Wars* (1977) eventually proved to have begun the saga *in medias res*, and on its reissue in 1981 was renamed *Star Wars: Episode IV – A New Hope*.

Luke Skywalker's simple farming life on a remote planet is dramatically changed when he intercepts a distress call from rebel leader Princess Leia. The message leads him to Ben (Obi-Wan) Kenobi and with the two robots C-3PO and R2-D2, and later Chewbacca and Han Solo, their journey to release the princess from the evil Empire begins. The first two sequels to be released follow in the sequence, then the next two instalments went back to the origins of the tale.

Now a quarter of a century old, Lucas's project has benefited from improvements in special effects technology, but his vision has remained the same: a naive, even childlike belief in absolute good and evil, a preference for action over character and spectacle over everything. Opinions may differ over the quality of the experience Lucas offers, but undoubtedly he has changed the face of Hollywood. No longer are box office receipts the only or even the main source of profit on such blockbuster films. The endless proliferation of products – toys, games, clothing – that spin off from *Star Wars* has made him a very wealthy man.

Country of Origin: USA
Production Company: Lucasfilm Ltd
Running Time: 121 mins

Producer: Gary Kurtz
Writer: George Lucas
Photography: Gilbert Taylor
Music: John Williams
Editors: Paul Hirsch, Marcia Lucas, Richard Chew
Production Designer: John Barry
Visual Effects: John Stears

Luke Skywalker: Mark Hamill
Han Solo: Harrison Ford
Princess Leia Organa: Carrie Fisher
Grand Moff Tarkin: Peter Cushing
Ben (Obi-Wan) Kenobi: Alec Guinness
C-3PO: Anthony Daniels
R2-D2: Kenny Baker
Chewbacca: Peter Mayhew
Darth Vader: David Prowse

Below: Chewbacca (Peter Mayhew), Luke Skywalker (Mark Hamill), Obi-Wan Kenobi (Alec Guinness) and Han Solo (Harrison Ford) up against the evil forces of Grand Moff Tarkin (Peter Cushing) and Darth Vader (David Prowse).

The galaxy is under threat from the Death Star controlled by the Imperial forces under the command of Grand Moff Tarkin and Darth Vader. The four journey to the Death Star in order to rescue Princess Leia (Carrie Fisher).

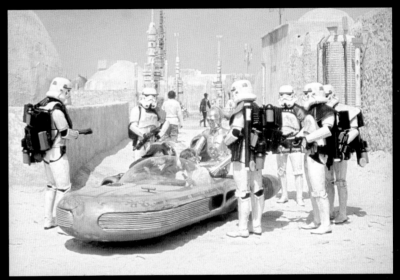

Above: Obi-Wan Kenobi and Luke Skywalker with the android C-3PO; menacing storm-troopers surround Luke Skywalker; Darth Vader threatens Princess Leia.

Left: Anakin Skywalker (Jake Lloyd), who lives on the Outer Rim desert planet of Tatooine, contemplates his destiny in *Star Wars: Episode I – The Phantom Menace* (1999). Below left: Podracers reach speeds of over 500 mph in *Star Wars: Episode I – The Phantom Menace* (1999). The state-of-the-art special effects add a new dimension to this *Star Wars* prequel. Dir: George Lucas

SHMI:	All slaves have transmitters placed inside their bodies somewhere.
ANAKIN:	I've been working on a scanner to try and locate them, but no luck.
SHMI:	Any attempt to escape ...
ANAKIN:	... and they blow you up ... poof!
JAR JAR:	How wude.
PADMÉ:	I can't believe there is still slavery in the galaxy. The Republic's anti-slavery laws ...
SHMI:	The Republic doesn't exist out here ... we must survive on our own.
ANAKIN:	Have you ever seen a Podrace?
QUI-GON:	They have Podracing on Malastare. Very fast, very dangerous.
ANAKIN:	I'm the only human who can do it.

Shmi Skywalker (Pernilla August), Anakin Skywalker (Jake Lloyd), Jar Jar Binks (voice, Ahmed Best), Queen Padmé Amidala (Natalie Portman), Qui-Gon Jinn (Liam Neeson), *Star Wars: Episode I – The Phantom Menace* (George Lucas, 1999)

was released in 1980; three years later came *Episode VI – The Return of the Jedi*, directed by Richard Marquand. George Lucas directed the prequels *Episode I – The Phantom Menace* (1999) and *Episode II – Attack of the Clones* (2002). Each new release provides further opportunities for merchandising and the re-release of previous episodes. Even Martin Scorsese, the least accommodating of the talents of the 1970s, eventually succumbed to Hollywood's determination to repeat itself, making *The Color of Money* (1986), a sequel to Robert Rossen's 1961 film *The Hustler*, and *Cape Fear* (1991), a remake of a thriller from 1961.

An equally important development at the beginning of the 1980s was the growth of video and television markets. In the United States the number of households with a video recorder went from 1.85 million in the early 1980s to 62 million by the end of the decade. Sales of pre-recorded video cassettes went from 3 million in 1980 to 220 million in 1990.[4] There was a similar explosion in Europe. By the end of the 1990s, receipts from theatrical release made up only 31.3 per cent of a film's total revenue. Video sales and rentals comprised 34.6 per cent.[5] The remaining 34 per cent came from sales to television, now a major factor not only in the domestic market but abroad; in Europe, for example, the privatization of much of the public television service has made for increased reliance on Hollywood products in the schedules.

Foreign markets have always been important to Hollywood, at least since World War I when the US film industry capitalized on the weakness of European cinema to edge French, Scandinavian, German and British films out of the markets they had previously enjoyed. However, whereas foreign sales were a useful additional source of revenue during Hollywood's 'classical' period, by 1994 the revenue from overseas surpassed that of the US market. The development of multiplex cinemas in Western Europe, and the opening up of markets in the former Soviet bloc, in China and elsewhere in the Far East have greatly boosted the export earnings of US films. So although the proportion of a film's income derived from ticket sales in theatres has decreased, the absolute total of such sales has greatly increased.

All these factors have had a dramatic effect on Hollywood's business. More to the point, they have had far-reaching effects on the kinds of film produced. From the 1980s onward Hollywood increasingly turned its attention to the perfection of a certain kind of film, dubbed 'high concept' – in essence a refinement of the blockbuster. Its characteristics follow from the changes in the nature of the business: principally, the new marketing strategies, in which the success of a film depends crucially on saturation advertising, especially on television and radio, plus an equally saturated release pattern; the growth of video; the vastly increased importance of ancillary sales, especially in merchandising; the globalization of the market, so that Hollywood comes increasingly to depend on foreign sales to supply the revenue to fund its inflated budgets; and the move towards a younger audience, less tolerant of orthodoxies, whether political or sexual, and with increasing amounts of money to spend on fashion and media products, especially music.

The 'high-concept' film has, in the first place, a narrative that is easily comprehended and summarized. As Steven Spielberg remarked in 1978, 'What interests me more than anything else is the idea. If a person can tell me the idea in twenty-five words or less, it is going to be a good movie.'[6] This means that the film can cross cultural and linguistic boundaries, and can be readily packaged in promotional material. Frequently such narratives reprocess or recombine traditional elements from horror or science fiction, or other genres with traditionally low cultural status. Thus *Star Wars* recycles the narratives and iconography of the Western and the war film. *Jaws* is a combination of small-town melodrama and monster picture. A corollary of this kind of narrative is a set of characters who are simple rather than complex, whose essence can readily be communicated through physical typing, as in muscle-men such as Arnold Schwarzenegger and Sylvester Stallone and their equally hyperbolic, silicone-enhanced female opposites.

While character and narrative are pared down, the visual style of such films is refined. Sleek and glossy, the high-concept film has a brilliant surface marked by easily recognizable and exploitable iconic images, often obtained through the manipulation of special effects, increasingly computer-generated. Such films are designed as much as they are written, and contemporary Hollywood has been eager to recruit directors and others from the advertising industry: for example, the Scott brothers, Ridley and Tony, responsible for some of Hollywood's most spectacular and profitable films in recent years, such as *Alien* (Ridley Scott, 1979), *Blade Runner* (Ridley Scott, 1982), *Top Gun* (Tony Scott, 1986), *Enemy of the State* (Tony Scott, 1998), *Gladiator* (Ridley Scott, 2000) and *Hannibal* (Ridley Scott, 2001).

Sound is also an important element in these films, both for the opportunities it offers for advertising (where would *Jaws* have been without John Williams's music?) and

Above: Director Ridley Scott, the master of the high-budget special effects spectacular, shooting *Alien* (1979).

Right: High flier Pete 'Maverick' Mitchell (Tom Cruise) (r) in the action-packed movie *Top Gun* (1986). Dir: Tony Scott

Previous pages and right: *Titanic* (1997), the most expensive film ever made when it was produced in 1997, is the perfect example of the high-concept blockbuster. The idea could not be simpler and has universal appeal: poor stowaway Jack Dawson (Leonardo DiCaprio) meets rich girl Rose Dewitt Bukater (Kate Winslet) on the doomed Atlantic liner; they fall in love, he drowns. It is the money spent on the spectacle of the shipwreck that gives the film its unique selling point.
Dir: James Cameron

Opposite: John Williams at work. His Oscar-winning music for *Jaws* (1975) highlights the important role that music plays in many films. A successful soundtrack album is a useful marketing tool and a guaranteed income generator.
Dir: Steven Spielberg

also for the sale of soundtrack albums, a powerful attraction to the multimedia conglomerates that now run Hollywood. In the high-concept film, both image and soundtrack are pumped up in excess of what is strictly required to communicate the narrative. It is as if the attenuated story and characterization release image and sound to take on an autonomous status which is then available both for marketing and for exploitation as ancillary products.

One further dimension characterizes this new kind of film. Made primarily for the young, whose minds are steeped in the manifold images and sounds sedimented by the mass media, and created by film-makers who often have a self-conscious awareness of the cinema's past (or at least its recent past), contemporary high-concept films exhibit a kind of ironic detachment. Older critics often see such films as somewhat 'camp', deliberately poking fun at the absurdities of their excesses. Yet it is hard to observe such intentions on the part of such film-makers as George Lucas or Steven Spielberg if their public pronouncements are to be believed. What their films display is a kind of knowingness which at the same time is innocent of a desire to parody – what Thomas Elsaesser has called 'sophisticated naivety',[7] which may on occasion be a naive sophistication. Such an air of detached 'cool', combined with pervasive allusions to other films and other media, seems to call for the description 'postmodern'. Some critics, disdainful of dignifying movies they despise, have dismissed contemporary Hollywood films as 'emptily expensive, aesthetically impoverished spectacles' which betray the traditional Hollywood virtues of well-told stories.[8] Yet these movies, while they may not satisfy the tastes of critics raised on more traditional fare, are representative of important shifts in contemporary culture which need to be taken into account.

The high-concept movie is not the whole story, and indeed film historian Thomas Schatz has divided contemporary US cinema into three main categories of production.[9] There is the calculated high-concept blockbuster, designed to exploit to the full its potential for profit in the world market: a prime example would be *Titanic* (James Cameron, 1997). There is the mainstream star-vehicle: for example, *Runaway Bride* (Garry Marshall, 1999), a comedy starring Julia Roberts and Richard Gere; and finally there is the lower-cost 'independent' feature looking for a niche, such as Neil LaBute's *Your Friends and Neighbors* (1998), an off-beat, edgy film with no major stars. Yet even if the high-concept film is not the be-all and end-all of the film business, it is the thing which pulls the rest along. It is in the blockbuster that new ideas, new technologies, new sales strategies are tried out. Those made uncomfortable by these tendencies may take solace in the indisputable fact that even massive marketing budgets cannot make a success out of a poor film. What is inescapable, however, is that marketing now governs the production of even modest films. The need to find a hook, an angle, a unique selling point, exerts pressure at all levels, in scripting, casting, design and editing. For Hollywood, it has never been simply a matter of the author's self-expression.

HOLLYWOOD AND THE RISE OF THE BLOCKBUSTER

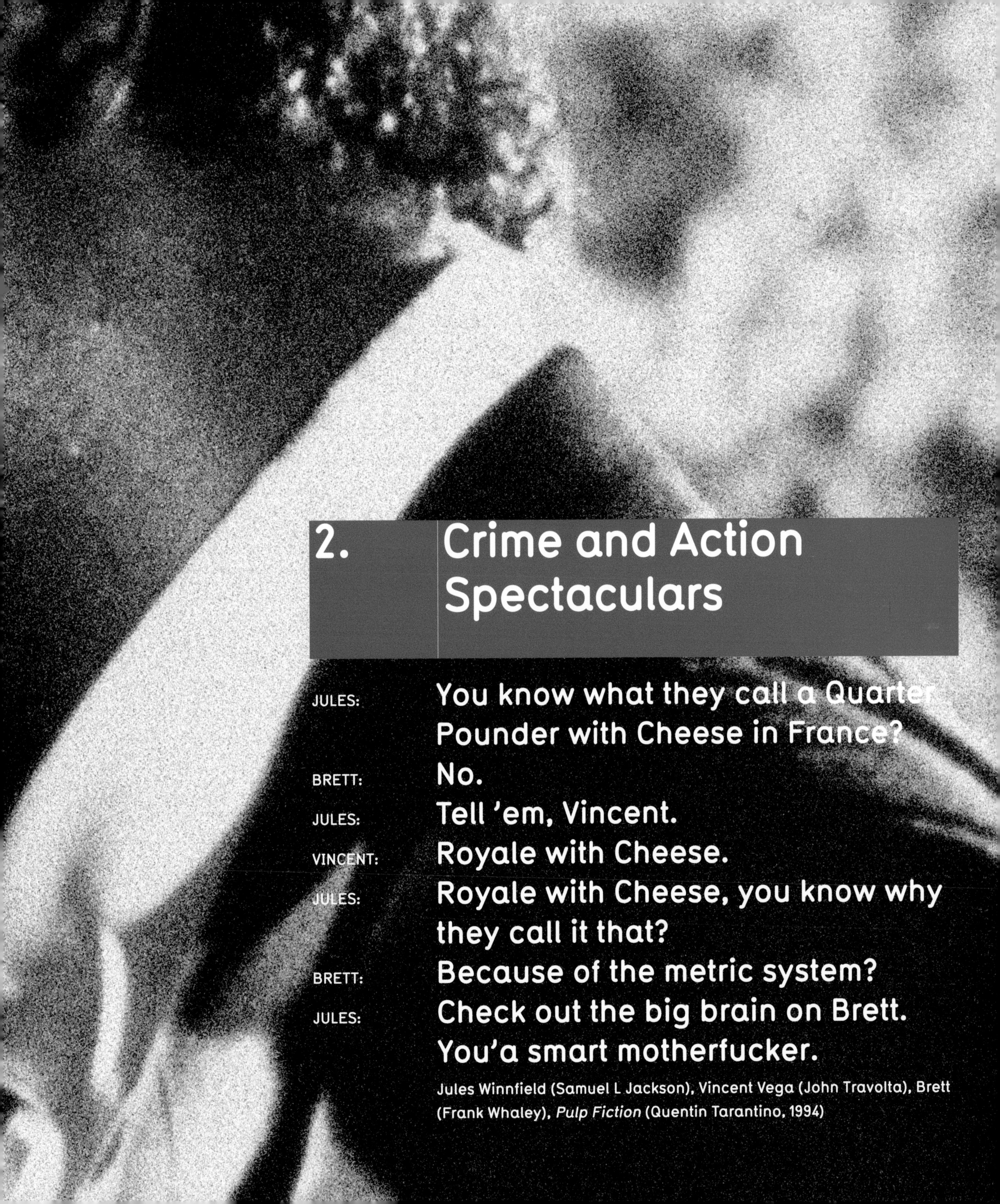

2. Crime and Action Spectaculars

JULES:	You know what they call a Quarter Pounder with Cheese in France?
BRETT:	No.
JULES:	Tell 'em, Vincent.
VINCENT:	Royale with Cheese.
JULES:	Royale with Cheese, you know why they call it that?
BRETT:	Because of the metric system?
JULES:	Check out the big brain on Brett. You'a smart motherfucker.

Jules Winnfield (Samuel L Jackson), Vincent Vega (John Travolta), Brett (Frank Whaley), *Pulp Fiction* (Quentin Tarantino, 1994)

In the cinema, crime always pays. The exploits of criminals and attempts to catch them were a staple of nineteenth-century popular fiction, upon which early cinema drew for much of its inspiration. The gangster films of the 1930s, the films noirs of the 1940s, the police procedurals of the 1950s, including television shows such as *Dragnet*, all proved reliable formulas which could be extended through appropriate modifications into the later part of the century. At the beginning of the 1970s two films proved particularly influential. *The French Connection* (William Friedkin, 1971) starred Gene Hackman as Popeye Doyle, a pugnacious but dogged New York cop on the track of drug-traffickers. Spectacular action, including a furious car chase, made the film a huge hit and led to a sequel in 1975. The figure of the disgruntled cop, battling not just the crooks but bureaucracy and often corruption on his own side, was also the basis of *Dirty Harry* (Don Siegel, 1971), in which Clint Eastwood plays a policeman whose impatience with legal niceties leads him to adopt his own more robust methods in the pursuit of a psycho killer. Harry's anti-establishment grudges, plus the charisma of Eastwood and the excellent direction of veteran Don Siegel, made the film a big success. Eastwood eventually completed four sequels, including *Sudden Impact* (Clint Eastwood, 1983). It was in this film that Eastwood, inviting a captured criminal to reach for his gun, coined the catchphrase 'Make my day' – which became so popular that it was later used by Ronald Reagan.

In the wake of the youth revolt of the late 1960s, films about the police tended to focus on wrongdoing within the force as much as outside, as in *Serpico* (Sidney Lumet, 1973), in which Al Pacino battles corruption, and *Prince of the City* (Sidney Lumet, 1981). It became almost a cliché that the rogue cop, even if not himself corrupt, has in his manner and world-view much in common with the criminals he pursues, a perception at the heart of Michael Mann's *Heat* (1995), in which Al Pacino tracks career criminal Robert De Niro.

Film noir, a shadowy world of double cross, disillusioned heroes and dangerous women, in which no one is what they seem, is a style that continues to exert fascination. Roman

Above: Al Pacino
in *Heat* (1995).
The complexity of
characterization and
the dynamism of the
action raise the film
above cliché.
Right: Cop Al Pacino
(l) and crook Robert
De Niro (r) have much in
common, as suggested
by the *mise-en-scène*,
seating them as
mirror images of
each other. *Heat* (1995)
also puts into play
other conventions of
the genre; for example,
as so often, the cop's
marriage is collapsing
under the strain of
his job.
Dir: Michael Mann

HANNA:	You ever wanted a regular type life?
McCAULEY:	What the fuck is that? Barbeques and ballgames?
HANNA:	Yeah.
McCAULEY:	This regular type life. That your life?
HANNA:	No. My life is a disaster zone. I got a step-daughter who's fucked up because her real father's this large type asshole. My wife and I are passing each other on the downsteps of our marriage, my third, 'cause every moment I got I spend chasing guys like you around the block.
McCAULEY:	A guy told me one time, don't let yourself get attached to anything you're not willing to walk out on if you feel the heat coming round the corner, in 30 seconds flat.

Vincent Hanna (Al Pacino), Neil McCauley (Robert De Niro), *Heat* (Michael Mann, 1995)

Above: In *Chinatown* (1974) Jack Nicholson's snappy clothes contrast with his conspicuously damaged nose, slit open by Roman Polanski playing a bit part as a nasty little thug.

Dir: Roman Polanski
Right: Jack Nicholson having adulterous sex on the kitchen table with Jessica Lange in *The Postman Always Rings Twice* (1981).
Dir: Bob Rafelson

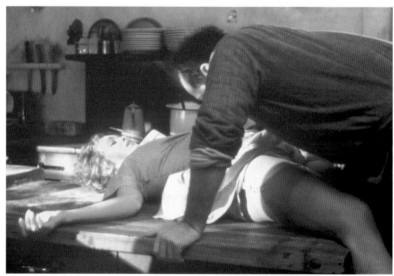

CRIME AND ACTION SPECTACULARS

Polanski's *Chinatown* (1974) is a masterpiece of neo-noir, with Jack Nicholson giving the performance of his life as J J Gittes, a seedy private eye who gets in much too deep when he stumbles across the truth about massive civic corruption in 1930s Los Angeles. Like other successful examples of the form, the film pays great attention to its look, in this case establishing through lighting, costumes and décor a milieu of seductive glamour. *The Postman Always Rings Twice* (Bob Rafelson, 1981), a remake of the 1946 film based on James M Cain's hard-boiled novel, starred Jack Nicholson and Jessica Lange as adulterous lovers in circumstances more gritty than glamorous; the film convincingly explored lust as a motivation for murder. In the 1990s neo-noir continued to offer not only the surety of good plots and strong characters but also plentiful opportunities for stylistic display. *L.A. Confidential* (Curtis Hanson, 1997), adapted from the novel by James Ellroy, produced a richly textured re-creation of 1950s Los Angeles in its story of criminal conspiracies and scandal in high places, with a superb performance by Russell Crowe as a brutal policeman. In Bryan Singer's *The Usual Suspects* (1995), based on a script by Christopher McQuarrie, it is not so much the visuals that impress as the almost sadistic tortuousness of the plot, which delights in its array of red herrings and mistaken identities, and perplexes the audience with flashbacks and sub-plots.

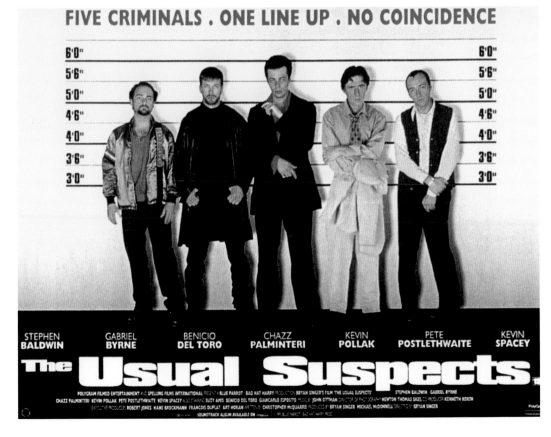

Above left and right: In *L.A. Confidential* (1997) Russell Crowe is compelling as Bud White, a brutal cop smashing through the Los Angeles underworld of the 1950s, and ensnared in the mystique of femme fatale Kim Basinger. Dir: Curtis Hanson. **Left:** The poster for *The Usual Suspects* (1995). Five criminals have one thing in common, an association with master crook Keyser Soze. But does he even exist? (l to r) Kevin Pollack, Stephen Baldwin, Benicio Del Toro, Gabriel Byrne, Kevin Spacey. Dir: Bryan Singer

Above and right: Hell hath no fury: Michael Douglas and Glenn Close conduct a passionate affair in *Fatal Attraction* (1987), which turns nasty when Douglas tries to end it and arouses his lover's homicidal impulses. Dir: Adrian Lyne

CRIME AND ACTION SPECTACULARS

The taste for 'retro' shared by these modern-day films noirs was perhaps less the result of a genuine interest in the past, and more a desire on Hollywood's part to retrieve its own former glories, to make films like they used to. Neo-noir also afforded opportunities for strong female characters. The femme fatale, as embodied by Barbara Stanwyck and Rita Hayworth, had been an essential ingredient of the films noirs of the 1940s. In *Body Heat* (Lawrence Kasdan, 1981) Kathleen Turner has all the essential qualities of the type: devious, manipulative and sexy. The dangerous woman may be an avenger, as in *Ms .45* (1981), Abel Ferrara's low-budget shocker in which Zoë Tamerlis goes on a murderous rampage after being raped; or she may be a mother protecting her son, like Anjelica Huston in *The Grifters* (1990), Stephen Frears's film of Jim Thompson's novel about confidence tricksters. In *The Last Seduction* (John Dahl, 1993) Linda Fiorentino has no motivation in her machinations other than getting rich, but in other manifestations of the strong woman character there is a powerful element of hysteria, even madness. Theresa Russell in *Black Widow* (Bob Rafelson, 1987), Jennifer Jason Leigh in *Single White Female* (Barbet Schroeder, 1992), Rebecca De Mornay in *The Hand That Rocks the Cradle* (Curtis Hanson, 1992) and, most notoriously, Sharon Stone in *Basic Instinct* (Paul Verhoeven, 1992) are all over the edge. It is an open question as to whether such characters represent a feminist advance towards equality (anything men can do women can do too, including murder), or whether they are part of a male reaction against feminism – a demonization of women. The role of Glenn Close in *Fatal Attraction* (Adrian Lyne, 1987) certainly leaned towards the latter. Cast aside by Michael Douglas after a brief affair, hers is the fury of the woman scorned. Her violent end, after she has tried to murder Douglas and his wife, has the feel of a harpy getting her just desserts. By comparison there have been few heroines like that played by Jamie Lee Curtis in Kathryn Bigelow's *Blue Steel* (1990), a New York policewoman battling both crooks and prejudice by her male superiors. In *Point of No Return* (John Badham, 1993), a remake of Luc Besson's French movie *Nikita* (1990), Bridget Fonda becomes a trained assassin; but it is not a career move, just the result of being blackmailed by a government agency.

Crime has attracted many of the best directors in the United States. Several Woody Allen films play around with crime and criminals: *Manhattan Murder Mystery* (1993), *Bullets over Broadway* (1994) and *Small Time Crooks* (2000). Dennis Hopper gives a disturbing performance as a demented hoodlum in David Lynch's *Blue Velvet* (1986). Terrence Malick's *Badlands* (1973) observes a young couple who embark on a Bonnie and Clyde-like killing spree. Malick's complex narrative strategy presents the events refracted through the unfeeling consciousness of the perpetrators. The Coen brothers' first film, *Blood Simple* (1983), was a noirish thriller shot through with black humour, and several of their subsequent

CRIME AND ACTION SPECTACULARS

Crime and the city have long been the centre of the Hollywood action film, focusing many of our most pressing concerns. In the quarter-century since the appearance of *Taxi Driver*, the damaged psyche of its hero, Travis Bickle, has come to seem more than ever symptomatic of our times. The opening images of the yellow taxi cab moving slowly through clouds of steam, seems an authentic vision of the city as netherworld, a landscape of gaudy nightmares. Bickle himself is an unnerving combination of psychopath and naive innocent, a victim whose attempts to put the world to rights produce yet more victims.

Like other troubled Hollywood heroes of the era, Bickle is a Vietnam veteran, working nights as a New York taxi driver, observing with increasing disgust the human flotsam that comes into his cab. His attempts at human contact are a failure. A young political campaigner whom he takes on a date (Cybill Shepherd) is repelled by his taste for porno films. He attempts to rescue Iris, a twelve-year-old prostitute (Jodie Foster), but increasingly his mind is under strain, and, thwarted in his attempt to assassinate a Presidential candidate, he murders Iris's pimp and a client in an orgy of what he intends as redemptive violence. In an ironic twist, his attempt to kill himself fails and he is hailed as a hero for handing out justice to the sleazy criminals he executes.

Robert De Niro standing in front of the mirror practising his insults ('Are you talking to me?') is one of the landmarks of contemporary Hollywood cinema. It helped to make the film a box office hit and show that feel-good films were not the only ones that could find a market.

Country of Origin: USA
Production Company: Bill/Phillips/Columbia Pictures Corporation/Italo/Judeo Productions
Running Time: 113 mins

Producers: Julia Phillips, Michael Phillips
Writer: Paul Schrader
Photography: Michael Chapman
Music: Bernard Herrmann
Editors: Tom Rolf, Melvin Shapiro
Art Director: Charles Rosen

Travis Bickle: Robert De Niro
Betsy: Cybill Shepherd
Wizard: Peter Boyle
Iris Steensma: Jodie Foster
Sport Matthew: Harvey Keitel

Opposite: Jodie Foster as Iris, the child prostitute, with Robert De Niro as Travis Bickle.
Left and below: The several faces of Robert De Niro, as the increasingly deranged Vietnam veteran.
Below left: The poster for the film illustrates the dark world inhabited by Travis Bickle.

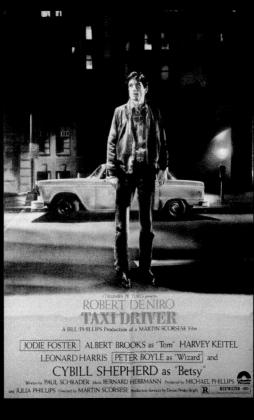

COLUMBIA PICTURES presents
ROBERT DE NIRO
TAXI DRIVER
A BILL/PHILLIPS Production of a MARTIN SCORSESE Film
JODIE FOSTER ALBERT BROOKS as "Tom" HARVEY KEITEL
LEONARD HARRIS PETER BOYLE as "Wizard" and
CYBILL SHEPHERD as "Betsy"
Written by PAUL SCHRADER Music BERNARD HERRMANN Produced by MICHAEL PHILLIPS
and JULIA PHILLIPS Directed by MARTIN SCORSESE Production Services by Devon-Persky-Bright R RESTRICTED

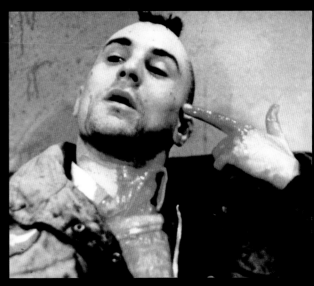

films, such as *Miller's Crossing* (1990) and *Fargo* (1996), have returned to a criminal milieu. But of all contemporary directors, Martin Scorsese is the one most closely associated with criminality. *Mean Streets* (1973), *Taxi Driver* (1976), *GoodFellas* (1990) and *Casino* (1995) are unrivalled in the intensity and profundity with which they explore the underworld.

The very different personalities of Clint Eastwood and Quentin Tarantino have also made crime their business. Tarantino shot to fame as director of *Reservoir Dogs* (1991). Its witty script about a heist that goes wrong was brilliantly interpreted by Tim Roth, Steve Buscemi and Harvey Keitel (the last an icon of the American crime film), but what gave the film notoriety was its violence, in particular a scene where a member of the gang tortures a policeman. Tarantino's next feature, *Pulp Fiction* (1994), was a work of considerable complexity and panache, a story of small-time crooks in several complex interlocking narratives, and with a modish intertextuality in its wide range of cultural references, plus lots of humour and violence. Tarantino also wrote the script for *True Romance* (1993), a road movie stylishly directed by Tony Scott in which a young couple with a bag of cocaine are chased by the mob. Tarantino's *Jackie Brown* (1997), based on a novel by Elmore Leonard, the premier crime writer in the United States, was a competent but altogether more conventional work, leading to suspicions that Tarantino had run out of steam.

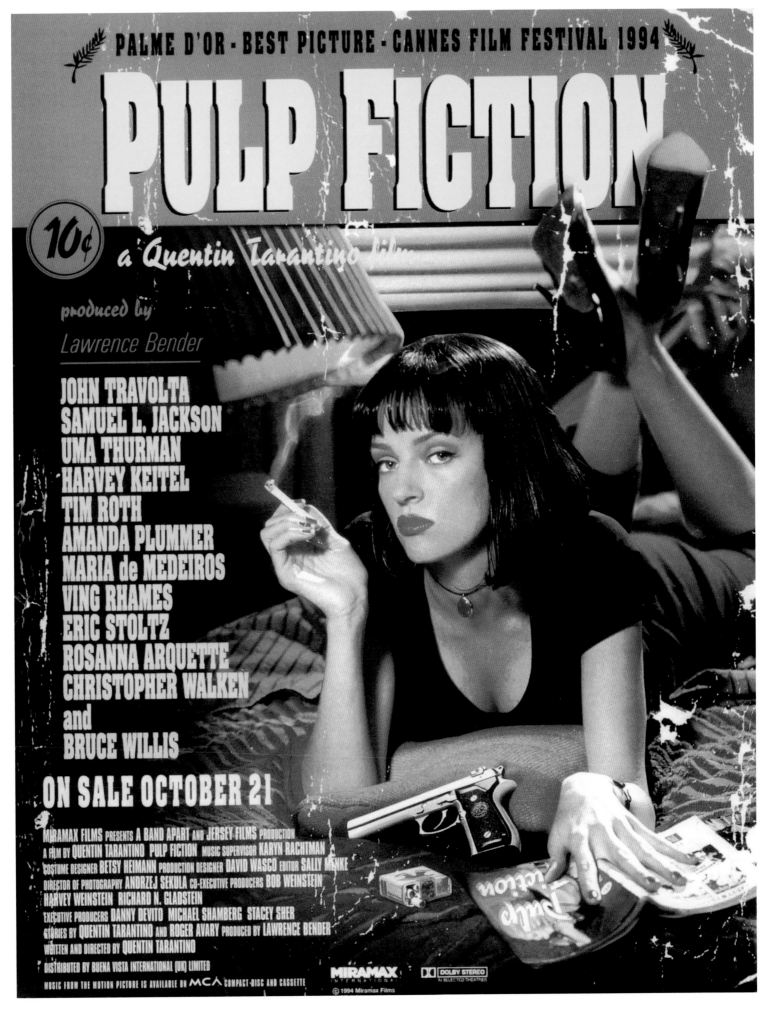

Almost overnight, Tarantino became a cult figure among young male cinephiles. Clint Eastwood, by contrast, is remarkable for the longevity of his screen presence, having been a major star for nearly forty years and an important director since the early 1970s. Though he has almost single-handedly kept the Western alive, in fact only five of the twenty-two films he has directed since 1971 are in this genre, and they are outnumbered by his crime films. Dirty Harry's opposition to authority structures, his refusal to conform, position him as a perpetual outsider, a stance that has rubbed off on many of Eastwood's other roles. As a veteran secret service agent he argues with his superiors throughout *In the Line of Fire*

Above and below:
In *Rocky* (1976)
Sylvester Stallone is
small-time boxer and
debt-collector Rocky
Balboa, billed as 'The

Italian Stallion', who
gets a crack at the
Heavyweight Champion
of the World Apollo
Creed (Carl Weathers).
Dir: John G Avildsen

(Wolfgang Petersen, 1993); in *Absolute Power* (Clint Eastwood, 1996) he is a burglar who by chance observes the US president in flagrante and is sucked into the cynical world of high politics, compared to which burglary seems an honest profession. In *True Crime* (Clint Eastwood, 1999) Eastwood is an ageing newspaper man whose career has been damaged by his lack of team spirit and whose personal life implodes under the weight of his infidelities and his obsession with work, but who single-handedly fights against the injustice being done to a black man.

Eastwood is a canny reader of how the wind is blowing. The tough-guy persona of Dirty Harry has become progressively tempered by a degree of self-mockery, an undercutting of the macho male's omnipotence. This is especially evident in a film like *The Gauntlet* (Clint Eastwood, 1977), in which Eastwood is a cop who has to escort a sassy young prostitute (Sondra Locke) across country, pursued by a gang bent on their destruction. Though there is never a doubt that Eastwood is up to the physical action, in the battle of wits with Locke he is continually bested.

Eastwood's accommodation with feminism may be one reason why his screen persona has survived for so long, well past the age at which his body can still plausibly deal with the rough stuff. In the mid-1970s, however, a new type of action hero arrived. Sylvester Stallone

Above: As protector
of the current First
Executive, Secret
Service agent Frank
Horrigan played by
Clint Eastwood
maintains a human
shield. Haunted by his

failure to stop the bullet
that killed President
Kennedy, he has a
chance to redeem
himself against another
assassin in *In the Line
of Fire* (1993).
Dir: Wolfgang Petersen

CRIME AND ACTION SPECTACULARS

in *Rocky* (John G Avildsen, 1976), with his pumped-up muscles and triangular outline, the huge shoulders tapering down to a narrow waist, represented a kind of hyper-masculinity whose appeal lay in almost superhuman strength. Such a type can be traced back to the action heroes of comic books, and indeed these became the source of many action films of the next two decades. *Rocky* and its four sequels were not crime films (though boxing films have frequently involved a criminal milieu), but they delivered many of the same satisfactions. In this case, a working-class protagonist (billed as 'The Italian Stallion'), ethnically different from Eastwood's WASP persona, takes on all odds and by force of character and brute strength wins through. The kind of spectacular body that Stallone incorporated found its apotheosis in Arnold Schwarzenegger, an even more massively built-up figure who achieved stardom in a couple of sword and sorcery films, *Conan the Barbarian* (John Milius, 1982) and *Conan the Destroyer* (Richard Fleischer, 1984), before finding his definitive role in *The Terminator* (James Cameron, 1984), in which he played a virtually indestructible robot. In his subsequent films Schwarzenegger alternated between science fiction – *The Running Man* (Paul Michael Glaser, 1987), *Total Recall* (Paul Verhoeven, 1990) and *Terminator 2: Judgment Day* (James Cameron, 1991); cop films – *Raw Deal* (John Irvin, 1986) and *Red Heat* (Walter Hill, 1988); and military adventures – *Commando* (Mark L Lester, 1985) and *Predator* (John McTiernan, 1987).

Stallone also moved between cop roles – *Cobra* (George Pan Cosmatos, 1986), *Tango & Cash* (Andrei Konchalovsky, 1989); science fiction – *Demolition Man* (Marco Brambilla, 1993), *Judge Dredd* (Danny Cannon, 1995); and the military. It was as Vietnam veteran John Rambo that he made his greatest impact, appearing in *First Blood* (Ted Kotcheff, 1982) and two sequels. Rambo undoubtedly caught the mood of the early 1980s, or at least the mood of those who voted for Ronald Reagan and Margaret Thatcher. Injured national pride is his motivation: as a character remarks in *Rambo: First Blood, Part Two* (George Pan Cosmatos, 1985), he is 'a pure fighting machine with only a desire to win a war

Above: Arnold Schwarzenegger hides from a deadly alien hunter in *Predator* (1987). An elite Special Forces team is picked off one by one as their jungle exercise becomes a fight for survival.
Dir: John McTiernan

Below: Arnold Schwarzenegger and bloody sword in the epic *Conan the Destroyer* (1984).
Dir: Richard Fleischer

someone else lost'. Events in the film confirm the sense of betrayal felt by the paranoid right, that the failure in Vietnam was the result of a sell-out, not a military defeat. Rambo is sent in to rescue American POWs in a hell-hole jungle camp. Just when the helicopter is about to winch them to safety there is an order to abort the mission. Those at the top do not want prisoners found; it would only lead to calls to restart the war, or else require money to buy them out.

The attempt to re-establish male power is evident enough in the large phallic knife that Rambo waves in front of his Vietnamese girl companion, and in the huge machine gun he wields, characteristically held pointing upwards like a monstrous erection. Yet the sexual significance of these films is perhaps a little more complex than this. Film theory has long argued that in Hollywood movies it is the female who is there to be looked at, the spectacle, while it is the man who carries the narrative – the active agent controlling the passive female. How, then, to explain the fact that Stallone and Schwarzenegger are patently on display, their huge bodies gleaming with sweat, their massive muscles rippling? Stallone as Rambo has long, hippie-length hair, and in the second film wears a girl's ornament around his neck. This feminization even extends to breaking down in tears at the end of *First Blood* and putting his arms around the Colonel, an obvious father figure, like a baby holds its mother. 'Hard bodies' is the term used to describe these films, but these same bodies are vulnerable, constantly shot at, cut, beaten, penetrated, bleeding. Marlon Brando had made something of a career out of physical suffering: beaten in *On the Waterfront* (Elia Kazan, 1954), whipped in *One-Eyed Jacks* (Marlon Brando, 1961), beaten again in *The Chase* (Arthur Penn, 1966). However, the masochism revealed in the contemporary action film goes beyond the psychopathology of an individual star. It is a more pervasive hysterical symptom, a kind of wallowing in self-pity that accompanies the paranoia about the masculinity lost in the jungles of Vietnam.

Stallone and Schwarzenegger were successful enough to spawn a host of imitators. Chuck Norris starred in *Missing in Action* (Joseph Zito, 1984), which repeated the missing POWs plot, though the lugubrious Norris with his rather hangdog moustache lacked the charisma of his rivals. The Belgian Jean-Claude Van Damme (tagged 'the muscles from Brussels'), the Swede Dolph Lundgren and US Steven Seagal are other cut-price action heroes who have demonstrated their expertise in kick-boxing or other martial arts in a string of pictures, many of which bypassed a theatrical release and went straight to video. *Universal Soldier* (Roland Emmerich, 1992), which unites Van Damme and Lundgren, is representative. It combines a military and science fiction plot; both stars are killed in Vietnam, but are resurrected by a secret military programme, becoming androids with

Left: Muscles bulging and machine gun at the ready, Sylvester Stallone attempts to rescue American POWs in *Rambo: First Blood, Part Two* (1985). Dir: George Pan Cosmatos

Opposite: In *Universal Soldier* (1992) Jean-Claude Van Damme is half-human, half-robot, in a film that blends a military-action scenario with science fiction. Dir: Roland Emmerich

superhuman strength and endurance, roles entirely appropriate to their wooden acting styles. There are attempts at humour: at one point Van Damme tells a blonde journalist to search his naked body for an embedded tracking device. 'Look for something hard,' he says as she simpers. For the most part, though, the film is a series of bloody encounters between the two stars, punctuated by gunfire and explosions.

It has been argued that the over-emphasis on male physique, on what has been termed 'musculinity', far from being a recuperation of the feminism of the 1970s, is rather a hysterical over-reaction to it, one that betrays its own inner uncertainty. It would be difficult, however, to show that this is how the films were actually read by the millions who bought tickets for them, and this argument may only be a means for politically correct film critics to justify their enjoyment. On the other hand, it does not necessarily follow that audiences wholeheartedly swallowed the right-wing agenda that Vietnam was lost through the betrayal of a liberal conspiracy, or that kicking ass is the only diplomacy that foreigners understand. It seems likely that the public's delight in these films was derived more from their visual and aural impact than their political ideology.

The fashion for the absurdly enhanced physiques of Stallone and Schwarzenegger soon waned, and each tried to reinvent himself in comedies that sent up his hard-man image; Schwarzenegger in *Kindergarten Cop* (Ivan Reitman, 1990), Stallone less successfully in *Stop! Or My Mom Will Shoot* (Roger Spottiswoode, 1992). But Hollywood had learned from its action spectaculars, and by the late 1980s the US crime film had undergone a change. In essence the hero remained the same, as famously defined by Raymond Chandler in his book *The Simple Art of Murder*, 'Down these mean streets a man must go who is not himself mean, who is neither tarnished or afraid'. The independents and the 'auteurs' (see Chapter 7) went for stylish retro décor, labyrinthine plots and complexity of characterization, but mainstream Hollywood went in the other direction. Two films were highly influential. In both *Lethal Weapon* (Richard Donner, 1987) and *Die Hard* (John McTiernan, 1988), the

The All-Action Thriller
Lethal Weapon (1987)
Dir: Richard Donner

As a film *Lethal Weapon* is a highly successful fusion of elements originating in other action films. Its success led to sequels in 1989, 1992 and 1998.

Mel Gibson's character of Martin Riggs works a variation on the 'rogue' cop syndrome, which dates back to Clint Eastwood in *Dirty Harry* (Don Siegel, 1971) and well beyond. Like Rambo, Riggs's violence derives from his experience with the Special Forces in Vietnam, and the death of his wife has rendered him incapable of re-adjusting to civilian life. His partner Roger Murtaugh (Danny Glover) is also a Vietnam veteran, but is well adjusted because of his secure family life, presented with rather cloying insistence. The fact that Roger is black (in the comparable *Die Hard*, directed by John McTiernan in 1988, Bruce Willis also chums up with a black cop) means that Martin, though delinquent, can be accorded moral credit through his lack of racism.

Issues of masculinity also surface, though the film seems uncertain how to resolve them. As usual in buddy films, *Lethal Weapon* skates around the sexual implications of male bonding, but the scene in which Gibson and Glover are captured by the crooks and tortured dramatizes male vulnerability in a manner that became familiar in the action film.

The bad guys are also Vietnam veterans, who have now turned to heroin dealing. Presumably we are intended to see the war as the source of dislocation in American society, but the real success of the film is in grafting onto the traditional cop thriller the explosive visual and aural effects that had become the norm in earlier science fiction and action films starring Sylvester Stallone and Arnold Schwarzenegger.

Country of Origin: USA
Production Company: Silver Pictures/ Warner Bros.
Running Time: 112 mins

Producers: Richard Donner, Joel Silver
Writer: Shane Black
Photographer: Stephen Goldblat
Music: Michael Kamen, Eric Clapton
Editor: Stuart Baird
Production Designer: J Michael Riva
Special Effects Coordinator: Chuck Gaspar

Martin Riggs: Mel Gibson
Roger Murtaugh: Danny Glover
Joshua: Gary Busey
General McAllister: Mitchell Ryan

Far left: Danny Glover as Roger Murtaugh interviews a witness with partner Mel Gibson as Martin Riggs.
Centre: Riggs and Murtaugh get in some target practice. As an ex-member of the Special Forces in Vietnam, Riggs is an

Below centre: Riggs putting flowers on his wife's grave.
Above: Riggs's unconventional manner of dealing with a would-be suicide is typical of his disregard for danger and of the film's set-piece action scenes.

hero is a policeman whose personal life is a failure and who finds problems adapting to the bureaucratic rules of contemporary policing. He battles against a criminal gang, virtually on his own save for his buddy. His personal style is crumpled, informal, his social origins humble. The line of descent from Dirty Harry is clear enough, and indeed goes back much further. What is new is the visual presentation of the conflict. The stakes have been upped, with production values far higher in a series of elaborate set pieces. Characteristically these involve crashing cars or other vehicles; sustained gunfire delivered by high-powered weapons wreaking wholesale destruction of the décor, bursting open TV sets or computer screens, smashing windows, ripping through walls and furniture; and – the *sine qua non* – huge explosions producing a massive red-gold fireball, usually shot in multiple camera set-ups to ensure the audience gets to see in detail an event that happens quickly. Plots and characterization are pared down to the minimum necessary to conduct the audience from one such scene to the next. Thus narrative becomes subordinated to spectacle in the manner of the very earliest 'cinema of attractions' (that is, a kind of cinema that relies more on spectacle than plot), before the story film had properly established itself.

Lethal Weapon and *Die Hard* were both extremely popular, each spawning several sequels, becoming, as the industry has it, a 'franchise'. The James Bond cycle began with *Dr. No* (Terence Young, 1962) and has now clocked up a score of titles, the most successful franchise in the history of contemporary Hollywood. Sean Connery was the first actor to play Bond and brought to the role a combination of suave good looks and underlying menace. Bond is an agent in the British Secret Service, his 'OO' designation giving him a 'licence to kill' on behalf of his country. Ian Fleming, the author of the books on which the films are based, had intended his hero to be, like himself, a product of English public schools and West End clubs, but Connery, a Scotsman, lent a more classless aspect that doubtless increased the character's international appeal.

Roger Moore, who took over the role in *Live and Let Die* (Guy Hamilton, 1973), softened the menace and played up the self-mockery which went some way towards mitigating the brazen sexism in Bond's attitude to women, whom he habitually treats as commodities to be consumed. Spectacular action sequences, exotic locations and vast, ever more expensive sets designed by Ken Adam ensured the films' popular appeal. Moore was eventually replaced by Timothy Dalton in *The Living Daylights* (John Glen, 1987) and *Licence to Kill* (John Glen, 1989) but he too was replaced by Pierce Brosnan in *GoldenEye* (Martin Campbell, 1995). Brosnan had no trouble maintaining Bond's sex appeal, but after the end of the Cold War, when Russia was no longer the enemy, the films had to reorient their ideological perspective. Thus in *Tomorrow Never Dies* (Roger Spottiswoode, 1997) the power of the media is portrayed as being a dangerous threat. In *Die Another Day* (Lee Tamahori, 2002) Bond is confronted by North Korean terrorists. There have been suggestions of casual racism in Bond's attitude to the non-white world, though the throw-away, self-deprecating humour is, as with the sexism, a useful tactic in deflecting criticism.

Race is an interesting issue in *Lethal Weapon*. Mel Gibson has a black policeman (Danny Glover) as his partner. Whereas Gibson is single, his personal life a disaster, Glover is happily married, as domesticated as Gibson is wild. Glover's bourgeois respectability is the antithesis of the racist stereotype of the black male, and his role in the film is to provide a more civilized role model for Gibson. In *Die Hard* Bruce Willis's only ally as he battles with a gang who have taken possession of a high-rise building is a black policeman with whom he develops a bond over the radio. In both films the white hero ends up embracing his black buddy, which has led to suggestions of a homoerotic sub-text, though one which the films go to some lengths to disavow. Race as an issue is not discussed; the assumption is that the white hero, despite his redneck tendencies, is colour-blind. But of course blacks still play the subordinate roles; a black cop with a white side-kick would be a very different matter.

Since the late 1980s, the action film in which narrative is subordinate to spectacle has become the dominant form in Hollywood, spreading across a range of formerly distinct genres, including crime, science fiction, adventure and historical epic. Steven Spielberg's *Raiders of the Lost Ark* (1981) anticipated the basic elements, transforming a narrative typical of the Saturday morning serials of the 1940s into a roller-coaster ride of thrills. Brian De Palma graduated from Hitchcock pastiche – with *Obsession* (1976), a homage to *Vertigo* (1958), and *Dressed to Kill* (1980), borrowing from *Psycho* (1960) – to a makeover of the classic gangster film in *Scarface* (1983) and *The Untouchables* (1987). In each, one suspects, the total number of bullets fired must exceed those in all the gangster films of the 1930s combined.

Opposite and above: Bruce Willis as the ordinary man in extraordinary circumstances in *Die Hard* (1988).
Dir: John McTiernan
Overleaf left: Roger Moore as James Bond desperately trying to escape from the clutches of Jaws (Richard Kiel) in *The Spy Who Loved Me*

(1977), one of the best James Bond adventures starring Moore.
Dir: Lewis Gilbert
Overleaf right: Michelle Yeoh as Wai Lin shares the driving with the current James Bond Pierce Brosnan in the media mogul thriller *Tomorrow Never Dies* (1997).
Dir: Roger Spottiswoode

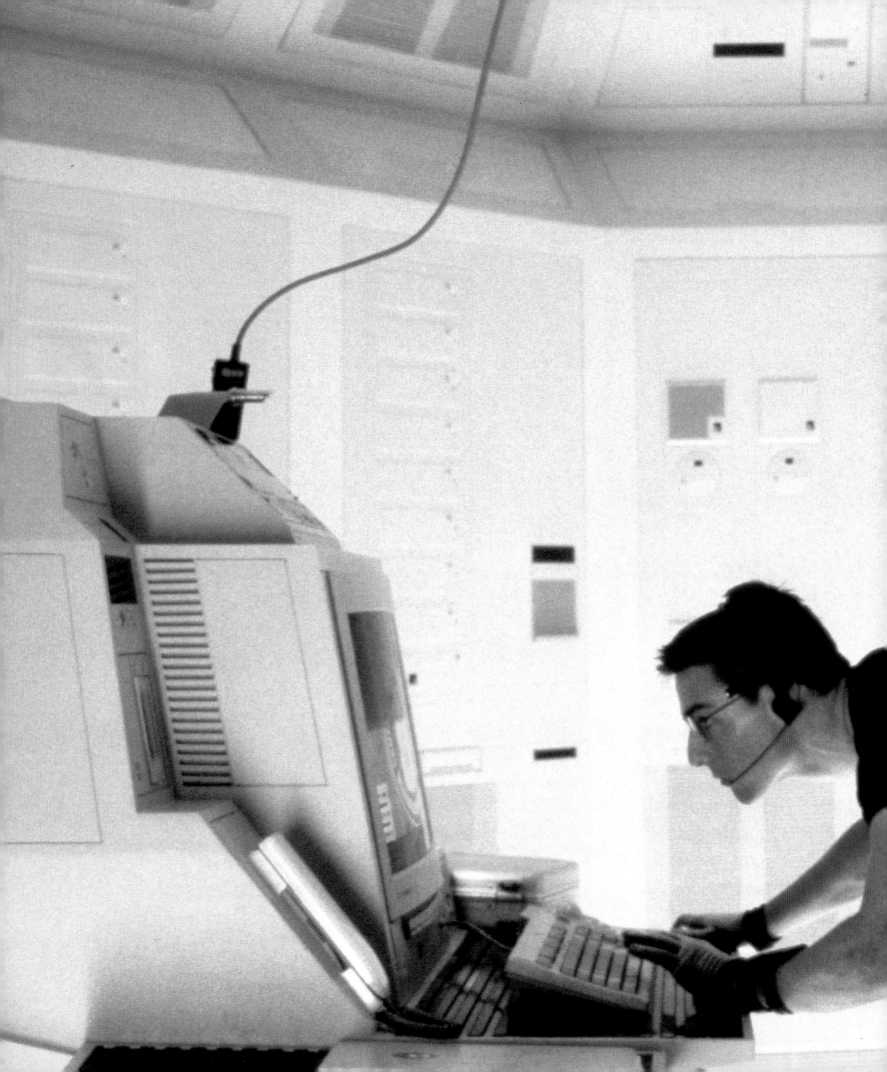

Like *The Untouchables*, De Palma's *Mission: Impossible* (1996) was based on a popular television series. The hero, played by Tom Cruise, has none of the emotional baggage of Bruce Willis or Mel Gibson, being merely a slick, sleek cipher connecting De Palma's clever series of plot surprises and spectacular set pieces. In the 1990s, the increasing sophistication of computerized special effects reinvigorated genres that had fallen out of favour. *Titanic* (1997) is a cross between a woman's film of the 1930s and 1940s, the kind of film that would have starred Bette Davis or Joan Crawford, and the disaster film, a genre that had taken on a new lease of life in the 1970s with *The Poseidon Adventure* (Ronald Neame, 1972), in which a cruise liner sinks, and *The Towering Inferno* (John Guillermin/ Irwin Allen, 1974), about fire in a high-rise building. Whereas in these films strong and confident male heroes save the day, in *Titanic* it is these very figures who are either responsible for the disaster or powerless to prevent it. The mawkish love story enacted between Leonardo DiCaprio and Kate Winslet is grafted on to state-of-the-art computer effects permitting the reconstruction of the liner's sinking in satisfying detail.

Other countries have their own tradition of crime films. The importance of the genre to French cinema is discussed in Chapter 12. In the Philippines, Lino Brocka's *Angela Markado* (1980) is a rape-revenge film as brutal as anything directed by Abel Ferrara.

Latin America, too, especially Mexico and Brazil, has produced notable contributions to the genre, most recently in the Mexican film directed by Alejandro González Iñárritu, *Amores perros* (2000), in which the brutal dog-fighting scenes act as a metaphor for the savagery of social life, and in the Brazilian film directed by Beto Brant, *The Trespasser* (*O invasor*, 2001), about dirty goings-on in the construction industry. In Japan the role of the Yakuza in organized crime can be equated to that of the Mafia, and this has generated a host of films. But it is Hong Kong that has supplied the most distinctive input, and its recent influence upon the US action film is marked. Several of its stars have made the transfer to Hollywood. Jackie Chan, whose combination of acrobatic action and good-natured humour made him the major figure in the Chinese martial arts film, appeared in *Rush Hour* (Brett Ratner, 1998) paired with a US cop in a story set in Los Angeles. The formula was repeated in *Rush Hour 2* (Brett Ratner, 2001), while in the neatly titled *Shanghai Noon* (Tom Dey, 2000) Chan visits the Wild West. Chow Yun-Fat was the star of *City on Fire* (*Longhu Fengyun*, Ringo Lam, 1987), a film which Quentin Tarantino acknowledged as an influence on *Reservoir Dogs* (1991). He also appeared in *Hard-Boiled* (*Lashou shentan*, John Woo, 1992), which featured some spectacular gunfights as the hero goes up against a gang of smugglers, ending with the virtual destruction of a hospital in the final confrontation. Chow Yun-Fat then appeared as a Chinese-American cop in New York in the Hollywood-produced *The Corruptor* (James Foley, 1999), before achieving international stardom in *Crouching Tiger, Hidden Dragon* (*Wo Hu Zang Long*, 2000), a film by director Ang Lee which achieved the difficult feat of making martial

CRIME AND ACTION SPECTACULARS

arts appeal to an art-house audience. Jet Li is the most recent Hong Kong action star to succeed in the West. After a series of very successful kung fu films, including *Once Upon a Time in China* (*Huang Feihong*, Tsui Hark, 1991), which had several sequels, Jet Li had a role as the villain in *Lethal Weapon 4* (Richard Donner, 1998), and then took the lead in *Kiss of the Dragon* (Chris Nahon, 2001), playing a Chinese government agent working with the French police in Paris. It is a Franco-American production, produced by Luc Besson.

Hard-Boiled was directed by John Woo, who subsequently directed Jean-Claude Van Damme in *Hard Target* (1993). Woo rapidly graduated from the martial arts film into the domain of the high-tech, big-budget action movie, with correspondingly bigger stars. *Broken Arrow* (1996) featured John Travolta and Christian Slater in a story about nuclear terrorism. *Face/Off* (1997) again featured Travolta, this time as a cop tracking down the criminal (Nicolas Cage) who has shot his son. In order to discover the location of a bomb, Travolta agrees to have his face replaced by that of Cage, who in turn is transformed into Travolta. This improbable plot is the thread on which hangs a succession of plane crashes, car chases, gunfights with splintering glass, and a final battle aboard a speeding motor boat. On the strength of this Woo was chosen to make the sequel to *Mission: Impossible* (1996). The plot of *Mission: Impossible 2* (2000) is taken from Hitchcock's *Notorious* (1946), in which Cary Grant falls in love with Ingrid Bergman but as a CIA man is obliged to make her marry a former boyfriend in order to bring a gang of spies to justice. There is even a straight steal of the racecourse scene from the earlier film. It is one of Hitchcock's most beautiful and moving works, but Tom Cruise is no Cary Grant. *Mission: Impossible 2* fails to arouse any emotion whatsoever; its series of chases and battles give it unsurpassed production values, but its human values are negligible. Woo's most recent picture, a war film entitled *Windtalkers* (2002), has plenty of money and technical expertise expended on its battle scenes, but it demonstrates all too clearly that pyrotechnics are not enough. In *Dirty Harry*, *Lethal Weapon* and *Die Hard* we care about the characters. That is why the physical action is interesting.

Above: Actor/director John Woo honed his skills in Hong Kong on such films as *Hard-Boiled* (*Lashou shentan*, 1992), starring Chow Yun-Fat and Tony Leung (featured).
Above right: John Woo (r) on the set of *Broken Arrow* (1996), a big-budget Hollywood action thriller about nuclear weapons.
Right: In *Face/Off* (1997) John Travolta (l) and Nicolas Cage (r) are cop and crook who exchange faces and a hail of bullets. Dir: John Woo

3. New Science Fiction

BATTY: I've seen things ... seen things you little people wouldn't believe ... Attack ships on fire off the shoulder of Orion bright as magnesium ... I rode on the back decks of a blinker and watched c-beams glitter in the dark near the Tanhauser Gate. All those moments ... they'll be gone.

Roy Batty (Rutger Hauer), *Blade Runner* (Ridley Scott, 1982)

DAVE:	Open the pod bay doors, HAL.
HAL:	I'm sorry Dave, I'm afraid I can't do that.
DAVE:	What's the problem?
HAL:	I think you know what the problem is just as well as I do.
DAVE:	What are you talking about, HAL?
HAL:	This mission is too important for me to allow you to jeopardize it.

Dr Dave Bowman (Keir Dullea), HAL 9000 (Douglas Rain), *2001: A Space Odyssey* (Stanley Kubrick, 1968)

Until the end of the 1960s science fiction in the cinema had low cultural prestige: it was a genre notorious for cheap special effects conjuring up giant spiders and other improbable monsters, the mutated offspring of scientific experiments gone wrong. If the science fiction of the 1950s and 1960s had any significance, it was as a symptom of the paranoia engendered by the Cold War, yet its nightmares were generally more laughable than disturbing. Stanley Kubrick's *2001: A Space Odyssey* (1968) announced in its very title, with its classical allusion, a more serious purpose. The precise meaning of Kubrick's allegorical excursion into the future has puzzled his fans ever since, but the technical achievements of the film revolutionized the genre, even if, more than thirty years later, when we have already passed the future that Kubrick foresaw, we now take them for granted.

At the heart of science fiction film is a paradox. On the one hand, the films of the last thirty years or so demonstrate the ever-increasing capacity of cinema to imagine and depict new worlds. Kubrick used computers to plot and control the movements of models of spaceships, thereby achieving a new precision and clarity in the process shots. Since the 1980s computers have increasingly been used in the actual generation of the images that appear on the screen. *Tron* (Steven Lisberger, 1982), a Disney production, was the first film with an entire sequence of images produced by a computer. Since then the power of computers has increased hugely, making it possible to generate sequences, indeed whole films, which can approximate, and even equal, the realism of photographic images. As a consequence, science fiction cinema has increasingly not only come to reflect technological improvements but to celebrate them. Like action films in other genres (crime films, war films), science fiction films now centre on elaborate and spectacular sequences designed to show off technology, with narratives and characters pared down to the minimum necessary for narrative coherence.

On the other hand, while these films glory in the power and sophistication of the technology they display, on a thematic level they often reveal profound disquiet about where that technology is leading us. *Westworld* (1973) is an early example. Written and directed by Michael Crichton, it is set in an amusement park which offers customers the opportunity to play out such fantasies as being a Western gunfighter. When the technology goes wrong, the robotic gunman (played by Yul Brynner, star of *The Magnificent Seven*, 1960) begins to shoot in deadly earnest. The aggressive and libidinous desires which the technology unleashes (customers can also have sex with female robots) have disastrous effects. Crichton's work would later form the basis for Steven Spielberg's *Jurassic Park* (1993), another film about an amusement park where technology gets out of control.

For a time at the end of the 1970s it appeared as if misgivings about science and

NEW SCIENCE FICTION

technology had given way to a sunnier view, a sense of wonder at what the future might bring. George Lucas's *Star Wars* (1977) was a cross between the fantasies of J R R Tolkien and science fiction serials from the 1930s such as *Buck Rogers* and *Flash Gordon*. It would be hard to say that technology, or indeed anything at all, is the underlying theme in Lucas's film, in which evil comes from an array of wicked wizards and other figures from comic-book fantasy. What the film did show was what could be achieved by dazzling the audience with state-of-the-art visual and aural effects. To date, according to the Internet Movie Database,[1] *Star Wars* and its four sequels have amassed a staggering $3.5 billion at the world box office, and this does not include video rentals or retail, nor income from the vast array of merchandised products.

In the same year as *Star Wars* Steven Spielberg directed *Close Encounters of the Third Kind* (1977), in which aliens land in the Midwest. In the final thirty minutes of the film, with a bravura display of light and sound, Spielberg achieves a tour de force in the meeting between humans and aliens, creating a sense of awe quite unlike anything previously realized in the cinema. Spielberg's *E.T. The Extra-Terrestrial* (1982) explores a similar theme. A creature from another world takes up residence in the home of a suburban US family, to the delight of its children. As in *Close Encounters*, the alien is benevolent, in contrast to the

<u>Opposite</u>: A dazzling display of light and sound as the aliens arrive creates a sense of awe during the last thirty minutes of *Close Encounters of the Third Kind* (1977).
Dir: Steven Spielberg
<u>Above</u>: Darth Vader (David Prowse) and Obi-Wan Kenobi (Sir Alec Guinness) battle it out with light sabres amid state-of-the-art visual and aural effects in *Star Wars: Episode IV – A New Hope* (1977).
Dir: George Lucas
<u>Right and below right</u>: Loveable alien E.T. and lonely boy Elliott (Henry Thomas) share a special friendship and appeal to the child in all of us in *E.T. The Extra-Terrestrial* (1982).
Dir: Steven Spielberg

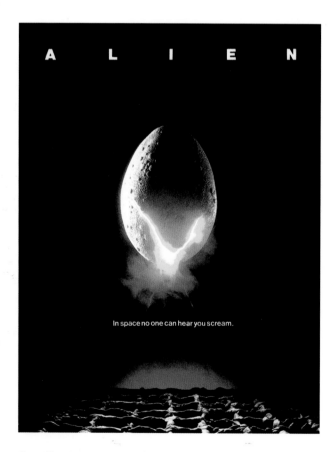

ALIEN

In space no one can hear you scream.

suspicious and aggressive forces of the state. Spielberg's cinema, as has been frequently remarked, often adopts the point of view of the child. While this can at times produce a cinema of arrested development, at his best Spielberg captures a sense of innocent wonder.

In later films Spielberg has succumbed to a darker mood. *Jurassic Park* features some lovely scenes of the genetically-cloned dinosaurs gambolling in the theme park that has been created for them, but it is not long before the technology goes wrong and the dinosaurs run amok. Spielberg's *AI: Artificial Intelligence* (2001) is based on an idea by Stanley Kubrick. Once again a child is at the centre, but this time he is a robot, created as a replacement for bereaved parents. In a dismal conclusion, a new race of ethereal beings find him buried at the bottom of the sea millennia after humans have been wiped out. Neither this nor Spielberg's *Minority Report* (2002) lighten the general gloom with much enjoyment.

Before the 1970s were out, a very different science fiction film arrived. *Alien* (1979), directed by Ridley Scott, combined several currents that were flowing through popular cinema at the time. Ripley is a female crew member on a spaceship, employed in routine work processing minerals. On an unknown planet they detect signs of life. One of the crew members (played by John Hurt) falls ill, and in a brilliantly shocking scene he 'gives birth' to a monster, a creature which has introduced its seed through his mouth and which emerges by bursting through his stomach. The monster is fearsomely aggressive and almost indestructible. Eventually Ripley proves herself to be the strongest of the crew; the last survivor, she ejects the monster from the ship in a final desperate battle.

As well as harking back to the 'creature-features' of the 1950s such as *The Creature from the Black Lagoon* (Jack Arnold, 1954), *Alien* draws on John Carpenter's low-budget *Dark Star* (1974), another film in which a group of discontented space travellers have trouble with an alien on board; Dan O'Bannon was the writer on both films. *Alien* was a huge success (with its tag line, 'In space no one can hear you scream'), and to date there have been three sequels: *Aliens* (James Cameron, 1986), *Alien³* (David Fincher, 1992) and *Alien Resurrection* (Jean-Pierre Jeunet, 1997), all starring Sigourney Weaver as Ripley. In each, the view of the future is dystopian – it is a world in which the social divisions and inequalities of late capitalism have taken a sinister turn. In the first film the crew are dissatisfied with their lot, grumbling about the food, the pay and conditions. Those who do the dirtiest work get the least money. The company that owns the space vehicle has a cynical disregard for the crew's welfare, their only concern being to capture the alien for weapons research, even if this results in the death of their employees. In the final film we discover that the company is now routinely using humans to breed the monsters, and we see the grisly genetic mutations that are the results of previous experiments.

NEW SCIENCE FICTION

It is the presentation of sexuality in the *Alien* films, however, which has most interested commentators. The crew first discover the alien life form by entering a crashed spaceship through an opening whose shape suggests a vagina. As they penetrate into the ship's 'womb' they find some large eggs. John Hurt is in effect raped by a kind of sucker that comes out of the egg and 'impregnates' him. When the resulting creature emerges, its appearance is unmistakably phallic: a kind of penis but with sharp teeth. Yet the creature is always referred to as female. Some critics see it as a representation of the vagina dentata,[2] the ultimate male nightmare; what undoubtedly creates a special kind of horror is that the alien is both male and female, reflecting the monstrosity of overturning normal human sexual difference.

This redeployment of sexual characteristics is reproduced in the figure of Ripley. In the opening film we never learn her first name and, unusually in a film dominated by a female star, Ripley has no romantic involvement. We discover that she has a daughter back on Earth, but in the second film time has advanced fifty-seven years (though Ripley herself has not aged) and her daughter has died in the meantime. She acquires a substitute child in the form of a little girl whom she rescues from the planet where the alien was discovered, and at the end Ripley is again bereaved when this girl dies. In the third film Ripley does have sex with a man, but only briefly and after she has been defeminized by having her head shaved.

Ripley's courage and determination make her the equal of any man. But the films compensate for this gesture towards feminism by dramatizing the disquiet it brings, projecting onto the monster – the phallic female, the 'bitch' as Ripley refers to it – our fears surrounding the upsetting of traditional sex roles. Ultimately Ripley's lack of conventional feminine attributes itself becomes monstrous: in *Alien*[3] Ripley is impregnated by the alien and commits suicide rather than give birth, and in the final instalment she is resurrected as a cyborg, a creature half human and half alien. This time Ripley does give birth to a monster, and describes herself as its mother; only half human, she has ambivalent

Below left: The heroine of *Alien* (1979) is Ripley (Sigourney Weaver). In the first film, though she forms no romantic relationships and is strong enough to defeat the monster, she is on occasion sexualized by her clothes.

Dir: Ridley Scott
Below right: In the second film, *Aliens* (1986), although time has advanced fifty-seven years, Ripley shows no sign of ageing as she rescues a little girl, Newt (Carrie Henn).
Dir: James Cameron

NEW SCIENCE FICTION

RIPLEY: Okay. It's important to understand this organism's life cycle. It's actually two creatures. The first form hatches from a spore ... a sort of large egg, and attaches itself to its victim. Then it injects an embryo, detaches and dies. It's essentially a walking sex organ. The ...

HUDSON: Sounds like you, Hicks.

RIPLEY: The embryo, the second form, hosts in the victim's body for several hours. Gestating. Then it ... then it ... emerges. Moults. Grows rapidly ...

VASQUEZ: I only need to know one thing.

RIPLEY: Yes?

VASQUEZ: Where they are.

Ripley (Sigourney Weaver), Private Hudson (Bill Paxton), Private Vasquez (Jenette Goldstein), Aliens (James Cameron, 1986).

feelings towards the race of aliens, which by the end of the film are themselves mutating to take on an appearance more like humans.

Though the four *Alien* films are of uneven quality, taken together they constitute a rich cluster of cultural meanings. They have also been read as an allegory about the AIDS virus, a seemingly unstoppable disease that threatens humanity's existence, and which itself has been the focus of sexual paranoia. Dangerous diseases are no stranger to science fiction. *The Andromeda Strain* (Robert Wise, 1970), also based on a Michael Crichton story, worried away at the implications of a disease for which there was no cure, and more recently *Outbreak* (Wolfgang Petersen, 1995) had a similar theme. What seems to give the *Alien* films a particular connection to AIDS is the sexual dimension. AIDS is most notoriously spread by sexual contact, and the aliens reproduce by implanting themselves in human bodies through a deadly kind of intercourse.

Like many science fiction films, the *Alien* series explores the difference between the human and the non-human, especially between humanity and the machine.[3] In each film one of the characters is an android, a machine whose outward appearance is human. In the first, the android Ash (played by Ian Holm) is cold and distant, and Ripley is right to be suspicious of him when he proves to be working for the company, trying to get the alien back to Earth even at the cost of the crew's lives. In *Aliens* there is another android, Bishop, of whom Ripley is again suspicious, but this time he proves benevolent. Though partly destroyed, Bishop survives in *Alien³* and is again useful. In *Alien Resurrection* the android is played by Winona Ryder and is once more benevolent, at one point complimented by Ripley, with whom she forms an alliance, for being more humane than the humans.

The figure of the android raises fundamental questions, ones which have continually concerned science fiction cinema. Is the human body itself a kind of machine? If not, what makes it different? Are machines evolving to the point where they can rival human

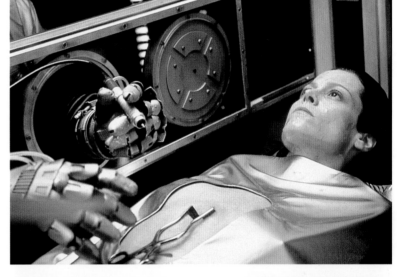

Above: In the third film, *Alien³* (1992), Ripley is desexualized, her head shaved and is impregnated by the alien. She commits suicide rather than give birth.
Dir: David Fincher
Above right and right: In the last film, *Alien Resurrection* (1997),

Ripley is resurrected by the humans as a cyborg. Only as half-human does she finally give birth to an alien. The android she befriends, played by Winona Ryder (r), turns out to be more humane than the humans.
Dir: Jean-Pierre Jeunet

Previous pages: In
Blade Runner (1982) the
reserved and distant
Deckard (Harrison Ford)
searches for runaway
androids. But is he
perhaps an android
himself?
Above: Futuristic flying
vehicles journey
through the fog of the
dingy, dystopian city in
Blade Runner (1982).
This vision of the future

is in complete contrast
to the clean and
ordered cities
portrayed in earlier
science fiction films.
Dir: Ridley Scott
Opposite: Michael
Keaton as Batman and
Jack Nicholson as the
Joker in *Batman* (1989),
another dark vision of
the city of the future.
Dir: Tim Burton

capabilities? The robot that runs amok is a recurring figure, dramatizing the fear that technology may not only escape our control but may eventually replace us. Such questions are at the heart of *Blade Runner* (1982), directed by Ridley Scott. Harrison Ford plays Deckard, whose job it is to track down runaway androids, or 'replicants'. To the outward eye they are indistinguishable from humans. Their essential difference – that they have no empathy, no emotions for others – appears in certain cases, particularly that of Roy Batty (Rutger Hauer), to be on the point of being erased. Near the end of the film Batty seems to take pity on Deckard and holds back from killing him. Deckard himself, by contrast, is a man who shows little emotion; we are left with the tantalizing thought that he too may be a replicant. The film explores the implications not only of machines that are like men but also of men who have become like machines – who experience what the postmodern theorist Fredric Jameson calls the 'waning of affect', the loss of our ability to truly feel, which he sees as a symptom of contemporary civilization.[4]

Blade Runner was a landmark not only for the philosophical implications of its narrative but also for the brilliance of its design. Early science fiction films such as *Metropolis* (Fritz Lang, 1926) and *Things to Come* (William Cameron Menzies, 1936) had presented a vision of future cities as being clean, functional and high-tech, even if below the surface all was not well. In *Blade Runner* the city (based on Los Angeles) is grimy and dark, its streets crowded and dangerous. Just as *Alien* was a hybrid of horror and science fiction, so *Blade Runner* incorporates elements of film noir in its visual atmospherics. Such a vision also inspired Tim Burton's *Batman* (1989), in which the masked crusader has to venture down streets in the mythical Gotham City as mean as any traversed by Philip Marlowe. John Carpenter's *Escape from New York* (1981) presents a similarly nightmarish vision of the dark cities of the future.

Androids reappear in two films directed by James Cameron, *The Terminator* (1984) and *Terminator 2: Judgment Day* (1991). In the first, Arnold Schwarzenegger is a cyborg, sent back from a future in which machines have achieved almost complete domination, in order to kill Sarah, the mother of a man who is leading a revolt. His mission is to rearrange the past to ensure the final victory of machines. The mission fails, but in the sequel 'Arnie' is reborn as another cyborg; this time he has been sent back by the humans in order to protect Sarah and her son against a still more powerful machine which has been programmed to finish the job. As Sean French has pointed out, the plot of the second film is a paradox.[5] The cyborg actually prevents the nuclear war which has led to the supremacy of machines; there is therefore no revolt and so no human leader to be protected; the cyborg thus renders both himself and his mission redundant.

The Special Effects Hit
Terminator 2: Judgment Day (1991)
Dir: James Cameron

For once audiences were not left disappointed when *Terminator 2: Judgment Day*, the big budget sequel to the original 1984 film *The Terminator*, was released. This exciting Sci Fi film follows the fortunes of Sarah Connor (Linda Hamilton) who is being pursued by a Terminator sent back in time to kill both her and her son, who will lead the rebellion against Skynet, the computer waging war against the humans. Only Sarah knows about the existence of the Terminators and she is in a state mental hospital. But Sarah's son, John (Edward Furlong), has sent back a re-programmed friendly T-800 cyborg (Arnold Schwarzenegger) from the future, to stop the evil T-1000 (Robert Patrick) from killing the young John and his mother. In *T2* Arnie is no longer a bad Terminator. He is now T-800 – the protector up against the more deadly threat from the liquid metal shape-changing T-1000 super cyborg.

With a massive budget reportedly of $80–100 million at his disposal, writer/director James Cameron exploited this battle of the cyborgs to the full with a new generation of special effects. The fear experienced while being pursued, which made the first film so exciting, is intensified with the introduction of these new dangerous threats to the heroes' survival.

It was the biggest box office success of 1991, taking over $514 million worldwide and was awarded an Oscar for Visual Effects and for Make-up.

Country of Origin: USA
Production Company: Carolco Pictures/ Le Studio Canal +/ Lightstorm Entertainment/ Pacific Western
Running Time: 137 mins

Producer: Joseph Nemec III
Writers: James Cameron, William Wisher
Photography: Adam Greenberg
Music: Brad Fiedel
Editors: Richard A Harris, Mark Goldblatt, Conrad Buff
Production Designer: Joseph Nemec III
Special Effects: Fantasy II Film Effects, Industrial Light and Magic

The Terminator (T-800 Model 101): Arnold Schwarzenegger
Sarah Connor/Narrator: Linda Hamilton
John Connor: Edward Furlong
The T-1000: Robert Patrick
Dr Peter Silberman: Earl Boen

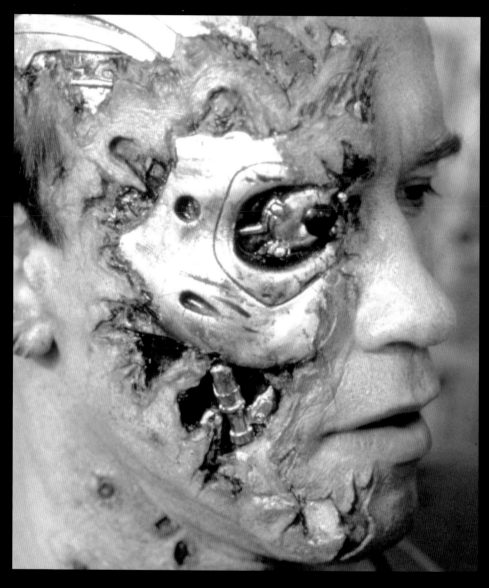

Above left: Android
Arnie: Arnold
Schwarzenegger
reveals his unique
features as The
Terminator.
Far left: Some running
repairs are required as
Arnie tries to outwit his
pursuer, the T-1000.
Left: A friendly T-800
Arnie shoots his way
out of trouble.

Above: Stunning special
effects allow the evil
Terminator T-1000
(Robert Patrick) to
shape-shift his way out
of a tight spot. But here,
the special effects
create his spectacular
death.
Right: The real T-1000:
no longer using the
bodies of the dead as a
disguise.

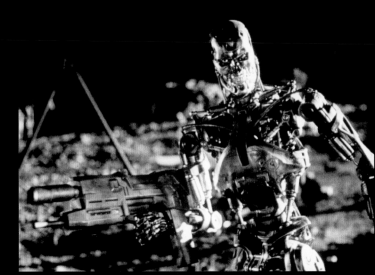

Previous pages: Eye-catching special effects made *The Matrix* (1999) a huge hit. Keanu Reeves as computer hacker Neo 'flies' towards his adversary Agent Smith (Hugo Weaving).
Dir: Andy and Larry Wachowski

MORTON: RoboCop, what are your prime directives?
ROBOCOP: Serve the public trust. Uphold the law.
           Protect the innocent.
MORTON: Very good.

Robert Morton (Miguel Ferrer), RoboCop (Peter Weller), *RoboCop* (Paul Verhoeven, 1987)

Above: *RoboCop* (1987), with its half-human, half-robot policeman played by Peter Weller, turns on the question of what is the difference between men and machines.
Dir: Paul Verhoeven

Right: In *Starship Troopers* (1997) director Paul Verhoeven presents the human soldiers as near-Fascists. The bugs, though terrifying, turn out to have feelings too.
Dir: Paul Verhoeven

In the first film the Terminator is terrifying because of his mechanical strength and durability. He is superior to humans both because of his power and because he is not constrained by emotion. In *Terminator 2: Judgment Day* the new cyborg, known as T-1000, is even more frightening. It has the ability to assume the shape and properties of anything it comes into contact with. Thus it can appear as a human, but also take the shape of a knife or a crowbar. The improvement in special effects technology between 1984 and 1991 is graphically demonstrated as we see the T-1000 morphing before our very eyes. What is truly disturbing is not just its implacable urge to kill, but the fact that it seems to have no essence, no real identity, nothing that can be grasped.

If in the future machines become like humans, humans may become like machines. That is the real danger. In *Terminator 2: Judgment Day*, Sarah has become transformed from the rather ditzy female of the first film. Traumatized by her experiences, she has grown a carapace over her emotions, dehumanized herself to the point that she has been incarcerated as mentally ill. By the end her human emotions have been rekindled as she fights passionately to save her son.

Three films directed by Paul Verhoeven provide further reflection on the human/non-human divide. In *RoboCop* (1987) policing in Detroit has been handed over to a private company, which is intent on replacing cops with robots. Murphy is a policeman who has been deliberately exposed to danger and killed. He is then reconstructed as a cyborg, half man, half armoured machine programmed to do the bidding of the company. Fortunately, the technology is flawed; Murphy's memories of his past life resurface and his humanity reasserts itself, albeit in his mechanical body. In *Total Recall* (1990) Arnold Schwarzenegger is Quaid, a security guard on Mars who has had artificial memories implanted in his brain in order to further the schemes of the evil Cohaagen. Strictly speaking Quaid is not a cyborg, though the wooden style of Schwarzenegger's acting, his association with *The Terminator* and the fact that there is something unnatural about the star's pumped-up body, imparts something of the non-human to his character.

In these films human identity is shifting and uncertain. Is Murphy in essence a man or a robot? If Quaid has false memories, who exactly is he, really? As he himself cries in despair, 'If I'm not me, who the hell am I?' In Verhoeven's subtle and subversive *Starship Troopers* (1997), humanity is becoming dehumanized. Earth is fighting a war against a race of monstrous insects. The aliens have knife-like incisors capable of dismembering a man in seconds and Verhoeven does not stint in providing satisfyingly violent battles against them. But the human society he depicts is one which appears close to Fascism. Its clean-cut soldiers are devoid of any individuality, their massed ranks filmed in a style that evokes the Nazi rallies at Nuremberg. In a bizarre finale the huge, grossly fat 'queen' which rules the insects is captured; the tears of the flabby blob are oddly affecting, contrasting with the triumphalism of the storm-troopers from Earth.

Science fiction films such as Verhoeven's have often been vehicles for social commentary, offering a blueprint for the future, or more often an awful warning. But advances in film technology have also allowed unprecedented opportunities for enjoyable displays of bravura effects, as in Tim Burton's *Mars Attacks!* (1996), a delirious pastiche of 1950s science fiction, and Barry Sonnenfeld's *Men in Black* (1997), starring Tommy Lee Jones and Will Smith as a couple of government agents hunting down a bizarre collection of

illegal aliens. Science fiction films have been among the most successful of all Hollywood films (they need to be, given what is spent on their special effects), and *Men in Black* at present stands in eighth place in *Variety*'s list of 'top sci-fi grossers', making over $250 million in the US market alone. Two of the *Star Wars* films occupy the first two places, with Spielberg's *E.T.* and *Jurassic Park* next.

Another film that claims a place in this list is *Independence Day* (Roland Emmerich, 1996), ranked sixth making over $300 million. It is a film of no great subtlety or originality. An alien invasion threatens Earth but is finally defeated by the US Air Force launching nuclear weapons against the aliens' spacecraft. Recruited into the struggle are a black pilot (Will Smith) and a Jewish scientist (Jeff Goldblum), thus testifying to the multiculturalism that gives the United States its right to assume moral leadership of the world, in whose name it acts to defeat the aliens – on the fourth of July! Chauvinism in the United States has rarely been so openly paraded. As Michael Rogin has argued, the film also manages to pick up some of its agenda from action and war genres.[6] Like Rambo, one of the pilots in *Independence Day* is a Vietnam veteran, still nursing the bitter taste of defeat. Victory over the aliens offers a healing of the wounds.

For a time, with the science fiction films of Steven Spielberg, Ridley Scott, James Cameron and Paul Verhoeven, the genre was intellectually the most vital in Hollywood. But just as it used to be thought that dinosaurs became extinct because their bodies outgrew their brains, so something similar seems to be happening to science fiction films, which are becoming ever more elaborate, expensive and empty-headed. *The Matrix* (Andy and Larry Wachowski, 1999) employs state-of-the-art special effects in its presentation of a virtual reality world, but its philosophical ideas are flimsy and pretentious, and like so many the film collapses into a series of routine gunfights. Is it too much to hope that the verve and ingenuity that are devoted to special effects might once more also be applied to a film's conceptual framework?

Below: Agent J (Will Smith) and Secret Agent K (Tommy Lee Jones) deal with some extra-terrestrials in the Sci Fi comedy *Men in Black* (1997). Based on a 1980s comic strip, K's task is to control alien activity on Earth while saving the planet from destruction.
Dir: Barry Sonnenfeld

Overleaf:
Independence Day (1996), in which the menace of an alien spaceship threatened the world, was an unabashed celebration of US nationalism, though directed by a German.
Dir: Roland Emmerich

4. Horror

DR LECTER: You're sooo ambitious, aren't you ...? You know what you look like to me, with your good bag and your cheap shoes? You look like a rube. A well-scrubbed, hustling rube with a little taste ... Good nutrition has given you some length of bone, but you're not more than one generation from poor white trash, are you – Officer Starling ...? That accent you're trying so desperately to shed – pure West Virginia. What was your father, dear? Was he a coal miner? Did he stink of the lamp ...? And oh, how quickly the boys found you! All those tedious, sticky fumblings, in the back seats of cars, while you could only dream of getting out. Getting anywhere – yes? Getting all the way – to the F ... B ... I.

Dr Hannibal Lecter (Anthony Hopkins), Clarice Starling (Jodie Foster), *The Silence of the Lambs* (Jonathan Demme, 1991)

Like science fiction, horror had traditionally been regarded as a low-status genre. Even the Universal pictures of the 1930s such as *Dracula* (Tod Browning, 1931) and *Frankenstein* (James Whale, 1931), now considered classics, were made with second-rank stars and small budgets by a studio near the bottom of the Hollywood pecking order. In the 1950s and 1960s horror was kept alive by Roger Corman's Edgar Allan Poe adaptations, such as *The Tomb of Ligeia* (1964) and *The Masque of the Red Death* (1964), and by the Hammer studio in England, for whom Terence Fisher directed *The Curse of Frankenstein* (1957) and many more. Although they benefited from Technicolor and skilled art direction, these films too were cheaply made, without important stars.

In 1968 two films set horror on a different course. George Romero's *Night of the Living Dead*, shot in black and white, was made even more cheaply than Corman's films. But instead of the nineteenth-century period settings which Corman and Hammer favoured, Romero's film was set in the present day. A small group find themselves besieged in a lonely farmhouse by hordes of flesh-eating zombies. What is remarkable, besides the inventiveness and energy of Romero's direction, is the unrelieved pessimism of the film. Previously, evil had been defeated by human courage and ingenuity or by divine intervention. In Romero's film there is no salvation. At the end, a black man, the most admirable character among the embattled group, is stupidly shot by rescuers.

Roman Polanski's *Rosemary's Baby* is a story of satanic possession. Mia Farrow plays a young woman who fears she has been impregnated by the devil. Polanski skilfully sustains our uncertainty about whether her fears are merely a fantasy. It is a classy production, well acted by an impressive cast. Unlike *Night of the Living Dead* there is little graphic violence; instead, Polanski conjures up an atmosphere of strangeness and menace.

Rosemary's Baby showed that there was a market for high-class horror, which could break out from the drive-in theatres into the mainstream. William Friedkin's *The Exorcist* (1973), made for a major studio, mined the same seam of demonic possession, but this time

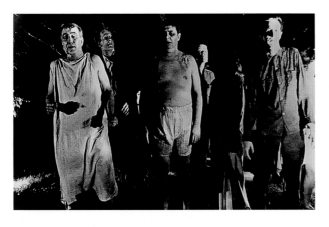

Opposite: Mia Farrow
helped give *Rosemary's
Baby* (1968) more class
than was usual in the
horror film.
Dir: Roman Polanski
Above: *Night of the
Living Dead* (1968)
had a cast of relative
unknowns, low
production values and
was shot in black and
white. But it had radical
implications for the
horror genre.
Dir: George Romero
Right and overleaf: Like
Rosemary's Baby, *The
Exorcist* (1973) was a
story of demonic
possession, but made
extensive use of special
effects in order to
visualize the abnormal
behaviour of its young
heroine (Linda Blair).
Dir: William Friedkin

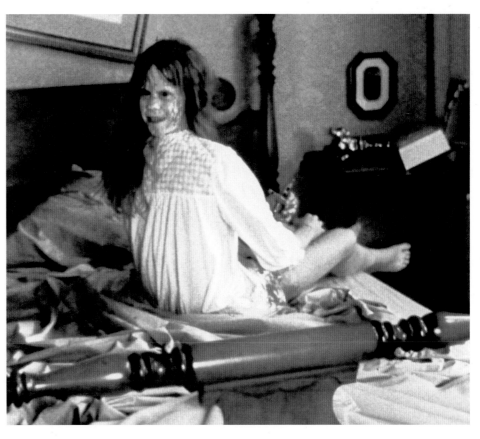

PSYCHIATRIST:	If I ask him to tell me, will you let him answer?
REGAN:	No.
PSYCHIATRIST:	Why not?
REGAN:	I'm afraid.
PSYCHIATRIST:	If he talks to me, I think he'll leave you. Do you want him to leave you?
REGAN:	Yes.

Psychiatrist (Arthur Storch), Regan MacNeil (Linda Blair), *The Exorcist* (William Friedkin, 1973)

there was plenty of explicit violence. In his story of the attempted exorcism of a young woman, Friedkin makes use of recent advances in special effects techniques: the main character levitates and walks upside down like a crab, and at one point her head revolves through 360 degrees. The film was a huge success and attracted a cult following, leading to a reissue in 1999.

But it was *Night of the Living Dead* which was to have more immediate consequences for the development of the genre. Romero jettisoned the whole baggage of traditional horror: the haunted castle, the moonlight and the sinister aristocratic figures. He created a home-grown variety, one that took place in suburban locations, the characters ordinary Americans; his sequel *Dawn of the Dead* (1979) was set in a vast shopping mall, and was read by some as a critique of consumerism. Nowhere is more American than Texas, and in 1974 Tobe Hooper's *The Texas Chain Saw Massacre* took up where Romero had left off. A party of young people chance upon a dysfunctional family who had once worked in a slaughterhouse; laid off as a result of mechanization, they now take up their trade in earnest, laying waste to the youngsters with chain saws. One of them, Leatherface, wears a mask of human skin, and the family maintains a grisly museum of human body parts grotesquely decorated like modernist sculpture, an allusion to the infamous case of Ed Gein, an elderly Wisconsin farmer arrested in 1957 when his house proved to be a repository of human remains.

The film has touches of black humour. Sally, the only victim left alive, escapes but is captured again. Grandfather, in appearance a living corpse, is revived by a taste of her blood and is encouraged by the rest of the family to beat her brains out, but farcically cannot muster strength to raise the hammer. Though we never see it penetrate a victim's flesh, the whirring chain saw is undeniably disturbing and the film was a box office hit, paving the way for sequels and a cycle of so-called 'slasher' films. Its centrality to the serial killer tradition is confirmed in *American Psycho* (Mary Harron, 2000), an elegant and witty film of Bret Easton Ellis's novel about a wealthy young Wall Street stockbroker and multiple murderer. The hero works out to a videotape of *The Texas Chain Saw Massacre*, does some chain-saw killing himself and amuses his friends by quoting Ed Gein to the effect that when he sees a pretty girl part of him wants to take her out and treat her nice, and part of him is thinking what her head would look like on a stick.

Some critics have made a distinction between slasher films and 'stalker' films, the latter finding their definitive form in John Carpenter's *Halloween* of 1978. It is, perhaps, a distinction without a difference. All of them can trace their origin back to Alfred Hitchcock's *Psycho* (1960), a film which also drew on the Ed Gein story (Norman Bates, like Gein, has an unhealthy interest in taxidermy). The essence is the stalking and murder of

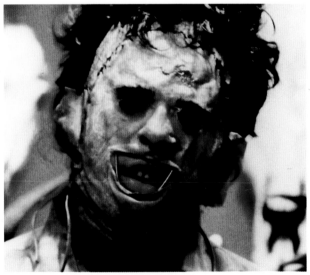

Opposite: *American Psycho* (2000), set among the world of Manhattan yuppies, is a more sophisticated version of the serial killer theme. Christian Bale is the suave but demented hero. Dir: Mary Harron
Above left and right:

The Texas Chain Saw Massacre (1974) helped establish the cycle of low-budget slasher films with teenage victims. Leatherface (Gunnar Hansen) wears a mask evocative of Alfred Hitchcock's *Psycho* (1960). Dir: Tobe Hooper

attractive young people by a homicidal maniac, usually in the confined setting of a house, a summer camp or a small town. The plot frequently hangs on some incidence of cruelty or mental disturbance in the past which re-surfaces, the narrative structure thus replicating that 'return of the repressed' which Freudian critics have identified as fundamental to the genre. Typically the weapons used to despatch the victims are knives, hooks or other sharp implements, never guns; the phallic implications are often explicit. Though victims may be both male and female, almost invariably the final survivor is a young woman, more sensible than the others, who manages to defeat or at least escape the predator. Authority, whether parents or police, is usually sceptical and ineffectual.

As in other contemporary genres, seriality is built-in. *The Texas Chain Saw Massacre* has so far produced two sequels and *Halloween* has had five. Other franchises include *Friday the 13th* (Sean S Cunningham, 1980), now up to ten editions, and *A Nightmare on Elm Street* (Wes Craven, 1984), with six sequels. Such generic stability is remarkable, and an indication that the structure of these films struck a chord with audiences. The conventional view is that they crudely exploit man's inhumanity to man (and woman), that they uncover savage instincts best left buried deep in our psyches. The more intellectual moral guardians have linked the films' violence to the brutality of the Vietnam War. Such films have also been read as an attack on the cosy nuclear family so dear to the heart of Hollywood. In *Night of the Living Dead* a child murders and eats her mother; critic Robin Wood has gone so far as to see the recurrent theme of cannibalism as a critique of the entire social system, since cannibalism is 'the logical end of human relations under capitalism', a statement in which Wood's political zeal perhaps gets the better of his critical judgement.[1]

Although some horror films do have a level of general social commentary, it is evident enough that most of these films are fundamentally about sex. Because the slasher is almost invariably a man, it is tempting for feminists to see these films as crude expressions of male hostility towards women, a backlash against the women's movement of the 1960s. But critics of horror like to dig deeper. Not surprisingly, Freudian psychoanalysis has been the privileged tool of analysis.

The most sustained investigation of the slasher cycle has been made by Carol Clover. Her book, forthrightly titled *Men, Women and Chain Saws*, identifies three related sub-genres: the slasher film proper, as described above; the demonic possession film, whose modern prototype is *Rosemary's Baby*, other notable examples being *Don't Look Now* (Nicolas Roeg, 1973), *Carrie* (Brian De Palma, 1976), *The Omen* (Richard Donner, 1976), *The Shining* (Stanley Kubrick, 1980) and *Poltergeist* (Tobe Hooper, 1982); and the rape-revenge film, examples of which are *Lipstick* (Lamont Johnson, 1976), *I Spit on Your Grave* (Meir Zarchi,

MARGE: You're not falling asleep are you?
            You could drown, you know.
NANCY: Mother, for petesakes.
MARGE: It happens all the time. I've got some
            warm milk all ready for you. Why don't
            you jump into bed? I'm gonna turn on
            your electric blanket, too. C'mon, now.
NANCY: Warm milk. Gross.
NANCY (cont.): One, two, Freddy's coming for you, three
            four, better lock your door, five six grab
            your crucifix, seven eight gonna stay up
            late, nine ten, never sleep again ...

Marge Thompson (Ronee Blakley), Nancy
Thompson (Heather Langenkamp), *A Nightmare
on Elm Street* (Wes Craven, 1984).

Top: Tony Moran as the escaped mental patient Michael Myers, wielding his phallic knife in *Halloween* (1978). Dir: John Carpenter
Above: Robert Englund as Freddy Krueger, the dreamworld killer in *A Nightmare on Elm Street* (1984).
Right: Heather Langenkamp as Nancy is threatened in the bath by Freddy's razor-sharp hand in *A Nightmare on Elm Street* (1984). Dir: Wes Craven

HORROR

Above: Michael Rooker as a killer with no inner life, in *Henry: Portrait of a Serial Killer* (1986). Drifting from city to city, no one knows he is a seemingly motiveless mass murderer. That is, until he lets his flatmate and fellow ex-con Otis (Tom Towles) in on his secret.
Dir: John McNaughton

1978) and *Ms .45* (Abel Ferrara, 1981).[2] Clover's argument is that in all these films the distinction between male and female is elided, and that to see them as merely affirmations of society's misogyny is a fundamental misreading. In the case of the slasher film, Clover believes that the audience is predominantly male (in fact, this seems doubtful; there is plenty of evidence that young women attend these films in large numbers), and that their viewing experience is an example of what Freud calls 'female masochism', a response in which males place themselves in a 'female' position and indulge their fear of being beaten, castrated or penetrated. (In *I Spit on Your Grave*, for example, the heroine cuts off the penis of one of the rapists as they take a bath together.)

Clover also sees the role of the Final Girl, the one who stands up against the killer, as crucial. Not only does she adopt a traditionally 'male' role by fighting back, but she is often represented as androgynous, slightly masculinized. In *Friday the 13th* Alice, the crop-haired lone survivor who cuts off the killer's head at the end, does not have sex, unlike her female companions, and avoids disrobing during a game of strip Monopoly. In *A Nightmare on Elm Street* Nancy (Heather Langenkamp) is rather dumpy, less glamorous and blonde than her friend Tina (Amanda Wyss), and unlike Tina she does not have sex with her boyfriend (promiscuity is invariably punished). At the end Nancy constructs a system of elaborate booby-traps to ensnare the monster Freddy Krueger, with no help from her boyfriend who keeps falling asleep.

Though the concept of the serial killer did not become popularized until the mid-1970s (*Psycho* is a pioneering film), by the 1980s it had become such a staple of horror that the commission of a single murder was hardly a worthy subject. In this plethora of multiple murderers, one film stood out. *Henry: Portrait of a Serial Killer* (1986), directed by John McNaughton, has the seeming objectivity of a documentary, yet it never delivers the coherent portrait of its protagonist that the title promises. Henry commits a series of murders, some in the course of robberies, some without any seeming motive, but he has

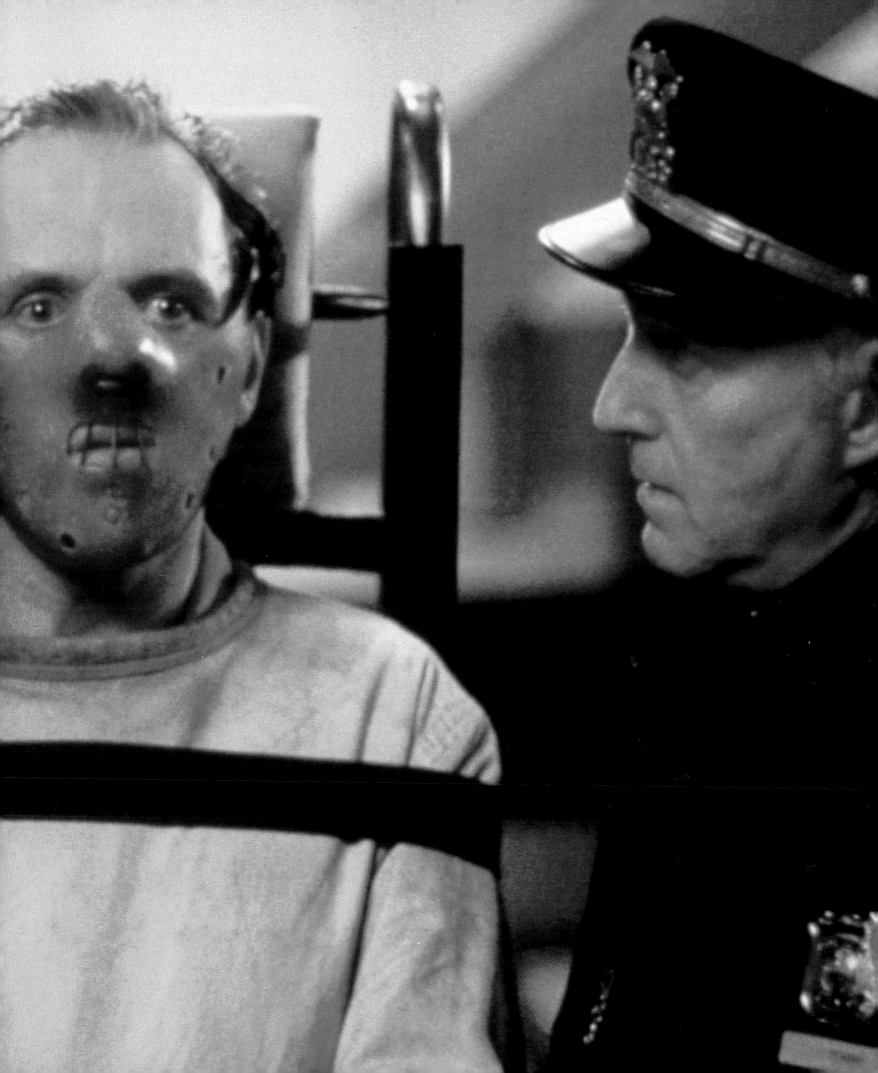

Previous pages:
Anthony Hopkins as
the charismatic killer
Hannibal Lecter,
imprisoned in his
sinister, rat-like mask,
in *The Silence of the
Lambs* (1991).
Dir: Jonathan Demme
Below: Marion Crane
(Janet Leigh) is murdered in the
shower in *Psycho* (1960).
Dir: Alfred Hitchcock
Right, from top: Kate
Miller (Angie Dickinson)
fantasizes an
encounter in the
shower with a stranger
in *Dressed to Kill* (1980).
Dir: Brian De Palma

no inner life. At one point he recounts a tale of childhood abuse which would seem to explain his life, yet the story of how he killed his abusive mother is inconsistent, since at different times he claims to have beaten or stabbed or shot her to death. Some of the murders have a grisly humour to them (an unpleasant purveyor of television sets is electrocuted when his head is forced into one), but other murders are shocking in their graphic violence, particularly the killing of his flatmate Otis, who is stabbed in the eye before Henry cuts off his head. The film ultimately resists any explanation of Henry's actions, and, in a strategy that is more art-house than Hollywood, rejects the satisfaction of closure; after killing Otis's sister Becky, we assume with a razor, Henry dumps her body by the road and drives off. Cue end credits.

Less interesting from a purely aesthetic point of view, Spike Lee's *Summer of Sam* (1999) has its own particular take on the serial killer. It is set in 1977 and David Berkowitz, dubbed 'Son of Sam', is terrorizing New York with his murders of courting couples. We learn almost nothing of the killer himself, but lots about the vigilante hysteria that the killings engender in the hot city streets. Lee's central character, a foul-mouthed young Italian misogynist who obsessively cheats on his new wife, is thoroughly repellent; he, unfortunately, narrowly escapes being a victim. The film is a convincing depiction of a city at the end of its tether.

More central to the development of the serial killer story was *The Silence of the Lambs* (1991), directed by Jonathan Demme. Jodie Foster is an FBI operative who tries to recruit the jailed multiple murderer Hannibal Lecter into the search for another serial killer. The film can be read as a study of both sexual and class difference: Foster's character is not only a woman but is of lower class origins, whereas Lecter is cultivated and charming. But it was Anthony Hopkins's bravura performance as the cannibalistic Lecter that mesmerized audiences, creating a genuinely chilling monster. The sequel *Hannibal* (2001), based on a later novel in Thomas Harris's sequence, was directed by Ridley Scott, but despite some frissons, it dissipated the horror of the original by tipping over into camp. A more worthy successor in the serial killer tradition was David Fincher's *Se7en* (1995), in which a novice detective (Brad Pitt) is teamed with an older and wiser cop (Morgan Freeman) to solve a series of murders linked to the seven deadly sins. The conclusion, in which the killer makes his final attack personal, is a truly horrifying moment.

Brian De Palma's early career worked systematically through the horror sub-genres, including the slasher film. *Sisters* (1973), like *Carrie* (1976), is a story of possession, while *Phantom of the Paradise* (1974) is a reworking of the classic *Phantom of the Opera* (Rupert Julian, 1925). *Obsession* (1976) owes much to Hitchcock's *Vertigo* (1958) in a story about a dead wife apparently restored to life, and in *The Fury* (1978) a young man has devastating

Above: Bebe Neuwirth (Gloria) and John Leguizamo as the foul-mouthed Vinnie read about the latest killings in *Summer of Sam* (1999).
Dir: Spike Lee
Right: Morgan Freeman as Lieutenant William

Somerset expounds on the seven deadly sins in *Se7en* (1995).
Overleaf: Morgan Freeman and Brad Pitt as Detective David Mills try to make sense of the killer's motives in *Se7en* (1995).
Dir: David Fincher

psychic powers. *Dressed to Kill* (1980) is another Hitchcock borrowing, this time from *Psycho* (a male serial killer dresses as a woman; there is a murder in the shower), and *Body Double* (1984) is a slasher film which foregrounds the theme of voyeurism in a story about an actor sacked from a horror film because of his fear of being buried alive, who witnesses the murder of an attractive young woman.

Carrie can be read in two ways. The heroine is a young woman on the brink of sexual maturity. At the beginning of menstruation, she starts to exhibit symptoms of demonic possession and acquires the power of telekinesis, which eventually breaks out in vengeful pyrotechnic attacks against those who bully her at school. Far from aiding her transition to womanhood, Carrie's mother is a bitter, sexually repressed puritan who does her best to deny Carrie a normal sexual development. Thus the film can be read as being about how if sex is denied it returns in a monstrous form. Or does the film present female sexuality as in itself monstrous? Carrie takes a shower just as her first period is beginning. Her horror at the blood emerging between her legs (her mother has not prepared her for this event) could be read as the response of the male spectator to this manifestation of the natural female body; as Freudians might say, a reaction to the female 'wound' which threatens him with castration.

Like De Palma, David Cronenberg has been both attacked and defended by film critics. Some see his films as an expression of fundamental disgust at the human body, particularly in its sexual functions. Others see the films as social critiques. In his early shocker, *Shivers* (1975), parasites invade human bodies, turning their victims into sex-crazed monsters. In one scene, horror icon Barbara Steele is lying in her bath when a parasite, an unpleasant turd-like object, swims between her legs and enters through her vagina. In *Rabid* (1977), Marilyn Chambers develops a growth like a penis in her armpit, with which she penetrates people and sucks their blood. In both films sexual desire is a kind of infection which drives people mad. In *Videodrome* (1983) there is a similar obsession with orifices, this time married to a wide-ranging if not always coherent critique of the media. James Woods plays an unscrupulous television executive looking for sensational content for his channel, whose mind is taken over by a sinister new form of television. As a result he develops a vagina-like opening in his stomach into which videotapes can be inserted. The media are also a target in *The Fly* (1986), in which scientist Jeff Goldblum gets his genes entangled with a fly and mutates into a monster. Geena Davis is a reporter who falls for him and is encouraged to exploit the story by her venal and cynical editor. The later stages of the hero's transformation are appropriately disgusting, and Cronenberg's obsession with orifices and penetration is evident in Davis's dream, in which she gives birth to a giant maggot. Rarely for this director's work, some emotion is generated by Davis, who feels genuine pity for the mutant, despite the rampant male egoism Goldblum exhibits in the early stages of his condition, including increased libido. Once again sex appears to be a pathological symptom.

Cronenberg's *Dead Ringers* (1988) has an ingenious plot in which identical twins, both gynaecologists played by Jeremy Irons, are each having an affair with an actress (Geneviève

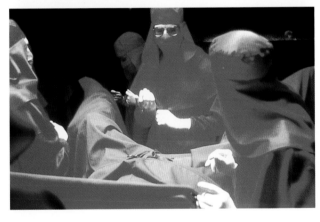

Opposite: Sissy Spacek turns her telekinetic powers on to her tormentors at the high school prom, with bloody results in *Carrie* (1976), a study of teenage sexual disturbance.
Dir: Brian De Palma

Top: James Woods and Deborah Harry (on TV screen) in the futuristic *Videodrome* (1983).
Dir: David Cronenberg
Above and right: Jeremy Irons plays twin gynaecologists in *Dead Ringers* (1988).
Dir: David Cronenberg

Horror meets Science Fiction
The Fly (1986)
Dir: David Cronenberg

Country of Origin: USA
Production Company:
Brooksfilms
Running Time: 95 mins

Producer: Stuart Cornfeld
Writers: Charles Edward
Pogue, David Cronenberg
Photography: Mark Irwin
Music: Howard Shore
Editor: Ronald Sanders
Production Designer:
Carol Spier
The Fly was created
and designed by Chris
Walas, Inc.

Seth Brundle: Jeff Goldblum
Veronica Quaife: Geena
Davis
Stathis Borans: John Getz
Tawny: Joy Boushel

David Cronenberg's version of *The Fly* has little in common with Kurt Neumann's 1958 film of the same title, one of the cheaply made 'creature-features' of the 1950s. Instead, it reveals many of the director's obsessions. Jeff Goldblum is Seth, a scientist who is working on 'teleporting', a means of transporting objects through space. Geena Davis is Veronica, a magazine writer who becomes interested in his work, and in him. They start an affair, but Seth believes Veronica is still seeing her former lover. In a rage he tries to teleport himself, and his genes become entangled with a fly that gets into the machine. Slowly Seth takes on the features of an insect.

As in other Cronenberg films, sexuality is seen as a dangerous force that leads to disaster. Seth cannot get his machine to transport living creatures until he has experienced the delights of sex with Veronica, but then almost immediately his jealousy leads to the genetic catastrophe. As Seth grows more like a fly he develops a raging libido; the more physically repulsive he is, the more he wants sex.

Like many successful films of the 1980s, *The Fly* is a hybrid, fusing elements of both horror and science fiction. Whereas the plot (technology gone wrong) is from the latter genre, the elements of fear and disgust with the human body are traditional to horror. Both genres, as this film well exemplifies, benefited enormously from the increasing sophistication of contemporary special effects techniques, and the make-up skills of Chris Walas and Stephen Dupuis won an Oscar. The success of the film led to a sequel in 1989, directed by Chris Walas, in which the son of Seth and Veronica begins to display familiar symptoms.

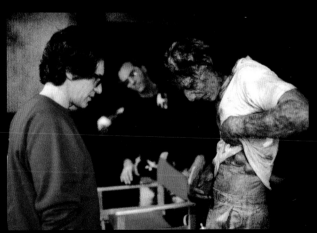

Opposite, top and top right: After exchanging genes with a fly, Seth (Jeff Goldblum) becomes more and more repulsive with the help of special effects and some gruesome make-up.
Above: Director David Cronenberg (l) checks the all-important make-up effects with actor Jeff Goldblum.

Above: *Blood and Black Lace* (*Sei donne per l'assassino*, 1964) was a breakthrough in Italian horror, marrying gore and sex with visual panache.

Dir: Mario Bava
Below: Cristina Marsillach is the young opera singer being tortured in *Terror at the Opera* (*Opera*, 1987).
Dir: Dario Argento

Right: Zombie witches prowling the corridors of a German ballet school terrorize Suzy Bannion (Jessica Harper) in *Suspiria* (1976).

Dir: Dario Agento
Opposite: Horror Japanese-style in *Tetsuo: The Iron Man* (*Tetsuo*, 1988), shot in black and white.
Dir: Tsukamoto Shinya

Bujold). Only later does she discover that there are two of them. Under the influence of drugs one of the twins becomes mentally disturbed and has a set of weird gynaecological instruments made for him under the delusion that his patients are mutant women. Though the film can be read as a critique of male arrogance as manifested in the medical profession, the initial disturbance in the sick twin's mind is set off by the fact that the actress has three uteruses. At the end, he performs a 'gynaecological' operation on his brother, a scene that combines Cronenberg's personal fixations with a classic instance of the horror film transgressing the boundary between male and female, and between normal and monstrous.

Horror has been a popular genre internationally, often drawing on indigenous folk or literary traditions. In Italy the so-called 'giallo' (literally meaning yellow, derived from the colour of the covers of a literary crime series in the 1930s) became a major genre at about the same time as the Italian Western emerged in the mid-1960s. Mario Bava's *Blood and Black Lace* (*Sei donne per l'assassino*, 1964) was a landmark film, depicting in stylish detail the murder of young women in a fashion house. The giallo is typified by a complex murder-mystery plot with multiple suspects in which the baroque sets and extreme elaboration of violence offer plentiful opportunities for directors and special effects technicians to show off their skills. Dario Argento, the most illustrious film-maker to have worked in this area, made a striking debut with *The Bird with the Crystal Plumage* (*L'uccello dalle piume di cristallo*, 1970), but *Suspiria* (1976), with witchcraft and multiple 'baroque' murders in a ballet school, is generally regarded as his masterwork. The film is a cult classic, appreciated for the inventiveness of the gruesome detail (at one point the camera enters the body of a victim to show a beating heart stabbed by a knife; at another a woman falls into the agonizing embrace of coils of barbed wire), and for Argento's flamboyant camera style, which in playing fast and loose with cinematic time and space evokes art-house rather than commercial cinema. *Terror at the Opera* (*Opera*, 1987) centres on a production of Verdi's *Macbeth* at La Scala, Milan. The multiple killer proves to be a policeman investigating an earlier murder; he is revealed as the lover of the heroine's mother, a sadist who had forced him to torture and murder women for her pleasure. At one point the villain binds the heroine and tapes needles under her eyes so that she cannot close them and is forced to watch a graphically enacted murder. Another Italian with a cult reputation is Lucio Fulci, whose zombie trilogy *City of the Living Dead* (*Paura nella città dei morti viventi*, 1980), *The Beyond* (*E tu vivrai nel terrore – L'aldilà*, 1981) and *The House by the Cemetery* (*Quella villa accanto al cimitero*, 1981) has its admirers.

In the East, Chinese cinema has its share of ghost stories and Chinese vampires, named 'jiangshi'. Tsui Hark has been a strong influence, directing the bloodthirsty *The Butterfly Murders* (*Die bian*, 1979) and producing the series *A Chinese Ghost Story* (*Xiannü Youhun*, 1987, 1990, 1991) in Hong Kong. Ghosts and vampires are also popular in Japan: for example, in Yamamoto Michio's trilogy *The Vampire Doll* (*Yureiyashiki no kyofu: chi o suu ningyoo*, 1970), *Lake of Dracula* (*Noroi no yakata: chi o suu me*, 1971) and *Evil of Dracula* (*Chi o suu bara*, 1975). The series of Japanese films based on the sea-monster Godzilla, beginning in 1954, are as much science fiction as horror (the monster is originally released from the depths by nuclear tests in the Pacific), though by the time of Hollywood's own version of the story, *Godzilla* (Roland Emmerich, 1998), the generic distinctions had become blurred. Perhaps the most extraordinary of all Japanese forays into the world of nightmare is *Tetsuo: The Iron*

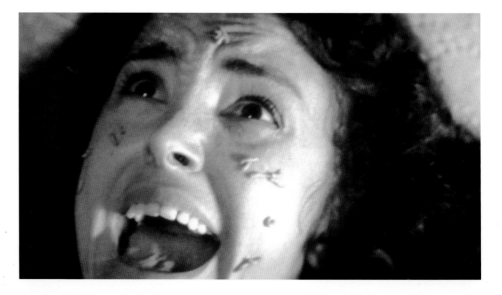

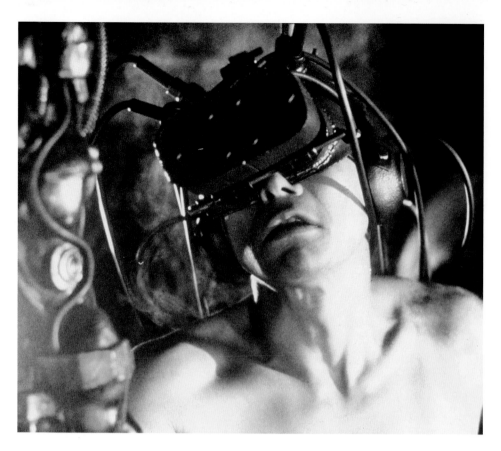

Man (*Tetsuo*, 1988), directed by Tsukamoto Shinya, with a sequel *Tetsuo II: Bodyhammer* (1991), a kind of glorified home movie in which a man finds himself turning into a grotesque metal robot. Based in part on Japanese horror comics but virtually dispensing with plot, it is a virtuoso exercise in eye-popping grotesquerie as the man's flesh splits and steel bars grow from his body.

Elsewhere in the Pacific, the Philippines has a lengthy tradition of horror films, drawing on a rich tradition of local folklore, which teems with monsters, ghosts and demons, tapped into by Peque Gallaga in *Shake, Rattle & Roll* (1984); the film's grisly if not totally convincing special effects pleased audiences enough for several sequels. Local comic books form the basis for many Filipino horror films, such as *The Killing of Satan* (Efren C Pinon, 1979), a fantasy in which the hero meets a number of strange monsters before encountering Satan himself. In the mid-1980s there was a short-lived horror boom in the Hindi cinema of Bombay, set off by Tulsi and Shyam Ramsay's *Purana Mandir* (1984). To the mix of monsters and mayhem was added as much sex as the censor would allow. Mohan Bhakri followed suit with a series of low-budget horror films, of which *Kabrastan* (1988) was typical, with its cast of dancing skeletons. In Latin America, the Brazilians have been making cheap and gory films since the 1960s, but nothing quite as strange as Santo, the masked wrestler of Mexican cinema played by Rodolfo Guzman Huerta, who fought with the full range of horror monsters, including zombies, werewolves and vampires, in a series of films from the late 1950s up to 1981.

The vampire is a staple of the horror genre. Like the zombie, it provokes terror because it is neither alive nor dead. Some see this as the essential characteristic of horror, that the monster is in some sense human and in some sense not; 'interstitial', to use Noël Carroll's term.[3] Robin Wood places the emphasis elsewhere, arguing that the vampire can stand for sexual potency (the vampire is irresistible), for promiscuity (he has numerous mates), for abnormal sexuality (sucking blood as a metaphor for oral sex or other 'perversions') and, even more transgressive, for bisexuality (vampires infecting both male and female victims).[4]

Surprisingly, contemporary vampire films have not always pursued this line. Werner Herzog's *Nosferatu the Vampire* (*Nosferatu: Phantom der Nacht*, 1979) is a remake of F W Murnau's silent classic, *Nosferatu – eine Symphonie des Grauens* (1922). Klaus Kinski is the aristocratic vampire terrorizing the town of Delft in the eighteenth century. Despite Kinski's bravura performance, the film, like much New German Cinema (see Chapter 12), sacrifices narrative focus for the expression of the director's personal artistic style. Neil Jordan's *Interview with the Vampire* (1994) also contains cinematic references, the vampire taking in screenings of Murnau's *Nosferatu* and *Sunrise* (1927). Based on the novel by Anne Rice, doyenne of contemporary vampirologists, the film begins in New Orleans

HARKER: Count Dracula?

DRACULA: I am Dracula, and I bid you welcome, Mr Harker, to my house. Come in. You will, I trust, excuse me that I do not join you but I have already dined and I never drink ... wine.

HARKER: An ancestor? I see a resemblance.

DRACULA: The Order of the Dracul ... the Dragon ... an ancient society pledging my forefathers to defend the church against all enemies of Christ. That relationship was not entirely successful.

HARKER: Oh, yes.

DRACULA: It is no laughing matter. We Draculs have a right to be proud. What devil or witch was ever so great as Attila whose blood flows in these veins? Blood is too precious a thing in these times. The warlike days are over. The victories of my great race are but a tale to be told. I am the last of my kind.

Jonathan Harker (Keanu Reeves), Prince Vlad Dracula (Gary Oldman), *Bram Stoker's Dracula* (Francis Ford Coppola, 1992)

in 1791, where the long undead Tom Cruise recruits Brad Pitt. Once again the sexual potential of vampirism is neglected, in favour of a rather torpid world-weariness.

The title of Francis Ford Coppola's *Bram Stoker's Dracula* (1992) announces itself as a return to basics, back to Stoker's literary classic which is the foundation of modern vampire stories, though Coppola made a number of changes, including the addition of an opening which explicitly links Dracula to the fifteenth-century historical figure of Vlad the Impaler, the defender of Christianity against the Turks. Coppola's film is a sophisticated and highly self-reflexive work, full of references to cinema itself (it is set in 1897, when Dracula comes to London to view the Lumières' Cinématographe). This made some critics reach for the term 'postmodern', particularly because of the peculiarly ironic tone of the work; we are never quite sure how seriously to take it. However, the film seems to reject the potentially liberating implications of the myth. Not only is Dracula identified with Christianity, but his polymorphous lust is ultimately redeemed by romantic love. By contrast, it is Lucy, the young woman he has vampirized, who becomes consumed by sexual desire, inappropriate in a well-brought-up Victorian young lady, and is punished with extermination.

Hollywood returned again to the foundational classics in *Mary Shelley's Frankenstein* (Kenneth Branagh, 1994), co-produced by Coppola, as well as reincarnating monster stalwarts from the past, as in *Wolf* (1994). This was an ambitious attempt at a werewolf film, starring Jack Nicholson, although not as much fun as the earlier *An American Werewolf in London* (John Landis, 1981). More recently, the figure of the mummy, memorably incarnated, like Frankenstein's monster, by Boris Karloff in 1932, has been revived in *The Mummy* (Stephen Sommers, 1999). Taking advantage of advances in special effects, this was a box office success with, inevitably, a sequel, *The Mummy Returns* (Stephen Sommers, 2001).

Pastiche and irony are held to be marks of postmodernism, the condition to which all art ultimately seems destined, and the most recent development in the horror film has been towards a degree of self-reflexiveness that threatens to consume the genre itself. In *Wes Craven's New Nightmare* (Wes Craven, 1994) the director of *A Nightmare on Elm Street* appears as himself, observed in the process of making a new film about his monster Freddie. The film deftly mixes reality and fiction, with the star of the original film (Heather Langenkamp) playing both herself and the character of Nancy. In Craven's *Scream* (1996) a group of young people are the victims of a crazed slasher, but this time they are all fans of the genre. In the video store where one of the teenagers works, there is a learned discussion about character motivation. Later a boy lists the rules, such as that sexual activity brings swift retribution. Sydney, the heroine (Neve Campbell), thinks horror films are silly, but no sooner has she allowed her boyfriend to make love to her than they are attacked. Craven's *Scream 2* (1997) and *Scream 3* (1999) further racked up the degree of self-reflexivity by incorporating a movie ('*Stab*') made about the original murders. This may be horror's last gasp, but such has been the box office appeal of the genre that it is hard to believe that Hollywood will not try once more to reinvent it.

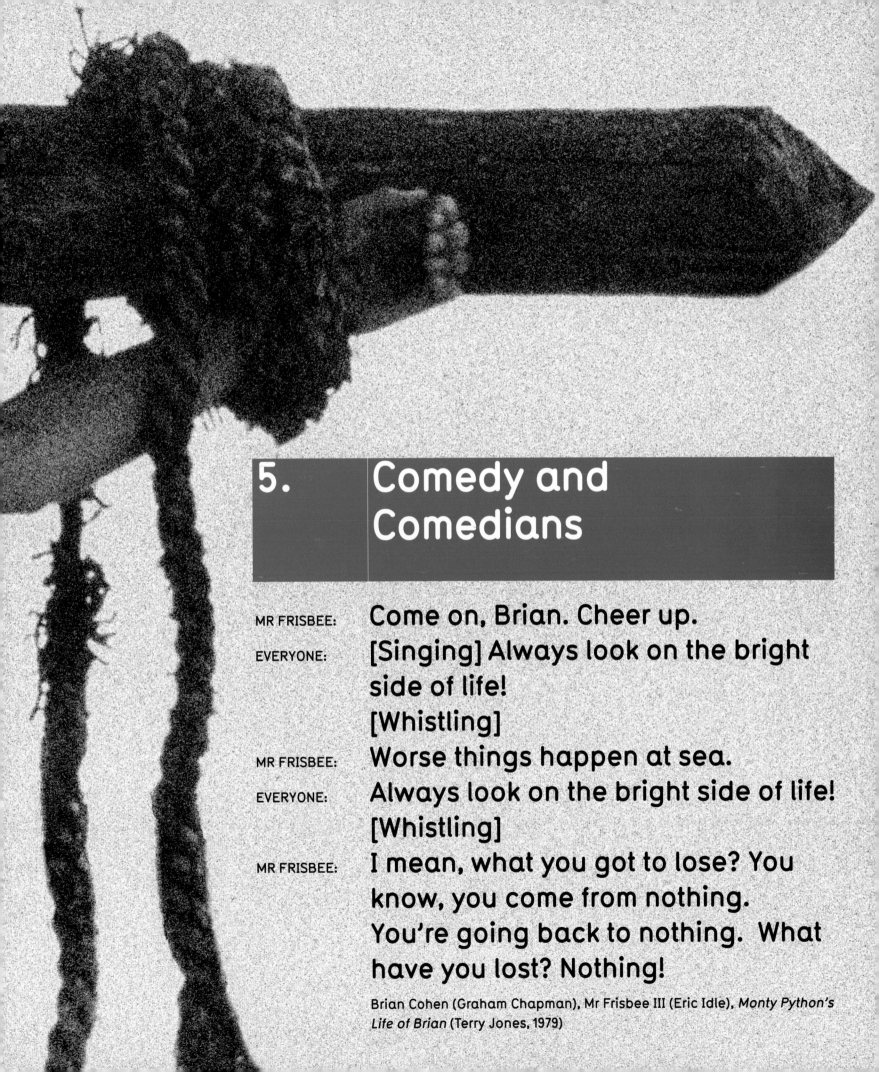

5. Comedy and Comedians

MR FRISBEE:	Come on, Brian. Cheer up.
EVERYONE:	[Singing] Always look on the bright side of life! [Whistling]
MR FRISBEE:	Worse things happen at sea.
EVERYONE:	Always look on the bright side of life! [Whistling]
MR FRISBEE:	I mean, what you got to lose? You know, you come from nothing. You're going back to nothing. What have you lost? Nothing!

Brian Cohen (Graham Chapman), Mr Frisbee III (Eric Idle), *Monty Python's Life of Brian* (Terry Jones, 1979)

Previous pages:
Graham Chapman as
the unfortunate Brian
in the iconoclastic
comedy of religion,
*Monty Python's Life
of Brian* (1979). Recent
comedies such as
Four Weddings and

a Funeral (Mike
Newell, 1994) and
The Full Monty (Peter
Cattaneo, 1997) have
been some of the most
successful British films
to have been made.
Dir: Terry Jones

Comedy, like the horror film, brings to the surface feelings which social controls have repressed, especially sexual desire, or infantile and aggressive urges. Not surprisingly, in view of his interest in the mechanisms of psychic repression, Freud devoted an entire work, *Jokes and their Relation to the Unconscious* (1905), to the subject. Moreover, comedy and horror both produce a bodily effect in the spectator: we laugh, we scream, we even scream with laughter. Though our initial response to horror may be fear, often this is followed by laughter in order to divest the horrific of its threat.

In the 1960s and 1970s, the greatest name in Hollywood comedy was Billy Wilder, who had followed his 1959 hit *Some Like It Hot* with a string of films in which his distinctive Jewish Middle-European wit, unsentimental, even cruel, was given perfect expression by the deft comic timing of actors such as Jack Lemmon and Walter Matthau. The two appeared together in *The Front Page* (1974), Wilder's remake of the 1931 film of Charles MacArthur and Ben Hecht's stage play satirizing the newspaper business. Lemmon and Matthau were reunited for Wilder's last film, *Buddy Buddy* (1981), not a triumph in itself but a film which shows traces of former glories.

Wilder's films do not only have wit; they also have narrative shape and subtle characterization. Another director who, like Wilder, was also a screenwriter before turning director, was Blake Edwards. Having spent the late 1970s trying to repeat the success of *The Pink Panther* (1964), in which Peter Sellers found his perfect role, at the end of the decade Edwards hit his stride with a series of clever and funny films. In *10* (1979) Dudley Moore was brilliant as a Hollywood composer in a mid-life crisis. Much of the humour consists of satirical swipes at the lives of the rich and famous, but Edwards excels at visual comedy. One sequence in which a decrepit old housekeeper staggers in with a tray piled perilously high with crockery is particularly deft and funny.

S.O.B. (1981) is another showbiz satire with some elaborate visual jokes. Like *10* it starred Edwards's wife, Julie Andrews, who also appeared in Edwards's masterpiece, *Victor/Victoria*

Above right: Jack
Lemmon and Walter
Matthau engage in
repartee in the remake
of Lewis Milestone's
1931 film *The Front
Page* (1974).
Dir: Billy Wilder
Above: Bo Derek and
Dudley Moore, playing
a randy Hollywood

composer who marks
women on a scale of
one to ten, in *10* (1979).
Dir: Blake Edwards
Opposite: Blake
Edwards cast his wife,
Julie Andrews, in
Victor/Victoria (1982),
a comedy of sexual
uncertainty.
Dir: Blake Edwards

COMEDY AND COMEDIANS

(1982). This also has a showbiz theme; Andrews plays a singer in 1930s Paris who, down on her luck, finds fame and fortune when she decides to pass as a man doing female impersonations. Edwards gets full value from the gender-bending possibilities of this scenario. In one sequence a troupe of dancers are dressed either at the front as men and at the back as women, or vice versa. The unsettling of sexual certainties that this provokes wittily anticipates the sexual displacements of what would be later called 'queer cinema'.

The greater licence of the 1970s facilitated such films as *Shampoo* (Hal Ashby, 1975), with Warren Beatty as a Hollywood hairdresser seducing all his clients. Set in 1968 as the United States is about to elect Richard Nixon as President, the film is politically savvy as well as sexually sophisticated. But by the end of the decade sophistication was becoming old-fashioned. The success of the Monty Python films, particularly *Monty Python and the Holy Grail* (Terry Gilliam/Terry Jones, 1975) and *Monty Python's Life of Brian* (Terry Jones, 1979) was an indication that the social basis of film comedy was shifting. Originating on British television, Monty Python appealed especially to the upper teens and lower twenties age bracket, particularly those either in or recently departed from full-time education, with a mixture of anarchic social satire, boisterous farce, black humour and scatological jokes.

Above: Julie Christie getting a blow-dry from Warren Beatty in *Shampoo* (1975). Dir: Hal Ashby
Below: Spying on the girls: Dan Monahan and Wyatt Knight in *Porky's* (1982). Dir: Bob Clark
Right: Michael Palin, Graham Chapman,

John Cleese and Terry Jones in the irreverent *Monty Python's Life of Brian* (1979). Dir: Terry Jones
Opposite: An end to sophistication: Tom Hulce and John Belushi in *National Lampoon's Animal House* (1978). Dir: John Landis

This was also the audience for *National Lampoon's Animal House* (John Landis, 1978). Based on stories originally appearing in the humorous magazine *National Lampoon*, the film is set on a college campus in 1962. *Animal House* set a pattern in which a group of characters with some institutional attachment – a frat house in *Animal House*; the police force in *Police Academy* (Hugh Wilson, 1984) – are set loose in an episodic plot. These films reject the previously dominant form of Hollywood comedy which centres on a romantic attachment between boy and girl. Instead the male characters, though seemingly driven by their sexual urges, bond with their colleagues, not with women. The humour, freed from constraint by the relaxation of the Production Code in the late 1960s, relies heavily on dirty words, nudity and toilet jokes. Thus John Belushi, a kind of low-life Falstaff, gorges on food and drink, at one point draining a whole bottle of Jack Daniels at a stroke, and introduces himself to two of the principal characters by urinating on their shoes. Similarly, the seven episodes so far of the *Police Academy* series are plentifully strewn with jokes about farting and penises. William Paul has suggested that these films should be included within Bakhtin's category of 'grotesque realism', a type of humour that ignores all that is spiritual to concentrate on the material, especially bodily functions below the waist.[1]

One of the best-known films of this type was *Porky's* (Bob Clark, 1982), reviled for its bad taste by critics but hugely successful at the box office. It is set in 1952, even further back in the past than *Animal House*, for no very evident reason except that the desperate attempts of the film's high-school boys to lose their virginity might be less believable in the permissive age. The humour is largely visual. Verbal wit may be more mature, but at a time when Hollywood was increasingly aware of the foreign market, visual humour has the advantage of overcoming language differences. Thus in a notorious scene, three of the boys spy on a group of girls in the showers. Pee Wee, a nerd who is perpetually teased about the size of his penis, finds his view through the peephole blocked by the bottom of a particularly fat girl. His protest alerts the girls to the boys' presence. Trying to brazen it out, another of the boys

COMEDY AND COMEDIANS

Above: Macaulay Culkin as Kevin McCallister takes aim at Daniel Stern as would-be robber Marv in *Home Alone* (1990). Dir: Chris Columbus

Below: Actors Christian Slater and Winona Ryder in the high-school black comedy *Heathers* (1989). Dir: Michael Lehmann

JD:	Veronica knew you'd have a hangover. So I whipped this up. Family recipe.
HEATHER:	Did you put a phlegm globber in it or something? I'm not drinking that piss.
JD:	I knew this stuff would be too intense.
HEATHER:	Intense? Grow up. You think I'll drink it just because you call me chicken. Just give me the cup, jerk. Corn nuts!
JD:	Something tells me you picked up the wrong cup.
VERONICA:	No shit, Sherlock. I can't believe it. I just killed my best friend.
JD:	And your worst enemy.

Jason 'JD' Dean (Christian Slater), Heather Chandler (Kim Walker), Veronica Sawyer (Winona Ryder), *Heathers* (Michael Lehmann, 1989)

sticks his tongue through a peephole. A girl responds by pouring soap on it. Upping the stakes, the boy then sticks his penis through the hole. At this point a fat and unpleasant teacher appropriately named Miss Balbricker enters the shower room. The girls leave and Miss Balbricker advances on the exposed penis, finally grabbing it with an exultant cry. The two other boys run away laughing, leaving their unfortunate colleague to his fate. Nothing in this scene requires translation; the basis of its humour is as old as drama itself.

The films have moments of social and political satire. In *Animal House* one of the students seduces the willing wife of the obnoxious college dean in what is more a political than a sexual act. In *Porky's* a scene in the principal's office where Miss Balbricker goes to demand an identity parade so she can pick out the offending penis ends in a close-up of a photograph of President Eisenhower. One strand of the plot concerns prejudices against Jews, and in the sequel *Porky's II: The Next Day* (Bob Clark, 1983) this is extended in a scene where the Jewish boy, supported by half the Seminole nation (the films are set in Florida), shaves the hair off members of the Ku Klux Klan. *Porky's II* also exposes the hypocrisy of the local school board (which includes a fundamentalist preacher), who want to ban Shakespeare for immorality but who are caught watching porn films.

Yet for all the obsession with sex, the sexual act itself is rarely followed to a conclusion. Belushi spies on half-naked college girls from a ladder (giving the audience a hilariously knowing wink as he does so) but, just as one of the girls is about to reveal all, his ladder (symbolically?) tips over. The most nerdy of the frat boys finally gets a girl to bed, but before she is fully undressed she falls asleep. On each side of the boy's face appear tiny figures: one the devil urging him to take advantage of her comatose condition, the other his mother threatening dire consequences if he does. The boy delivers the girl intact back to her house. The films are attracted to the idea of total abandon but when faced with its realization they retreat; their sexual timidity has much in common with Britain's long-running *Carry On* series, which began in the late 1950s but staggered on into the 1990s, marking the quincentennial with *Carry On Columbus* (Gerald Thomas, 1992).

John Hughes had been a writer on *National Lampoon* magazine and had scripted two sequels to *Animal House* before directing his first film, *Sixteen Candles* (1985), a comedy about a teenage girl coming up to her sixteenth birthday. In quick succession he made *The Breakfast Club* (1985), *Weird Science* (1985), *Pretty in Pink* (1986), for which he wrote the script only, and *Ferris Bueller's Day Off* (1986). All these films deal with the problems of youth, mostly involving the opposite sex, but for the coarseness and occasional genuine anarchy of *National Lampoon* they substitute acute observation of teen tribulations and at times a surprising delicacy of feeling. In *Planes, Trains and Automobiles* (1987) Hughes moved up an age bracket. Starring Steve Martin and John Candy, it is a farcical story, fast-paced and ingeniously plotted, of a disastrous cross-country journey after all flights are grounded by snow. But for his biggest success, *Home Alone* (1990), Hughes chose a pre-teen protagonist. Played by Macaulay Culkin, Kevin is accidentally left behind when his family travels to Paris. The film combines farce, as Kevin finds increasingly ingenious ways to repel a couple of incompetent burglars, with some affecting moments as the small boy, initially pleased to have the run of the house, begins to feel lonely.

It is hardly surprising, given changing audience demographics and the preponderance of teens and twenty-somethings in the audience, that films set in high schools and colleges should prove so popular, forming a sub-genre governed by the rituals of dating and the pressures of the battle for popularity and prestige. A particularly acerbic example was *Heathers* (Michael Lehmann, 1989), a black comedy which subverted many of the clichés of the form, with Winona Ryder attempting to overturn the tyranny of the dominant school clique, with literally murderous results. Most of the successful examples of high school and college comedy are satires, if affectionate ones. *Clueless* (Amy Heckerling, 1995), loosely based on Jane Austen's *Emma*, has Alicia Silverstone as a scholar at Beverly Hills High whose preoccupations are shopping, boyfriends and popularity, in any order. *The Opposite of Sex* (Don Roos, 1998) is set further down the social scale, with Christina Ricci as a ruthlessly manipulative teenager who moves in with her gay brother, a high-school teacher, and seduces his boyfriend. Cynicism and power games are also at the heart of *Cruel Intentions* (Roger Kumble, 1999), based on *Les Liaisons dangereuses*, the eighteenth-century French novel by Choderlos de Laclos which had been filmed by both Stephen Frears and Milos Forman at the end of the 1980s. In the teen version Ryan Phillippe and Sarah Michelle Gellar plot to seduce the daughter of the headmaster, played by Reese Witherspoon. If Phillippe can bed her, Gellar will allow him to have sex with her too. If the film draws back from the crueller machinations of the original, it derives much enjoyment from pushing the conventions of teenage sexual manoeuvres to their logical conclusion.

COMEDY AND COMEDIANS

Above: Jim Levinstein (Jason Biggs) discusses centrefolds with his father (Eugene Levy) in *American Pie* (1999). Dir: Paul Weitz
Above right: Kathryn Merteuil (Sarah Michelle Gellar) and Sebastian Valmont (Ryan Phillippe) discuss the fate of their dupes in *Cruel Intentions* (1999). Dir: Roger Kumble
Below: Actress Cameron Diaz in a sticky situation in *There's Something about Mary* (1998). Dir: Bobby and Peter Farrelly

Reese Witherspoon also stars in *Election* (Alexander Payne, 1999); an unscrupulously ambitious candidate in the school's popularity contest, she spurns the attentions of teacher Matthew Broderick, who in turn plots revenge. Not once does the film threaten to fall back into sentimentality, remaining sharp, witty and relentlessly cynical to the end. Witherspoon continued in similar vein with *Legally Blonde* (2001), in which she plays a ditzy college student who to spite her snobbish boyfriend enrols at Harvard Law School and manipulates everyone to her advantage. Two other high-school films from 1999 are worth noting: *10 Things I Hate about You* (Gil Junger), yet another adaptation, this time from Shakespeare's *The Taming of the Shrew*; and *She's All That* (Robert Iscove). Rather in the manner of *Les Liaisons dangereuses*, both films turn on a bet. In the first, one boy is bribed by another to woo the combative Kat so that he may then romance her younger sister Bianca, who has been forbidden by her father to have a boyfriend until Kat has been paired off. In the latter film, the most popular boy in school takes a bet that he can get the least attractive girl in school voted prom queen.

If on occasion there is a happy ending of sorts, the sardonic stance of these films is at odds with the previous history of Hollywood. The boy–girl romance leading inexorably to marriage, once the firm foundation of traditional comedy, is now a kind of game, in which the ultimate goal is not true love, but rather the achievement of power, fame or influence. The romantic comedy has not completely disappeared, but in a society where divorce rates continue to rise inexorably the formerly unchallengeable dogma of everlasting love may no longer pass unexamined.

American Pie (Paul Weitz, 1999) is also a high-school story. Four boys vow to lose their virginity before prom night. As often in these films, female sexuality is something mysterious, difficult if not impossible for the male to fathom. Women are either prudes, citadels of chastity to be conquered by fair means or (usually) foul, or else they are creatures of infinite sophistication, capriciously bestowing their favours, and then usually to boys whose wealth, looks or savoir-faire are out of the heroes' reach. Even if, after painstaking and dedicated work, the boy does manage to persuade a girl to have sex, as often as not consummation will be interrupted by a farcical intrusion.

American Pie is also a return to the 'gross-out' films of the era of *Animal House*, ratcheted up a notch or two. The humour is now at an extreme level of physicality centred on the excretory and reproduction systems. Not only are there jokes about farting and masturbation; one boy drinks beer from a cup into which another has previously ejaculated; another boy has intercourse with an apple pie (hence the title). In the late 1990s a series of such films hit box office gold: for example, *There's Something about Mary*

Above: Jim Carrey and feathered friend in *Ace Ventura, Pet Detective* (1994).
Dir: Tom Shadyac

Below: Tom Hanks playing a game of high-speed ping-pong in *Forrest Gump* (1994).
Dir: Robert Zemeckis

(1998), in which star Cameron Diaz gets her hair stuck up with dried sperm. The Farrelly brothers, Bobby and Peter, who wrote and directed, had earlier made *Dumb & Dumber* (1994), in which Jim Carrey and Jeff Daniels outdo one another in stupidity and crassness. The title provoked critics to pronounce such films the culmination in a process of dumbing-down which had been going on ever since the audience became dominated by teens and twenties. Such a claim was also made against Robert Zemeckis's *Forrest Gump* (1994), in which Tom Hanks plays a man of limited intelligence who in a series of happy accidents becomes a Vietnam war hero and champion sportsman; in making a virtue out of stupidity, it was alleged, Hollywood was implicitly attacking intelligence and education. Yet there is nothing in these films which could not be found in Chaucer or Rabelais. Those who take the long view might argue that at the beginning of the twenty-first century we are only just emerging from a 200 year era of prudery imposed by the Romantic revolution, Victorian clergymen and the innate censoriousness of the Anglo-Saxon middle classes.

Jim Carrey also stars in the Farrelly brothers' *Me, Myself & Irene* (2000), which contains politically incorrect jokes about the handicapped and ethnic minorities, as well as a scene in which a chicken is stuffed up a policeman's bottom. In his first hit, *Ace Ventura, Pet Detective* (Tom Shadyac, 1994), Carrey is a well-meaning but accident-prone chaser of lost animals. The film set the pattern for the star's relentless mugging; Carrey cannot speak a single line without a dozen different facial contortions. Funny in themselves some of them might be, but this sheer determination to extract a laugh can be wearing. In his next feature, *The Mask* (Charles Russell, 1994), Carrey finds an ancient mask which transforms him into a cartoonish character capable of manic feats. With the aid of special effects the trademark mugging is exaggerated into Tex Avery-type bulging eyes and other bodily distortions. Carrey has kinetic energy in abundance, and in *The Cable Guy* (Ben Stiller, 1996) and *Liar Liar* (Tom Shadyac, 1997) there are some effective moments of manic, almost surreal

COMEDY AND COMEDIANS

The High-School Comedy
Election (1999)
Dir: Alexander Payne

High-school comedies became popular because the milieu was familiar to a large proportion of the film-going audience. But the best examples of the genre in the 1980s and 1990s satirized not only the perennial battle of the sexes, but other elements in American life. The frequent struggles between jocks and nerds were a kind of microcosm of the class difference which is supposed not to exist in the United States. In *Election*, one of the best examples of this popular genre, much of the humour is at the expense of the 'democratic' process. The film's guiding insight is that in practice democracy reduces to a popularity contest, in which dirty tricks are the norm.

Tracy is a squeaky-clean blonde paragon standing for election as student president. Played by Reese Witherspoon, Tracy is as brittle as glass, eaten up by ambition and her ruthless determination to win. She is loathed by a teacher, Jim McAllister, for her self-righteousness, and also for her role in the dismissal of his fellow teacher Dave after a sex scandal. Jim encourages student football star Paul to stand against Tracy. Though Tracy wins the election Jim, as supervisor, rigs the count, only to be discovered. As a result he loses his job and his marriage collapses.

One of the most pleasurable aspects of the film is its total lack of sentimentality. Tracy is the least likeable character in the film but ends up with a top job in politics (Republican, naturally), while Jim's attempt to seduce Dave's wife Linda ends in excruciating embarrassment, and by the end of the film his career is in ruins. For once, nobody gets their just desserts.

Country of Origin: USA
Production Companies: Bona Fide Productions/ MTV Films/Paramount Pictures
Running Time: 103 mins

Producers: Albert Berger, Ron Yerxa, David Gale, Keith Samples
Writers: Alexander Payne, Jim Taylor, based on a novel by Tom Perrotta
Director of Photography: James Glennon
Music: Rolfe Kent
Editor: Kevin Tent
Art Director: Tim Kirkpatrick

Jim McAllister: Matthew Broderick
Tracy Flick: Reese Witherspoon
Paul Metzler: Chris Klein
Tammy Metzler: Jessica Campbell
Dave Novotny: Mark Harelik
Linda Novotny: Delaney Driscoll

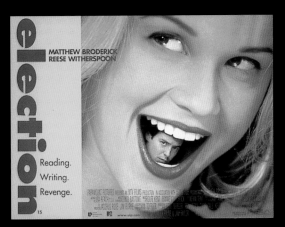

Top: Matthew Broderick as the hapless teacher Jim McAllister.
Above: Reese Witherspoon as the squeaky-clean Tracy Flick, ruthlessly ambitious and without compassion. A satirical microcosm of contemporary American politics.
Left: This poster for the film promotes the three 'Rs' – Reading, Writing and Revenge.

humour. Peter Weir's *The Truman Show* (1998) allowed him to calm down a little and play a more nuanced role.

Like Jim Carrey, Robin Williams came out of television and in the 1990s developed as a major comedy star. His first significant role was as an army DJ in Vietnam in *Good Morning, Vietnam* (Barry Levinson, 1987). Like Carrey, Williams seems almost to bully us into laughter, his non-stop repartee an attempt to beat the audience into submission. Unlike Carrey, Williams has mixed comedy with serious films. It is a cliché that all clowns want to play Hamlet, and Williams came close by appearing as Osric in Kenneth Branagh's 1996 screen version of the play. In Peter Weir's *Dead Poets Society* (1989) Williams is a schoolteacher who inspires his pupils with a love of culture; in Terry Gilliam's *The Fisher King* (1991) he is a former professor of history gone mad on the death of his wife, and in Gus Van Sant's *Good Will Hunting* (1997) he is a psychiatrist treating a brilliant maths student. This devotion to education may be evidence of Williams's good intentions, and in *Patch Adams* (Tom Shadyac, 1998) he plays a doctor who believes, literally, that laughter is the best medicine. But there is something cloying about Williams's sincerity; his desperate desire to be liked is ultimately unlikeable. When he devotes himself whole-heartedly to a comic part, masquerading as a middle-aged female housekeeper in *Mrs. Doubtfire* (Chris Columbus, 1993), he is genuinely funny.

Another star comedian who started in television, where he was a regular on *Saturday Night Live*, is Steve Martin. Several of his earlier films were parodies of one sort or another. *Dead Men Don't Wear Plaid* (Carl Reiner, 1982) recycled clips from 1940s film noir in a spoof of hard-boiled detective films; *The Man with Two Brains* (Carl Reiner, 1983) has a science fiction basis; *The Little Shop of Horrors* (Frank Oz, 1986) is a cod horror film-cum-musical; and *Three Amigos!* (John Landis, 1986) is a Western. In all of them Martin is a likeable presence whose most characteristic look is of blissful innocence while around him chaos reigns. Martin is also a writer, often collaborating with Carl Reiner. Though capable of pathos in *Pennies from Heaven* (Herbert Ross, 1981), where he is a small-time music salesman in the Depression, and in *Roxanne* (Fred Schepisi, 1987), a modern-day version of the Cyrano de Bergerac story, he lacks Robin Williams's compulsion to pluck the heartstrings. In the 1990s Martin became less a comedian, more an actor playing comic roles in such films as *L.A. Story* (Mick Jackson, 1991), where he plays a weatherman in love, and *Father of the Bride* (Charles Shyer, 1991), a remake of the 1950 film in which Martin plays the role originally performed by Spencer Tracy. This, its sequel *Father of the Bride Part II* (Charles Shyer, 1995) and the earlier *Parenthood* (Ron Howard, 1989) show Martin orienting his appeal to the middle-aged suburban middle class, an audience which younger comedians seem to have deserted.

COMEDY AND COMEDIANS

Above: Do you want fries with that? Kevin Kline and Michael Palin in *A Fish Called Wanda* (1988).
Dir: Charles Crichton
Above right: Andie MacDowell as Carrie adding Hollywood star power to Hugh Grant's

Charles in *Four Weddings and a Funeral* (1994).
Dir: Mike Newell
Opposite: Dustin Hoffman plays the inventive Hollywood producer Stanley Motss in *Wag the Dog* (1997).
Dir: Barry Levinson

Television was also the forcing ground for Eddie Murphy, who made his name on *Saturday Night Live* before breaking into movies with *48 Hrs.* (Walter Hill, 1982), in which he plays the fast-talking side-kick of tough cop Nick Nolte. Murphy's almost maniacally ebullient personality was packaged in a series of films, most notably *Beverly Hills Cop* (Martin Brest, 1984), in which he is sassy, quick-witted, unafraid of giving offence. In his more recent roles, such as *The Nutty Professor* (Tom Shadyac, 1996) and *Dr. Dolittle* (Betty Thomas, 1998), with sequels in 2000 and 2001 respectively, Murphy has calmed down a little. He now has competition from younger black comic actors such as Will Smith and Chris Tucker, but Murphy was the first Afro-American comic actor to achieve genuine international stardom.

The United States can export its comedy even when it depends on verbal wit or ethnic and regional stereotypes, because the long-term dominance of Hollywood has familiarized audiences the world over with its sense of humour. Other countries have comedy films, but often they struggle to export them. One of the greatest French comedians, Fernandel, never achieved the fame abroad which he found in France. Finland has its Uuno films, Denmark its 'Olsen Gang' series, but they do not travel far beyond those countries' borders. On the other hand, comedy is an important aspect of the international appeal of many contemporary Spanish directors, including Pedro Almodóvar and Bigas Lunas. In France, too, Bertrand Blier has made a string of successful comedies, some of which helped to make Gérard Depardieu an international star.

Humour has been a vital ingredient in the international success of Hong Kong cinema, especially in the films of Jackie Chan (discussed in Chapters 2 and 17). Britain has found comedy the easiest genre to export. *Four Weddings and a Funeral* (Mike Newell, 1994) is one of the most successful British films ever, credited by the Internet Movie Database as number 155 in the list of all-time box office hits, with a worldwide gross of $244 million by 2002. It exploited the quintessentially English charms of Hugh Grant in some cleverly contrived situations. The follow-up, *Notting Hill* (Roger Michell, 1999), repeated the formula of a middle-class Englishman in love with an American, this time played by Julia Roberts. *The Full Monty* (Peter Cattaneo, 1997), about a group of unemployed steel workers who take up stripping for a living, achieved equivalent international success. In the previous decade *A Fish Called Wanda* (1988) was, as its zany title suggested, in the Monty Python tradition, utilizing Python regulars John Cleese and Michael Palin and directed by Charles Crichton, a veteran of the great days of Ealing Studios in the 1940s.

Good comedy relies on directors and writers as much as stars. Of contemporary US writer-directors, Barry Levinson stands out. With early experience in television on *The Carol Burnett Show* and in the movies writing several Mel Brooks films, Levinson first directed *Diner* (1982), about adolescents growing up in his native Baltimore. *Good Morning, Vietnam* was dominated by Robin Williams, but *Tin Men* (1988) is more of an ensemble piece about deadly and hilarious rivalry between aluminium-siding salesmen Richard Dreyfuss and Danny DeVito. Not all Levinson's films are comedies – *Rain Man* (1990) has Dustin Hoffman as an autistic man, and in *Bugsy* (1992) Warren Beatty is gangster Bugsy Siegel – but there

Above: Gene Wilder
squares up to Cleavon
Little in the Western
parody *Blazing Saddles*
(1974).
Dir: Mel Brooks
Below right: Meg Ryan
and Billy Crystal in the
famous 'faking orgasm'
scene in *When Harry*

Met Sally (1989).
Dir: Rob Reiner
Opposite: Elizabeth
Hurley and Mike Myers
star in the smash-hit
James Bond spoof
Austin Powers:
International Man
of Mystery (1997).
Dir: Jay Roach

SALLY:	... Most women at one time or another have faked it.
HARRY:	Well they haven't faked it with me.
SALLY:	How do you know?
HARRY:	Because I know.
SALLY:	Oh, right, that's right, I forgot, you're a man.
HARRY:	What is that supposed to mean?
SALLY:	Nothing. It's just that all men are sure it never happened to them and that most women at one time or another have done it so you do the math.
HARRY:	You don't think that I could tell the difference?
SALLY:	No.
HARRY:	Get outta here.
SALLY:	Ooh ... Oh ... Ooh ...
HARRY:	Are you okay?
SALLY:	Oh ... Oh God ... Ooh Oh God ... Oh ... Oh ... Oh ... Oh God ... Oh yeah right there Oh! Oh ... Yes Yes Yes Yes Yes Yes ... Oh ... Oh ... Yes Yes Yes ... Oh ... Yes Yes Yes Yes Yes Yes ... Oh ... Oh ... Oh ... Oh God Oh ... Oh ... Huh ...

LADY AT ANOTHER TABLE:

I'll have what she's having.

Sally Albright (Meg Ryan), Harry Burns (Billy Crystal),
When Harry Met Sally (Rob Reiner, 1989)

is humour in all of them. With *Wag the Dog* (1997) Levinson is on top form. The film is a sophisticated and penetrating satire of the US political system, and anything but dumb. The US President, in an uncanny anticipation of real-life events, is discovered in a sexual peccadillo. Robert De Niro is a fixer who contrives to divert attention from the President's misdeeds by paying Hollywood producer Dustin Hoffman to 'create' a war against Albania.

One might see Hollywood's exploitation of parody as evidence of a decline, making fun of its own product a symptom of a lack of confidence in old narrative forms, and a failure to develop new ones. Or has comedy, like everything else, become postmodern in its preference for irony? Yet parody has always been part of Hollywood's comic arsenal. In the 1920s Buster Keaton was making fun of virtually every genre, including the Western, the Civil War picture, the horror film and D W Griffith's historical films. Beginning in the late 1960s, Mel Brooks made a career of spoofing familiar genres. *The Producers* (1968) guys the Broadway musical, *Blazing Saddles* (1974) is a comedy Western, *Young Frankenstein* (1974) a comic horror film, *High Anxiety* (1977) is a Hitchcock parody and *Spaceballs* (1987) makes fun of *Star Wars*. Brooks's humour is often no more sophisticated than the *National Lampoon* variety (cowboys eating beans in *Blazing Saddles* provides an opportunity for farting jokes), and his parodies were soon outdone in wit and popularity by *Airplane* (Jim Abrahams/David and Jerry Zucker, 1980), a spoof on disaster movies, and *The Naked Gun: From the Files of Police Squad* (David Zucker, 1988), a parody thriller which spawned two sequels. More recently, *Austin Powers: International Man of Mystery* (Jay Roach, 1997) and its sequel, *Austin Powers: The Spy Who Shagged Me* (Jay Roach, 1999), written by and starring Mike Myers, have been long-overdue parodies of the James Bond films.

In a society in which sexuality threatens to replace romantic love as the basis for a 'healthy' relationship, it is not surprising that the traditional 'boy meets girl' formula which sustained so many Hollywood comedies should be in decline. Yet some of the most successful films of recent years have relied on a modified form of this plot. Frank Krutnik has coined the term 'nervous romance' for a film in which the heterosexual couple is still the basis for the story, but in which simple-minded assumptions about the stability of this pillar of the social edifice are no longer to be counted on.[2] Films as various as *Annie Hall* (Woody Allen, 1977), *Something Wild* (Jonathan Demme, 1986), *Peggy Sue Got Married* (Francis Ford Coppola, 1986), *When Harry Met Sally* (Rob Reiner, 1989), *Pretty Woman* (Garry Marshall, 1990) and *My Best Friend's Wedding* (P J Hogan, 1997) can all be included in this category. As Virginia Wright Wexman has argued, traditional Hollywood comedy had to manage the contradiction between love as an all-consuming passion and love as the cornerstone of an enduring marriage.[3] It did this by ending the picture at the altar steps, fading out at the point where difficulties begin, thus avoiding a collision between fantasy and reality. In the 'nervous romance', sexual relationships are not necessarily a stepping stone to marriage, and marriage is itself not synonymous with commitment and sexual contentment. The famous scene in *When Harry Met Sally* where Meg Ryan demonstrates how to fake an orgasm is an acknowledgement that heterosexual relationships involve a good deal of deception. Love must now coexist with a degree of disillusion.

COMEDY AND COMEDIANS

<table>
<tr><td>6.</td><td>Classic Genres Revived</td></tr>
</table>

DUNBAR:	Actually sir, I'm here at my own request.
FARNBROUGH:	Really! Why?
DUNBAR:	I've always wanted to see the frontier.
FARNBROUGH:	You want to see the frontier.
DUNBAR:	Yes sir, before it's gone.

Lieutenant John G Dunbar (Kevin Costner), Major Farnbrough (Maury Chaykin), *Dances with Wolves* (Kevin Costner, 1990)

CLASSIC GENRES REVIVED

There is a tendency to think of film genres, the building blocks of popular cinema, as fixed and unchanging. As a category, the Western may be fuzzy round the edges (is *Thelma & Louise* a kind of Western?), but its essence remains the same. In fact, as recent discussion of genre has shown, not only do genres mutate over time but they fall in and out of favour.[1] Since the 1970s genres that were once minor have come to prominence, while others have gone into decline. One such genre is the historical epic, which in the 1950s and 1960s led Hollywood's fight-back against television by making films on the grand scale, employing the new technologies of CinemaScope and stereophonic sound, and the legendary 'cast of thousands'. But a series of much-publicized financial disasters such as *Cleopatra* (Joseph L Mankiewicz, 1963) caused the genre to expire. In the 1990s there were occasional efforts to revive it, including a brace of Scottish epics in 1995, Mel Gibson's *Braveheart* and Michael Caton-Jones's *Rob Roy*, each of which allowed Hollywood to indulge its fondness for bashing British – or rather English – imperialism. The most whole-hearted and impressive attempt to revive the sword and sandals epic is Ridley Scott's *Gladiator* (2000). Russell Crowe is a powerful presence, carving his way through ancient Rome, and Scott uses digital technology to augment the crowd numbers in the scenes in the Colosseum.

In the 1940s and 1950s the Western was the most important genre in US cinema, comprising around twenty per cent of all features released and constituting the bedrock of solid box office performance upon which the edifice of Hollywood economic dominance was built. But in the 1960s the genre suffered a precipitous decline in the face of the shifting demographics of audiences. Younger spectators favoured genres with more spectacular effects and in which the patriarchal authority of such figures as John Wayne did not weigh so heavily. Hollywood was reluctant to abandon such a proven money-spinner as the Western without a fight, and attempts were made in the 1970s to resuscitate the basic formula, though some, such as Mel Brooks's *Blazing Saddles* (1974), a crude if at times inspired farce, were dancing on its grave.

The Western's myth of the onward march of civilization led by strong men and loyal women was looking rather threadbare. In particular, it was difficult to sustain in the light of revisionist histories which subverted the white supremacist view. Robert Altman's *Buffalo Bill and the Indians, or Sitting Bull's History Lesson* (1976), based on Arthur Kopit's stage play, laid bare the naked commercialism behind one of the founders of the myth of the West, Buffalo Bill Cody. Altman's *McCabe & Mrs. Miller* (1971) was a similarly disenchanted tale of a gambler and a prostitute in a gold camp, drawing a sad beauty from the frozen landscapes. Another heroic figure to be debunked was Jesse James: in Phil Kaufman's *The Great Northfield Minnesota Raid* (1971) the heroic outlaw is reduced to a half-crazed

Far left: Russell Crowe battles in the Colosseum in a revival of the sword and sandals epic, *Gladiator* (2000). Dir: Ridley Scott
Left: *Buffalo Bill and the Indians, or Sitting Bull's History Lesson* (1976) stars Paul Newman as Buffalo Bill Cody, the man who made the Wild West into a paying proposition. Dir: Robert Altman

eccentric. Jesse James appears again in Walter Hill's *The Long Riders* (1980), riding a West in which only family ties can protect against brutality and exploitation, and even those not for long. Some of the myths surrounding Wyatt Earp were stripped away in Frank Perry's *Doc* (1971), though two films of the 1990s, *Tombstone* (George P Cosmatos, 1993) and *Wyatt Earp* (Lawrence Kasdan, 1994), in which Earp is played respectively by Kurt Russell and Kevin Costner, attempted to patch up the earlier iconoclasm. Another legendary gunfighter, Wild Bill Hickok, is savagely satirized in Arthur Penn's *Little Big Man* (1970), in which the hero, Jack Crabbe (played by Dustin Hoffman), has a series of picturesque adventures, leading a double life as he constantly crosses the racial divide between whites and Indians. The film's bitterest denunciation is reserved for General Custer, seen as a crazed militarist bent on genocide.

Even Clint Eastwood, whose career began in the Italian or spaghetti Westerns of the 1960s and who transposed their tough and cynical view of the West to his own productions such as *High Plains Drifter* (1973), felt obliged to acknowledge that times had changed. In *The Outlaw Josey Wales* (1976) he befriends an ancient Indian, played by Chief Dan George, who had become something of a star after performing a similar role as Old Lodge Skins in *Little Big Man*. Eastwood has revealed himself a crafty negotiator between the traditional demands of the Western and the new political realities. *Pale Rider* (1985), a loose reworking of George Stevens's classic *Shane* (1953), pursues an ecological theme in scenes which document the devastation caused by hydraulic mining, while in *Unforgiven* (1992) Eastwood plays William Munny, an ageing former gunfighter who has renounced violence at his wife's insistence. Munny is persuaded out of retirement to avenge a prostitute who has been cruelly abused by a customer. Munny also has a black friend (Morgan Freeman), thus adding racial consciousness to the film's quasi-feminism.

The Westerns of the 1970s had many elegiac refrains for the passing of an era. Sam Peckinpah, the inheritor of John Ford's mantle, seemed intent on polishing off the genre single-handed. *The Wild Bunch* (1969) marked the passing of the old West in an orgy of destruction, as its heroes go down with all guns blazing. *The Ballad of Cable Hogue* (1970) was a gentler lament for a vanishing past, while in *Pat Garrett & Billy the Kid* (1973) Peckinpah did his bit for the demolition of the heroic figures of legend. Eastwood's mentor, Don Siegel, crafted a milestone along the trail to the last sunset with *The Shootist* (1976), in which John Wayne, himself stricken with the disease, plays an aged lawman dying of cancer.

One film seemed to sound the final death knell of the genre. Michael Cimino's *Heaven's Gate* (1980), a sprawling epic of the Johnson County War in Wyoming in the 1890s, was a not unimpressive achievement, radical in its denunciation of wealth and power and its

Above: The changing West. William Holden, Ernest Borgnine and Robert Ryan starred in *The Wild Bunch* (1969), a violent elegy. Dir: Sam Peckinpah
Below: Dustin Hoffman is Jack Crabbe, a white man who goes native in *Little Big Man* (1970) Dir: Arthur Penn
Below right: In *Pale Rider* (1985) Clint Eastwood is a fighting preacher who helps poor miners battle a big corporation. Dir: Clint Eastwood
Opposite: Clint Eastwood is poacher turned gamekeeper in *Unforgiven* (1992), a reformed gunfighter who takes up the cause of a wronged prostitute. Dir: Clint Eastwood

CLASSIC GENRES REVIVED

Above: 'Regulators' assemble to throw immigrants off the open range in the expensively produced *Heaven's Gate* (1980). Dir: Michael Cimino
Below: Lothaire Bluteau as Father Laforgue, a Jesuit priest among the native peoples of Canada in *Black Robe* (1991).
Dir: Bruce Beresford
Opposite: Union officer Lieutenant John Dunbar (Kevin Costner) opts for a remote posting and the life of a native American in *Dances with Wolves* (1990). Dir: Kevin Costner
Overleaf: Daniel Day-Lewis is frontiersman Hawkeye, here fighting the French with his Indian companion Uncas (Eric Schweig) in *The Last of the Mohicans* (1992). Dir: Michael Mann

defence of landless immigrants. But it was so expensive to produce and such a box office disaster when released that it dissuaded Hollywood executives from ever green-lighting a Western again. Only at the end of the decade did the Western struggle back on its feet. *Young Guns* (Christopher Cain, 1988), which retooled the story of Billy the Kid for a youth audience with Brat-Pack stars such as Emilio Estevez and Charlie Sheen, was successful enough to warrant a sequel, *Young Guns II* (Geoff Murphy, 1990). Then Kevin Costner surprised everyone with *Dances with Wolves* (1990), a three-hour film about a Civil War soldier who joins the Sioux. Sentimental and naive in many ways, it nevertheless achieved an epic narrative sweep and made full use of the landscape of the rolling plains.

Dances with Wolves was one of a trio of films in the early 1990s about Indians, or Native Americans as it was now correct to call them, which show Hollywood adapting the genre just enough to accommodate new attitudes without destroying its basic premises. *Black Robe* (Bruce Beresford, 1991), based on a novel by the Irish Catholic writer Brian Moore, tells the story of a seventeenth-century Jesuit priest among the native peoples of Canada. A coproduction between Canada and Australia, it attempts to show the strangeness of Indian life to a European, without either idealization or denigration. By contrast, Michael Mann's version of the much-filmed *The Last of the Mohicans* (1992) plumbs largely for excitement and romance, which it delivers in large measure. Despite some changes to James Fenimore Cooper's book, the film remains faithful to its central concept of a white hero 'gone native', who prefers the company of Indians to his own kind. In this way Hollywood seeks to adapt the Western to a society more aware of racial prejudice. Now that Native Americans are making their own films, we shall get a different take on these topics, but the results will not fit comfortably within the Western genre.

If the decline of the Western may be laid at the door of changing social and political consciousness, the eclipse of the musical surely derives from changes within the media. Both Fred Astaire and Gene Kelly had retired from dancing by 1970. That they were not replaced is the result of the radical transformation in popular music since the 1950s, with Cole Porter and Rodgers and Hammerstein usurped by rock music. Since the film audience was getting younger, Hollywood was obliged to adapt the musical to their tastes. But the raw energy and iconoclasm of rock was ill-suited to the narrative and social conventions of the musical. Rock found its natural outlet in live performance, in domestic consumption through records and, from 1981, in the format of MTV, which offered a new way of combining music and visuals.

Attempts were made to harness rock to film. Ken Russell's *Tommy* (1975), a version of The Who's 'rock opera', was too flashily eccentric to lead anywhere, but *Rock 'n' Roll High School*

CLASSIC GENRES REVIVED

Opposite: John Travolta disco-dancing in *Saturday Night Fever* (1977).
Dir: John Badham
Above: Liza Minnelli and Robert De Niro get it on 1940s-style in *New York, New York* (1977).
Dir: Martin Scorsese
Below: An energetic and expensive attempt to revive the tradition of the Hollywood musical:

Nicole Kidman and Ewan McGregor in *Moulin Rouge!* (2001).
Dir: Baz Luhrmann
Below right: A big production number in *Pennies from Heaven* (1981), counterpointing glamour and despair, and based on a BBC television series by Dennis Potter.
Dir: Herbert Ross

(Allan Arkush, 1979) and *Footloose* (Herbert Ross, 1984) catch something of the authentic feel of the music (in the former case supplied by the Ramones). *Grease* (Randal Kleiser, 1978) was a self-conscious exercise in nostalgia, set in a 1950s high school, successful enough to warrant a sequel *Grease II* (Patricia Birch, 1982). *Saturday Night Fever* (John Badham, 1977) owed its success mainly to the Bee Gees's disco music and John Travolta's energetic if unsophisticated dancing; it spawned a sequel, *Staying Alive* (Sylvester Stallone, 1983), but by that time music had moved on.

Bob Fosse had been choreographer on such classic musicals as *The Pajama Game* (Stanley Donen, 1957), and his two musicals of the 1970s, *Cabaret* (1972) and *All That Jazz* (1979), were in the tradition of the Broadway show. Musicals have continued to be popular in the theatre; witness the astonishing success of Andrew Lloyd Webber. But the audience for such productions – older, more middle class – cannot sustain the musical film, and Alan Parker's *Evita* (1996) shows why. The show-stopping numbers seem bombastic in the cinema, while the lack of narrative drive makes the film's two-hour span seem endless.

Two of Hollywood's heavyweights tried to swim against the tide. Martin Scorsese directed *New York, New York* (1977), a recreation of the MGM musical, casting Judy Garland's daughter Liza Minnelli opposite Robert De Niro in a reconstruction of the musical world of the 1940s, with Scorsese's usual mixture of powerful emotion and visual flair. By contrast, *The Last Waltz*, which he directed the following year, is a restrained but meticulously staged film of a performance by The Band. Francis Ford Coppola's *One from the Heart* (1982) is a commonplace, even banal love story but makes wonderful use of the resources of Hollywood studio technology in creating a highly artificial but beautiful neon-lit space. Coppola's *The Cotton Club* (1984) was an expensive reconstruction of Harlem in the Prohibition era. Though more of a gangster film than a musical, its best moments are the staging of the numbers in the famous club of the title.

When a genre loses its confidence it may either ironize or naturalize its conventions.

Jane Feuer has shown how *Pennies from Heaven* (1981) 'systematically deconstructs' the genre.[2] Based on Dennis Potter's series for BBC Television, the film counterpoints the downbeat tale of a salesman during the Depression with songs of the era, their easy optimism contrasted with the protagonist's increasingly desperate plight. This was one solution to the awkwardness that contemporary audiences seem to feel when the music and dancing are introduced into the story. Another is to use the biographical format, thus realistically anchoring the songs in the story. *Lady Sings the Blues* (Sidney J Furie, 1972), about Billie Holiday; *Bound for Glory* (Hal Ashby, 1976), about Woody Guthrie; *The Buddy Holly Story* (Steve Rash, 1978); *Coal Miner's Daughter* (Michael Apted, 1980), about Loretta Lynn; *La Bamba* (Luis Valdez, 1987), about Richie Valens; *Great Balls of Fire!* (Jim McBride, 1989), about Jerry Lee Lewis; *The Doors* (Oliver Stone, 1991), about Jim Morrison; and *What's Love Got to Do with It?* (Brian Gibson, 1993), about Tina Turner, were films of no great cinematic distinction but the biographical narrative gave a strong peg on which to hang the musical numbers. However, Hollywood's most recent attempt to revive the musical, *Moulin Rouge!* (Baz Luhrmann, 2001), shows how not to do it. The stars, Nicole Kidman and Ewan McGregor, show little aptitude for singing or dancing, a fact barely disguised by frenzied camerawork and editing.

The biopic was a mainstay of classical Hollywood, reserved for some of its most earnest eruptions of social conscience, as for example in the 1937 Warner Bros. production *The Life of Emile Zola* (William Dieterle). Though Hollywood seems increasingly reluctant to deal with serious issues, biography can still offer a way of leavening a film about politics with human interest. *Blaze* (Ron Shelton, 1989) starred Paul Newman in a story about the maverick governor of Louisiana, Huey Long, and his affair with a stripper. More substantial political biopics were Oliver Stone's brace of presidential lives, *JFK* (1991) and *Nixon* (1995). Like most of Stone's pictures they tended towards the bombastic, but the 'conspiracy' of Kennedy's assassination and the tragi-comedy of Nixon's fall were treated in exhaustive and exhausting detail, each film running over three hours. More entertaining purely as a film was Alan J Pakula's *All the President's Men* (1976), which employed the visual style and narrative tension of film noir to uncover the complexities of Watergate. Robert Redford, who played *Washington Post* reporter Bob Woodward, had also been the star of Michael Ritchie's *The Candidate* (1972), playing a politician whose ideals are eroded by electoral pressures. Unashamedly scabrous in tone is Larry Cohen's muck-raking *The Private Files of J. Edgar Hoover* (1978), which combined fierce attacks on the illiberal regime of the former head of the FBI with revelations about his unorthodox sexual tastes. The most radical of Hollywood's biopics is Warren Beatty's *Reds* (1981), perhaps the closest Hollywood ever came to endorsing an anti-capitalist philosophy. A tale of the Russian Revolution using the life story of US journalist John Reed to focus its sprawling panorama, the film deals even more impressively with the radical socialist tradition in the United States than with the political convulsions of Russia in 1917.

Specific social problems, rather than politics in general, tend to be the preserve of the made-for-TV movie, but there are notable exceptions. *Bob Roberts* (1992), about an unscrupulous right-wing politician, had already shown Tim Robbins to be an actor-director prepared to confront serious subject matter, and his *Dead Man Walking* (1995), which starred his partner, Susan Sarandon, is a protest against capital punishment which does not load the dice by absolving the condemned man of his anti-social attitudes. Alan Parker's *Mississippi Burning* (1988), about the civil rights protests of the 1960s, was criticized for its view of the blacks as victims needing to be rescued by noble whites, but produced an uninhibited portrait of southern racism. Barry Levinson's *Rain Man* (1988), in which Dustin Hoffman plays a gifted autistic, is perhaps less about a problem than it is an opportunity for the stars (Tom Cruise plays his brother) to go through their tricks. Much the same could be said about *Kramer vs. Kramer* (Robert Benton, 1979), in which Hoffman is again the star, this time divorcing from Meryl Streep in a melodrama that plays up the personal rather than

Top left: Dustin Hoffman as Carl Bernstein and Robert Redford as Bob Woodward, investigating conspiracy in *All the President's Men* (1976). Dir: Alan J Pakula
Above left: Warren Beatty as the intrepid John Reed among the Soviets in *Reds* (1981). Dir: Warren Beatty
Left: Kevin Costner (standing) as New Orleans District Attorney Jim Garrison, investigating the Kennedy assassination in *JFK* (1991). Dir: Oliver Stone

Above top: Sean Penn
as convicted killer
Matthew Poncelet and
Susan Sarandon as
Sister Helen Prejean in
Dead Man Walking
(1995).

Dir: Tim Robbins
Above: Divorced father
Ted Kramer (Dustin
Hoffman) in *Kramer vs.
Kramer* (1979).
Dir: Robert Benton

developing the issues. *Clean and Sober* (Glenn Gordon Caron, 1988) has Michael
Keaton as an alcoholic forced to confront the consequences of his addiction. It avoids the
melodramatics of some earlier Hollywood films on the topic such as *The Lost Weekend* (Billy
Wilder, 1945) and *Days of Wine and Roses* (Blake Edwards, 1962), but is not so entertaining.
A less fashionable subject was the plight of small farmers in the United States as depicted
in *Country* (Richard Pearce, 1984), in which two glamorous stars, Jessica Lange and Sam
Shepard, give moving performances as a couple whose farm is caught in the tightening
vice of economic forces.

Throughout World War II war films had been a staple in Hollywood, and they continued
to be so into the 1970s and beyond. *Tora! Tora! Tora!* (Richard Fleischer, 1970) was an old-
fashioned example of the genre, an 'epic' (i.e. expensive) reconstruction of the attack on
Pearl Harbor. But as with the Western, irreverence set in. Robert Altman's *MASH* (1970), set
in a US field hospital during the Korean War, rejects conventional heroics, making farcical
humour from the absurdities of conflict. Its spirit doubtless owed something to Joseph
Heller's novel *Catch-22*, first published in 1961 but filmed by director Mike Nichols in the
same year as *MASH*. But most war films continued to be set in World War II, and it took
Hollywood a long time to catch up with Vietnam. The Tet offensive of 1968 signalled
the beginning of the end for US involvement, the reverses suffered by US troops a clear
indication that things on the ground were getting worse, not better. Yet it would be at least
a decade before Hollywood could bring itself to address the foreign and domestic policy
issues which the Vietnam War raised. When at last Vietnam films arrived, they came not
as single spies but in battalions. *The Boys in Company C* (Sidney J Furie, 1977) was actually
produced by Golden Harvest, a Hong Kong company, but it conformed to the stereotype
of World War II movies, following a group of raw recruits, played by unknown US actors,
as they experience combat for the first time. *Go Tell the Spartans* (Ted Post, 1978) had the
advantage of Burt Lancaster in the principal role of a disillusioned veteran, with a group

<u>Opposite</u>: Willem Dafoe as Sergeant Elias, one of the foot-soldiers in *Platoon* (1986). Dir: Oliver Stone <u>Right</u>: Games of Russian roulette with the Vietcong: John Savage in *The Deer Hunter* (1978). Dir: Michael Cimino <u>Below</u>: Rehabilitation therapy: Jon Voight and Jane Fonda in *Coming Home* (1978). Dir: Hal Ashby

of Americans trying to make sense of a war they do not really understand. Oliver Stone's *Platoon* (1986) at least had the advantage that its director was himself a Vietnam veteran, and it captures the physical feel of the country like no other. But like virtually all its companions it presents the war simply as it affected the US combatants. John Irvin's *Hamburger Hill* (1987), Stanley Kubrick's *Full Metal Jacket* (1987) and Brian De Palma's *Casualties of War* (1989) all focus on the experiences of foot soldiers in combat, with the latter, despite its melodramatic excesses, quite radical in confronting the degradation of the US fighting man. The cinema, of course, is uniquely well-equipped to portray what fighting looks like, even what it feels like. What is missing from these films, and even more from the gung-ho heroics of Sylvester Stallone in *First Blood* (Ted Kotcheff, 1982), *Rambo: First Blood, Part Two* (George Pan Cosmatos, 1985) and *Rambo III* (Peter MacDonald, 1988), not to mention the cut-price imitations of Chuck Norris in *Missing in Action* (Joseph Zito, 1984), is any real sense of what the war was about.

Francis Ford Coppola's epic *Apocalypse Now* was released in 1979. The story of its production has been extensively documented: the interminable shooting schedule (238 days); the disasters (storms that wrecked the sets, a heart attack suffered by the film's star, Martin Sheen); Coppola's lengthy attempts at the editing stage to wrestle his unwieldy monster into a coherent film. What emerged was a series of impressive set pieces (the helicopter attack cut to Wagner's *Ride of the Valkyries*, the hideous incongruity of the Playboy Bunnies performance in the jungle, the final revelation of the horrors of Kurtz's camp), but also something more than that. If Coppola did not supply a political analysis, he at least provided a fuller portrait of the war: expensive, wasteful, good intentions vitiated by confusion, the military-industrial complex out of control.

The Deer Hunter (Michael Cimino, 1978) was extravagantly praised on its release and is undeniably powerful in its depiction of a blue-collar worker's initiation into warfare and its after-effects. The sequence in which the Vietcong force their captives to play Russian roulette demonizes the enemy but makes for memorable cinema. If ultimately the film cannot carry the weight of its allegorical significance as a statement about the United States, strong performances by Robert De Niro and Christopher Walken make it never less than watchable.

What is most striking about Hollywood's treatment of Vietnam is not the absence of political analysis; after all, how many World War II films seriously discuss what the war was about? Rather, it is that even when the films take a critical view of the conflict, the drastic effects of the war on the Vietnamese – both North and South – simply do not register. By contrast, a whole sub-genre of films (which *The Deer Hunter* anticipates) deal with the after-effects of the war on US combatants. In Hal Ashby's *Coming Home* (1978) Jane Fonda plays a nurse whose sexual favours rehabilitate a crippled veteran (Jon Voight) at the same time as his understandably anti-war sentiments help her question her previous unexamined affirmation of the military values espoused by her husband. Karel Reisz's *Dog Soldiers/Who'll Stop the Rain?* (1978) begins in Vietnam, where two US military men

The Epic War Film
Apocalypse Now (1979)
Dir: Francis Ford Coppola

After the success of the first two *Godfather* films in 1972 and 1974 respectively, Francis Ford Coppola embarked on an ambitious attempt to bring home the reality of the war in Vietnam, which had concluded with the fall of Saigon to the Vietcong in 1975. It was to be as disaster-prone as the American war effort itself. As a consequence of a typhoon which wrecked the sets, a heart attack to star Martin Sheen and other problems, the shooting schedule, much of it in the Philippines, eventually extended to sixteen months and the budget inflated to $30 million.

The plot was loosely based on the book *Heart of Darkness*, a story by Joseph Conrad about Kurtz, a trading company agent in the African jungle who has acquired mysterious powers over the natives. Coppola retains much of this, including such details as the severed heads outside Kurtz's headquarters and his final words, 'The horror, the horror...'. In the film Sheen plays an army captain given the job of 'terminating with extreme prejudice' Kurtz, a US soldier who has become an embarrassment to the authorities. On his journey up the river to Kurtz's camp he experiences the demoralization of the US forces, high on dope or drunk with power.

Although, as a result of cuts forced on Coppola, the film was accused of incoherence when first released, it was by far the most serious attempt to get to grips with the experience of Vietnam and a triumphant reinvention of the war film genre. In 1980 the film won an Oscar for Best Cinematography and Best Sound. *Apocalypse Now* was re-released in 2001 with fifty minutes restored. As a result, the film can now be seen as the epic masterpiece it is.

Country of Origin: USA
Production Company: Zoetrope Studios
Running Time: 153 mins (Re-release 203 mins)

Producer: Francis Ford Coppola
Writers: John Milius, Francis Ford Coppola
Director of Photography: Vittorio Storaro
Music: Carmine Coppola, Francis Ford Coppola
Production Designer: Dean Tavoularis
Editors: Walter Murch, Gerald B Greenberg, Lisa Fruchtman

Colonel Walter E Kurtz: Marlon Brando
Lt-Col Bill Kilgore: Robert Duvall
Captain Benjamin L Willard: Martin Sheen
'Chef' Hicks: Frederic Forrest
Chief Phillips: Albert Hall
Lance B Johnson: Sam Bottoms
'Clean': Lawrence Fishburne
Photojournalist: Dennis Hopper
Colonel Lucas: Harrison Ford

Above: Despite huge material resources, the Americans are losing the war.
Left: Actor Marlon Brando (l) with director Francis Ford Coppola.
Top right: Stunning poster conveying the drama and spectacle of this truly outstanding film.

Above right: 'I love the smell of napalm in the morning': Robert Duvall as the gung-ho Lieutenant-Colonel Kilgore.
Right: Martin Sheen as Captain Willard plumbs the depths, physically and mentally.

SCHINDLER: He wants to kill everybody? Great. What am I supposed to do, bring everybody over? Is that what you think? Yeah, send them over to Schindler, send them all. His place is a 'haven', didn't you know? It's not a factory, it's not an enterprise of any kind, it's a haven for people with no skills whatsoever. You think I don't know what you're doing? You're so quiet all the time? I know.

STERN: Are you losing money?

SCHINDLER: No, I'm not losing money, that's not the point.

STERN: What other point is –

SCHINDLER: It's dangerous. It's dangerous, to me, personally.

Oskar Schindler (Liam Neeson), Itzhak Stern (Ben Kingsley), *Schindler's List* (Steven Spielberg, 1993)

Above: Liam Neeson as Oskar Schindler confronts Ben Kingsley as Itzhak Stern in *Schindler's List* (1993), shot in black and white.

Left: Black and white realism: entering the concentration camp in *Schindler's List* (1993). Dir: Steven Spielberg

Above: Tom Cruise plays crippled Vietnam veteran Ron Kovic in *Born on the Fourth of July* (1989). Dir: Oliver Stone
Below: Christian Bale as the young boy Jim Graham in Japanese-occupied China in *Empire of the Sun* (1987). Dir: Steven Spielberg
Below right: Sean Penn and comrades pinned down under Japanese fire in *The Thin Red Line* (1998). Dir: Terrence Malick

smuggle a shipment of heroin back to the States. The subsequent story, involving their attempts to outwit FBI narcotics investigators, owes more to the crime genre, except that the war appears to function as a kind of catch-all explanation of why good people turn bad. The junkie/criminal/psychotic veteran would become something of a cliché in the crime film: in *Lethal Weapon* (Richard Donner, 1987) cop Mel Gibson's psychological disturbance is largely the result of his experiences in Vietnam.

Oliver Stone returned to the subject in *Born on the Fourth of July* (1989), about a crippled veteran, played by Tom Cruise. Based on the autobiography of Ron Kovic, it is a moving story, told with some passion though suffering from Stone's increasingly florid and overblown style. His third Vietnam film, *Heaven & Earth* (1993), traces the path of a Vietnamese woman through the war and beyond. Her eventual marriage to a US marine emerges as some kind of solution to the 'problem' of the war.

One of the greatest casualties of the Vietnam War was Cambodia, and *The Killing Fields* (1984) is an attempt to tell what happened under the Pol Pot regime. Though the film is clumsily structured and Roland Joffé's direction is uncertain, it is an honourable piece of work which takes a steady look at horror. By the end of the 1980s Hollywood felt it had done Vietnam. But, surprisingly perhaps, the war film did not, like the Western, wither away. Instead, it returned to the more comforting certainties of World War II. Steven Spielberg's *Empire of the Sun* (1987) is based on J G Ballard's novel about a young boy imprisoned by the Japanese in China during World War II. The film has some extraordinary images and successfully renders the whole business of war strange by showing it through the eyes of a child. Spielberg's *Schindler's List* (1993) is again based on a major novel, by the Australian Thomas Keneally, about a German who saves Jews from the concentration camps. Shot in black and white (perhaps to denote this is a serious piece of work), the film demonstrates Spielberg's desire to be seen as something more than a mere entertainer. It manages largely to avoid sentimentality without becoming the masterpiece its director wished for (and some of his audience thought he had achieved). Much the same might be said of *Saving Private Ryan* (1998), which begins on the beaches of Normandy with some graphic sequences of combat but suffers from a clichéd story line not saved by Tom Hanks's dogged performance.

The pretensions of *Saving Private Ryan* were exposed by another World War II film in the same year, this time set in the Pacific. Terrence Malick's return to film-making following a twenty-year absence after *Days of Heaven* in 1978 was a triumph. Shot through with images of stunning delicacy and power, with brilliant performances from Nick Nolte and Jim Caviezel, *The Thin Red Line* (1998) might claim to be the best war film Hollywood ever produced. One sequence, in which a group of fearful GIs try to advance up a hill under murderous fire from the Japanese, is unsurpassed in its representation of the sheer terror of armed combat. But there are extra dimensions to Malick's film, in the mysterious images of nature he intercuts and in the conversations of those fighting and those supposedly in control. By contrast, Ridley Scott's *Black Hawk Down* (2001), about the US debacle in

Somalia in 1993, though made with undeniable technical skill and giving a vivid sense of combat, lacks insight into the events it describes.

One of the most securely established of all Hollywood genres has been the animated feature for children. From its first brilliant success with *Snow White and the Seven Dwarfs* (David Hand, 1937), Disney has led the way, and until recently had no rivals. By the 1970s the company was a Goliath in the entertainment business, having diversified into theme parks, publishing, television, merchandising and other spin-offs. But, just at the time that Hollywood was renewing itself, it appeared as if Disney had lost its way. Its feature-length cartoons such as *Robin Hood* (Wolfgang Reitherman, 1973) and *Pete's Dragon* (Don Chaffey, 1977) were lacklustre, abandoning the previously labour-intensive methods of production, which involved thousands of hand-produced drawings, for cheaper, less detailed processes. The company revived in the mid-1980s by starting up an ancillary, Touchstone Pictures, to make live-action films aimed at adults. *Splash!* (Ron Howard, 1984), a comedy about a modern-day mermaid, starring Tom Hanks and Daryl Hannah, was an early fruit of this policy. Disney has continued to make live-action features for both adults and children; *Honey I Shrunk the Kids* (Joe Johnston, 1989), a popular comedy about a man who accidentally miniaturizes his family, made clever use of special effects. *Who Framed Roger Rabbit* (Robert Zemeckis, 1988) ingeniously integrated cartoon characters into real-life sequences in a loving pastiche of the films noirs of the 1940s.

In the 1990s Disney came triumphantly back to form with animated features, making full use of the advances in production techniques achieved by computers. *Beauty and the Beast* (Gary Trousdale, 1991), *Aladdin* (John Musker/Ron Clements/Ted Elliott/Terry Rossio, 1992), *The Lion King* (Roger Allers/Rob Minkoff, 1994) and *The Hunchback of Notre Dame* (Gary Trousdale/Kirk Wise, 1996) were technically assured and dramatically inventive, if not always avoiding the winsome sentimentality which the company seems to believe essential in addressing children. *Pocahontas* (Mike Gabriel/Eric Goldberg, 1995) also showed a belated attempt to get to grips with the problem of racial stereotyping which had dogged the company from its earliest days, though Pocahontas's physique owes as much to contemporary ideas of fashionable beauty as to the actual appearance of any Native American, and tying the release of the film to a promotion by McDonalds for its 'McChief burger' took a little of the gloss off Disney's new-found political correctness. In the 1990s a dozen or so animated features were released by Hollywood each year, but Disney's supremacy was challenged only by the new studio DreamWorks, with *Shrek* (Andrew Adamson/Vicky Jenson, 2001), and by *Chicken Run* (Peter Lord/Nick Park, 2000), made by British company Aardman Animations.

Previous pages: Spaceman Buzz Lightyear and cowboy Woody, two characters from *Toy Story* (1995), the first animated feature to be entirely computer-generated. Dir: John Lasseter
Top: Actor Bob Hoskins and the animated bunny in *Who Framed Roger Rabbit* (1988). Dir: Robert Zemeckis

Above: Characters from *Shrek* (2001), a popular animated film from the DreamWorks studio. Dir: Andrew Adamson and Vicky Jenson
Right: *The Lion King* (1994), one of the most successful of Disney's animated films of the 1990s, was later turned into a stage musical. Dir: Roger Allers and Rob Minkoff

CLASSIC GENRES REVIVED

Top: A British challenge to Disney: a scene from *Chicken Run* (2000). Dir: Peter Lord and Nick Park
Above: (l to r) Emma Watson as Hermione Granger, Rupert Grint as Ronald 'Ron' Wesley and Daniel Radcliffe as Harry Potter in *Harry Potter and the Philosopher's Stone* (2001), a combination of state-of-the-art special effects and traditional British acting. Dir: Chris Columbus

In the 1980s the merchandising tail began to wag the dog in children's films; with *The Care Bears Movie* (Arna Selznick, 1985) the cuddly toys came first and the film was a spin-off. Yet imaginative works continued to emerge, not always from the obvious sources. Wolfgang Petersen's *The NeverEnding Story* (1984) was a German production, a fairy-tale fantasy which was successful enough to warrant two sequels, in 1990 and 1994. *Babe* (Chris Noonan, 1995) was an Australian film about a talking pig which used state-of-the-art effects to animate its animal characters and integrate them into the live action. *Toy Story* (John Lasseter, 1995) was the first feature whose animation was entirely computer-generated, but more importantly it made believable characters of the toys that populated its narrative. Its technical quality, the texture of the images being a huge advance on the flatness of previous animation, drew high praise. Inevitably there was a sequel, *Toy Story II* (John Lasseter/Lee Unkrich, 1999). Nicolas Roeg's *Witches* (1990), more conventional technically, managed to capture the genuine cruelty and menace which made its author, Roald Dahl, such a favourite with children. In 2001 another British author, J K Rowling, was the basis for a huge box office hit, *Harry Potter and the Philosopher's Stone* (Chris Columbus), swiftly followed by a sequel, *Harry Potter and the Chamber of Secrets* (Chris Columbus, 2002). Over 100 million Harry Potter books have been sold worldwide, providing the film with a ready-made audience. Both films rely heavily on computer-generated effects for their most spectacular sequences, but also benefit from the traditional strengths of British character actors such as Maggie Smith, Robbie Coltrane and Alan Rickman.

The huge revenues generated by the Harry Potter films, likely to be a long-running franchise, mean that children's films – so long, to coin a phrase, the Cinderella of the film industry – are now at the cutting edge of technical achievement, because of the resources that can be deployed. It also means that risks can more readily be afforded, thus offering the prospect that the genre becomes increasingly a site of artistic creativity and daring.

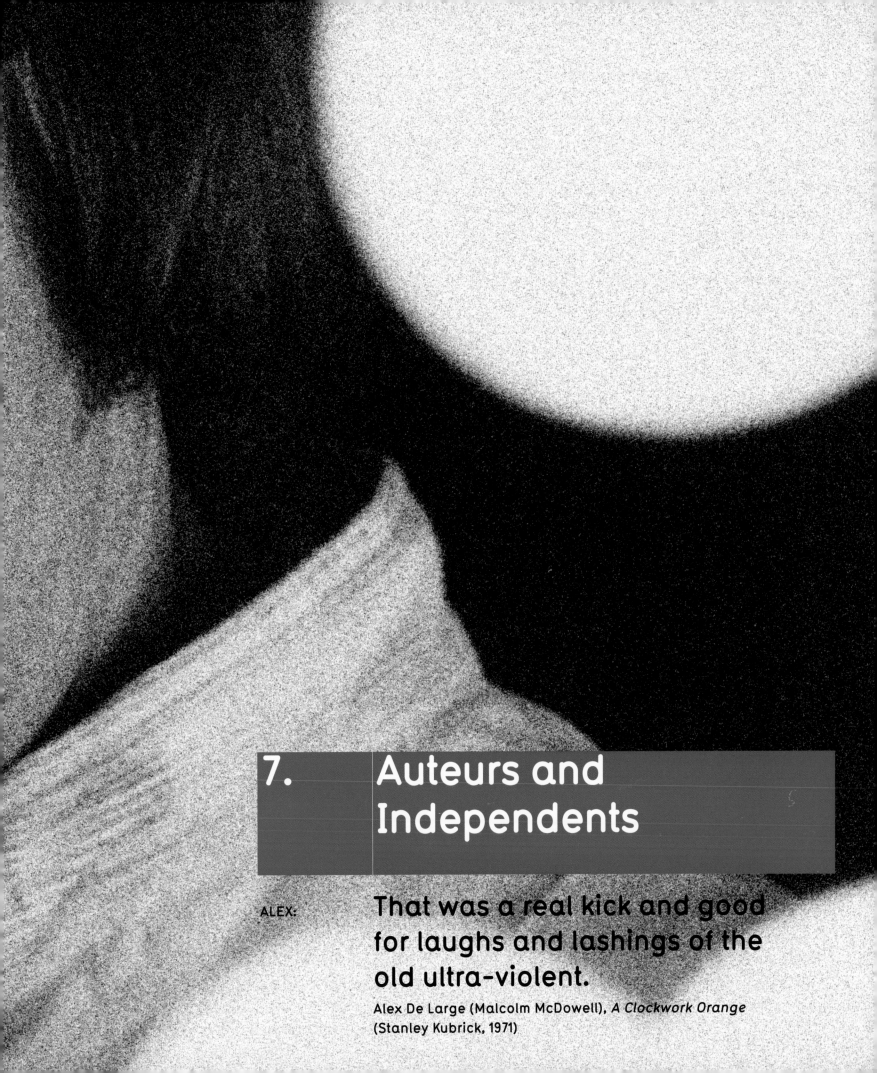

7. Auteurs and Independents

ALEX: **That was a real kick and good for laughs and lashings of the old ultra-violent.**

Alex De Large (Malcolm McDowell), *A Clockwork Orange*
(Stanley Kubrick, 1971)

ALVY:	Sure, I got ... I got nothing, uh, nothing till my analyst's appointment.
ANNIE:	Oh, you see an analyst?
ALVY:	Y-y-yeah, just for fifteen years.
ANNIE:	Fifteen years?
ALVY:	Yeah, uh, I'm gonna give him one more year and then I'm goin' to Lourdes.

Alvy Singer (Woody Allen), Annie Hall (Diane
Keaton), *Annie Hall* (Woody Allen, 1977)

Top: *Husbands and
Wives* (1992) was full of
insights into modern
marriage. Here director
Woody Allen's on-
screen wife Judy (Mia
Farrow) listens to friend
Michael (Liam Neeson).
Above: Woody Allen
with Mia Farrow and
Judy Davis on the set of
Husbands and Wives
(1992).
Dir: Woody Allen
Right: Ronee Blakley

as Barbara Jean in
Nashville (1975) a blend
of country and western
music, comedy and
tragedy.
Dir: Robert Altman
Opposite: Writer,
director and actor
Woody Allen appears
as Alvy Singer in his
first great hit, *Annie Hall*
(1977), with his co-star
Diane Keaton, who
takes the title role.
Dir: Woody Allen

In the Hollywood cinema of genres, the expression of the creative personality has to take second place to the fashioning of a commercial product. Yet such is the size of Hollywood that, systematic as its mechanisms are, they are bound to be leaky. Films get made which break the mould, which refuse to conform to the prevailing conventions. And such is Hollywood's wealth that it can afford a certain amount of experimentation, can indulge a talented but eccentric minority. For a moment in the 1970s it looked as if the mould might be broken altogether, as a new kind of cinema emerged in the work of Francis Ford Coppola, Bob Rafelson and others, as discussed in Chapter 1. Though the system soon reasserted itself, a few seized their chance to pursue a singular course, if not independent of Hollywood then at least at arm's length.

Physically removed by the width of the continent is the comedian Woody Allen, who has used New York as his base for a steady stream of films which, though increasingly well-crafted, retain their roots in Allen's distinctive New York Jewish humour. Originally a stand-up comic and scriptwriter, Allen appears in nearly all his films as the nerdy, insecure anti-hero who aspires to worldly success, especially with women. His first great hit was *Annie Hall* (1977). Since then he has averaged nearly a film a year. Always cinematically literate (his great hero is Ingmar Bergman), films such as *Zelig* (1983), *The Purple Rose of Cairo* (1985) and *Shadows and Fog* (1992) play with filmic conventions, while others such as *Deconstructing Harry* (1997) satirize the pretensions of the artist. One of his most successful is *Husbands and Wives* (1992), in which Allen and his long-time companion Mia Farrow play a Manhattan husband and wife, Gabe and Judy, happily married despite underlying tensions. They are shocked when their best friends Jack and Sally announce their separation. In a series of deft and witty scenes punctuated by the characters' interviews with an off-screen investigator, we see Jack and Sally eventually stitch their marriage back together while Judy leaves Gabe for Sally's former boyfriend. Unable to commit himself to a young student he is attracted to, Gabe ends sadder if not wiser. The jokes are clever and funny, and the insights into modern marriage penetrating and often uncomfortable. Immediately afterwards Allen was involved in an acrimonious split with Farrow after it emerged he had been conducting an affair with Farrow's adopted daughter. But the scandal has done little to harm the success of his stylish and economically produced films.

Equally as productive, though more protean, is Robert Altman. His first big success, *MASH* (1970), established his distinctive style, with its naturalistic use of sound and fast-paced action. In the 1970s Altman worked in several genres, though always against the grain, including the Western – *McCabe & Mrs. Miller* (1971) and *Buffalo Bill and the Indians* (1976); the crime film – *Thieves Like Us* (1974); and science fiction – *Quintet* (1979), but

apart from *Nashville* (1975), a dazzlingly complex and highly entertaining story of the country music industry, he had little success at the box office. His frequently declared hostility to studio methods of working led to him becoming estranged from Hollywood in the 1980s (he lived in Paris for much of the time), but made him the ideal director for *The Player* (1992), a satire on the film industry. The 1990s have seen much of Altman's best work, including *Prêt-à-porter* (1994), set in the Paris fashion industry, and what is perhaps his masterpiece, *Short Cuts* (1993), an intricately structured series of overlapping narratives of Los Angeles.

Stanley Kubrick is another who physically separated himself from Hollywood, living in England from the early 1960s. His sudden death in 1999 ended a career which had huge influence over contemporary cinema. Kubrick was the supreme technician, his films taking longer and longer to prepare and execute, but he was also a thinker in a world of dilettantes. *2001: A Space Odyssey* (1968) is a founding text of the science fiction boom that has sustained much of Hollywood in recent years. *A Clockwork Orange* (1971) was a stylistically original and intellectually challenging film about urban alienation. If *Barry Lyndon* (1975) was not much more than an elegant costume saga, *The Shining* (1980), from a Stephen King novel, was an influential contribution to the horror genre. Few will forget the scene where

AUTEURS AND INDEPENDENTS

Above and right: Malcolm McDowell leads a gang of young thugs engaged in orgiastic violence in a bleakly dystopic Britain portrayed in *A Clockwork Orange* (1971). Dir: Stanley Kubrick

The tide of terror that swept America
IS HERE

THE SHINING

A STANLEY KUBRICK FILM

STARRING
JACK NICHOLSON SHELLEY DUVALL "THE SHINING" WITH SCATMAN CROTHERS DANNY LLOYD

BASED ON THE NOVEL BY   SCREENPLAY BY   PRODUCED AND DIRECTED BY   EXECUTIVE PRODUCER
STEPHEN KING   STANLEY KUBRICK & DIANE JOHNSON   STANLEY KUBRICK   JAN HARLAN

PRODUCED IN ASSOCIATION WITH THE PRODUCER CIRCLE CO. From Warner Bros. W A Warner Communications Company. © Warner Bros. Inc.1980 All Rights Reserved

Opposite: 'Here's Johnny!'. Adapted from a Stephen King novel, *The Shining* (1980) had many frightening moments, as when the demented Jack

Nicholson breaks through the door with an axe while his terrified wife (Shelley Duvall) cowers inside.
Dir: Stanley Kubrick

a demented Jack Nicholson, supposedly writing a novel, is discovered typing out the same sentence over and over again. Kubrick's film about the Vietnam War, *Full Metal Jacket* (1987), avoids the sentimentality of many Hollywood war films, though is too cold-hearted for some. His final film, *Eyes Wide Shut* (1999), a teasing mystery starring Tom Cruise and Nicole Kidman, was disliked by some for its sexual content but looks set to grow in stature as the beauty of its style and subtlety of its content become acknowledged.

If Hollywood repelled some, it drew in many. One of the most successful immigrants is Milos Forman. Arriving in the United States after his career in Czech cinema was cut short by the Russian invasion of 1968, Forman achieved both commercial and critical success with *One Flew Over the Cuckoo's Nest* (1975), a powerful, at times harrowing story set in a mental hospital, with an outstanding performance by Jack Nicholson. *Ragtime* (1981) was an ambitious attempt to realize E L Doctorow's dense historical portrait of the United States in 1906. Forman scored another success with *Amadeus* (1984), a flamboyant film of Peter Shaffer's play about Mozart. Forman dug into the social life of his adopted country with his portrait of a pornographer in *The People vs. Larry Flynt* (1996). *Man on the Moon* (1999), starring Jim Carrey in a life of the manic comedian Andy Kaufman, is another venture into the byways of US culture.

Above: Czech-born Milos Forman on the set of *Hair* (1979), the psychedelic musical that was his third Hollywood feature.
Dir: Milos Forman
Right: Actor Jack Nicholson (in blue shirt) in the ward of the mental hospital in *One Flew Over the Cuckoo's Nest* (1975), based on

Ken Keysey's novel.
Dir: Milos Forman
Below right: Tom Hulce as Wolfgang Amadeus Mozart conducting the orchestra. Adapted from the play about Mozart by Peter Shaffer, *Amadeus* (1984) was both visually powerful and commercially successful.
Dir: Milos Forman

An Auteur Par Excellence
Casino (1995)
Dir: Martin Scorsese

Martin Scorsese is an American auteur par excellence, and as one would expect *Casino* has much in common with his earlier crime films such as *Mean Streets* (1973), *Taxi Driver* (1976) and *GoodFellas* (1990). All of them star Robert De Niro, an icon of the contemporary Hollywood crime film, and *Casino* is written by Nicholas Pileggi, who wrote *GoodFellas*. But where Scorsese's earlier films focused on the pathology of the individual criminal, *Casino* lays bare a whole system.

The film traces the career of 'Ace' Rothstein (De Niro), charged by the mob with running the Tangiers casino in Las Vegas in the 1970s. *Casino* has a brilliant surface glitter and extraordinary performances (not least from Sharon Stone as the hooker 'Ace' marries), but it also meticulously presents the mechanisms whereby organized crime drains money from the gaming system.

Perhaps the Scorsese film *Casino* most resembles is *Gangs of New York* (2002), a similarly sprawling narrative of a city's development which reveals the violence and criminality welling up from the depths. But Scorsese's thematic concerns, with the paranoia which constantly hovers at the edge of contemporary urban life, and with masculinity pushed to the point of hysteria, surface in other, non-crime films such as *Raging Bull* (1980) (about a boxer Jake La Motta) and *The King of Comedy* (1983), in which Jerry Lewis is stalked by an obsessive fan. In both films Robert De Niro, Scorsese's favourite actor, exudes the barely controlled menace which gives the director's films much of their characteristic edge.

Based in New York, Scorsese has kept some distance both physically and artistically between himself and the Hollywood mentality, while remaining resolutely American in his sensibility and style.

Country of Origin: USA
Production Company: De Fina-Cappa/ Légende Enterprises/ Syalis DA/ Universal Pictures
Running Time: 178 mins

Producer: Barbara De Fina
Writers: Nicholas Pileggi, Martin Scorsese
Director of Photography: Robert Richardson
Music Editor: Bobby Mackston
Editor: Thelma Schoonmaker
Art Director: Jack G Taylor, Jr

Sam 'Ace' Rothstein: Robert De Niro
Ginger McKenna: Sharon Stone
Nicky Santoro: Joe Pesci
Lester Diamond: James Woods

Above from top: A difference of opinions: Joe Pesci as right-hand man Nicky Santoro and Sharon Stone as Ginger McKenna; Robert De Niro in a contemplative mood as 'Ace' Rothstein; Director Martin Scorsese (l) on set with Robert De Niro and Sharon Stone; and Martin Scorsese with Robert De Niro, dressed in the height of 1970s fashion Vegas-style.
Opposite: A roll of the dice: Sharon Stone as Ginger.

Above: *Mean Streets* (1973), with Robert De Niro (l) and Harvey Keitel, was an early exploration of the criminal milieu to which Scorsese has frequently returned.
Dir: Martin Scorsese
Right: A hard-hitting but brilliant piece of film-making, *GoodFellas* (1990)

starred (l to r) Ray Liotta, Robert De Niro and Joe Pesci (with gun).
Dir: Martin Scorsese
Below: Richard Gere as Julian, the elegant young man who sells himself to rich women, including Lauren Hutton, in *American Gigolo* (1980).
Dir: Paul Schrader

Though the child of Sicilian immigrants, no one is more American than Martin Scorsese. Several of his films have been set in a specifically Italian-American milieu, such as his first success, the crime drama *Mean Streets* (1973). *Taxi Driver* (1976) starred Scorsese's favourite actor Robert De Niro, another Italian-American, in a violent and disturbing story of New York lowlife (see Chapter 2). De Niro was also the lead in Scorsese's boxing drama *Raging Bull* (1980), a powerful study of the inarticulate rage behind machismo. Even Scorsese's lighter works such as *The King of Comedy* (1983), in which Jerry Lewis is stalked by De Niro as an eccentric fan, and *After Hours* (1985), a frenetic comedy of New York life, are tinged with menace, but *GoodFellas* (1990) surpasses any of the director's films both in the intensity of its violence and the brilliance of its camera technique. Scorsese was marking time with *Cape Fear* (1991), a remake of a 1961 crime thriller, and *The Age of Innocence* (1993), a lavish period piece based on Edith Wharton's novel, though each was made with great style. *Casino* (1995) saw Scorsese revert to more familiar subject matter in a story of Las Vegas mobsters, to which he brought a wonderful surface polish while losing nothing of his excoriating intensity. In *Gangs of New York* (2002) Scorsese has gone back to his roots in a story of ethnic violence set in the lawless New York City of the nineteenth century, with a mesmerizing performance by Daniel Day-Lewis.

Scorsese's scriptwriter on some key films (*Taxi Driver*, *Raging Bull* and the highly personal *The Last Temptation of Christ*, 1988) was Paul Schrader, whose strict Calvinist upbringing was an unusual preparation for Hollywood. Like Scorsese a cinephile (he wrote a book on Ozu Yasujiro, Robert Bresson and Carl Dreyer), but also like

AUTEURS AND INDEPENDENTS

BYTES:	Out!
MERRICK:	Bytes! Bytes, please! NO! I AM NOT AN ELEPHANT! I AM NOT AN ANIMAL!! I AM A HUMAN BEING! I ... AM ... A MAN! I AM A MAN!!
DWARF:	You alright?
MERRICK:	y-y-yes.
DWARF:	Want to come out?
MERRICK:	You're English.
DWARF:	Of course! You want out?
MERRICK:	Yes.

Bytes (Freddie Jones), John Merrick (John Hurt), Plumed Dwarf (Kenny Baker), *The Elephant Man* (David Lynch, 1980)

Scorsese compelled to plunge into the lower depths, Schrader first directed *Blue Collar* (1978), a slice of US working-class life. *Hardcore* (1979) descends into the murky world of commercial pornography, while *American Gigolo* (1980) is a brilliant study of sex for sale, with Richard Gere in the title role as a coldly beautiful gigolo. *Mishima: A Life in Four Chapters* (1985) was an uncommercial but ambitious biography of the right-wing Japanese novelist. A coolness often tending to bleakness is Schrader's most characteristic mode, as in *Affliction* (1997), a painful examination of family strife set in an appropriately wintry landscape, and *Auto Focus* (2002), a wickedly funny but disturbing chronicle of 1960s TV star Bob Crane, whose life disintegrates in a welter of porn and promiscuity.

Born in the same year as Schrader (1946), and for a time personally involved with Scorsese's former wife Isabella Rossellini, David Lynch has an artistic personality far removed from either of those directors. His first feature, *Eraserhead* (1977) was a highly eccentric work, full of surreal, even repellent imagery, which became a cult success. *The Elephant Man* (1980), the story of a deformed Victorian who achieves celebrity, continued Lynch's interest in the abnormal. *Dune* (1984) was an ill-advised venture into big-budget science fiction, but his masterpiece to date, *Blue Velvet* (1986), was a great success. Set in the small-town middle America that has become his preferred milieu, it recounts the misadventures of an innocent plunged into a world of drugs, masochistic sex and crime. *Wild at Heart* (1990), a freewheeling road movie, similarly exploited the terror of what lurks beneath the surface of everyday life, a theme explored at length in Lynch's television series *Twin Peaks* (1990). Some felt that Lynch had gone soft with *The Straight Story* (1999), a disarmingly naive tale about an elderly man who drives a lawn mower across two states, but *Mulholland Dr.* (2001) is a triumphant return to form, a mystery thriller set in a nightmarish Los Angeles full of cold-eyed killers and cowboys, eccentric movie folk and lipstick lesbians.

Right: Terrence Malick at work on his second feature, *Days of Heaven* (1978).
Below: Robert Wilke and Sam Shepard during a restful moment in the visually stunning *Days of Heaven* (1978).
Dir: Terrence Malick
Bottom: Sarah Jessica Parker and Johnny Depp, as an amusingly

untalented film director in *Ed Wood* (1994), shot in black and white, with occasional effects in colour.
Dir: Tim Burton
Opposite: Michael Keaton in *Beetlejuice* (1988), a visually inventive ghostly comedy.
Dir: Tim Burton

Like Lynch, Terrence Malick was a fellow at the American Film Institute's Center for Advanced Film Studies in the early 1970s, though his introduction to feature-film-making was more conventional. Whereas Lynch's *Eraserhead* was essentially a home movie, Malick wrote Hollywood scripts before directing his first film, *Badlands*, in 1973. The story of a young couple on a crime spree, it had an assured style and a very contemporary, non-judgemental distance from its subject. Malick's next film, *Days of Heaven* (1978), was a work of great visual beauty set around the time of World War I, but its story of city workers migrating to the wheatfields did not hold the public. As a result Malick withdrew from active film-making for the next twenty years, resurfacing in 1998 with the masterly *The Thin Red Line*, a visually stunning and philosophically profound depiction of World War II in the Pacific.

Alan Rudolph began as a protégé of Altman. His first film as director, *Welcome to L.A.* (1977), follows Altman's preference for a large cast of characters, in this case inhabitants of the Los Angeles rock scene. More of a visual stylist than Altman, Rudolph showed again with *Choose Me* (1984) his skill with ensemble playing and his sense of décor. *Mortal Thoughts* (1991) was a rare outing into working-class life, but *Afterglow* (1997), in which Julie Christie plays an ageing B-movie star, was a return to the show-business or artistic milieux Rudolph favours. A true child of Hollywood (his father was a director), Rudolph has the kind of detachment from his world that only an insider can achieve.

Tim Burton, too, was born in Hollywood, and was apprenticed early to the Disney cartoon factory. His films display an intimate, playful relationship to US popular culture. *Beetlejuice* (1988) showed astonishing visual inventiveness in a contemporary ghost story, and *Batman* (1989) was a brilliant dystopian vision of the modern city and its discontents. *Edward Scissorhands* (1990) combined surreal visuals with a satire on suburbia in its tale of a man with scissors for hands. Burton, doubtless seduced by huge amounts of money, had another go at Batman with *Batman Returns* (1992), then reverted to his animation roots with *The Nightmare before Christmas* (1993), a children's film for grown-ups. His most successful film to date is *Ed Wood* (1994), a clever and very funny reconstruction of the world of Hollywood B-films, based on the career of the man generally considered the worst director Hollywood ever produced. Burton's continuing re-creations of Hollywood genres – science fiction with *Mars Attacks!* (1996), horror with *Sleepy Hollow* (1999) and science fiction again with the remake of *Planet of the Apes* (2001) – hardly mark him out as an industry rebel, but his commercial success has enabled him to choose his own projects and to a remarkable extent put his visions on the screen unadulterated.

The Coen brothers, Joel and Ethan, have also, by dint of working within careful budgets,

Above: Frances McDormand as Marge Gunderson, the heavily pregnant police officer in *Fargo* (1996), set in a snowy North Dakota. Dir: Joel and Ethan Coen

JERRY: Ma'am, I answered your question.
            I answered the darn – I'm cooperating
            here, and I ...

MARGE: Sir, you have no call to get snippy with me.
            I'm just doin' my job here.

JERRY: I'm not, uh, I'm not arguin' here. I'm
            cooperating ... There's no, uh – we're doin'
            all we can ...

MARGE: Sir, could I talk to Mr. Gustafson? ...
            Mr. Lundegaard?

JERRY: Well, heck, if you wanna, if you wanna
            play games here! I'm working' with ya on
            this thing, but I ... Okay, I'll do a damned
            lot count!

MARGE: Sir? Right now?

JERRY: Sure right now! You're darned tootin'!

Jerry Lundegaard (William H. Macy), Marge
Gunderson (Frances McDormand), *Fargo* (Joel and
Ethan Coen, 1996)

Above: Billy Bob Thornton as the murderous barber with his adulterous wife (Frances McDormand) in the noirish *The Man Who Wasn't There* (2001), shot in black and white.
Dir: Joel and Ethan Coen
Above right: John Turturro, Tim Blake Nelson and George Clooney escape from the Depression prison farm in *O Brother, Where Art Thou?* (2000).
Dir: Joel and Ethan Coen
Below: Damián Delgado as Domingo, the soldier in *Men with Guns* (1997).
Dir: John Sayles

managed a close degree of control over their output. Like Burton, they feed off Hollywood's traditional genres, not quite subverting them but giving them a new, more self-conscious face. *Blood Simple* (1984) was a film noir which sucked the audience into an enjoyable but perplexing labyrinth of double-crossing, with a grisly climax. *Raising Arizona* (1987) was a madcap comedy about an incompetent kidnapper. *Miller's Crossing* (1990) was another crime film, set at the time of Prohibition and darker in tone. The Coens' next two films, *Barton Fink* (1991), a kind of Hollywood biopic which mutates into a horror film with political overtones, and *The Hudsucker Proxy* (1994), a pastiche of Frank Capra, were not successful commercially, but *Fargo* (1996) was a triumph. Set in a wintry North Dakota, it is the story of a car salesman whose plans to solve his money worries by arranging the kidnapping of his wife go badly astray. Frances McDormand (Joel's wife) is exceptional as a heavily pregnant police officer; the scenes of her domestic life display a tenderness the Coens had not previously revealed. *The Big Lebowski* (1998) featured yet another kidnapping and owed much to the hard-boiled detective fiction of the 1930s and 1940s, though even more to the Coens' distinctive sense of humour. *O Brother, Where Art Thou?* (2000) was another visit back to the 1930s, a prison-escape drama that worked variations on Warner Bros. crime films of the era, with the Coens' trademark mix of the comic and the macabre. *The Man Who Wasn't There* (2001) is a black and white thriller in the style of film noir, in which a small-town barber (Billy Bob Thornton) murders his wife's lover, lets his wife be charged with the crime, then is executed for a murder he did not commit – a plot strongly reminiscent of James M Cain's *The Postman Always Rings Twice*, first published in 1934.

John Sayles has found his own way of negotiating with the system. Beginning by writing screenplays for Roger Corman, he has worked on commercial productions as a means of financing his own more personal projects. Appearing at the same time as a couple of horror films, *Alligator* (Lewis Teague, 1980) and *The Howling* (Joe Dante, 1981), both of which he scripted, Sayles's first film as director, *Return of the Secaucus Seven* (1980), was a portrait of a group of 'thirty-somethings' with a lot more political edge than would find its way into mainstream Hollywood. Sayles's personal films since then have explored 'issues': lesbianism in *Lianna* (1983), race in *Brother from Another Planet* (1984) and again in *Lone Star* (1995), labour unions in *Matewan* (1987), political corruption in *City of Hope* (1991), the plight of indigenous peoples in Latin America in *Men with Guns* (1997). In *City of Hope* Sayles weaves a densely structured plot involving inner-city development projects into a clear-sighted commentary on local politics, in which any attempt to change the system involves the massaging of special interests. In *Men with Guns*, an elderly doctor in an unnamed Central American country goes to visit his former students, who have gone to work with the Indians. Naive and well-intentioned, he is shocked to find how cruelly the Indians are oppressed by the army, the 'men with guns' who murder, rape and torture. A voyage of discovery that progressively peels away the fictions disguising the true nature of third-world politics, the film is as radical as any directed by an American in the 1990s. As usual in Sayles's films, there is a lucid and literate script (in Spanish), with polished performances and direction, proving that political cinema need not be an excuse for boring the audience. *Sunshine State* (2002) is another dissection of local politics and development, this time in Florida.

Australian cinema experienced a renaissance in the 1970s, and Peter Weir was one of its

Above: Jeff Bridges walks away from a plane crash in the philosophically challenging *Fearless* (1993). Dir: Peter Weir

Below: Julianne Moore is the wife of TV producer Earl Partridge (Jason Robards), who is dying of cancer; two of the intertwined lives in *Magnolia* (1999). Dir: Paul Thomas Anderson

Opposite: Jim Carrey fast asleep, live on television, before an audience of millions, in *The Truman Show* (1998). Dir: Peter Weir

leading lights. His films in Hollywood have often explored a clash of cultures, a theme the immigrant director is well placed to observe. *Witness* (1985) was a thriller set among the Amish community of Pennsylvania, while *The Mosquito Coast* (1986), from Paul Theroux's novel, pitched Harrison Ford into the jungles of Africa. *Dead Poets Society* (1989) relied overmuch on the charm of Robin Williams as a charismatic teacher, but *Fearless* (1993), about the survivor of an air-crash forced to re-examine his life, was wholly original, even if its philosophical underpinnings do not wholly achieve lift-off. Weir's most solid achievement so far is *The Truman Show* (1998), in which Jim Carrey is at last given a role to stretch his talents, as an innocent whose life has, unbeknown to him, been turned into a television soap opera. The scene where he at last breaks through to discover the real world outside his artificial one is a typically Weir moment of mystical revelation.

Born on Hollywood's doorstep in Studio City, California, Paul Thomas Anderson is another who shows that sizeable budgets and established stars are not a barrier to intelligent, hard-headed film-making. A college dropout who worked as a production assistant in television, Anderson entered the Sundance Institute's Filmmakers' Workshop on the strength of a short film, *Cigarettes and Coffee*, in 1993. *Boogie Nights* (1997), about the hard-core film industry of the 1970s, exploits the sexual frankness which independent cinema had done so much to open up, but within a complex narrative of shifting viewpoints. This quality, skilfully piecing together a kaleidoscope of characters and story lines, is seen to great advantage in *Magnolia* (1999), a picture of contemporary Los Angeles in some ways reminiscent of Robert Altman's *Short Cuts*, but with a darker, deeper vision.

Hollywood does not contain the totality of US cinema. In the past twenty years a kind of parallel universe has emerged, of so-called 'independent cinema'. Independence is always relative, but the term has taken on a fairly precise meaning, designating a cinema that does not depend directly on the studios for financing. Independent film-makers draw support from charitable foundations, entrepreneurs, even family and friends. They work this way in order to make films which the studio system would not make because their subjects are too political, or too explicitly sexual, or drugs-related, or because they depart from Hollywood stylistic norms, at least up to a point. Independent cinema still has stories and recognizable characters; only the avant-garde rejects them entirely.

Several factors have proved favourable to the rise of independent cinema. Hollywood's single-minded pursuit of the largest possible audience has tended to an artistic blandness in which all films seek the lowest common denominator. Inevitably this leaves room for those who want something with more substance, or more aesthetically adventurous. Secondly, the rise of MTV and the music video has provided a training ground and source

AUTEURS AND INDEPENDENTS

Top: Catherine Zeta-Jones as the wife of a drugs dealer who takes on his business when he is arrested in *Traffic* (2000).
Above: Michael Douglas as the newly appointed drugs supremo who discovers his daughter is a heroine addict, in *Traffic* (2000).
Dir: Steven Soderbergh

of employment for aspiring young film-makers. However, these factors would count for nothing if there were no outlets for their work. The growth of video and cable TV, with their voracious appetites for product, has increased the possibilities for exposure, even if for small reward. And the prestige of the independent sector has been greatly enhanced by the annual Sundance Film Festival. Brought into existence in the mountains of Utah by Robert Redford's Sundance Institute in 1985, the festival showcases over a hundred new feature films every year.

Among those whose early work was exhibited at Sundance were John Waters, Steven Soderbergh, Neil LaBute, Todd Haynes, Todd Solondz, Whit Stillman, Kevin Smith and David O Russell. Such a roll call gives some idea of the diversity of the independent sector. Of course independence is only a relative term. Many film-makers have used Sundance as a jumping-off point into mainstream cinema, and indeed one can see a certain consolidation of the sector: Miramax, formerly a key independent distributor, is now allied with Buena Vista, an offshoot of Disney.

It is hard to imagine the camp sensibility of John Waters ever fully succumbing to the mall mentality of the Hollywood majors, though there are signs he is mellowing. *Hairspray* (1988) premiered at the 1988 Sundance Festival and was something of a breakthrough film, a satire on the Hollywood musical and on life in Waters's home town of Baltimore, a more coherent and careful production than the director's early somewhat hit-or-miss affairs. It starred Waters's favourite performer Divine, a fat transvestite who notoriously ate dog shit in Waters's earlier film *Pink Flamingos* (1972). In his more recent features, such as *Serial Mom* (1994) and *Cecil B DeMented* (2000), Waters has had bigger budgets and the use of Hollywood stars (Kathleen Turner in the former, Melanie Griffiths in the latter), but still retained most of his bad taste.

In 1989, Sundance saw the screening of Steven Soderbergh's *sex, lies and videotape*. It went on to win the Palme d'Or at Cannes and at the age of only twenty-six Soderbergh's career seemed made. Largely self-taught, he had experimented with Super-8mm and video, and his first feature was based in part on his early film-making experiences. Through the mechanism of a young man who for a hobby tapes women talking about their sex lives, the film explores with subtlety and ingenuity the levels of deceit involved in the relationships of the four principal characters. As if to avoid too easily being sucked into Hollywood, Soderbergh's next feature, *Kafka* (1991), was an ambitious attempt to find a film equivalent for Kafka's novels. Shot in black and white, the film is self-consciously arty, with odd camera angles and a labyrinthine plot. It was followed by two more conventional films, *King of the Hill* (1993), about a young boy growing up in the Depression, and *Underneath* (1995), a remake of the 1940s film noir *Criss Cross* (Robert Siodmak, 1948) that while reproducing the narrative complexities typical of the genre drained them of suspense. Soderbergh's *Schizopolis* (1996), a kind of glorified home movie which largely abandons plot altogether, suggested he had lost interest in commercial film-making. Yet within two years he bounced back to become one of the most successful mainstream directors in

AUTEURS AND INDEPENDENTS

Above: Ageing hitman
Charlie (Morgan
Freeman; centre) with
sidekick Wesley (Chris
Rock) eat breakfast in
Nurse Betty (2000),
served by waitress
Betty Sizemore (Renée
Zellweger), who is
unaware they have
murdered her husband.
Dir: Neil LaBute

Hollywood. *Out of Sight* (1998) was an accomplished version of an Elmore Leonard thriller, with a big star, George Clooney. *The Limey* (1999) was another crime film, with Terence Stamp as an English gangster on the loose in LA. Julia Roberts was a hit in *Erin Brockovich* (2000) as a working-class single mother who fights a legal case against a large corporation. *Traffic* (2000) also has big stars (including Michael Douglas), in a story of the international drugs trade. Though Soderbergh has now moved decisively into the mainstream, *Traffic* shows that he has lost none of his interest in complex, interlocking narrative, and its different colour tinting for different locations indicates that his aesthetic adventurousness persists, even if *Ocean's Eleven* (2001), an aimless remake of the Frank Sinatra vehicle with George Clooney, Brad Pitt and Julia Roberts, was a waste of star-power.

A similar trajectory, from 'independent cinema' towards bigger budgets and stars, seems likely to be followed by another Sundance alumnus, Neil LaBute. Converting to the Mormon faith at Brigham Young University, LaBute developed his theatrical writing skills in student drama and one of his plays became his first feature film, *In the Company of Men* (1997). It is a cold-eyed look at male behaviour. Two junior executives amuse themselves by getting off with a pretty girl with a speech defect; once they have hooked her they dump her, just to see how it feels. *Your Friends & Neighbors* (1998) is a similarly misanthropic portrait of young suburbanites. Shallow, self-obsessed, they provide a very funny but bleak view of modern marriage. Both written and directed by LaBute, these films are sharp, full of insight and completely without sentimentality. LaBute's next film, *Nurse Betty* (2000), starred Renée Zellweger and Morgan Freeman in the story of a waitress obsessed with a TV soap opera who, when her drug-dealer husband is murdered, goes into shock and believes she inhabits the world of the soap. In theme not unlike *The Truman Show*, the film has its share of cynicism and satire, but the near Swiftian savagery of LaBute's earlier films has waned to something gentler in its portrait of the central female character.

Some might discern a similar movement in the career of Todd Haynes. *Poison* (1991),

Previous pages: Jonathan Rhys Myers as glamrock star Brian Slade in a re-creation of the 1970s music scene in *Velvet Goldmine* (1998). Dir: Todd Haynes
Above: Cynthia Stevenson plays the wife and Dylan Baker the husband who is revealed as a child-abuser in *Happiness* (1998). Dir: Todd Solondz
Below: Long shots as the equivalent of moral objectivity: actress Julianne Moore in *Safe* (1995). Dir: Todd Haynes

Above: Actress Isabelle Huppert (l) as the former nun turned pornographer in the off-beat *Amateur* (1994), with Martin Donovan and Elina Lowensohn. Dir: Hal Hartley
Opposite: Johnny Depp is William Blake, an easterner out of his depth in the anti-Western *Dead Man* (1995). Dir: Jim Jarmusch

a big success at Sundance, was heralded as a founding text of the new 'Queer Cinema', films which seek to be insidiously, even perversely subversive of the 'straight' world rather than campaigning for tolerance towards homosexuality (see Chapter 10). Haynes's next feature, *Safe* (1995), is about a rich woman from southern California (Julianne Moore) with a mysterious wasting illness. It owes something to Haynes's first film, *Superstar: The Karen Carpenter Story* (1987), a pseudo-documentary about the Carpenters, the pop duo of the 1970s, in which the two singers are played by Barbie dolls and which delves into the social causes of Karen Carpenter's death from anorexia. At times *Safe*, too, achieves a documentary quality in the scenes when the heroine's various ailments are investigated. What makes it cinematically original is its resolute refusal of any point of view. Is the film an indictment of bourgeois life, a feminist protest, a public information film on toxic chemicals, a treatise on new-age medicine? The frequent long shots of Moore are the visual equivalent of its moral objectivity. Haynes's *Velvet Goldmine* (1998) is very different, a flamboyant account of the 1970s rock music scene shot in garish colour and with a complex flashback structure. Androgyny is the sexuality of choice, with Oscar Wilde as a kind of patron saint. While undoubtedly brilliant in parts, the film is often self-indulgent and lacks the discipline that would underpin its ambition. These faults have been fully corrected in *Far from Heaven* (2002), Haynes's homage to the 1950s melodramas of Douglas Sirk. Its story, of a conventional housewife who discovers that her husband is having a homosexual affair and who seeks solace in the arms of a black gardener, is beautifully controlled and exquisitely mounted, a re-creation of an era of film-making that miraculously avoids camp and parody.

Like several of his contemporaries, Todd Solondz is a graduate of the film-making school of New York University. His *Welcome to the Dollhouse* (1996), a sharp and funny account of a teenage girl's anxieties, was another success at Sundance. His following film, *Happiness* (1998), is one of the masterworks of 'independent cinema', a beautifully mounted satire of middle-class life in which the father of a pre-teen boy, just beginning to explore his own sexuality, proves to be abusing his son's best friend. Shocking but with moments of black humour, the film is a triumphant vindication of the independent sector, dealing with subject matter of pressing social concern which Hollywood, in its obsession with the feel-good factor, would never touch. Solondz's follow-up, *Storytelling* (2001), challenges pious assumptions about race and sex, as well as mounting a very funny but penetrating satire on the ethics of documentary film-making.

Henry Jaglom, born in 1941, is part of an older generation of independents, one who has worked largely outside the studio system while often using big-name actors. His first film, *A Safe Place* (1971), starred Tuesday Weld and Jack Nicholson, while *Tracks* (1976) starred Dennis Hopper – Jaglom had been a consultant on *Easy Rider* (1969). His successful comedy *Can She Bake a Cherry Pie?* (1983) featured Karen Black. Women get good roles in Jaglom's films, and *Last Summer in the Hamptons* (1995) stars Jaglom's wife Victoria Foyt, with Viveca Lindfors in her last role as a faded Hollywood star.

Both Hal Hartley and Jim Jarmusch made their first films in the 1980s, which makes them veterans of the independent movement. Hartley, a former art student who worked in commercials and local television, has established a reputation as the artist of a rootless hip world whose characters speak a desultory, enigmatic dialogue expressive of an inner half-life. *Simple Men* (1992) follows a small-time crook and his brother on the road, searching for their father. *Amateur* (1994) features Isabelle Huppert as a nun turned pornographer and Martin Donovan as a crook who cannot remember his past. Though criminality is part of Hartley's milieu, narrative and action always takes second place to philosophical musings.

Jarmusch, too, has remained resolutely within the independent frame. More formally experimental than many American independents, Jarmusch has strong links with European art cinema, in part through a connection to Wim Wenders established when he worked on Wenders's *Lighting Over Water* (1980), a documentary about director Nicholas Ray. Though never forsaking narrative, his films explore a world of loners struggling to find

DANTE:	Did you ever notice all the prices end in nine? Damn, that's eerie.
RANDAL:	You know how much money the average jizz-mopper makes per hour?
DANTE:	What's a jizz-mopper?
RANDAL:	He's the guy in those nudie-booth joints who cleans up after each guy that jerks off.
DANTE:	Nudie booth?
RANDAL:	Nudie booth. You've never been in a nudie booth?
DANTE:	I guess not.

Dante (Brian O'Halloran), Randal (Jeff Anderson),
Clerks (Kevin Smith, 1994)

direction. In *Down by Law* (1986) three ill-assorted prisoners in a New Orleans jail make an escape into the bayou. *Mystery Train* (1989) links a series of stories set in a Memphis hotel, and features Steve Buscemi, practically a *sine qua non* of American independent cinema in the 1990s. The five stories of *Night on Earth* (1991) are set in taxi cabs in different cities of the world. *Dead Man* (1995) is an anti-Western, with Johnny Depp playing William Blake, a naive easterner who encounters a Native American who believes him to be his namesake, the English Romantic poet; together the two take a journey through the wilderness. Like Jarmusch's *Ghost Dog: The Way of the Samurai* (1999), in which Forest Whitaker plays a professional hit-man and pigeon-fancier, *Dead Man* has a postmodern take on genre, playfully but seriously pressing against the conventions.

Whit Stillman's *Metropolitan* (1989) was a hit of the 1990 Sundance Festival. Made on a budget of only $80,000, it is a surprisingly stylish view of a group of rich young New Yorkers. Stillman's own origins are in the world of old money, but after graduating from Harvard he worked in publishing and journalism before becoming a foreign sales rep for Spanish films. As in all Stillman's films, the elevated social standing of his subjects in *Metropolitan* does not disguise their insecurities and vanities, which are observed with cool, ironic detachment. *Barcelona* (1994), set in the Catalan capital, follows a couple of young Americans in their encounters with the natives. *The Last Days of Disco* (1998) stars Chloë Sevigny, something of an icon of independent cinema, and centres on a New York club, focus for the loves and lives of the yuppies who frequent it. Once again, Stillman's visual elegance is matched by the perception and precision with which he dissects his characters.

There could scarcely be a greater contrast to this than the films of Kevin Smith. *Clerks*, premiered at the 1994 Sundance Festival, was made for even less money than Stillman's opening feature, a mere $27,000. A day in the life of two young men serving in a convenience store in New Jersey, the film is equally scatological and funny. Shot in grainy black and white, with no great visual sophistication, the brilliance of the dialogue, giving the impression of spontaneity, makes the film's low-grade visuals unimportant. Smith's next feature, *Mallrats* (1995), merely repeated the formula, but *Chasing Amy* (1997) has a more structured narrative and more developed characters. The hero, a comic-book artist, falls for a girl who proves to be lesbian. Somehow they manage a relationship, but through his inability to jettison his prejudices, and his male friend's jealousy, it all ends in tears. Shot with a good deal more visual brio, in bright colours, the film is as scabrous and funny as *Clerks*. Smith's *Dogma* (1999) got a mixed reception. A comedy about two angels, it has a lot of jokes about the Catholic church which may have passed by those indifferent to Christianity. It is clear by now that the strength of Smith's cinema is in the writing, with lots of funny dialogue. In the longer term this may be a weakness too.

The films of David O Russell perfectly encapsulate what independent cinema can do at its best. *Spanking the Monkey* (1994), another Sundance success, covers familiar indie territory with its satire of the bourgeoisie and its breaking of sexual taboos. The youthful hero, sex-obsessed yet uncertain of himself, is drawn into incest with his mother, the latter laid up

Above: Masquerading as a big-budget action film set in the Gulf War, *Three Kings* (1999), starring (l to r) George Clooney, Mark Wahlberg and Ice Cube, is a subtle satire on American militarism and the media. Dir: David O Russell

with a broken leg and disillusioned with her marriage to her salesman husband, a domestic tyrant who cheats on her during sales trips. What could have been an uncomfortable subject is saved by Russell's black sense of humour. The title of the film is slang for masturbation; the hero's attempt to perform this act is constantly interrupted by an inquisitive dog. This did little to prepare audiences for Russell's *Three Kings* (1999), a big-budget production starring George Clooney and set during the Gulf War, though Russell's early career as a full-time political activist might have given a clue to its intentions. On the surface a gung-ho action movie, it is perhaps the most subversive American war film ever made, undermining stereotypes and questioning ideological certainties while delivering plenty of thrills and not a few laughs. Whether most of the audience got the joke is another story.

The future of independent films will be greatly influenced by the new technological developments outlined in the final chapter of this book. Potentially there are large savings in production costs to be made through the use of cheap, lightweight video cameras and the digitization of other stages in the production process. Digital methods of distribution, whether employing satellite and cable links or high-quality software such as DVDs, which are cheap to manufacture, can also offer savings over conventional film technology. These savings will be available to Hollywood too, but it is likely to plough them into more expensive special effects and increased promotional expenditure. Thus the division between Hollywood and the independent sector seems destined to continue, with Hollywood aiming at the mass market, and a younger, leaner, more adventurous kind of film-making finding the niches. It is a mutually beneficial relationship. Hollywood can draw on a continually replenished pool of talent, while independents enjoy some trickle-down effect of Hollywood money, either directly through the part-financing of their productions or indirectly through investment in infrastructure. And for those independents who want it, there is always the chance of being discovered.

8. X-Rated

A candy-colored clown they call
  the Sandman
Tiptoes to my room every night
Just to sprinkle stardust and
  to whisper
Go to sleep everything is all right.

Roy Orbison, 'In Dreams', soundtrack, *Blue Velvet* (David Lynch, 1986)

Sex sells, and film-makers know this better than most. While the early film industry developed the stories of romantic love which have served cinema so well down the years, a parallel but undercover pornographic industry flourished. These clandestine 'stag' films existed almost wholly in isolation from their more respectable cousins, despite occasional rumours about the pornographic pasts of movie stars.

The sexual revolution of the 1960s threatened Hollywood with a major change. The machinery of censorship, the Production Code, which in one form or another had been in place since the 1920s, was swept away. No longer was every film required to conform to a uniform standard of morality. By 1970 the industry had decided on a system of ratings graded according to age: henceforth films were to be categorized as G – suitable for general viewing; PG – suitable for all ages but parental guidance advised; R – restricted to over-17s unless accompanied by a parent; X – no admittance to 17s and under (in 1990 this rating was designated NC-17). Film-makers were now free to show on the screen things that mainstream audiences had never seen before. More radical still was the report of a Presidential Commission on Pornography in 1970 which stated that pornography had no observable deleterious effects on those who consumed it. Overnight, pornographic films which depicted in full detail intercourse and other sexual acts came out of the shadows and on to Main Street. *Deep Throat* (Gerard Damiano) opened in New York in 1972 and attendance became fashionable. Linda Lovelace became a star in the role of a woman whose clitoris is improbably located in her throat, a disability which conveniently necessitated numerous scenes in which she performed 'blow jobs' or oral sex upon men, a staple ritual of the heterosexual porn film. When the anonymous source in the Watergate conspiracy was christened 'Deep Throat', pornography completed its passage into popular consciousness. In the same year came *The Devil in Miss Jones*, a more sophisticated piece of film-making in which after suicide a woman is sent back to Earth with the chance to experience the sex pleasures she had previously denied herself. This, like *Deep Throat*, was

Previous pages: Dennis Hopper as the sinister criminal Frank Booth and Isabella Rossellini as Dorothy Vallens in a weird sexual encounter in *Blue Velvet* (1986). By the mid-1980s American films were benefiting both from a more liberal ratings system and from the sexual frankness of European art cinema.

Dir: David Lynch

Right: The first outright pornographic film to be shown in mainstream theatres in the US: Linda Lovelace and Harry Reems in *Deep Throat* (1972). Lovelace subsequently claimed she performed under duress, suffering abuse from her husband.
Dir: Gerard Damiano

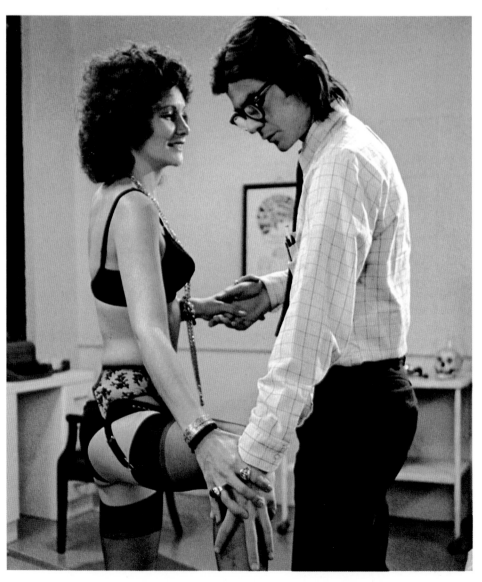

X-RATED

hugely successful in the hard-core cinemas which were opening up across the United States, as was another film of 1972, *Behind the Green Door* (Artie and Jim Mitchell), which starred Marilyn Chambers, a model who had advertised soap in television commercials. Chambers was later to make what had previously seemed an impossible leap, from porn into mainstream, by starring in David Cronenberg's horror film *Rabid* (1976).

For a period in the early 1970s it seemed as though the enormous success of pornographic films might force Hollywood itself to embrace them. But then came a setback. When elected US president in 1968 Richard Nixon had effectively packed the Supreme Court with right-wing lawyers opposed to the prevailing mood of liberalism. In 1973 they handed down a series of decisions which, though they did not outlaw pornography, allowed local authorities to make their own rulings. The reasoning behind the Production Code and its successor, the ratings system, was the need for a uniform system of regulation across the United States. Hollywood could not afford to engage in a series of expensive arguments while every local community attempted to establish its own standards. As soon as it became clear that this is exactly what would happen in the case of X-rated films, Hollywood lost interest. Henceforth it would sail as close to the wind as the ratings allowed, but hard-core pornography would be left to marginal producers. (The accepted definition of 'hard-core' is that the sexual activity on display, if it involves men, must show erect, 'hard' penises, thus guaranteeing that the activity being filmed involves real and not just simulated desire. Hard-core is thus distinguished as the only cinematic genre which can actually guarantee to deliver on cinema's age-old claim to represent reality instead of illusion.)

By 1981 there were over 1,000 hard-core cinemas in the United States. Screenings were mainly confined to large cities, but in the mid-1980s the porn industry embraced video. Not only were productions much quicker and cheaper to make in the new format, but domestic consumption – for viewing in the safety and privacy of the home – hugely increased the potential market, with a rental system making viewing cheap. Public theatres for porn films withered away, and at this point the porn film industry proper journeys beyond the scope of this book, even if its effects do not, for the existence of a parallel industry, a kind of cinematic equivalent of the dark matter which makes up a large proportion of the physical universe, exerts a constant gravitational pull. After all, the audience for porn films, by now a large one, also consumes the products of mainstream Hollywood, which must feel itself in competition and thus impelled to constantly push back the barriers of what is permissible in the multiplex.

Porn film has not been the only source of pressure on Hollywood to offer more open depictions of sexuality. It is a fact perhaps not sufficiently acknowledged that during the late 1960s and early 1970s the success of European art cinema in the international, especially English-speaking, market was in no small measure due to the audience's expectation that there would be more sex on display than in the home-grown product. Before Hollywood adjusted to the new sexual freedoms, it was Europe that made the running. Intellectual directors such as Ingmar Bergman made films like *The Silence* (1963), in which nudity was commonplace and sexual desire, even in its less conventional manifestations, frankly accepted. Its heroine, played by Gunnel Lindblom, oppressed by her guilt-ridden and censorious sister, demonstrates her liberation by picking up a stranger and fucking him in the back seat of a cinema. *Belle de jour* (1967), by the Spanish master surrealist Luis Buñuel, deals with the gap between fantasy and reality in female desire in its tale of a middle-class woman (played by the immaculate Catherine Deneuve) who spends her afternoons working in a brothel.

The loosening of censorship in the 1970s was equally rapid in Europe, which continued to exploit its reputation for greater sexual licence. The fourth feature of the Yugoslav director Dusan Makavejev, *WR: Mysteries of the Organism* (*WR: Misterije Organizma*, 1971), was a clever and playful investigation of the teachings of the sexologist Wilhelm Reich, stylistically complex in its mix of documentary and feature film techniques and with

Above: Jagoda Kaloper as Jagoda licking the pages in *WR: Mysteries of the Organism* (*WR: Misterije Organizma*, 1971).
Dir: Dusan Makavejev

Sex in the Art Movie
Last Tango in Paris
(*Ultimo tango a Parigi,* 1972)
Dir: Bernardo Bertolucci

A worldwide *succès de scandale* when first released, *Last Tango in Paris* astutely melded together a heterogeneous mix of ingredients. In essence the film is a typical European art movie dealing with familiar themes of alienation and the loss of the capacity to feel emotion. Paul is a middle-aged American living in Paris and trying to get over the suicide of his wife. He meets Jeanne by chance in an empty apartment. Without telling each other anything about themselves, even their names, they have a series of meetings during which they have sex. But eventually their outside lives intrude and Jeanne shoots Paul to rid herself of him.

Bernardo Bertolucci injected two elements into this situation. Firstly, as Paul he cast Marlon Brando. Although Brando's career had been in decline (even if, unknown to Bertolucci, it was about to revive with *The Godfather*, released in the same year), he was still one of the world's most famous movie stars; the idea of him appearing in a film containing explicit sex was news in itself.

Then there was the sex itself. Bertolucci was able to take advantage of the freedoms which had opened up at the beginning of the 1970s by filming sex scenes of unprecedented explicitness, with copious shots of the nude body of Maria Schneider, the unknown who had been cast as Jeanne. In the event, the film went too far for some. The British censor snipped out a ten-second shot where Brando's fingers, smeared with butter, go between Schneider's buttocks prior to an act of sodomy. In Italy the film was banned and the film-makers condemned to a two-month suspended prison sentence. Naturally, all this notoriety made the film a hit at the box office, eclipsing its very real qualities as a piece of film-making.

Opposite, above and left: Marlon Brando as Paul and Maria Schneider as Jeanne, the lovers who meet for anonymous sex.
Below left: Brando and Schneider crash a tango competition, incurring the wrath of the judges.
Below right: Director Bernardo Bertolucci in discussion with his two stars.

Country of Origin: Italy/France
Production Companies: Les Productions Artistes Associés/Produzioni Europee Associati (PEA)
Running Time: 129 mins

Producer: Alberto Grimaldi
Writers: Bernardo Bertolucci, Franco Arcalli
Photography: Vittorio Storaro
Music: Gato Barbieri
Editor: Franco Arcalli
Supervision of Set Design: Ferdinando Scarfiotti

Paul: Marlon Brando
Jeanne: Maria Schneider
Tom: Jean-Pierre Léaud
Concierge: Darling Legitimus

frequent shots of naked women. Also from Eastern Europe was Walerian Borowczyk, who had begun as an animator in Poland before moving to France to make live-action features. Borowczyk's *Blanche* (1971), *Immoral Tales* (*Contes immoraux*, 1974) and *The Beast* (*La Bête*, 1975) are elegantly photographed stories of lust and perversion set in a fairy-tale land in which the nude bodies of beautiful young women are refracted through the director's highly individual, often surreal sensibility; in *The Beast* a woman has sex in the woods with a strange creature whose huge penis gushes semen, while another young woman masturbates with a rose.

A different kind of sensibility – cool, modern, cosmopolitan – was revealed in Bernardo Bertolucci's *Last Tango in Paris* (*Ultimo tango a Parigi*, 1972). Bertolucci's coup was in persuading Marlon Brando into giving what is probably his last great performance, as a lonely middle-aged man who embarks on a frenzied affair with a much younger woman. The pair meet anonymously in an empty apartment for bouts of desperate sex, portrayed by Brando with almost embarrassingly raw emotion. It is a film of great insight into the power that sex can exert; the notoriety of its most daring moment, in which Brando smears butter up the backside of his partner (Maria Schneider) before having anal intercourse with her, not only guaranteed the film a huge box office success but also some unwanted mockery.

In the 1970s the Italians plunged into the soft-core market, none with a bigger splash than Tinto Brass. *Salon Kitty* (1978) was set in a Nazi-run brothel, a crude attempt to exploit the association between Fascism and deviant sex which Italian cinema had already explored in Luchino Visconti's *The Damned* (*La caduta degli dei*, 1969), Bertolucci's *The Conformist* (*Il conformista*, 1969) and Liliana Cavani's *The Night Porter* (*Il portiere di notte*, 1973). Brass (the name seems oddly symptomatic in its associations of money and brazenness) also directed *Caligula* (1979), an attempt by the owner of *Penthouse* magazine to break into the market for sex films, which was laughed out as a tasteless and overblown farrago despite the presence of such actors as John Gielgud and Peter O'Toole.

Below: Eroticism in the European art cinema: Sirpa Lane as Romilda de L'Esperance having sex with the creature in *The Beast* (*La Bête*, 1975) Dir: Walerian Borowczyk

X-RATED

Above: Beautiful young
men and women
imprisoned by the
Fascists in the
disturbing *Salò or the
120 Days of Sodom* (*Salò
o le 120 giornate di
Sodoma*, 1975).
Dir: Pier Paolo Pasolini
Below: The elegant
Sylvia Kristel in a highly
commercial piece of

French soft-core;
Emmanuelle (1974)
had several sequels.
Dir: Just Jaeckin
Overleaf: Matsuda Eiko
and Fuji Tatsuya as the
couple who take their
passion to the ultimate
in *In the Realm of the
Senses* (*Ai No Corrida*,
1976).
Dir: Oshima Nagisa

The furthest point to which the European art film has yet ventured comes in *Salò or the
120 Days of Sodom* (*Salò o le 120 giornate di Sodoma*, Pier Paolo Pasolini, 1975). Loosely based
upon the writings of the Marquis de Sade, the film is set in the short-lived Fascist republic
of Salò at the end of the war. A group of middle-aged men with dictatorial power brutalize,
rape, torture and murder their beautiful young male and female prisoners while Pasolini's
camera coldly observes. The scatophagous tastes and anal fixations of the Fascists clearly
function as a metaphor for totalitarianism, and the film replaces the prurience of much
cinema sex with a kind of fascinated disgust.

In Europe, the Far East and Latin America sex films spread like weeds, often driving out
other kinds. Each country produced films in its own image: earnest sex education films in
Germany and Scandinavia, Japanese *ero-guro* films featuring rape and other violence, more
cheerful Brazilian *pornochanchadas*. But for the Anglo-Saxon mind, France has always been
the home of Eros. In the 1960s Brigitte Bardot had been the cinematic embodiment of free
sexuality. In the 1970s France virtually abandoned censorship altogether and hard-core
films such as *Exhibition* (Jean-François Davy, 1975) were permitted in cinemas on payment
of a special tax which was ploughed back into mainstream production. Soft-core films
flourished too. *Emmanuelle* (Just Jaeckin, 1974), an enervated but artfully photographed
tale of sexual adventures in Thailand, starred the Dutch model Sylvia Kristel and had an
astonishing international success. As often in the classics of literary pornography, the
protagonist is a young woman embarking on a voyage of erotic discovery. Newly married to
a husband who encourages her to experiment, she is seduced by several women (lesbianism
being *de rigueur* in the genre) and later by an elderly guru (the veteran actor Alain Cuny)
who regales her with his 'philosophy' of free love and procures her as the prize to the
winner of a Thai kick-boxing match. A seemingly interminable series of sequels followed.
Just Jaeckin also made a soft-core version of the classic novel of female masochism, *Histoire
d'O* (1975), though it failed to capture the austere eroticism of the original. Bertrand Blier's
Les Valseuses (1974) – the title is slang for 'testicles' – presents a kind of *menage à trois* in
which Gérard Depardieu, Patrick Dewaere and Miou-Miou spend a lot of time in bed
together. Depardieu is also the star of Barbet Schroeder's *Maîtresse* (1976), playing a burglar
who breaks into the apartment of a dominatrix and becomes her assistant. The film does
not flinch from depicting some of the excruciating 'tortures' which the dominatrix (Bulle
Ogier) inflicts upon her clients. It was also to France that the Japanese director Oshima
Nagisa came in order to make *In the Realm of the Senses* (*Ai No Corrida*, 1976). The film
reconstructs a love affair in pre-war Japan between a servant girl and her master. Doomed
by their incompatible class positions, the pair enact a series of highly explicit sexual

encounters before the woman ritually castrates her lover. In showing the man's erect penis the film stepped over the line marking art cinema from pornography, or perhaps more accurately erased it, which ensured that it was denied a certificate in Britain until 1991.

French cinema has continued to show what is still forbidden to mainstream English-speaking cinema, and an erect penis and female genitals both appear in Catherine Breillat's ironically titled *Romance* (1999), in which a disillusioned young woman finds sex and love hard to bring together. Breillat's *A ma sœur* (2001) is an equally grim tale about two teenage sisters, one pretty, the other fat, groping their way towards sexual knowledge only for an act of brutal violence to cut them short. Breillat's films feature nudity, male and female, and explicit discussion of sexual acts, but watching them is more gruelling than erotic.

Even British cinema has recently moved a step closer to pornography with *Intimacy* (Patrice Chéreau, 2001), a down-market version of the story of *Last Tango in Paris*, in one scene of which the female protagonist, played by Kerry Fox, takes into her mouth the erect penis of her male counterpart, played by Mark Rylance. It may be significant that this 'first' in British cinema was directed by a Frenchman.

Pushed by the emergence into the limelight of hard-core pornography, and the increasing sexual openness of European art cinema, Hollywood made a determined move if not towards a genuinely liberated sexuality then to more sexual content, especially nudity, on screen. French director Louis Malle, who had made films with Brigitte Bardot, was imported to make *Pretty Baby* (1978), in which the twelve-year-old Brooke Shields played the role of innocent at large in a New Orleans brothel. Nicolas Roeg's *Don't Look Now* (1973) contained, within the context of its Venice-based melodrama, a scene of love-making between Donald Sutherland and Julie Christie that went some way further than Hollywood had previously dared. The same director's *Bad Timing* (1980) copiously displays the body of Theresa Russell (later Roeg's wife) in a grimly pessimistic tale of suicide and sexual angst, and in his *Castaway* (1986) – set on a desert island – though there is little actual sex, Amanda Donohoe spends almost the entire film naked.

In 1986 two films ventured into what had been largely unexplored territory for Hollywood. *9¹/₂ Weeks* (Adrian Lyne) has Mickey Rourke and Kim Basinger engage in some soft-focus, rather half-hearted sado-masochism. The film raises an occasional frisson, but draws back from the real thing. More adventurous and genuinely disturbing is David

Lynch's *Blue Velvet* (1986), a study of the dark forces that lurk beneath the apparently placid surface of a small American town, in which Dennis Hopper and Isabella Rossellini enact a scene which one critic has described as 'a compound of frottage, rape, sadism, torture, fetishistic obsession, helpless incestuous anxiety and infantile rage'.[1] By the 1990s Hollywood felt impelled to go further. *Basic Instinct* (1991) was a neo-noir thriller in which Sharon Stone became notorious. The infamous scene in which, facing interrogation by a battery of aggressive policemen, she shows her disdain by crossing her legs to reveal her absence of underwear, ensured the film worldwide box office success. Its director, the Dutchman Paul Verhoeven, tried to upstage himself in *Showgirls* (1995), set in Las Vegas and featuring a parade of nude or near-nude dance numbers. Despite its high degree of sexual content, the film flopped badly. Whereas *Basic Instinct* had a gripping plot and exceptional star performances (Michael Douglas on top form), *Showgirls* had neither, proving that sex is no guarantee of success.

Philip Kaufman has directed a trilogy of intelligent and sophisticated films based on the work of authors preoccupied with sex. *The Unbearable Lightness of Being* (1987), from the novel by Milan Kundera, explores the sexual affairs of a Czech surgeon during the so-called Prague Spring of 1968 and the subsequent invasion of Soviet troops. It manages to be serious about both sex and politics and yet preserve a delicate touch. *Henry and June* (1990), the first film released under the NC-17 rating, is about Henry Miller and Anaïs Nin, having an affair as they compete to write pornographic novels in the Paris of the 1930s. *Quills* (2000) recounts the life in prison of the Marquis de Sade, conducting a kind of guerrilla war against the authorities while trying to smuggle his scandalous writings out of jail.

Two films of the later 1990s made serious attempts to investigate the sex industry. Milos Forman's *The People vs. Larry Flynt* (1996) was a biography of the publisher of *Hustler*, a pornographic magazine. Without whitewashing the crudities and excesses of Flynt, the film scored some notable hits against the narrow-mindedness and hypocrisy of the American authorities who tried to suppress his activities. *Boogie Nights* (1997), directed by Paul Thomas Anderson, is a funny and open-minded account of the pornographic film business just at the moment when it moved from film to video. The film cleverly postpones until the last moment a full view of the prodigious penis of the young stud whose progress through

Above: Daniel Day-Lewis and Lena Olin enjoy the sexual liberation of the days before the Soviet invasion of Czechoslovakia in *The Unbearable Lightness of Being* (1987).
Dir: Philip Kaufman
Right: Woody Harrelson as pornography publisher Larry Flynt, under restraint during a court hearing in *The People vs. Larry Flynt* (1996).
Dir: Milos Forman
Opposite: Sharon Stone as the dangerous Catherine Tramell, facing the music in one of the most notorious scenes in the history of Hollywood: *Basic Instinct* (1991).
Dir: Paul Verhoeven

LT. WALKER: You describe a white silk scarf in your book.
CATHERINE: I've always had a fondness for white silk scarves. I have a very vivid imagination.
NICK: But you said you liked men to use their hands.
CATHERINE: No. I said I liked Johnny to use his hands. I don't give any rules, Nick. I go with the flow.

Lieutenant Walker (Denis Arndt), Catherine Tramell (Sharon Stone), Detective Nick Curran (Michael Douglas), *Basic Instinct* (Paul Verhoeven, 1991)

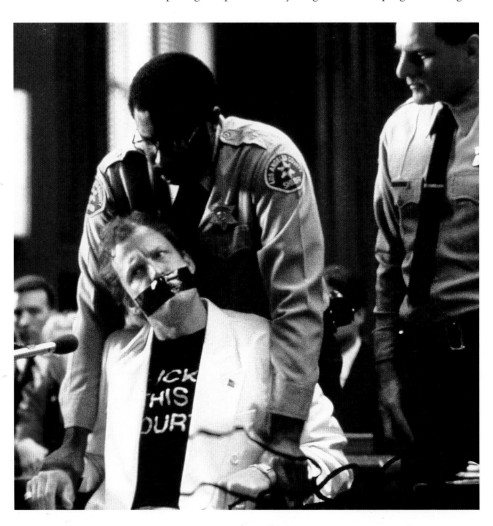

X-RATED

the industry we have observed, thus delivering an authentic shock of exposure which is the essential mark of the sex film. These films take advantage of the frankness now possible in Hollywood films without offering gratuitous displays of nudity or sexual activity.

By the late 1990s 20 million people in the United States subscribed to cable TV channels offering 'adult' (i.e. pornographic) content, and the yearly sales of adult videos amounted to $4 billion, fifteen per cent of the entire market.[2] There are about 700 million rentals of adult movies per year. To give some idea of the relative size of the porn industry, over 11,000 adult movies (i.e. videos) were made in Los Angeles in 2000, compared to about 600 Hollywood features. After backing off in the 1970s, Hollywood is now openly flirting with the adult industry; hard-core star Asia Carrera had a walk-on part in the Coen brothers' *The Big Lebowski* (1998). Stanley Kubrick's final film, *Eyes Wide Shut* (1999), which stars Tom Cruise and Nicole Kidman, two of Hollywood's biggest names, contains an orgy sequence previously unthinkable in a mainstream film. The expectation must be that once the Internet is engineered to offer full-length films at an acceptable level of definition, the appetite for pornography will grow – unless, which seems unlikely, the authorities find both the will and technical means to censor it. The sheer volume of this material seems likely to exert pressure on Hollywood to increase the sexual content of its films, even if the full-scale conversion to hard-core which the more apocalyptic prophecies foretell does not come to pass.

Beyond Hollywood, the cinema continues to open itself up to experience it had previously ignored. The films of Pedro Almodóvar (see Chapter 12) display a dizzying range of alternative lifestyles and sexual orientations, including gays, lesbians, transsexuals and porn actresses. Meanwhile in Russia the collapse of Communism has freed up the censorship regime even if production cash is hard to come by. *Of Freaks and Men* (*Pro urodov ì lyudei*, 1998), directed by Alexei Balabanov, is set in pre-Revolutionary St Petersburg. Photographed in sepia-tinted black and white in a style that brilliantly recreates the early cinema, the film details the work of pornographers who specialize in the flagellation of young girls. Surreal at times (not least in its portrayal of the sex life of a pair of Siamese twins), it is an elegant and witty film which shows that sexual freedom in the cinema has produced real benefits.

Opposite: Tom Cruise and Nicole Kidman as the married couple at the centre of Kubrick's last film, *Eyes Wide Shut* (1999).
Dir: Stanley Kubrick
Above: Burt Reynolds as a porn director and Mark Wahlberg as star performer Dirk Diggler in *Boogie Nights* (1997).
Dir: Paul Thomas Anderson
Right: Turn-of-the-century erotica, taking advantage of a more liberal regime in Russia in *Of Freaks and Men* (*Pro urodov ì lyudei*, 1998).
Dir: Alexei Balabanov

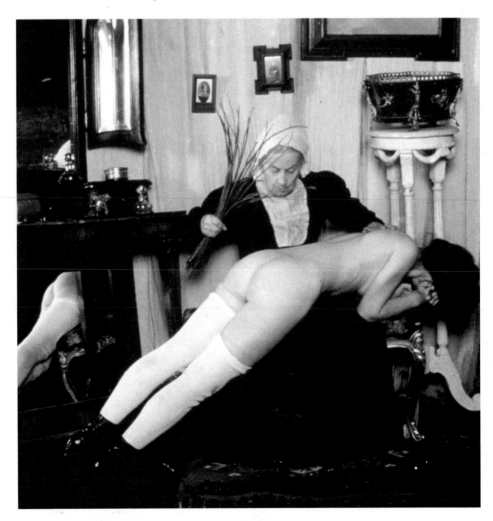

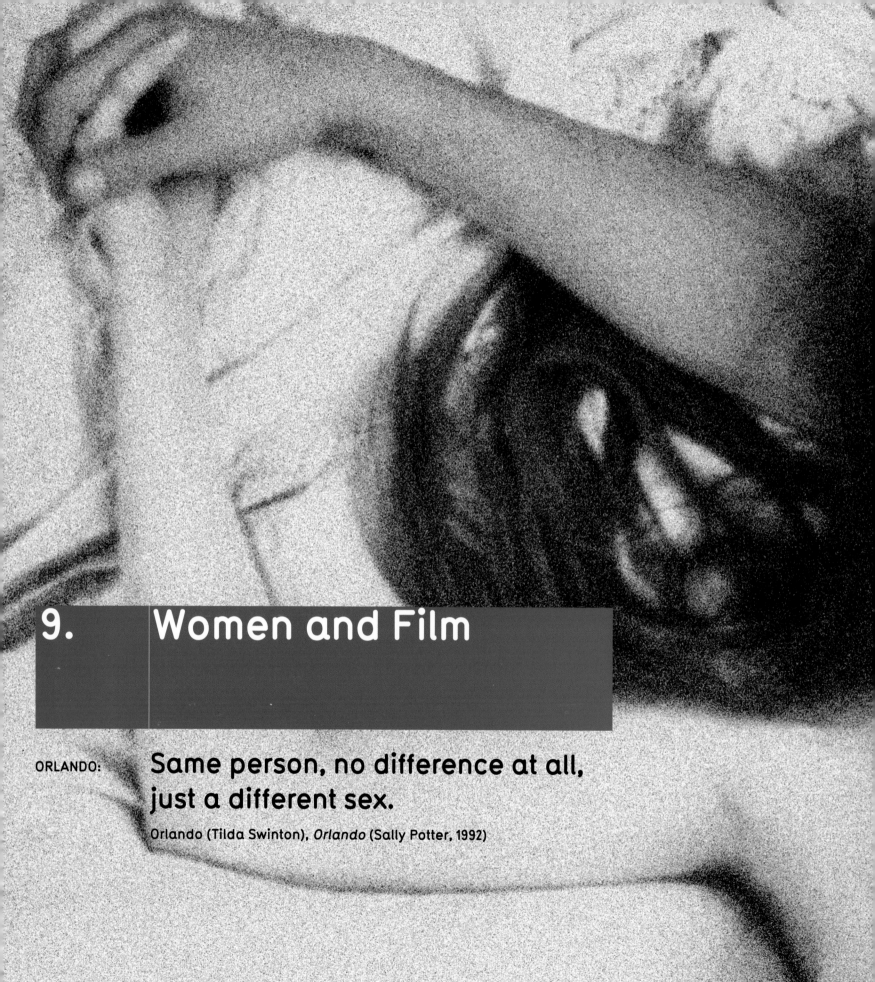

9. Women and Film

ORLANDO: **Same person, no difference at all, just a different sex.**

Orlando (Tilda Swinton), *Orlando* (Sally Potter, 1992)

Previous pages: Tilda
Swinton as Orlando,
who lives for 400 years,
changing into a woman
during the eighteenth
century, and Billy Zane

as Shelmerdine. Based
on the Virginia Woolf
novel, Orlando (1992)
is challenging yet
appealing.
Dir: Sally Potter

In *What Women Want* (Nancy Meyers, 2000) – an echo of Sigmund Freud's notorious question, 'What do women want?' – Mel Gibson discovers that he can suddenly read women's minds. Hollywood's (almost exclusively male) executives have been trying to pull off the same trick for years, not without success. Classic films such as *Stella Dallas* (King Vidor, 1937), *Mildred Pierce* (Michael Curtiz, 1945) and *Imitation of Life* (Douglas Sirk, 1959) have a special appeal to women not just because they have strong, even dominant female characters, or because they are about love and marriage, but because they are concerned with motherhood and other matters of particular interest to a female audience. Even so, Hollywood's view of women was a conventional one, offering few role models to those who aspired to something beyond domesticity.

By 1970, however, things were stirring in the wider world. One of the founding texts of the women's movement, Betty Friedan's *The Feminine Mystique*, had been published in 1963. Kate Millett's *Sexual Politics* came in 1969, Germaine Greer's *The Female Eunuch* in 1970. Feminism was on the march, even if Hollywood, rarely in the forefront of social progress, was slow to take notice. Ahead of its time, one swallow that did not make a summer was *Wanda* (1971), about a female misfit, aimless and hapless but sympathetically played by Barbara Loden, who directed herself. More typical of Hollywood's portrayals of women was *Klute* (Alan J Pakula, 1971), in which Jane Fonda plays a prostitute. Though there is an intimation of resistance in Fonda's quick glance at her wristwatch as she services a client, it scarcely constitutes empowerment. As film historian Yvonne Tasker has remarked, the prostitute is a key figure within Hollywood representations of women, since she foregrounds the extent to which sexuality is the dominant aspect of women's roles in films. In selling her body, she is only taking to its logical conclusion the process whereby in film narratives women are almost invariably required to be sexually available.[1] Twenty years later, the huge success in supposedly more liberated times of *Pretty Woman* (Garry Marshall, 1990), in which Julia Roberts plays a happy and successful prostitute, is evidence of the deep-rooted nature of this syndrome.

Other isolated attempts in the 1970s to shift the representation of women include Martin Scorsese's *Alice Doesn't Live Here Anymore* (1974), a surprising film from a director not normally associated with female-centred stories, about a woman (wonderfully played by Ellen Burstyn) searching for a new life for herself and her young son. In *Julia* (1977), the central relationship in Fred Zinnemann's film is between playwright Lillian Hellman (Jane Fonda) and her lifelong friend Julia (Vanessa Redgrave), and this might be a working definition of the Hollywood woman's film, one in which the relationships between women are more important than those between women and men.

Above: A poster for
Klute (1971), which
starred Jane Fonda as
a prostitute, a figure
who makes explicit
what is usually implicit
in Hollywood roles for
women; that the woman
is sexually available.

Dir: Alan J Pakula
Right: Ellen Burstyn in
*Alice Doesn't Live Here
Anymore* (1974), which,
for Scorsese, provides
an unusually positive
female role.
Dir: Martin Scorsese

WOMEN AND FILM

Below: Jill Clayburgh as Erica, finding her way after her husband leaves her, and Alan Bates as a new man in her life in *An Unmarried Woman* (1977).

Dir: Paul Mazursky
Right: Leading lady Sally Field standing up for women as the union organizer in *Norma Rae* (1979).
Dir: Martin Ritt

Feminist film studies have been a huge growth area over the past twenty-five years, much of it dedicated to revealing the fundamental sexism of mainstream cinema. Much of this work has been too abstruse to percolate through to Hollywood, but two books aimed at the general reader were influential at the beginning of the 1970s. Marjorie Rosen's *Popcorn Venus* (1973) and Molly Haskell's *From Reverence to Rape* (1974) surveyed the long and inglorious history of Hollywood's representation of women. Slowly the changes taking place in society at large began to make an impact. *An Unmarried Woman* (Paul Mazursky, 1977) starred Jill Clayburgh as a middle-class wife who is jolted into standing on her own two feet when her husband leaves her and who finds herself taking an increasing critical look at the men who offer themselves as substitutes. Truer to the experiences of the mass of women was *Norma Rae* (Martin Ritt, 1979), in which Sally Field plays a trade union organizer in a small southern town, working towards liberation from her husband's expectations while seeking a decent wage for her members.

An entire book could be written on the representation of women within mainstream Hollywood cinema since the 1970s; indeed, several already have been and are listed in the bibliography. Two related but separate issues are the employment of women in the film industry, and the continuance of a separate genre of the 'women's picture', a film

ROBERTA: Here it is, a message from Jim. 'Desperately seeking Susan. Meet me, four o'clock, Battery Park. Keep the faith. Love, Jim.'

LESLIE: Jim? Susan? Do you know these people?

ROBERTA: They send messages through the personal ads, that's how they hook up. Last year she was in Mexico City, then Los Angeles, now New York. Desperate. I love that word.

LESLIE: Everybody I know is desperate, except for you.

ROBERTA: I'm desperate.

LESLIE: Ha!

ROBERTA: Well, sort of.

Roberta Glass (Rosanna Arquette), Leslie Glass (Laurie Metcalf), *Desperately Seeking Susan* (Susan Seidelman, 1985)

Opposite: Robert Joy as Jim, the boyfriend that Susan (Madonna) contacts through the personal ads in *Desperately Seeking Susan* (1985).
Dir: Susan Seidelman

Above: Director Kathryn Bigelow at work.
Right: Jamie Lee Curtis as a cop under suspicion in the tough thriller *Blue Steel* (1990).
Dir: Kathryn Bigelow

aimed primarily at a female audience. Women are never likely to achieve a balanced representation on screen unless they are better represented behind it. At the end of the 1970s *Time* magazine reported that of 7,332 feature films made in Hollywood between 1949 and 1979, only fourteen were directed by women. Twenty years later, things had scarcely improved. The Directors Guild of America reported that in 1999 DGA women theatrical film directors worked 6.1 per cent of the total days worked by Guild directors as a whole, down from 6.3 per cent in 1998.[2] Nevertheless, by the 1980s women started to become more visible. At Twentieth Century Fox, Sherry Lansing became the first woman to head a major studio, and in 1987 Dawn Steel was made President of Columbia Pictures. Women directors began to get a foot in the door. Bette Gordon's *Variety* (1983) is a one-off. Scripted by Kathy Acker, it is a product of the New York avant-garde, a film about a woman who takes a job selling tickets at a porn cinema. More mainstream, and more successful at the box office, was Susan Seidelman's *Desperately Seeking Susan* (1985), which starred Madonna as a kooky young woman accidentally brought into contact with a bored housewife (Rosanna Arquette). The relationship between the two provides the film with plenty of sparks.

Barbra Streisand used her stardom as a stepping stone to the director's chair when she made *Yentl* (1983), following with *The Prince of Tides* (1991). Other female stars to follow suit include Jodie Foster with *Little Man Tate* (1991) and Diane Keaton with *Unstrung Heroes* (1995). Successful screenwriters such as Nora Ephron have also become directors, notably with *Sleepless in Seattle* (1993), a romantic comedy with strong female appeal in which a small boy tries to find his widowed father a new wife. Not all the new breed of women directors chose material specially aimed at a women's audience. Amy Heckerling is a comedy specialist, whose *Fast Times at Ridgemont High* (1982) is a sharp and amusing high-school story with some real insight into teenage angst, a genre Heckerling revisited with *Clueless* (1995). It is worth noting, though, that the issue at the heart of her comedy *Look Who's Talking* (1989) – what sort of father single mother Kirstie Alley should seek for her new baby – looms larger in the picture than the question of what man the leading lady should fall in love with. Parenting, not romance, is the issue. Penny Marshall has also specialized in comedies, such as *Big* (1988), with Tom Hanks, who also appeared in *A League of Their Own* (1992), Marshall's appealing comedy about a women's baseball league. Penelope Spheeris made a couple of pictures about violent teenagers, *Suburbia* (1984) and *The Boys Next Door* (1986), before also moving into comedy with *Wayne's World* (1992) and *The Beverly Hillbillies* (1993).

One of the most distinctive women directors in Hollywood today, Kathryn Bigelow, has worked in male-centred genres, to which she has sometimes been able to give a female twist. *Near Dark* (1987) is an eerie horror film about a group of vampires travelling the roads of the Midwest. *Blue Steel* (1990) has Jamie Lee Curtis as a New York cop chasing a serial killer. As often in pictures with female investigators, it is the heroine's sexuality which is under scrutiny as much as the crime; see for example Sondra Locke's *Impulse*

Above: Laura Dern as the naive but sexually active Rose with Robert Duvall as her kindly employer in *Rambling Rose* (1991).
Dir: Martha Coolidge
Right: Edda Barends, Nelly Frijda and Henrietta Tol as the three accused women in *A Question of Silence* (*De stilte rond Christine M,* 1982).
Dir: Marleen Gorris

(1990), with Theresa Russell as a cop going undercover as a hooker while, like Curtis, being investigated for shooting a suspect. Bigelow's science fiction film *Strange Days* (1995) explores issues of sexual voyeurism, taking cinema to its logical extreme in a near-future Los Angeles. The choice of Bigelow to direct *K-19: The Widowmaker* (2002), a big-budget action film about a stricken Russian nuclear submarine – not exactly female-friendly material – may be a significant step in the progress of women directors.

Martha Coolidge began making films in the 1970s, but not until *Rambling Rose* (1991) did she connect with the wider women's audience. Laura Dern plays a young woman taken on as a servant by a southern family in the 1930s. Her sexually generous nature is regarded by the local (male) doctor as requiring drastic surgical intervention but she is protected by her female employer in a gesture of womanly solidarity. More explicitly feminist is Lizzie Borden's independent feature *Working Girls* (1986), which takes a clear-eyed look at life in a New York brothel from the point of view of the employees.

For a still more radical agenda, one must look beyond Hollywood. No American feature film of the 1980s had the cutting edge of *A Question of Silence* (*De stilte rond Christine M*, 1982), by the Dutch director Marleen Gorris. Three women murder the manager of a shop. At their trial they refuse to cooperate, but the case is reconstructed for us, tracing the pattern of male

oppression that has triggered the attack. Gorris has a sharp line in humour (the film ends with the women laughing out loud) but makes her feminist points with chilling accuracy. Her follow-up film, *Broken Mirrors* (*Gebroken Spiegels*, 1984), connects two stories: in one a brutal kidnapper and rapist is finally brought to justice, while in the other a woman signs on at a brothel. In her later work, such as a dramatization of Virginia Woolf's *Mrs Dalloway* (1997), Gorris's feminism has a softer edge, but she has maintained a unique voice.

Sally Potter is a British director whose early work was within an avant-garde tradition. *Orlando* (1992) is more mainstream and stars Tilda Swinton as the immortal hero/heroine of another Virginia Woolf novel. At the start of the film, in the year 1600, Orlando is a man, albeit a rather androgynous one, which allows for a scene of giddily subversive sexual role-play, with Swinton (a woman playing a man) encountering a man (Quentin Crisp) playing Queen Elizabeth. In the eighteenth century Orlando changes sex. Looking at her naked

Right: Quentin Crisp
as Queen Elizabeth I
and Tilda Swinton as
the sexually mutating
hero/heroine in
Orlando (1992).
Dir: Sally Potter
Below top: Jutta Lampe
(l) as Julianne visiting
Marianne (Barbara
Sukowa), the sister who
becomes a terrorist, in
The German Sisters
(*Die bleierne Zeit*, 1981).
Dir: Margarethe

von Trotta
Below bottom: Picking
over the ruins in
*Germany, Pale
Mother* (*Deutschland,
bleiche Mutter*, 1980).
Dir: Helga Sanders-
Brahms
Overleaf: Jodie Foster
(l) as the gang-raped
woman and Kelly
McGillis as her lawyer
make their way to court
in *The Accused* (1988).
Dir: Jonathan Kaplan

body in the mirror she observes: 'Same person, no difference at all, just a different sex.'
One cannot imagine Hollywood being comfortable with such an assertion.

In Germany feminist film-making has been a strong tradition. The film journal *Frauen und Film*, founded in 1974, provided a focus for the work of a group committed to leftist causes and to women's liberation, and who benefited from the government's financial support of auteurist film-making. Helke Sander (the first editor of *Frauen und Film*) directed a loosely connected trilogy tracing the evolution of a young woman's political consciousness: *The All-round Reduced Personality* (*Die allseitig reduzierte Persönlichkeit REDUPERS*, 1977), *The Subjective Factor* (*Der subjektive Faktor*, 1981) and *Love Is the Beginning of All Terrors* (*Der Beginn aller Schrecken ist Liebe*, 1984). More accessible is Margarethe von Trotta's *The Lost Honour of Katharina Blum* (*Die verlorene Ehre der Katharina Blum*, 1975), co-directed with her husband Volker Schlöndorff, about a young woman whose life is destroyed when she unknowingly sleeps with a terrorist. One of Von Trotta's most impressive works, *The German Sisters* (*Die bleierne Zeit*, 1981), also explores women's experience of terrorism, based on the case of Gudrun Ensslin, a member of the Baader-Meinhof terrorist group. Von Trotta's *Rosa Luxemburg* (1986) stars Barbara Sukowa as the German revolutionary leader, murdered in 1919. Like Sander and Von Trotta, Helga Sanders-Brahms links the personal and the political through the exploration of women's experience in German history, most notably in *Germany, Pale Mother* (*Deutschland, bleiche Mutter*, 1980), which traces her autobiography before, during and after World War II. Less severe are the films of Doris Dörrie, offering a breezily satirical and unconventional look at the state of sexual relations in *Men* (*Männer*, 1985) and *Paradise* (*Paradies*, 1986).

To discuss all important women film-makers in a single chapter would be to imply a uniformity of approach that their work does not possess. Directors in Muslim countries, such as Rakhshan Beni-Etemad and Moufida Tlatli, confront issues rather different from their counterparts in Hollywood or Western Europe, just as those in Eastern Europe such as Vera Chytilová and Márta Mészáros share a common experience of a unique film-making system. Some, such as French directors Claire Denis or Agnès Varda, do not neatly conform to a women's agenda. Their achievements, like those of Gillian Armstrong, Maria Luisa Bemberg, Jane Campion, Safi Faye, Agnieszka Holland, Ann Hui, Pilar Miró, Mira Nair, Euzhan Palcy, Liv Ullmann and Kira Muratova, are dealt with in other chapters.

Women's issues are not confined to films directed by women. Two mainstream Hollywood films which confronted the issue of rape were *The Accused* (1988) and *Thelma & Louise* (1991). Both were directed by men, Jonathan Kaplan and Ridley Scott respectively. In the former, Jodie Foster plays a young woman who is raped by a group of men in a bar.

Women and the Road Movie
Thelma & Louise (1991)
Dir: Ridley Scott

The road movie is traditionally a male genre, relying on the sense of freedom and independence that having one's own transport endows and which has usually been the prerogative of men. What is innovatory about *Thelma & Louise* is the way it retools the genre for women. Thelma (Geena Davis) is a housewife trapped in a meaningless marriage, Louise (Susan Sarandon) is a waitress in a not very significant relationship. They decide to give themselves a little space by taking off for a weekend. But when Louise shoots a man who is trying to rape Thelma, they are precipitated into a far more radical break with their past lives.

The setting of the action in the American southwest and the acts of outlawry the women are obliged to commit in order to keep on the run give the film some of the feel of a Western. What makes it nevertheless a women's film is that the relationship between the two principals is at the centre of the story. The various men they encounter, both the ones they leave behind and those they meet on the road, have less importance for Thelma and Louise than the two women do for each other.

Predictably, the film met with hostility from some male viewers, on the grounds that the men were caricatured and that the film encouraged violence. Scriptwriter Callie Khouri, who won an Oscar for the film, countered this by pointing to the numerous stereotypical characterizations of women in male-centred Hollywood films, and the vastly greater violence present in the contemporary *Terminator 2: Judgment Day* (James Cameron, 1991).

The ending, in which, trapped by the forces of law, the intrepid duo drive their car clean over the edge of the Grand Canyon, is an affirmation of the freedom they have won, a rare moment in cinema of the total rejection of the rule of law and patriarchy.

Country of Origin: USA
Production Companies: Metro-Goldwyn-Mayer (MGM)/Pathé Entertainment
Running Time: 129 mins

Producers: Ridley Scott, Mimi Polk
Writer: Callie Khouri
Photography: Adrian Biddle
Music: Hans Zimmer
Editor: Thom Noble
Production Designer: Norris Spencer

Louise Sawyer: Susan Sarandon
Thelma Dickinson: Geena Davis
Hal Slocombe: Harvey Keitel
Jimmy: Michael Madsen
Darryl: Christopher McDonald
Max: Stephen Tobolowsky
JD: Brad Pitt

Opposite above: Ridley Scott directs Brad Pitt and Geena Davis.
Opposite below: Geena Davis as Thelma Dickinson and Susan Sarandon as Louise Sawyer driving through the southwest.
Above: Geena Davis as Thelma takes aim at a policeman.

Left: It is the task of Hal Slocombe (Harvey Keitel) to track down the fleeing Thelma and Louise. Throughout the journey he attempts to understand their motives and gain their trust but is the ultimate cause of their dramatic exit.

Above right: Female
solidarity: Sally Field,
Darryl Hannah, Olympia
Dukakis, Shirley
MacLaine and Dolly
Parton rally round in
Steel Magnolias (1989).
Dir: Herbert Ross
Opposite: Friendship is

the most important
thing: Jessica Tandy
as Ninny Threadgoode
and Kathy Bates as
housewife Evelyn
Couch in *Fried Green
Tomatoes at the Whistle
Stop Café* (1991).
Dir: Jon Avnet

Kelly McGillis is the lawyer who brings a case against them. Opinions were divided about the inclusion of a fairly explicit scene of the actual attack; was it necessary to show the violence involved, or was it titillating? A woman director might have done it differently. In *Thelma & Louise* two women (played by Susan Sarandon and Geena Davis) go on the run after Sarandon shoots a man who is trying to rape Davis. The gutsy performances and Ridley Scott's fluent direction ensured that the film was a big success. It was also controversial, spawning heated debate on the implications of the women's violent retaliation. However, despite their male directors, what is central in these films is not so much the issue of male violence as the solidarity of the women with each other.

Westerns such as *The Ballad of Little Jo* (1993), directed by Maggie Greenwald (in which the heroine spends the film disguised as a man), and science fiction films such as *Alien* (Ridley Scott, 1979) (see Chapter 3), have shown the possibilities for reworking male-centred genres. But it is clear that women can constitute a distinct audience, one that Hollywood has sought out by creating a sub-genre in which the woman's sphere is supreme and in which male–female relations become subordinate. Examples are *Crimes of the Heart* (Bruce Beresford, 1986), which united Diane Keaton, Jessica Lange and Sissy Spacek, offering each other support through the disappointments of life, and *Beaches* (Garry Marshall, 1988), in which Bette Midler and Barbara Hershey play lifelong friends whose deep affection survives all their ups and downs. The title of *Steel Magnolias* (Herbert Ross, 1989) alludes to the strength that lies below the feminine exterior of a group of southern women who rally round one of their number (Sally Field) when her daughter (Julia Roberts) dies after a kidney transplant. *Fried Green Tomatoes at the Whistle Stop Café* (Jon Avnet, 1991), also set in the South, again shows women winning through their troubles by drawing inspiration from each other. As Jessica Tandy says at the end, friendship is the most important thing. A black variation was *Waiting to Exhale* (Forest Whitaker, 1995), in which Whitney Houston, Angela Bassett, Loretta Devine and Lela

NINNY:	Did you know they took my gallbladder out?
EVELYN:	Uh, no I didn't.
NINNY:	Oh yes, still in the hospital in a jar. I guess that's where they keep them.
EVELYN:	I guess.

Ninny Threadgoode (Jessica Tandy), Evelyn
Couch (Kathy Bates), *Fried Green Tomatoes at the
Whistle Stop Café* (Jon Avnet, 1991)

WOMEN AND FILM

Rochon pool complaints about the men in their lives, while in *The First Wives Club* (Hugh Wilson, 1996) Goldie Hawn, Bette Midler and Diane Keaton plan revenge on the men who have traded them in for younger models.

That the women's film is still alive and well was proved by the success of *Erin Brockovich* (Steven Soderbergh, 2000), with Julia Roberts as a feisty working-class woman turning herself into a lawyer. What gives the film a special resonance for women is the prominence given to Roberts's child-care problems as she struggles to combine career and motherhood. The quality of these films varies, but all of them work on the premise that women can ultimately rely only on each other. This may fall somewhere short of fully-fledged feminism (all these films were directed by men, though women had a hand in some of the scripts), but it undeniably strikes a chord with the women's audience.

Once again, though, it is to Europe that we have to turn for a more radical development. *Baise-moi* (2000), a French film directed by Virginie Despentes and Coralie Trinh Thi, is surely the *ne plus ultra* of the women's picture, a kind of *Thelma & Louise* from hell in which two women go on a murderous rampage. Crammed with pornographic sex and violence, it is undoubtedly a story of female empowerment, and though hardly a comforting one, may be a sign of things to come.

Opposite: Julia Roberts as a working-class single parent turned lawyer in *Erin Brockovich* (2000). Dir: Steven Soderbergh
Below: Sexual violence in the women's film: Karen Bach and Raffaëla Anderson on the rampage as they shoot up a sex club in *Baise-moi* (2000). Dir: Virginie Despentes and Coralie Trinh Thi

10. Gay and Lesbian Cinema

MIKE: Oh. Have you ever. Uh ... I mean, don't you ever get horny?

SCOTT: Yeah. But ...

MIKE: Oh, yeah ... not for a guy.

SCOTT: Mike. Two guys can't love each other. They can only be friends.

Mike Waters (River Phoenix), Scott Favor (Keanu Reeves),
My Own Private Idaho (Gus Van Sant, 1991)

In the comedy *In & Out* (Frank Oz, 1997) Kevin Kline plays a schoolteacher who is 'outed' by a former pupil at an Oscar ceremony, much to his discomfort. Over the past few years, an extraordinary amount of scholarly effort has been expended on rewriting the history of Hollywood in order to bring 'out' its hidden homosexual sub-texts and claim a wide range of actors, directors and writers for gay and lesbian audiences. Some, such as director Dorothy Arzner and actor Montgomery Clift, were homosexuals or bisexuals who spent their careers passing for straight; others, such as the actor Rock Hudson, eventually acknowledged the true nature of their sexuality. Others again, such as Joan Crawford or Judy Garland, though straight, have had their screen images reinterpreted as gay or lesbian icons. Still others, like Jodie Foster, inhabit a space somewhere in the middle; undoubtedly a figure of interest for lesbian audiences, especially in such films as *Foxes* (Adrian Lyne, 1979) and *The Hotel New Hampshire* (Tony Richardson, 1984), in which her character has an affair with Nastassja Kinski's, Foster herself has consistently declined to be outed as a practising lesbian. The most entertaining example of this process of historical recovery is itself a film, *Gods and Monsters* (Bill Condon, 1998), in which Ian McKellen gives a memorable performance as James Whale, the gay director of such horror classics as *Frankenstein* (1931).

Gay and lesbian cinema proper dates from the beginning of the 1970s, when film censorship became liberal enough to permit the depiction of homosexual relationships, including sex acts, on screen. Even so, Hollywood dragged its feet. Although *Dog Day Afternoon* (Sidney Lumet, 1975), in which Al Pacino plays a gay man who robs a bank in order to buy a sex-change operation for his lover, presents a fairly sympathetic view of homosexuality, more typical of Hollywood's attitude was another Pacino film, *Cruising* (William Friedkin, 1980), in which he plays a cop venturing into a murky world of S&M gay sex. The negative stereotypes in the film produced a storm of gay protest, but instead of persuading Hollywood into a full-scale reassessment of its attitudes, it made it wary of touching the subject at all.

Beyond Hollywood things were moving a little faster. In Britain, Derek Jarman's *Sebastiane* (1976) was ground-breaking in its presentation of the life of the martyred saint, portrayed as an icon of gay masochism. It was also the first film with Latin dialogue. Jarman's films display a talent for visual experimentation which was fostered by the director's art school background, and included further historical re-creations such as

Caravaggio (1986) and *Edward II* (1991). All of them expressed a distinctive and engaging gay sensibility, increasingly marked by Jarman's experience of AIDS, which caused his death in 1994.

In France, *La Cage aux folles* (Edouard Molinaro, 1978) was a hugely successful farce which had fun at the expense of the moral majority when in the finale a strait-laced politician representing the 'Union for Moral Order' is obliged to disguise himself in drag. There is a funny if not very politically correct scene in which a gay man tries to teach his partner to act straight, including walking like John Wayne. Sequels followed in 1980 and 1985, and the film was remade in Hollywood as *The Birdcage* (Mike Nichols, 1996). Elsewhere in Europe the art cinema tradition, always more open about sexuality, threw up a number of adventurous films. Hungary produced *Another Way* (*Egymásra nézve*, 1982), directed by Károly Makk, in which two female journalists conduct an affair; in the context of the 1950s, when the film is set, this can lead only to tragedy. Germany in particular has been a forcing house of both gay and lesbian cinema. Ulrike Ottinger's *Madame X – An Absolute Ruler* (*Madame X – eine absolute Herrscherin*, 1977) comically deconstructs the swashbuckling genre in its tale of a lesbian pirate. Monika Treut's films resist easy classification and scandalize the orthodox, both gay and straight. In *The Virgin Machine* (*Die Jungfrauenmaschine*, 1988) a German female reporter visits San Francisco, where sex expert Susie Bright shows off her collection of dildos and she has an affair with a performer in a strip-club for women. The prevailing tone is light-hearted. Frank Ripploh's *Taxi zum Klo* (1981) is a disarmingly cheerful film about a gay 'odd couple', one of whom prefers domestic life while the other charges around public lavatories (the Klo of the title) in search of excitement. Rainer Werner Fassbinder, always drawn to unorthodox sexuality, made an out-and-out gay film in *Querelle* (1982). Shot in Fassbinder's characteristic lurid lighting style, heavy with pinks and blues, it is a stylized version of the work by Jean Genet about a young bisexual sailor who finds murder a turn-on. Visually the sex is restrained, though the dialogue is explicit enough ('You have a solid, heavy, massive prick, not elegant but strong,' remarks Jeanne Moreau, a brothel-keeper, to Brad Davis, the hero). Rosa von Praunheim (the pseudonym of Holger Mischwitzki) began his career as a gay film-maker at the end of the 1960s; in the new century he is still working. His *A Virus Knows No Morals* (*Ein Virus kennt keine Moral*, 1985) was a pioneering feature about AIDS, relying on provocative caricatures and garish images. Werner Schroeter, too, began late in the 1960s, but his films are almost the opposite of Von Praunheim's, full of excessively beautiful images, gorgeous operatic music, tragic, larger than life figures, as in *The Rose King* (*Der Rosenkönig*, 1986).

In the United States it was the avant-garde and independent cinema which made the running. Andy Warhol's 'factory' was making gay films in the 1960s, moving into features with *Flesh* (1968) and *Trash* (1970), both of which starred the languidly good-looking Joe Dallesandro. John Waters's *Pink Flamingos* (1972), starring 300-pound transvestite Divine, was the product of an authentically if camp gay sensibility with a consciously 'trash' aesthetic. For Hollywood's rare ventures into homosexual subjects, lesbianism was always

GAY AND LESBIAN CINEMA

Right: Divine with a succulent morsel in *Pink Flamingos* (1972). This film not only defined bad taste but simply revelled in it.
Dir: John Waters
Below left: James Wilby and Hugh Grant as the nearly lovers in *Maurice* (1987).
Dir: James Ivory
Below right: Sonia Braga as the Spider Woman and Raúl Julia as Valentin in *Kiss of the Spider Woman* (1985).
Dir: Hector Babenco

BABS: Kill everyone now! Condone first degree murder! Advocate cannibalism! Eat shit! Filth is my politics! Filth is my life!

Babs Johnson (Divine), *Pink Flamingos* (John Waters, 1972)

likely to offer a less troubling subject than male homosexuality. *Personal Best* (Robert Towne, 1982) had Mariel Hemingway as a runner discovering her desire for another female athlete in a series of soft-focus encounters. Like John Sayles's *Lianna* (1982) and Donna Deitch's *Desert Hearts* (1985), the narrative has a straight woman (in the last two cases married) being initiated into homosexuality by an experienced lesbian, suggesting that the films were made less for those who were already lesbians than for a straight audience who were curious.

Richard Dyer, the doyen of gay film critics, has remarked that whereas lesbian films tend to show women happily discovering their sexuality, films about gay men are full of angst. In *Kiss of the Spider Woman* (1985), directed by the Brazilian, Hector Babenco, William Hurt plays a camp gay imprisoned for the corruption of a minor and who escapes his self-loathing by retreat to a fantasy world of old films. Eventually his straight cell-mate, Raúl Julia, a political prisoner on whom he is spying for the authorities, teaches him self-respect. Once released, Hurt redeems himself by refusing to betray Julia's associates to the police and is shot. Another Latin American film, Jaime Hermosillo's *Doña Herlinda and Her Son* (*Doña Herlinda y su hijo*, 1984), in which a mother takes her son's gay relationship in her stride, is less agonized. Dyer has also remarked on the irony that Britain, the only European country to enact anti-gay legislation in the past twenty years, should have been the source of so many gay films in the late 1980s, during the high point of Thatcherism. This was Jarman's most productive period; it also saw a 'heritage' variation of gay cinema in *Maurice* (1987), based on E M Forster's posthumously published novel, produced by the team of James Ivory and Ismail Merchant and handsomely set in Edwardian England.

Previous pages: (l to r)
Freda Dowie, Dean
Williams, Angela
Walsh and Lorraine
Ashbourne in *Distant
Voices, Still Lives* (1988).
Dir: Terence Davies
Above: River Phoenix on
the road in *My Own
Private Idaho* (1991).
Dir: Gus Van Sant

Below: A touching
moment for Daniel Day-
Lewis as Johnny and
Gordon Warnecke as
Omar, who dreams of
owning the most
dazzling laundrette in
London in *My Beautiful
Laundrette* (1985).
Dir: Stephen Frears

Hugh Grant and James Wilby are two Cambridge students who fall just short of consummating their love affair. Grant eventually denies his sexuality, opting for marriage and respectability, but Wilby, after much soul-searching, follows his true nature and finds happiness with a gamekeeper, played by Rupert Graves. Stephen Frears's near-contemporaneous *My Beautiful Laundrette* (1985) features a gay affair between a violent white racist and a young Asian. The same director made *Prick Up Your Ears* (1987), the story of the doomed relationship between playwright Joe Orton and his lover Kenneth Halliwell. Arguably Britain's most talented gay director is Terence Davies, though in films such as *Distant Voices, Still Lives* (1988) and *The Long Day Closes* (1992), largely autobiographical accounts of a working-class childhood shot in a mesmerizing visual style, sexual orientation emerges more by implication than directly.

The 1990s saw the emergence within US independent film-making of what has been termed 'queer' cinema. Recuperating a previously derogatory term for homosexual, critics used 'queer' to signal a type of film which did not seek to stake a place for gays in the mainstream of popular culture or provide positive role models, but which insisted instead on its marginal, transgressive position. Queer cinema was unsettling, insidious, elusive in its identity. Typical was Todd Haynes's *Poison* (1991). Its three-part structure contains a kind of spoof television documentary, a pastiche of 1950s science fiction films, and a version of Jean Genet's *The Thief's Journal*. The connections between the three strands are elliptical, but all are concerned in some way with sexuality outside social 'norms', and AIDS is clearly the subject of the allegorical science fiction section.

Gus Van Sant was another US director labelled 'queer', initially on the strength of his early feature *Mala Noche* (1985), about a liquor-store clerk who pursues a migrant worker, but more particularly because of *My Own Private Idaho* (1991), in which River Phoenix plays a gay hustler who meets a well-connected young man (Keanu Reeves) and goes on the road. Beautifully shot, the film playfully works in documentary-like sequences and an ingenious

Above: From the episode 'Homo', based on Jean Genet's *The Thief's Journal*, in *Poison* (1991). Dir: Todd Haynes
Above right: Romane Bohringer, Cyril Collard and Carlos López make a threesome in *Savage Nights (Les Nuits fauves*, 1992). Dir: Cyril Collard
Below: Tom Hanks as the gay lawyer in a rare Hollywood film about AIDS, *Philadelphia* (1993). Dir: Jonathan Demme

version of Shakespeare's *Henry IV* with Reeves doing Prince Hal. Van Sant's subsequent career, including the amusing satire about television, *To Die For* (1995), seemed to move away from his queer origins.

By the 1990s, AIDS had come to dominate the gay agenda. In Gregg Araki's indie feature *The Living End* (1992) a young movie critic picks up a hitchhiker soon after testing positive for HIV; he too is positive. When the hitchhiker shoots a gay-basher they go on the run. Though laced with humour the film conveys their desperation: 'We're not like them, we don't have much time. We have to grab life by the balls.' The French film *Savage Nights* (*Les Nuits fauves*, 1992) was directed by Cyril Collard, who also stars in the film. It tells the story of Jean, HIV-positive, who simultaneously conducts tempestuous and complex love affairs with a young girl, Laura, and a young man, Samy, all the time having anonymous gay sexual encounters in back alleys. The film brilliantly conveys Jean's state of mind in a series of highly charged emotional crises which drive his girlfriend into a mental institution: 'Sometimes I'll do anything just to forget I'm wasting away.' Three days before the film won a César Award, the French equivalent of an Oscar, Collard died of an AIDS-related disease.

Hollywood felt it had to respond. *Philadelphia* (Jonathan Demme, 1993) stars Tom Hanks as a gay lawyer with AIDS who sues his firm when he is sacked. It is a decent film but a lot less progressive than it thinks, mainly because Tom Hanks's performance is dedicated to persuading us what a nice guy he is, rather than convincing us that he is gay. Since that time, with very few exceptions, Hollywood has preferred that gay characters, if they exist at all, are marginal eccentrics like the outrageous transvestite Lady Chablis in Clint Eastwood's *Midnight in the Garden of Good and Evil* (1997). Not a single major gay star has

Subverting Gender
Boys Don't Cry (1999)
Dir: Kimberly Peirce

Teena Brandon (Hilary Swank) is a girl who wishes to become a boy. Arriving in the small Nebraska town of Falls City, Teena binds her breasts, cuts her hair and calls herself Brandon Teena. When Brandon meets Lana (wonderfully played by Chloë Sevigny), a love affair develops, in the course of which sexual identities and gender stereotypes are turned upside down. Eventually Lana comes to realize Brandon is anatomically female, but by then she does not care. Brandon offers her a caring relationship such as she has never known. Unfortunately, Brandon's secret is eventually discovered by two young men, John and Tom, who have befriended him. The knowledge that they have been deceived is deeply disturbing to their male pride. They beat Brandon and rape him, then when he presses charges against them they kill him.

The film is based on a true story, which was also the subject of a documentary, *The Brandon Teena Story* (1998). But it is less its status as a true-crime document, more its subtle power to subvert our usual assumptions about sexuality that makes this a notable film, and a key text of the so-called 'queer' cinema. Unlike militant films which proselytize for homosexuality, 'queer' films adopt a more insidious strategy, seeking to undermine such rigid categories as gay and straight. Thus Brandon, in Hilary Swank's excellent interpretation of the role, alert to all the ambiguities, is not a lesbian though he/she has sex with women. And while he/she has adopted some of the physical attributes of a man (clothes, hair-style, certain mannerisms), Brandon has retained a softness and sensitivity which implies a critique of conventional masculinity, and which is the secret of his/her sexual success with women. No wonder he arouses the rage of other men.

Country of Origin: USA
Production Companies: Hart-Sharp Entertainment/ Independent Film Channel/Killer Films
Running Time: 118 mins

Producers: Jeff Sharp, John Hart, Eva Kolodner, Christine Vachon
Writers: Kimberly Peirce, Andy Bienen
Photography: Jim Denault
Editors: Lee Percy, Tracy Granger
Production Designer: Michael Shaw
Music: Nathan Larson

Brandon Teena: Hilary Swank
Lana Tisdal: Chloë Sevigny
John Lotter: Peter Sarsgaard
Tom Nissen: Brendan Sexton III
Candace: Alicia Goranson

Above: Hilary Swank as the ultimately tragic Teena Brandon, who after cutting her hair and binding her breasts passes herself off as Brandon Teena.
Left: A shared moment: Brandon's girlfriend Lana (Chloë Sevigny) maintains their relationship knowing that Brandon is anatomically female. In real life, Lana tried to prevent the film's release.

emerged, and Anne Heche is the only top-billing female star to admit to being lesbian, giving, perhaps, a queer inflection to Gus Van Sant's otherwise inexplicable shot-for-shot remake of *Psycho* (1998) starring Heche.

It has been left to the independent sector and to the rest of the world to reflect social realities. Much of the most interesting work lies in documentary – for example the interview film *Word Is Out* (Rob Epstein, 1977) – or in avant-garde video, and is thus outside the scope of this book. But the 1990s saw a significant number of low-budget lesbian features such as *Bound* (1996), a thriller from the Wachowski brothers in which Jennifer Tilly and Gina Gershon play two lesbians who steal money from the mob, and *High Art* (1998), directed by Lisa Cholodenko, about a young woman photographer who is drawn into the bisexual world of an older woman. *The Incredibly True Adventures of Two Girls in Love* (1995), directed by Maria Maggenti, is a charming if occasionally awkward first feature about two high-school girls from different social backgrounds who defy family and friends to fall in love. Probably the best, certainly the most forceful, of recent lesbian-themed US features is *Boys Don't Cry* (1999), directed by Kimberly Peirce, with an extraordinary performance by Hilary Swank as Brandon Teena, a girl passing as a boy in small-town Nebraska. Except that Brandon is not a lesbian at all but a transgendered individual, thus blurring the sexual divide in the best queer tradition.

Julian Schnabel's American-made *Before Night Falls* (2000), starring Javier Bardem as the Cuban poet Reinaldo Arenas, imprisoned by the Castro regime in the 1970s, is a convincing reconstruction of gay life under a homophobic regime. But Europe has continued to be the source of many of the most enjoyable films on gay and lesbian subjects. In the French comedy *French Twist* (*Gazon maudit*, 1995), a neglected wife is seduced by a burly but personable lesbian, to the chagrin of her husband. Directed by Josiane Balasko, who also plays the lesbian, the film is full of incisive and hilarious sallies against the male ego. *J'embrasse pas* (1991), directed by André Techiné, is about a young man who leaves the country for Paris and, finding himself without a job, drifts into male prostitution. Very effectively Techiné shows the pain beneath the youth's bravado. Lukas Moodysson's *Show Me Love* (*Fucking Åmål*, 1998) is set in a small town in Sweden, where two schoolgirls tentatively embark on an affair. Elin and Agnes suffer all the usual tribulations of teenagers (boredom, embarrassment at parents) plus the difficulties of being lesbian when all their friends are obsessed with boys. The film brilliantly captures Agnes's pain when Elin rejects her advances because she cannot face her sister's derision.

Gays and lesbians are well to the fore in the films of Spanish director Pedro Almodóvar, as in *The Law of Desire* (*La ley del deseo*, 1987), in which a gay film director is pursued by

Previous pages:
Outrageous in the
outback: Terence
Stamp as transsexual
Bernadette (centre)
with Hugo Weaving (l)
and Guy Pearce as the
drag queens in *The
Adventures of Priscilla
Queen of the Desert*
(1994).
Dir: Stephan Elliot

Right: Parents over
from Taiwan to attend
his wedding unaware
it is a marriage of
convenience: no
wonder Winston
Chao as Gao Wai-
Tung (second from
the left) looks worried
in *The Wedding
Banquet* (1993).
Dir: Ang Lee

Below: Heather
Juergensen as Helen
Cooper and Jennifer
Westfeldt as journalist
Jessica Stein who
answers an
advertisement placed
in a 'lonely hearts'
column by Helen, in
Kissing Jessica Stein
(2001).
Dir: Charles Herman-
Wurmfeld

Opposite: Shabana
Azmi (l) as Radha, the
sister-in-law of Sita
(Nandita Das), who
is looking for a more
sustaining relationship
than that with her
faithless husband in
Fire (1996).
Dir: Deepa Mehta

JESSICA: But I had such a wonderful time with you
           the other night. I've been 'marinating' on
           things. Anyway, I have taken the liberty
           to get some informational material on the
           topic and I wondered if I might ...
HELEN: Of course.
JESSICA: This one leaflet was particularly intriguing
           to me: 'Lesbian sex: hot safe and sane'.
           Do you know it?
HELEN: No, but please share, I'd love to see it.
JESSICA: Ok, well, I was surprised to learn that
           lesbians accessorize, I didn't know that.
           So for example, on page 11, I dog-eared it,
           they show some of the high-tech lesbian
           accoutrement ...

Jessica Stein (Jennifer Westfeldt), Helen Cooper
(Heather Juergensen), *Kissing Jessica Stein* (Charles
Herman-Wurmfeld, 2001)

Antonio Banderas while his brother, now a transexual lesbian (played by Carmen Maura), has problems of his/her own. Britain, too, has continued to make gay films of quality, including *Beautiful Thing* (Hettie MacDonald, 1996), a charming if slight study of gay awakening on a suburban housing estate. Given its vibrant gay culture, Australia might have been expected to follow up the worldwide success of the outrageously camp *The Adventures of Priscilla Queen of the Desert* (Stephan Elliot, 1994) with something more substantial, but this has not been the case. Elsewhere in the Pacific region, gays are finding a voice. Ang Lee's *The Wedding Banquet* (1993) is a comedy of acute social observation about a Taiwanese man living happily in New York with his boyfriend and who is obliged to enter a marriage of convenience. Chen Kaige's *Farewell My Concubine* (*Ba Wang Bie Ji*, 1993) is set in the Peking Opera, where a gay actor falls for a straight colleague. Stanley Kwan's *Lan Yu* (2001) follows the love affair of a male student and an older businessman in Beijing. From Thailand comes *Iron Ladies* (*Satree Lex*, Youngyooth Thongkonthun, 1999), a comedy about a volleyball team of gays and transvestites which was an unexpected international success. In *Fire* (1996), directed by Deepa Mehta, an Indian director based in Toronto, a young Indian wife whose husband neglects her for another woman begins a lesbian affair with her sister-in-law, whose husband has renounced sex on religious grounds.

The annual London Lesbian and Gay Film Festival was founded in 1987. The 2002 Festival offered a comprehensive overview of the state of gay and lesbian cinema around the world. Over fifty feature-length films were screened, about half of them documentaries. The majority originated in North America, with over thirty from the American independent sector and half a dozen from Canada. Doubtless this reflects the economic dominance of the United States, as well as the fact that gay and lesbian activism has a longer and stronger history there than in most countries. Surprisingly perhaps, given the traditional imbalance between men and women in the film industry, lesbian subjects made up about half of the total. One of the most successful lesbian films was *Kissing Jessica Stein* (Charles Herman-Wurmfeld, 2001). Written by and starring Heather Juergensen and Jennifer Westfeldt, it is a sharp and witty story about a woman who, disillusioned with men, answers a 'woman seeks woman' advertisement in the personal columns.

Another notable film was *Stranger Inside* (2001), about a young African-American woman who is united with her mother inside a woman's prison. It is the second feature by Cheryl Dunye, an African-American lesbian film-maker (a rare combination) whose first feature, *The Watermelon Woman* (1996), a witty and ingenious 'mockumentary' about a black actress of the 1930s, was a worldwide festival hit. Other recent successes at the London Festival have included *Come Undone* (*Presque Rien*, 2000), about a summer-long romance between two young men, directed by Frenchman Sébastien Lifshitz; and *Lost and Delirious* (2001), about the agonies of lesbian first love in a girls' boarding school, the first English-language feature by Canadian Léa Pool, whose *Anne Trister* (1986) was one of the most thoughtful lesbian films of the 1980s. As well as films from Western Europe, the 2002 Festival also included features from Japan, the Philippines and Hong Kong, among them *Peony Pavilion* (*Youyuan jingmeng*, 2001), directed by Yonfan, about a beautiful courtesan and her cross-dressing cousin, described in the programme notes as 'a sumptuous and bold melodrama'. Hollywood seems miles behind, still unable fully to come to terms with gay and lesbian subjects; but who cares, if the films keep coming from elsewhere?

11. Hollywood and Ethnicity

BEN: I have some dead brothers laying out there ... and this ain't where I should be.

SHAFT: 'Til we find out why they dead this is the only place for you to be.

BEN: You think like a white man.

SHAFT: And you don't think at all. Do you want to get wasted?

Ben Buford (Christopher St John), John Shaft (Richard Roundtree), *Shaft* (Gordon Parks, 1971)

The starry galaxy of Hollywood has always exerted a strong gravitational pull on other cinemas. From the 1920s onwards film-makers from other lands have been drawn to the United States by its combination of high salaries and excellent technical facilities. Greta Garbo, Marlene Dietrich with her directorial guru Josef von Sternberg, and Ingrid Bergman were among the most illustrious, but many now half-forgotten names such as the Japanese Sessue Hayakawa, the Polish Pola Negri, the Russian Nazimova, the Mexican Ramon Novarro, not to mention the Italian Rudolph Valentino, were major stars recruited to Hollywood during the silent era.

Foreign directors were recruited from early days. Since 1970 Hollywood has benefited from the talents of Poles (Roman Polanski, *Chinatown*, 1974), Czechs (Ivan Passer, *Cutter and Bone* 1981; Milos Forman, *One Flew over the Cuckoo's Nest*, 1975), Australians (Peter Weir, *Witness*, 1985), Germans (Wolfgang Petersen, *The Perfect Storm*, 2000), Dutch (Paul Verhoeven, *Basic Instinct*, 1991). But to what extent they have imparted an identifiable ethnic quality to their Hollywood films, or whether it has disappeared into the melting pot, is an open question. One might argue that there is more ethnic specificity in the films of American-born directors such as Martin Scorsese and Francis Ford Coppola.

Performers are always likely to retain at least some element of their origins, though Hollywood was slow to develop its own pool of ethnically differentiated performers. Actors often had to mask their origins, the Jewish Issur Danielovitch Demsky becoming Kirk Douglas, the Latina Margarita Cansino becoming Rita Hayworth. Black actors, unable to pass as anything else, fared especially badly, relegated to roles as sleeping car attendants and janitors or guest appearances in musicals, as was the case with the incredibly talented tap-dancing Nicholas brothers. The civil rights movement of the 1960s could not help but have an effect on Hollywood, and at the end of the decade Hollywood produced some earnest pictures which tried to take race seriously. Several of them, such as *Guess Who's Coming to Dinner* (Stanley Kramer, 1967) and *In the Heat of the Night* (Norman Jewison, 1967), starred Sidney Poitier, the biggest black star of his day.

US cinema had produced ethnically specific films before the 1970s, with films made for Latino, Yiddish and African-American audiences in the 1930s. But the 1970s saw the rise of a self-confident black cinema no longer confined to the ghetto, forcing its ethnically specific attitudes into the mainstream but wanting to stay distinct. A harbinger was Melvin Van Peebles's *Sweet Sweetback's Baad Asssss Song* (1971), an unclassifiable mélange of avant-garde effects and fractured narrative, with frequent scabrous sexual interludes which caused censorship problems. Cinematically it was a dead end but it deserves its status as a pioneering piece of consciousness-raising, miles away from the staid liberalism of the Poitier vehicles, which nervously inched towards political correctness. No such inhibitions marked the wave of so-called 'Blaxploitation' movies inaugurated by *Shaft* (1971), directed by Hollywood's first major black director, Gordon Parks. Richard Roundtree emerged as a new style of black actor – loud, brash, unapologetic. Sequels and imitations followed, including *Superfly* (1972), directed by Parks's son, Gordon Parks, Jr: crime melodramas in which the black characters gave as good as they got, and usually better. There were female equivalents, too, such as *Cleopatra Jones* (Jack Starrett, 1973) with Tamara Dobson, and *Coffy* (Jack Hill, 1973) with Pam Grier. These were the ancestors of a new wave of black films in the 1990s such as *Boyz N the Hood* (1991), John Singleton's convincingly mounted drama

Hotter than Bond,
Cooler than Bullitt.

SHAFT's his name.
SHAFT's his game.

HOLLYWOOD AND ETHNICITY

of black gangs in Los Angeles, *New Jack City* (Mario Van Peebles, 1991), *Juice* (Ernest R Dickerson, 1992), *Menace II Society* (Allen and Albert Hughes, 1993) and a remake of *Shaft* (John Singleton, 2000), films whose milieu is the world of drugs, crime and ghetto life. If for some they merely confirm white stereotypes of black youth, they nevertheless actualize facets of black experience which more earnest films ignore.

That this is not the entirety of black American life is obvious enough, and the films of Spike Lee have sought a broader canvas. For one thing, they have more complex roles for women. Lee's first film, *She's Gotta Have It* (1986), centres on a young black woman who maintains her independence by refusing to settle with any one man. In *Jungle Fever* (1991) Lee explored the theme of inter-racial sex. Wesley Snipes plays a young black architect, apparently happily married, who begins an affair with an Italian-American woman (Annabella Sciorra). Sex between black men and white women is still a rare thing in US cinema, and Lee's film is ground-breaking in its depiction of the racism such unions arouse.

Lee's most ambitious project to date is *Malcolm X* (1992), a biography of the black Muslim leader, played by Denzel Washington. It is a serious film, illuminating and informative about black experience, and not afraid to experiment stylistically. As the most talented black film-maker working today, and the only one with a sustained career in the industry, Lee suffers from the burden of expectation that his every film should be the definitive statement about the black experience. When he does deal with the problems of life in the ghetto, as in *Clockers* (1995), he is supposed to provide not only analysis but solutions. In fact, the story of a small-time drug-pusher accused of murder by the racist police, who by the skin of his teeth manages to make an escape from the grim prospects that await him, gives a frighteningly real picture of how drugs, crime and guns can dominate the life of poor, black men. The young hero's fascination with his electric train set points to a childlike and imaginative side to his nature, and lends an apt symbolism to the ending in which he escapes by riding the train west – but it is a film-maker's resolution, not a politician's.

Above: Annabella Sciorra and Wesley Snipes as the inter-racial couple Angie Tucci and Flipper Purify in *Jungle Fever* (1991). Dir: Spike Lee

Below: Denzel Washington as the charismatic black leader of the Nation of Islam in *Malcolm X* (1992). Dir: Spike Lee

HOLLYWOOD AND ETHNICITY

Lee's *Bamboozled* (2000) is an ambitious satire on media images of blacks. A young TV producer wants to demonstrate the racism of his network and proposes a new format, based on the old minstrel shows, reincarnated in glorious colour. He cannot believe it when his ironic suggestion is taken up by the company and becomes a huge hit. In a sharp, almost Brechtian exposé, Lee shows us both what is wrong with stereotypes of blacks, and just how easily even black people can be seduced by them. Unfortunately, Lee is not wholly in control of his material and the film ends quite inappropriately in a hail of bullets, but until then there are plenty of laughs and much food for thought.

A different sensibility appears in the films of Charles Burnett. Where Lee's style is flamboyant, at times excessive, Burnett is restrained, almost to a fault. *Killer of Sheep* (1977) is about a black man living in Watts, Los Angeles, and working in a slaughterhouse. It is a quiet though heartfelt study of lower middle-class life. In *To Sleep with Anger* (1990) Danny Glover plays a charming but menacing intruder into the lives of a black middle-class family. Burnett's carefully composed images and measured pacing mean that the film is slow to reveal its surprises, and it resists easy genre classification. *The Glass Shield* (1994), dealing with racism in a California police force, is more familiar territory, but again Burnett avoids the more obvious elements of his subject matter in favour of a serious look at a black policeman's predicament.

Burnett was part of the so-called LA School, a loosely associated group of independent film-makers attempting to put authentic black experience on the screen without the compromises that Hollywood inevitably demanded. Another member of the group was Julie Dash, whose *Daughters of the Dust* (1991) is more experimental, stretching the confines of conventional narrative in its story of a black family about to leave their island home off the coast of Georgia to emigrate to the mainland. Dash treats with respect the mystical beliefs of a traditional culture in a film that uses symbolism to convey the lived experience of an unfamiliar milieu.

Above: Alva Rogers, Barbara-O and Cora Lee Day in the low-budget feature *Daughters of the Dust* (1991).
Dir: Julie Dash
Right: Danny Glover as Harry Mention, the menacing intruder in *To Sleep with Anger* (1990). Harry is a drifter who shows up one day at the Los Angeles home of friends Gideon (Paul Butler) and his wife Suzie (Mary Alice), with whom he grew up in the South. His arrival soon turns from fun to the sinister.
Dir: Charles Burnett
Overleaf: Savion Glover as Manray Mantan in one of the satirical minstrel numbers in *Bamboozled* (2000).
Dir: Spike Lee

Carl Franklin appears to have done his best to avoid being typecast as a black director. His first assignment, *Full Fathom Five* (1990), was an action film about a stolen Russian nuclear submarine. *One False Move* (1991) was a crime thriller in which most of the characters are white. After committing a violent drug theft, a group of criminals arrive in a small Arkansas town. Franklin handles the interaction between the Los Angeles police and the local force with great deftness and insight, in a film that is both thrilling and rooted in a fully realized world. *Devil in a Blue Dress* (1995), based on a novel by the black thriller writer Walter Mosley, managed the 1940s setting and the dynamics of film noir with great facility, aided by a strong performance by Denzel Washington.

Washington is one of a new generation of black male actors who have made the transition to being stars in their own right, capable of carrying a film intended for the mainstream audience. No longer are black actors only featured in films with black subjects. Eddie Murphy, a successful stand-up comic, was teamed with Nick Nolte in *48 Hrs.* (Walter Hill, 1982), playing a streetwise crook who is persuaded to help cop Nolte track down a gang. It is not irrelevant that Murphy is black: he has the complete range of urban black mannerisms and an initially pugnacious attitude to the white cop. But it is a thriller, not a problem picture, which with only slight modification could have used a white actor in the part. Murphy repeated the performance in *Beverly Hills Cop* (Martin Brest, 1984) and its two sequels, before mellowing into more conventional comedy with *The Nutty Professor* (Tom Shadyac, 1996).

Will Smith is another actor who has become a major star without trading on his blackness. Beginning in television in *The Fresh Prince of Bel-Air*, he had a huge hit as a young pilot in *Independence Day* (Roland Emmerich, 1996), and another in the science fiction comedy *Men in Black* (Barry Sonnenfeld, 1997). *Enemy of the State* (Tony Scott, 1998), a conspiracy thriller, and *The Wild Wild West* (Barry Sonnenfeld, 1999), an action fantasy, offered further roles in which blackness was not a major constituent. Blackness can

hardly be ignored in *Ali* (2001), Michael Mann's biography of Muhammad Ali, the most charismatic black man of his age, but Smith's performance is star quality and gives the film universal appeal.

Both Wesley Snipes and Denzel Washington appeared in Spike Lee's *Mo' Better Blues* (1990). Since then Washington has alternated between specifically black subjects such as *The Hurricane* (Norman Jewison, 1999), in which he plays a black boxer wrongly imprisoned, and genre films such as *Crimson Tide* (Tony Scott, 1995), a submarine drama, and *The Bone Collector* (Phillip Noyce, 1999), in which he is a homicide detective. Snipes has largely favoured action films such as *Rising Sun* (Philip Kaufman, 1993), *Demolition Man* (Marco Brambilla, 1993) and *Blade* (Stephen Norrington, 1998), a vampire fantasy. More interesting, both as a film and as a cultural shift, was *One Night Stand* (Mike Figgis, 1997), in which he plays an advertising man who spends a night with another woman. The woman

HOLLYWOOD AND ETHNICITY

is white (played by Nastassja Kinski), and Snipes's wife in the film is Asian (played by Ming-Na Wen). Perhaps the most interesting feature of the film is that race is scarcely mentioned.

Inter-racial sex remains a problem for Hollywood. In action films the romantic involvements are secondary, and so black male actors do not necessarily require a female opposite, thus avoiding a decision about whether she should be black or white. For black female performers, it is more likely that the romantic life of the character will be central, and therefore the decision about who to cast against them is crucial. As a result, there are fewer major black women stars. Of course they could be cast against Will Smith or Wesley Snipes, but then the film would appear to situate itself largely towards a black audience, thus narrowing its box office potential. Despite their obvious talent, Angela Bassett or Halle Berry have waited long to make an impact, though both have appeared in major science fiction productions, Berry in *X-Men* (Bryan Singer, 2000) and Bassett in *Supernova* (Walter Hill, 2000). Berry's role in *Monster's Ball* (Marc Forster, 2001), in which she has a romance with a white racist played by Billy Bob Thornton, proved to be her breakthrough.

There has been a small but significant number of films aimed at a black female audience. *The Color Purple* (1985) and *Beloved* (1998) were based on books by noted black women writers Alice Walker and Toni Morrison respectively, though directed by white men (Steven Spielberg and Jonathan Demme). Directed by the black actor Forest Whitaker (who memorably played saxophonist Charlie Parker in Clint Eastwood's 1988 film *Bird*), *Waiting to Exhale* (1995) stars Whitney Houston and Angela Bassett in a film about four successful black women who compensate for the inadequacies of the men in their lives by bonding together. Black cinema still sets itself to work against the old damaging stereotypes, but is at the same time evolving towards a more confident black consciousness – one that no longer needs to assert an essence of black experience, and can rather celebrate a heterogeneity in which, like the white majority, sexual, class and other cultural variations are in play. As Ed Guerrero has noted, the increasingly visible presence of blacks in other cultural arenas, especially music, has spilled over into cinema, providing high-profile performers and writers.[1] Such a beneficial spin-off for black cinema seems likely to increase.

Other ethnic minorities have been slower to assert themselves. Latinos have yet to establish a substantial presence on screen beyond menial roles such as servants or criminals, a position from which blacks began to extricate themselves a generation ago. This seems surprising given that at 12.5 per cent of the US population, Latinos have now taken over from African-Americans as the largest ethnic minority. The Directors Guild of America reported that in 1999 DGA Latino film directors worked only 1.1 per cent of the total days worked by Guild directors. However, the early 1980s saw the beginnings of a Chicano or Latino cinema with *The Ballad of Gregorio Cortez* (1982), directed by Robert M Young, a kind of anti-Western about a Mexican folk hero battling the Texas Rangers, and *El Norte* (1983), directed by Gregory Nava, about migrant workers crossing from Mexico into the United States. Later in the decade Luis Valdez's *La Bamba* (1987), a biopic about the singer Richie Valens, did well at the box office, and in Rámon Menéndez's *Stand and Deliver* (1988) Edward James Olmos gave an excellent performance as a charismatic schoolteacher in a Los Angeles barrio. But Latino cinema in Hollywood is still a marginal affair. Native Americans, too, have yet to make an impact. Numerically much smaller than African-Americans or the Latino group, their socio-economic position is also far weaker.

HOLLYWOOD AND ETHNICITY

Above: Bringing a bride to the new country: newly-weds Ben Loy (Russell Wong) and Mei Oi (Cora Miao) are welcomed to New York in *Eat a Bowl of Tea* (1989).
Dir: Wayne Wang
Below: Dancing cheek-to-cheek in *The Joy Luck Club* (1993). Stories of the Chinese-born mothers are compared with those of their American-born daughters in this witty but weepie film.
Dir: Wayne Wang

But there are signs of a change. Sherman Alexie is a celebrated Native American writer who wrote the script for *Smoke Signals* (Chris Eyre, 1998), a quirky and engaging film about family dislocation, set on the Cœur d'Alene reservation, which won a prize at the Sundance Film Festival in 1998.

Apart from blacks, the ethnic group that has so far made the most accomplished contribution in Hollywood has been the East Asians. The American career of John Woo, from Hong Kong, is discussed in the chapter on action films (Chapter 2), since his Hollywood features such as *Mission: Impossible 2* (2000) show no trace of his ethnic origins. By contrast, Wayne Wang's most successful films take his background as subject matter. Born in Hong Kong but in the United States since the age of eighteen, Wang made *Dim Sum: A Little Bit of Heart* (1985) and *Eat a Bowl of Tea* (1989), each set among the Chinese community, in San Francisco and New York respectively. In *Eat a Bowl of Tea* a young Chinese-American goes back to China after World War II and returns to the United States with a new bride. She soon finds everything in the United States is not rosy, and, feeling neglected by her new husband, embarks on an affair. The culture clash is explored with exquisite irony as a night-club singer performs 'I'd Like to Get You on a Slow Boat to China', and as the young marrieds discuss their life at an outdoor screening of *Lost Horizon* (1937), Frank Capra's classic film about an idealized fantasy of the Orient. Wang's most fully realized film on this theme is *The Joy Luck Club* (1993), based on Amy Tan's best-selling novel about mother–daughter relations as observed at a mah-jong club. Wang's *The Center of the World* (2001), in which a white computer engineer pays a stripper to go to Las Vegas with him, is a study of the connections between sex and money. Whether this signals a decisive move away from ethnic subjects remains to be seen.

Ang Lee was born in Taiwan but educated in the United States at the New York University film school. His first three films are firmly set in his native culture. *Pushing Hands* (*Tui shou*, 1992) is about the tensions that arise when an elderly Chinese man comes

HOLLYWOOD AND ETHNICITY

to the United States to stay with his son and his American wife. In *The Wedding Banquet* (*His yen*, 1993) a young gay Chinese man in New York has to contract a marriage of convenience when his conventional parents come to visit. *Eat Drink Man Woman* (*Yin shi nan nu*, 1994) is set in Taipei, the story of a generational clash in which the three unmarried daughters of a widowed chef are all looking to escape the family nest. All these films combine acute social observation with subtle comedy and good ensemble playing, qualities which Lee brought to his next project. *Sense and Sensibility* (1995), based on Jane Austen's novel with a script by its star, Emma Thompson, was a surprising project for a Chinese-born director, but Lee carried it off with style. *The Ice Storm* (1997) was Lee's first entirely American subject, a cool, at times bleak look at white middle-class Americans in the suburbs of the early 1970s. *Ride with the Devil* (1999), a Civil War western, did not quite catch the raw violence of the original novel, but Lee's *Crouching Tiger, Hidden Dragon* (*Wo hu cang long*, 2000) was a sophisticated Chinese-language martial arts drama filmed with great visual brio. Shot in mainland China but largely financed by Columbia Pictures, it illustrates the problem of cross-over, making a film based in one culture which is deliberately intended to appeal to another. Despite its huge success, the suspicion remains that *Crouching Tiger* is a martial arts film for those who do not like martial arts films, its stylistic panache not covering for its lack of sufficient character development and complexity. Nevertheless, actors and directors of Chinese origin are more visible in Hollywood films than they have ever been. Chow Yun-Fat has several Hollywood projects on the go after his appearance in *Crouching Tiger*, while Hong Kong martial arts star Jackie Chan has had two highly successful American outings in *Rush Hour* (Brett Ratner, 1998) and the neatly titled Western *Shanghai Noon* (Tom Dey, 2000). Jet Li, after a hit with *Lethal Weapon 4* (Richard Donner, 1998), made *Kiss of the Dragon* (Chris Nahon, 2001) with Bridget Fonda. It is more than a dozen years since Sony bought Columbia Pictures in 1989, but at last there is a discernible Eastern component in the content of Hollywood Films.

Below: Lung Sihung as the father and chef Mr Chu in *Eat Drink Man Woman* (*Yin shi nan nu*, 1994). Family dinners are the last surviving ritual as romance intrudes upon their close-knit family. Dir: Ang Lee

The Martial Arts Epic
Crouching Tiger, Hidden Dragon (Wo hu cang long, 2000)
Dir: Ang Lee

Chinese martial arts films had found a market in the West during the kung fu boom initiated by Bruce Lee in the early 1970s. But *Crouching Tiger, Hidden Dragon* represents a new departure, an attempt to produce a sophisticated, big-budget Chinese film that would appeal both to mainstream Western audiences and to audiences in the Far East. Through their quest to find the stolen sword of Green Destiny, warriors Yu Shu Lien (Michelle Yeoh) and Li Mu Bai (Chow Yun-Fat) explore themes of love, loyalty and sacrifice.

Ang Lee was an astute choice as director. Born in Taiwan but educated in US film schools, he made a trilogy of Taiwanese family comedies, then three widely differing films in Hollywood: Jane Austen's *Sense and Sensibility* (1995), *The Ice Storm* (1997), a family drama set in the 1970s, and *Ride With the Devil* (1999), a Civil War action film.

Crouching Tiger, Hidden Dragon was largely financed by Sony through its Columbia Pictures Asian venture. The location shooting was on the Chinese mainland and the actors came from Malaysia, Hong Kong and Taiwan, as well as China. Instead of the Shaolin school of martial arts favoured by Bruce Lee, Ang Lee opted for the more spiritual form of Wudan; brute force is replaced by scenes of balletic grace as opponents shin up walls or flit through tree-tops. The fight scenes were choreographed by Yuen Woo-Ping, who also worked on *The Matrix* (Andy and Larry Wachowski, 1999).

The widespread success of the film in both East and West, together with the breakthrough into Hollywood of other Far East stars such as Jackie Chan and Jet Li, is a firm indication that Chinese culture is making its mark.

<u>Country of Origin</u>:
China/Taiwan/USA
<u>Production Companies</u>:
Sony Pictures Classics and Columbia Pictures Film Production Asia
<u>Running Time</u>: 120 mins

<u>Producers</u>: Bill Kong, Hsu Li-Kong, Ang Lee
<u>Writers</u>: James Schamus, Wang Hui-Ling, Tsai Kuo-Jung
<u>Photography</u>: Peter Pau
<u>Editor</u>: Tim Squyres
<u>Production Designer</u>: Tim Yip
<u>Music</u>: Tan Dun

<u>Master Li Mu Bai</u>: Chow Yun-Fat
<u>Yu Shu Lien</u>: Michelle Yeoh
<u>Jen</u>: Zhang Ziyi
<u>Lo</u>: Chang Chen

<u>Below</u>: Zhang Ziyi and Michelle Yeoh in one of the dazzling sword fights. Director Ang Lee made extensive use of special effects to produce such memorable scenes.

<u>Bottom</u>: Michelle Yeoh and Chow Yun-Fat in a tender moment.
<u>Right</u>: Zhang Ziyi as the teenage thief Jen with Chang Chen as Lo viewing a stunning landscape.

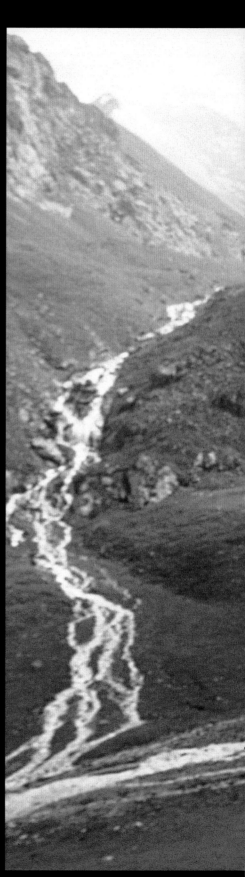

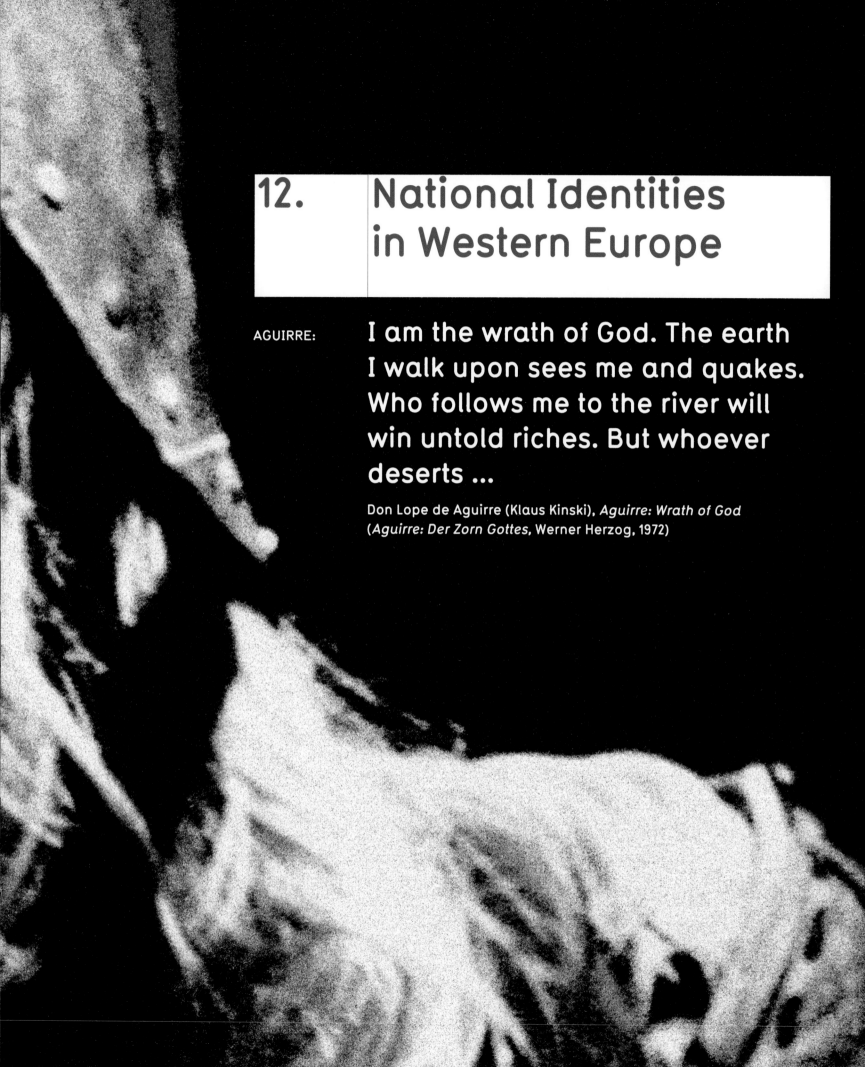

12. National Identities in Western Europe

AGUIRRE:

I am the wrath of God. The earth I walk upon sees me and quakes. Who follows me to the river will win untold riches. But whoever deserts ...

Don Lope de Aguirre (Klaus Kinski), *Aguirre: Wrath of God*
(*Aguirre: Der Zorn Gottes*, Werner Herzog, 1972)

Western Europe's cinematic legacy is a proud one. The roll call of great masters is long. Still active in 1970 were Jean-Luc Godard, François Truffaut, Ingmar Bergman, Luis Buñuel, Michelangelo Antonioni, Frederico Fellini and Luchino Visconti. Among directors of world class to make their name since 1970 are Bernardo Bertolucci, Lars von Trier, Rainer Werner Fassbinder, Theo Angelopoulos and Pedro Almodóvar. All these are figures from art cinema, auteurs whose films have been supported in one way or another by the state. Measures of subsidy and of protection have ensured that their unique and gifted voices are heard. But European popular cinema, the cinema that supplied the mass audience with its comedies and thrillers in their native tongue, has been virtually driven out of existence in most Western European countries by the combined effect of ever more intense competition from Hollywood and of television, which now supplies the mass entertainment that indigenous cinemas once provided. Yet even the relatively small amount of state support that Europe can muster is regarded with hostility by Hollywood, whose lobbyists exert continuous pressure on the US State Department to bring artistic products fully under the free trade provisions of the World Trade Organization. Western Europe, particularly France, fought a rearguard action in the late 1980s to get culture excluded from such provisions, so that domestic production might retain some share of the market, but for how long these 'concessions' by the US will remain is uncertain.

By the end of the twentieth century Hollywood was making half its money from sales abroad, with fifty-five per cent of this coming from Western Europe. Three-quarters of all the money taken at the Western European box office goes back to Hollywood, so that national cinemas now capture on average only a quarter of their own domestic markets – even though production, at just over 600 titles, was almost equivalent to that of the US in 2001. Despite widespread subsidies and in some countries minimum exhibition quotas for domestically produced films, the decline has been precipitous; only ten years ago Western Europe still had half of its home market, though there were marked variations nationally.[1]

Contemporary Western European cinema, then, is an endangered species. Yet it continues to show itself full of invention, alive to the urgent social and political questions of the day, daring in its exploration of new cinematic styles. Though some productions have the artificial look of hot-house flowers doomed to wilt when exposed to the open air of the international market, at their best the cinemas of Western Europe express the inner life of their nations in ways that it is impossible for Hollywood to reach.

The French have always considered cinema an essential part of their culture and crucial to national identity. French cinema, the largest on the Continent with 218 films produced in 2001, has consistently received firm government support.[2] At the beginning of the 1970s French films enjoyed high prestige internationally, in the wake of the success of the *Nouvelle Vague*, whose star directors were still going strong and many of whom continue to be active today. Beginning in 1959, the *Nouvelle Vague*, or New Wave, had been an iconoclastic movement that rejected the so-called 'cinéma du papa' in favour of a more freewheeling, eclectic style, and fresh subject matter chiefly located in the life and loves of the younger generation. Though more concerned with cinematic than social revolution, some of the moving spirits of the New Wave became radicalized during the 'événements' of 1968, and one, Jean-Luc Godard, adopted Maoist politics and an avant-garde aesthetic. Though *Tout va bien* (1972) had stars (Jane Fonda and Yves Montand, no less), its narrative, concerning a factory strike, is fractured and full of self-reflexive devices. As the 1970s progressed Godard all but abandoned narrative altogether, though he returned to it with *Every Man for Himself* (*Sauve qui peut la vie*, 1980), an interrogation of contemporary sexual relations including prostitution, one of Godard's recurrent themes. In recent years Godard has continued to make films which playfully test the limits of cinematic representation while retaining his radical edge, as in *For Ever Mozart* (1990), his take on the Balkan conflict. *In Praise of Love* (*Eloge de l'amour*, 2001) once more combines politics (an elderly couple is negotiating the sale of their wartime Resistance experiences

Above: Stars Yves Montand and Jane Fonda among the factory workers in the political drama *Tout va bien* (1972).
Dir: Jean-Luc Godard

Opposite: Director Jean-Luc Godard, founder-member of the New Wave movement, is still radical in his seventies.

NATIONAL IDENTITIES IN WESTERN EUROPE

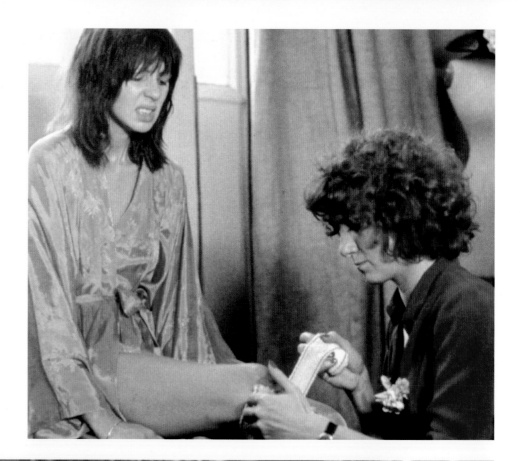

Above: French director Jacques Rivette at work on *La Belle Noiseuse* (1991).
Below: Emmanuelle Béart as Marianne posing for painter Frenhofer (Michel Piccoli) in *La Belle Noiseuse* (1991), a film which explores the nature of creativity.
Dir: Jacques Rivette
Right: Juliet Berto as Céline and Dominique Labourier as Julie in *Céline and Julie Go Boating* (*Céline et Julie vont en bateau*, 1974).
Dir: Jacques Rivette

to a Hollywood studio; should people's memories be traded in this way?) with playful, teasing reflections on the nature of the film-making process.

Jacques Rivette and Alain Resnais, less overtly political, also maintained a foothold in the avant-garde. Rivette's most celebrated film is *Céline and Julie Go Boating* (*Céline et Julie vont en bateau*, 1974), a film of humour and charm in which two female 'buddies', Juliet Berto and Dominique Labourier, attempt to solve the mystery behind certain events in an old house. At times they actively take a hand in the construction of the narrative, at others they are passively swept along. The length of Rivette's films (sometimes four hours or more) has counted against him commercially, though *La Belle Noiseuse* (1991), an exhaustive but fascinating exploration of a painter and his model, was released in both long and short versions. In *Who Knows?* (*Va savoir*, 2001) Rivette produced one of his most engaging works, a witty tale of an actress who revisits a former boyfriend, setting off a chain of events which end in a happy but farcical manner. Resnais, meanwhile, has pursued the philosophical investigations he broached in *Last Year at Marienbad* (*L'Année dernière à Marienbad*, 1961), venturing into English with *Providence* (1977), which starred John Gielgud, and making *Smoking/No Smoking* (1993) from plays by Alan Ayckbourn.

Despite its notable auteurs, French cinema has been heavily reliant on genres. One of the most important has been the thriller or crime film, known in France as the 'polar'. As befits the co-author of a book on Alfred Hitchcock, Claude Chabrol has specialized in the creation of well-crafted thrillers exposing the greed and lust that seethe beneath the complacent surface of French bourgeois life. In *Violette Nozière* (1978) Isabelle Huppert gives a powerful performance as a young woman who poisons her parents. Huppert is again brilliant in *Story of Women* (*Une affaire de femmes*, 1988), playing an abortionist in Nazi-occupied France who is sent to the guillotine, and in *A Judgement in Stone* (*La Cérémonie*, 1995) she is once more outstanding, as a village postmistress who sets a housemaid on a path of confrontation with her employer in a plot reminiscent of Genet's play *The Maids*.

Below: Isabelle Huppert as the young poisoner, Violette, with a pin-up of silent film star Lilian Gish in *Violette Nozière* (1978). This French film was based on a real murder case of the 1930s. Dir: Claude Chabrol

Some of Robert Bresson's films could be considered crime films including his last, *Money* (*L'Argent*, 1983). Yet Bresson can scarcely be confined to genre; his films are austere disquisitions on fate, grace and redemption, rather than thrillers or sociological studies. In *Money* the passing of a forged note leads with deadly logic to the incarceration of an innocent man and his transformation into a murderer. The spareness of Bresson's style, nothing but what is necessary, makes other film-makers appear prolix and self-indulgent.

François Truffaut worked in the 'polar' genre, and indeed his last film before his untimely death in 1984 was *Finally, Sunday* (*Vivement Dimanche!*, 1983), based on a book by the US crime writer Charles Williams. But Truffaut's major contribution in the later part of his career was to another important genre, the 'heritage' film. Often drawing on highbrow literary sources, usually set in the past, these films consciously re-create France's historical legacy. Ironically, they can be seen as a development of the 'tradition de qualité' which the New Wave had set out to overthrow. Truffaut's *Anne and Muriel* (*Les Deux Anglaises et le continent*, 1971) is set around 1900, *The Story of Adèle H.* (*L'Histoire d'Adèle H.*, 1975) is about the daughter of Victor Hugo, and *The Green Room* (*La Chambre verte*, 1978) is based on a Henry James story and is set in the 1920s. One of Truffaut's most successful films was *The Last Metro* (*Le Dernier Métro*, 1980), a story about French theatre in wartime Paris, with outstanding performances by an energetic Gérard Depardieu and the austerely beautiful Catherine Deneuve. Wistful, at times fey, these films are all imbued with Truffaut's evident love of cinema.

Truffaut had worked with Godard and Rivette on the influential magazine *Cahiers du cinéma* in the 1960s, helping to formulate the critical principles which informed the New Wave. So, too, did Eric Rohmer, who was Chabrol's co-author for the book on Hitchcock. Rohmer hit on his method and style from the beginning. His films, simply but elegantly shot, are made in series, such as the six *contes moreaux* with which he began, among them *Claire's Knee* (*Le Genou de Claire*, 1970). In each, Rohmer explores the gap between what his intelligent, middle-class protagonists say, and what is actually going on in their heads as they manoeuvre through their complicated love affairs. These sophisticated films about *amour* might almost serve as a definition of French cinema itself. At the age of eighty Rohmer shows with *The Lady and the Duke* (*L'Anglaise et le Duc*, 2001), a story of the French Revolution, that his method works as well as ever, and that, with the use of digital technology to create the historical settings, he remains alive to fresh ideas.

Period films are not necessarily exercises in nostalgia. Louis Malle, another New Wave veteran, set *Lacombe, Lucien* (1974) during the German occupation and raised uncomfortable questions about French collaboration. His *Goodbye, Children* (*Au revoir les enfants*, 1987) is in a similar vein, set in a wartime boys' school in which a Jewish pupil is betrayed to the Nazis. A much more agreeable take on the past was provided with Claude Berri's brace of adaptations from the pre-war playwright and director, Marcel Pagnol: *Jean de Florette* (1986) and *Manon des sources* (1986). The lush re-creations of Provence proved a big hit both in France and abroad. Berri also directed a version of Emile Zola's classic tale of coal miners,

Above: Jean-Claude Brialy and Laurence de Monaghan in *Claire's Knee* (*Le Genou de Claire*, 1970), a tale of a forty-something man who falls in love with a young girl. Dir: Eric Rohmer
Right: Gérard Depardieu and Catherine Deneuve in

The Last Metro (*Le Dernier Métro*, 1980), a bittersweet tale of wartime Paris. Dir: François Truffaut
Opposite: Yves Montand as cunning French peasant Soubeyran with his son (Daniel Auteuil) in *Jean de Florette* (1986). Dir: Claude Berri

NATIONAL IDENTITIES IN WESTERN EUROPE

CÉSAR:	Now let's talk about other things. I'm going to write to Scratcher.
UGOLIN:	Who's she?
CÉSAR:	You don't know her because she left here before you were born. She had the body of an angel. They called her Scratcher because when the boys tried to kiss her she scratched their faces. She used to sharpen her nails especially. But because of this she ended up a spinster and when her parents died she went to work for the priest at Mimet. About four or five years ago the Pope moved him to Crespin and she should still be with him.
UGOLIN:	So long as she didn't scratch him.
CÉSAR:	Oh, at her age you don't scratch people, and because she was a friend of Florette she must still visit her. I'm going to write immediately.
UGOLIN:	And if she's dead?
CÉSAR:	Not everyone my age is dead.

César Soubeyran (Yves Montand), Ugolin Soubeyran (Daniel Auteuil), *Jean de Florette* (Claude Berri, 1986)

Previous pages:
Feelings run high
as Toussait Maheu
(Gérard Depardieu)
confronts authority in
the big-budget film
Germinal (1993).
Dir: Claude Berri
Above: Betty Blue with
her boyfriend Zorg
(Jean-Hugues Anglade)

in Betty Blue (37,2
le matin, 1986).
Opposite: Béatrice
Dalle as the lively
waitress Betty in Betty
Blue (37,2 le matin,
1986), a strongly visual
film in bright colours.
Dir: Jean-Jacques
Beineix

Above left: Anne
Parillaud plays
a trained assassin in
the slick and violent
Nikita (1990).
Dir: Luc Besson
Left: (l to r) Vincent

Cassel as Vinz, Saïd
Taghmaoui as Saïd
and Hubert Koundé
as Hubert in the black
and white crime movie
La Haine (1995).
Dir: Mathieu Kassovitz

Germinal (1993). This film became the standard around which the defenders of French culture, including the culture minister Jack Lang, could rally against the encroachments of Hollywood. (In 1986 receipts of US films in France had overtaken those of domestic films for the first time.) Another director who has successfully mined this vein is Bertrand Tavernier, whose *Daughter of d'Artagnan* (*La Fille d'Artagnan*, 1994) is a charming and spirited addition to the Musketeer canon. Films with a more prestigious literary pedigree include Jean-Paul Rappeneau's *Cyrano de Bergerac* (1990) and Chabrol's *Madame Bovary* (1991). *La Reine Margot* (1994), directed by Patrice Chéreau, is a stylish and lurid account of the Saint Bartholomew's Day Massacre of Protestants in the sixteenth century, which has been read by some as a commentary on ethnic cleansing in the Balkans.

In 1970 two of French cinema's greatest male stars, Jean-Paul Belmondo and Alain Delon, had a huge success with *Borsalino* (Jacques Deray), a modish gangster film set in the 1930s. Delon was something of a specialist in the crime genre, appearing as a cop in the last film of Jean-Pierre Melville, *Un flic* (1972), as well as several films directed by Jacques Deray, including *Flic Story* (1975) and *Le Gang* (1976). Frequently drawing on the rich tradition of the French 'série noir', a form of popular fiction that owed something to the American 'hard-boiled' school of Dashiell Hammett and Jim Thompson, the French crime film has long remained a box office staple, with 'polars' representing no less than fifteen per cent of all French films in 1980. As in the United States, the requirement of the genre to produce a quota of thrilling action did not preclude a certain level of social observation. Thus *La Balance* (1982), whose director, Bob Swaim, of US origin, was a veteran of advertising commercials, depicts the casual brutality and racism of a police force far removed from the comfortable image of Inspector Maigret.

Genre divisions are never absolute, and the crime film overlaps at times with films centred on the youth problem, as with Maurice Pialat's *Police* (1985), in which a detective competes with a drug dealer for the affections of a young woman. Mathieu Kassovitz's *La Haine* (1995) is set in the Paris suburbs, where three young men spend the night in aimless skirmishes with police and bands of skinheads. One of the youths has Arab origins, which connects the film to a small but significant group of so-called 'beur' films, concerned with the experience of those of North African descent. Born in 1967, the son of a film director and an editor, Kassovitz was submerged in cinema from an early age, and appeared as a child actor. Shot in black and white, *La Haine* has clear US influences, with its references to *Lethal Weapon* (Richard Donner, 1987) and with one of the characters imitating Robert De Niro in *Taxi Driver* (Martin Scorsese, 1976). But the elegance of *La Haine*'s visual style also has something in common with the 'cinéma du look', a movement associated with the directors Jean-Jacques Beineix, Luc Besson and Léos Carax.

Beineix's *Diva* (1981) is a kind of a chase thriller with a dual plot involving police corruption and a pirate recording of an opera singer. But it is the surface of the film which got it noticed, a bravura display of eye-catching sets and dazzling architecture. *Betty Blue* (*37,2 le matin*, 1986) told its tale of *amour fou* with a stylistic flourish in which saturated colours assault the eye. Besson's *Nikita* (1990) is about a young woman blackmailed by the police into becoming a professional killer. Its slick technique owed much to the aesthetics of the television commercial and rock video, in which style is all. As if in recognition of his aesthetic and thematic influences, Besson's next picture, *Leon* (1994),

NATIONAL IDENTITIES IN WESTERN EUROPE

also about a professional assassin, was shot in English in New York. His ambitious and expensive science fiction film *The Fifth Element* (*Le Cinquième élément*, 1997) also had a largely English-speaking cast, including Bruce Willis. Besson then ventured into heritage cinema with a version of France's greatest national myth, *Joan of Arc* (*Jeanne d'Arc*, 1999). Carax's *Les Amants du Pont-Neuf* (1991), by contrast, is set on a bridge across the Seine, where Juliette Binoche, an artist who is going blind, conducts a love affair with a homeless man. Made on a large budget, the film contains stunning visual effects, not least in a scene of water-skiing down the Seine, but its relentless romanticism fails to convince.

Though many of these films were popular with the young, French critics were rather snooty about the 'look', accusing it of a fashionably postmodern emptiness behind the technical wizardry. By contrast, many of the most popular films have been comedies, usually of modest aesthetic ambition. Indeed, in the 1980s five out of the six best-attended French films were comedies. Among the most successful directors in this genre has been Bertrand Blier, whose *Les Valseuses* (1974) has Gérard Depardieu and Patrick Dewaere as a couple of petty crooks who share some high-spirited adventures as well as a girlfriend (Miou-Miou). Blier's films often make play with sexual identity and in *Evening Dress* (*Tenue de soirée*, 1986) Depardieu is again a crook, who this time develops a homosexual relationship with

Above: (l to r) Gérard Depardieu, Miou-Miou and Patrick Dewaere as partners in crime and much else in *Les Valseuses* (1974). Dir: Bertrand Blier
Right: *Les Amants du Pont-Neuf* (1991) was a romantic drama set in Paris which starred Juliette Binoche and Denis Lavant. Dir: Léos Carax
Below right: Issach de Bankolé and Cécile Ducasse in a childhood vision of West Africa: *Chocolat* (1988). Dir: Claire Denis

NATIONAL IDENTITIES IN WESTERN EUROPE

the husband of a couple caught up in his criminal activities. *Trois hommes et un couffin* (1985) was directed by a woman, Coline Serreau. Its story of three men unexpectedly landed with looking after a baby provided laughs at the expense of men's domestic ineptitude, and was remade by Hollywood as *Three Men and a Baby* (1987). Jean-Pierre Jeunet's whimsical, at times cloying, comedy *Amélie* (*Le Fabuleux destin d'Amélie Poulain*, 2001), set in an idealized Paris, was a huge hit in France and a considerable success abroad, helping French films to a remarkable forty-one per cent of the domestic market share for 2001.

Serreau is not the only woman to have achieved success in contemporary French cinema. Nelly Kaplan's *Dirty Mary* (*La Fiancée du pirate*, 1969) is a direct and often very funny assault on sexual convention and hypocrisy in the person of Bernadette Lafont, who deliberately seduces the men of her village to expose its bigotry. Kaplan's *A Young Emmanuelle* (*Néa*, 1976) is another passionate plea for sexual liberation. Diane Kurys's first feature, *Peppermint Soda* (*Diabolo menthe*, 1977), was an engaging and unsentimental look at the adolescence of two teenage girls. Her later film *Entre Nous* (*Coup de foudre*, 1983) is about the friendship of two women, which provides solace for their unhappy marriages. Their relationship stops just short of a sexual expression, though in the United States the film found an audience among lesbians as well as others.

Though Agnès Varda is undoubtedly a political radical, her feminism does not always conform to orthodoxy. *One Sings, the Other Doesn't* (*L'une chante, l'autre pas*, 1977) traces the relationship of two women through the formative years of the late 1960s and early 1970s. It does not always escape the warm glow of sentimentality; on the other hand, *Vagabonde* (*Sans toit ni loi*, 1985) is a clear-eyed, tough-minded portrait of a young female drifter, with a scathing performance by Sandrine Bonnaire.

Claire Denis seems almost wilfully to have avoided the usual women's subjects. Her first film, *Chocolat* (1988), is set in the Cameroons, where a young woman remembers her childhood idyll disrupted by a group of plane passengers who are billeted in her house. Africa is again a theme in *S'en fout la mort* (1990), about two West Africans in France who make a living cock-fighting, and once more in *I Can't Sleep* (*J'ai pas sommeil*, 1994), in which a mixed group of immigrants, including some Africans and a girl from Latvia, become involved with a serial killer. *Beau travail* (1999) is set among the Foreign Legion in Djibouti, a tale of suppressed desire and sadism in which, as usual in Denis's films, motives have to

Below: Sandrine Bonnaire gives a powerful performance as Mona, a young drifter, in *Vagabonde* (*Sans toit ni loi*, 1985). Dir: Agnès Varda

Bottom: Audrey Tatou in the metro, playing the title role in *Amélie* (*Le Fabuleux Destin d'Amélie Poulain*, 2001). Dir: Jean-Pierre Jeunet

Above: Anna Karina as the beautiful housekeeper in the Belgian film *Rendez-vous à Bray* (1971). Dir: André Delvaux
Below: Delphine Seyrig played the domesticated prostitute leading a quiet life in *Jeanne Dielman, 23 quai du Commerce,*

1080 Bruxelles (1975). Dir: Chantal Akerman
Bottom: Delphine Seyrig (r) as the vampire Countess Bathory and Danielle Ouimet as a young wife who becomes her victim in *Daughters of Darkness* (*Le Rouge aux lèvres*, 1971). Dir: Harry Kümel

be inferred. Denis refuses the easy psychological explanations of most cinema, preferring her films to make their effects by visual means and through music. Her most recent work, *Trouble Every Day* (2001), similarly denies the audience a simple explanation for its tale of ghoulish blood-lust.

The relative strength of contemporary French cinema derives from the size of the country, its cinematic tradition and the determination of successive governments to maintain French culture. Smaller countries have more difficulty, particularly those in which the potential audience is further reduced by language divisions. Yet despite Belgium's bilingualism (French in one half of the country, Flemish in the other), there is a distinctive film culture, making about a dozen films a year. Belgium has a strong surrealist tradition (René Magritte was a Belgian), and this manifests itself both in the avant-garde and in more mainstream production. Roland Lethem is an example of the former; his film *Bande de cons!* (1970) was described as an extended insult to the audience. Within the mainstream, André Delvaux has produced a series of beautifully composed, dream-like films which hover on the border between reality and fantasy. In *Rendez-vous à Bray* (1971) the setting is a country house during World War I. A young man arrives to meet a friend, who does not appear. Instead he has a series of enigmatic encounters with the beautiful housekeeper. In *Belle* (1973) Delvaux explores a similar situation. Landscape, especially the flat, misty vistas of Belgium, is always prominent. Delvaux's *The Abyss* (*L'Œuvre au noir*, 1988) has a stronger narrative, in which a doctor seeks to resist the Inquisition in Spanish-ruled Flanders in the sixteenth century.

Chantal Akerman also began in the avant-garde with a series of films that were as interesting for their aesthetic approach as for their feminism. *Jeanne Dielman, 23 quai du Commerce, 1080 Bruxelles* (1975) plays with our expectations of narrative in a four-hour-long drama meticulously recording the domestic life of a prostitute. *All Night Long* (*Toute une nuit*, 1982) is far more animated, a series of micro-romances strung together during a hot night in Brussels. Never one to repeat herself, Akerman then made a musical, *Golden Eighties* (1986), set in a shopping mall. Her recent films have put her more centrally in the tradition of the art movie, with *The Captive* (*La Captive*, 2000) an admirable adaptation of a work by Proust.

A more conventionally commercial talent is Harry Kümel, who made a reputation in the 1970s for sophisticated and stylish horror films such as *Daughters of Darkness* (*Le Rouge aux lèvres*, 1971) and *Malpertuis* (1972). More recently, two outstanding talents have emerged. Jan Bucquoy's *The Sexual Life of the Belgians* (*La Vie sexuelle des Belges 1950–1978*, 1995) is the sexual odyssey of a gormless young Belgian, played by the director. Bucquoy's fascination and horror at the sheer awfulness of Belgian provincial life gets further expression in *Camping Cosmos* (1996), a satire on Belgians on holiday, full of scatological vulgarity. Jaco Van Dormael's *Toto the Hero* (*Toto le héros*, 1991) was a big hit internationally, a film about a man who, believing he was switched at birth and deprived of his inheritance, sets out to plot revenge. Van Dormael's *The Eighth Day* (*Le Huitième jour*, 1996) concerns a businessman who, rather against his will, develops a relationship with a Down's syndrome man (a brilliant performance by Pascal Duquenne). Van Dormael's films at times have an excess of feeling, but they explore original territory with charm and insight.

Man Bites Dog (*C'est arrivé près de chez vous*, 1992), directed by Rémy Belvaux, André Bonzel and Benoît Poelvoorde, is perhaps the strangest of all Belgian films, a pseudo-

Above: Thomas Godet as the young Thomas, who comes to believe he was switched at birth in *Toto the Hero* (*Toto le héros*, 1991). Dir: Jaco Van Dormael
Below left and right: Benoît Poelvoorde as

Ben, the serial killer in the spoof documentary *Man Bites Dog* (*C'est arrivé près de chez vous*, 1992). Dir: Rémy Belvaux, André Bonzel and Benoît Poelvoorde

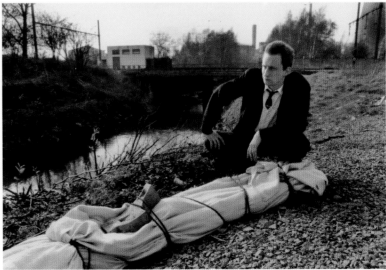

documentary about a serial killer. We watch in fascinated horror as, observed by a film crew, he performs his increasingly grisly crimes. It is offensive, disturbing and blackly comic, in the best surrealist tradition.

As with Belgium, the difficulties of production in Switzerland are complicated by the linguistic divisions of the country, which has four separate languages – French, German, Italian and Romansch. Most film-making has been within the French- and German-speaking cultures. In the early 1970s two French-speaking directors shot to prominence, taking inspiration from the stylistic freedoms of the French New Wave. Alain Tanner's *The Middle of the World* (*Le Milieu du monde*, 1974) tells of an affair between a small-time politician and a waitress. More ambitious was *Jonah Who Will Be 25 in the Year 2000* (*Jonas qui aura 25 ans en l'an 2000*, 1976), a kind of microcosm of Swiss society seen through the eyes of eight interconnecting characters. The film was co-scripted by John Berger, the British art historian. Tanner followed this with *Messidor* (1979), a more jaundiced view of Swiss society in which two young female dropouts embark on a crime spree. Tanner has remained active, working in Spain during the 1990s, though his films have not had the same exposure in later years.

Tanner had collaborated with Claude Goretta on *Nice Time*, a documentary short made for the British Film Institute in 1957. Like those of his countryman, Goretta's films have much of the élan of the New Wave, especially such early comedies as *L'Invitation* (1973), in which a number of revelations come to light in the course of an office party. In *Pas si méchant que ça* (1974) Gérard Depardieu is a businessman who resorts to holding up banks when his business fails, and recruits one of the female cashiers. More sombre was *The Lacemaker* (*La Dentellière*, 1977), in which Isabelle Huppert gives a remarkable performance as a young girl who, disappointed in love, withdraws from the world.

Daniel Schmid represents the German side of Swiss cinema, in a more florid style, full of melodrama. He worked with Rainer Werner Fassbinder and other figures from New German Cinema in the 1970s, and his film *Schatten der Engel* (1975) was based on a controversial play by Fassbinder, the story of a consumptive prostitute and her client, a rich Jew. Schmid's recent work, *Beresina oder Die letzten Tage der Schweiz* (1999), is a black comedy in which a Russian prostitute trying to become a naturalized Swiss gets involved with the head of a shadowy right-wing organization.

In Germany itself, the film industry was dismantled by the Allies at the end of the war and German cinema struggled, in the West producing unambitious comedies and thrillers, and in the East, at the nationalized DEFA studios, trying to flog some life into the doctrine of socialist realism. In 1962 at the Oberhausen Film Festival twenty-six young West German film-makers signed a manifesto demanding a fresh start, with the state as a sponsor for a new cinema in which artistic quality was to be the criterion for subsidy. By the early 1970s a new generation of West German film-makers had brought into existence the *Autorenfilm*, an art cinema which elevated the personal vision of the director. One of the main driving forces behind the movement was Alexander Kluge, whose films such as *Occasional Work*

Opposite: Clémentine Amouroux and Catherine Rétoré as the two dropouts on a crime spree in the Swiss Alps in *Messidor* (1979). Dir: Alain Tanner
Above: Isabelle Huppert as Béatrice and Yves Beneyton as François Beligne in *The Lacemaker* (*La Dentellière*, 1977). Dir: Claude Goretta
Right: Yelena Panova as Russian call girl Irina receives some special attention in *Beresina oder Die letzten Tage der Schweiz* (1999). Dir: Daniel Schmid

The 'Auteur'
Fitzcarraldo (1982)
Dir: Werner Herzog

Werner Herzog's films are perfect examples of the European tradition of the 'auteur' film, in which the director is seen as the originating and creative force behind the work. But there is also a sense that Herzog's visionary monomaniacs function as the director's alter ego, embodying the heroic status of the auteur, always struggling against recalcitrant reality to fulfil his dream. Herzog not only directs but writes and produces his films, ensuring total control. His films are deeply personal, visually exciting and uncompromising.

This seems especially true of *Fitzcarraldo*, which, set a hundred years ago, begins with an Irish colonialist who has a passion for opera rowing 1,200 miles down a South American river, accompanied by the madam of a brothel, in order to hear the great Caruso perform. Inspired by this experience, Fitzcarraldo embarks on a grandiose plan to open up the Amazonian jungle to river transport, providing access to new rubber plantations and thereby making enough money to build an opera house.

Herzog's favourite actor, Klaus Kinski, is as appropriately manic as Fitzcarraldo, eyes glittering madly as he pursues his vision. In the central sequence he organizes a tribe of Indians to help him pull a steamboat across a mountain in order to by-pass dangerous rapids.

The shooting of these scenes became an epic story in itself, with tensions among Herzog's crew, problems from snakebites, weather and a war that erupted between Peru and Ecuador. As if this was not enough, the Indian extras rebelled and Jason Robards, originally cast as the lead, had to retire through illness, necessitating re-shooting the film after nearly half had been completed.

Fitzcarraldo seems by turns admiring of its hero's megalomania and mocking of his hubris, with no illusions about the cynical exploitation of the region's riches by the rubber barons whom Fitzcarraldo tries to outwit. Ultimately though, it is the sheer spectacle which we remember.

Above: Director Werner Herzog with actors Claudia Cardinale and Klaus Kinski.
Left and below: Klaus Kinski as Fitzcarraldo supervising the pulling of the boat over the mountain, a feat actually carried out for the making of this film. A documentary *Burden of Dreams* was also made, following the filming of this extraordinary film.
Bottom: Fitzcarraldo plays opera to the jungle.

Country of Origin: West Germany
Production Companies: Werner Herzog Filmproduktion/Pro-ject Filmproduktion/Zweites Deutsche Fernsehen
Running Time: 158 mins

Producer: Werner Herzog
Writer: Werner Herzog
Photography: Thomas Mauch
Editor: Beate Mainka-Jellinghaus
Production Designers: Ulrich Bergfelder, Henning von Gierke
Music: Popol Vuh

Fitzcarraldo: Klaus Kinski
Molly: Claudia Cardinale
Don Aquilino: José Lewgoy
Cholo: Miguel Angel Fuentes
Paul: Paul Hittscher

Right: The attractive poster featuring Klaus Kinski as the predatory and reptilian vampire in the eighteenth-century setting of *Nosferatu the Vampire* (*Nosferatu: Phantom der Nacht*, 1979).

Dir: Werner Herzog

WARDEN: The patient that came in yesterday is having a fit.

VAN HELSING: Which one?

WARDEN: The one that bit the cow.

Warden (Dan van Husen), Dr Van Helsing (Walter Ladengast), *Nosferatu the Vampire* (*Nosferatu: Phantom der Nacht*, Werner Herzog, 1979)

of a Female Slave (*Gelegenheitsarbeit einer Sklavin*, 1973) and *Germany in Autumn* (*Deutschland im Herbst*, 1978), a collective work to which he contributed, have been dedicated to a painstaking political analysis of post-war Germany. Many directors were drawn to making films about the socially ostracized, including immigrant workers, alcoholics, the mentally ill or handicapped. In part this reflected their left-wing sympathies, but it also corresponded to their sense of themselves as outsiders. Werner Herzog's heroes are often over-reachers, larger than life characters whose ambitions usually end in disaster, especially when played by the manic Klaus Kinski, as in *Aguirre: Wrath of God* (*Aguirre: der Zorn Gottes*, 1972), *Nosferatu the Vampire* (*Nosferatu: Phantom der Nacht*, 1979), *Fitzcarraldo* (1982) and *Cobra verde* (1987). *Aguirre*, shot in difficult conditions in the Amazon jungle, follows a monomaniac sixteenth-century Spanish explorer on a nightmare journey. *Nosferatu* is an atmospheric remake of Murnau's classic vampire film. Herzog returned to South America for *Fitzcarraldo*, in which an Irish entrepreneur tries to bring grand opera to the jungle, while in *Cobra verde* Kinski is a Brazilian adventurer in Africa. Herzog's films are stylish and handsomely mounted, if overwrought emotionally.

Though the new film-makers rejected the crass commercialism of earlier German cinema, this did not necessarily involve a turning away from Hollywood, and two of the

most successful directors maintained a dialogue with US culture. While Fassbinder's early films such as *The Bitter Tears of Petra von Kant* (*Die bitteren Tränen der Petra von Kant*, 1972) and *Fear Eats the Soul* (*Angst essen Seele auf*, 1974) are concerned with unconventional sexuality, his later work centres on Germany during the Nazi and post-war years. *The Marriage of Maria Braun* (*Die Ehe von Maria Braun*, 1979) and *Lili Marleen* (1980) both feature Hanna Schygulla, the nearest thing the New German Cinema got to a genuine star. Like *Lola* (1982) and *Veronika Voss* (*Die Sehnsucht der Veronika Voss*, 1982), they are female-centred narratives whose combination of stylized décor, intense emotional moments and social criticism owe much to the Hollywood melodramas of Douglas Sirk, an influence Fassbinder readily acknowledged. There is a slight whiff of trashiness about even Fassbinder's best films, but that is not the worst thing to be accused of if you are working in a popular genre. His early death in 1982 took much of the steam out of the New German Cinema movement.

Wim Wenders has had an even closer, though highly ambiguous, involvement with US culture. *The American Friend* (*Der amerikanische Freund*, 1977) was an adaptation of a crime novel by Patricia Highsmith starring Dennis Hopper. Wenders then went to Hollywood to make *Hammett* (1982) for Francis Ford Coppola. A thriller about an episode in the life of crime writer Dashiell Hammett, the film had a tortuous production history. Despite the director's fascination with the United States, *Hammett* contained, like other Wenders films, long passages of tedium, surely a cardinal sin in his Hollywood models. Far more successful was *Paris, Texas* (1984), like other Wenders films a kind of road movie, in which Harry Dean Stanton searches for his lost wife (Nastassja Kinski, daughter of Klaus) in the deserts of the American West.

Volker Schlöndorff pursued the status of 'author' less single-mindedly, establishing a reputation as a skilled adapter of literary classics, starting with *The Lost Honour of Katharina Blum* (*Die verlorene Ehre der Katharina Blum*, 1975), based on Heinrich Böll's novel and co-directed with his wife, Margarethe von Trotta (whose work, with other German women directors, is discussed in Chapter 9). Schlöndorff followed this with *The Tin Drum* (*Die Blechtrommel*, 1979), from Günther Grass's novel, which presented a child's-eye view of German history and garnered much praise on the international circuit. Schlöndorff's international coproduction *Swann in Love* (1984) was another adaptation, based on Proust.

Opposite: Hanna Schygulla and Margit Carstensen in *The Bitter Tears of Petra von Kant* (*Die bitteren Tränen der Petra von Kant*, 1972), an elegantly designed study of possessiveness among an all-female cast.

Dir: Rainer Werner Fassbinder
Above: Hanna Schygulla as Willie Bunterberg giving a starry performance in *Lili Marleen* (1980). Dir: Rainer Werner Fassbinder

TRAVIS: Yeah, but you can really see them if you want, can't you? I mean, you can go home with them, if you want to, all these places say that. How much extra money do you make? How much, huh? How much money do you make on the side?!

JANE: I'm sorry, sir, but I think maybe you wanted to talk to one of the other girls. I'll see if I can find one for you.

Travis Anderson (Harry Dean Stanton), Jane (Nastassja Kinski), *Paris, Texas* (Wim Wenders, 1984)

Above left: Harry Dean Stanton wanders the West in search of his wife in *Paris, Texas* (1984).
Above: Nastassja Kinski as Jane, the lost wife in *Paris, Texas* (1984), discovered working

in a peep-show. Dir: Wim Wenders
Overleaf: David Bennent as Oskar, the boy with a child's view of German history in *The Tin Drum* (*Die Blechtrommel*, 1979). Dir: Volker Schlöndorff

Above: The poster for *Hitler – A Film from Germany* (*Hitler – Ein Film aus Deutschland*, 1977), a lengthy and demanding portrayal of Adolf Hitler.
Dir: Hans Jürgen Syberberg
Above right: A dramatic moment beneath the waves in the submarine epic *Das Boot* (1981).
Dir: Wolfgang Petersen
Below: Franka Potente as Lola in full flight in *Run Lola Run* (*Lola rennt*, 1998).
Dir: Tom Tykwer

Hans Jürgen Syberberg, originally a maker of documentaries, directed a trilogy of films which dramatized German history through the lives of three key figures. *Ludwig – Requiem for a Virgin King* (*Ludwig – Ein Requiem für einen jungfräulichen König*, 1972) was about the nineteenth-century king of Bavaria; the subject of *Karl May* (1974) was the hugely popular German writer of Westerns; and *Hitler – A Film from Germany* (*Hitler – Ein Film aus Deutschland*, 1977) was a meditation on the significance of the Nazi dictator. Syberberg's films are serious, intellectual, formally innovative in their combination of documentary and dramatic material, and sometimes hard to watch. Their unwillingness to compromise with the audience (*Hitler* is 400 minutes long) is an indication that the New German Cinema contained within it the seeds of its own decline. The importance accorded to the director, whose duty of self-expression is paramount, could only be sustained on the back of government financial support. Though the films were successful at international film festivals, in Germany the audiences mostly stayed away. A change of government in the 1980s undermined the subsidy system. As a result the German cinema of the 1990s is a far more mainstream affair, unashamedly seeking audiences with a string of comedies appealing to the youth market (there are not many laughs in the New German Cinema), poking fun at contemporary lifestyles in a manner akin to television sitcoms. A deregulated, more commercial television has encouraged this tendency, though recent German films have not managed an audience share of more than about twelve per cent of the domestic market. Many of these comedies have not travelled well either, and the international profile of German cinema is now lower than fifteen years ago, though there are occasional box office hits such as Tom Tykwer's *Run Lola Run* (*Lola rennt*, 1998), a fast-paced and visually inventive story of contemporary urban youth.

Instead of maintaining a detached, ambiguous relationship with US culture, contemporary German film-makers are more likely to swallow it whole, if the careers of Wolfgang Petersen and Roland Emmerich are any indication. After directing the wartime submarine drama *Das Boot* (1981), a huge box office hit in Germany and abroad, and the big-budget children's film *The NeverEnding Story* (*Die unendliche Geschichte*, 1984), Petersen moved to Hollywood to direct such mainstream movies as *In the Line of Fire* (1993), a Clint Eastwood vehicle, while Emmerich, after two films in Germany, went on to make the science fiction blockbuster *Independence Day* (1996).

Austria suffers not only from competition with the US colossus but also from sharing a language with a larger near-neighbour. Down the years, Germany sucked in a good deal of Austrian film talent, Fritz Lang included. Despite this, Austria has managed to put out about twenty films a year and has maintained a distinctive voice, not least in its avant-garde film-makers such as Peter Kubelka. Angry polemics against a comfortable bourgeois society reluctant to acknowledge its guilty past mark feature film production as much as the avant-garde. Austria's most important woman director, Valie Export, has made a couple of features, *Invisible Adversaries* (*Unsichtbare Gegner*, 1978) and *The Practice of Love* (*Die Praxis der Liebe*, 1984), which have achieved international exposure for their radical feminist agenda. Niki List's *Helden in Tirol* (1998) is a kind of exposé of the rural charms that the Austrian tourist industry promotes. Designated the 'new Heimatfilm' – a reference to the German genre which celebrated the countryside as homeland – this kind of film has become something of a speciality for Austrian film-makers. Wolfram Paulus's *Heidenlöcker* (1985) is in a similar vein. Even in the thriller genre, such as Peter Patzak's *Killing Blue* (1988), the story of a cynical detective and his female assistant chasing drug pushers through the Berlin underworld, the genre accommodates plenty of comment on society's corruption and racism. Whether this kind of cinema will survive Austria's lurch to the right politically and the consequent cuts in subsidy remains to be seen.

Michael Haneke's films, though less rooted in specifically Austrian situations, also take a cool look at contemporary society and the coldness and detachment he observes in human relations. In *Benny's Video* (1992) a young man obsessed with watching the world through video kills a young woman 'to see what it felt like'. His uncomprehending parents try to help by disposing of the body, but he then confesses to the police. In *Funny Games* (1997) two young psychopaths hold a family hostage and subject them to random acts of violence. Haneke forces his audience to question its response, via nods and winks from the two youths; at one point he shows us the family fighting back, only to rewind the camera, change the action and deny the viewer a cathartic moment. *Code Unknown* (*Code inconnu*, 2000) stars Juliette Binoche as a Parisian actress connected by a chain of coincidences with the city's immigrants. The film observes, in a spare and impeccable style, the difficulties of relationships, both economic and personal, within contemporary urban life. *The Piano*

Above top: An idyllic scene in the Austrian film *Helden in Tirol* (1998).
Dir: Niki List
Above: Isabelle Huppert as the teacher and Benoît Magimel as the pupil with whom she embarks on a obsessive affair in

The Piano Teacher (*Le Pianiste*, 2001).
Dir: Michael Haneke
Right: Juliette Binoche as Anne, who gets involved in an altercation with immigrants in *Code Unknown* (*Code inconnu*, 2000).
Dir: Michael Haneke

Teacher (*La Pianiste*, 2001) is a bleak but compelling story of a repressed music teacher who begins an affair with a younger pupil. Isabelle Huppert gives an excoriating performance as a woman who can only find sexual expression in pain and humiliation, and who fails to draw the conventional young man into her fantasies, with tragic results. With these two international successes (significantly, made in French rather than his native German), Haneke has propelled himself into the first rank of European film-makers.

Few countries are as internationally minded as Holland, and, as with Germany, some of their most talented contemporary film-makers have relocated to Hollywood. The established veterans of Dutch film-making, Bert Haanstra and Fons Rademakers, continued working well into the 1980s, Haanstra drawing on his documentary background, Rademakers making well-crafted literary adaptations such as *Max Havelaar* (1975), set in Indonesia under Dutch rule, and *The Assault* (*De Aanslag*, 1986), in which a man works through the trauma of having seen a wartime Dutch collaborator shot in front of him as a child. The war has been a frequent theme in Dutch cinema. Ben Verbong's first feature, *The Girl with Red Hair* (*Het Meisje met het rode haar*, 1981), celebrated the exploits of a famous Resistance heroine. But younger film-makers have also embraced the thriller, whether from a genuine fascination with popular genres or a need to work with stories that will

Above: Eric Visser (Huub Stapel) on the trail of a serial killer who is taking revenge on an uncaring society, responsible, he believes, for his disfiguring scars, in *Amsterdamned* (1988).

Dir: Dick Maas
Opposite: Martin (Rutger Hauer) and Agnes (Jennifer Jason Leigh) kneel before a gruesome scene in the medieval epic *Flesh and Blood* (1985).
Dir: Paul Verhoeven

Above: Director Paul Verhoeven, with loud-hailer, on the set of *Flesh and Blood* (1985).
Right: Renée Soutendijk

and Jeroen Krabbé in the noirish thriller *The Fourth Man* (*Die vierde man*, 1983).
Dir: Paul Verhoeven

find a more international audience. In Dick Maas's first film, *The Lift* (*De Lift*, 1983) the occupants of a lift are subject to malevolent forces. In Maas's *Amsterdamned* (1988), fast-paced and stylishly shot, a serial killer works underwater in the canals. George Sluizer's *The Vanishing* (*Spoorloos*, 1988) was a powerful, at times harrowing, film about the kidnapping of a young woman. Sluizer was invited to direct the Hollywood remake, which appeared in 1993. The result was disappointing, but Sluizer has continued to work in the English-speaking cinema.

Sluizer's compatriot, Paul Verhoeven, has made a similar but more spectacular transition. Verhoeven's Dutch films span a number of genres. *Business Is Business* (*Wat zien ik?*, 1971) is a sex film which follows a cheerful prostitute and her frequently ridiculous customers. *Turkish Delight* (*Turks fruit*, 1973) also has plenty of sex in a tale of a crazy sculptor and his wife, who eventually dies of a brain tumour. Verhoeven takes gleeful pleasure in rubbing the audience's nose in the dirt (at one point a dog licks up a woman's urine). *Cathy Tippel* (*Keetje Tippel*, 1975) is the story of a young female servant who uses her body to gain upward mobility in nineteenth-century Amsterdam, while *Soldier of Orange* (*Soldaat van Oranje*, 1977) is Verhoeven's contribution to the war film. *Spetters* (1980) gained Verhoeven some notoriety, a commodity he has assiduously sought, in its portrayal of contemporary youth culture. The in-your-face depiction of sexuality and other bodily functions has ensured his work high visibility, though in his Dutch films Verhoeven inclines to a slapdash style. Scenes follow each other at breakneck speed, the narrative structure is disjointed, and characterization is two-dimensional. *The Fourth Man* (*Die vierde man*, 1983) was a more complex work, a kind of film noir. *Flesh and Blood* (1985) was a transitional film, a tale of medieval Europe, shot in Spain, starring Jennifer Jason Leigh and Rutger Hauer (who appeared in many of Verhoeven's early films before going on to international fame). Once again there was plenty of sex and violence, Verhoeven's calling card when he moved to Hollywood, where after a couple of science fiction spectaculars he graduated to *Basic Instinct* (1992).

In contrast to Germany, cinema in Italy was thriving in the 1960s. In the post-war period neo-realism became the national style, exploring social realities with an unadorned visual repertoire, taking its stories and often its actors from the streets. Then came modernism, which directors of genius such as Michelangelo Antonioni, Federico Fellini and Luchino Visconti used to propel Italian cinema to the first rank. At the same time commercial Italian films were holding their own against imported Hollywood productions, achieving fifty per cent of the domestic box office. Italian stars such as Sophia Loren and Marcello Mastroianni were internationally famous.

In the 1970s it all went wrong. Hollywood competition, with its new blockbuster mentality and emphasis on foreign sales, was stronger than ever and Italian cinema attendance dropped as television became more popular. The short-lived boom in the spaghetti Western, which had sustained production in the late 1960s, was coming to an end; Sergio Leone's last was *A Fistful of Dynamite* (*Giù la testa*) in 1971. He would later

change genres for his gangster epic, *Once upon a Time in America* (1984), shot partly in the United States and with US stars. The national identity of Italian cinema became diluted as foreign stars were imported in an attempt to give Italian films appeal in the world market: Marlon Brando in *Last Tango in Paris* (*Ultimo tango a Parigi*, Bernardo Bertolucci, 1972), Dirk Bogarde in *Death in Venice* (*Morte a Venezia*, Luchino Visconti, 1971).

And yet many excellent Italian films were made in the 1970s. Working in English, Michelangelo Antonioni made *Zabriskie Point* (1970), about the student movement, using Death Valley as a location, and *The Passenger* (1975), with Jack Nicholson exploring the murky world of international gun-running. In each film political analysis is combined with Antonioni's coolly beautiful visual style. By contrast, Federico Fellini's style is nothing if not extravagant, at times seeming to take on the features of the excitable Italian of caricature. Like previous films such as *8½* (1963), his works of the 1970s are often autobiographical. *Roma* (1972) gives his impressions of the capital, *Amarcord* (1973) revisits his birthplace of Rimini under Fascism. By the 1980s Fellini was undoubtedly the best-known Italian film-maker in the world, though his idiosyncrasies produced few disciples.

Luchino Visconti, who had long since left his neo-realist roots behind him in favour of an almost operatic grandeur, had an international triumph with *Death in Venice*, based on

Opposite: Dirk Bogarde (l) and Italian director Luchino Visconti, on the set of *Death in Venice* (*Morte a Venezia*, 1971). Above and right: Scenes evoking Rimini during the Fascist era in the comic satire *Amarcord* (1973). Dir: Federico Fellini Overleaf: Protest in 1970s America: the student love-in in the desert in *Zabriskie Point* (1970). Dir: Michelangelo Antonioni

Thomas Mann's novel, a stately study of an elderly composer who falls for a beautiful young boy. Visconti's filming of a wintery Venice lido was too slow for some, but Dirk Bogarde's performance brought universal praise. Visconti's *Ludwig* (1972) came out in the same year as Syberberg's film on the same subject; in each, the mad artist king of Bavaria functions as a kind of metaphor for the director himself. In Visconti's last two films, *Conversation Piece* (*Gruppo di famiglia in un interno*, 1974) and *The Innocent* (*L'innocente*, 1976), a patrician figure (in the first a professor, in the second a nineteenth-century aristocrat) struggles to cope with the forces of social change.

Visconti's 1969 film *The Damned* (*La caduta degli dei*) was a flamboyant portrait of the decadence of Nazi Germany. The attempt to understand history has been a consistent theme in contemporary Italian cinema. Pier Paolo Pasolini began making films in the neo-realist tradition in the 1960s, then discovered semiotics and a deconstructivist cinema before making a trilogy which abandoned such experiments and returned to traditional film-

making in utopian recreations of the medieval era. *Il Decameron* (1971), *The Canterbury Tales* (*I racconti di Canterbury*, 1972) and *The Arabian Nights* (*Il fiore delle mille e una notte*, 1973) celebrate a world of frank and unashamed hedonism. In yet another lurch in a different direction, Pasolini's final feature was a savage and deeply disturbing view of Fascism which equated its political amorality with sexual libertarianism. *Salo, or the 120 Days of Sodom* (*Salò o le 120 giornate di Sodoma*, 1975), like Visconti's *The Damned*, sees sexual decadence as both a symbol and a symptom of an evil political creed.

Bernardo Bertolucci had been Pasolini's assistant on *Accatone* (1961) and his early work was committed to left-wing political positions. His *The Conformist* (*Il conformista*, 1969) is one of the most successful films about Italy's recent past. Jean-Louis Trintignant plays an elegant but hollow young man whose career is set against the grandiloquent and even more hollow backdrop of Fascism. Bertolucci's *1900* (1976) was an ambitious rendering of an entire swathe of Italian history, a family saga starring Gérard Depardieu and Robert De Niro in which Bertolucci's liking for visual display leads him into vulgar excess, though there are some memorable set pieces. *The Tragedy of a Ridiculous Man* (*La tragedia di un uomo ridicolo*, 1981), about a farmer whose son is kidnapped by terrorists, is Bertolucci's contribution to a sub-genre of Italian cinema, the film about the contemporary political situation. But at the end of the 1980s Bertolucci abandoned his engagement with Italian social realities for a series of increasingly showy international co-productions such as *The Last Emperor* (1987), set in early modern China.

The most sustained analysis of the social and political state of the nation has been produced by Francesco Rosi, whose rigorous and clear-sighted films are exemplary. *The Mattei Affair* (*Il caso Mattei*, 1972) and *Lucky Luciano* (1973) follow the model Rosi perfected in *Salvatore Giuliano* (1962), about a Sicilian bandit. It is a cinema of investigation, which in the manner of a forensic inquiry pieces together the evidence connecting an individual crime or criminal to a wider political and social context. *Illustrious Corpses* (*Cadaveri eccellenti*, 1976), about the systematic murder of magistrates investigating the Mafia, has all the suspense qualities of a thriller in addition to intelligence and visual elegance. One would not have supposed that Rosi was well suited to the magical realism of Gabriel García Marquez, but his version of *Chronicle of a Death Foretold* (*Cronaca di una morte annunciata*, 1987) proves that Rosi's lucid style, both in narrative and visuals, does not lead to the evacuation of Marquez's poetry.

Rosi's cinema is concerned with the issues of modern, mainly urban society; by contrast the Taviani brothers, Paolo and Vittorio, set many of their films in the past, and instead of Rosi's elegantly spare style they go for broader effects, though *Padre padrone* (1977), about a young Sardinian peasant who through education frees himself from a tyrannical father, was relatively restrained in its execution. *The Night of San Lorenzo* (*La notte di San Lorenzo*, 1982) has the citizens of a small Tuscan town in wartime trapped between the Americans and the Germans. The story is seen through the eyes of a child and mixes fantasy with realism. *Night Sun* (*Il sole anche di notte*, 1990) is set in the eighteenth century; a young

Above: The Italian version of an English classic: Ninetto Davoli in *The Canterbury Tales* (*I racconti di Canterbury*, 1972). Dir: Pier Paolo Pasolini
Below: Max von Sydow as a judge in *Illustrious Corpses* (*Cadaveri eccellenti*, 1976), a political thriller about the murder of magistrates.
Dir: Francesco Rosi
Below right: Jean-Louis Trintignant as a young man seeking to be normal in the decadent world of Fascism in *The Conformist* (*Il conformista*, 1969).
Dir: Bernardo Bertolucci

NATIONAL IDENTITIES IN WESTERN EUROPE

nobleman, disappointed in love, becomes a hermit priest. Tempted by a beautiful young woman, he cuts off his finger in an act of symbolic castration. The Tavianis' *Good Morning, Babylon* (1987), shot partly in English, follows two Italian brothers to the United States, where they find work in 1915 constructing the sets for DW Griffith's *Intolerance*. The American scenes have charm, but World War I intrudes and after the melodramatic death of one brother's wife, the two of them perish together on the battlefield, not before filming each other's dying words. It is a ludicrously over-the-top finale, the sort of thing that gives Italian cinema a bad name.

This was one of a quartet of Italian-made films about the cinema produced in 1986–8, all tinged with nostalgia. Fellini made *Ginger and Fred* (*Ginger e Fred*, 1986), in which the great Marcello Mastroianni and Giulietta Masina, Fellini's wife and star of his early films, play a couple of ageing dancers who do Astaire and Rogers numbers. Their appearance on a TV show is the occasion for Fellini to satirize the vulgarity of television compared to the greatness of cinema. In Giuseppe Tornatore's *Cinema Paradiso* (1988) a fatherless boy is taken under the wing of a cinema projectionist. Told largely in flashback, the film contains some gentle satire of the Catholic Church's censorship, but small-town cinema-going is cocooned in a warm glow which contrasts with the emptiness of the boy's adult life in the

Right: Set in the late 1940s, *Padre padrone* (1977) follows the story of a young Sardinian boy left to look after the sheep in the mountains. The boy, Gavino Ledda, is played by Saverio Marconi and his father is played by Omero Antonutti.
Dir: Paolo and Vittorio Taviani
Below right: Giulietta Masina and Marcello

Mastroianni impersonate Ginger Rogers and Fred Astaire in *Ginger and Fred* (*Ginger e Fred*, 1986).
Dir: Federico Fellini
Overleaf: Philippe Noiret as the elderly projectionist who inspires Salvatore (Salvatore Cascio) with a love of cinema in *Cinema Paradiso* (1988).
Dir: Giuseppe Tornatore

city. Ettore Scola's *Splendor* (1988) also stars Mastroianni, as the owner of a small-town cinema threatened with redevelopment. Television, held responsible for the cinema's decline, is again a target. Mastroianni's world-weary, melancholy demeanour is used to great effect by Scola in *A Special Day* (*Una giornata particolare*, 1977), where he stars with Sophia Loren in a story set during Hitler's visit to Rome in 1938. Scola had made his name as a writer of *commedia all'italiana*, a typically Italian mix of humour and social criticism, of which *We All Loved Each Other So Much* (*C'eravamo tanto amati*, 1974) is a good example, a good-natured tale of three men who become friends in the war but then have to cope with the problems of peace.

Two Italian women directors achieved international success in the 1970s. Lina Wertmüller made a series of films, many starring Giancarlo Giannini, in which the characters' fevered sexual encounters, often tinged with sado-masochism, are set against some kind of political crisis. In *Swept Away ... by an Unusual Destiny in the Blue Sea of August* (*Travolti da un insolito destino nell'azzurro mare d'Agosto*, 1975) two castaways play out the sex and class war on an island. Wertmüller's taste for the grotesque was indulged to the full in *Seven Beauties* (*Pasqualino settebellezze*, 1975), with Giannini as an Italian seducer who ends up in a Nazi concentration camp; it was a hit with art-house audiences, but her attempts to out-do Fellini (she had been his assistant on *8½*) soon palled with the public. Liliana Cavani's sensational *The Night Porter* (*Il portiere di notte*, 1974) paired Dirk Bogarde and Charlotte Rampling in a story which once again linked Fascism with the dangerous fascination of sado-masochism. But her attempt to repeat the formula in *Berlin Interior* (*Interno berlinese*, 1985), about an affair in Berlin in 1938 between a diplomat's wife and the daughter of the Japanese ambassador, was indifferently received.

Ermanno Olmi, originally a documentary-maker, produced his masterpiece in 1978. *The Tree of Wooden Clogs* (*L'albero degli zoccoli*) shows the unmistakable trace of neo-realism in its understated style and use of nonprofessionals to re-create the lives of the peasantry of a hundred years ago. But by the 1990s Italy required something different, and found it in a new breed of comedians. Roberto Benigni began in theatre and television before transposing his gadfly personality to the cinema in such films as *Johnny Stecchino* (1991), a Mafia comedy, and *Life Is Beautiful* (*La vita è bella*, 1997); the latter, a satire set in a concentration camp, though a hit internationally, was thought by some critics to be in bad taste. Nanni Moretti has evolved a distinctive genre of his own, a kind of freewheeling documentary which combines a running commentary on Italian social and political life with more personal material. *Dear Diary* (*Caro diario*, 1994) includes gags, social observation and a contemplation of the death of Pasolini, as Moretti buzzes around Italy on his scooter. *Aprile* (1998) is more political, commenting on Berlusconi's electoral success, but also documenting the birth of Moretti's son. At one point he gives the infant exercises so that he does not grow up with the feeble arms of Italian tennis players, always full of excuses when they lose, says Moretti. *The Son's Room* (*La stanza del figlio*, 2001) is more conventional in form, the story of a psychoanalyst (played by Moretti) whose son is killed in an accident. Moretti's precise and lucid *mise-en-scène* serves as counterpoint to the almost unbearable grief of the family. He is a director who may be poised on the brink of great things, but Italian cinema generally, which produced 103 films in 2001 but captured only nineteen per cent of the domestic market, is likely to find itself starved of funds by the right-wing Berlusconi government.

Above: Ana Torrent as the lonely child who befriends a soldier in *The Spirit of the Beehive* (*El espíritu de la colmena*, 1973). Dir: Victor Erice

Spanish cinema since 1970 separates into two distinct periods: before Franco and after. In the early 1970s films could only criticize Spanish society in an oblique and coded manner. In Victor Erice's *The Spirit of the Beehive* (*El espíritu de la colmena*, 1973), set in the Civil War period, a child, remote from her parents but liberated by her imagination, takes pity on a runaway soldier (whose political allegiance is not disclosed). In José Luis Borau's *Poachers* (*Furtivos*, 1975) a provincial governor encounters his former nurse who, her mind unhinged by a lifetime of sexual and social repression, goes mad and murders her son's wife. Carlos Saura's *Cría cuervos* (1975) is another coded study of a repressed family. In these films the enclosed world of an authoritarian society threatens to come apart at the seams, but social criticism had to be guarded. Spain's greatest director, Luis Buñuel, had been allowed back into Spain to film *Viridiana* in 1961, but its religious satire caused it to be banned. Though Buñuel set *Tristana* (1970), a typically wry study of sexual repression, in Toledo in the 1930s, he concluded his career in France. His last great film, *The Discreet Charm of the Bourgeoisie* (*Le Charme discret de la bourgeoisie*, 1972), starred Buñuel stalwart Fernando Rey; otherwise the cast was French, though the film had all the merciless sardonic humour at the expense of middle-class respectability and piety which distinguished Buñuel's best work. As the director was fond of remarking, 'Thank God I am still an atheist.'

The death of the Fascist dictator in 1975 and the resultant abolition of censorship in 1977 released the floodgates. Spanish film-makers were now free to work over the past at will, and to explore the new society which emerged. Thus Saura's *Ay, Carmela!* (1990) deals far more explicitly with the Civil War, in a story about music-hall performers trapped behind Fascist lines and forced to put on a show for the troops. The heroine, unable at the last to hide her loyalties to the Republican cause, is shot. *Cows* (*Vacas*, 1992), directed by the Basque, Julio Medem, cuts a wide swathe through Spanish history, from the Carlist War in 1875 to the Civil War of the 1930s. Its tale of two feuding peasant families echoes in their tragedy the political and social divisions of Spain itself. Fernando Trueba's *Belle*

NATIONAL IDENTITIES IN WESTERN EUROPE

époque (1992) is a more light-hearted affair. Just before the outbreak of the Civil War a young soldier is taken in by an elderly artist, whose four daughters each seduce him in turn. Besides the comic twists in the romantic plot, there is some good-natured satire at the expense of the priesthood and other forces of conservatism. José Luis Cuerda's *Butterfly's Tongue* (*La lengua de las mariposas*, 1999) shows that this theme is far from exhausted. A shy little boy is taken under the wing of a kindly old teacher, who is then denounced by his parents as a Communist when the Civil War breaks out.

The young soldier in *Belle époque* is taken aback by the forwardness of the four daughters, and sexually assertive women are a feature of contemporary Spanish cinema. In Vicente Aranda's *Lovers* (*Amantes*, 1990) Victoria Abril plays the mature lover of a young soldier; consumed by jealousy of his virginal fiancée, she provokes him to murder her. The sexual encounters in the film are frank even by Spanish standards; to control her lover's orgasm Abril pushes a handkerchief into his anus. Sexual desire is also the motor that drives the plots of *Jamón, jamón* (1992) and *Golden Balls* (*Huevos de oro*, 1993), two rumbustious exposés of contemporary Spanish life by the Catalan director Juan José Bigas Luna. In the first, a bourgeois young man is prevented from marrying the attractive daughter (Penélope Cruz) of the local whore by his bossy mother, who enlists a ham salesman (Javier Bardem) to seduce the girl, only to fall for the salesman herself. Predictably it all ends in tears, somewhat farcically, with her son killed by a blow from a ham-bone and the now-pregnant girl in the arms of the bossy woman's husband. Similar farcical goings-on occur in *Golden Balls*, in which Bardem plays a building worker who claws his way up to become a property developer by getting his girlfriend to sleep with clients, then dumps her and marries a banker's daughter. Made in a slapdash, anarchic style, with plentiful references to surrealism (Bardem draws on his girlfriends' bodies replicas of Dalí's paintings of women as chests of drawers), the film produces a telling commentary on a get-rich-quick society. Bigas Luna's *The Tit and the Moon* (*La teta y la luna*, 1994) is a less frenetic affair, about a young boy

Above: Trapped behind enemy lines: Carmen Maura and Andrés Pajares (centre) as the entertainers Carmela and Paulino caught up in the Civil War in *Ay, Carmela!* (1990). Dir: Carlos Saura

Right: Javier Bardem as the unscrupulous builder turned property speculator Benito Gonzalez in *Golden Balls* (*Huevos de oro*, 1993). Dir: Juan José Bigas Luna

pushed out of his mother's affections by the arrival of a baby brother, and who fantasizes about the breasts of a young Frenchwoman. It is an engaging mix of psychoanalytic insights, popular culture (the Frenchwoman works in a cabaret) and the clash of nationalisms; at one point the Catalan audience at the cabaret waves little European flags in time to the prodigious farts of a professional petomane (the Frenchwoman's husband).

Freedom, however, did not in itself arrest the long-term decline of Spanish cinema. Movie attendance went down from 331 million in 1970 to 101 million in 1985; worse still, Spanish films took an ever-decreasing share of the box office, declining from thirty per cent in 1970 to only seven per cent in 1994. Since the 1980s government subsidies had been directed towards the creation of a prestige, art-house cinema, which gained considerable recognition abroad but often failed to find audiences at home. In the mid-1990s the system was changed, and subsidy redirected towards films that were successful at the box office. By 2001, with around 100 films produced, including coproductions, Spanish films had climbed back to eighteen per cent at the domestic box office.

Spanish cinema has plenty of genre pictures, such as Juanma Bajo Ulloa's thriller *The Dead Mother* (*La madre muerta*, 1994), about a hardened criminal kidnapping a young woman who years before had been witness to a robbery he committed. Comedies are popular, especially those that poke fun at the lifestyles of young urban sophisticates. But Spanish cinema continues to be one in which the distinctive mark of the artist is valorized. Victor Erice, the auteur par excellence, made only two features in the twenty years after *The Spirit of the Beehive*. Both *The South* (*El sur*, 1982) and *The Quince Tree Sun* (*El sol del membrillo*, 1992) have the same minimal narrative subordinated to Erice's calm, pensive visual style. Julio Medem has followed *Cows* with films that reflect upon Spanish society in an elliptical style. In *The Red Squirrel* (*La ardilla roja*, 1993) a female motorcyclist loses her memory after a crash. Or does she? The film plays teasingly with issues of identity and truth, while packing a powerful sexual charge. In *Earth* (*Tierra*, 1995) there is a clash of old and new as a pest controller arrives in a remote community and gets involved with two women, one a leather-clad motorcycle rider (something of a Medem motif), the other the wife of a macho boar-hunter. The hero has a dual personality: at times the two sides of his nature debate with each other on the screen. In *Lovers of the Arctic Circle* (*Los amantes del Círculo Polar*, 1998) two children, Ana and Otto, meet by chance. Their paths cross in a series of coincidences: they become lovers, are separated, and meet again inside Finland's Arctic Circle only for chance to snatch away the anticipated happy ending. Medem playfully teases the audience with narrative twists in a film whose primary interest is the relation between passion and the arbitrary nature of fate. Yet even in such a film, resolutely

Above: Fele Martínez as Otto and Najwa Nimri as Ana in *Lovers of the Arctic Circle* (*Los amantes del Círculo Polar*, 1998). Although having loved each other since childhood, fate intervenes and they spend long periods apart. With a complex narrative structure the audience is teased and ultimately denied a happy ending.
Right: Najwa Nimri in *Lovers of the Arctic Circle* (*Los amantes del Círculo Polar*, 1998). Dir: Julio Medem

NATIONAL IDENTITIES IN WESTERN EUROPE

Above: Julieta Serrano as Lucia points the gun at Carmen Maura, who as Pepa has been dumped by her married lover in *Women on the Verge of a Nervous Breakdown* (*Mujeres al borde de un ataque de nervios*, 1988).
Dir: Pedro Almodóvar
Below: Victoria Abril as Marina, the porn star kidnapped by mental patient Ricky (Antonio Banderas) in *Tie Me Up, Tie Me Down!* (*Átame!*, 1990).
Overleaf: Marina falls in love with her captor Ricky adding to the controversy of *Tie Me Up, Tie Me Down!* (*Átame!*, 1990).
Dir: Pedro Almodóvar

contemporary, the Spanish past continues to reverberate, since the bond that unites the lovers' two families goes back to an encounter in the Civil War, between a German pilot involved in the bombing of Guernica and a Spanish peasant woman he meets when he is shot down. Medem's *Sex and Lucia* (*Lucía y el sexo*, 2001), about an affair between a writer and a waitress, is another fractured narrative punctuated with flashbacks, fantasies and dreams, centred on obsessional love.

Though Spain has few women directors, Pilar Miró has been an influential figure. Her early films ran foul of Franco's censors, with the melodrama *The Engagement Party* (*La petición*, 1976) banned; *The Cuenca Crime* (*El crimen de Cuenca*, 1979), about abuses by the Civil Guard, proved provocative even though censorship had in theory been abolished. In 1982 Miró became Minister for Film in the socialist government, helping to inject subsidies into the ailing industry before resigning three years later to return to film-making.

No one has profited more from the post-Franco freedoms and from Spain's structural bias towards an auteur cinema than Pedro Almodóvar. *Women on the Verge of a Nervous Breakdown* (*Mujeres al borde de un ataque de nervios*, 1988) was a dazzling mix of comedy and melodrama exploring a range of sexual identities, packaged in a garish, eclectic visual style and told with great narrative élan. The film was a huge hit internationally. Almodóvar's next film, *Tie Me Up, Tie Me Down!* (*Átame!*, 1990) concerned a porn actress (Victoria Abril) who is kidnapped by a recently-released mental patient (Antonio Banderas). As often in Almodóvar, the film skates on thin ice in its depiction of a sado-masochistic relationship, leavened with characteristic black humour. *Live Flesh* (*Carne trémula*, 1997) was a more sombre affair, a story about a wrongfully accused man seeking revenge, based on a Ruth Rendell novel. Almodóvar returned to a mix of emotional drama, comedy and sexual outrageousness with *All About My Mother* (*Todo sobre mi madre*, 1999), in which a woman grieving for her dead son becomes involved with a motley group of fringe characters including a nun, an ageing actress, her lesbian lover and a transsexual. *Talk to Her* (*Hable*

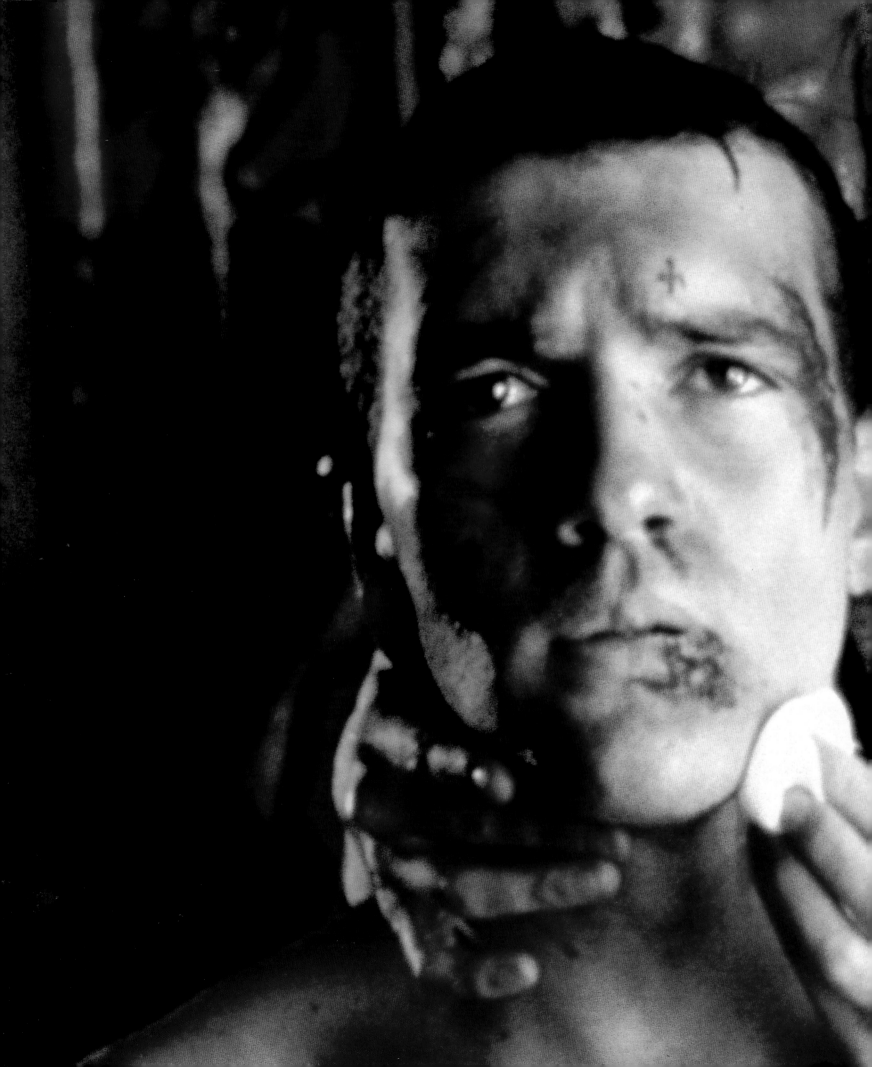

An Art Cinema Classic

Talk to Her
(Hable con ella, 2002)
Dir: Pedro Almodóvar

Spanish director Pedro Almodóvar was propelled to the top rank of art cinema directors with his critically acclaimed film *All About My Mother* (1999). But unlike other directors of equivalent status who have been beguiled by Hollywood, or chosen to work within the rootless world of the international coproduction, Almodóvar has remained planted in the rich culture of his native Spain.

In *Talk to Her* (*Hable con ella*) the two main protagonists are men, unusually for Almodóvar, whose films have been notable for a succession of strong and striking female roles. Benigno is a male nurse who is employed to care for Alicia, in a coma after a car accident. At the clinic he meets Marco, a journalist who is in love with Lydia, a female bullfighter also in a coma after being attacked by a bull. They become friends and Benigno persuades Marco that he must talk to Lydia, even if she cannot hear (hence the title). But then we learn that the gentle and sympathetic Benigno has raped Alicia. Sent to prison, he kills himself, but Alicia is pregnant and in the trauma of giving birth she recovers consciousness. Thus from a bad deed comes a happy outcome, a moral conundrum typical of this most surprising director.

European art cinema has a great tradition but an uncertain future in a world increasingly dominated by Hollywood. Almodóvar is an ornament of European culture who proves that the form still has much to say about the human condition and can say it with grace and beauty.

Country of Origin: Spain
Production Company: El Deseo SA
Running Time: 112 mins

Producer: Agustín Almodóvar
Writer: Pedro Almodóvar
Photography: Javier Aguirresarobe
Editor: José Salcedo
Music: Alberto Iglesias
Art Director: Antxón Gómez

Benigno: Javier Cámara
Marco Zuloaga: Darío Grandinetti
Alicia: Leonor Watling
Lydia: Rosario Flores

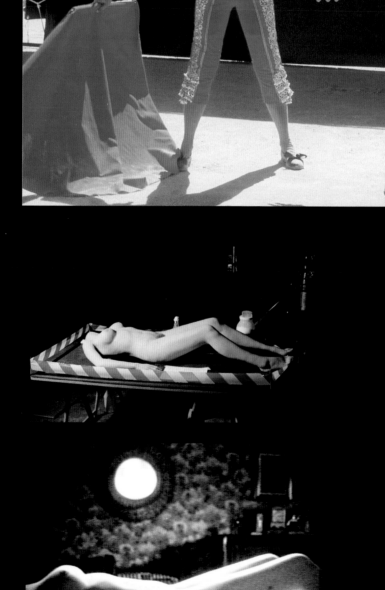

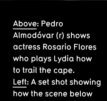

Above: Pedro Almodóvar (r) shows actress Rosario Flores who plays Lydia how to trail the cape.
Left: A set shot showing how the scene below was staged.
Below left: A shot from the silent film-within-the-film which Benigno (Javier Cámara) recounts to entertain Alicia (Leonor Watling).

Un Film de Almodóvar

El Deseo S.A. presenta con la colaboración de A3 Tv y Vía Digital

hable con ella

Javier Cámara
Leonor Watling
Darío Grandinetti
Rosario Flores
Con la participación de
Geraldine Chaplin

Maquillaje: Karmele Soler Peluquería: Francisco Rodríguez Sonido: Miguel Rejas Vestuario: Sonia Grande Montaje: José Salcedo Música: Alberto Iglesias Director de Arte: Antxón Gómez Director de Fotografía: Javier Aguirresarobe A.E.C. Directora de Producción: Esther García Productor Ejecutivo: Agustín Almodóvar

Guión y Dirección: Pedro Almodóvar

Left: Benigno and Marco (Darío Grandinetti) with the comatose Alicia and Lydia (Rosario Flores). **Above:** The film poster showing Leonor Watling and Rosario Flores. **Below:** Hoping to gain a reaction, Benigno shows Alicia a signed picture of dancer Pina Bausch.

con ella, 2002) is a triumph, a constantly surprising and moving film in which the two chief female characters are both in a coma.

In the new century Spanish cinema is becoming more internationally minded, a tendency illustrated in the career of Chilean-born Alejandro Amenábar. His first film, *Thesis* (*Tesis*, 1996), was a Spanish thriller in which a young media student stumbles upon evidence that someone in her college is making snuff movies. In *Open Your Eyes* (*Abre los ojos*, 1997) a young philanderer finds his life changed when his face is disfigured in a car crash. The film starred Penélope Cruz, who, now a Hollywood star, appeared in the remake, *Vanilla Sky* (2001), directed by Cameron Crowe and starring Tom Cruise. Amenábar moved to Hollywood for his next feature, *The Others* (2001), a stylishly mounted and atmospheric ghost story set in Jersey at the end of the war, starring Cruise's former wife, Nicole Kidman.

How can a small country such as Portugal, producing less than a dozen films a year, punch above its weight on the international film scene? Cinema was given a fillip by the revolution of April 1974, which swept away the remnants of the Salazar regime and brought democracy. A national institute for cinema made production subsidies available, essential since the domestic box office could not generate enough finance for even modest films. A Portuguese art cinema was the result. Directors such as João César Monteiro and João Botelho found success on the festival circuit. Monteiro's *Recollections of the Yellow House* (*Recordações da Casa Amarela*, 1989) is a slow, austerely stylish film about a tenant of a seedy Lisbon boarding house. Botelho's *Hard Times* (*Tempos Difíceis*, 1988) is an updating of Dickens's novel to contemporary Lisbon, the melodrama counterpointed by the elegant black and white photography. In his *A Portuguese Goodbye* (*Um Adeus Português*, 1985), a couple whose son has been killed in Portuguese West Africa visit their remaining children in an attempt to find peace in their grief.

Success abroad was not always repeated at home, and some films failed to win a release in the domestic market. Fortunately, Portugal boasts one of the great names of European

Above: Penélope Cruz in the teasing thriller *Open Your Eyes* (*Abre los ojos*, 1997). Cruz also appeared in the Hollywood remake *Vanilla Sky* (2001), directed by Cameron Crowe and starring Tom Cruise.
Dir: Alejandro Amenábar
Below: Nicole Kidman as Grace, the mother of two children in the creepily atmospheric *The Others* (2001). Dir: Alejandro Amenábar

NATIONAL IDENTITIES IN WESTERN EUROPE

cinema. Manoel de Oliveira's first feature, *Aniki-Bóbó*, was made in 1942 and is a recognized classic, but thereafter he made few films until the 1980s. Since then Oliveira has been astonishingly productive for a man born in 1908. Representative is *Abraham Valley* (*Vale Abraão*, 1993), a three-hour-long version of the story of Flaubert's Emma Bovary set in the valley of the Douro in a present day which seems timeless. It is a stately, densely textured film, given added resonance by a voice-over that provides a subtle and ironic commentary. Oliveira's *The Convent* (*O Convento*, 1995) is less successful; despite the presence of international stars such as Catherine Deneuve and John Malkovich, the story of a search for evidence that Shakespeare was a Spanish Jew does not avoid the pretentiousness into which Oliveira's fondness for philosophical digressions can lead him. A more recent film, *I'm Going Home* (*Je rentre à la maison*, 2001), made in France when Oliveira was over ninety, is far more rewarding, a tale about an ageing actor (wonderfully played by Michel Piccoli). There is some deftly-handled comic business about buying shoes and getting the right table at a café, and a sense of serenity achieved despite the recent death of the actor's family in a car crash. *The Uncertainty Principle* (*O Princípio da Incerteza*, 2002) is another teasingly complex melodrama about class and wealth, immaculately filmed. Sooner or later this remarkable man will have made his last film;

Above right: Leonor Silveira as the heroine trapped in a bourgeois marriage in *Abraham Valley* (*Vale Abraão*, 1993).
Dir: Manoel de Oliveira

Right: Michel Piccoli as the elderly actor who gets his favourite café table in *I'm Going Home* (*Je rentre à la maison*, 2001).
Dir: Manoel de Oliveira

Portuguese cinema will find him hard to replace.

Like Spain and Portugal, post-war Greek cinema was deformed by political repression, first in the Civil War immediately after World War II, and later under the rule of the 'Colonels', the military junta that seized power in 1967. When the military was overthrown in 1974 cinema underwent a renaissance and a New Greek Cinema emerged. Melina Mercouri, world-famous star of *Never on Sunday* (1959), became socialist Minister of Culture and introduced state subsidies. For a time there was a steady output of films dealing with Greece's social and political problems, including a reassessment of the past, in a style derived from the model of European art cinema. Nikos Koundouros's *1922* (*To Noumero*, 1978) is about a group of Greek prisoners on a forced march to a prison camp in Turkey. The same director's *Bordello* (1985) deals with a dozen women stranded on Crete in 1897 during its revolt against the Turks. In Pantelis Voulgaris's *Stone Years* (*Petrina Chronia*, 1985) two young Communists maintain their love affair despite imprisonment during the Civil War.

As in other European countries, the spread of television undermined the market for popular cinema in Greece, especially comedy, while subsidized cinema, though it increased prestige abroad, struggled to find an audience at home. Fortunately, like Portugal, Greece has been blessed with one of the undoubted masters of modern world cinema, Theo Angelopoulos. His first feature, *Reconstruction* (*Anaparastassi*, 1970), a murder mystery, was made under the Colonels, as was his next, *Days of 36* (*Meres Tou 36*, 1972), part of a loosely associated historical trilogy which included *The Travelling Players* (*O Thiassos*, 1975) and *The Hunters* (*Oi Kynighoi*, 1977), all dealing with events during the troubled years preceding and following World War II. Angelopoulos has a highly personal style, characterized by measured, stately tracking shots, a cinema not slow but certainly unhurried. His films of the later 1980s are concerned with exile. In *Landscape in the Mist* (*Topio stin omichli*, 1988) two children try to get to Germany, where they believe their father lives. They have strange, surreal encounters: a bride rushes from a wedding party into the snow, a dying horse is towed by a tractor, a giant stone hand is winched from the sea by a helicopter. Yet this is no mythical Greece, but a succession of railway waiting-rooms, cheap cafés and rainswept roads. The camera stares helplessly at the back of a truck while inside the girl is raped.

In the 1990s Angelopoulos directed himself to the fundamental European problem of borders, of asylum and refugees. In *Ulysses' Gaze* (*To Vlemma tou Odyssea*, 1995) Harvey Keitel plays a Greek-American director who returns to his homeland in search of a film made by two pioneer Balkan film-makers in the early years of the century. His search takes him on a journey through the Balkans, taking in Skopje, Bucharest and Belgrade, at one point getting a lift on a barge transporting a huge statue of Lenin that has been sold to

Above: Actress Agapi Manoura with a group of stranded women in the period drama *Bordello* (1985).
Dir: Nikos Koundouros
Below left and right: Scenes from *Ulysses' Gaze* (*To Vlemma tou Odyssea*, 1995), with Maia Morgenstern and Harvey Keitel as the Greek film-maker who embarks on a journey of discovery.
Dir: Theo Angelopoulos
Opposite: The stone hand being transported by helicopter in *Landscape in the Mist* (*Topio stin omichli*, 1988).
Dir: Theo Angelopoulos

NATIONAL IDENTITIES IN WESTERN EUROPE

a collector. Ultimately he reaches Sarajevo, where his search is rewarded but at the cost of tragedy. *Eternity and a Day* (*Mia aiwniothta kai mia mera*, 1998) is a kind of archetypal European art film, about an elderly intellectual (Bruno Ganz) facing a terminal illness who reassesses his life, in particular the sacrifice of his family to his career. Inadvertently he becomes responsible for a small Albanian boy, an economic refugee exploited by his countrymen. It is the fate of great directors in small countries to bear almost single-handedly the burden of their national cinema, but Angelopoulos has the genius to sustain it. Fortunately, there are signs of life elsewhere. The 2001 Thessaloniki film festival showed no fewer than thirty-six new Greek films, most of them financed by the government's Greek Film Centre.

At least Greece has the advantage that no one else is making films in its own language. Britain shares the difficulties of all European cinemas, with the added one of a common language with the United States, which means that Hollywood films are absorbed direct into the bloodstream of the British audience. In 2001 American films, including American–British coproductions, secured nearly ninety per cent of the British box office. Measures of protection and support have been attempted down the years, but not consistently and not sufficiently. The Thatcher government of the 1980s swept away many of the tax incentives that had been in existence, and also the box office levy which provided an important source of finance. In the later 1990s the Labour government made new money available from the National Lottery, and attempted to restructure the industry to create larger production units. Production is running at about 100 films a year, but the results in terms of the quality of films have not justified this initiative.

For a time in the 1970s it looked as though Nicolas Roeg would be Britain's answer to the great modernist directors of France and Italy. *Performance* (1970), co-directed with Donald Cammell, was a visually striking gangster film with a fractured narrative and a mix of drugs, sex and rock 'n' roll, starring Mick Jagger. In *Don't Look Now* (1973) Roeg exposed the raw emotions of a marriage within the framework of a thriller set in Venice. Previously a cameraman, Roeg gave all his films a dazzling surface. *Bad Timing* (1980) upset its financiers, the Rank Organization, with its explicit sex, especially in a scene where Art Garfunkel rapes a comatose Theresa Russell (later Roeg's wife), but the film crackles with ideas and emotion. Yet these have ebbed away in Roeg's later films, leaving only the brilliant surface.

The British have always been suspicious of visual style, but in the 1970s two other directors of talent made films with bravura. Ken Russell's *The Music Lovers* (1971) and *The Devils* (1971) – the first a biography of Tchaikovsky, the second a tale of demonic possession – spurned the diffident good taste of earlier British films, with brash camerawork and in-your-face sexuality. But in later years Russell, once the *enfant terrible* of British cinema, has become more *enfant* than *terrible* in his desire to shock with his (rather innocent) sexual fantasies. John Boorman went early to Hollywood, and had a huge hit with the action film *Deliverance* (1972). The later 1970s were a disappointment, but with *Excalibur* (1981), an Arthurian romance, and *The Emerald Forest* (1985), set in the Amazon, Boorman showed

Previous pages: Ben
Cross as Harold
Abrahams, a Jewish
student, and Ian
Charleson as Eric

Liddell, a Scottish
missionary, both
Olympic runners in
Chariots of Fire (1981).
Dir: Hugh Hudson

himself as a director with a wonderful eye. *Hope and Glory* (1987) was a return to his roots, a charming if soft-edged memory of his wartime childhood, after which there was another fallow period before *The General* (1998), a deftly-told story about a Dublin criminal who falls foul of the IRA.

Those responsible for supporting British cinema have never made up their minds whether, given the shared language, it was better to challenge Hollywood with films of popular appeal, or construct a minority but viable art cinema. From time to time the mirage of international success has seduced film-makers and administrators alike into a belief that a breakthrough was imminent. One such moment came with the success of *Chariots of Fire* (Hugh Hudson) in 1981, about a British triumph at the 1924 Olympics. A film of no cinematic distinction, it nevertheless pleased audiences, aided by Vangelis's syrupy score, and led to a number of other productions in the genre of 'heritage' cinema, a celebration of the national past characterized by period locations, authentically detailed costumes, quality acting (in Britain, this means the use of theatrically trained players) and a sumptuous if not taxing visual style. Richard Attenborough's *Gandhi* (1982) displayed all this with the addition of some liberal sentiments in its biography of the Indian leader, and was rewarded with great international success. James Ivory and Ismail Merchant, as director and producer respectively, made a series of 'heritage' films, including *Heat and Dust* (1983), *A Room with a View* (1986), *Maurice* (1987) and *Howards End* (1992), the last three from novels by E M Forster, whose literary credentials ensured an extra dimension of cultural respectability. Ironically, the makers of these quintessentially English films are foreign: Ivory is an American and Merchant an Indian.

Above left and right:
Geraldine Muir and
Sebastian Rice-
Edwards as wartime
evacuees, and cheering
the returning pilots in
Hope and Glory (1987).
Dir: John Boorman
Right: Julian Sands
and Helena Bonham-
Carter as lovers in the

'heritage' drama
A Room with a View
(1986).
Dir: James Ivory
Opposite: Ben
Kingsley as the
spiritual leader of
Indian Independence
in *Gandhi* (1982).
Dir: Richard
Attenborough

Art cinema, though precarious, has its achievements. Many of them were in part due to the support of the British Film Institute (BFI), whose Production Fund pursued a coherent policy during the 1970s and 1980s of coaxing promising talent through to the point where feature production became feasible. Working often with Film on Four, the feature production arm of Channel Four Television, the BFI began backing innovative low-budget features, an early example of which was Peter Greenaway's *The Draughtsman's Contract* (1982), an elegantly shot and intricately constructed tale of sexual intrigue in a seventeenth-century country house. Superficially the film has something in common with heritage cinema, but its experiments with narrative and point of view place it apart. Greenaway's films often feature sexual stratagems; *The Cook, the Thief, His Wife & Her Lover* (1989) adds a darker note in a lurid tale of a brutal London underworld boss whose wife extracts a terrible revenge for her humiliation.

In the 1970s the BFI supported Bill Douglas, whose trilogy of films – *My Childhood* (1972), *My Ain Folk* (1974) and *My Way Home* (1979) – offers an intensely personal account of a deprived childhood, achieved with minimal resources. Later, the BFI and Channel Four helped finance films by Derek Jarman, Britain's foremost gay director, and by Terence Davies, who like Douglas has explored his working-class upbringing in *Distant Voices, Still Lives* (1988) and *The Long Day Closes* (1992), though in a far more deliberate style, using elaborate tracking shots and layered soundtracks. Most recently Davies has directed *The House of Mirth* (2000), superficially another slice of heritage (from a novel by Edith Wharton) but with an acerbic sense of class conflict which counter-matches its elegant visuals.

Class is central to the work of two of Britain's most distinctive film-makers. Both Ken Loach and Mike Leigh worked in television before making their first features. In Loach's *Kes* (1969) a novice child actor (David Bradley) plays a young boy who finds consolation for the tedium of school and family life in the care of a kestrel. Loach has continued to use nonprofessional actors in the belief that they will provide unmediated access to social reality. His films achieve undeniable power in expressing the struggles of the dispossessed against the economic and institutional forces of capitalism, but they suffer from an aesthetic poverty, a visual flatness which some have ascribed to the influence of television but which seems equally to derive from Loach's suspicion of anything so bourgeois as stylistic panache. Films such as *Riff-Raff* (1990), *Raining Stones* (1993) and *My Name Is Joe* (1998) have also been criticized for being restricted to the world of the white, male working class, unwilling to face the new politics of ethnicity and gender. Recently, though, Loach has looked further afield. *Land and Freedom* (1995) is set during the Spanish Civil War, *Carla's Song* (1996) in Nicaragua and *Bread and Roses* (2000) in Los Angeles.

By contrast, Mike Leigh places huge demands on the professional skill of his actors, devising his films in extensive sessions with his cast, during which director and actors develop both character and plot. This has sometimes been misrepresented as improvisation, but in fact once the production moves to the floor of the studio the script is relatively fixed. Leigh's first feature, *Bleak Moments* (1971), set the tone for much of what was to follow in its study of suburban hopelessness. Leigh's world is mainly that of the lower middle classes, about whose pretensions he is devastatingly funny. For the next seventeen years he worked exclusively in television, until *High Hopes* (1988), in which an ill-matched inner London couple manage to achieve a modus vivendi. *Naked* (1993) achieves a raw edge in its portrayal of sexuality; some critics tried to lay the misogyny exposed at the director's door. It had superlative performances from David Thewlis and the late Katrin Cartlidge. The more squeamish have accused Leigh's satire of patronizing his characters, but *Secrets & Lies* (1995), perhaps his best film so far, offers one of the best parts ever to a black English actress, Marianne Jean-Baptiste, as an adopted optometrist who tracks down her natural mother and discovers she is white. As with many of Leigh's later films, it also features a wonderful performance by the rotund Timothy Spall. *Topsy-Turvy* (1999) is Leigh's first non-contemporary story, about the Victorian light-opera team of Gilbert and Sullivan. Visually richer than his previous work, it suggested Leigh might be ready to move away from his television roots, though *All or Nothing* (2002), with Timothy Spall as a lugubrious south London taxi driver, is a return to earlier milieux.

Neither Loach nor Leigh has been tempted by Hollywood, whose economic power and prestige have drained away many other British talents. Among them is Terry Gilliam, an inventive and quirky mind whose *Brazil* (1984) was a blackly comic, often surreal vision of a future distopia, but whose later Hollywood work such as *Fear and Loathing in Las Vegas* (1998) has disappointed. Alan Parker is a confectioner of commercial entertainments whose early British successes such as *Bugsy Malone* (1976) and *Midnight Express* (1978) propelled

CYNTHIA: This is stupid. I don't understand. I mean, I can't be your mother, can I?
HORTENSE: Why not?
CYNTHIA: Well, look at me.
HORTENSE: What?
CYNTHIA: Listen, I don't mean nothing by it, darling, but I ain't never been with a black man in my life. No disrespect nor nothing. I'd have remembered, wouldn't I?

Cynthia (Brenda Blethyn), Hortense (Marianne Jean-Baptiste), *Secrets & Lies* (Mike Leigh, 1995)

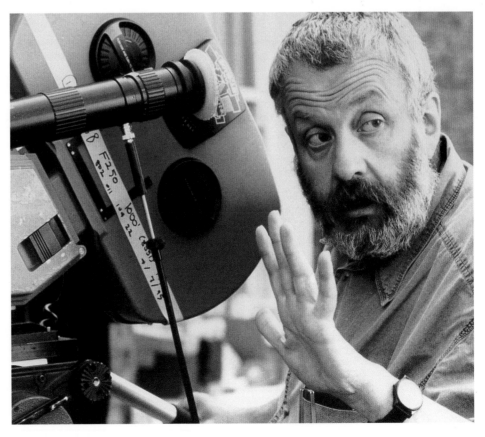

him to Hollywood, though it may be that his best film is *The Commitments* (1991), a story about an Irish rock band which has a real feel for working-class Dublin life. Ridley Scott, a visually assured director with an eye for hit material, is another who, like Parker, came from the world of advertising. After his British debut with *The Duellists* (1977), an elegantly-mounted tale of Napoleonic times, he has worked exclusively in Hollywood.

In the middle of the 1980s British cinema found another distinctive voice, one that could talk about British experience in a way that had international resonance. *My Beautiful Laundrette* (1985), in which a National Front sympathizer and a young Asian have an unlikely gay affair, was a big hit, but shortly afterwards its director Stephen Frears was also called to Hollywood. He has made regular forays back, however, directing *Liam* (2000), set in Liverpool in the 1930s, for the BBC.

In the 1990s there were some international successes, most of them comedies. *Four Weddings and a Funeral* (Mike Newell, 1994) (as discussed in Chapter 5), found a formula in the romantic comings and goings of the young middle class, later repeated in *Notting Hill* (Roger Michell, 1999), an even bigger box office hit, currently rated as number fifty-nine in the all-time worldwide hit list with total takings of $363 million.[3] Unfortunately, as with *The Full Monty* (Peter Cattaneo, 1997), in which a group of unemployed men take up

Above: Andrew Strong as Deco, lead singer of an Irish rock band in *The Commitments* (1991). Dir: Alan Parker
Right: Hugh Grant as bookshop owner William Thacker and Julia Roberts as actress Anna Scott in the smash-hit comedy *Notting Hill* (1999). Dir: Roger Michell
Below right: An unlikely hit: *The Full Monty* (1997) was a comedy about unemployed steel workers. Dir: Peter Cattaneo

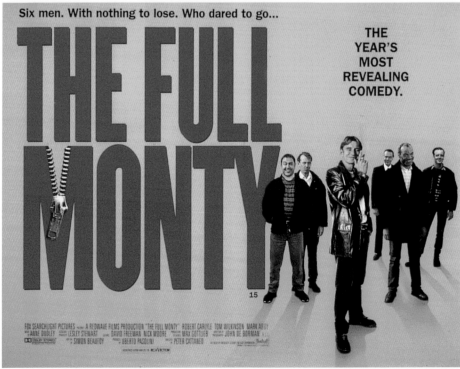

NATIONAL IDENTITIES IN WESTERN EUROPE

"HOLLYWOOD COME IN ... YOUR TIME IS UP
TRAINSPOTTING IS HERE AND IT'S TOE-CURLINGLY GOOD"
★★★★★

Trainspotting

Above right: The poster for *Trainspotting* (1995) is a little over-optimistic about its challenge to Hollywood.
Dir: Danny Boyle

Right: Steve Coogan as pop entrepreneur Tony Wilson in *24 Hour Party People* (2002).
Dir: Michael Winterbottom

Below: Vinnie Jones as an enforcer for an East End crook in *Lock, Stock and Two Smoking Barrels* (1998).
Dir: Guy Ritchie

Overleaf: Is this the end for junkie Renton (Ewan McGregor) in *Trainspotting* (1995).
Dir: Danny Boyle

stripping, the profits went to the films' American backers. *Trainspotting* (1995), directed by Danny Boyle, was a shocking and intermittently brilliant plunge into Edinburgh's drug culture that successfully tapped the youth market, but its makers have subsequently failed to sustain such high quality. *Lock, Stock and Two Smoking Barrels* (1998), a stylishly-shot crime film, directed by Guy Ritchie with an engaging mix of violence and black comedy, has a lot to answer for. With lottery money now available, a rush of ill-prepared scripts went into production seeking to emulate its success. None has done so, and many were so abysmal as not even to find a distributor. At the end of the decade British cinema seemed capable of throwing up an isolated hit, such as *Billy Elliot* (Stephen Daldry, 2000), about a miner's son who becomes a dancer, but it was a poor place in which to build a career. It would be hard to say that any true auteurs have emerged in the past decade, with the possible exception of Michael Winterbottom, whose films have a formal assurance and a distinctive emotional climate, at best bittersweet, as in the ironically titled *Wonderland* (1999) about the lives of three sisters in contemporary London, or outright tragic, as in his two Thomas Hardy adaptations, *Jude* (1996) and *The Claim* (2000). *Welcome to Sarajevo* (1997) also deals with characters on the edge in a story about a British television reporter in Sarajevo who gets emotionally involved to the point of adopting a traumatized child of the besieged city. The most productive of the younger British film-makers, Winterbottom has recently explored subjects as diverse as the Manchester club scene in *24 Hour Party People* (2002) and asylum-seekers with *In This World* (2002).

In what was until very recently a poor country, Irish cinema largely meant foreign films about Ireland, of which the most influential was John Ford's *The Quiet Man* (1952), or films shot at Dublin's Ardmore Studios to take advantage of favourable tax regimes and exchange

Opposite: Helen Mirren and John Lynch as lovers from opposite sides of the sectarian divide, Marcella and Cal in *Cal* (1984). Dir: Pat O'Connor
Left: Jaye Davidson as Dil and Stephen Rea as IRA man Fergus in *The Crying Game* (1992). Dir: Neil Jordan
Below: Liam Neeson in the title role as the Irish republican leader in the biopic *Michael Collins* (1996). Dir: Neil Jordan

rates. Since 1970 a more authentic Irish cinema has been taking shape, though of the twenty or so films made each year only a handful will be truly indigenous. Kieran Hickey was one of the first to emerge, with the short features *Exposure* (1978), a thriller set on the West Coast, and *Attracta* (1983), about an elderly teacher. Bob Quinn's *Lament for Art O'Leary* (*Caoineadh Airt Uí Laoire*, 1975) was the first fiction film shot in Gaelic, and his later feature *The Bishop's Story* (1994), also in Gaelic, is a thinly disguised version of the scandal concerning the Bishop of Galway, who resigned when it emerged that he had fathered a child. Cathal Black's *Pigs* (1984), set in a Dublin squat, is a downbeat film enlivened by some black comedy. Joe Comerford's *High Boot Benny* (1993) centres on a teenage dropout who gets sucked into the politics of the north–south conflict.

Not surprisingly, the 'Troubles' loom large in contemporary Irish cinema. Pat O'Connor, one of the most successful Irish directors, made his feature debut with *Cal* (1984), in which a young Catholic falls for the widow of a policeman in whose murder he has been implicated. In *Fools of Fortune* (1990) a family is torn apart by a murderous attack by the infamous Black and Tans, though the film's handsome setting gives it more than a touch of heritage cinema. *Dancing at Lughnasa* (1998) slipped back into the sentimental 'Oirishness' from which film-makers have tried hard to escape.

Neil Jordan is the most talented of contemporary Irish directors, and *Angel* (1982) was a brilliant debut. Stephen Rea plays a saxophonist who witnesses a sectarian murder and is drawn into pursuit of the killers. Jordan has a highly visual imagination, and his films are shot through with surprising images. *The Crying Game* (1992) concludes with a stunning 'coup de théâtre' when an IRA man meets the girlfriend of a black British soldier he has kidnapped. Much of Jordan's work has been in Britain and the United States, but in 1996 he attempted an Irish epic. *Michael Collins* (1996), with Liam Neeson as the Irish republican hero, was accused of inaccuracies, as every film on the Irish question inevitably is, but it achieved an epic sweep, if dutiful at times, and introduced some of the complexities of

Irish politics to a wide audience. Jordan has often worked abroad, and *The Butcher Boy* (1997) is technically an American film, but its story of a disturbed young boy who becomes a killer has a densely realized sense of small-town Irish life in the 1960s.

The cinemas of the Nordic countries have in common a lengthy period of social democratic government, which resulted in a high level of state subsidy, and a film-making tradition stressing a respect for national identity and social decency. Recently, however, some governments have become more right-wing, leading to a reduction in subsidies, while there are signs, as in the films of Lars von Trier in Denmark or the productions of the Finnish Kaurismäki brothers, that young film-makers are kicking over the traces.

As with some other small countries, the perception of Swedish cinema abroad has been dominated by a single director, in this case Ingmar Bergman. His films, with their brooding heroes tormented by metaphysical dilemmas and by the seductive sexuality of Bergman's radiant actresses – among them Harriet Andersson, Liv Ullmann and Bibi Andersson – fixed an indelible image of Swedish cinema in the minds of a generation. But by the 1970s Bergman's best years were behind him, although *Cries and Whispers* (*Viskningar och Rop*, 1972), an intense study of female suffering, was an international success. He had left Sweden, complaining of harassment by the tax authorities, and worked in Germany, mainly in the theatre, but also directing *Autumn Sonata* (*Herbstsonate*, 1978) starring Ingrid Bergman as a concert pianist and Liv Ullmann as the daughter with whom she has a difficult relationship. His homecoming in the 1980s led to the production of *Fanny and Alexander* (*Fanny och Alexander*, 1982), a lengthy and opulent family saga set at the beginning of the twentieth century which drew heavily on Bergman's memories of his own family.

One who reacted against Bergman's dominance was Bo Widerberg. His early films owed much to the French New Wave, but after international success with the romantically tragic *Elvira Madigan* (1967) Widerberg produced a brace of films about labour history: *Ådalen '31* (1969) is set in Sweden in the Depression, and *Joe Hill* (1971) is about the American labour organizer. Widerberg then made some successful thrillers, including *The Man from Majorca* (*Mannen från Mallorca*, 1984), before embarking on his last venture, *All Things Fair* (*Lust och fägring stor*, 1995), about a young boy's relationship with a woman teacher, set in World War II and starring Widerberg's own son.

Two directors who made their mark in the early 1970s were Vilgot Sjöman and Jan Troell. Sjöman's *I Am Curious (Yellow)* (*Jag är nyfiken – en film i gult*, 1967), a kind of pseudo-documentary investigation into Swedish sexuality, was just what the international market expected from Sweden. But though he continued to work the sexual theme with *Till Sex Us Do Part* (*Troll*, 1971) and *Taboo* (*Tabu*, 1977), none of his later films achieved the same success. Troell made a pair of films, *The Emigrants* (*Utvandrarna*, 1971) and *The New Land* (*Nybyggarna*, 1972), about Swedish emigrants to America in the nineteenth century. Benefiting from the redoubtable presence of Max von Sydow and Liv Ullmann, the films combined epic sweep with domestic intimacy. Troell revisited the American West for *Zandy's Bride* (1974), a downbeat drama in which Gene Hackman takes a mail-order wife.

NATIONAL IDENTITIES IN WESTERN EUROPE

ALEXANDER: You'd better return to heaven. You can't help us anyway.

OSCAR: I lived my life with you children and Emilie. Death makes no difference. What is it, Alexander?

ALEXANDER: Why can't you go to God and tell him to kill the Bishop? Or doesn't God give a damn? Have you ever seen God over there? There's no one here who can even think. Idiots the whole lot.

Alexander Ekdahl (Bertil Guve), Oscar Ekdahl (Allan Edwall), *Fanny and Alexander* (*Fanny och Alexander*, Ingmar Bergman, 1982)

Below: Ing-Marie Carlsson as the beautiful artist's model Berit and Anton Glanzelius as Ingmar, a small boy who loses his mother in *My Life as a Dog* (*Mitt liv som hund*, 1985). Dir: Lasse Hallström

Above: Lars Nordh as Kalle, the salesman whose business is collapsing in *Songs from the Second Floor* (*Sånger från andra våningen*, 2000). Dir: Roy Andersson

The Swedish Film Institute had been the mainstay of Swedish film production in the 1970s and 1980s, not only channelling funds but actively involved in production itself until 1993. Since then, under a more right-wing government, subsidies have decreased. Two directors of note show in different ways the difficulties of working in small countries. Lasse Hallström had a huge success domestically and internationally with *My Life as a Dog* (*Mitt liv som hund*, 1985), a fresh, inventive and unsentimental story about a young boy's response to the death of his mother. Hallström used this as a stepping stone to Hollywood, where he has made a series of films, most recently *The Cider House Rules* (1999), *Chocolat* (2000) and *The Shipping News* (2001) which, while displaying some of the charm of his Swedish work, have fatally succumbed to American soft-centredness.

Roy Andersson, on the other hand, was unable to get funding for twenty-five years following the failure of *Giliap* (1975), and abandoned feature films for commercials. Finally in 2000 he produced *Songs from the Second Floor* (*Sånger från andra våningen*), an utterly individual film that could not be less like Hollywood. A series of scenes in an unnamed city in the throes of an economic crisis, it follows furniture salesman Kalle as his business collapses (due to his own arson) and he visits his son in a mental hospital. The method of the film borrows something from absurdist theatre, something from Bergman in its sense of guilt, and also something from Buñuel's savage attacks on the bourgeoisie in such films as *The Exterminating Angel* (*El ángel exterminador*, 1962).

Among women directors, Suzanne Osten has made her mark, not confining herself to the usual subjects of the woman's film. *The Guardian Angel* (*Skyddsängeln*, 1990) is set in the 1910s, about a young revolutionary who infiltrates the house of a government minister and plans to assassinate him. Among distinguished actresses who graduated to directing are Mai Zetterling and Gunnel Lindblom. Zetterling's early films such as *Night Games* (*Nattlek*, 1966) scandalized with their sexual frankness; *Scrubbers* (1982), made in England, and about young women in a reformatory, was also controversial. Lindblom,

NATIONAL IDENTITIES IN WESTERN EUROPE

memorable in such Bergman films as *The Silence* (*Tystnaden*, 1963), directed *Summer Paradise* (*Paradistorg*, 1977), a sensitively handled drama of family tensions.

Currently, Swedish cinema is picking up, producing twenty-five films in 2001. In 2000 domestic productions secured twenty-five per cent of the box office. Lukas Moodysson is perhaps the most promising of the younger directors. His first feature, *Show Me Love* (*Fucking Åmål*, 1998), is about two schoolgirls starting a lesbian affair. *Together* (*Tillsammans*, 2000) is set in a commune in the mid-1970s. Deftly filmed, it observes the political earnestness and emotional naivety of the inhabitants with affectionate amusement, contrasting them with their uptight bourgeois neighbours.

The Danish Film Institute, based on the Swedish model, was set up in 1972 and has subsidized films of artistic merit, but, in addition, any film that could get fifty per cent of its financing from other sources was entitled to receive the other half of its budget from the state. Funding has recently been increased, and production is currently running at just under twenty films a year. The abolition of censorship in 1969 led to a spate of sex comedies, of which John Hilbard's *Danish Dentist on the Job* (*Tandlæge på sengekanten*, 1971), a hit in sex-starved England, was a representative title. Popular cinema also flourished with a series of genial comedies based on the crime capers of the 'Olsen Gang', which were successfully remade in Norway and in Sweden (where they were renamed the Jönsson gang). More substantially, Nils Malmros made a series of films about adolescents, including *The Tree of Knowledge* (*Kundskabens træ*, 1981) and *Beauty and the Beast* (*Skønheden og udyret*, 1983).

Denmark has had no single dominant figure, but a number of talented film-makers. One of them, Bille August, belongs as much to Swedish cinema as to Danish. His first major success, *Pelle the Conqueror* (*Pelle Erobreren*, 1987), was a coproduction between the two countries, starring Sweden's Max von Sydow as a poor labourer who emigrates with his young son from Sweden to Denmark in search of work. The film details the unremitting hardship and occasional brutality of nineteenth-century farm work, relieved only by sex and drunkenness. No face in European cinema is more eloquent of suffering than von Sydow's, and the film captures a Hardyesque bitterness of crushed ambitions. August has gone on to an international career, making *Smilla's Feeling for Snow* (1997) from the Danish best seller, with a largely British cast, and a remake of *Les Misérables* (1998), but these films have lacked the impact of his earlier work.

Two veteran Danish directors continued into the 1990s. Gabriel Axel, born in 1918, worked in France for much of the 1970s, returning to Denmark to make *Babette's Feast* (*Babettes Gæstebud*, 1987), in which Stéphane Audran starred as a Frenchwoman widowed

Above: A playful moment at the commune in *Together* (*Tillsammans*, 2000). Dir: Lukas Moodysson
Below: Stéphane Audrun as the servant who spends all her money on a dinner in *Babette's Feast* (*Babettes*
Gæstebud, 1987). Dir: Gabriel Axel
Right: Pelle Hvenegaard as Pelle and Max von Sydow as his father Lasse, poor farm workers in *Pelle the Conqueror* (*Pelle Erobreren*, 1987). Dir: Bille August

during the uprising of the Paris Commune in 1871 and who comes to work for the two spinster daughters of an austere Danish minister. Winning the lottery, she elects to spend her money on a French dinner for the circle of ascetic parishioners, astonishing them – and us – by its magnificent luxury. Not a Euro-pudding but a Euro-feast, the film can be read as an allegory of narrow provincialism contrasted with a wider, more generous culture.

Henning Carlsen (born 1927) produced an impressive tour de force with *Hunger* (*Sult*, 1968), from Knut Hamsun's classic novel about a writer's descent into destitution. Carlsen has specialized in studies of those on the edge of despair, such as *Did Somebody Laugh* (*Hør, var der ikke en som lo?*, 1978), about an unemployed man in the Depression, and *The Wolf at the Door* (*Oviri*, 1986), a coproduction with France, a spare but compelling film about the struggles of Paul Gauguin.

Undoubtedly the most arresting development in Danish cinema has been the rise of the Dogme school. Rejecting the excesses of big budgets, the self-imposed rules of this

KATHY: You cheated the doctor. You shouldn't be working here. How dare you! How much can you see?

SELMA: We could do it with our eyes closed. So could you.

KATHY: No.

SELMA: It's just because I was daydreaming.

KATHY: Daydreaming. Daydreaming about what?

SELMA: I just hear music.

KATHY: Come on, Selma. Music? You could cut off your hand. You have to watch out. Promise me you'll stay awake.

SELMA: I promise I will stop daydreaming.

Kathy (Catherine Deneuve), Selma (Björk), *Dancer in the Dark* (Lars von Trier, 2000)

NATIONAL IDENTITIES IN WESTERN EUROPE

Above: Enjoying a drink together: the three wives from left to right, Kaja (Katja Medbøe), Mie (Anne Marie Ottersen) and Heidrun (Frøydis Armand) in the Norwegian film *Wives* (*Hustruer*, 1975). Dir: Anja Breien

Overleaf: Stellan Skarsgård as the husband, Emily Watson as the wife, with Katrin Cartlidge (r) as Dodo, her sister-in-law in *Breaking the Waves* (1996). Dir: Lars von Trier

self-selected club dictate that stories be set in the present, that camerawork must be hand-held, and that there should be no special lighting, post-recorded sound or constructed sets. The directors of the films are not credited, though it is hardly a secret that the principal exponent is Lars von Trier. He had already made a name as a startlingly innovative film-maker with *Element of Crime* (*Forbrydelsens element*, 1984), a noirish thriller; a path-breaking television series *The Kingdom* (*Riget*, 1994); and the British-made *Breaking the Waves* (1996), a film of raw emotional power about an inhibited young woman (Emily Watson) who discovers sexual fulfilment when she marries a worker on the North Sea oil rigs, only to have it snatched away when he is paralysed in an accident. Unable to have sex, her husband persuades her to make love with other men, an experience she finds both exciting and degrading. Von Trier's first Dogme film, *The Idiots* (*Idioterne*, 1998), concerns a group of radical young people who dedicate themselves to *épater les bourgeois* by pretending to be mentally handicapped. Some scenes of nudity ensured the film a *succès de scandale*, and von Trier once again achieved considerable emotional turbulence. *Dancer in the Dark* (2000) is a musical in which the Icelandic singer Björk, sadly miscast, plays a poor factory-worker who is hanged for the murder of a thief. The combination of singing and dancing with such a downbeat story divided critics, some still convinced of von Trier's genius, others ready to call him a fraud; the director appears to thrive on the controversy.

In the 1970s Norwegian film production, heavily subsidized by the state, was marked by a rejection of Hollywood in favour of politically-conscious films in a realistic style, such as Oddvar Bull Tuhus's *Strike!* (*Streik!*, 1975). Norway also saw the rise of some talented woman directors. In Anja Breien's *Wives* (*Hustruer*, 1975) three thirty-year-old women let their hair down in an enjoyably feminist comedy. Breien managed to secure the same three actresses for her sequels, *Wives: Ten Years After* (*Hustruer ti år etter*, 1985) and *Wives III* (*Hustruer III*, 1996). In between Breien made *Next of Kin* (*Arven*, 1979), in which family tensions rise to the surface when a wealthy member dies. It is an acerbic look at the

Above: A drama of
family strife, made
according to Dogme
rules: Gørild Mauseth
as the daughter
and Zbigniew
Zamachowski as the
brother-in-law in *Cabin
Fever* (*Når nettene blir
lange*, 2000).
Dir: Mona J Hoel
Below left: Special
delivery: Robert
Skjærstad as a
postman who gets

mixed up with crooks
in *Junk Mail*
(*Budbringeren*, 1997).
Dir: Pål Sletaune
Below right: The horrors
of war: *The Winter War*
(*Talvisota*, 1989).
Dir: Pekka Parikka
Opposite: Marianne
O Ulrichson and Stellan
Skarsgård in the fast-
paced thriller *Insomnia*
(1997), later remade
by Hollywood.
Dir: Erik Skjoldbjærg

Norwegian middle classes; as the family carry off their loot from the rich man's house, Rossini's 'Thieving Magpie' overture plays on the soundtrack.

Other successful films by women include Laila Mikkelsen's *Little Ida* (*Liten Ida*, 1981), a touching and deeply felt story set in World War II about a child ostracized because her mother is having an affair with a German officer. Vibeke Løkkeberg's *Kamilla* (*Løperjenten*, 1981) is another film about childhood, while Mona J Hoel's *Cabin Fever* (*Når nettene blir lange*, 2000) is a gruelling but brilliantly-handled drama made according to Dogme rules, in which a family gathers for Christmas and tears itself apart. Liv Ullmann, who made a name for herself appearing in Bergman's films, returned to Norway to direct *Kristin Lavransdatter* (1995), a medieval epic. *Faithless* (*Trolösa*, 2000), a forceful if traditional drama about an ageing playwright which she directed from a Bergman script, was made in Sweden.

Norway's popular cinema had been largely sustained by comedy. *The Olsen Gang* (*Olsenbanden*, 1969) was the first in a long-running series of crime capers adapted from the Danish originals. But in the 1980s came a change of mood. Audiences had failed to respond to the worthier films of the previous decade, and there was a push towards action-oriented genres. *Orion's Belt* (*Orions belte*, 1985), directed by Ola Solum, was a Cold War thriller about Soviet espionage, which made up for weak characterization with a relentless narrative drive and excellent use of the icy locations. Nils Gaup's big-budget *Pathfinder* (*Ofelas*, 1987) is set in twelfth-century Lapland and filmed in the Sami language. A boy takes revenge on intruders who have murdered his family; the sudden eruption of violence from a malevolent band of raiders emerging out of the landscape gives it the feel of a Western. There is a stark beauty in the 70 mm location shooting: the snow waist-deep, the trees encrusted with frost.

The film of social consciousness still survives in Norway, while the directing team of Svend Wam and Petter Vennerød has entertained audiences with its frequently comic looks at modern life. In *The Wedding Party* (*Bryllupsfesten*, 1989) a man devises an insurance scam to take place during his daughter's wedding. It is a breakneck farce with plentiful vulgarity and running jokes, but not the sort of film likely to travel. More international in appeal is *Junk Mail* (*Budbringeren*, 1997) directed by Pål Sletaune, a black comedy about a postman who gets sucked into the sleazy world of Oslo's petty criminals. Uneven but quirky and original, it reached the same market as films like *Trainspotting*. Erik Skjoldbjærg's stylishly shot *Insomnia* (1997), in which a Swedish cop searches for the killer of a young girl (remade in Hollywood in 2002 with Al Pacino), confirms that the move towards more internationally viable genres continues.

Earth Is a Sinful Song (*Maa on syntinen laulu*, 1973) is probably most people's idea of a Finnish film, a heartfelt portrait by Rauni Mollberg of the impoverished inhabitants of the bleak northern region of Lapland, with their harsh living conditions, spare but beautiful landscapes and the religious and sexual intensities they generate. Finland has also made some notable films about its war with Russia, such as Jaakko Pakkasvirta's *Sign of the Beast* (*Pedon merkki*, 1980), Mollberg's *The Unknown Soldier* (*Tuntematon sotilas*, 1985) (a remake of a 1955 version of a Finnish classic), and *The Winter War* (*Talvisota*, 1989) by Pekka Parikka, reputedly the most expensive Finnish film ever made. Equally typical but less exportable are the comedy films based on a character named Uuno Turhapuro, the first appearing in 1973. Coarse, idle and scruffy, Uuno is a fart in the face of respectability.

NATIONAL IDENTITIES IN WESTERN EUROPE

No less disrespectful of upright and uptight Finnish culture are the Kaurismäki
brothers, Aki and Mika. Their films are an unstable mixture of influences from
European art cinema (their production company is called Villealfa, after Godard's
Alphaville), with genre pastiche, social commentary, deadpan humour and much else
besides. Aki's *Crime and Punishment* (*Rikos ja rangaistus*, 1983) is a version of Dostoyevsky's
novel that begins in a slaughterhouse, while *Hamlet Goes Business* (*Hamlet liikemaailmassa*,
1987) updates Shakespeare to an analysis of Finland's economic crisis, in which Hamlet's
family firm manufactures rubber ducks. Aki's *I Hired a Contract Killer* (1990) has a typically
Kaurismäki situation; a man wishes to kill himself but cannot face suicide. He hires
a killer to do the job, then, too late, changes his mind; Jean-Pierre Léaud, veteran of Godard
and Truffaut, plays the lead. Mika Kaurismäki's *Highway Society* (1998) is a kind of road
movie set in Germany. Best known of all Aki Kaurismäki's films is *Leningrad Cowboys Go
America* (1989), in which members of the 'worst rock band in the world', failures in Finland,
embark on a tour of the United States, taking with them the frozen body of their assumed
dead guitarist. The group's absurd quiffs and long pointed boots created an iconic image
that ensured the film cult status (when they visit the father of the 'dead' guitarist even the
family dog and a baby have the trademark quiff) and was reprised in *Leningrad Cowboys
Meet Moses* (1994). Aki Kaurismäki's *The Man Without a Past* (*Mies vailla menneisyyttä*, 2002),
about a man who loses his memory after a blow to the head and finds a new life among
the down-and-outs, is wonderfully droll as well as affecting.

Iceland's tiny population (only a quarter of a million) sets limits to film production.
In the 1990s, while Norway and Finland each made a dozen films a year, Iceland could
manage only one or two. But when a film fund was set up in 1979 the results were
immediate. Ágúst Guðmundsson's *Land and Sons* (*Land og synir*, 1979), about a lonely
farmer and his son in the Depression, was seen by nearly thirty per cent of the populace.
The same director's version of the Icelandic sagas, *Outlaw* (*Útlaginn*, 1981), drew on material

NATIONAL IDENTITIES IN WESTERN EUROPE

central to Iceland's national identity and in its mythical qualities was ideal for the cinema. Hrafn Gunnlaugsson's *When the Raven Flies* (*Hrafninn flýgur*, 1984) and *The Shadow of the Raven* (*Í skugga hrafnsins*, 1988) mined the same sources, producing a violent, unheroic, at times surreal vision of the medieval world. In a different mode, comedy and youth culture have also been a mainstay, with Guðmundsson's *On Top* (*Með allt á hreinu*, 1982) combining both, in a popular film about a male and a female pop group battling for supremacy in the Icelandic music scene. Baltasar Kormákur's *101 Reykjavik* (2000) had some international success trading on Iceland's reputation as a centre of youthful hedonism, with a story of a rootless young man who embarks on an affair with his mother's lesbian lover (played by Spanish star Victoria Abril).

It seems appropriate to conclude with one of Europe's smallest nations. In an age of globalization it is heartening to find that such countries accord so important a place to national cinema. Realistically, countries such as Iceland or Portugal can never hope to dominate their domestic film markets, yet few things contribute so much to a sense of national identity as a film that reflects directly the lives of its citizens and speaks to them in their own language. Western European nations are virtually unanimous in believing that the amount of subsidy required to preserve indigenous film-making is a small price to pay to keep culture alive.

Above right: Markku Peltola as the man who loses his memory and Kati Outinen as the Salvation Army worker who helps him in *The Man Without a Past* (*Mies vailla menneisyyttä*, 2002). Dir: Aki Kaurismäki
Below right: Hilmir Snær Guðnason as the son

Hlynur who discovers Lola (Victoria Abril, left) in bed with his mother (Hanna María Karlsdóttir) in *101 Reykjavik* (2000). Drunk, Hlynur, too, ends up in bed with Lola, resulting in her becoming pregnant.
Dir: Baltasar Kormákur

HLYNUR: Lola will be his mum, and my mum will be his dad. And I'll be his brother, but his father too, and the son of his dad and of his grandmother and his mother's ex-lover.
Hlynur (Hilmir Snær Guðnason) *101 Reykjavik* (Baltasar Kormákur, 2000).

ANNOUNCER: **Mateusz Birkut's feat may launch a revolution in construction techniques. It's not only a building foundation which is being laid but the foundations of a new life and prosperity for working people as well.**

Announcer (Anon.), Mateusz Birkut (Jerzy Radziwilowicz),
Man of Marble (Człowiek z marmuru, Andrzej Wajda, 1977)

Previous pages: Jerzy Radziwilowicz in *Man of Marble* (*Człowiek z marmuru*, 1977), a satire on state-controlled propaganda. Before the collapse of Communism, cinema in Eastern Europe tested the limits of censorship with a series of films criticizing the authorities.
Dir: Andrzej Wajda
Below: Actresses Irina Muraviova and Vera Alentova in *Moscow Does Not Believe in Tears* (*Moskva slezam ne verit*, 1979).
Dir: Vladimir Menshov

EASTERN EUROPE AND THE FORMER SOVIET UNION

Since the collapse of Communism the countries of Eastern Europe and the former Soviet Union can no longer be thought of as a single coherent entity; they now develop in different directions, at different speeds. But in 1970 their film industries shared a number of crucial features. As with other forms of economic production under socialism, cinema was tightly controlled by a highly centralized apparatus. Decisions on the allocation of resources, and even on the kinds of films to be made, were handed down from above. Moreover, the role of the cinema was different from that in the West. The purpose of films was above all to instruct the population, to improve them as citizens and as economic performers. Accordingly, commercial considerations did not loom large in production decisions. Cinema attendance was high in any case, since there were few other forms of entertainment, but the most important test of a film was its capacity for raising consciousness among its audience.

Following the lead of the Soviet Union, where it was initially developed in the 1930s, 'socialist realism' was the approved aesthetic model for Communist cinema. (A statute of the Soviet Film-Makers' Union decreed that 'only those film-makers who stand for the principles of 'socialist realism' may be members'.) Fundamentally conservative, it demanded that films be easily intelligible as representations of the real world, that they deal in material and styles with which audiences feel comfortable. In the words of Andrei Zhdanov, one of the architects of the policy, 'Not everything that is accessible is great, but everything that is authentically great is accessible, and the greater it is, the more accessible to the masses.' Criticism was possible, but only in the interest of realizing the future utopia to which Communism was leading. However, the tendency towards banality which such an aesthetic encouraged was countered by the tradition, common throughout the territories under consideration, to accord high status to the arts and to intellectuals. As a result, cinema under Communism was often earnest and dull, but its exceptional films displayed an intellectual sophistication and stylistic bravura that rivalled anything the West had to offer.

Moreover, the actual system of production in Communist countries allowed more leeway than might be thought. The notion that a censor would sit next to the director, supervising every shot, is erroneous. Film-makers, including directors, scriptwriters and editors, were usually salaried employees of production units, which submitted scripts to a central authority. If approved, finance was then made available to the unit, and production normally proceeded free from interference. But then the film had to pass another hurdle: distribution and exhibition were state monopolies also, and each film required further approval before being shown. It was therefore not unknown for a film to be made but then shelved, or else receive only a limited distribution in one or two prints. Yet this would not necessarily affect the future career of the makers of the film.

The homogeneity of production systems under socialism was counteracted by national variations. The diverse artistic tradition of each country could not but have an influence on its films. Particular political histories had a profound effect. The events of 1956 left a lasting mark on Hungarian cinema; the so-called Prague Spring radically changed Czech cinema, if only for a moment. Partly as the direct result of such political events, there were significant variations in the degree of central control and the manner in which it was exercised.

In the Soviet Union cinema was highly popular. Lenin had called it 'the most important art', because of its potential for influence over the masses. Even though cinema-going declined slightly in the 1970s as a result of competition from television, the main problem, given the cumbersome nature of the production process, was keeping up with demand. In 1972 Alexei Romanov, the elderly and conservative head of Goskino, the state cinema company, was replaced by Filipp Yermash, an avowed admirer of Hollywood who sought to turn the industry towards efficiency and the production of more upbeat entertainment films. Typical was Vladimir Menshov's *Moscow Does Not Believe in Tears* (*Moskva slezam ne verit*, 1979), which follows three women, first seen living in a hostel and looking for husbands; twenty years later, their fortunes have varied. Despite some heartache for the protagonists, it is a cheerful picture with a breezy style that made it popular both in Russia

Top: Anatoli Solonitsyn as The Writer, taken to The Room where truth and desire can be gained in the science fiction film *Stalker* (1979).

Dir: Andrei Tarkovsky
Above: Andrei Boltnev as the title character in *My Friend Ivan Lapshin* (*Moj drug Ivan Lapshin*, 1983). Dir: Aleksei German

Right: Mikhail Ulyanov as Kim Yesenin the writer and Inna Churikova as Sasha in a snowy cemetery in *Theme* (*Tema*, 1979).

Dir: Gleb Panfilov
Opposite: Director Andrei Tarkovsky at work on *The Sacrifice* (1986), his last film.

and the West, without rocking the ideological boat. Yet Soviet cinema was not devoid of challenging works. Andrei Tarkovsky's *Andrei Rublev* (1966), about a fifteenth-century painter of icons, had raised issues of artistic freedom, as well as being stylistically inventive. Although it encountered difficulties, it was eventually released in 1971. Tarkovsky's next film was *Solaris* (*Solyaris*, 1972), a kind of science fiction film for intellectuals. His later films such as *The Mirror* (*Zerkalo*, 1974) and *Stalker* (1979) were partly autobiographical metaphysical speculations, shot in a meticulous style, and a long way from being accessible to all. Eventually Tarkovsky, a prickly character, found the difficulties put in his way too great to overcome and finished his career in Western Europe.

Other film-makers who fell foul of the authorities during the Brezhnev years from the late 1960s to the early 1980s include Aleksei German, whose *Trial on the Road* (*Proverka na dorogakh*, 1971) is about a Red Army officer who is captured by the Germans and then recaptured by the Soviets. The treatment of returning prisoners touched a raw nerve with the censors, and the film was banned. Yet German was still allowed to work, and in 1983 made *My Friend Ivan Lapshin* (*Moj drug Ivan Lapshin*), set in a drab provincial town in the early 1930s, just before Stalin's terror was unleashed. The hero is a policeman chasing a gang of thieves, the leader of whom he finally shoots in cold blood. Along the way he tries and fails to win the affections of an actress, who has to play a prostitute in a play and has come to him looking for a real-life model on which to base her performance. The style is remarkable, with lots of hand-held camera (mainly in black and white) and an elliptical narrative. Even more surprising to its contemporary Russian audience was the picture of life it offered: the cramped, grubby flat where the policeman lives, the combination of idealism and grimness in his work. Again German had his film banned, but it was eventually shown in 1985, to wide acclaim. His recent film *Khrustalyov, My Car!* (*Khrustalyov, mashinu!*, 1998) is a bizarre comedy set at the time of Stalin's death, again shot in black and white with a restless camera, with much of the action taking place in a lunatic asylum where the inmates are no more mad than those outside.

Another banned film was Gleb Panfilov's *Theme* (*Tema*, 1979). Again set in the provinces, it follows a celebrated but cynical playwright, Kim, visiting from Moscow. He encounters a woman, Sasha, who, unlike everyone else, refuses to tell him how marvellous he is. Drawn to her, he discovers she is conducting an affair with a young writer who, despairing of being published and reduced to working as a gravedigger, has decided to leave Russia. Despite its rather theatrical staging, the film starkly contrasts the hypocrisy of toeing the line with the integrity of protest.

The various national republics that made up the Soviet Union had their own film production centres. One of the most active was in Georgia, where *Repentance* (*Monanieba*, 1984) was directed by Tengiz Abuladze. Its protagonist, Varlam, is an amalgamation of sinister dictator figures, with a Hitler moustache, the rimless glasses of Beria (the notorious chief of Stalin's secret police) and Mussolini's blackshirt uniform. He is fond of sententious statements such as 'Nothing is more beautiful than a working person'; meanwhile, his

EASTERN EUROPE AND THE FORMER SOVIET UNION

opponents are arrested and forced into ludicrous confessions, such as plotting to build a tunnel from London to Bombay. After Varlam's death his supporters produce justifications all too familiar in totalitarian societies: 'It was different then. We were surrounded by enemies. What is one life when so many were in danger?'

The Armenian director Sergo Paradzhanov evolved a highly stylized form of film-making, seen at its best in *The Colour of Pomegranates* (*Sayat Nova*, 1969), a film about an eighteenth-century Armenian poet, told in a series of stunningly beautiful iconographic images. Paradzhanov was imprisoned for much of the 1970s on trumped-up charges of homosexuality and dealing in religious objects, but eventually emerged to make *Legend of the Suram Fortress* (*Legenda o Suramskoi kreposti*, 1984), with equally sumptuous visuals.

In Kazakhstan, a 'new wave' emerged in the late 1980s. Rashid Nugmanov's *The Needle* (*Igla*, 1988) starred legendary rock idol Viktor Tsoi in a thriller exploring the world of drugs and youth culture. More recent Kazakh films include Serik Aprymov's *Aksuat* (1997) and *Three Brothers* (*Tri brata*, 1998), documenting the continuing rigours of daily life. In the past ten or so years state regulation in the former republics of the Soviet Union has to a great extent been dismantled, but private capital has failed to replace public support and film production is spasmodic.

The winds of *perestroika* (restructuring) and *glasnost* (openness), which had commenced in earnest when Gorbachev replaced Chernenko as General Secretary of the Communist Party in March 1985, blew away the leadership of the Film-Makers' Union in the following year. At its fifth Congress the old guard was replaced by a respected group of younger film-makers, including Vadim Abdrashitov, Eldar Shengelaya and, as First Secretary, Elem Klimov. Immediately films that had been banned, around sixty in all, were taken 'off the shelf'. One beneficiary was Kira Muratova, whose work had suffered severely from the censors, including *A Long Farewell* (*Dolgie provody*, 1971), a deeply-felt film about the relationship between a single mother and her teenage son. Since the momentous changes

Above: Rock idol Victor Tsoi in *The Needle* (*Igla*, 1988).
Dir: Rashid Nugmanov
Right: Sergei Popov as the teacher Nicolai, being inspected for signs of life in *The Asthenic Syndrome* (*Astenicheskij sindrom*, 1989).
Dir: Kira Muratova

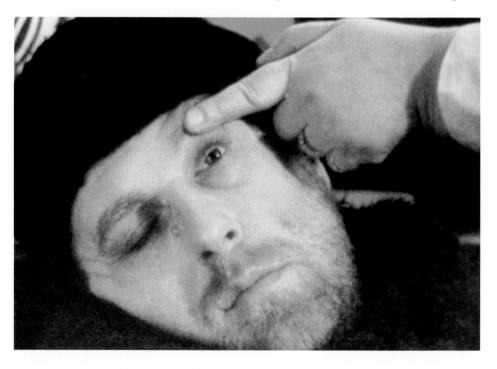

of the late 1980s, Muratova has found her career revitalized. *The Asthenic Syndrome* (*Astenicheskij sindrom*, 1989), made just before the break-up of the Soviet Union, is a vision of Soviet society on the brink of disintegration. At the beginning Natasha loses her husband and is distraught with grief. Yet this proves to be only a film within the film, as the screen changes from black and white to colour and follows a teacher, Nikolai, through a series of disconnected episodes expressing the lack of purpose or pity in society (several scenes show cruelty to animals). At one point Nikolai falls over in a crowded underground station; passers-by ignore him as they rush past. The film ends without redemption, with Nikolai on a train going nowhere: life is absurd, directionless. Muratova's subsequent films, such as *The Sentimental Policeman* (*Chuvstvitelnyi militsioner*, 1992) and *Enthusiasms* (*Uvlecheniya*, 1994), present an equally absurdist view of the world.

Klimov himself had suffered more than most at the hands of the censors, having no fewer than five of his films 'arrested', as the phrase was, including *Farewell* (*Proshchanie*,

EASTERN EUROPE AND THE FORMER SOVIET UNION

1981), about a village which is to be flooded by a new dam. Klimov lovingly details the life of the doomed village (in one sequence people joyfully participate in a last hay-making), in contrast to the bleak housing estate to which they will be moved. In a moving scene an old woman washes her house then decorates it with wild flowers before abandoning it. One can only assume that the censors thought Klimov insufficiently enthusiastic about 'progress'. *Come and See* (*Idi i smotri*, 1985) was delayed at the script stage. It is an almost unbearably harrowing film about German wartime atrocities in Belarus. The young hero, Flyor, somehow manages to preserve his sanity even while watching the entire population of a village burned alive by SS troops.

The thaw resulting from Gorbachev's reforms in the late 1980s gave Soviet film-makers a renewed confidence in cinema's ability to confront the true nature of their society. No longer need they strive to be upbeat. Vadim Abdrashitov's *Plumbum, or A Dangerous Game* (*Plyumbum, ili opasnaya igra*, 1986) is about a teenage boy (Plumbum, meaning lead, he explains; not hard like steel – 'Stalin' in Russian), who spies on crooks and reports them to the police. His declared motive is idealistic. 'I hate evil. I'll give my life in the struggle,' he declares melodramatically. But he seems propelled more by a naive desire for power. His parents refuse to believe his accounts of his exploits, until the moment when he shops his own father. The ending is shocking, as Plumbum's teenage girlfriend falls to her death during a rooftop chase. Abdrashitov's *Time of the Dancer* (*Vremya tantsora*, 1998) is set in an unspecified region to the south where a Muslim couple seek revenge on three Russian former soldiers for the near-murder of the husband and the theft of the couple's house.

A film which created a sensation was Vasili Pichul's *Little Vera* (*Malenkaya Vera*, 1988). In a decaying southern port, a young woman, played by Natalia Negoda, shares a cramped little flat with her parents. Life seems devoid of purpose or enjoyment and even upbeat moments are blighted; when Vera becomes engaged, her father gets drunk, is beaten up by her fiancé and then stabs him. But Vera is an appealing and convincing figure, with

Right: Sergei Bodrov, Jr
as Danila, the youthful
contract killer in St
Petersburg in *Brother*
(*Brat*, 1997).
Dir: Alexei Balabanov
Below: Sergei Bodrov,
Jr as Ivan 'Vania' Zhilin
and Oleg Menshikov as
Sacha Kostylin in *The*

Prisoner of the
Mountains (*Kavkazskii*
plennik, 1996).
Dir: Sergei Bodrov
Bottom: Off-duty
soldiers while away
the time in *Checkpoint*
(*Blokpost*, 1998).
Dir: Aleksandr
Rogozhkin

her blonde highlights, short skirt and garish top. The film has great honesty, refusing to gloss over the desperation of what it reveals. It was hugely successful in the Soviet Union, doubtless in part because of two scenes where the heroine is seen topless, a rarity in Russian cinema at that point.

Releasing banned films proved a simple matter compared to restructuring the film industry. As the Soviet state crumbled (Boris Yeltsin replaced Gorbachev in 1991), film production abandoned its systems of ideological and economic control. Film-makers were no longer salaried, but freelance. Managerial control was devolved, and film enterprises were supposed to become self-financing in a free market. At first production boomed, the annual number of features rising from about 150 in the Soviet era to twice that number at the end of the 1980s. But this proved a short-lived episode, the figures inflated by dubious enterprises using the film industry to launder money. Production dropped dramatically in the later 1990s, with fewer than fifty Russian films released in 1997. Distribution and exhibition were the last sectors to be reformed, and when they were it became evident that indigenous film-makers were ill-equipped to compete with the twin threats of television and foreign film imports.

Absolved of the obligation to be constantly optimistic, some Russian film-makers wanted at last to show the realities of daily life in the new era: mafia crime, prostitution, beggars, drug abuse, shabby housing, the alienation of the young. Such themes were known collectively as *chernukha*, literally 'what is dark'. Typical is Alexei Balabanov's *Brother* (*Brat*, 1997), in which a young man, fresh out of the army, becomes a professional killer in St Petersburg. Danila has no higher purpose in life than listening to the music of rock group Nautilus, but he is resourceful and brave and that makes him a hero of sorts. In the sequel *Brother 2* (*Brat 2*, 1999), Danila travels to the United States to help a Russian ice-hockey player who is being swindled by an American crook. Danila has no compunction about shooting people, but mostly they deserve it (the bad guy makes snuff movies).

At the same time, the past was being interrogated. Pavel Chukhrai's *The Thief* (*Vor*, 1997) is set in the Stalinist period after World War II, when a personable young man, masquerading as a soldier, takes up with a woman and her young son. Through the child's eyes we see the man revealed as a practised thief who eventually is caught and imprisoned. The criminal underbelly of Soviet society is revealed. Also set in the Soviet period is Lidiya Bobrova's *In That Land* (*V toj strane*, 1997), in which a harassed overseer attempts to cope with a drunken peasantry and a distant bureaucracy, amid moments of farce and pathos.

Sergei Bodrov's *The Prisoner of the Mountains* (*Kavkazskii plennik*, 1996) is very much of the present, set in a conflict not specifically identified but similar to that in Chechnya. Two Russian soldiers are captured by Muslim insurgents. Trying to exchange their captives, the Muslims are double-crossed. At the end one of the prisoners is killed for murdering a shepherd. The film is remarkable for giving equal weight to the predicament of captors and captives, all of them victims of war. Comparable is Aleksandr Rogozhkin's *Checkpoint* (*Blokpost*, 1998), in which a group of young conscripts combating Muslim rebels are beset by do-gooders on their own side investigating an incident in which troops have shot a village woman. The soldiers lark about, play football, have sex with local girls, one of whom turns out to be a sniper herself. The reasons for the conflict are never stated. Alexei Balabanov's *War* (*Voina*, 2002) is yet another view of the Chechen conflict, which makes a point of rubbing the noses of the audience in the brutalities of both sides; in an early scene Chechen rebels cut the head off one of their captives.

'Why such gloomy films?' asks a man in the audience watching the film within the film in Muratova's *The Asthenic Syndrome*. Many critics and older spectators, still hung up on the notion that cinema should be improving, disliked the new stance of staring reality in the face. Though younger film-goers appreciated movies like *Brother* for their honesty and narrative drive, Russian film-makers have found it hard to respond to a market-based film economy. Giving the audience what it wants still remains an alien concept. In 1998, for example, no comedies at all were made in Russia.

Contemporary Russian cinema has two directors who have held to the ideal of cinema's social purpose. Nikita Mikhalkov is a key figure who has imparted a nationalist impulse to his film-making. His most celebrated feature, *Burnt by the Sun* (*Utomlennye solntsem*, 1994), is set in the 1930s. The idyllic family life in a country dacha of Kotov, an army general (played by Mikhalkov himself), is brutally interrupted by the arrival of a member of the secret police, Mitia (the former lover of the general's wife). The general is arrested. Ashamed of himself as a tool of Stalinist terror, Mitia cuts his wrists in his bath. A richly textured film full of extraordinary images (at one point a balloon lifts a huge portrait

Right: The image of Stalin carried by a balloon rises ominously in a stunning scene from *Burnt by the Sun* (*Utomlennye solntsem*, 1994). Dir: Nikita Mikhalkov

of Stalin over the fields), it sees the past as a tragedy for victims and oppressors alike.

An advocate of strong cinematic heroes who will lift Russian cinema from its obsession with dirt and gloom, Mikhalkov is something of a hero himself to many, voted chairman of the Film-Makers' Union in 1997 and elected a member of the Russian parliament (though he declined his seat). In *The Barber of Siberia* (*Sibirskii tsiriul'nik*, 1999), a lavish and nostalgic coproduced epic with foreign stars, set in the nineteenth century and a celebration of Mother Russia, Mikhalkov himself plays Tsar Alexander III.

Alexander Sokurov has been seen as the heir of Tarkovsky, an uncompromising film-maker with a markedly spiritual bent most of whose early works ended up 'on the shelf'. *Mother and Son* (*Mat y syn*, 1997) is an extraordinary film, in which the minimal narrative (about a son ministering to his dying mother in an old house in the country) becomes the opportunity for a stylistic tour de force of long tracking shots, through a landscape imbued with the dense texture of an oil painting. There is a distinct nationalist tinge to Sokurov's rejection of both conventional film aesthetics and commercialism, and his current project, a trilogy of films about Hitler, Lenin and Churchill, is nothing if not ambitious. *Russian Ark* (*Russkij Kovcheg*, 2002) offers vignettes from Russian history via a conducted tour of the Hermitage Museum in St Petersburg, shot in a single take, using advanced digital technology. Such film-making can only survive with public support, or else, as with Sokurov's later films, through international coproduction. The Russian state continues to fund cinema, but had only $10 million to invest in 2000. Serious problems remain. Film-going has undergone a disastrous decline, from twenty attendances a year per head of population in the 1960s down to eight in 1990 and less than one by 1998, as a result of competition from television and video (with widespread piracy) and the lack of modernized theatres. More recently there have been signs of a pick-up thanks in part to the refurbishment of many cinemas and to new piracy laws, but a viable commercial production sector has yet to emerge in the absence of any

Above: Aleksei Ananishnov as the son and Gudrun Geyer as the mother in the painterly *Mother and Son* (*Mat y syn*, 1997). Dir: Alexander Sokurov
Right: Sergei Dontsov as the guide to history in *Russian Ark* (*Russkij Kovcheg*, 2002). Dir: Alexander Sokurov
Below right: Nicholas II (Vladimir Baranov) and family enjoying tea in *Russian Ark* (*Russkij Kovcheg*, 2002). Dir: Alexander Sokurov

EASTERN EUROPE AND THE FORMER SOVIET UNION

Above: Director Andrzej Wajda.
Above right: Solidarity demonstrations in the shipyards in *Man of Iron* (*Człowiek ż zelaza*, 1981).

Director Andrzej Wajda manages to combine fiction with the current events surrounding the Solidarity movement.

system of tax breaks such as those that sustain film-making elsewhere.

During the 1950s and 1960s cinema in Poland had major achievements to its credit. Andrzej Wajda's films about the war, including the stunning *Kanał* (1956), were widely seen in the West, and in the 1960s he continued to make distinctively personal works, shot through with striking, even surreal images, such as *Everything for Sale* (*Wszystko na sprzedaż*, 1969), about the early death of the charismatic actor Zbyszek Cybulski, star of several Wajda films. At the start of the 1970s the political climate improved somewhat after riots led to the replacement of the Stalinist Gomułka as head of government, and Wajda was put in charge of 'X', one of the semi-autonomous production units which organized Polish film-making. He began work on *Man of Marble* (*Człowiek z marmuru*, 1977), in which a young film-maker investigates the fate of a hero of labour from the 1950s. The film is a damning account of Communist propaganda practice. In 1980 the Solidarity movement began in the Gdansk shipyards, and Wajda made a follow-up film, *Man of Iron* (*Człowiek z żelaza*, 1981), in which a drunken hack is detailed to smear one of the Solidarity activists, who turns out to be the son of the labour hero from the earlier film. Wajda is scathing about the corruption and cynicism of Polish political life. Later the same year the liberalization process was stopped in its tracks when martial law was declared by General Jaruzelski and Solidarity banned. During the 1980s Wajda largely worked abroad in France and Germany, making *Danton* (1982), about the French Revolution, and *A Love in Germany* (*Eine Liebe in Deutschland*, 1983), the story of a wartime love affair between a Polish prisoner of war and a German woman. Following the demise of Communism at the end of the decade, Wajda became a member of parliament, but kept up his film career.

Exile, whether temporary or permanent, has been the fate of many East European film-makers, and some of Poland's most talented have pursued their careers abroad. Roman Polanski departed in the mid-1960s, initially to Britain then to Hollywood, latterly to France. Jerzy Skolimowski also went to Britain after the banning of his anti-Stalinist film *Hands Up* (*Ręce do góry*, 1967). Walerian Borowczyk, the possessor of a quirky, at times disturbing imagination, began making short animation films, but moved to France in the 1960s, returning only once to Poland to make *Story of a Sin* (*Dzieje grzechu*, 1975), a period melodrama.

The late 1970s saw the rise of the so-called 'cinema of moral concern', films which took a clear-eyed look at the corruption and political manipulation that characterized Polish life under Communism. Prominent among directors of such films was Krzysztof Kieślowski. Beginning with documentaries, Kieślowski made *Blind Chance* (*Przypadek*, 1981), in which a young man faces three alternative political choices: Stalinism, radicalism and a quiet life.

Politics and Film
Three Colours Blue
(*Trois couleurs bleu*, 1993)
Dir: Krzysztof Kieślowski

One of Polish director Krzysztof Kieślowski's most successful and best-known films, *Three Colours Blue* (*Trois couleurs bleu*) is the first part of his *Three Colours* trilogy. *Blue* is set in France, *White* in Poland and *Red* in Switzerland, but all production was based in France. Not only are the colours of the trilogy those of the French national flag; the original intention was a meditation on the ideals of the French Revolution: freedom, equality and fraternity. This suggests a political dimension to the work. But though like most Polish film-makers Kieślowski had his difficulties with the Polish Communist system, its collapse by the early 1990s meant that he was not only free to work where he pleased, but liberated from the necessity for his films to engage directly in the political process.

In *Three Colours Blue* Juliette Binoche plays a woman whose husband and daughter are killed in a car crash. Overcome by melancholy, she progressively withdraws from life, divesting herself of possessions and refusing relationships, a state of mind conveyed in part by the director's subtle use of the colour blue. But eventually she is able to accept the attentions of a lover and even to offer friendship to another woman who is pregnant with her husband's child. Finally, she completes the piece of music which her husband had been commissioned to write.

The result is a work that has less in common with the Polish 'Cinema of moral concern' of the late 1970s than with the tradition of the mainstream European art cinema, in its concerns with alienation and the loss of feeling, countered by the transcendent power of love. Kieślowski's work, therefore, represents the development of the cinema of Eastern Europe towards integration into a more international movement. At the same time, the political changes of Eastern Europe, resulting in the introduction of market forces, made the production of art cinema much more difficult in those territories. Kieślowski therefore chose to move to capitalist France to make his *Three Colours* trilogy – ironically, perhaps the last bastion of state-supported cinema.

Country of Origin: France/Switzerland/ Poland
Running Time: 98 mins

Production Companies: MK2 Productions SA/CEO Productions/France 3 Cinéma/CAB Productions/ 'Tor' Production
Producer: Marin Karmitz
Writers: Krzysztof Piesiewicz, Krzysztof Kieślowski
Photography: Slawomir Idziak
Editor: Jacques Witta
Art Director: Claude Lenoir
Music: Zbigniew Preisner

Julie: Juliette Binoche
Olivier: Benoît Régent
Sandrine: Florence Pernel
Lucille: Charlotte Véry

Above: Juliette Binoche as Julie watching her daughter get into the car unaware of her family's impending fate.
Right and below right: Trying to cope with her immense grief, Julie tries to live anonymously in the city, leaving her past behind.
Opposite: Juliette Binoche gives a sensitive performance as the sole survivor of a car crash, learning to live with the deaths of her daughter and husband.

The film was banned, but Kieślowski's series of ten films for television, *Dekalog*, in particular *A Short Film about Killing* (*Krótki film o Zabijaniu*, 1988), won him great praise, especially abroad. His next feature, *The Double Life of Véronique* (*Podwójne życie Weroniki*, 1992), was coproduced with a French company. It is a film of great subtlety and ingenuity, the story of two identical-looking women – one French, one Polish – linked by a common love of music. His final work before his untimely death in 1996 was the masterful trilogy *Three Colours Blue* (*Trois couleurs bleu*, 1993), *Three Colours White* (*Trois couleurs blanc*, 1993) and *Three Colours Red* (*Trois couleurs rouge*, 1994). In these works (the colours are those of the French flag, and also of the Polish) Kieślowski explores in turn the lives of a recently bereaved widow, a divorced Polish hairdresser and a young model who encounters a mysterious and manipulative judge. Stylistically assured, full of unexpected narrative twists and moments of numinous insight as well as black comedy, these films represent the apotheosis of European art cinema just at the moment when its very existence seemed most precarious.

Another important contributor to the cinema of moral concern was Krzysztof Zanussi, who was head of the 'Tor' production unit which coproduced *The Double Life of Véronique*. Zanussi's *Illumination* (*Iluminacja*, 1973) observed the narrowing horizons of a young man as maturity encroaches. In *The Contract* (*Kontrakt*, 1980) a bride-to-be runs off just before the wedding. The party goes ahead anyway, a microcosm of Polish society with drunkenness, sexual peccadilloes and petty pilfering. Zanussi's films are highly intelligent, though too spartan in style for some tastes.

Agnieszka Holland, a former assistant of Zanussi whose early films were made in Wajda's 'X' unit, is also associated with the cinema of moral concern. *A Woman Alone* (*Kobieta samotna*, 1981) is the tragic story of a female postal worker struggling to bring up her young son. Its desolate view of contemporary Poland, from which the protagonist wants to emigrate, ran foul of the authorities and the film was banned. Holland appeared as an actress in Ryszard Bugajski's *The Interrogation* (*Przesłuchanie*, 1981), about the arrest

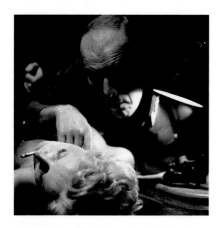

Above: Teresa Ann Savoy, fully dressed as Baroness Mary Vetsera, amid the frolics in *Private Vices, Public Virtues* (*Vizi privati, pubbliche virtù*, 1975). Dir: Miklós Jancsó

Below: Krystyna Janda as cabaret artist Antonia Dziwisz is brutally cross-questioned in *The Interrogation* (*Przesłuchanie*, 1981). Dir: Ryszard Bugajski

of a young woman under Stalinism. It is a brilliant and disturbing study of physical and psychological torture, edgy and intelligent, which not surprisingly upset the regime. (The film was not generally seen until 1989.) As a consequence of increasingly oppressive political control, Holland became another emigré, working in Western Europe and more recently in Hollywood, making literary adaptations such as *The Secret Garden* (1993) and *Washington Square* (1997).

While offering contemporary film-makers unprecedented freedom, the radical political changes of the 1990s, in which the institutions of Communism were swept away as it seemed almost overnight, have been a mixed blessing. The collapse of a centralized funding system has thrown film-makers onto the market. As a result, across the region new film starts fell precipitously in the early 1990s, with Polish production down to a mere dozen by 1999. Those films that did get made tended to be in commercial genres such as comedies and crime films, or safe literary adaptations. The auteur-based cinema which state funding had created seemed everywhere under threat, salvaged only by those who could attract coproduction deals with Western companies or make films for television. Increasingly studios looked to make their facilities available at preferential rates to foreign companies, while the exhibition circuits were opened up to imports, almost exclusively from Hollywood. By 1991 all top twenty box office hits in Poland were American.

The same story could be told of contemporary Hungary, though its history is different. The traumatic events of 1956, when a revolution was bloodily suppressed by Soviet troops, may have made both authorities and film-makers wary of the dangers of open confrontation. In the 1960s a singular form of political film-making emerged, most notably in the work of

Miklós Jancsó. Censorship, though never welcome, can on occasion call forth subtlety and ingenuity in film-makers. *The Round-up* (*Szegénylegények*, 1965) notionally concerns the revolt against Austrian rule in 1848, but it was widely interpreted as a commentary on the events of 1956. Jancsó's heightened stylization, his use of long takes, elaborate tracking shots and visual symbolism found ready acceptance on the festival circuit, while possibly serving to disguise the political message. In the early 1970s Jancsó worked in Italy, making *Private Vices, Public Virtues* (*Vizi privati, pubbliche virtù*, 1975), a film about the Mayerling scandal which developed Jancsó's interest in the relationship between the political and the erotic.

In the early 1970s the institutional structures of the Hungarian film industry were reformed, loosening the bonds of bureaucracy and creating two new companies, Budapest and Hunnia, which were to engage in creative rivalry. In all, about twenty films a year were produced during the 1970s. Among these were works by István Szabó, who was much influenced by the French New Wave and whose early films were personal, sensitive, at times remote. In the 1980s Szabó changed gear dramatically. *Mephisto* (1981) was a compelling and convincing depiction of Nazi Germany through the eyes of an ambitious actor, played by the Austrian Klaus Maria Brandauer. *Colonel Redl* (*Redl Ezredés*, 1985) used the same star in a story of the rise up the army hierarchy of a part-Jewish officer, dissecting the poisonous politics of the Austro-Hungarian empire. It is a film of visual panache, dramatic power and intellectual distinction, making crystal clear the insidious gradations of class, and nationalist and ethnic hostility. Despite availing himself of coproduction finance, Szabó has continued to mine the intricacies of Hungarian history, ambitiously in *Sunshine* (*A napfény íze*, 1999), a multi-generational saga, shot in English, which follows the fortunes of a Jewish family through the Hapsburg empire, the years of Fascism, World War II and Communism.

Despite Communist rhetoric about equality, the proportion of women film-makers was not appreciably greater than in the West, but Márta Mészáros is one who made her mark, initially with a trio of films in the mid-1970s. In *Adoption* (*Örökbefogadás*, 1975) a woman whose relationship is going nowhere decides to adopt a child. In *Nine Months* (*Kilenc hónap*, 1976) a woman chooses between an unexciting suitor and life on her own. *The Two of Them* (*Ök ketten*, 1977) centres on two women of very different personalities who find comfort in their friendship. Formerly married to Jancsó, Mészáros has a very different style – sober, restrained, almost documentary. In the 1980s she began a series of 'diary' films, semi-autobiographical works, including *Diary for My Loves* (*Napló szerelmeimnek*, 1987) in which her heroine Juli becomes a film director just before the 1956 uprising. Mészáros's own father was a victim of Stalin's purges, and the portrait of Stalinism has unquestionable authenticity.

That the personal is political was a dictum of Western feminism in the 1970s, and Hungarian films in the 1970s and 1980s, even those directed by men, frequently made the connection. Pál Gábor's *Angi Vera* (1978), set in the Stalinist era, is about a young woman

Above: Veronika Papp as Vera Angi, the young nurse who is sent to a correction centre after complaining about hospital conditions in *Angi Vera* (1978).
Dir: Pál Gábor
Right: Jan Nowicki (Janos) being led by the guards watched by Zsuzsa Czinkoczi (Juli) in *Diary for My Loves* (*Napló szerelmeimnek*, 1987).
Dir: Márta Mészáros
Overleaf: Klaus Maria Brandauer as Hendrik, the actor taken up by the Nazis in *Mephisto* (1981).
Dir: István Szabó

CONTESTANT: Sorry I'm late but I went to get my swimsuit.
HEAD OF COMMITTEE:
    You've got it with you? What are you doing?
COMMITTEE MEMBER:
    Don't stop her.
HEAD OF COMMITTEE:
    She can't undress in here.
HEAD OF COMMITTEE (cont.):
    Lock the door then.
    Head of Committee (Jan Vostreil), *The Firemen's Ball*
    (*Hoří, má panenko*, Miloš Forman, 1967)

sent for political education who learns how to accommodate herself to the system, even to the extent of betraying her lover. The film was a big hit in the West, which welcomed its political implications but also responded to the film's undoubted quality. In a very different style is Pál Sándor's work: for example, the extraordinary *Improperly Dressed* (*Herkulesfürdöi emlék*, 1976), in which a beautiful young man, on the run from the authorities in the wake of the failed revolution of 1919, dresses as a woman in order to take refuge in a sanatorium. Sándor's dreamy photography of the androgynous boy creates a disturbingly compelling film. Other distinctive work was done by Péter Gothár, whose *Time Stands Still* (*Megáll az idö*, 1981) is, like so many Hungarian films, set against a historical background. Two young men grow up in the wake of 1956. Both seek freedom, but only Pierre decides to leave. His friend, Dénes, chooses to remain in Budapest, having apparently found domestic contentment. But in a final flash forward, we see how badly things have turned out for him.

As the 1980s progressed, the difficulties of the Hungarian economy put pressure on film-making structures, with subsidy increasingly tied to box office performance. Television and foreign film imports made the position of Hungarian cinema precarious. By 1992 each of the ten most popular films was imported from abroad. Yet excellent films continued to be made: for example, Gyula Gazdag's *A Hungarian Fairy Tale* (*Hol volt, hol nem volt*, 1987), a brilliantly executed fantasy about a young man seeking his lost father, a kind of Hungarian version of magical realism. Perhaps the most individual of contemporary Hungarian directors is Béla Tarr. Beginning in the early 1980s with documentary-style films about people on the margins of society, he ran foul of the authorities and moved to Berlin, only returning after the end of Communism. Since then he has made films in which landscape is as important as narrative, as in *Damnation* (*Kárhozat*, 1988). Filmed in black and white, it starts with seemingly endless shots of cable cars moving across a grimy industrial wasteland. Its story of double-cross takes place in dreary bars against a background of melancholy accordion music. Tarr's *Sátántangó* (1994), over six hours long, is a strange tale of a rural community deceived by a charismatic trickster. Whether the small amounts of money the state finds to support cinema can sustain such work seems open to doubt; the twenty Hungarian features released in 2000 took only 3.9 per cent of the box office total.

The most productive period in the history of Czechoslovak cinema came to an abrupt end just before the point at which this book begins. From about 1963 to the end of the decade, Czechoslovak cinema experienced an extraordinary outburst of creativity. Encouraged by liberalization in politics and in artistic life, film-makers came up with a series of works, some of which departed from the officially approved aesthetics of 'socialist realism' and most of which ignored the dogma of party ideology. Among the best-known films of this period are *The Firemen's Ball* (*Hoří, má panenko*, 1967), directed by Miloš Forman, a very funny satire about official pomposity and venality, and *Daisies* (*Sedmikrásky*, 1966), directed by Věra Chytilová (one of the country's few women directors), a visually inventive, almost plotless pot-pourri of gags in which two teenage girls expose hypocrisy and materialism in Czech society.

The flowering of this 'New Wave' was brutally cut short when, after the heady events of the Prague Spring in 1968 – during which for a brief period it looked as though the liberal reforms might achieve an unstoppable momentum – the Soviet invasion of August that same year restored orthodox Communism. Many films were banned, including *The Firemen's Ball*. An official history of Czech cinema, published in 1982, proclaimed that the film-makers of the New Wave were 'characterized by their pessimism, destructiveness, aridity and negativeness. Because some film-makers belonging to this period of Czechoslovak cinema viewed the society without the necessary class-consciousness, they were at variance with the cultural policy of the Party and with the cinema-goers' thoughts and taste.'[1] Faced with such attitudes, several of the brightest film-making talents, including Forman, Ján Kadár and Ivan Passer, left the country soon after 1968, along with over 170,000 of their fellow citizens. Henceforth, only films on safe subjects were to be made: stories about heroes of industry, tales of World War II resistance, versions of the classics and fairy tales.

Some film-makers of talent remained in Czechoslovakia, in particular Jiří Menzel and Chytilová. Menzel's *Seclusion Near a Forest (Na samotě u lesa*, 1976) is a comedy about a city family trying to buy a house in the country. Its deft observation of human foibles avoids any political overtones. *Those Wonderful Movie Cranks (Báječni muži s klikou*, 1978) was a well-received re-creation of the days of silent movies, while *My Sweet Little Village (Vesničko má, středisková*, 1985), another comedy, about an oddly assorted pair of rural workmates, is also largely innocent of ideology, though not always staying the right side of whimsy. Chytilová's freewheeling style was out of favour and she was not permitted to work until the mid-1970s, when she made *The Apple Game (Hra o jablko*, 1976), a satire on sexuality, and *Prefab Story (Panelstory*, 1981), set in a large apartment block. *The Wolf's Lair (Vlčí bouda*, 1986) was a psychological thriller about a group of young people at a ski resort.

After the collapse of Communism, the Czechoslovak film industry, like others in Eastern Europe, declined precipitously as state support was withdrawn and imports grew. Yet veterans such as Menzel and Chytilová kept working, Menzel with *The Life and Extraordinary Adventures of Private Ivan Chonkin (Život a neobyčejná dobrodružství vojáka Ivana Conkina*, 1994), a comedy of a novice soldier in Russia during World War II. In 1998 Chytilová made *Traps (Pasti, pasti, pastičky*), a black comedy about a woman who is raped and extracts a painful revenge, peppered with jokes at the expense of the male ego, and *Expulsion From Paradise (Vyhnání z ráje*, 2001), a comedy about a film unit trying to make a movie on a nudist beach, which *Variety* considered only 'intermittently funny'.

In 1993 the country split in two, with the formation of the Czech Republic and Slovakia. The best known Slovak director is probably Martin Sulík, whose *The Garden (Záhrada*, 1995) is an allegorical story of a teacher's return to the countryside. Film-making in the Czech Republic has made a strong comeback, with seventeen features released in 2000. Jan Sverák's *Kolya* (1996) is about a grouchy musician who is landed with caring for a small Russian boy. It was a big hit in the West, partly because it articulated Czech resentments over Russian occupation, though its ultimate, slightly sentimental, moral is one of reconciliation. *Divided We Fall (Musíme si pomáhat*, 2000), directed by Jan Hřebejk, is about an unheroic Czech couple who shelter a Jew during the war; in order to prevent a pro-Nazi neighbour being billeted on them, the wife has to get pregnant. Since her husband is sterile the Jew must father the child. Like many of the best Czech films it is by turns farcical and bittersweet. Hřebejk's *Cosy Dens (Pelísky*, 1999) was one of the first films to deal fully with the tragedy of the Prague Spring. *Eeny Meeny (Ene Bene*, 2000), directed by Alice Nellis, is reminiscent of *The Firemen's Ball*, a comedy about a group of civil servants supervising a election. While a student struggles through Joyce's *Ulysses* in between tearful phone-calls to her American academic boyfriend, her mother laments that everyone claims they want democracy to work, but cannot be bothered to take part. *Way Through the Bleak Woods (Cesta pustým lesem*, 1997), directed by Ivan Vojnár, is utterly different. Shot in black and white, it is set in the country, where a city doctor has come to live just before World War I. The narrative is often elliptical, but the woods are dark and deep and the film has a hypnotic power.

Two promising Czech directors are Saša Gedeon and Petr Zelenka. Gedeon's *Indian Summer (Indiánské léto*, 1994) is a slight but deftly-handled story about two girls, Marie worldly, Klára gauche and withdrawn. Mostly shot in an unobtrusive style, it has some oddly surreal touches, as when Klára, after another failed episode with a boy, submerges herself in a bath of floating apples. *Return of the Idiot (Návrat idiota*, 1999) is loosely based on Dostoyevsky; *Time Out* called it 'immaculately acted and controlled'.[2] Zelenka's *Buttoners (Knoflíkáři*, 1997) has six linking stories mining the seam of surrealism that

is never far below the surface of Czech cinema. Zelenka also wrote *Loners* (*Samotáři*, 2000), a delightfully odd look at the loves and lives of Prague youth.

In the context of surrealism, one can hardly leave out Jan Švankmajer, who although beginning with animated shorts has now moved into the production of full-length features which combine live action with a variety of animation techniques, including puppets and clay models. His grotesque and sadistically comic tales, with an undertone of sexual perversity, mark him as a true original; *Little Otik* (*Otesánek*, 2000), about a husband who carves a monstrous child from a tree-trunk, is representative.

In the smaller countries of south-eastern Europe, cinema has always struggled to compete for economic resources. Things were particularly difficult in Romania in the 1970s, with the economy under stress and political power increasingly concentrated in the hands of the dictator Nicolae Ceaușescu. Lucian Pintilie's *The Reconstruction* (*Reconstituirea*, 1969), an allegorical comment on the political situation, though successful abroad, encountered hostility at home and Pintilie went into exile, along with other talented film-makers such as Radu Gabrea, whose *Beyond the Sands* (*Dincolo de nisipuri*, 1973), about an anarchist, also had trouble with the censors. Nevertheless, some films of distinction were made in the 1970s and 1980s, including Alexandru Tatos's *Red Apples* (*Mere rosii*, 1976), about a young doctor struggling against the system in a small town, and Mircea Daneliuc's *Special Issue* (*Editie speciala*, 1978), a war film, and *Microphone Test* (*Proba de microfon*, 1979), a look at the insular world of Romanian television; Daneliuc also starred in both films.

Plenty of genre films, about thirty a year, appeared in Romania, too, with comedies, thrillers and patriotic historical epics (many directed by the veteran Sergiu Nicolaescu, who also starred in some of them) being turned out at the giant Buftea film studios outside Bucharest, in addition to Romanian 'Westerns' shot in Transylvania. The 1989 Revolution, in which Ceaușescu was executed, led to a rapid decline in feature production, which was down to single figures by 1998, as state support withered and competition from commercial

Above: The young doctor is shown the exit in *Red Apples* (*Mere rosii*, 1976). Dir: Alexandru Tatos Below and right: The

grotesque and the comic: surrealism in Švankmajer's live-action film *Little Otik* (*Otesánek*, 2000). Dir: Jan Švankmajer

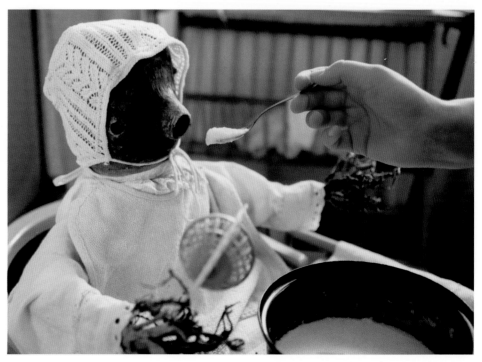

television and foreign film imports grew. However, Pintilie returned to an appointment as Director of Film at the Ministry of Culture and to make a series of films, mostly coproductions such as *The Oak* (*Balanta*, 1992), dramatizing life in the later years of the dictatorship, and *An Unforgettable Summer* (*O Vara de neuitat*, 1994), with Kristin Scott-Thomas as the wife of an army officer caught up in inter-ethnic violence in the 1920s.

In Bulgaria, the formerly rigid censorship relaxed somewhat in the 1970s and a series of films on social issues appeared, including Georgi Dyulgerov's *Advantage* (*Advantazh*, 1977), about a petty crook living on the margins of society; Lyudmil Staykov's *Affection* (*Obitch*, 1972), about contemporary youth; and Hristo Hristov's *The Last Summer* (*Posledno lyato*, 1972), about a villager who refuses to leave his home despite the encroaching waters of a new dam. *The Last Summer* was held up by censors and not released until 1974. Metodi Andonov's *The Goat Horn* (*Koziyat rog*, 1972) was set in the seventeenth century, a tale in

EASTERN EUROPE AND THE FORMER SOVIET UNION

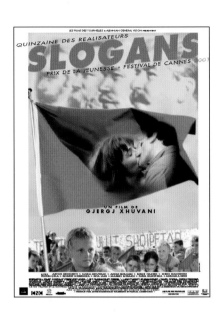

Above: Poster for the
Albanian film set in the
Hoxha era: *Slogans*
(2001).
Dir: Gjergj Xhuvani

Right: Katya Paskaleva
as the avenging
daughter in *The Goat
Horn* (*Koziyat rog*, 1972).
Dir: Metodi Andonov

which a father trains his daughter to kill the men who raped her mother. It proved to be
a huge hit, and was remade in the 1990s, though its director had unfortunately died in an
accident in 1974.

In the early 1980s the government decreed that the film industry commemorate the
anniversary of the founding of Bulgaria, and a series of expensive epics were produced,
including Dyulgerov's *Measure for Measure* (*Mera spored mera*, 1981) and Staykov's *Khan
Asparuh* (*Han Asparuh*, 1981). There was further government direction of film content
in Staykov's *Time of Violence* (*Vreme na nasilie*, 1988). It deals with the enforced conversion
of Bulgarians to Islam during the years of Ottoman rule, and appeared in the middle
of an official campaign to pressurize Muslims in Bulgaria to assimilate. The long-time
Communist leader Todor Zhivkov was overthrown in 1989, but freedom led, as elsewhere,
to state neglect of the cinema, with production falling from about twenty films a year to
a mere handful by the end of the century.

The most backward country in this part of Europe, Albania, did not produce its first
feature film until 1958. Under the repressive Stalinist regime of Enver Hoxha cinema had
to be instrumental in the building of socialism. Many films celebrated Albania's struggle
against Fascism in World War II, with production creeping up to fourteen in 1984. The
following year Hoxha died and the regime grew weaker, until a form of democracy was
established in 1990. Albania's chronic economic instability reduced film production to
a mere five in 1990 and fewer in the following years. Nevertheless, some significant films
have been made that interrogate the legacy of the past, including *Death of the Horse* (*Vdekja e
kalit*, 1992), directed by Saimir Kumbaro; *Colonel Bunker* (1996), directed by Kujtim Çashku;
and more recently *Slogans* (2001), coproduced with France and directed by Gjergj Xhuvani,
a wry comedy set in the late 1970s. Children in a village school spend their time laying out
political slogans on a hillside, while the local party secretary pursues his petty vendettas.
In a moment of black humour, one elderly teacher has to be informed that his slogan so
painstakingly pieced together, 'Vietnam Will Win', is years out of date.

The German Democratic Republic, by contrast, was the richest economy of Eastern
Europe. DEFA, the production and distribution monopoly set up in the German Democratic
Republic after the war, had the advantage of inheriting the giant Babelsberg film studios
which had once housed the Ufa company, producer of so many German classics. Though
East Germany was always one of the most orthodox Communist states, in the mid-1960s
there was something of a thaw in film-making. Subsequently a number of productions,
including *The Rabbit Is Me* (*Das Kaninchen bin ich*, 1965), directed by Kurt Maetzig, and *Just
Don't Think I'm Crying* (*Denk bloss nicht, ich heule*, 1965), directed by Frank Vogel, were singled

out for attack by Erich Honecker, later to become Party leader. The first film was critical of the country's legal system, the second dealt with youth culture. Evidently they touched a raw nerve, for Honecker accused them of propagating 'nihilistic, defeatist and immoral philosophies'. These and other films were banned and their makers' careers put on hold. A few years later, in 1971, Honecker seemed to relent, offering his opinion that 'Providing one starts from an established socialist standpoint, there cannot, in my opinion, be any taboo subjects for art and literature.' But this did not mean what it appeared to. The Party continued to keep film-makers on a tight rein, with the result that in the later 1970s and the 1980s many – actors in particular – voted with their feet and left the country.

Popular comedies, costume dramas and even a series of Westerns shot in the mountains of Yugoslavia all avoided contentious ideological issues. Yet some thoughtful film-makers persisted in the attempt to make honest and interesting films that tried to take account of social reality. Konrad Wolf's *Solo Sunny* (1980) is about a female singer in a band (excellently played by Renate Krössner) who tries to build a career in the face of sexual harassment and betrayal by her lover, a snobbish and self-righteous intellectual. Rejecting the tedium of life in a factory, she struggles against the indifference of audiences and her own self-doubts. The film provides fascinating glimpses of what passed for popular entertainment in the GDR; it also gives a real sense of the difficulties experienced by those who would not fit into the norm. It was widely popular.

Films about contemporary life (*Gegenwartsfilme*) often had women as protagonists, who could be used to represent the private sphere, the world of personal feelings which the official state seemed so often to ignore. In *The Bicycle* (*Das Fahrrad*, 1982), directed by Evelyn Schmidt, one of the few women working at DEFA, Susanne is a single mother with no qualifications and a boring job, struggling to bring up her child. Despite the film having considerable success abroad it was disliked in official quarters. Once again, it seemed, though criticism was fine in theory, in practice the system could not accommodate any works that showed the regime in a poor light. The end of the East German state, symbolized by the pulling down of the Berlin Wall in November 1989, came as a surprise to some film-makers, who thought right up to the end that their leaders could be persuaded that greater tolerance would give the regime legitimacy. But things had gone too far for that.

Of the important film-making countries of Eastern Europe, Yugoslavia at one time appeared to be best placed to develop its cinema. By the end of the century it was the worst. The 1960s had seen a move towards economic decentralization in the so-called self-managing structures of Yugoslav industry. There was also a dispersal of authority and financial resources towards the six separate republics of the Yugoslav state. Production expanded to about thirty features a year, although thanks mainly to the growth of television, cinema admissions fell steadily throughout the 1960s. Political liberalization permitted the emergence of films critical of contemporary society, in a movement subsequently dubbed the 'Black Wave'. The term was at first pejorative, a label attached to films that were accused by the critic Vladimir Jovicic of presenting 'visions of violence, moral degeneracy, misery, lasciviousness and triviality'.[3] Prominent in this grouping was Dušan Makavejev, whose *Switchboard Operator* (*Ljubavni slučaj ili tragedija službenice PTT*, 1967) – a clever mixture of melodrama (the love affair of a telephone worker and a rat catcher) and documentary material, including newsreels and a lecture on sexuality – was a hit on the international art-house circuit. But Makavejev got into trouble with *WR: Mysteries of the Organism* (*WR – Misterije organizma*, 1971), which took his interest in sexuality a stage further by combining a study of the theories of sexologist Wilhelm Reich with extracts from a Stalinist documentary and a love story between an uptight Russian skater and a Yugoslav woman. Makavejev's combination of sexual audacity and impudent disrespect for the Stalinist past was intensely disliked by the authorities, who refused to distribute his film, and Makavejev was forced to move abroad. He continued his explorations of sexual liberation with *Sweet Movie* (1974), made in France and too scandalous to be much seen, and *Montenegro* (1981), made in Sweden, in which Susan

Above: Renate Krössner as the aspiring singer in *Solo Sunny* (1980). Dir: Konrad Wolf
Opposite: Ivica Vidović as Vladimir Ilyich, Jagoda Kaloper as Jagoda and Milena Dravić as Milena engage in dialectics in *WR: Mysteries of the Organism* (*WR – Misterije organizma*, 1971).
Dir: Dušan Makavejev

Anspach, as all Makavejev heroines, searches for sexual fulfilment. But the director's career spluttered fitfully outside his native land.

Despite an increasingly restrictive political and economic climate (production fell to under twenty features a year in the mid-1970s), by the end of the decade a group of directors known as the Prague group (all had been educated at the Czech film school) emerged with films of visual distinction and social bite. Srdjan Karanović, a Serb, directed *Petria's Wreath* (*Petrijin venac*, 1980), a moving portrait of an illiterate peasant woman whom life subjects to a series of tragedies. The Croatian, Lordan Zafranović, made *Occupation in 26 Scenes* (*Okupacija u 26 slika*, 1977), about three friends – a Jew, an Italian and a Croat – living in Dubrovnik during World War II. When the Fascists arrive their idyllic life is torn apart as they are set against each other. In a horrific scene, Ustashi irregulars torture and massacre a bus-load of prisoners while an accordion plays.

Emir Kusturica, in origin a Bosnian, has become the best known of the Prague Group, winning the Palme d'Or at Cannes for *When Father Was Away on Business* (*Otac na službenom putu*, 1985). *Time of the Gypsies* (*Dom za vešanje*, 1989) was widely admired for its unsentimental look at gipsy life, a compelling mixture of comedy and tragedy acted mostly by non-professional Roma. But Kusturica, like all Yugoslav film-makers, was swept

Previous pages and above: Scenes from the saga of Roma life, *Time of the Gypsies* (*Dom za vešanje*, 1989). Dir: Emir Kusturica
Right: Crni (Lazar Ristovski), Natalija (Mirjana Joković) and Marko (Miki Manojlović) get drunk in *Underground* (*Bila jednom jedna zemlja*, 1995). Dir: Emir Kusturica

up in the war that broke out at the beginning of the 1990s. As Yugoslavia disintegrated into its constituent nationalities, people were obliged to take sides or go into exile. Kusturica at first went to the United States, but *Arizona Dream* (1993) was a failure, his quirky, often magical touch in earlier films descending into whimsy. He returned to Belgrade to make *Underground* (*Bila jednom jedna zemlja*, 1995), a sprawling narrative of Yugoslav history from World War II up to the present. Its 'heroes' are a couple of con men, one of whom becomes an important official in Tito's Yugoslavia. Though the film lays bare the deceptions of Communism, it is not at all clear what or whom Kusturica thinks is responsible for the disasters of the 1990s. As Dina Iordanova reports, the director's expressed view is that it was an 'earthquake', the kind of natural disaster to which the Balkans are prone.[4] This of course ignores the political actions of individuals, some of whom are now in prison at The Hague.

Despite *Underground* winning another Palme d'Or, Kusturica was criticized by some for making Serbian propaganda, and his next film, *Black Cat, White Cat* (*Crna macka, beli macor*, 1998), once again set among gipsies, was deliberately non-political. Another film from Serbia was Srdjan Dragojević's *Pretty Villages, Pretty Flame* (*Lepa sela lepo gore*, 1996). A group of Serb soldiers and a female American journalist are besieged in a tunnel by Bosnian forces. Full of black humour, the film certainly does not set out to glorify the Serbs, who include a pickpocket, a junkie, a corrupt *apparatchik* and a ridiculous long-haired nationalist who believes that the Serbs are superior because they invented eating with forks; yet since its effect is inevitably to humanize its protagonists, it too has been accused of taking sides.

No Man's Land (2001), directed by the Bosnian Danis Tanović, is another war story, characteristically avoiding the heroics of the Hollywood war genre. A Serb and two Bosnians are trapped in a trench; one is lying on a mine which will explode if he moves. Again there is plenty of gallows humour, and satire against the international media circus that descends on them, asking the usual ridiculous questions such as 'How do you feel?' *Powder Keg/Cabaret Balkan* (*Bure baruta*, 1998), directed by Goran Paskaljević, another member of the Prague Group, deals, like Dragojević's *Wounds* (*Rane*, 1998), with the society that war had created in Belgrade, a community close to breakdown, in which acts of sudden and arbitrary violence break out even between friends.

Finally, Milcho Manchevski has directed two films set in his native Macedonia. *Before the Rain* (*Pred dozhdot*, 1994) is a beautifully shot story of an expatriate Macedonian photographer, based in London, who returns home and is caught up in the age-old cycle of ethnic violence. In *Dust* (2002), two cowboys from the American Wild West take part in the Macedonian struggle for independence against the Turks. The film has an ingenious narrative structure, but the historical scenes are given little political context. Violence against someone or other, it seems, is the Balkan way – or was. The slow return to political stability in the territory of the former Yugoslavia at last offers some hope that its talented film-makers will have a better climate in which to practise.

Above: Rade Serbedzija as the Macedonian photographer Aleksandar and Katrin Cartlidge as his lover Anne in *Before the Rain* (*Pred dozhdot*, 1994). This was the first film to be produced in the newly formed Republic of Macedonia. Dir: Milcho Manchevski

14.   **The Middle East and the Muslim World**

Break the windows so that the birds can set themselves free.

Provisional title for the film *The Way* (*Yol*, Şerif Gören, 1982)

Previous pages: Actors
Tarik Akan and Şerif
Sezer struggle
through the snow in
an epic scene from
the Turkish film *The
Way* (*Yol*, 1982). The
film, about a group
of prisoners allowed
home on leave, was
written by Yilmaz
Güney while in
prison. Güney was
subsequently granted
leave and did not
return.

Dir: Şerif Gören
Below: Ahmed Marei
as Wanis in *The
Mummy: The Night of
Counting the Years*
(*al-Mumya'*, 1969).
Dir: Chadi Abdessalam
Bottom: A poster from
the first of Youssef
Chahine's
autobiographical
trilogy *Alexandria,
Why?* (*Iskindiriyya,
Lih?*, 1978).
Dir: Youssef Chahine

A geographical area that ranges from Morocco's Atlantic coast to the border of Pakistan spans not only several thousand miles but many different contexts for cinema. What the countries in this chapter most evidently have in common, with the single exception of Israel, is the religion of Islam. Yet, as the West is slowly coming to realize, Islam is not a monolithic culture, but contains within itself separate, sometimes conflicting traditions. Nor do these countries comprise the whole of Islam; the most populous Islamic nation is in fact Indonesia, while black Africa and India also contain sizeable Muslim populations.

Nevertheless, this region has been at times profoundly marked by religion; or, to be more precise, by the politicization of religion. At its most extreme, as under the Taliban regime in Afghanistan, cinema has been proscribed altogether on the grounds that the Koran forbids making images of humans and animals. Saudi Arabia, too, forbids public performances. Though this interpretation is a minority view, it is true that the visual arts within Islam have been mainly decorative rather than representational, so that cinema does not grow organically out of a visual artistic tradition, even if it draws on music and literature. Yet across the region films have been made, often in considerable numbers, if rarely without obstacles.

Three countries – Egypt, Iran and Turkey – are large enough to have had a viable popular cinema, though, as elsewhere, it increasingly suffers from competition from Hollywood and television. The smaller countries are obliged to offer their film industries state support if they are to survive at all. This generally results in a socially conscious cinema, often – as elsewhere in the Third World – following a neo-realist style, shooting on location, telling stories of ordinary life, sometimes with non-professional actors. In some cases, however, notably Iran, a more sophisticated style has emerged.

In a region where democratic regimes are the exception, both popular and art cinema are obliged to keep one eye on the censors. But this need not result in dull conformity to a restricted set of social prescriptions. In particular, it is surprising, given Islam's reputation in the West regarding the emancipation of women, how many films put women at centre stage, and indeed how many women directors in the region have achieved prominence.

Egypt has always been the powerhouse of Arab cinema. By the end of the last century it had produced nearly 3,000 features, mostly within popular genres such as the melodrama, comedy (with the ever-popular star 'Adil Iman), various kinds of thrillers, and especially musicals starring a series of redoubtable women singers and belly dancers such as Tahiya Caricoca. From early days its films were exported all around the Middle East, with the result that the Egyptian form of colloquial Arabic became a kind of cinematic lingua franca. Following the abolition of the monarchy in the 1950s Egypt became a socialist state and the cinema was taken into public ownership. Production then entered a slow decline, and by the time the Sadat government began to dismantle the structures of state ownership in 1971 the General Film Organization was deeply in debt. Much of the technical infrastructure remained under public control even though private companies were increasingly responsible for production.

In recent years, Egypt's export market has been affected by political and technological developments. The *rapprochement* with Israel led to a ban on Egyptian films in Syria, for example, and the Gulf War in the early 1990s also affected its markets. The growth of satellite television led to a further decline, and Egyptian cinema has been slow to take advantage of this new distribution system. In addition, Egyptian cinema has found itself under increasing pressure to conform to the prudish requirements of some of its foreign markets, and to Islamic fundamentalism at home. The number of Egyptian films released for public screenings fell from seventy in 1992 to a low of sixteen in 1997. However, investment in infrastructure increased in the late 1990s and thirty-one films were released in 2000. Despite continuing problems with fundamentalist groups, some courageous films have been made, including Magdy Ahmad Ali's *A Girl's Secret* (*Asrar El-Banaat*, 2000), in which an unmarried schoolgirl gives birth in the bathroom, to the consternation of her parents. Taken to hospital, she is then circumcized by a zealous Muslim doctor.

In earlier years, a more committed and socially conscious cinema was largely overshadowed by the popular star- and genre-based cinema, until the rise of the so-called New Realism in the early 1980s, often working within traditional forms such as the gangster movie but preferring to shoot on the streets rather than in the studio, and dealing with the materialism, corruption, social dislocation and abuse of power that were seen as symptomatic of the Sadat regime. Typical of this type of production is *People from the Top* (*Ahl al-Qumma*, 1981), directed by 'Ali Badrakham, about a policeman caught up in a world of sharp practice and fraud.

One of the landmarks of auteur cinema in Egypt is *The Mummy: The Night of Counting the Years* (*al-Mumya'*, 1969), the only feature directed by Chadi Abdessalam, who had a successful career as a production designer, including working on the Hollywood spectacular *Cleopatra* (Joseph L Mankiewicz, 1963). Set near Thebes in the 1880s, *The Mummy* is a work of stately pace and monumental visual style. Wanis discovers that his tribe make their living robbing the nearby tombs of the pharaohs. He tries to balance his people's need for money against the immorality of looting their historical inheritance. The allegorical significance is clear, but not banally schematic. Unfortunately, the film found only a small audience and Abdessalam was never able to get finance for a second proposed feature on the pharaoh Akhenaton.

By far the most celebrated of Egyptian auteurs is Youssef Chahine, who began directing in 1950 but is still active. In his early career he worked in many of the popular genres, including comedies, thrillers, melodramas and even a historical epic, *The Victorious Saladin* (*al-Nasir Salah al-Din*, 1963), about the great Muslim leader of the twelfth century. *The Sparrow* (*Al-'Usfur*, 1973) is set during the Six Day War of 1967; a police officer discovers mounting corruption in the armaments industry. In the late 1970s Chahine's films display an increasing stylistic sophistication, especially in the autobiographical trilogy *Alexandria, Why?* (*Iskindiriyya, Lih?*, 1978), *An Egyptian Fairy Tale* (*Hadduta Misriyya*, 1982) and *Alexandria Now and Forever* (*Iskindiriyya Kaman Wa Kaman*, 1990). In the last, Chahine himself plays a veteran film director whose favourite male star has abandoned his production of *Hamlet* for a more lucrative role in a TV soap opera. The film contains some hilarious historical sequences in a life of Alexander conjured up in the imagination of the director, intercut with scenes of a strike by film-workers and the director's memories of happier times winning an award at an international film festival (after which director and star dance in the street à la Gene Kelly to the music of Nat King Cole singing 'Walking My Baby Back Home').

Chahine's *The Emigré* (*al-Muhaji*, 1994) is, like many of his later works, a coproduction, using European money. Not for the first time, he had censorship problems. Fundamentalists

objected that the story of Ram – based on the Biblical Joseph and Koranic Yusuf, who leaves the land of his birth and journeys to ancient Egypt in search of agricultural knowledge – infringed prohibitions against the representation of the prophets. It is a work of considerable narrative and thematic complexity, raising issues of national identity and religion as Ram achieves rank and influence in his adopted land but becomes embroiled in religious and political struggles, as well as being torn emotionally between Shemit, the wife of the Egyptian commander, and Hati, a peasant girl.

Chahine's films have been celebrated around the world and he received a lifetime achievement award at the 1997 Cannes Film Festival. Despite their visual and narrative sophistication, his films have never lost the love for music, spectacle and comedy which root them in Egyptian popular cinema. *Silence, We're Rolling* (*Sukut hansawwar*, 2001) is a jolly comedy set in the film world in which the story of a con man's seduction of an ageing movie star contains many subtle digs at the vanities and absurdities of showbiz.

Elsewhere in North Africa, all three countries of the Maghreb – Algeria, Morocco and Tunisia – were marked by their experience of French occupation, but cinema has been variously affected by their differing histories since independence. In Algeria, the 1970s saw mostly dramatizations of pre-colonial oppression and of the long and bitter war against the French. An ambitious film on this theme was *Chronicle of the Years of Embers* (*Waqai Sanawat al-Jamr*, Mohamed Lakhdar Hamina, 1975), a visually impressive epic of the struggles of the 1940s and 1950s. *The Charcoal Burner* (*al-Faham*, Mohamed Bouamari, 1972) is a typical third-world story, about a charcoal burner whose profession is overtaken by new technology and who migrates to the city in search of work. Merzak Allouache's *Omar Qatlato* (*Umar Gatlatu*, 1976) was a break from this tradition, exploring instead the sexual frustrations of a young office worker. Finding the voice of a young woman on his cassette recorder, he obsessively tracks her down, but at the crucial moment cannot summon up the courage to speak to her.

Algerian film production continued at the rate of about three or four films a year until the mid-1990s. In 1993 the nationalized film industry was privatized, but this experiment was rendered void by the catastrophe which overtook the country as the confrontation between the secular authorities and Islamic militants escalated into horrifying violence. Since then Algerian cinema has all but collapsed, with many of its most talented film-makers, including Allouache, retreating into exile.

Though Tunisia had a less traumatic experience of liberation from French colonial rule, which was achieved in 1955, production has been low, with no more than one or two films in some years, although occasionally more. In the 1970s the government attempted to monopolize both production and exhibition. But by the 1980s the state film organizations were virtually bankrupt. A more pragmatic approach was instituted, leading to a greater emphasis on independent producers and on coproductions with other countries, mainly European, with some financial support from the state. Work of genuine quality began to emerge. Among the best known of Tunisian directors is Férid Boughedir, who has also written extensively and made documentaries about African and Arab cinema. In *Halfaouine* (*Halfawin 'Usfur Stah*, 1990) a young boy, Noura, is taken frequently to the public baths by his mother. His growing interest in women's bodies results in his eventual ejection from a feminine milieu, in which he has hitherto felt comfortable, into the unaccustomed realities of a man's world. Surprisingly frank in its depiction of sexuality (eavesdropping on a group of women as they make ribald jokes about cucumbers), the film offers a stylish and attractive take on the rigid sexual divide of Arab society, and was a considerable hit in its country of origin.

Man of Ashes (*Rih al-Sad*, 1986), directed by Nouri Bouzid, also centres on sexuality. Hachemi, a young carpenter, is getting married, but reluctantly. It emerges that he has been abused as a young boy by Ameur, to whom he had been apprenticed. Unable to articulate his trauma, he is beaten by his exasperated father. On the eve of the wedding his friends take him to a brothel, where a prostitute dresses as a bride, but Hachemi is

Above: Hachemi as a young boy in a flashback scene from *Man of Ashes* (*Rih al-Sad*, 1986).
Above right: Khaled Ksouri (centre) as Farafat, Hachemi's friend and a fellow victim of abuse in *Man of Ashes* (*Rih al-Sad*, 1986).
Dir: Nouri Bouzid
Right: Selim Boughedir as Noura, at the baths with his mother (Rabia Ben Abdallah) in *Halfaouine* (*Halfawin 'Usfur Stah*, 1990).
Dir: Férid Boughedir

unable to have sex with her. Hachemi's glum inarticulateness makes the film heavy-going at times, but undeniably it provides powerful insights into the male psyche in a predominantly patriarchal society.

Tunisia's foremost woman director, Moufida Tlatli, was the editor of such films as *Omar Qatlato* and *Halfaouine* before directing *The Silences of the Palace* (*Samt al-Qusur*, 1994). Alia remembers her life as the illegitimate daughter of Khedija, who was sold to the rulers of Tunisia by her parents. The film creates an intense and vivid sense of life in the enclosed world of the palace in colonial times. When the French impose a curfew, one woman responds that her life is a curfew anyway; she wants to run in the street but is unable to. Now, Alia has achieved a measure of independence as a singer, but being pregnant she is being pressured by her boyfriend to have an abortion. Women have still not found their voice. Tlati's second feature, *Season of Men* (*Mawsim al-Rijal*, 1999), is another study of women's domestic lives told in flashback. Aicha, separated from her husband, remembers her life as a carpet weaver; her autistic son Aziz has become a carpet weaver too, finding a role within what is traditionally a female occupation. In Tlati's films women make a space for themselves, but only within limits ultimately defined by men. By contrast, *Fatma* (2001), directed by a man, Khaled Ghorbal, is more radical: the heroine refuses to accept her lot. Raped by her cousin, she undergoes an operation to restore her virginity in order to marry an apparently modern-minded doctor. But when he finds out her deception he runs home to mother, who advises divorce. Fatma asks if he would have married her had she been honest with him; when he replies he does not know, she walks out on him. It is a slow, rather stolid film which nevertheless makes a powerful protest against dictatorial patriarchy.

Feature film-making did not begin in Morocco until 1968. Since then around seventy films have been made. Production received a considerable stimulus in 1980 when the government introduced a state support system, with around fifteen films made since 1999. As elsewhere, the contrast between urban and rural life has offered a major theme, as for example in Ahmed al-Maanouni's film *The Days, the Days!* (*al-Ayyam, al-Ayyam*, 1978), about a young peasant who wants to emigrate, and Mohammed Abderrahman Tazi's *The Big Trip* (*Ibn al-Sabil*, 1981), in which a lorry driver undertaking a trip to Casablanca also decides to emigrate, with disastrous consequences.

Much Moroccan film-making has been achieved in a realist style, dealing with social issues of pressing importance. The position of women was notably explored in *Reed Dolls* (*'Ara'is Min Qasab*, 1981), directed by Jillali Ferhati. Aicha is married very young to her cousin. When he dies she rejects the advances of her brother-in-law and instead becomes pregnant by her employer. In revenge the brother-in-law, who has inherited most of her husband's property, has her brought before a court, which takes her children away. Despite attempts to rebuild her life, at the end Aicha is left disconsolate by her husband's grave. The film adopts an uncompromising position. 'We're lost as soon as we cross the threshold,' says one woman, deploring the lack of freedom outside the home. But Western customs are not necessarily the answer. When Aicha envies the life of Spanish women of the city (presumably Ceuta), her mother-in-law, a sympathetic character, calls them promiscuous. The film is scripted by Ferhati's former wife, Farida Benlyazid, who directed *Gateway to Heaven* (*Bab al-Sama' Maftuh*, 1987), in which a young Moroccan woman living in France returns home and rediscovers her Islamic roots.

One of the younger Moroccan directors is Nabil Ayouch, born and educated in Paris. His first feature, *Maktub* (1997), was a thriller about an Arab-American doctor whose wife is kidnapped in Tangier. It was a big hit at the Moroccan box office and won the prize for best Arab film at the 1997 Cairo Film Festival. His next film, *'Ali Zawa* (2000), was a story

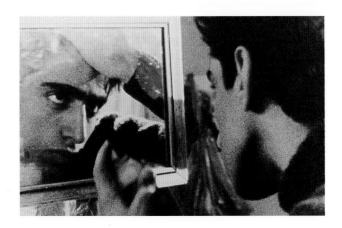

of street children in Casablanca which combines social realism (not avoiding the question of sexual abuse) with a strain of mystical symbolism initiated in Hamid Benani's *Traces* (*Washma*, 1970), an earlier story of delinquents.

In the 1970s Turkish cinema was booming, with production up to no fewer than 298 films in 1972. Turkish popular cinema was genre- and star-based, churning out melodramas, comedies, historical adventures and crime films starring tough-guy heroes such as Cüneyt Arkin. In *Karamurat, the Sultan's Warrior* (*Karamurat*, 1973) Arkin leads the Turks against a brutal Hungarian Christian leader who personally chops off the heads of Turks who refuse to convert. At the end of the decade the advent of television and severe social unrest in Turkey caused the mass audience to desert film theatres for video viewing at home. Many cinemas closed. Turkish cinema declined rapidly and Yesilçam (as popular cinema was designated, after the street in Istanbul where its main companies were based) turned to the production of cheap sex films, of which 131 were made in 1979, with the actress Zerrim Egeliler disrobing in no fewer than thirty-seven of them.

Despite strict censorship, a form of art cinema emerged in Turkey as popular cinema declined, interrogating the role of women and minorities, and exploring migration to the cities and abroad as a major theme, as in Lütfi Ömer Akad's *The Bride* (*Gelin*, 1973), in which a move to the city leads to the death of a child and the disintegration of a family. Other notable directors of this more personal cinema include Erden Kiral, whose *A Season in Hakkari* (*Hakkari' de Bir Mevsim*, 1982), about a school teacher in a small village, won a prize at the Berlin Film Festival. Also a winner at Berlin was Yeşim Ustaoğlu, a woman director whose *Journey to the Sun* (*Güneşe Yolculuk*, 1999) is a heart-rending story about a Turk who befriends a Kurd, gets mistaken for a terrorist by the police, loses his job, and ends up taking the body of his friend back to his village for burial only to discover it abandoned.

Undoubtedly the major figure of Turkish cinema is Yilmaz Güney, who had a foot in both the popular and art cinema camps. Originally he made his name as an actor in low-

Above: Newroz Baz as Mehmet in *Journey to the Sun* (*Güneşe Yolculuk*, 1999). Dir: Yeşim Ustaoğlu
Below: Turkish director Yilmaz Güney.
Below right: Captured by the army: a scene from *The Way* (*Yol*, 1982). But as the five prisoners on leave soon find out, the outside world can be as brutal and restrictive as life in prison. Dir: Şerif Gören

budget action films, turning to directing in the late 1960s, by which time his left-wing sympathies had already led to spells in jail. Films such as *Hope* (*Umut*, 1970), *The Father* (*Baba*, 1971) and *The Friend* (*Arkadaş*, 1974) all drew on Güney's sympathy for the underdog fighting a corrupt and oppressive system, whether in the harsh landscape of Anatolia or in city slums. In 1974 he was convicted of the murder of a judge and sentenced to a further eighteen years in jail. While in prison Güney managed to continue his film career, scripting *The Herd* (*Sürü*, 1978), a story of Anatolian shepherds directed by Zeki Ökten, who also directed Güney's script of *The Enemy* (*Düşman*, 1979). Güney's best-known film is *The Way* (*Yol*, 1982), directed from his script by Şerif Gören. It follows five prisoners on leave, as they each in their different ways discover that iron bars are not the only kind of prison. It contains some extraordinarily affecting moments, as when Mehmet, on the run with his wife from her family, who hold him responsible for their son's death in a robbery, desperately seeks a moment of comfort by having sex with his wife in the toilet of a train.

Discovered by one of the passengers, the wretched couple are publicly humiliated. Like the subjects of his film Güney took leave from jail but never returned and died in exile in France at the age of forty-seven in 1984. He is buried in Paris's Père Lachaise cemetery, his grave marked with a striking chrome-plated steel structure.

The phenomenal box office success of Yavuz Turgul's *The Bandit* (*Eşkiya*, 1997), an action film in which an ageing bandit released from jail finds himself disconcerted by modern life, led to hopes that Turkish popular cinema might revive. But with only fifteen films made in 2000, the industry is a shadow of its former self. Meanwhile, some Turks have taken advantage of European coproduction finance: for example, Ferzan Özpetek, whose *The Turkish Bath* (*Hamam*, 1997) is about an Italian who inherits a traditional Turkish bath in Istanbul and is drawn into the life of the city. Özpetek, now based in Rome, subsequently directed *Le fati ignoranti* (2002), in which a woman discovers that her dead husband was engaged in a homosexual affair. In Germany the large Turkish community is beginning to throw up some interesting work, such as Kutluğ Ataman's *Lola und Bilidikid* (1999), in which a young man uncertain of his sexuality gets taken up by Lola, a transvestite performer in Berlin. As Turkey seeks to draw closer to Europe by pursuing its application to join the European Union, its cinema may be expected to develop its multicultural concerns.

The countries to the south of Turkey have been in the forefront of the conflicts that have racked the Middle East. Not surprisingly, film-making has been difficult. In the Lebanon, Baalbek Studios was from the mid-1950s an important centre of production for Egyptian and other films. The civil war which broke out between Christians and Muslims in the

Above: Walking to freedom in *The Bandit* (*Eşkiya*, 1997).
Dir: Yavuz Turgul
Above right: Rami Doueiri and Mohamad Chamas as the two Muslim boys in *West Beirut* (1998).

Dir: Ziad Doueiri
Below: Family tensions, love and sacrifice are all explored in *Sacrifices* (*Sunduq al-Dunya*, 2002).
Dir: Oussama Mohammad

1970s and which later led to intervention by Syria and Israel severely disrupted cinema production and exhibition. Directors such as Maroun Baghdadi moved abroad; his film *Outside Life* (*Kharij al-Hayat*, 1991) is the story of a French journalist kidnapped in Beirut and was filmed partly in Italy and France. In *West Beirut* (1998), directed by Ziad Doueiri, two teenage Muslim boys form a friendship with a Christian girl as war breaks out. Youthful high jinks combine with the growing dislocation of their families. Lebanese films are rare events, but *When Mariam Spoke Out* (*Lamma hikyit Maryam*, 2002), a film about a young couple's difficulties in conceiving a child, directed by Assad Fouladkar, was shown at the 2002 London Film Festival and may be a sign of things to come.

Syria, too, had a film at the LFF in 2002: *Sacrifices* (*Sunduq al-Dunya*, 2002), the second feature by Oussama Mohammad. During the Cold War, Syria was closely aligned with the Soviet bloc and its film industry was rigidly controlled by the state. Production is currently no more than three or four films a year. As in many authoritarian regimes with multiple levels of regulation, films may get made but not released. Such was the fate of *Daily Life in a Syrian Village* (*al-Hayat al-Yaumiyya fi Qarya Suriyya*, 1974), a gritty picture of village life conveyed with a documentary realism that apparently told too many home truths for the censors. Yet despite economic and political obstacles, a kind of auteur cinema has emerged in Syria, typified by Mohammed Malass. His *Dreams of the City* (*Ahlam al-Medina*, 1984) is a semi-autobiographical story of a young boy growing up in Damascus against the background of Nasser's nationalization of the Suez Canal. History is also the backdrop to Malass's *The Night* (*al-Layl*, 1991). Set in Kuneitra, it traces events from 1936 to the period following Syria's independence from France, with the fate of Palestine constantly

THE MIDDLE EAST AND THE MUSLIM WORLD

intruding. The narrative is highly fractured, weaving together past and present in its story of a young boy and his parents' battles against a dictatorial grandfather.

For a brief moment at the end of the 1970s Iraq seemed to have a chance of becoming a major player in Arab cinema, with films such as *The Walls* (*Al-Asuar*, 1979), directed by Mohamed Shukri Jameel, about three students and their differing political responses to the monarchy that ruled Iraq until 1958. But the war with Iran which broke out in 1980 overwhelmed any chance of serious films. Instead, cinema was put at the service of the war with pompous epics such as *al-Qadissiyah* (Salah Abu Seif, 1982), about the battle in AD 636 between the Arabs and the Persian king Yazdigird, one of the most expensive Arab films ever made; and *The Big Question* (*al-Mas'ala al-Kubra*, Mohamed Shukri Jameel, 1983), about the rebellion against the British in the 1920s, which co-starred the British actor Oliver Reed. Iraq's economic and political situation since the Gulf War has inevitably had a damaging effect on its cinema.

If in a sense all films are political, Israeli films are liable to be more political than most, unable to avoid a commentary on Israel's condition of permanent conflict. In the 1970s, however, Israeli cinema moved away from naively nationalist films, in particular taking notice of the Sephardi Jews of eastern extraction, who up until then had been dominated in Israel by the Ashkenazi Jews from Europe. Films such as *Light out of Nowhere* (*Or Min Hahefker*, Nissim Dayan, 1973) painted a grim picture of urban deprivation in a grainy neo-realist style. Following Israel's 1973 war against its neighbours and a move to the right in Israeli politics, the cinema felt emboldened to mount a critique of the Zionist project, buttressed after 1979 by the finance made available by the Fund for the Promotion of Israeli Quality Films. *Paratroopers* (*Massa Alunkot*, Yehuda Ne'eman, 1977) and *Wooden Gun* (*Roveh Chuliot*, Ilan Moshenson, 1979) were forcefully anti-militaristic. In *On a Narrow Bridge* (*Gesher Tsar Me'od*, 1985), directed by Nissim Dayan, a member of the occupying Israeli forces in the West Bank falls in love with a Palestinian woman. Another dramatization of the Israeli–Palestinian conflict is *Smile of the Lamb* (*Chyuch Hagdi*, Shimon Dotan, 1986), which explores the relationship between an army doctor and an elderly Arab. Such films gained Israeli cinema prestige abroad, even if they did not always do well at the box office. More popular was *Beyond the Walls* (*Me'achorei Hasoragim*, 1984), a prison drama directed by Uri Barabash in which an Israeli criminal joins forces with a Palestinian political prisoner against sadistic prison authorities.

More recently some film-makers have attempted to move away from direct engagement with politics, concentrating instead on the perennial themes of art cinema such as the frustrations of youth. *Tel Aviv Stories* (*Sipurei Tel-Aviv*, Ayelet Menahemi/Nirit Yaron, 1992) recounts three tales of contemporary young women in the city. Nor is all Israeli cinema high-minded. *Lemon Popsicle* (*Eskimo Limon*, Boaz Davidson, 1978), a teenage sex comedy, did record business both at home and abroad, developing into a long-running series and propelling its producers, Menahem Golan and Yoram Globus, to Hollywood.

Right: A titillating moment: Huey (Zachi Noy), Nikki (Anat Atzmon) and Bobby (Jonathan Sagall) in *Lemon Popsicle* (*Eskimo Limon*, 1978). Dir: Boaz Davidson

Perhaps Israel's only director of international status is Amos Gitai, who began as a documentarist but has now directed several feature films that have achieved success abroad. In *Kadosh* (1999) two sisters, Rivka and Malka, struggle against the suffocating constrictions of ultra-orthodox Judaism. Malka has sex with her boyfriend before undertaking an arranged marriage with a man she does not love and who later beats her; Rivka's husband Meir is forced by the rabbi to divorce her because they are childless and the faith needs to expand its numbers, even though it is Meir who is subsequently proved infertile. Eventually Malka runs away, telling her sister there is a big world outside the narrow confines of their enclave. It is a film which exposes the harshness of orthodox patriarchy without resorting to caricature. A new art cinema may be emerging in Israel, judging by Gitai's films and from Dover Kosashivili's acerbic *Late Marriage* (*Hatouna Mehuheret*, 2001), which explores somewhat similar territory to *Kadosh*.

The difficulties of making cinema in Palestine can readily be imagined. On top of the usual problems of production finance and the lack of adequate distribution comes the fact that the Palestinian people have been in a constant struggle for national identity and even existence. Most of the films that have been made are, not surprisingly, documentaries designed to further their cause. In both fiction and non-fiction the revolutionary male hero has been the focus, with as little nuance and complexity in the representation of masculine certainties as in the portrayal of the conflict with Israel. All of which makes Michel Khleifi's *Wedding in Galilee* (*'Urs al-Jalil*, 1987) all the more remarkable. In order to celebrate his son's wedding during the curfew, a father must obtain permission from the occupying Israeli forces. The condition is that the Israelis be invited. He accepts this despite objections from his family and friends. At the wedding a female Israeli soldier faints. She is looked after by the women of the family; she awakes to find herself in a feminized interior, her uniform replaced with a brightly coloured Arab dress. An old man provides comic moments in his confused memories of former occupiers, the Turks and the British. Two boys let the father's prize stallion escape into a minefield; the Israelis have to help negotiate a route out. Most significantly, the bridegroom cannot accept the authoritarianism of his father, which ultimately renders him impotent at the moment of consummation. In a scene of powerful symbolic significance, the bride takes matters into her own hands and deflowers herself lest the son be shamed. It is a film of assured style and considerable complexity, which has so far found few imitators, though *Rana's Wedding* (*al Quds fi Yaum Akhar*, 2002), a coproduction with the Netherlands directed by Hany Abu-Assad, may indicate that a Palestinian cinema is emerging against all odds.

Despite Iran having fought a disastrous war with Iraq in the 1980s, Iranian cinema has prospered. Before the fall of the Shah in 1979, the film industry in Iran had been mainly a commercial affair, turning out large numbers of 'tough-guy' films in which stars such as Mohammad Ali Fardin battled against the gangsters of the urban jungle. But there were signs of an art cinema movement in *The Cow* (*Gav*, 1969), directed by Dariush Mehrjui, a story about a poor peasant and the death of his cow, his only source of livelihood. Things looked bleak for cinema when the Islamic government took control. Many cinemas were burned in early outbursts of revolutionary fervour, the import of foreign films was severely restricted, there was a purge of film-makers and a rigorous censorship was imposed. Even today, Iran has only 315 cinemas for a population of nearly 70 million.

Given this inauspicious beginning, it is remarkable that between 1980 and 1998 a total of 851 films were made in Iran, and that Iranian cinema today has an international prestige that is second to none. This is of course entirely due to its art films, but like most industries of any size there is both a popular and an elite sector of production. Strictly speaking there are three domains, since there is also a kind of official cinema, charged with making films about the war with Iraq and other approved subjects.

The art cinema, which comprises about ten per cent of total output in Iran, has evolved as a cinema of auteurs whose unique vision gives the films their special quality. Censorship is never welcomed by film-makers, but in certain circumstances (one thinks of Poland under Communism, for example) the result can be a cinema rich in symbolic meaning, a cinema which does not directly challenge the regime but which points to ironies and absurdities. Thus *A Taste of Cherry* (*Ta'm-e Gilas*, 1997), directed by Abbas Kiarostami, one of Iran's foremost directors, is ostensibly about a middle-aged man's search for someone to assist his suicide (an act forbidden to Muslims). But the subtext can be read as a commentary on the nature of male friendship, a subject even more taboo.

Kiarostami's early films draw, like many in the underdeveloped world, on the aesthetics of neo-realism. Filming is on location, with little or no studio work, lighting is naturalistic, camera movements are simple, the actors are mainly non-professionals and the stories are drawn from everyday life. As often in Iranian films, children are at the centre, standing for optimism and innocence in a harsh world. In *Where Is My Friend's House?* (*Khaneh-ye Doust Kojast?*, 1986) a young boy has to return a schoolbook to his friend, who otherwise faces punishment. An old man recounts how his father gave him a penny every week and a beating every fortnight; sometimes he forgot the penny, but never the beating. Kiarostami's films have increasingly taken on an intriguingly self-reflective dimension. In *And Life Goes On* (*Zendegi Va Digar Hich*, 1991) the director (played by an actor) of *Where Is My Friend's House?* goes back to the region where it was shot after it has been hit by an earthquake. The film is both a document of ordinary people's courage in the face of disaster and also a subtle commentary on a film-maker's relationship with his material. In *Through the Olive Trees* (*Zir-e Darakhtan-e Zaitun*, 1994) the commentary is further elaborated, as the director of *And Life Goes On* (played by Mohammed Ali Keshavarz) now reconstructs the making of his film. In Kiarostami's *Close-Up* (*Kelosup, Nama-ye Nazdik*, 1989) an obsessive movie fan, playing himself in real life, pretends to be the Iranian director Mohsen Makhmalbaf. In *The Wind Will Carry Us* (*Bad Ma Ra Khahad Bord*, 1999) a director goes to a remote village to film the mourning ceremony for an old woman. By the time she actually dies the crew have been recalled to Tehran. The film *10* (2002) is a stylistic tour de force, consisting of ten sequences shot in a car as a woman drives it around Tehran. Minimalist in technique, it says much about contemporary Iran while seeming to say very little.

Kiarostami's films are punctuated by philosophical and religious enigmas, such as the meaning of earthquakes. Are they sent by God, asks the director's son? If not, why do they happen? Mohsen Makhmalbaf began as a strictly Islamic film-maker, but he too has moved to question the certainties of the official line. *Marriage of the Blessed* (*Arusi-ye Khuban*, 1989) is the story of a shell-shocked photographer who returns from the war with Iraq and whose photographs of the seamier side of urban life are then rejected by his newspaper. Makhmalbaf's recent film *Kandahar* (*Safar e Ghandehar*, 2001) reconstructs the journey

Above top: Babek Ahmed Poor as Ahmed in *Where Is My Friend's House?* (*Khaneh-ye Doust Kojast?*, 1986). Dir: Abbas Kiarostami
Above: The remote village in the mountains visited by the camera crew in *The Wind Will Carry Us* (*Bad Ma Ra Khahad Bord*, 1999). Dir: Abbas Kiarostami

TABIB SAHID: What can I do for you?
NAFAS: I don't know. Maybe you can say something for my sister. You can say something about life, about hope for her.
TABIB SAHID: About hope? Hope? You know a person needs a reason for living, and in difficult circumstances, hope is never easy. Of course it's abstract but for the thirsty it's water; for the hungry it's bread; for the lonely it's love; for a woman living under full cover hope is the day she will be seen.

Tabib Sahid (Hassan Tantai), Nafas (Nelofer Pazira), *Kandahar* (*Safar e Ghandehar*, Mohsen Makhmalbaf, 2001)

A Woman's Story of Our Time

Kandahar
(Safar e Ghandehar, 2001)
Dir: Mohsen Makhmalbaf

Kandahar's great success with audiences was in part due to the timing of its release, at a moment when Afghanistan had been catapulted into the headlines by the activities of the Taliban and the attacks of 11 September 2001. But the film, directed by one of Iran's most prominent film artists, is much more than a story plucked from the headlines. It stars Nelofer Pazira, an Afghan woman based in Canada, playing Nafas, who is trying to get into Afghanistan to reach her sister who lives in Kandahar. Nafas's sister is threatening suicide because of the intolerable oppression of women by the Taliban. Like many films from Muslim countries, *Kandahar* is vitally concerned with female emancipation.

In the course of her long and dangerous journey, Nafas encounters a mixed array of Afghan people, many of them refugees. An old man agrees to take her into the country disguised as his fourth wife. Later she acquires a young boy, Khak (Sadou Teymouri), as her guide after he has been expelled from a religious school. On the way she meets Tabib Sahid, an African-American who had come to fight the Soviets but who is now practising medicine. (The actor playing this role, Hassan Tantai, was later accused of committing the murder in the United States of an Iranian opposed to the regime of Ayatollah Khomeini.)

Kandahar mixes documentary authenticity with extraordinary moments of visual strangeness and beauty. At one point an aircraft drops sets of artificial limbs from the sky and amputees rush out to collect them. The burka is an ever-present symbol of women's subjugation, yet underneath women wear varnished nails and lipstick, and their brightly-coloured robes affirm their individuality. At the end, ominously, Nafas is detained by the Taliban. Widely recognized at the major European film festivals, *Kandahar* placed the suffering of the Afghan people, particularly the women, on an international stage.

Country of Origin: Iran
Running Time: 84 mins

Production Company: Makhmalbaf Film House
Producer: Mohsen Makhmalbaf
Writer: Mohsen Makhmalbaf
Photography: Ebrahim Ghafouri
Editor: Mohsen Makhmalbaf
Set Designer: Akbar Meshkini
Music: Mohammad Reza Darvishi

Nafas: Nelofer Pazira
Tabib Sahid: Hassan Tantai
Khak: Sadou Teymouri
Hayat: Hayatalah Hakimi

Left: The restrictions placed upon the Afghan women in particular is yet another reason to condemn the Taliban regime. Yet the film asserts that the strength of this sisterhood can overcome patriarchal repression.

Above top: Amputees rush out into the desert to pick up artificial limbs dropped by a helicopter.
Above: Hassan Tantai as Tabib Sahid, a doctor with whom Nafas is obliged to communicate from behind a screen.

Above: The oppression of a male-controlled society where a simple telephone call is scrutinized in *The Circle* (*Dayereh*, 2000). Dir: Jafar Panahi

back into Taliban-controlled Afghanistan by a Canadian-based Afghan woman. Its narrative of a grim and dangerous trek is shot through with strange, even surreal images, such as a parachute drop of artificial limbs, a parade of dazzlingly coloured clothes against the drabness of the desert, and a woman putting on lipstick under her all-encompassing burka.

Iranian cinema has brought extraordinary intensity to its depiction of life in the poorer parts of the country, as in Majid Majidi's *The Colour of Paradise* (*Rang-e Khoda*, 1999), about a blind boy and his father, and Bahman Ghobadi's *A Time for Drunken Horses* (*Zamani Baraye Masti Asbha*, 2000), about a young Kurdish orphan struggling to support his siblings, including a severely handicapped brother, in a harsh mountain village. Iranian films have also provided radical insights into the condition of women. Jafar Panahi's film *The Circle* (*Dayereh*, 2000) links half a dozen female characters in present-day Tehran, all of whom suffer from the oppression of a male-controlled society. Some of the women have just been released from prison for unspecified crimes, one needs an abortion, another is accused of prostitution. Nor are Iranian women denied a place behind the camera. Women directors include Rakhshan Beni-Etemad with *The Blue Veiled* (*Rusari-ye Abi*, 1994), about a widower falling for a young woman, and *The May Lady* (*Banu-ye Ordibehesht*, 1997), about a widow documentary film-maker whose desire to remarry is opposed by her son. Beni-Etemad's *Under the Skin of the City* (*Zir-e poost-e shahr*, 2000) deals with issues such as illiteracy, homelessness and prostitution in a drama about a mother with three sons and an unemployed husband.

Mohsen Makhmalbaf's daughter, Samira, directed *The Apple* (*Sib*, 1997), which re-creates, using the actual people involved, the extraordinary story of two girls kept imprisoned by their father for eleven years in order to preserve them from contamination by the outside world. Eventually they are 'liberated' by their friendship with a neighbouring boy, who offers them an apple. Makhmalbaf himself wrote the script for his wife Marziyeh Meshkini's *The Day I Became a Woman* (*Roozi khe zan shodam*, 2001), three stories in which women of different generations seek to realize their desires. In the most unusual, a young woman takes part in a cycle race, against the wishes of her brothers; horsemen race beside the sea pursuing a long line of black-clad women cycling for all they are worth.

Despite its concern for women's conditions, there are problems for a strict Islamic cinema in the representation of erotic love, as the critic Hamid Naficy explains. Since a woman acting in a film is deemed to be in public ('in the movies all private spaces were considered to be public spaces'[1]), she must wear the chador, which envelops her from head to toe. This remains the rule even if the scene shows a wife and husband alone together in the privacy of their bedroom, when in reality the woman would not be so covered. Any realistic depiction of heterosexual relations is thus made difficult, but this can result in highly subtle or eroticized displacements, as in Mohsen Makhmalbaf's *Gabbeh* (1995) when a woman milks a goat as a man stands nearby watching intently. In Hassan Yektapanah's *Djomeh* (2000) a young Afghan refugee falls for the daughter of the local shopkeeper. Anxious to ingratiate himself he goes to the shop while she is there alone and orders a long list of items, but convention does not allow her to give him any indication of her feelings. Some children run off with his bike; he gives chase, then breathlessly returns to pursue his suit, but instead finds her stern father has taken over. Finally, the audience is given a sign of the girl's emotions, as we catch a glimpse of the girl (visible to us but not to the father) waiting behind the back door.

The achievements of contemporary Iranian cinema are all the more remarkable given the fierce political struggle between traditionalists and modernizers which has had its casualties within the media, with newspapers closed and editors imprisoned. Despite its international success, Panahi's *The Circle* encountered considerable censorship problems at home. Though Iranian films have earned the country cultural prestige abroad, as well as foreign exchange, there are undoubtedly those who are annoyed by the increasing liberalism of many of the films. Depending on who gets the upper hand, Iranian cinema may achieve even greater things, or be reined in by a more restrictive censorship.

In late November 2001, after the Taliban had been expelled from Kabul, the capital of Afghanistan, the 'Bakhtar' cinema re-opened after five dark years. The first film was *Uroj* (date uncertain), described as a tale about heroic Afghan mujahedin fighters defeating the Russians. 'It was the first time I have ever seen a film and I loved it,' said Omaid, aged seventeen.[2] In 2002, several Afghan film-makers who had remained in their homeland under the Taliban regime joined together to produce Afghanistan's first local film in ten years, *The Speculator*. Director Sayed Faruk Haybat told Agence France Presse that while making his previous film in 1992, a rocket landed on the set and killed eight people.

Below left: Children representing optimism and innocence: Massoumeh Naderi and Zahra Naderi in *The Apple* (*Sib*, 1997).
Below right: Azizeh Mohamadi in *The Apple* (*Sib*, 1997).
Dir: Samira Makhmalbaf

15. Bollywood and New Indian Cinema

Those falling leaves were our
   hearts.
Where there is a heart there will
   be suffering.
Where there is suffering there
   is a heart.
The seasons go by ...

Lyricist Sampooran Singh Gulzar, 'From the Heart' (Dil Se Re),
soundtrack, *Dil Se* (Mani Rathnam, 1998)

The sheer size of the Indian cinema, with production reaching eight or nine hundred films a year in the 1990s, makes it more akin to a region such as Western Europe than to a nation state. The fact that films are produced in a dozen different languages makes the analogy even more apposite. Yet within this diversity one form of cinema has become dominant, the Hindi-speaking cinema based in Bombay and popularly known as Bollywood.

The allusion to Hollywood derives from a number of striking resemblances. In cultural prestige and influence, if not strictly in numbers of films produced, Hindi cinema dominates Indian production, just as Hollywood dominates that of the world, not only in terms of the size of its output (about a quarter of all the films that India produces) but also because of its popularity in non-Hindi speaking regions, and indeed in the growing Indian diaspora in the West and elsewhere. The language spoken is in fact more properly described as Hindustani, a mix of Hindi and Urdu, which is more or less understood by up to half of India's population (which is rapidly approaching the one billion mark). Like Hollywood, too, Hindi cinema is unashamedly commercial, requiring no state aid and ensuring that India is one of the few countries in the world whose indigenous cinema outperforms all foreign – including US – competition. And like Hollywood, indeed like most truly popular cinema, it makes its appeal through genres and stars.

In earlier decades a number of distinct genres arose, including films based on India's rich mythological inheritance, and on its history, as well as social and romantic dramas, and comedies. Music and dance were important elements in many films, as they had been in Indian classical theatre and in the urbanized Parsi theatre centred on Bombay in the nineteenth and twentieth centuries. By the 1970s a new form was evolving, the so-called 'masala' film, incorporating a mixture of many ingredients. The separate genres merged into one, the characteristic form of Hindi cinema which now dominates the subcontinent. At the centre of the film is a romance between a personable, handsome hero and a beautiful girl. There are obstacles in the way of their fulfilment: their misunderstanding of each other, family objections, a prior attachment. Villainous forces will be at work, and the hero will have to fight them, but the plot will be leavened by comedy. The action will be punctuated by frequent songs accompanied by dancing, in which the emotions and aspirations of the principals will be articulated, albeit in fantastical form.

Music is even more vital to these films' success than was the case in earlier Indian cinema. The songs are released in advance of the film's opening; if successful they will ensure good box office returns. Almost invariably the songs are not sung by the film actors but by established playback singers who are stars in their own right. One of the most famous and prolific, Lata Mangeshkar, has recorded literally thousands of songs in a career going back to the 1940s. Increasingly, traditional Indian film music has absorbed a range of external influences, and traces can be found of anything from Hawaiian 'hapa haole' to flamenco, from rock 'n' roll to jazz.

Dancing, too, has evolved. Though still based on Indian folk and classical dance, increasingly the style incorporates a mix of disco gyration and aerobics. Notoriously, the strict Indian censors do not admit kissing on the screen (though this rule has been flouted on occasion), so in place of openly sexual contact the musical numbers offer a substitute. Dancing has become increasingly eroticized, with the camera closing in on the female star's erogenous zones, especially the navel, which traditional costume conveniently leaves bare. The heroine's clothes have become more provocative, miniskirts and bathing suits alternating with brightly coloured saris. Sometimes her clothes get wet, making them more revealing; in *Hum* (Mukul Anand, 1991) the heroine is hosed down by the hero and half her dress is washed away. Viewed alone, perhaps on video, these sequences can seem naive, even silly to a Western spectator, though the daring colour schemes and swirling music are seductive enough. But watching with an Indian audience it is difficult not to get caught up in the infectious enthusiasm they engender.

The musical numbers are not only the site of sexual display. They also articulate the fantasies that impel the hero and heroine. In *Dil Se* (Mani Rathnam, 1998) a young radio

BOLLYWOOD AND NEW INDIAN CINEMA

reporter, Amarkanth (Shah Rukh Khan), becomes involved with Meghna (Manisha Koirala), a member of a group of militants in Assam. She is torn between her love for the hero and her political commitment. In an extended dance number at the centre of the film she appears first in a black top and baggy trousers, her naked belly painted with a traditional henna design as she writhes to an insistent musical beat amid the ruins of an ancient fort. We cut to a snowy mountain top, where she is now dressed in flowing white robes, then to a desert where she appears in red, and next in yellow dancing in front of a burning tree that might symbolize her political mission or her passion or both. In subsequent shots her costume changes to purple, then to green, then she and the hero are beside a lake, covered by a billowing red cloth – the implication is that she is naked underneath. In the next shot her chest is bound round and round with a white rope as she and the hero dance beneath a net, doubtless symbolic of the emotional and political complexities in which they are enmeshed. Finally, after a brief shot of the heroine in purple, she is once more in flowing white robes, set against a backdrop of snow as she and the hero embrace.

Besides amply demonstrating the sexual allure of Meghna, the sequence foreshadows her fate. The initial black costume suggests the heroine's commitment to the grim business of revolutionary politics. The change from black to white (the colour of mourning in India) signals the heroine's eventual fate, since at the end she blows up both herself and her lover. Red, on the other hand, is the colour for a bride, and in the central part of the sequence this implies the sexual union with the hero to which she is drawn but which impedes her political commitment.

Dance numbers may express a more generalized conflict between the traditional and the modern. In *Hum* the hero's brother has begun a romance with the daughter of an army general. The general wants her to marry an army officer. He tells her to wear traditional clothes ('a girl's beauty comes from concealing her body, not displaying it') and encourages her to study the Bharat Natyam, 'our traditional dance'. But in the next sequence, a musical number, she is at the seaside with her boyfriend, wearing a skimpy beach dress, which soon gets wet as they cavort in the waves. There is a cut to the airport, where, clad in jeans, the boy plays electric guitar and the girl, in a brightly patterned dress, dances inside the engine cowling of a jumbo jet. Next we see her in a lilac-coloured dress with a spangled bodice dancing on a cabin cruiser and then in a speed boat, wearing black leather trousers. Back beside the sea the couple roll across the rocks, before ending up speeding through green fields on a motorbike.

Nothing could be plainer: the father wants a traditional daughter; she is rushing headlong into the modern world. This clash between the old and the new often forms the basis of the entire plot. In *Dilwale Dulhania Le Jayenge* (Aditya Chopra, 1995) a father living in London wants to take his daughter back home to India for an arranged marriage. Reluctantly the daughter, Simran (played by Kajol), agrees if she can be allowed a trip round Europe by rail before surrendering her freedom. On the journey she meets Raj, played by Shah Rukh Khan, currently one of Bollywood's biggest stars. Naturally she falls in love. Back home her mother says that she had to give up her own ambitions when she married. She is well aware of the unfairness, that it is never men who must sacrifice; nevertheless she urges Simran to give up the boy. Raj follows Simran to India. There seems no way of avoiding

SAMEER: I'm Sameer, you can call me Sam.
What's your name?
NANDINI: Nandini
SAMEER: Can I call you Nandu?
NANDINI: Only Nandini.
SAMEER: Oh, I see. Your name is different. Does it mean Nandini, the bull?
NANDINI: It's not necessary for every name to have a meaning.

Sameer (Salman Khan), Nandini (Aishwarya Rai), *Hum Dil De Chuke Sanam* (Sanjay Leela Bhansali, 1999)

Above right: In *Hum Dil De Chuke Sanam* (1999) modernity and tradition are not easily reconciled. Nandini (Aishwarya Rai) marries her parent's choice of husband, despite loving Sameer (Salman Khan). Dir: Sanjay Leela Bhansali

Above: Casually dressed, on a motorbike, man of the people Amitabh Bachchan rides into action on this poster for *Muqaddar Ka Sikandar* (1978). Dir: Prakash Mehra

Simran's forthcoming marriage to a man her father has selected, despite his obvious unsuitability, yet Raj refuses to take the obvious course of elopement. Though a progressive and sophisticated young man, when she gets drunk Raj declines to take advantage of Simran, asserting that he is an Indian 'and I know what honour means'. The film works hard to negotiate a compromise between traditional and modern ideas of marriage, though the ending is too convenient: the local suitor is disgraced and Simran's father comes around at last, blessing his daughter's choice of Raj.

Modernity and tradition are not always so easily reconciled. In *Hum Dil De Chuke Sanam* (Sanjay Leela Bhansali, 1999) Nandini (Aishwarya Rai) falls in love with Sameer (Salman Khan), a distant relative who has been studying to be an opera singer in Italy (Europe seemingly the place of origin for modern ideas). Nandini's father agrees to give him lessons in traditional Indian singing, and in one sequence Nandini herself expounds on the range of styles. 'You've a song for every occasion,' says Sameer. 'Yes,' she replies, 'from birth to death. Harvest songs, love songs, wedding songs, workers' songs, gipsy songs, Bhavai.' She demonstrates the latter, and then Garba, 'the one with the clapping'. But Nandini's parents have already selected a husband for her. When her sister's arranged marriage results in her being beaten by her husband, the father nevertheless orders her to go back to him. In this house, says the mother, no one has the right to fall in love. Nandini eventually marries her parents' choice, Vanraj. When Vanraj discovers she loves another, he offers to come with her to Italy to help her find Sameer. But at the end Nandini avows that love is sacrifice, renounces her love for Sameer and remains true to her marriage.

Family is at the centre of Hindi cinema. The hero will have a close relationship with his mother, invariably a saintly figure whose sole *raison d'être* is selfless love of her son. The father is frequently in opposition to the son, or absent altogether. In *Muqaddar Ka Sikandar* (Prakash Mehra, 1978), one of the most successful films of superstar Amitabh Bachchan, Sikander is a street urchin, an orphan who acquires a substitute mother who has lost her own son and who adopts him. His new mother dies and he promises to devote his life to looking after her daughter, his adopted sister. When he grows up he falls under the influence of a courtesan, Zohra, but renounces her when his sister's suitor threatens to pull out of marriage because of the shame of the association. Zohra poisons herself and Sikander dies fighting the villain, Dilawar, but Sikander's promise to his dying mother has been sustained and the honour of the family saved.

The heroine's role in Hindi cinema is to be the object of the hero's desire. Rarely does she have any other function in the plot, or any kind of occupation. Besides the mother and the heroine, a third female figure is the courtesan. In earlier Muslim culture, courtesans

were traditionally poets, singers and dancers, and their presence in a film offers plentiful opportunity for musical numbers, but usually the courtesan is doomed to sacrifice herself. She will love the hero but he, however dazzled by her gaudy charms (Zohra dances several seductive numbers), will not love her in return. In *Utsav* (Girish Karnad, 1984) Rekha plays Vasantsena, a beautiful courtesan of the classical period who, fleeing from Samasthanaka, the lustful brother-in-law of the king, falls in love with a married commoner. At the end of the film her lover returns to his wife and Vasantsena resigns herself to Samasthanaka. Not all courtesan films end in tragedy; in *Pakeezah* (Kamal Amrohi, 1971) Meena Kumari is rejected by her husband's family and dies giving birth to a child, but her daughter, who also becomes a courtesan, eventually finds happiness.

Just as in the 1970s Hollywood initiated new kinds of action films to please a more international and youthful audience, so Bollywood developed its own formula of action spectaculars, in which Amitabh Bachchan rapidly became the biggest star in Indian cinema. In *Deewar* (Yash Chopra, 1975) and *Sholay* (Ramesh Sippy, 1975) he played a type largely new to Bombay films, the streetwise character of lower-class origins, a man of the people forced to take the law into his own hands to avenge the evils done to his family. Tall, with strong rather than handsome features, Amitabh made a convincing working-class rebel or 'angry young man', as the type was labelled, especially in the frequent scenes of violence.

In *Sholay* Amitabh plays Jaidev, a rogue just out of prison who is recruited by Thakur, a policeman, to help fight a bandit preying on local villagers, a plot that owed much to the hit Hollywood Western *The Magnificent Seven* (John Sturges, 1960). In a flashback, the bandit cuts off Thakur's arms. Later Jaidev's friend, Veeru (Dharmendra), is captured by the bandit, who says he will keep him alive only for as long as Veeru's lover can dance, strewing broken glass beneath her bare feet in an especially villainous touch. Jaidev dies at the end in a heroic stand against great odds, but the bandit is defeated and nearly kicked to death by the armless Thakur.

Above: Dharmendra as Veeru and Amitabh Bachchan as Jaidev in *Sholay* (1975). Dir: Ramesh Sippy
Below: Amitabh Bachchan (centre), the Indian superstar who plays the streetwise man of the people, with Shashi Kapoor as the brother who becomes a policeman and Nirupa Roy as his mother in *Deewar* (1975). Dir: Yash Chopra

In *Deewar* Amitabh is Vijay, brought up by his mother in the slums of Bombay. He grows up to become a gangster, while his brother joins the police. Vijay falls for a nightclub singer (i.e. courtesan); when she becomes pregnant he decides to marry her, but she is killed by a rival gang and Vijay is himself gunned down by his brother. He dies in his mother's arms, declaiming, 'I never slept well away from you, mother.'

In *Amar Akbar Anthony* (Manmohan Desai, 1977), Amitabh for once survives to the end of the picture. Three brothers are separated in childhood: Amar grows up a Hindu, Akbar a Muslim, Anthony (Amitabh) a Christian. Amitabh is again a gangster, though an amiable one, who has several comic scenes, including a funny drunken conversation with himself in the mirror. The day when they were separated was 15 August, Indian Independence Day, and the eventual uniting of the three brothers of different religions is a sign of Hindi cinema's ambition to express a national identity united in diversity.

The extra-judicial violence meted out to bandits and gangsters in these films serves as a fantasy of revenge by the powerless against those who have corruptly seized society's wealth, and its appeal to the masses is hardly surprising. The vigilantism proposed as the solution to corruption and ineffective legal institutions has something in common with the *Dirty Harry* cycle of movies in Hollywood, and the films have been interpreted as implicitly supporting the suspension of civil liberties during the so-called Emergency imposed by Indira Gandhi's government in 1975. But, as in Hollywood cinema, the critique rarely extends to a radical analysis of the institutions themselves, confining itself to the unmaking of individual wrong-doers. Thus in *Hum* the chief villain is an unscrupulous police inspector, who manipulates the local gangsters and even the army. Once he has been bested, everything is all right.

The position of women is not immutable, and the assumption of passivity is sometimes challenged. Rape became a political issue in India in the course of the 1970s, and *Insaaf Ka Tarazu* (B R Chopra, 1980) was one of a number of films in which a rape victim, failing to

Below: Seema Biswas as Phoolan Devi, a victim who takes the law into her own hands in *Bandit Queen* (1994). Causing much controversy when released, this film condemns both the caste system and the subservient role of women in a modern Indian society.
Dir: Shekhar Kapur

BOLLYWOOD AND NEW INDIAN CINEMA

get justice, takes the law into her own hands as a kind of female equivalent of the Amitabh persona. However, such issues were more likely to find expression in Indian art cinema than in Bollywood, most forcefully in *Bandit Queen* (Shekhar Kapur, 1994), based on the true story of Phoolan Devi, a low-caste woman who sought revenge for rape by leading a gang of bandits. (Devi, who had become a member of the Indian Congress, was assassinated in 2001.)

Though popular Indian cinema is primarily dedicated to providing escapist entertainment, politics does intrude one way or another. As we have seen, *Dil Se* is about a young woman militant working for a separatist movement in Assam. Directed by Mani Rathnam, it is part of a trilogy that includes *Roja* (1992) and *Bombay* (1995). *Roja*, set partly in Kashmir, where Muslim groups have long fought against Indian administration, works up a kind of generalized pan-Indian nationalism, while the Kashmiri separatists are treated unsympathetically. As the *Encyclopaedia of Indian Cinema* notes, 'In one famous scene, the tied-up hero, offended by the Kashmiris' burning of the Indian flag, crashes through a window and tries to extinguish the flames with his body to the tune of a Subramanyam Bharati lyric.'[1] In *Bombay* a young Hindu falls in love with a Muslim girl. Both sets of parents object, so they move to Bombay, only to be caught up in the riots following the destruction of the mosque at Ayodhya by Hindu extremists in 1992. The powerful scenes of murderous destruction contrast with the lyricism of the love scenes and musical numbers. The message may be the usual one of popular cinema everywhere, that love conquers all, but the difficulties in its way are real enough.

Both *Roja* and *Bombay* are in the Tamil language, not Hindi (though *Bombay* was later dubbed into Hindi). Centred on Madras, Tamil is one of the most important regional cinemas, with an annual production now outstripping that of Hindi cinema. For many years the most prominent figure was Marudur Gopalamenon Ramachandran, or MGR as he was popularly known, a star of dozens of films in which he played the defender of poor peasants against evil moneylenders and grasping landlords. His populist politics were to

Above: Arvind Swamy as Shekhar and Manisha Koirala as Shehla Bano in *Bombay* (1995). Dir: Mani Rathnam

Right: Rishi Kumar (Arvind Swamy) is kidnapped by Kashmiri separatists in *Roja* (1992). Dir: Mani Rathnam

propel him to the position of chief minister of the state of Tamil Nadu in the 1970s.
Another actor who used his film fame as a stepping stone into politics was Nandamuri
Taraka Rama Rao, otherwise known as NTR, a megastar of the Telugu cinema centred on
Hyderabad, the only other regional cinema to rival the Hindi in output. The star of
countless 'mythologicals', stories of gods and goddesses, in which he frequently played
Krishna, NTR was chief minister of the state of Andhra Pradesh in the 1980s, at a time
when Ronald Reagan was parlaying film stardom into an even higher political office.

Other important regional cinemas include Bengali, based in Calcutta; Kannada in the
southern state of Karnataka; Malayalam, centred on Kerala; and Marathi, based, like Hindi
cinema, in Bombay. But none of these can command a national audience, unless its films
are dubbed into other regional languages. Hindi cinema is therefore the nearest thing that
India has to a genuinely national cinema. Recently there has been an attempt to break
out into a wider market. *Asoka* (Santosh Sivan, 2001), an epic based on the life of an early
Indian emperor, starring Shah Rukh Khan, and *Lagaan* (Ashutosh Gowariker, 2001), about
a cricket match against the British at the time of the Raj, both enjoyed a general release in
Britain. Like *Bombay*, *Lagaan* attempts within the framework of a popular drama to do
its bit for Indian national unity: the village team that achieves victory over the British
contains a Muslim, a Sikh and an untouchable.

In the 1960s the Indian government began making money available for film production
through the Film Finance Corporation (FFC). The resulting 'New Indian Cinema' set out
to create a different image of India, one which avoided the boisterous vulgarity of Hindi
popular films and more closely reflected the refined tastes of the educated elite who
controlled cultural policy. As Mira Reym Binford points out, New Indian Cinema differed
in almost every respect from popular Hindi films.[2] Not only was it state-supported instead
of commercial, but it drew its cultural models not from traditional Indian forms of theatre
or music but frequently from European cinema, especially the French New Wave and Italian
neo-realism. In keeping with the latter, Indian art cinema favoured the use of unknown and
even non-professional actors; it could not afford Bollywood stars in any case. Commentators
have pointed out the irony that in a sense the commercialized, 'vulgar' cinema of Bollywood
is therefore more authentically Indian, being based on traditional genres, music and dance.

Making a virtue out of necessity, New Indian Cinema preferred location shooting and
natural lighting to studio work, and, at least in the 1970s, black and white to the bright
colours and wide screens of popular cinema. Whereas Bollywood plots were melodramatic
fantasies, it took its stories from the everyday life of the Indian masses, and instead of
action and spectacle it focused on character, largely renouncing song and dance. In place

BOLLYWOOD AND NEW INDIAN CINEMA

A Bollywood Blockbuster
Lagaan (2001)
Dir: Ashutosh Gowariker

Lagaan conforms to the formula of the Bollywood blockbuster, with a love-triangle at the centre, a dastardly villain and plentiful singing and dancing. The setting is historical, the year 1893, with the British Raj imposing heavy taxes on the people of a rural backwater. An arrogant army captain, confident in his countrymen's ability, offers the villagers relief if they can beat the British at cricket. Unknown to him, his sister has fallen in love with Bhuvan (Aamir Khan), the captain of the village team, and decides to help the Indians. The second half of the film (in total nearly four hours in length) is taken up with the cricket match, which pits Indian ingenuity and solidarity against British over-confidence.

Despite its closeness to the conventions, *Lagaan* proved to be a break-out film and might almost have been designed to persuade British cinema-goers of the appeal of Bollywood cinema. Besides the usual attractions of music and movement, it has a plot carefully tailored to a cross-over audience. Though the British men are unsympathetic, they are minor characters compared to the captain's beautiful sister (Rachel Shelley), who not only upholds the British tradition of fair play but also loses her heart to the handsome Indian hero. Equally important, the cricket match is dramatized with great élan and suspense, even if the ultimate victory of the Indians is not in doubt.

As a result, the film was released to twenty-three screens in Britain and at one time was the UK's tenth best grossing film. Indian films are also achieving success in the North American market, where *Lagaan* was released on thirty-four screens, surprising in view of Americans' indifference to cricket. Perhaps most unpredictably of all, and unusually for an Indian film, *Lagaan* was given a wide release in China.

Country of Origin: India
Running Time: 223 mins

Production Company: Aamir Khan Productions
Producer: Aamir Khan
Writers: Ashutosh Gowariker, Kumar Dave, Sanjay Dayma
Photography: Anil Mehta
Music: A R Rahman
Editor: Ballu Saluja
Production Designer: Nitin Chandrakant Desai

Bhuvan: Aamir Khan
Gauri: Gracy Singh
Elizabeth Russell: Rachel Shelley
Captain Andrew Russell: Paul Blackthorne
Yashodamai: Suhasini Mulay

Above left: Aamir Khan as Bhuvan, captain of the village team.
Above: Poster advertising Lagaan, one of the most expensive films ever produced by Bollywood.
Left: The village eleven pose for the camera before the game.
Top right: Bhuvan and Gauri (Gracy Singh) perform a musical number on an ox-cart.
Centre right: Kulbhushan Kharbanda as the Rajah and Rachel Shelley as Elizabeth, sister of the English captain.
Below right: Gauri dancing in the village square with her true love Bhuvan.

of Bollywood's dependence on stars and genres, New Indian Cinema encouraged the emergence of auteurs.

Even before the 1960s this path had been marked out by Satyajit Ray, who until his death in 1992 was the world's most celebrated Indian director. With his roots deep in Bengali culture (the writer Rabindranath Tagore was a family friend), Ray made his first film, *Pather Panchali*, in 1955; it was a big success at the Cannes Film Festival. Over the next thirty years Ray completed about one film a year until ill health slowed him. His films are marked by a quiet but elegant shooting style, a deeply felt humanism and interest in the emotions and problems of ordinary people. Vittorio De Sica's *Bicycle Thieves* (*Ladri di biciclette*, 1948), a key work of Italian neo-realism, was a formative influence. In the 1970s Ray's films took on a sharper edge. *Jana Aranya* (1975) explores corruption in contemporary Calcutta as the hero seeks a prostitute in order to bribe a businessman. After this, Ray largely turned away from direct commentary on contemporary politics, making a series of successful children's films such as *Hirak Rajar Deshe* (1980).

Two films mark the onset of New Indian Cinema proper. Mrinal Sen's *Bhuvan Shome* (1969), financed by the FFC, was a comedy in black and white, shot on location, about an uptight railway official whose world is turned upside down by a lively village girl. By contrast, Mani Kaul's *Uski Roti* (1969), a story about a bus driver, also funded by the FFC, is formally experimental, playing with cinematic space, and deliberately rejects the norms of narrative cinema. Like Ray, Sen is from Bengal, and in the early 1970s he made a trilogy about Calcutta. Originally a Marxist, his films, such as *Oka Oorie Katha* (1977), have dealt with rural poverty, women's exploitation and the despair of the dispossessed. Mani Kaul has spent much of his career in documentaries, but in 1991 completed *Idiot*, an ambitious adaptation of Dostoyevsky's novel.

Another influential work of New Indian Cinema was Shyam Benegal's *The Seedling* (*Ankur*, 1973), about a young landowner who has an affair with the wife of a deaf-mute peasant. Benegal's style, realist yet fluid, married to themes of social disruption, proved popular, offering something of a middle way in Hindi cinema between the austerity of art cinema and the extravagance of Bollywood. *Junoon* (1978) was a story of the 1857 Indian Mutiny, filmed on a large scale, in which an Anglo-Indian girl suffers from being mistrusted by both sides.

Women have found it difficult to break into the Indian film industry as anything other than actresses, though Mira Nair's *Salaam Bombay!* (1988), shot in the slums of Bombay, had a deserved international success. Whether in search of greater social mobility or easier sources of finance, Nair moved to the United States to make *Mississippi Masala* (1991), in

Opposite: Satyajit Ray, the world's best-known Indian director, a native of Calcutta, Bengal.
Top: Sudeshna Das and Pradip Mukerji in *Jana Aranya* (1975).
Dir: Satyajit Ray
Above: Utpal Dutt as Bhuvan Shome and Suhasini Mulay as village girl Gauri in *Bhuvan Shome* (1969).
Dir: Mrinal Sen
Right: Shabana Azmi as Firdaus the betrayed wife in *Junoon* (1978).
Dir: Shyam Benegal
Overleaf: Shafiq Syed as Krishna/Chaipau and Chandra Sharma as Solasaal in *Salaam Bombay!* (1988).
Dir: Mira Nair

Below: Preparing for
the big day in *Monsoon
Wedding* (2001).
Dir: Mira Nair
Bottom: Zhora Sehgal,
Lalita Ahmed and
Sarita Khajuria
in *Bhaji on the Beach*
(1993), a comedy

following a group of
Indian women from
Birmingham on a trip
to Blackpool which
results in greater
understanding of
each other's problems.
Dir: Gurinder Chadha

JOE: Where do you normally play?
JESS: In the park.
JOE: I mean what position?
JESS: Oh, sorry. I usually play all over, but
          up front. On the right is best.

Joe (Jonathan Rhys Meyers), Jess (Parminder
Nagra), *Bend It Like Beckham* (Gurinder Chadha,
2002)

which her Indian immigrant heroine has a relationship with an African-American, played by Denzel Washington. Nair's *Monsoon Wedding* (2001), a slight though diverting comedy about a middle-class marriage in Delhi, was popular when released in Britain. The British-based Gurinder Chadha, part of the growing Indian diaspora, has had considerable success with her comedies *Bhaji on the Beach* (1993) and *Bend It Like Beckham* (2002). Another Indian director working in Britain is Shekhar Kapur, whose *Elizabeth*, starring Cate Blanchett as Elizabeth I, was a notable success in 1998, while London-born Asif Kapadia's *The Warrior* (2001), a dream-like tale making the most of Indian landscapes, won the prize for the best feature shown at London's National Film Theatre in 2001.

The sheer size of the Indian industry permits an art cinema to exist at the margins. Among notable current directors are Rituparno Ghosh and Jayaraj Rajasekharan Nair. Nair is from Kerala. His film *Karunam* (1999) concerns an elderly Christian couple whose son fails to appear on a visit from the United States. His most recent work, *Calmness* (*Shantham*, 2000), is about childhood friends whose political differences have tragic results. Ghosh, like Satyajit Ray, comes from Bengal, and his work has been compared to Ray in its realism and humanist stance. In *The Lady of the House* (*Bariwali*, 2000) a film company rents the house of an reclusive spinster, whose life is for a time transformed by the bustle of film production, only for her loneliness to return when the production has wrapped.

More recently a kind of Indian 'independent' cinema has evolved, sometimes in the form of international coproductions, which tries to be neither Bollywood nor art film, with ambitions to tell the truth about contemporary Indian society while providing a fast-paced narrative and rolling back the barriers to sexual and political expression. Dev Benegal's *Split Wide Open* (1999) exposes corruption in Bombay's water industry and probes the sexual underbelly of the city, while Kaizad Gustad's *Bombay Boys* (1998) takes a cool look at the city through the eyes of three Indian youths from New York, London and Sydney, again taking in crime and corruption, and the hitherto taboo subject of gay sex.

Cinema elsewhere on the subcontinent suffers from the economic might of Indian cinema, a powerful competitor. In Pakistan, the war between the two separate parts of the country in 1971, which resulted in the independence of Bangladesh, left an industry in the former West Pakistan struggling to rival the super-productions of Bollywood. Centred on Lahore (hence its designation as Lollywood), Pakistani cinema has suffered from economic woes compounded by political and religious interference. General Zia, who became Pakistan's military ruler in 1977, imposed Islamic law, revoking previously granted censorship certificates and closing many cinemas. As video, and later satellite television, became more widely available, competition from India (despite the hostility between the

Right: The new India:
in a daring television
show, participants are
encouraged to discuss
their sex lives in *Split
Wide Open* (1999).
Dir: Dev Benegal
Opposite: Another
contest between
tradition and modernity

in *Bend It Like Beckham*
(2002): Jesminder
(Parminder Nagra)
wants to play football
in imitation of her hero
David Beckham, but her
Indian-born parents
prefer she think about
marriage.
Dir: Gurinder Chadha

Above: A poster for the film *Maulajut* (1979), featuring Pakistan's biggest star, Sultan Rahi, in a bloodthirsty battle against lawlessness.
Dir: Yunus Malik
Below: The life of fishermen who make a living from the river Padma: their aspirations and dreams of a better life are skilfully explored in *Padma Nadir Majhi* (1993).
Dir: Goutam Ghose

Right: Nithyavani Kandasamy as the daughter of a wounded Tamil Tiger guerrilla and Pramudi Karunarathne as a Sinhalese girl who becomes her friend in *Saroja* (1999).
Dir: Somaratne Dissanayake
Opposite: Malini Fonseka is being attacked in *Village in the Jungle* (*Baddegama*, 1980).
Dir: Lester James Peries

two nations) became ever more detrimental to the home-grown product, which went ever further down-market in a desperate effort to find an audience. *Maulajut* (Yunus Malik, 1979) starred Sultan Rahi, Pakistan's biggest star until he was murdered in 1996, as a hero standing up against a corrupt clan in a country ruled by lawlessness, a role not unlike those favoured by Amitabh Bachchan. The film was hugely popular, leading to many cheap imitations.

Production is currently less than a tenth of India's annual total and consists almost entirely of action films aimed at a working-class male audience. Independent or art cinema has only a precarious foothold in Pakistan. Jamil Dehlavi's updating of a story from Muslim history, *The Blood of Hussain* (1980), remains banned, though the same director's *Jinnah* (1998), a biography of Pakistan's leader at the time of Partition, was given a respectful reception. In the autumn of 2001 the burning of cinemas by mobs opposed to Pakistan's support of the military campaign against the Taliban in Afghanistan did not augur well for the future of its film industry.

Bangladesh, a state created out of the former East Pakistan, managed the considerable total of about forty films a year during the first decade of its existence, with many titles reworking the experience of the war of independence. In later decades fantasy films and song and dance romances à la Bollywood have dominated, though there have been some notable literary adaptations, such as *Padma Nadir Majhi* (1993), directed by Goutam Ghose and based on the classic novel by Manik Bandopadhyay.

In Sri Lanka the film industry was nationalized in 1970 by the new socialist government. This ushered in a decade of serious debate about the nature of a national cinema and some important films, mainly in a social realist aesthetic, such as Dharmasena Pathiraja's *Ahas Gauwa* (1974). The doyen of Sri Lankan cinema, Lester James Peries, continued to make the deeply felt humanist dramas that won him an international reputation, such as *The Eyes* (*Desa nisa*, 1972), about an ungainly man who marries a blind woman and fears she may reject him if she regains her sight. *Village in the Jungle* (*Baddegama*, 1980) was based on a novel by Leonard Woolf and featured science fiction writer Arthur C Clarke, who settled in Sri Lanka, playing a judge. Peries's wife, Sumitra Gunawardena, previously an editor, launched her own directorial career in the 1970s; her most recent work is *A Mother Alone* (*Duvata Mawaka Misa*, 1997), about the troubles of a young woman, pregnant and unmarried.

In the 1980s the dead weight of government bureaucracy impaired the creativity of Sri Lankan film-makers, but some interesting directors emerged, including Tissa Abeysekera, later appointed chairman of the National Film Corporation (NFC). His *Viragaya* (1987) was one of Sri Lanka's highest grossing films. In 2000 the NFC ceased its monopoly of production and distribution, offering opportunities to new directors such as Somaratne Dissanayake, whose *Saroja* (1999), selected for the London Film Festival, is about a wounded Tamil Tiger given refuge in a Sinhalese village. Though some Tamils have criticized it as overly favourable to the Sri Lankan government, its message of reconciliation is timely now that there are concrete moves towards peace in the island's long-running conflict.

16. African Voices

PAPA WEMBA: **If I was not a musician of contemporary music and if I had lived in my village, I would be a griot.**

Papa Wemba, star of *La vie est belle*, quoted by director Ngangura Mweze in an interview with Mbye Cham, *La vie est belle* (Ngangura Mweze and Benoît Lamy, 1986)

African cinema was a child of the independence movement. In the late 1950s and early 1960s increasing numbers of countries freed themselves from their colonial masters and set about transforming their economic, social and cultural structures. But independence was not in itself a solution to the manifold problems that the newly emergent states inherited, and the new cinemas they tried to fashion were born into the difficulties of underdevelopment.

These obstacles, the legacy of colonialism soon compounded by the corruption of the local elites, were the root cause of the many disadvantages African cinema has had to overcome. For one thing, film distribution was largely in the hands of overseas companies. As a result, African audiences were fed a diet of commercial cinema, cheaply imported from Hollywood or India, which, while undoubtedly popular, bore no relation to their daily lives and, moreover, accustomed them to expensive production values unmatchable by indigenous film-makers. Attempts by some countries such as Guinea to assume state control over distribution resulted only in boycotts by foreign distributors.

African countries are among the poorest on Earth. Their governments have little money to spare for subsidizing film production. Infrastructure, too, is lacking. Studios if they exist at all are poorly equipped, training facilities very limited. Censorship, as in many other parts of the world, is a constant impediment to film-makers who take seriously their role as social commentators. African cinema also suffers acutely from the language problem. Even small countries may host a dozen or more language groups. If film-makers shoot in English or French to ensure wider comprehension, they not only risk confining their audience to the educated elite but also make it more difficult to escape the colonialist mentality.

As a result, film-making is a spasmodic activity, with directors sometimes spending years completing a project. 'You have to be crazy to make films in Africa,' says the elder statesman of African cinema, Ousmane Sembène. It takes the whole of Africa a decade to produce as many films as India makes in a year. Nevertheless, films do get made, some of them distinguished, and most of these will appear at the festival of African films (FESPACO), which began in Ouagadougou, capital of Burkina Faso, in 1969. Over the years this has been a vital showcase for African films and a rallying point for their makers. In 1970 a pan-African film-makers' organization (FEPACI) was set up to further facilitate cooperation.

The first major African film-maker, Ousmane Sembène, made his debut in 1963 with his short *Borom Sarret*, a story about a cart driver who loses his cart and therefore his livelihood. His film is reminiscent of Vittorio De Sica's *Bicycle Thieves* (*Ladri di biciclette*, 1948) in both theme and style. A novelist who had studied film in the USSR, Sembène was from Senegal, which has proved to be fertile ground for film-makers. Over the following ten years he made three feature films, before directing *Xala* in 1974. It is the story of El Hadji, a wealthy and well-connected businessman who decides to take a young and beautiful third wife. El Hadji dresses throughout in a suit and affects a Western lifestyle – he drinks only Evian mineral water. When his daughter Rama objects to his polygamy, she addresses him in Wolof, the local language; he angrily insists on speaking French. Yet his modernity is superficial. Before the wedding he refuses to ensure his potency by sitting in a large mortar, as folk wisdom decrees. But when he finds himself the victim of a 'xala' or curse and becomes impotent, he immediately resorts to a 'marabout' or traditional healer. The clash of tradition and modernity manifests itself in countless small details. When El Hadji's first two wives attend the

PRESIDENT: Gentlemen, to end this memorable day we are invited to the wedding of our colleague El Hadji Abdou Kader Beye who takes his third wife today. We must be African as well as modern. El Hadji, your turn to speak.

EL HADJI: By now the religious ceremony is over. Forgive me Mr President, Mr Minister, Deputies and honoured colleagues … I'm remarrying out of duty. You are all invited to tonight's festivities. There'll be lots of everything!

Mr President (Makhouredia Gueye), El Hadji (Thierno Leye), *Xala* (Ousmane Sembène, 1974)

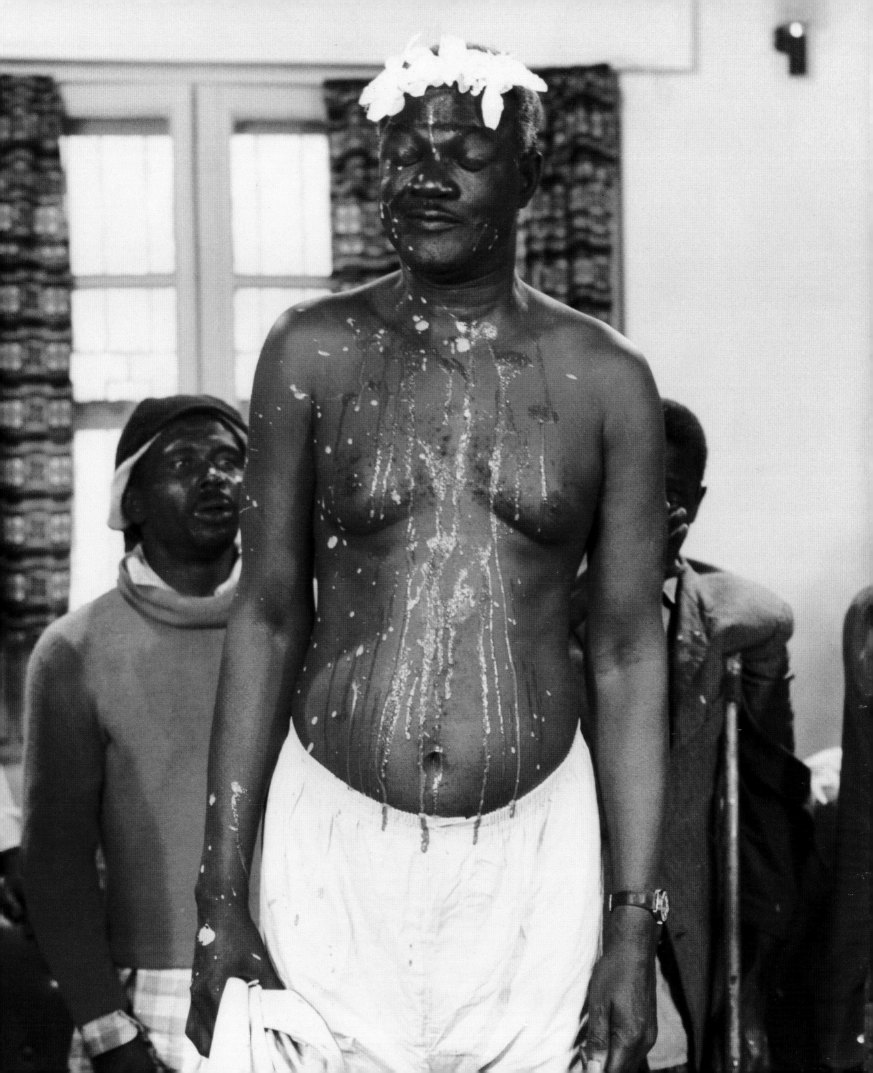

AFRICAN VOICES

wedding, the elder, Adja, wears traditional costume and sits on a sofa picking her teeth with a stick. The second wife, Oumi, sits beside her wearing Western clothes and a wig, chewing on her sunglasses.

Xala is a witty and engaging film, but its caustic satire of the elite and their Western paymasters caused censorship problems with the Senegalese government. Sembène's later films have continued his focus on the legacy of colonialism, and also on the position of women, so often caught at the sharp end of social conflicts. *Faat Kiné* (2000), directed by Sembène at the age of seventy-seven, is about a middle-aged businesswoman who runs a petrol station, and her struggles to achieve independence from men.

Given that women film-makers are few and far between in Africa, it is surprising how many films focus on the social position of women. *The Young Girl* (*Den Muso*, 1975), an early film by Souleymane Cissé, from Mali, is the tragedy of Ténin, the mute daughter of wealthy parents who is raped by her father's employee, Sékou. When she becomes pregnant her father disowns her. She goes to Sékou's house to plead with him to stand by her, but he is with another woman and throws her out. Ténin's inability to speak clearly has a metaphoric significance, for as Cissé remarked, 'To make the public understand the utter isolation experienced by these unfortunate young women, I chose to make my heroine a mute.' Overcome by rage and grief she burns Sékou's house down, then kills herself.

Finzan (1990), directed by Cheik Oumar Sissoko, also from Mali, is the story of Nanyuma, who when her husband dies is coveted by his brother Bala, a buffoonish figure. She resists bitterly but is forced into marriage. Meanwhile Fili, her young niece, is discovered to be not yet excised. Two girls debate the issue. The clitoris is dirty, says one. Nonsense, it is just an organ, like the tongue, says another. But eventually Fili is brutally mutilated. In all these films men's oppression of women is embedded in traditional attitudes that a modernized Africa should be leaving behind. 'The progress of our societies is linked to our emancipation,' says one of the women at the end of *Finzan*.

In *Tilaï* (1990), directed by Idrissa Ouedraogo, from Burkina Faso, Saga returns to his village after an absence to find that his fiancée, Nogma, has been married to his father. Saga and Nogma meet in secret. When this is discovered, Saga's brother Kougri is given the task of killing him, but allows him to escape. Nogma follows and the two runaways live happily until Saga returns home to see his dying mother and is finally killed by Kougri. Almost as in

Opposite: *Hyenas* (*Hyènes*, 1992): Ami Diakhate as Linguère Ramatou, a woman who returns to seek revenge on the man who abandoned her. Dir: Djibril Diop Mambéty
Above: Mgaye Niang and Miriam Niang in *Touki Bouki* (1973): a fantasy of leaving Senegal for Paris.

Dir: Djibril Diop Mambéty
Below: *Soleil O* (1970), is an experimental black and white exploration of an African's experience in France. Dir: Med Hondo
Bottom: Goundo Guissé and Fousseyni Sissoko in *The Wind* (*Finyé*, 1983). Dir: Souleymane Cissé

Greek drama, his death follows as the inevitable tragedy of implacable tradition, when love comes up against women's position as chattels.

Hyenas (*Hyènes*, 1992), by the Senegal director Djibril Diop Mambéty, is an African version of Friedrich Dürrenmatt's play *The Visit* (1956), in which a woman wreaks revenge for a wrong done in the past. Linguère Ramatou is seduced and abandoned in her youth by Dramaan, who hires two poor men to say that they had slept with her instead. She leaves the sleepy backwater of Colobane and becomes rich working as a prostitute. Years later she returns and with her money corrupts the village into joining in her revenge on Dramaan, now the prosperous owner of a bar.

Mambéty, who died in 1998 after completing only two features, was an important figure because his films mark a move away from the social realist style. *Hyenas*, at one level a caustic satire of greed and lust, is told in a manner reminiscent of the literary tradition of magical realism. Linguère has a golden leg and golden arm, ostensibly the result of an air crash but clearly symbolic of selling her body for money. At the end of the film Dramaan is literally consumed by the townspeople she has bribed, the 'hyenas', who leave nothing but a pile of clothes on the ground, as Linguère herself descends a flight of steps into the underworld. Mambéty's earlier feature, *Touki Bouki* (1973), is about two young people in love, Mory and Anta, whose fantasy is to leave Senegal for Paris. In one sequence they travel through the African countryside, with the black singer Josephine Baker on the soundtrack singing 'Paris … a little corner of paradise'. An animal is being slaughtered, there are shots of waves beating on the seashore, Anta takes off her shirt, there is a shot of the cow's horn that adorns their motorbike, another of a metal cross, then more shots of waves as on the soundtrack we hear the sounds of love-making. The meaning of this complex sequence is not easily reducible to words.

Soleil O (1970), an early film by the Mauritanian director Med Hondo, is also experimental in style, a series of incidents loosely strung together, in which a black worker in France experiences racism in its various forms. It mixes acute social observation with satire, both at the expense of the whites and of the black elite, seen living in luxury and enjoying white prostitutes. The films of Haile Gerima, from Ethiopia, also employ unconventional narrative strategies, mixing documentary with fictional reconstructions, as in the early *Harvest 3000 Years* (1974), made on return to his native country from the United States, and the later *Sankofa* (1993), about the Atlantic slave trade.

Med Hondo's *Sarraounia* (1987) explores the tradition vs. modernism conflict through a historical re-creation of the struggle against colonialism. Yet another film focused on a female character, it concerns a warrior queen of the Azna people of Niger who leads resistance both against the French invaders and against Muslim threats from the east. Queen Sarraounia is conceived on a heroic scale, tall, noble, passionate, inspiring, whether leading her troops into battle or asserting her independence from her lover. Brutally frank about the cruelties of the French, the film finds in history a role model for the modern African woman, while at the same time not despising cultural tradition. In her upbringing Sarraounia is initiated into the secrets of spiritual forces; at a crucial moment in a battle against the French she conjures up a thunderstorm.

Ousmane Sembène, too, has made several excursions into the past. His third feature, *Emitai* (1971), dramatizes an episode during World War II in which the women of an African village rebel when the French requisition their rice. *Ceddo* (1976) is about resistance, particularly on the part of women, to early attempts to convert Senegal to Islam, while *Campe de Thiaroye* (1988) recounts another true incident from World War II, in which a group of African soldiers are massacred by the French when, after fighting to liberate France, they demand their rights. (Sembène had himself fought for the French in the war.)

Freedom from the legacy of colonialism is understandably an African preoccupation. Souleymane Cissé's *The Wind* (*Finyé*, 1983), by contrast, deals with the struggle by students against a contemporary military regime. The father of one of the students, Batrou, is in charge of military action against the strike. His oppression of his daughter in the domestic sphere is inextricably linked to the political.

The relationship between the rural and the urban is another constant theme, as in *Letter to My Village* (*Kaddu Beykat*, 1975) by Safi Faye, a woman director from Senegal. Ngor's desire to marry Coumba is blocked by his lack of a bride price. He journeys to the city to make some money, but ultimately fails and returns home. Into the documentary-style presentation of village life is woven an argument about the effects on peasant ground-nut farmers of the cash-crop economy. In Idrissa Ouedraogo's *Samba Traoré* (1993) the eponymous hero begins in the city, taking part in a robbery. He flees back to his village and there attempts to reintegrate himself into community life.

A Film of Beauty and Magic
Yeelen (1987)
Dir: Souleymane Cissé

Yeelen is at once the most mystical and the most beautiful of African films. Its director, Souleymane Cissé, from Mali in West Africa, has expressed his desire to make films which are uniquely African in style rather than imitating those of the United States or Europe. To this end he relies on stories, true and mythical, told by old men and handed down through the generations.

Nianankoro (Issiaka Kane), threatened with death by his shaman father, goes on a journey where he learns the power of magic. Some Western critics have been tempted to interpret the film along psychoanalytic lines, with Nianankoro's struggle against his father analogous to that of Oedipus, and his taking of the King of Peul's wife reminiscent of Oedipus's marriage to his mother. But attempts to appropriate the film to Western ideas are surely misguided. The film inhabits a world of dreams, but not the kind described by Dr Freud.

However, the film's basis in a mystical tradition does not render it inaccessible to Western audiences. The structure of the narrative, based on a quest for magical knowledge and power, is clear and firm, and the consistent pattern of imagery based on the elements of fire, water, earth and light (the title translates as 'brightness') is not specific to African culture. The film's use of landscape, the spare, yellow spaces of the desert, is one of its chief glories. The performers too have great charm. Cissé worked with a non-professional cast whose naturalness is well suited to the elemental nature of the story. A visually stunning film, *Yeelen* won the 'Prix du Jury' at the Cannes Film Festival in 1987.

Country of Origin: Mali
Running Time: 105 mins

Production Company: Les Films Cissé
Producer: Souleymane Cissé
Writer: Souleymane Cissé
Photography: Jean-Noël Ferragut
Editors: Dounamba Coulibaly, Andrée Davanture, Marie-Cathérine Miqueau, Jenny Frenck, Seipati N'Xumalo
Production Designer: Kossa Mody Keita
Music: Salif Keita, Michel Portal

Nianankoro: Issiaka Kane
Attu: Aoua Sangare
Soma: Niamanto Sanogo
King of the Peul: Balla Moussa Keita

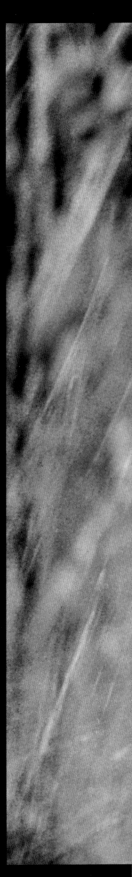

Top: The power of the mystical shaman. Nianankoro's father casts an evil spell.
Above: Nianankoro's son discovers some egg-like objects in the sand.
Left: Born in Mali, director Souleymane Cissé began his film career as a projectionist after Mali gained its independence in 1960.
Right: Attu (Aoua Sangare), the wife of the king, bathes in a desert spring.

Above: In an attempt to find her perfect match, Kabibi (Bibi Krubwa) consults a 'nyanga', or herbalist, along with Nvouandou (Kambu Kasongo) who is having marital problems in *La vie est belle* (1986). The medicine works for Kabibi, while the promise of a microwave oven for her mother persuades Kabibi to become Nvouandou's second wife, with disastrous results. Dir: Ngangura Mweze and Benoît Lamy

La vie est belle (1986) is a film from Zaire, directed by Ngangura Mweze and Benoît Lamy. The hero, Kourou, is a poor village musician whose traditional flute is broken in an accident. He journeys to the city (Kinshasa) in search of work. There, in a series of entertaining adventures, he finds success playing a modern style of African music with electric instruments. *La vie est belle* has something in common with *Xala* in its satire of the moneyed elite. Kourou's employer in Kinshasa, Nvouandou, is a wealthy bar owner who, like El Hadji, decides to take a new young wife, Kabibi. He too becomes impotent and goes to the witch doctor for help. The witch doctor tells him to perform certain rituals, and not to begin sexual relations with his new wife for a month. During that time Kabibi's affections turn towards Kourou and she leaves Nvouandou, telling her mother he is a 'fetisher'.

The Kinshasa of the film is a city of hardship for the poor but also a place of opportunity. Not the least of its attractions is its lively music scene; the hero is played by Papa Wemba, a popular music star in Zaire. It is also full of strong and independent women. Though Kabibi does little more than look pretty on screen, Nvouandou's first wife is a sturdy and forceful woman who spends much of her time having fun with a band of other jolly ladies. At the end, reconciled with her husband, she promises to renounce the company of 'liberated' women, but it is hard to see her husband keeping her in order for long.

Though *La vie est belle* provides a fascinating portrait of contemporary African urban life, its primary purpose is to entertain. By contrast, many of the films from French West Africa, such as those by Sembène, Sissoko and Cissé, have had a more explicitly didactic intent. Sembène has remarked that he looks upon cinema as 'a night school' for the audience. To an extent, African cinema has followed a pattern common in other areas of the world. Attempting to counter the deep penetration of their cultures by commercial films from overseas, West African governments and cultural elites have backed a form of counter-cinema.

The results are notably different from the commercial model. In the first place, this type of cinema makes a virtue out of necessity by shooting in real locations with natural lighting, frequently using non-professional actors. The camera style is often spartan, with few elaborate tracking or crane shots. In filming a dialogue sometimes the camera will simply move from side to side instead of cutting, preserving the unity of real space instead of constructing a specifically cinematic space. Screen time, too, is less broken up; the visual style is often more observational, actions being continued for longer than a strictly narrative imperative would consider necessary. Narrative itself is not always seamlessly integrated as it would be in a Hollywood picture. Characters who have an important function in the plot may be suddenly introduced without explanation; loose ends are not always tied up.

It is often remarked that the narrative style of African cinema owes much to the role of the 'griot', or storyteller, within traditional culture. Certainly this seems relevant to the 'folk-tale' quality of many films, which, unlike literary narratives such as the novel, often present characters who are emblematic types rather than fully developed individuals. Film historian Manthia Diawara remarks that cutaway shots are not always motivated by a relation to a character ('this is what x or y sees') but may be an intrusion of authorial comment by the director, in the same way that the griot might embellish the story he is telling.[1] However, trying to define an essence of African cinema does a disservice to its variety. In any case it is not always easy to say to what extent the stylistic features of African cinema are due to a cultural tradition different from the West, and to what extent they are the result of the extreme conditions in which African films are made. More time and money might lead to more elaborate script development. They might also result in a smoother, more conventional visual style.

As it is, the self-conscious attempt to create an African cinema distinct from all others can result in what have been called 'festival films', films that win prizes at Cannes but which, ironically, are scarcely ever seen in their countries of origin. The 2001 African Film Festival in Milan, for example, showed a dozen new African films; but how many will get a proper showing in their own country? The ironies of this phenomenon have been pointed out by the Tunisian director Férid Boughedir in discussing the role of magic in African films.[2] Whereas in the cinemas of the West the fantastic is wholly a realm of make-believe, relegated to a separate genre, the horror film, in African cinema the existence of supernatural powers may be no more than a conjuring trick, or else accepted as a matter of fact. In *Xala* El Hadji is made to appear ridiculous as he crawls towards his bride on all fours, a fetish in his mouth. Yet the curse placed upon him is real enough, whereas in *Saitane* (1972), a film from Niger directed by Oumarou Ganda, the fetishist is a swindler, and in *Finzan* the clownish Bala is tricked by the

AFRICAN VOICES

village boys into believing that a tree-god has spoken to him. Yet again, in Souleymane
Cissé's *Finyé* the god is real. Approached by an old man, Djandjo, for help when his son
is arrested by the military, the fetish in the tree replies that Djandjo must rely on the
wisdom he has acquired with his years. The god tells him to make an offering and depart.
At that moment a white cow magically appears. *La Chapelle* (1979), directed by the
Congolese Jean-Michel Tchissoukou, pits the village sorcerer as the defender of traditional
values against the school teacher, who sides with the French. In Idrissa Ouedraogo's *Yaaba*
(1989) two village children befriend a childless old woman, Sana, whom many believe
to be a witch. When one of the children, Nopoko, develops an infection, she is cured by
a friend of Sana who practises traditional medicine. The heroine of *Sarraounia* also has
genuine magical powers.

The most impressive of all the films that deal with traditional knowledge is Souleymane
Cissé's *Yeleen* (1987). Set in the dusty, sun-baked landscapes of the Sahel, the near-desert
region of northern West Africa, the film explores the conflict between Nianankoro and his
father, who blocks access to his knowledge of the secret society of Komo. Nianankoro is
sent on a pilgrimage by his mother. He comes to the land of the Fulanis, and uses his
supernatural powers to help them against their enemies, at one point working a spell with
the thigh bone of a horse which sets a swarm of bees on their foes. Nianankoro seduces the
king's youngest wife, Attu. In a beautiful scene they bathe in a desert spring. Nianankoro
eventually dies in a ritual confrontation with his father, but Attu bears him a son. In a sand
dune the boy discovers two sacred white orbs. He gives one to his mother, who in turn
gives him his father's cloak as a signal of succession.

Magic, as Boughedir points out, is a way for African cinema to get back to the roots of
its culture and its profoundly religious nature. Instead of simply rejecting traditional pre-
colonial beliefs in favour of Western rationality, some film-makers have taken them
seriously. Paradoxically, in doing so they have created a kind of cinema that finds ready

Previous pages:
Schoolchildren protest
in *A Dry White Season*
(1989).
Dir: Euzhan Palcy

acceptance in the West, which is always on the look out for the exotic, for something new and different. *Yeleen* can fit into a view of Africa as timeless, mysterious, enchantingly unknowable. 'So what started,' argues Boughedir, 'as a return to African spirituality in order to differentiate itself from Western models and affirm an African specificity has become, through some strange perversion in the system, an object of consummation for Western audiences in need of escape.'[3]

The festival films that Boughedir describes derive almost entirely from francophone West and Central Africa, which has produced around eighty per cent of all African films, in part because of the financial and other support made available by the French government. In 1963 the French Ministry of Cooperation began funding African film-making as part of a policy to tie its former colonies into the French sphere of influence. Though not without its critics (inevitably there have been charges of French interference), this policy has contributed to the high number and quality of francophone films. Historically, the British government has always had difficulty in seeing cinema as a genuine part of national culture. As a result, the former British colonies have so far made little impact on the stage of world cinema, though some of them have developed an indigenous popular cinema which if little seen or valued outside Africa has nevertheless demonstrated its commercial viability. In Nigeria there is a flourishing industry of up to thirty productions a month, according to Adewale Maja-Pearce;[4] *Variety* magazine estimates nearly twice as many. The films are quickly and cheaply made, both shot and distributed on video, with budgets of under £20,000 – often considerably less. The stories are lurid melodramas, full of violence and moralizing. *Wages* (2000) is typical. It stars Sandra Achums as Chetan, who goes to the city in order to be able to support her widowed mother but who soon succumbs to a life of easy virtue. She rejects her mother but after her mother dies they are reunited in a supernatural denouement. *Thunderbolt* (2000), directed by Tunde Kelani, reworks the Othello story with a tale of jealousy involving lovers from two different tribes, Yoruba and Ibo, and excursions into magic and traditional medicine.

Nigerian cinema is not entirely a matter of potboilers, but entertainment is well to the fore – for example, in the work of director Ola Balogun, who had great success with a series of films drawing on the resources of the popular Yoruba theatre. *Ajani-Ogun* (1976), described as Africa's first musical comedy, features the Yoruba star Ade Folayan performing several numbers in a story about a young man's struggles against a corrupt politician. At one point he kills a snake that has been threatening a pretty young woman, and she obligingly joins him in a cheerful song. In contrast to most other African films, stars are important in Nigerian cinema, and the following year Balogun directed the same performer in *Fight for Freedom* (*Ija Ominira*, 1977), about the overthrow of a tyrannical king. Balogun's 1982 film *Orun Mooru* has another popular Yoruba star, Baba Sala, in a fantasy about a villager who travels to the land of the dead intending to commit suicide, only to be refused admission. Magic, or juju, is an ever-present feature of these films, which whatever their weaknesses are undeniably part of a living popular culture.

In Ghana, two films by Kwaw Ansah combine comedy and music in dramatizing the perennial theme of tradition vs. modernity. *Love Brewed in the African Pot* (1980) is the tale of Aba, the daughter of a civil servant, who wants to marry Joe, a poor mechanic. Her father, Koffi, objects – as a Westernized middle-class man he wants her to better herself. The film points up the contradictions in the characters. Koffi thinks of himself as modern, yet has recourse to traditional medicine. Aba rejects his snobbery and class prejudice, but romanticizes Joe. Ansah's second film, *Heritage ... Africa* (1987) is set in the colonial period; the hero, Kwesi Atta Bosomefi, attempts to lose his African identity and become thoroughly Westernized, even to the point of changing his name to Quincy Arthur Bosomfield. This film was the first anglophone production to win the top prize at the FESPACO festival in Ouagadougou.

Until the collapse of apartheid in 1990 it was difficult for indigenous South African film-makers to truly reflect their society. Visitors such as Richard Attenborough, with *Cry Freedom* (1987), about the Steve Biko case, and Euzhan Palcy with *A Dry White Season* (1989), set at the time of the Soweto uprising, at least brought the iniquities of white rule to an international audience. Not so directly political but with an authentic feel for Johannesburg street life, *Mapantsula* (Oliver Schmitz, 1988), made under the last years of white supremacy, was co-written by its black star Thomas Mogotlane, who plays a petty crook trying to hustle a living. A later visitor was Les Blair, whose *Jump the Gun* (1996) is a brilliantly acted slice of more contemporary Johannesburg life.

The potential for cinema in South Africa, with its large market and capital resources,

Top: Mother and child
in a scene from the
musical film *Ajani-Ogun*
(1976).
Dir: Ola Balogun
Above: Thomas

Mogotlane as the
petty crook struggling
with the police in
Mapantsula (1988).
Dir: Oliver Schmitz

Above: A musical scene
from the exuberant
Sarafina! (1992).
Dir: Darrell James Roodt
Below: *Abouna* (2002).
Amine (Hamza Moctar
Aguid) and his older

brother Tahir (Ahidjo
Mahamat Moussa)
as the two boys who
think they saw their
missing father in a film.
Dir: Mahamat Saleh
Haroun

must be great. It has yet to be fully realized, but in the 1990s local film-makers such as
Darrell James Roodt found more freedom. His *Jobman* (1990) is a gritty story of a deaf and
dumb man's search for work, while *Sarafina!* (1992) stars Whoopi Goldberg and Leleti
Khumalo in a musical set in a Soweto school, where the students are becoming radicalized.
Dangerous Ground (1997) features Ice Cube and other American actors in a thriller aimed at
international audiences. In a significant development, some francophone directors are now
starting to shoot in southern Africa: for example, Idrissa Ouedraogo, whose *Kini and Adams*
(1997) was shot in English in Zimbabwe.

Lusophone cinema from the former Portuguese colonies has also trailed behind the
francophone, though *The Blue Eyes of Yonta* (*Udju Azul di Yonta*, 1991), directed by Flora
Gomes of Guinea-Bissau, is a striking reworking of the theme of post-revolutionary
disillusion, dramatized in a triangular love story.

Africa's grave social and economic difficulties make it hard for cinema to build on its
achievements. Every film-maker, it seems, must go back to scratch. *Dôlé* (2001), a first film
from Gabon by Imunga Ivanga, has a non-professional cast, natural lighting and real-life
locations, which give a lively sense of street life in Libreville, but the neo-realist style leaves
things pretty much where they were twenty years ago. However, a recent initiative by the
European Union offers a modest hope for continuity of production, providing €6 million
over three years from January 2000. Among the films that have already received such
assistance is *Abouna* (2002), a rare film from Chad, directed by Mahamat Saleh Haroun.
When their father deserts them, two young boys are sent by their mother to a harsh Koranic
school. The younger boy dies and the older escapes with a deaf-mute girl he has befriended.
The film has many echoes of European art cinema (the director is based in France), but is
firmly rooted in the rhythms and rigours of local life. Ironically, the film was selected for
showing at the 2002 Cannes Film Festival before it had been screened in its country of
origin. There is only one cinema in Chad.

KYOAMI:

In a mad world, only the mad are sane.

Kyoami (Peter), Lord Hidetora (Nkadai Tatsuya),
Ran (Kurosawa Akira, 1985)

Previous pages:
Nakadai Tatsuya as
the aged ruler in *Ran*
(1985), a Japanese
version of King Lear.
Period films or
jidaigeki have been
a staple of Japanese
cinema, projecting
an easily identifiable
image of Japanese
culture. But nowadays
they appeal less to
younger audiences.
Dir: Kurosawa Akira
<u>Above</u>: Chen Kaige

directing *Temptress
Moon* (*Fengyue*, 1996)
<u>Below right</u>: Gong Li as
the scarlet-clad wife in
a field of sorghum in
Red Sorghum (*Hong
Gaoliang*, 1987).
Dir: Zhang Yimou
<u>Opposite</u>: Xue Bai as
Cuiqiao, the young
peasant girl who falls
for the Communist
soldier in *Yellow Earth*
(*Huang Tudi*, 1984).
Dir: Chen Kaige

East Asia contains some of the most dynamic film industries in the world. Its populous societies, often economically vibrant and with rich cultural heritages, have mostly taken to cinema with enthusiasm and produced work of great distinction. But for many of these countries the twentieth century was one of political turmoil, often marked by war, and these convulsions have profoundly affected their films.

Every nation's cinema is influenced by its social and political history, but this is nowhere more true than in China. Since the Communist victory in 1949 the film industry has been under strict government control, with each turn in political policy reflected on the country's screens. In the 1950s and 1960s the Chinese made great efforts to bring cinema to their vast rural population. The films produced closely followed the dogma of 'socialist realism' first developed under Stalin – aesthetically conservative and dedicated to the improvement of the population. Then in 1966 came the tumult of the Cultural Revolution. Feature-film production was halted. Established figures in the industry were sent to the country for 're-education' or were imprisoned; some committed suicide. Though production resumed in the early 1970s, it was not until 1978 that the Beijing Film Academy, then the country's only film school, reopened to students. When this intake graduated, four years later, it was dubbed the Fifth Generation, indicating a distinct break with earlier generations of Chinese film-makers, both politically and aesthetically. Born after 1949, they had no personal memories of pre-revolutionary China to compare with the present, favourably or unfavourably. Nor did they have to serve the long apprenticeship of their predecessors; assigned to small regional studios, where there were few trained directors, they were able to make films straight away.

Yellow Earth (*Huang Tudi*, 1984), directed by Chen Kaige,[1] created a sensation when shown at foreign film festivals. Set in the 1930s, the film concerns a young Communist soldier sent to collect folk songs from the peasants. In a village he befriends a girl who is betrothed to an old man. With his tales of modern life in the areas under Communist rule the soldier raises the girl's expectations, but is unable to change the feudal ways of the village. This alone made the film a departure from political orthodoxy. But even more startling was its look. The bare landscape is filmed in static long shots, often empty of figures, a style which some critics have traced back to traditional, pre-socialist Chinese landscape painting. Instead of the conventional framing and lighting of previous Chinese cinema, Fifth Generation films often show characters off-centre, the lighting dark. Not every shot has a clear narrative function; ambiguity, so distrusted by Party ideologues, is common. The Fifth Generation were the first group of Chinese film-makers systematically exposed to the masters of European modernism such as Michelangelo Antonioni, Jean-Luc Godard and Rainer Werner Fassbinder, and it showed in their work.

Other, equally daring films followed. Hu Mei's *Army Nurse* (*Nü'er lou*, 1985), directed by a woman, explores the distinctively female point of view of its protagonist by means of voice-over and other subjective techniques, to the point of explicitly presenting her desire for a male patient. Tian Zhuangzhuang's *Horse Thief* (*Daoma Zei*, 1986) is set among Tibetan nomads. Visually stunning but narratively elliptical, it caused a stir, especially when the director, stung by criticism that the film was not popular, claimed to have made it for 'audiences of the next century'.

If Chinese audiences and officials were not always sympathetic, abroad the films of the

CINEMA IN THE FAR EAST

Fifth Generation were a hit. Zhang Yimou's *Red Sorghum* (*Hong Gaoliang*, 1987) won the Golden Bear award at the Berlin Film Festival. It is a story of peasant life, beginning in the 1920s, continuing into the Japanese invasion. A young woman is married to an elderly leper, then kidnapped by a man who has sex with her in a field of sorghum. Her husband dies, her kidnapper claims her as his wife and they build a successful business making sorghum wine, only for their lives to be brutally interrupted by the arrival of the Japanese. It is a film of visual splendour, but also, unusual in earlier Chinese cinema, of transgressive female desire. Red, a persistent motif in Zhang's films, clearly signifies something other than Communism. Zhang's subsequent films *Ju Dou* (1990) and *Raise the Red Lantern* (*Dahong Denglong Gaogao Gua*, 1991), both successfully shown in the West, form a kind of trilogy with *Red Sorghum*. Each is set in the 1920s, concerns a forceful young woman married to an older man and stars the beautiful Gong Li. *Ju Dou* takes place in a dye factory, which gives occasion for Zhang's brilliant use of colour in the story of how a young wife deceives her elderly husband. In *Raise the Red Lantern* Gong Li is the fourth wife of a rich man and has to struggle for power and position, symbolized in the red lantern which is hung outside the room of whichever wife enjoys the husband's favour that night.

The Fifth Generation were not the only ones attempting to break out of the strait-jacket of Party policy. Xie Jin, who was born in 1923 and began his career before the Cultural Revolution, made a number of melodramas in the 1980s which were critical of aspects of the Party's history. In *Hibiscus Town* (*Furong Zhen*, 1986) a woman builds up a good restaurant business through hard work only to have it destroyed in the excesses of the Cultural Revolution. But it was the younger directors who caught the eye of foreign critics, even if at home their films increasingly ran into trouble; both *Ju Dou* and *Raise the Red Lantern* (each funded with foreign money) were initially banned in China, where politics had lurched back towards repression in the wake of the Tiananmen Square massacre of 1989.

Without justifying the oppressive censorship exercised by the Chinese authorities, one can understand up to a point why many Fifth Generation films did not meet with approval. Some Chinese critics charged that the films encouraged an emphasis on the exotic, reinforcing stereotypes of Chinese 'backwardness', producing only those images of China that the West wished to consume. These films seemed less concerned with dramatizing the realities of Chinese life and more with China's place in the global film market. But their sexual openness was also a problem for official puritanism.

Chen Kaige's *Farewell My Concubine* (*Ba Wang Bie Ji*, 1993) is a case in point. It wove together the personal and the political in the story of two actors in the Peking Opera from the 1920s to the 1970s. Their increasingly intense homoerotic relationship is complicated both by outside events and by one falling for a prostitute, played by Gong Li. An opulent and subtle film, it garnered awards abroad but was questioned at home. Chen's later film, *The Emperor and the Assassin* (*Jing Ke Ci Qin Wang*, 1999), a historical epic, was also on a lavish scale, but more conventional in its characterization.

Zhang Yimou's next film after *Raise the Red Lantern* was *The Story of Qiu Ju* (*Qiu Ju Da Guansi*, 1992), in which a young peasant woman battles the legal system to get redress for her husband, who has been wrongfully assaulted. Though the film observes the obtuseness of the authorities, the wife's final victory serves to indicate that the system is fundamentally

Above: Gong Li as the young wife of an elderly owner of a dye factory and Li Baotian as her lover in *Ju Dou* (1990).
Dir: Zhang Yimou
Right: Zhang Yimou directing *Raise the Red Lantern* (*Dahong Denglong Gaogao Gua*, 1991).
Opposite top: Gong Li as Songlian, being prepared for her fifty-year-old husband in *Raise the Red Lantern* (*Dahong Denglong Gaogao Gua*, 1991).
Opposite below: Kneeling in the snow, a servant views the charred remains of the lanterns in *Raise the Red Lantern* (*Dahong Denglong Gaogao Gua*, 1991).
Dir: Zhang Yimou

CINEMA IN THE FAR EAST

Challenging Authority
Farewell My Concubine
(*Ba Wang Bie Ji*, 1993)
Dir: Chen Kaige

Farewell My Concubine was Chen Kaige's fifth feature film and his first with a large budget. Shot largely in the studio, with well-established stars such as Leslie Cheung, it paints on a broad canvas the story of two actors, from their first meeting at school in the 1920s through their success as stars of the Peking Opera, difficulties during the Japanese occupation, the Communist takeover in 1949 and the traumas of the Cultural Revolution in the 1960s. For the so-called Fifth Generation of Chinese film-makers, the film breaks new ground on two fronts. In the first place, though it does not shy away from recognizing the hardships of life under the old regime, it takes a jaundiced view of Communist society and of the Cultural Revolution in particular. The two friends, Xiaolou and Dieyi, adopt a young man, Xiao Si, who becomes one of the Red Guards and promptly denounces the political 'crimes' of his benefactors. (Chen Kaige had himself been a Red Guard and denounced his own father – who is the art director on this film.)

Second, the film is a love story of an unusual kind. Dieyi is homosexual and suffers rejection when Xiaolou begins an affair with Juxian (Gong Li), a beautiful prostitute. Emotional fulfilment and the problems of attaining it are at the heart of the film. They do not make the politics irrelevant, but politics makes love more difficult to achieve.

The film had a great success in the West, in no small measure due to the gorgeousness of its production, especially the splendid re-creations of the Peking Opera, with wonderfully fluid camerawork and rich art design. Back home the film was treated with suspicion by the authorities, nervous of both its politics and its presentation of homosexuality.

Country of Origin:
Hong Kong/China
Running Time: 156 mins

Production Company:
Tomson (HK) Films
Company Limited
Producer: Hsu Feng
Writers: Lilian Lee, Lu Wei
Photography:
Gu Changwei
Editor: Pei Xiaonan
Production Designer:
Chen Huaikai
Music: Zhao Jiping

Cheng Dieyi:
Leslie Cheung
Duan Xiaolou:
Zhang Fengyi
Juxian: Gong Li
Guan Jifa: Lu Qi
Na Kun: Ying Da
Xiao Si (Teenage): Li Chun
Xiao Si (Adult): Lei Han

A FILM BY CHEN KAIGE

霸王別姬

FAREWELL TO MY CONCUBINE

Left: Listening intently, Leslie Cheung as Cheng Dieyi, one of the stars of the Peking Opera.
Above: A poster depicting the intense passion of *Farewell My Concubine*.
Right: A great performance from Zhang Fengyi as Duan Xiaolou and Leslie Cheung as Cheng Dieyi. Initially banned in China the film explores the changing relationship between the two men against a political backdrop.

Above: Wei Minzhi as the thirteen-year-old teacher pitched into the classroom without experience in *Not One Less* (*Yi Ge Dou Bu Neng Shao*, 1999). Dir: Zhang Yimou

Above right: Li Bin as the schoolboy who steals a bicycle from a poor worker in *Beijing Bicycle* (*Shiqi Sui De Danche*, 2001). Dir: Wang Xiaoshuai

sound. Two films at the end of the 1990s show Zhang pulling back from the forthright and sexually assertive female characters of his earlier work. In *Not One Less* (*Yi Ge Dou Bu Neng Shao*, 1999) a shy young girl barely into her teens is obliged to take over at the village school from an experienced teacher who is called away. He admonishes her not to lose a single pupil. Working with a largely non-professional cast Zhang paints a charming rural tableau, one that shows traditional Chinese virtues overcoming hardship and poverty. *The Road Home* (*Wo De Fuqin Muqin*, 1999) contrasts the present (in monochrome) with the past of the 1950s (in glorious colour), in a story of a young country woman who falls in love with a visiting teacher. Again, Zhang produces a sympathetic portrait of rural life, but the teacher's absence during the period of 'Anti-Rightist' purges is rather glossed over, and the demure heroine is a far cry from those of his earlier work.

In the 1990s the chill winds of economic liberalization began to blow through the film studios. No longer could films be produced simply according to political principles. Now they had to perform at the box office. Unfortunately few in China had experience of such a regulatory mechanism and the studios were soon in trouble. Coproduction finance from abroad had been forthcoming for star directors such as Chen and Zhang, with as much as a quarter of Chinese production funded from abroad by 1993, but as the 1990s wore on the authorities tightened their political grip, insisting on total control of the negative, with the inevitable consequence that foreign producers became reluctant to invest.

Seeking to find a formula for popular success, the studios began making entertainment films in well-established genres such as kung fu or comedy, though the government continued to insist on a certain number of politically approved productions such as war films or stories of model workers. The Fifth Generation directors were still making 'art' films aimed at the international market. At the same time a new sort of cinema began to emerge, underground film-making carried on outside the official channels. Wang Xiaoshuai's *The Days* (*Dongchun De Rizi*, 1993) follows the relationship of a couple of unsuccessful artists dreaming of striking it rich while eking out a humdrum existence. Shot in black and white against a wintry Beijing background and an even bleaker north-eastern countryside, the film entirely resists the upbeat optimism enjoined by the Party. At one point the hero, asked about his plans for the future, remarks bitterly, 'Damn the future!' The film is not so much hostile to socialist ideology as uninterested, leading to some critics' description of such films as 'post-socialist'. Wang's later films *Frozen* (*Jidu Hanleng*, 1996) and *So Close to Paradise* (*Biandan Guniang*, 1998) are equally about marginal characters, though *Beijing Bicycle* (*Shiqi Sui De Danche*, 2001), made with official approval, is more mainstream, a kind of Chinese version of the neo-realist classic *Bicycle Thieves* (*Ladri di*

CINEMA IN THE FAR EAST

biciclette, Vittorio De Sica, 1948) which nevertheless contains implicit criticism of the continuing divide between rich and poor.

In the same vein, Jiang Wen's *In the Heat of the Sun* (*Yangguang canlan de rizi*, 1994) debunks the Maoist rhetoric surrounding the Cultural Revolution, as the hero looks back on the fights and sexual escapades he experienced. Another innovative young director is Zhang Yuan. *Mama* (1992) is a grim look at the difficulties of a single woman trying to care for her handicapped child. *Beijing Bastards* (*Beijing Zazhong*, 1993) takes a look at contemporary urban youth, drugs and all, incorporating performances by the radical rock

star Cui Jian. Most challenging to the official line was Zhang's *East Palace West Palace* (*Dong Gong Xi Gong*, 1996), in which a gay man's interrogation by a policeman develops disturbing sado-masochistic undertones. It led to the authorities tightening up on the production of unofficial films.

At the same time, China has been opening up its cinema screens to Hollywood, to an extent that would have previously been unthinkable, with the limit being raised to twenty films a year, with the possibility of forty before long. Imports during 2001 included Michael Bay's *Pearl Harbor*. To what extent this will lead to increasing financial pressures on domestic production, hovering at around 100 films a year, and to what extent Chinese film-makers will be increasingly influenced by Hollywood models, are questions that will become more pressing in future.

Hong Kong, meanwhile, has produced a quite exceptional cinema. This tiny former British colony has a population of only six million, yet its films have been exported all over the world, while at home Hong Kong was long one of the few countries where domestic output dominated the box office. From 1970 Hong Kong produced at least 100 films a year, and in the early 1990s twice that, its production equalling Japan – a country with a population twenty times as large – and often outstripping that of mainland China.

How has this been achieved? Certainly not with state support. Hong Kong's economy has been founded on unbridled capitalism, free trade and production for export. The country has been a copy-book demonstration of the apparent fact that if you give people what they want at the right price they will buy it. Export in cinema production was essential; though Hong Kong has a very high rate of cinema attendance (ten tickets sold per year per head of population), the domestic market alone is not enough to sustain its high levels of production.

The large Chinese diaspora in south-east Asia and elsewhere provides a ready market, but at the beginning of the 1970s there was also a boom in exports to Europe and the United States. The explanation can be given in two words: kung fu. This variant of Chinese unarmed combat was adapted into an individual style by the actor Bruce Lee in films produced by the newly formed Golden Harvest company. *Fist of Fury* (*Jingwu men*, 1972), titled *The Chinese Connection* in the United States to cash in on the smash-hit *The French Connection* (1971), was a great success internationally, leading to the rapid production of *Way of the Dragon/Return of the Dragon* (*Menglong guo jiang*, 1972), directed by Lee himself, and *Enter the Dragon* (1973), financed by Hollywood.

In these films Lee was the stern-faced, ascetic avenger. *Way of the Dragon* was set, improbably, in Rome, affording an opportunity for Lee and Chuck Norris, as an American hitman imported by the villains, to have a final confrontation in the Colosseum. Apart from Lee the acting is execrable and the attempts at comedy dismal, but neither affected the film's popularity, which turned entirely on Lee's ability as a fighter. The films ascribe his prowess to a monkish dedication, including the refusal of sexual overtures. In *Enter the Dragon* contestants at a martial arts competition organized by the villain Han are offered girls. Only Lee declines, set on revenging his sister, who had committed suicide when faced with rape by Han's men. Han's metal hand is a clear steal from the first Bond film, *Dr No* (Terence Young, 1962), whose eponymous oriental villain is similarly gifted.

Lee's style of fighting made him a star. Sudden, violent action is compressed into split-seconds, punctuated by moments of contemplative stasis. Kung fu became an international craze, inspiring pop songs, fashion and an American TV series. One can speculate that the worldwide patrons of Bruce Lee films were those same young urban males, from Mombasa to Manila, who in the previous decade had delighted in Italian spaghetti Westerns.

Lee's premature death in 1973 canonized him as the patron saint of kung fu. His mantle was inherited by Jackie Chan, whose screen persona was the opposite of Lee's. Chan was forever the underdog, with a rueful, self-deprecating expression. Kung fu comedy was his forte in such films as *Snake in the Eagle's Shadow* (*She xing diao shou*, Yuen Woo-ping, 1978).

Right: Jackie Chan as Detective Inspector Lee performing one of his many breathtaking stunts in the action-comedy *Rush Hour* (1998).
Dir: Brett Ratner

CINEMA IN THE FAR EAST

As the kung fu craze waned, Chan moved into other genres with such films as *Police Story* (*Jingcha Gushi*, Jackie Chan, 1984), a crime film in which Chan performed some astonishing stunts on a double-decker bus. By the late 1990s he had made a breakthrough in Hollywood with the action-comedy *Rush Hour* (Brett Ratner, 1998) and the comedy Western *Shanghai Noon* (Tom Dey, 2000).

Kung fu largely replaced the earlier swordplay or wuxia films, of which King Hu was the supreme director. His masterpiece, *A Touch of Zen* (*Xia nü*, 1969), actually made in Taiwan, is a dazzling display of editing technique and spectacular pageantry. Like Hollywood, Hong Kong cinema has been primarily genre-based and reliant on stars, though with a narrower range of genres, mainly martial arts, crime films and comedies. Genres, while ensuring the continuity that popular cinema requires for efficient production, also need to be constantly reinvented if the public is to stay interested. At the end of the 1970s came the so-called New Wave, which saw a new breed of younger directors reworking generic traditions. It was at this point that Hong Kong cinema really took off stylistically. Director and producer Tsui Hark brought brilliant technical skills and artistic élan to a range of popular formats: *The Butterfly Murders* (*Die bian*, 1979) reworked the martial arts film; *Zu: Warriors from the Magic Mountain* (*Shu shan*, 1983) updated the swordplay genre; *A Better Tomorrow* (*Yingxiong Bense*,

Above: A scene from the martial arts film *A Touch of Zen* (*Xia nü*, 1969). Dir: King Hu
Right: Jet Li limbering up in the martial arts spectacular *Once Upon a Time in China* (*Huang Feihong*, 1991). Dir: Tsui Hark

1986) was the film in which John Woo found his feet as Hong Kong's supreme director of hard-edged crime movies; Tsui's *Peking Opera Blues* (*Daoma Dan*, 1986) is a dazzling re-creation of the traditional Chinese theatrical entertainment, set in the early twentieth century. *A Chinese Ghost Story* (*Xiannü Youhun*, 1987), produced by Tsui Hark and directed by Ching Siu-Tung, was a not particularly scary horror film (its vampire-like ghosts are rather sweet), but it sparkled with spectacular swordplay and special effects, including a tree-spirit with an enormous tongue. Hardly a shot is not tilted, nor is any held for more than a few seconds. In *Once Upon a Time in China* (*Huang Feihong*, 1991) and its sequels Tsui revived the traditional kung fu story. Wong Fei-hung was the hero of a popular martial arts series in the 1950s, and Tsui's series has a strongly nationalist slant, set in a late nineteenth-century China struggling to free itself from foreign domination. The films also show that he has no superior as a director of intricate and inventive action. *Once Upon a Time in China 2* (*Huang Feihong zhi Yi: nan'r Dang Zi Qiang*, 1993) follows the celebrated fight on ladders of the first film with a battle between star Jet Li, armed with a bamboo pole, and an opponent who has ingeniously twisted a length of cloth into a flexible but dangerous whip that can knock lumps out of the wall.

John Woo's direction of Chow Yun-fat in *A Better Tomorrow* made both of them stars. Woo's *The Killer* (*Die xue shuang xiong*, 1989) and *Hard-Boiled* (*Lashou shentan*, 1992) continued the partnership, in which Woo married the bleak heroics of the American cop genre to stylistic bravura, using editing, framing, camera movement and the agility of actors to achieve unprecedented levels of aesthetic fluency, as in the dazzling shoot-out in a restaurant kitchen that opens *Hard-Boiled*.

Above: The look of defiance in *Boat People* (*Touben Nü Hai*, 1982). Dir: Ann Hui
Below: Tony Leung and Maggie Cheung, thrown together in an increasingly intimate friendship when they discover their spouses are having an affair. *In the Mood for Love* (*Hua yang nian hua*, 2000). Dir: Wong Kar-wai
Opposite: Faye Wong looks up from her reflection in the evocative and experimental *Chungking Express* (*Chongqing Senlin*, 1994). Dir: Wong Kar-wai

Another New Wave director, Ann Hui, Hong Kong's best woman director, has embellished traditional genres. *The Spooky Bunch* (*Zhuang dao zheng*, 1980) is an inventive and comic ghost story, *The Story of Woo Viet* (*Hu Yue de Gushi*, 1981) is a crime film, and *Boat People* (*Touben Nü Hai*, 1982) a realist drama set in Vietnam which explains why so many Vietnamese left to become refugees or 'boat people' in Hong Kong. *Romance of Book and Sword* (*Shujian Enchou Lu*, 1987) is a sumptuously filmed historical action spectacular. In the 1990s Hui revitalized the melodrama in such films as *Song of the Exile* (*Ketu qiuhen*, 1990), about a troubled mother–daughter relationship.

Stanley Kwan's *Rouge* (*Yanzhi kou*, 1987) is also a ghost story, but at the same time perhaps the closest Hong Kong cinema has got to an art-house movie, its story of a prostitute of the 1930s who haunts the present over-laid with lush and languorous images, evoking a powerful nostalgia for the passion of past times contrasting with the prosy hustle and bustle of present-day Hong Kong. *Actress* (*Ruan Lingyu*, 1992) also merges past and present in a highly self-reflexive manner: a biography of a Shanghai actress of the 1930s, it mixes interviews and film clips in its dramatization. Kwan's recent film *Lan Yu* (2001) is stylistically more orthodox but thematically innovative, the story of an affair between a boy up from the country and a successful businessman. It is not Kwan's first film to touch on gay sexuality, but it is his most explicit.

What characterizes all these film-makers and sets them off against Chinese cinema on the mainland and in Taiwan is a sense of playfulness, a delight, occasionally hyperactive, in the sheer visual and auditory possibilities of cinema, all in the cause of entertainment. The most inventive talent to appear in the 1990s was undoubtedly Wong Kar-wai, who has rapidly made himself the darling of the international festival circuit with barely more than half a dozen films, the best known of which is *Chungking Express* (*Chongqing Senlin*, 1994). Its two connected stories of love set around a fast-food café match a mood of melancholy romanticism, musing on the fleeting nature of love, always prey to the caprices of coincidence, to a virtuoso parade of stylistic devices. Shooting a huge amount of footage, with no fixed script, Wong Kar-wai plays with unsettling angles and bright colours, showing off a full box of technical tricks. A character in the foreground will move normally while in the background things whizz past at speed. Some shots are filmed at ultra slow-motion then stretched in the printing to bring them up to normal speed, creating a strangely hypnotic effect. And always there is music, never more memorably than in his highly successful *In the Mood for Love* (*Hua yang nian hua*, 2000), which tells the story of a doomed love affair against an incessantly repeated wistful musical motif. Though as carefully shot as any of his previous films, *In the Mood for Love* is less frenetically paced, as befits its elegiac memories.

Ironically, at a time when the international prestige of Hong Kong cinema was at its height, commercially it began to falter. In the early 1990s production reached over 150 films per year, and in 1992 the top dozen films at the Hong Kong box office were all domestic productions. Excessive production, piracy, competition in overseas markets, the exhaustion of its favoured genres and uncertainty about the consequences of the reversion of Hong Kong to mainland Chinese control in 1997 led to a decline in confidence in the later 1990s, with production barely expected to reach fifty features in 2002.

The cinema of Taiwan is in many ways a complete contrast. Whereas in Hong Kong the film industry was left to its own devices, treated as just another example of successful capitalism, in Taiwan it was for many years an instrument of government policy. On their defeat by the Communists in 1949 the Kuomintang or Nationalist forces had set themselves up in Taiwan, determined to assert their legitimacy as the rightful government of all China. Channelling funds to the film industry through the Central Motion Picture Corporation, established in 1963, the Nationalists ensured that cinema remained politically quiescent. Film-going and production expanded in the 1960s until Taiwan was making over 200 films a year. Many were in the approved genre of 'wholesome realism' designed, in the official definition, to 'promote good qualities of humanity such as sympathy, care, forgiveness, consideration and altruism'.

CINEMA IN THE FAR EAST

Other genres were permitted, however. It has been estimated that in the 1970s no fewer than forty-two per cent of all Taiwanese films were kung fu dramas, and costume pictures and romantic melodramas also proliferated, while studios directly under the control of the government made war films and anti-Communist propaganda. The economic boom of the 1980s, the growth of the cities and the rise of a younger generation of film-goers led to demand for new genres which could compete with the sex and violence emanating from Hong Kong and elsewhere. But as Taiwanese cinema went down-market in a search for new audiences, the authorities became concerned. The Government Information Office decided to encourage the more serious and talented of the younger directors, and in the early 1980s a New Taiwanese Cinema was born.

The most celebrated of these directors is Hou Hsiao-Hsien. His early work, such as *The Green, Green Grass of Home* (*Zai na hepan qingcao qing*, 1983), is still conditioned by the worthiness of 'wholesome realism', but *The Boys from Fengkuei* (*Fengqui Lei de Ren*, 1983), about a group of country youths encountering city life, shows signs of an independent point of view. *The Time to Live and the Time to Die* (*Tong nian wang shi*, 1985) is a masterly portrait of family life through the eyes of a young man growing up in the 1950s and 1960s. Like many of Hou's films it subtly mingles the political with the personal. The hero's father was born on the mainland, and has never lost the dream of one day returning, but at the time of his death the Nationalists and Communists remain locked in struggle. Hou's lucid, unhurried, elegant style, the usually static camera observing the minutiae of the household and its surroundings, allows a series of loosely related tableaux to build up a richly textured picture of daily life in several generations of one family.

A loosely connected trilogy on Taiwanese history allowed Hou to open up areas that up until that time the Nationalist government had preferred should remain unexamined. *City of Sadness* (*Beiqing chengshi*, 1989), which won the Golden Lion at the Venice Film Festival, covers the period 1945–9, from the end of Japanese occupation up until the Nationalists' defeat on the mainland by the Communists. It is set against the background of the events of 28 February 1947, when the Taiwanese rebelled against the Nationalist administrators. They were brutally repressed and thousands were killed, but for decades afterwards the government refused to recognize the scale of the atrocity. In Hou's film these events are refracted through the lives of four brothers, each of whom suffers as a result. In a scene at the end, the wife of the youngest son, who is deaf, receives a letter announcing the murder of her brother by the Nationalists. She and her husband weep silently as their baby son plays happily on the bed in front of them. It is a moment of profound emotion, achieved in a single long take.

The Puppetmaster (*Ximeng Rensheng*, 1993) is set during the Japanese occupation, which in Taiwan lasted half a century, from 1895 to 1945. An old man, the eponymous hero, who eventually joins a Japanese propaganda puppet show, recounts both family and political history without rancour. At the end of the war a Japanese commander invites him to lunch and tells him how much he will miss Taiwan. In the final film of the trilogy, *Good Men, Good*

Above top: The ever-widening generation gap seen through the eyes of a young man in *The Time to Live and the Time to Die* (*Tong nian wang shi*, 1985). Dir: Hou Hsiao-Hsien
Above: *Good Men, Good Women* (*Haonan Haonü*, 1995) follows the lives of a couple who are arrested when they return to Taiwan from China.
Dir: Hou Hsiao-Hsien
Right: The family group assembled for the wedding which breaks up in farce in *A One and a Two...* (*Yi yi*, 2000).
Dir: Edward Yang

CINEMA IN THE FAR EAST

Women (*Haonan Haonü*, 1995), an actress in a contemporary film begins to dig into the lives of a left-wing couple in the 1950s who were persecuted during the so-called 'White Terror', an anti-Communist purge in which thousands were arrested and executed.

A director whose career has been closely linked with Hou's is Edward Yang. Yang's *Taipei Story* (*Qingmei Zhuma*, 1985) actually stars Hou as an unsuccessful businessman trying to cope with the effects of rapid modernization. Yang's *The Terrorizer* (*Kongbu fenzi*, 1986) is a deeply impressive study of the modern city with all its complexity and arbitrary connections. *A Brighter Summer's Day* (*Guling die Shaonian Sha Ren Shijian*, 1991) is set in 1960. Schoolboys form gangs and immerse themselves in US culture (the title comes from a line in the Elvis Presley song 'Are You Lonesome Tonight?'). It is a measured, detailed portrait of youth struggling to find an identity between the United States and China, with ultimately tragic results. Yang's *A One and a Two...* (*Yi yi*, 2000) is perhaps his masterpiece. Beginning at a wedding which degenerates into a farce as the parties begin to row with each other, it follows a businessman forced to re-examine his life when an old girlfriend shows up. From such material, the small change of soap operas, Yang builds a dense, rich and moving panorama of modern urban life, its triumphs and tragedies.

The films of the New Taiwanese Cinema did not always do well at the box office, but the government – by now more liberal and democratic – has supported young, unknown directors. Though Taiwanese cinema in the 1990s has been scaled down to around twenty films a year, high-quality work has continued to appear, even if aimed mainly at a festival audience and often made with coproduction finance from abroad. Hou's recent films have not been his best. *Flowers of Shanghai* (*Hai shang hua*, 1998) is a supremely elegant period piece set in a high-class brothel within the British enclave in Shanghai at the end of the nineteenth century. 'Exquisite' was the adjective most often applied by critics, but the hothouse atmosphere, brilliantly filmed in a formally elegant style, with long mobile takes, is ultimately stifling compared to his earlier work. *Millennium Mambo* (*Qianxi manbo*, 2001) is another departure, Hou's attempt to say something about contemporary youth culture, but its story of a bar girl shacked up with an aimless loser fails to overcome the unattractiveness of the characters.

More closely in touch with contemporary youth is Tsai Ming-Liang's acute *Rebels of the Neon God* (*Qing Shaonian Nezha*, 1992), about a young drifter on the edges of the criminal world. His *Vive L'Amour* (*Aiqing wansui*, 1994) follows a lonely estate agent as she has loveless sex with a casual pick-up in an empty flat. Under the bed, masturbating, is a young man who makes a precarious living selling cremation containers, and who earlier had been intending to commit suicide after breaking in. In the final shot the woman sits on a park bench, crying. It is a disturbing yet elegant study of urban ennui. Tsai's *The River* (*Heliu*, 1997) – a story of a family, each of whom is miserable in their own way – shows how total has been the break with 'wholesome realism'. Its climax, in which the son encounters his father in a gay sauna, is a landmark moment in Taiwanese cinema, transgressive of the taboos of homosexuality and incest and expressive of a profound dislocation in contemporary urban family life.

In 1975, for the first time, foreign films out-performed domestic productions at the Japanese box office. Until then the Japanese had a film industry not unlike the United States', tightly controlled by a small number of film studios, who owned their own theatres. Films fell into a number of clearly defined genres. These included comedies, often in series such as the seemingly endless sequence of films entitled *Tora-san* (*Otoko wa tsurai yo*) churned out by the Shochiku studio from 1969 and starring Atsumi Kiyoshi as the amiable Tora-san. Period films, called *jidaigeki*, had long been a staple and the more artistic ones, many directed by Kurosawa Akira, were exported to the West as 'samurai' films, especially after his *Rashomon* (1950) won a prize at Venice. Science fiction was another major genre and included the redoubtable Godzilla series, begun in 1954. Yakuza or gangster films had become popular in the 1960s, especially at the Toei and Nikkatsu studios.

Yet overall production had been falling since 1960, when 547 films were produced; by the end of the century it was down to half that figure and the share of the audience commanded by indigenous films steadily declined as television made inroads and Hollywood grew ever more powerful. In the early 1970s, in an attempt to arrest the decline, Nikkatsu went over to the production of soft-core pornography, the so-called *roman poruno* genre, with such productions as *Street of Joy* (*Akasen tamanoi: Nukeraremasu, tamanoi*, 1974), directed by Kumashiro Tatsumi, and *A Woman Called Sada Abe* (*Jitsuroku Abe Sada*, 1975), directed by Tanaka Noboru, a version of the same story filmed by Oshima Nagisa as *In the Realm of the Senses* (*Ai No Corrida*, 1976). In the 1980s and 1990s more extreme erotic films appeared, the so-called *ero-guro* ('erotic-grotesque'), featuring rape and torture scenarios and increasingly

Above top: The hothouse atmosphere of the brothel: Carina Lau in *Flowers of Shanghai* (*Hai shang hua*, 1998).

Dir: Hou Hsiao-Hsien
Above: Li Kangsheng as Hsiao Kang and Miao Tan as his father in *The River* (*Heliu*, 1997). Dir: Tsai Ming-Liang

weird titles (a 1992 example is rendered into English as *Masturbation in Uniform: Virgins' Panties*). Increasingly these were produced for video consumption, though they provided useful training for such directors as Ishii Takashi, whose *Gonin* (1995), a frantically exciting yakuza film, was one of the hits of the 1990s.

By the end of the 1960s Oshima had established a reputation as an iconoclastic director with an anti-establishment attitude and a determinedly modernist technique, both shown to good effect in *Death by Hanging* (*Koshikei*, 1968), about the judicial execution of a young Korean. *The Ceremony* (*Gishiki*, 1971) shows the influence of social rituals on the Japanese character. *In the Realm of the Senses* featured a ritual castration (see Chapter 8). Unfortunately Oshima's later career has amounted to little more than a collection of curiosities, such as the war drama *Merry Christmas, Mr Lawrence* (1983), starring David Bowie, and *Max, mon amour* (1986), in which Charlotte Rampling falls in love with a chimpanzee. *Gohatto* (1999), about gay love affairs in a Japanese military academy in the nineteenth century, is a return to his earlier dissections of Japanese ritual and institutions.

During the 1980s established directors such as Imamura Shohei kept going despite the sense that Japanese cinema had become ossified. Imamura's films have usually had a high sexual content since his early days at Nikkatsu, but this is placed in the context of a subtle and often witty social analysis, as in *Ballad of Narayama* (*Narayama bushiko*, 1982), in which an elderly widow prepares herself for death by sorting out her family's marital and other problems. *Black Rain* (*Kuroi ame*, 1989), about a family that survives the atom bomb at Hiroshima, leaves little room for Imamura's quirky humour, but *The Eel* (*Unagi*, 1997) is a considerable achievement, a complex mix of comedy and menace. In a graphically presented opening sequence the hero catches his wife in bed with another man and murders her. Years later he comes out of prison and becomes a barber. He has a pet eel, to whom he talks (animal imagery is a constant in Imamura's films), and soon an assistant, a young woman whom he saves from suicide and then defends against a gang of incompetent gangsters who are trying to embezzle her mother's money. Meanwhile a young man prepares for the arrival of aliens. *Warm Water Under the Red Bridge* (*Akai hashi noshitano nurui mizu*, 2001) has the same lead actor, Yakusho Koji, as an unemployed 'salaryman' who begins an affair with a woman who gushes water whenever she has an orgasm. This unlikely tale, decked out with a parrot and shoals of fish, serves as a vehicle for reflection on Japanese economic stagnation and much else, leavened by the philosophy of an old tramp whom the salaryman has befriended: 'Enjoy life while you can still get a hard-on.'

Another veteran was Ichikawa Kon, who is still making samurai films in his late seventies. *The Forty-Seven Ronin* (*Shijushichinin no shikaku*, 1994) is a worthy if conventional

Above: Shimizu Misa as Keiko, who is befriended by reformed murderer and now barber Yamashita (Yakusho Koji) in *The Eel* (*Unagi*, 1997). Dir: Imamura Shohei **Right:** Director Kurosawa Akira (in dark glasses) on the set of *Kagemusha* (1980). **Opposite:** Epic in scale, and based loosely on Shakespeare's *King Lear*: a poster for the film *Ran* (1985). Dir: Kurosawa Akira

HIDETORA: A dream. Such a dream. I was in a strange
            land, a vast wilderness. I went on and
            on, without meeting anyone. I called and
            called, but no one answered. I was alone,
            alone in the whole, wide world. Chilled.
            Such nonsense ...Taro's voice pulled me
            back. I saw my dear children. Taro. Jiro.
            Saburo.
SABURO: Father, I've never see you like this before.
TARO: Saburo, be thankful he thinks of us.
JIRO: I too can scarcely believe my ears. Usually
            father demands our obedience; that is his
            affection.

Lord Hidetora (Nakadai Tatsuya), Saburo (Ryu Daisuke), Taro (Terao Satoshi), Jiro (Nezu Jinpachi), *Ran* (Kurosawa Akira, 1985)

CINEMA IN THE FAR EAST

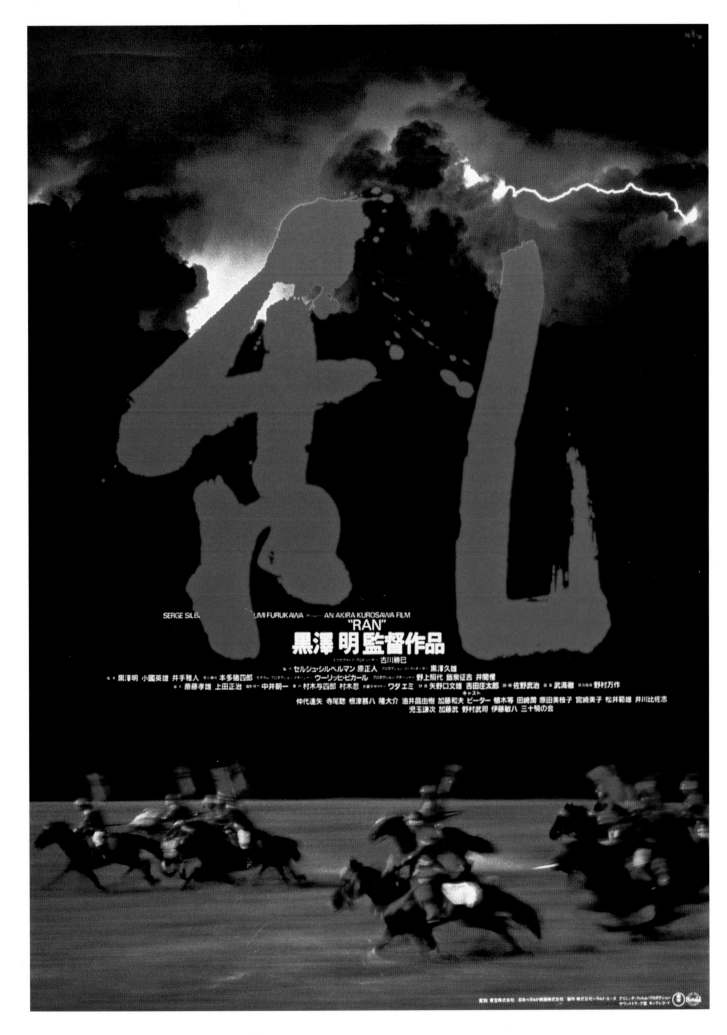

Above: Miyamoto
Nobuko as the female
tax inspector in
A Taxing Woman
(*Marusa no onna*, 1987).
Dir: Itami Juzo
Below: Hara Hisako
as an old lady who
remembers cherry
blossoms, one of the
dead in *After Life*
(*Wandarafu raifu*, 1998).
Dir: Koreeda Hirokazu
Right: Kusakari Tamiyo
with Yakusho Koji as the
'salaryman' who joins
a dancing school in
Shall We Dance? (1996).
Dir: Suo Masayuki

story of stoic resistance in the face of inevitable defeat. Kurosawa himself had begun the 1970s with a flop. When *Dodes'ka-den* (1970) – about down-and-outs in contemporary Tokyo – failed, he attempted suicide, but came back with *Kagemusha* (1980), a historical epic about a thief who becomes the double for a war lord. *Ran* (1985), based on *King Lear*, is similarly large in scale, and both these late films, though showing signs of lassitude, were rapturously received in the West, where Kurosawa received at times exaggerated veneration.

Comedy received a lift in the work of Itami Juzo, whose *Death, Japanese Style* (*Ososhiki*, 1985) extracted humour from the stilted formality of Japanese funeral rites. *Tampopo* (1986), about a quest for the perfect bowl of noodles, is a loosely structured series of comic turns, some of them parodies of Hollywood movies, including *Shane* (George Stevens, 1953). Perhaps Itami's most successful work, carefully plotted and directed with pace, is *A Taxing Woman* (*Marusa no onna*, 1987), about a female tax inspector who conducts a devastatingly effective campaign against tax dodgers. Itami's satire of the yakuza, *The Anti-Extortion Woman* (*Minbo no onna*, 1992), hit its target hard enough for Itami to be stabbed in the leg in retaliation. His suicide in 1997 deprived Japanese cinema of its most astringent social observer.

During the 1990s Japanese cinema tried to reinvent itself. Belatedly it woke up to the fact that the audience had changed. In consequence there were more films about rebels and marginal characters, as well as films aimed directly at the children's market. Major social issues or historical dramas were out; what was wanted were personal, quirky movies that chimed with the mood of the young. Typical was *Shall We Dance?* (Suo Masayuki, 1996), the most popular Japanese film ever released in the United States, a light-hearted story about a 'salaryman' who, sensing something missing in his life, joins a ballroom dancing school. Koreeda Hirokazu's *Maborosi* (*Maboroshi no Hikari*, 1995) shows many of the virtues of traditional Japanese film – impeccable framing, measured pacing, emotional delicacy – in the story of a widow coming to terms with her husband's suicide. But Koreeda's next film,

After Life (*Wandarafu raifu*, 1998), is highly original. The newly dead are called for an interview in a crumbling office block where they are asked to decide on the one memory they will keep for all eternity. This device allows Koreeda almost unlimited scope for comment on contemporary Japanese society, and a variety of types appear: a naive schoolgirl who remembers her trip to Disneyland (and is persuaded to recall something better), a prostitute, an old man who remembers starving as a soldier in the war, an old woman who remembers the Great Earthquake, a bolshie young man, a woman who remembers childbirth.

The decline of the studios led to the emergence of an 'independent sector'; two of its most prominent directors are Nagasaki Shunichi and Ishii Sogo. Nagasaki's *Heart, Beating in the Dark* (*Yamiutsu shinzo*, 1982), shot on Super-8 mm, is an intense examination of an edgy, compulsive love affair. *The Enchantment* (*Yuwakusha*, 1990) and *Some Kinda Love* (1995) also play with psychosexual complexities, while in *Shikoku* (1999) Nagasaki ventures into the horror film. His *A Tender Place* (*Yawaraka na hoo*, 2000) is a lengthy but subtle story of a woman's search for her missing child, and hailed already as Nagasaki's masterpiece. By the 1990s Ishii was something of a veteran, having begun his career in the 1970s, but a trilogy of films in the mid-1990s showed him consistently exploring the further reaches of narrative cinema. *Angel Dust* (1994) is a thriller that begins with killings on the Tokyo underground, *August in the Water* (*Mizu no Naka no Hachigatsu*, 1995) is a science fiction film of sorts, and *Labyrinth of Dreams* (*Yumeno Ginga*, 1997) is about a female bus conductor who falls for a murderer, but none of them conforms to strict generic codes.

By contrast, the most talented Japanese film-maker of the 1990s, Kitano Takeshi, began work within the tradition of the yakuza film. A stand-up comedian and popular personality on Japanese television, Kitano had appeared in half a dozen films before directing his first, *Violent Cop* (*Sono otoko, kyobo ni tsuki*), in 1989. Kitano himself plays Azuma, a Dirty Harry-type policeman, at odds with his superiors over his aggressive methods of combating crime.

Below: Kitano Takeshi in a bit of rough stuff in *Sonatine* (1993). Dir: Kitano Takeshi

With the face and rolling gait of a punch-drunk boxer, Kitano makes a convincing counter-hero, and when gangsters drug and gang-rape his mentally unstable sister, Azuma wreaks revenge. In his next two crime films, *Boiling Point* (*3-4x jugatsu*, 1990) and *Sonatine* (1993), Kitano elaborates his screen personality, a kind of very rough diamond, intolerant of bullshit, fond of practical jokes, his heart in the right place whichever side of the law he is on. The films alternate off-beat comedy with sudden outbreaks of violence and moments of tenderness. In *Sonatine* Kitano is an ageing yakuza who wants to quit. He forms a relationship of sorts with an admiring girl. 'It's great not to be afraid of killing,' she says, then takes off her T-shirt. 'It's great not to be afraid of showing your tits,' he answers.

Kitano's masterpiece to date is *Fireworks* (*Hana-bi*, 1997). Once more he is a cop. His daughter has died, his wife has an incurable disease, the yakuza are pursuing him for money he owes. One of his buddies is crippled in a shoot-out and starts doing paintings, strange but beautiful images of animals with flowers for heads. Menaced by the yakuza in a bar, Kitano stabs one in the eye with a chopstick, almost too quickly to see. On the run, he and his wife light fireworks by the sea. Putting two bullets in his gun, he shoots them both. Throughout the film, Buster Keaton-like, Kitano's expression never changes. Stoicism is his code; only an occasional facial twitch hints at the psychological cost. Kitano's later works have tended to move away from the crime milieu; although one of the characters in *Dolls* (2002) is an ageing yakuza, the film is essentially a series of interconnected tragic love stories.

It would be easy to make sweeping assertions about why Japanese cinema is so extreme, linking it to the brutal conquest of Japan's neighbours in the 1930s and 1940s, or to its experience as the only country ever to have been attacked with nuclear weapons. More relevant is Japanese literary and artistic tradition. As Ian Buruma explains in *Behind the Mask*, an investigation into the roots of Japanese culture, nineteenth-century Japanese painting is full of images of tortured women. 'Aesthetic cruelty, in Japan as elsewhere, is a way of relieving fear, of exorcising the demons. Because female passion is thought to be more demonic than the weaker, male variety … and because of her basic impurity and her capacity to lead men so dangerously astray, it is Woman who has to suffer most.'[2] Outside the cinema Japan is not a particularly violent country, but inside the violence is often extreme, nowhere more so than in the films of the highly prolific Miike Takashi. After a trilogy pitting Japanese criminals against the triads of Taiwan, Miike topped even their inventiveness and gruesomeness with *Audition* (*Odishon*, 1999), in which a widowed film producer pursues a disturbed young woman who exacts a terrible penalty for his presumption. Whether the film's international sales were buoyed by its stylish sense of menace or the climactic scene of grisly dismemberment, it showed Miike as a director of shocking power. *Ichi the Killer* (*Koroshiya Ichi*, 2001) is a yakuza film, drawn from a Japanese *manga* (comic books, frequently displaying extreme violence). Miike manages to surpass himself once again, with scenes in which victims are literally sliced in two and women have their nipples tortured.

By comparison, the highest grossing horror film in Japanese history, Nakata Hideo's *Ring* (*Ringu*, 1998), has little explicit violence, relying instead on a skilfully constructed sense of menace in its tale of a mysterious video tape that brings death to those who watch it. Only at the end, when horror crawls from the television screen, is the threat actualized.

The visual inventiveness and stylistic assurance of Japanese popular culture remains undimmed, and the thirty-two per cent of the box office secured by domestic productions in 2000 compares favourably with most countries. The question is whether anything can hold back the ever-rising tide of US imports. *Pearl Harbor* (Michael Bay, 2001) was a surprising hit in Japan, whose industry cannot compete with the vast budgets of Hollywood and whose government, beset by economic problems, is unlikely to provide any countervailing support.

The sad history of Korea in the twentieth century continues to affect its cinema. Annexed by the Japanese in 1910, the country was liberated in 1945 only to be divided between Western and Communist powers. The Korean War (1950–53) devastated the country and left it more divided than ever. Since then South Korea has enjoyed remarkable economic success, but until lately has done so under a series of repressive governments. In the North rigid Communist Party direction of the economy and political life led to stagnation and, by the end of the century, near-starvation.

Since 1968 film in the North has been under the direct control of Kim Jong-Il, the son and successor of Kim Il-Sung, leader of the country from 1948 to 1994. Author of a book of film theory (*The Theory of Cinematic Art*, published in 1973), Kim Jong-Il has a personal collection of 15,000 film titles, and such is his enthusiasm for cinema that in 1978 he organized the kidnapping of the leading South Korean director Shin Sang-Ok, forcing him to work in the North until Shin and his actress wife finally escaped in 1986.

Producing around thirty feature films a year, the North Korean industry is highly centralized, based on three main studios. Films are mostly screened at the place of work rather than in public theatres. North Korea is thus the only place in the world where film-going is compulsory. Consequently audience appeal is not a high priority, leaving film-makers free to pursue the official ideology, known as 'Juche'. Films must produce an idealized representation of the Korean working class and implant in the collective mind the revolutionary ideas of the 'dear leader'. Standard subjects are the struggle against the land-owning class during the feudal era, and the anti-Japanese resistance (in which Kim Il-Sung is deemed to have played a major role). There are also films about the Korean War: for example, *Wolmi Island* (*Wolmido*, 1982), directed by Cho Kyung-Sun, in which a small group of North Korean soldiers hold back a vastly superior force from the South, sustained, as ever, by thoughts of Kim Il-Sung.

The same director's *Bellflower* (*Torajikkot*, 1987) deals with the conflict between town and country that troubles so many third-world countries. The heroine, Songnim, devotes herself to working for the improvement of her remote village, but her boyfriend, Wonbong, dreams of the excitement of city life and leaves. Songnim is killed in an accident. Twenty years later Wonbong returns to the village and tries to make amends for his desertion. Though set in the 1950s, it is clearly addressed to a contemporary audience, justifying the policy of the Party in directing people to stay on the land.

South Korean cinema was at a low ebb in the 1970s. The military government imposed strict censorship and production declined from over 200 films a year in the previous decade to a mere 100 by the end of the 1970s. The assassination of President Park Chung-Hee in 1979 led to further repression and a massacre of protesters in Kwangju in 1980. But though most films were run-of-the-mill martial arts stories, war films, melodramas and soft-core porn, by the end of the 1980s distinctive voices began to be heard. The prolific Im Kwon-taek had begun his career in the early 1960s; his feature *Adada* (1987), a historical drama about a deaf-mute woman abandoned by her husband, won admiration for its portrayal of female suffering and the beauties of the landscape. Im's speciality is the melodrama, to which he brings a note of powerful sincerity. The 1990s saw some of his best work, including *Sopyonje* (*Seo-Pyon-Jae*, 1993), a tale of a travelling musician and his children, again making the most of the Korean landscape; *The Taebaek Mountains* (*Taebaek sanmaek*, 1994), set in the late 1940s, about a Communist revolt in the south which presaged the Korean War; and *Chunhyang* (2000), a version of a well-known Korean folktale about the daughter

Above: Lee Hyo-Jeong and Cho Seung-Woo as the married couple separated with cruel consequences in *Chunhyang* (2000). Dir: Im Kwon-taek

CINEMA IN THE FAR EAST

of a courtesan who marries the son of the governor, is separated from her husband and ill-treated by the new governor when she refuses his advances. Gorgeously mounted, in brilliant colours, the film exudes a subtle but seductive eroticism, as when the young man writes words of love on the girl's pink silk dress. Im's *Chihwaseon* (2002), a philosophical biopic about a Yi Dynasty painter, won the Best Director's prize at the 2002 Cannes Film Festival.

Despite the improving quality of South Korean films, and a quota system for domestic exhibition, production declined to about sixty films a year by 1993, with locally produced films taking a mere sixteen per cent of the market. But the second half of the 1990s saw a dramatic revival. Though production numbers remained steady, by 2001 South Korean films had secured no less than 49.5 per cent of the domestic box office, leading to a demand by US producers to drop the country's quota system. The improvement seems to have been largely the result of opening up the industry to a new breed of young directors, many of whom have come up through the radical, underground film scene, and a determination to make films that audiences wanted to see, such as the phenomenally successful *Friend* (*Chingu*, Kwak Kyung-taek, 2001), a coming-of-age drama with plenty of gangster violence.

Korean society, both North and South, is still in many ways strongly traditional, with Confucian values governing respect for authority, deference to elders and a resistance to women's equality. The new directors have found audiences by challenging this. South Korean Park Kwang-Su's *Black Republic* (*Keduldo urichurum*, 1990) inserts a highly dramatic personal story into a strongly political context. Han Tae-Yun is a student activist who comes to a mining town. As he experiences the harsh social realities of the miners' lives, he becomes involved with Song Young-Suk, a local callgirl. When he rescues her from a beating by Song-Chol, the son of a factory owner, he falls foul of the police. He decides to leave. Young-Suk wants to go with him, but is prevented by Song-Chol, whom she stabs with a knife. Park's later film, *A Single Spark* (*Jeon Tae-Il*, 1995), tells the story of a labour activist in the 1960s, and is a much more subtle work than such a bald outline suggests.

South Korean Hong Sang-Soo's *The Day a Pig Fell into the Well* (*Daijiga umule pajinnal*, 1996) is an engaging kaleidoscope of five contemporary urban lives, skilfully cut together. Hong's later film, *Virgin Stripped Bare by Her Bachelors* (*Oh! Soo-jung*, 2000), confirms his promise, as well as a liking for strange titles, in the story of a young woman who decides to get rid of her virginity. It is an amusing dissection of Korean sexual mores, cleverly structured. Strict censorship of erotic content was relaxed in 1985, allowing Korean film-makers considerable leeway. A notable first was *Broken Branches* (*Naeil ui hyahae hurunun kang*, 1995), directed by Park Jae-Ho, South Korea's first gay movie. Another director to take advantage has been Jang Sun-Woo. *To You, From Me* (*Neoege narul bonaenda*, 1994) and *Timeless Bottomless Bad Movie* (*Nappun Yeonghwa*, 1997) take a frank look at Korean youth, the former film described by Tony Rayns in *Time Out* as 'one of the most gleefully offensive films ever made anywhere', the latter as 'shocking and disturbing'.[3] In *Lies* (*Gojitmal*, 1999) a sculptor engages in a sado-masochistic affair with a schoolgirl while his wife is in Paris. The scenes in which they whip each other are performed with convincing rigour, but it is the hypocrisy of conventional relationships that Jang intends us to find most shocking.

Not all the films achieving box office success in South Korea are of the quality of Lee Myung-se's *Nowhere to Hide* (*Injong sajong polkot opta*, 1999), which though routine in narrative (the cops chasing a killer are dedicated but 'fucked up', with no family life), is astonishingly dynamic visually. Some are potboilers like *Shiri* (*Shwiri*, Kang Je-gyu, 1999), an action thriller about North Korean terrorists, and *Whispering Corridors* (*Yeogo goedam*, Park Ki-Hyung, 1998), a horror film set in a girls' school, where the most frightening thing is the way the teachers are allowed to beat up the students. But a thriving commercial cinema, while no guarantee of artistic quality, provides a launching platform for those more ambitiously inclined.

Not surprisingly, the Vietnam War had a serious effect on cinema in south-east Asia. In Laos, despite peace and reunification after 1975, no feature films were produced until 1983, and the State Cinematographic Company went bankrupt in 1992. Cambodia saw some film-making activity in the early 1970s before the Khmer Rouge takeover in 1975. Cinema-going revived when the Vietnamese ousted the Khmer Rouge, but by the early 1990s video had ruined the market for theatrical screenings. Perhaps the strangest aspect of cinema in Cambodia is the career of Prince Norodom Sihanouk, who assumed the throne of Cambodia in 1941 and has since made no fewer than forty-six films. Despite more than once being removed as head of state in the abrupt swings of Cambodian politics, he made a comeback in the 1990s, being once more crowned king in 1993. Sihanouk's films, in which he frequently stars as well as directing, draw on traditional Khmer stories, adapted

Above: Top Korean movie star Park Joong-Hoon as Detective Woo in *Nowhere to Hide*

(*Injong sajong polkot opta*, 1999). Dir: Lee Myung-se

into thinly disguised allegories of Sihanouk's role in the nation's history. *An Ambition Reduced to Ashes* (1995) is typical – the tale of a sorcerer who tries but fails to come between the people and their king.

During the war Vietnam made a large number of documentaries, but feature production was almost nil. After 1975 features stepped up to nearly twenty a year, but the move to a more market-oriented economy from 1985, plus competition from video and television, cut production back to only five features in 1993. Coproduction has become increasingly important, and is reflected in the work of Tran Anh Hung. Though of Vietnamese birth he is based in France, where his first feature, *The Scent of Green Papaya* (*Mui du du Xanh*, 1993), was shot. However, it is hard to imagine anything more authentically Vietnamese than this story of a servant girl, Mui, whom we see first as a child in 1951 and later as a young woman forming a relationship with (and being taught to read by) a young composer. The rituals of cooking and cleaning are lovingly detailed, as is Mui's fascination with the natural world, movingly expressed in a scene where she slits open a papaya and stares with wonder at the delicate white seeds within. *Cyclo* (*Xich lo*, 1995) is less idyllic. In contemporary Ho Chi Minh City, formerly Saigon, a poor young man is forced into a criminal gang and his sister is prostituted by the gang's head. It is a film of striking images, some lyrical, some brutal: the girl having her toenails painted by a client; her brother left for dead covered in blue paint, an ornamental fish stuck in his mouth. Tran's third film, *At the Height of Summer* (*A la verticale de l'été*, 2000) again displays his interest in family, in the story of three sisters in present-day Hanoi, offering exquisite images of domestic work as the sisters prepare an elaborate meal for the anniversary of their mother's death.

Despite military control and strict censorship, Thailand managed to produce some films in the 1970s which reflected the realities of Thai society. Prince Chatri-Chalerm Yukol, a member of the Thai royal family, made *The Citizen* (*Thongpoon Kokpo*, 1977), about a taxi driver whose cab is stolen, an echo, like *Cyclo*, of the neo-realist *Bicycle Thieves*. But most Thai films fell into the popular genres of fantasy, action dramas and comedy, with production reaching over 100 films a year in the early 1980s, without any direct government support, though towards the end of the 1980s taxes on foreign imports were raised. Later the market turned to youth, with a profusion of films about teenage romance and pictures featuring recording stars. There were some exceptions, such as Euthana Mukdasanit's *Butterfly and Flowers* (*Peesua lae Dokmai*, 1985), an exquisitely shot picture of rural life. In the mid-1990s the government lowered the tax on film imports, leading to a predictable surge in the audience for Hollywood films; all top ten performers at the Thai box office in 1998 were American. Local production was only eleven films in 2001. Nevertheless, Thai cinema has continued to turn out ambitious works of some style. Two that have achieved success abroad recently are *Tears of the Black Tiger* (*Fa talai jone*, Wisit Sasantieng, 2000), a stylishly shot Thai Western, and *Jan Dara* (Nonzee Nimibutr, 2001), a steamy melodrama set in the 1930s which works a contemporary variation on the Thai genre of 'nang chiwit', which typically raises issues of female sexuality and family and property relations.[4]

Malay cinema was productive in the 1950s and 1960s, especially in the Singapore studio run by the Shaw brothers, Chinese producers who were also important players in the Hong Kong film industry. But competition from television, plus the loss of Indonesian markets during the political confrontation that began in the mid-1960s, led to the closure of the studio in 1967. From that time Malaysia, as it became in 1963, has struggled to make films for the majority Malay population, and only four were produced in 1999. U-Wei bin Hajisari's melodramas such as *Woman, Wife & ...* (*Perempuan Istri & ...*, 1991) and *The Arsonist* (*Kaki Bakar*, 1995) have a powerful realism at odds with the more lurid traditions of earlier Malay cinema. Singapore pulled out of the new Malaysian federation in 1965. The tiny city-state of only three million people produced little of note in the 1970s and 1980s, but in 1998 the Singapore Film Commission was set up to offer funding. As a result the country managed five films in 1998 and six in 1999. Eric Khoo's *Twelve Storeys* (*Shi-er lou*, 1997), selected for the Cannes Film Festival, takes the lid off a buttoned-up society in a government-owned block of apartments, in one of which an uptight schoolteacher is trying to repress his sister's sex life.

In Indonesia, the upheavals of 1965–6, when there was a violent seizure of power by the army, led to the massacre of thousands of Communists and the eventual overthrow of Sukarno, who had led the country to independence from the Dutch in 1949. Several leftist film directors were imprisoned, film organizations were purged and indigenous production collapsed, partly due to a surge of imports. But in the 1970s it revived, in part through a government requirement that distributors must finance one domestic production for every

Above: May Yee Lum as Trixie and Boon Pin Koh as Meng in *Twelve Storeys* (*Shi-er lou*, 1997).
Dir: Eric Khoo
Right: Chartchai Ngamsan as Dum, who joins a gang when his father is murdered, with fellow gang member Mahesuan (Supakorn Kitsuwon), in the Western-inspired *Tears of the Black Tiger* (*Fa talai jone*, 2000).
Dir: Wisit Sasanatieng

Above: Street children
beyond control in *Leaf
on a Pillow (Daun di*
atas bantal, 1997).
Dir: Garin Nugroho

three imported. The number of features made rose from twenty-two in 1970 to 122 in 1977, but many were cheaply made comedies, musicals and horror films with tawdry special effects offering gory decapitations and the like. Cinema was also used to flatter Suharto, who had replaced Sukarno: *Janur Kuning* (1979) shows him as a heroic leader of the struggle against the Dutch.

Despite strict government censorship of leftist political ideas, some films paid regard to social realities. *Si Mamad* (1973), directed by Syuman Djaya, is a satire on government corruption, in which a poor clerk, desperate for money for his expanding family, steals stationery from his office, only to find that the shop that deals in such stolen property is run by his boss. *November 1828* (1978), directed by Teguh Karya, is an epic about the 'Java War' against the Dutch in the nineteenth century. *The Village Virgin* (*Perawan Desa*, 1978) is about the rape of a village girl by a group of privileged young men.

During the 1980s Indonesian film-making declined again. The requirement to support domestic production was abandoned and foreign film imports were monopolized by a company run by the family of Suharto, which also controlled the new multiplex cinemas in urban areas. These were much more profitable than the smaller cinemas in the provinces, which, showing mostly Indonesian films, began to close, shrinking the market for local films. Television was also taking its toll, and by 1992 only thirty-seven Indonesian films were made, falling to twenty in 1999. Some younger directors had success in festivals, including Garin Nugroho with *Love on a Slice of Bread* (*Cinta dalam sepotong roti*, 1991), a kind of youth movie on the road, and *Leaf on a Pillow* (*Daun di atas bantal*, 1997), about street children running wild in the city. But the political turmoil that led to the overthrow of Suharto has not run its course, and Indonesian cinema will struggle to achieve a revival.

At the beginning of the 1970s Filipino cinema was buoyant, with 220 features produced in 1971. It was a cinema of popular genres, adventure films of various kinds, musicals, horror films, melodramas and soft-core porn films or 'bombas', though the last were curtailed under martial law in 1972. The most prominent Filipino director, at least internationally, was Lino Brocka, once a trainee Mormon missionary, who chose to work largely within the genres of thriller and the melodrama while adapting them to his own ends. In *Insiang* (1976) a teenage girl in the slums of Manila is raped by her mother's lover; the mother murders the man. In *Bona* (1981) an obsessive fan devotes herself to a small-time movie actor, but when he ultimately rejects her she douses him with boiling water. The desperation that drives Brocka's characters derives from the extreme circumstances of their social positions. *Manila: In the Claws of Darkness* (*Maynila, sa mga kuko ng liwanag*, 1975) follows a young country boy's search for a girl through the Manila underworld, presenting a powerful indictment of poverty under the Marcos regime. *Macho Dancer* (1988) daringly exposed male prostitution in Manila. Brocka's films are often raw, even crude, but have an undeniable energy and immediacy. His death in a car crash in 1991 robbed Filipino cinema of a talent.

Other interesting Filipino directors of the period include Eddie Romero, whose *As We Were* (*Ganito kami noon, paano kayo ngayon?*, 1976) tells the story of a simple country peasant in Manila during the revolt against the Spanish at the end of the nineteenth century. Mike De Leon's *The Rites of May* (*Itim*, 1976) is a ghost story in which elegant long takes are concluded by a burst of action as a family's secrets are revealed. Family repression is also at the heart of his *Kisapmata* (1981). Ishmael Bernal's *City after Dark* (*Manila by Night*, 1981) is a painfully honest look at Manila lowlife. More recently younger film-makers have come through, including a rare woman director, Marilou Diaz-Abaya, whose *Milagros* (1997) is about a young prostitute who becomes the maidservant of a family of four men. Jeffrey Jeturian's *Larger Than Life* (*Tuhog*, 2001) is a satire on sex and the cinema in which a mother and daughter's story of sexual abuse is turned into a cheap erotic movie. It was shown at the Venice Film Festival, though *Variety* magazine thought it 'shallow'. Lavrente Diaz's *Naked under the Moon* (*Hubad Sa Illalim Ng Buwan*, 1999) is a feverish melodrama dealing with rape and impotence, featuring the soft-core porn star Klaudia Koronel. By the end of the 1990s cinema in the Philippines was showing the effects of political and economic uncertainty, with production declining from 200 titles in 1997 to eighty-nine in 2000. Though a former movie actor, Joseph Estrada, was elected president, two years later he was deposed on the grounds of corruption. Yet, despite the increasing dominance of the United States, both culturally and economically, the Philippines continues, like most of east Asia, to display a remarkable energy and self-confidence in its cinema which, whatever the political storms ahead, must augur well for its future production.

Above: A moment of tenderness in *Manila: In the Claws of Darkness* (*Maynila, sa mga kuko ng liwanag*, 1975). Dir: Lino Brocka

Right: Alan Paule as Pol, a country boy lured into the sex clubs of Manila, performing with Bobby Sano as Greg in *Macho Dancer* (1988). Dir: Lino Brocka

ADA: My husband said my muteness does not bother him. He writes and hark this: God loves dumb creatures, so why not he! Were good he had God's patience for silence affects everyone in the end.

Ada (Holly Hunter), *The Piano* (Jane Campion, 1993)

Australia, Canada and New Zealand have all found, like their one-time ruler Britain, that sharing a language with the United States has made their film industries peculiarly vulnerable both to import penetration by Hollywood and to having their best talents lured away. The result was that up to the 1970s in each of these countries the cinematic tradition was impoverished. It required an act of political will to construct a cinema capable of reflecting national identity.

Following prolonged discussion and a government report on the arts, an Australian film industry was legislated into existence in 1970, when the Film Development Council was set up to lend money to local film-makers. Becoming the Australian Film Commission (AFC) in 1975, it conjured up a series of films which raised the profile of Australian cinema both at home and abroad. An early success was *The Adventures of Barry McKenzie* (Bruce Beresford, 1972), an example of what has been dubbed 'ocker' comedy, mobilizing the stereotype of the hard-drinking, philistine, macho Australian male. The film raised in acute form the dilemmas of any government-funded cinema. Was the rationale largely economic, providing seed money from which would grow a fully self-supporting commercial cinema able to create jobs and exports? If so, the success of such a film could only be welcomed. Or was the intention cultural? At a time when Australia was beginning to find its voice politically there was intense discussion of what exactly it meant to be an Australian and how Australian cultural identity might be fostered by a national cinema. But if this was the object, did films like *The Adventures of Barry McKenzie*, with its scenes of alcoholic excess, create the right impression?

From the mid-1970s the AFC encouraged a more high-minded production policy. The result was 'the AFC genre', a series of films often set in the past, many based on novels, displaying the distinctive Australian landscape and in a style deriving from the European art cinema, with elusive narratives, slow motion and soft focus. Typical is Peter Weir's *Picnic at Hanging Rock* (1975), in which a group of nineteenth-century schoolgirls mysteriously disappear in the countryside. Others include Bruce Beresford's *The Getting of Wisdom* (1977), another period piece about schoolgirls, and Gillian Armstrong's *My Brilliant Career* (1979), in which a country girl has ambitions as a writer. Landscape also featured strongly in Fred Schepisi's *The Chant of Jimmie Blacksmith* (1978), an early attempt at getting ethnic minorities on the screen, albeit made by a white director.

The ocker comedy moderated into a series of films that centred on male camaraderie – the 'mateship' that some commentators have seen as one of the defining elements of the Australian national character. In Beresford's *Breaker Morant* (1979) three Australian soldiers are accused of murdering prisoners during the Boer War. Weir's *Gallipoli* (1981) dramatizes

CINEMA IN AUSTRALIA, CANADA, NEW ZEALAND

the ill-fated military campaign against the Turks in World War I. Training in Egypt, Australians of different origins display their solidarity by playing Australian rules football in the shadow of the Sphinx. In both films Australian men bonding together (women are largely absent) are contrasted with the less egalitarian British. Later, *Romper Stomper* (Geoffrey Wright, 1992), a rather thin story about a group of neo-Nazi skinheads in Melbourne, showed the dark side of male bonding. The female character, sexually abused by her father (an opera lover), is seen by the chief male character (Russell Crowe) as an encumbrance, and she finally brings about his death.

In 1981 the emphasis moved from direct financial involvement by the government to a system of tax relief, known as 10BA after the relevant clause in tax legislation. Cultural worthiness was no longer the only criterion. *Crocodile Dundee* (Peter Faiman, 1986) trades heavily on the ocker stereotype in the tale of a cheeky and resourceful backwoodsman who is taken up by a US journalist and carries all before him in New York. It became the highest grossing Australian film of all time.

One way to combine economic and cultural imperatives is to give Hollywood genres a distinctively local feel, and Peter Weir's *The Cars That Ate Paris* (1974), set in a small town where passing motorists are preyed on by local psychopaths, has something in common with the rural menace of *Psycho* or *The Texas Chain Saw Massacre*. Steve Jodrell's *Shame* (1987) is another film that uncovers brutish behaviour in the outback, this time in a tale of gang rape. In Phillip Noyce's *Heatwave* (1981) it is the urban jungle that is the focus of terror as a monstrous conspiracy hatched by rapacious developers unfolds. Australian cinema's most arrestingly dystopian vision, drawing on science fiction, is George Miller's *Mad Max* (1979), a nightmarish view of a future in which armed gangs scavenge among the ruins of civilization. The film's huge success spawned two sequels and, together with his role in *Gallipoli*, raised Mel Gibson to international stardom.

Not all Australian film-making falls neatly into genre categories. Paul Cox, born in Holland, is Australia's nearest equivalent to the European model of an art-house director, and his *Man of Flowers* (1983), about the relationship between an elderly art collector and an artist's model, is an early example of his distinctive style, conveying genuine eroticism and unafraid of visual extravagance.

No cinema has had its cultural credentials so much picked over as the Australian. As a counterbalance to its perceived bias towards the experience of white males, a Women's Film Fund was set up in 1976. A number of women directors emerged. Gillian Armstrong made *High Tide* (1987) and *The Last Days of Chez Nous* (1992), both with complex female interactions, before moving on to Hollywood to do a version of Louisa May Alcott's *Little*

<u>Above:</u> A cultural clash: Paul Hogan as the man from the outback on the look-out in New York in *Crocodile Dundee* (1986).
Dir: Peter Faiman
<u>Right:</u> Future nightmare in *Mad Max* (1979), with Mel Gibson (standing) as cop Max Rockatansky and Tim Burns as one of the tearaways, Johnny the Boy.
Dir: George Miller

Above: Kerry Fox as Vicki in a complex story of shifting family relationships in *The Last Days of Chez Nous* (1992).
Dir: Gillian Armstrong
Left: Based on the true story of Australian pianist David Helfgott (here played by Noah Taylor as the adolescent David), *Shine* (1996) portrays David's traumatic childhood through a series of flashbacks. His recovery from a breakdown to his ultimate success in the concert hall is handled with great skill.
Dir: Scott Hicks

CINEMA IN AUSTRALIA, CANADA, NEW ZEALAND

Above: Paul Mercurio and Tara Morice as the two young dancers who take on the establishment in *Strictly Ballroom* (1992). Dir: Baz Luhrmann

Below: Temuera Morrison and Rena Owen as the Maori married couple in *Once Were Warriors* (1993). Dir: Lee Tamahori

Women (1994). Among other successful women directors are Ann Turner, whose *Celia* (1988) imaginatively explores the fears and superstitions of a small girl, and Jocelyn Moorhouse, whose *Proof* (1991) is an unorthodox study of blindness. Women have also benefited from the effort to move Australian cinema towards multiculturalism by supporting Aboriginal film-making. Tracey Moffat's experimental work in *beDevil* (1993) found critical support, and Rachel Perkins's *Radiance* (1998), which observed three Aboriginal sisters at their mother's funeral, achieved success with audiences as well as critics, though the climactic scene, in which the sisters burn down their mother's house while an aria from *Madame Butterfly* plays on the soundtrack, shows the director straining for effect.

By the end of the 1990s Australian cinema had moved beyond the worthy if occasionally dull kind of 'heritage' cinema of the 1970s, achieving international success in a quartet of films that deviate sharply from the national stereotypes. *The Adventures of Priscilla Queen of the Desert* (1994), directed by Stephen Elliott, is an outrageously camp comedy about a troupe of drag queens touring the outback. Baz Luhrmann's *Strictly Ballroom* (1992) is a deftly-made comedy about a ballroom dancing championship. The charming *Muriel's Wedding* (1994), directed by P J Hogan, is about an ambitious wallflower from the backwater of Porpoise Spit who turns the tables on those who despise her taste in music and fashion. In Scott Hicks's *Shine* (1996) Geoffrey Rush delivers an extraordinary performance as an eccentric and disturbed pianist. None of these films seems deliberately aimed at forging Australian cultural identity, a fact that surely argues for maturity.

Unfortunately, despite the success of these productions, in 1999 Australian films could only command a three per cent share of the domestic box office. This fact, coupled with the flight of talent (among the actors lost to Hollywood are Mel Gibson and Russell Crowe; among the directors Peter Weir, Phillip Noyce, Baz Luhrmann, Gillian Armstrong and Fred Schepisi), means that even if cultural identity now rests on a firmer footing, economic viability is still a long way off.

New Zealand's geographical isolation and a population of only four million make a precarious environment for film-making. The establishment of the New Zealand Film Commission in 1978 provided financial support and produced immediate results, with two films sent to the Cannes Film Festival in 1980. Loopholes in the tax laws brought in more finance, with production up to fourteen features in 1984. After the loophole was closed the number declined to about five a year in the 1990s, but despite a shift to the right in New Zealand politics, leading to a bias in favour of the 'free market', subsidy has continued, with the provision of funds from the state lottery.

Simultaneous with the expansion of the film industry came changes in New Zealand's sense of itself. Maori demands for justice and equity led to the reassessment of colonial history. Immigration from the Pacific Islands and Asia forced New Zealand to acknowledge a new, more complex cultural identity than that provided by its British inheritance, while in the field of popular culture US imports were increasingly influential. This fluid cultural mix has proved fertile ground for film-makers. Paul Maunder's *Sons for the Return Home* (1979) is about the relationship between a white woman and a young man from Western Samoa. Roger Donaldson's *Smash Palace* (1981), about an emotional crisis in the life of the owner of a car-wrecking yard, dramatizes the white male ego under stress. Geoff Murphy explores similar terrain with *Goodbye Pork Pie* (1980), a road movie exploring the relationship between a couple of regular guys, zestfully shot and enlivened by comedy. It was the first New Zealand film to recover its costs from the domestic market.

Murphy's *Utu* (1983) explores different territory, a historical drama about the conflict between white settlers and Maori. Owing something in format to the Western, it is alert to the complexities of the situation while siding unequivocally with the dispossessed. *Ngati* (1987) was the first feature to be largely made by Maori, and *Mauri* (1988) was the first film to be directed by a Maori woman, Merata Mita. *Once Were Warriors* (1993), directed by Lee Tamahori, is a raw, violent film about an urban Maori family tearing

itself apart despite the struggles of a heroic matriarch.

New Zealand's most original director is Jane Campion. Made in Australia, *Sweetie* (1989) is about two strange sisters and achieves an unsettling but exhilarating mix of tragedy and farce. *An Angel at My Table* (1990) recounts the struggle of Janet Frame to become a writer, brilliantly rendering the processes of a mind under strain. In *The Piano* (1993) a mute Scottish piano teacher forms an erotic relationship with a New Zealand settler gone native. Its powerful emotions and stunning visuals (such as the piano marooned upon a wind-swept beach) won the film international awards. Like many New Zealand talents, Campion has gravitated to Hollywood. *The Portrait of a Lady* (1996), a costume drama based on Henry James's novel, was disappointingly conventional, but Kate Winslet is splendid in *Holy Smoke* (1999), adding another to Campion's gallery of unorthodox but determined female characters.

After a couple of low-budget horror films – *Bad Taste* (1987) and *Braindead* (1992) – Peter Jackson directed *Heavenly Creatures* (1994), about a true-life case of the 1950s in which two teenage girls murder the mother of one of them. Jackson brilliantly re-creates the intensely emotional fantasy life that gives rise to the crime. In *The Lord of the Rings: The Fellowship of the Ring* (2001) Jackson dramatized J R R Tolkien's literary epic in a multimillion dollar production which made use of New Zealand's spectacular scenery and most of the country's film production personnel. The second part of what is proving to be a highly popular trilogy, *The Two Towers*, premiered in 2002, with *The Return of the King* released in 2003.

Vincent Ward has made only four features in nearly twenty years, but has a distinctive vision. *Vigil* (1984) is set in a remote sheep-farming valley in which a twelve-year-old girl and her mother are confronted by a mysterious stranger. It is a film of haunting images, replete with symbolism. *The Navigator: A Medieval Odyssey* (1988) is a fantasy about a group of medieval peasants who, escaping the plague, tunnel through to present-day New Zealand. Despite striking imagery and strange juxtapositions, it at times strains after significance. Ward's most ambitious film, *Map of the Human Heart* (1992), in which a cartographer befriends a young Inuit boy in Canada before participating in the Allied bombing of Dresden, was an international coproduction, after which Ward went to Hollywood to make *What Dreams May Come* (1998), a fantasy of the after-life with Robin Williams.

Canada, where *Map of the Human Heart* begins, shares not only a common language with the United States but also an easily traversed border, making its domestic film industry especially vulnerable to Hollywood imports. Only two per cent of Canadian screen time is devoted to domestic product, one of the lowest rates in the world. Not surprisingly, Canadian legislators have long sought ways of encouraging home-grown cinema, and in

BAINES: Those 80 acres, that cross the stream,
what do you think of them?

STEWART: On your property?

BAINES: Yes.

STEWART: Good, flatish land with reliable water, why?
I don't have money. What are you about?

BAINES: I'd like to make a swap.

STEWART: What for?

BAINES: The piano.

STEWART: The piano on the beach? Ada's piano?

Baines (Harvey Keitel), Stewart (Sam Neill), *The
Piano* (Jane Campion, 1993)

CINEMA IN AUSTRALIA, CANADA, NEW ZEALAND

Above: One of many
moments of spectacle
in *The Lord of the Rings:
The Fellowship of the
Ring* (2001), New
Zealand's biggest
ever production.

Dir: Peter Jackson
Below: Maxime Collin as
Léolo being comforted
by his mother (Ginette
Reno) in *Léolo* (1992).
Dir: Jean-Claude
Lauzon

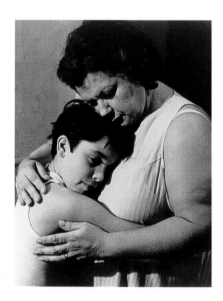

1967 established the Canadian Film Development Corporation to invest in Canadian feature films. But production is only half the problem. Canadian film distribution has been almost entirely controlled by US companies, who have little incentive to show Canadian films, and pressure from Hollywood meant that exhibition quotas were rejected. Tax shelter legislation and lower costs have led to a healthy production sector in Canada, but it is mainly devoted to making Hollywood films. Canada's most commercially successful contemporary director, David Cronenberg, is now essentially a Hollywood film-maker; his work is discussed in the chapter on horror films (see Chapter 4).

Despite this, Canadian cinema has managed to find some distinctive voices, especially in that part of the country which is non-English-speaking. *Mon oncle Antoine* (1971), directed by Claude Jutra, is an early example of Cinéma Québécois – a story about an asbestos miner grounded in the politics of Québec nationalism, which came to a head with the rise of the Front de Libération du Québec (FLQ) at the beginning of the 1970s. Robert Lepage's *The Confessional* (*Le Confessionnal*, 1995) is an ingenious mystery set in Québec as Alfred Hitchcock films his thriller *I Confess* (1953). Lepage's *Nô* (1998), set in 1970, is a subtle and comic meditation on Québec nationalism in which an actress goes to Japan to appear in a French theatrical farce somehow intended to represent Canadian culture, while back home her boyfriend is involved in a hamfisted terrorist plot with the FLQ.

One of the most striking French-Canadian films of the 1990s was *Léolo* (1992), directed by Jean-Claude Lauzon, about a sensationally dysfunctional family whose youngest member rejects his Québec identity on the grounds that his mother was impregnated by semen contained in imported Italian tomatoes! The film has been read as an allegory of Canada itself, desperately seeking an identity while its regions squabble among themselves. Perhaps the best known French-Canadian director is Denys Arcand, whose *Decline of the American Empire* (*Le Déclin de l'empire américain*, 1986) is a witty and penetrating satire on middle-class mores. Arcand's *Jesus of Montreal* (*Jésus de Montréal*, 1989) was equally sharp, its story about

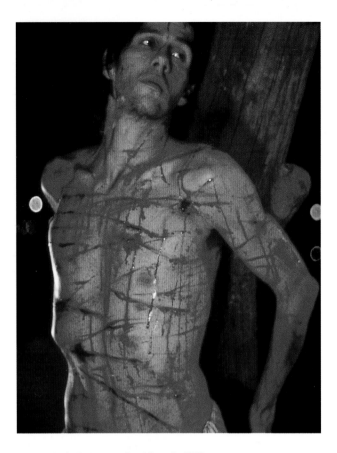

an actor producing a revisionist Passion Play affording plentiful opportunities to score points off the religious establishment.

Canada's most celebrated art-house director is Atom Egoyan, of Armenian extraction. Formally exact, austere in tone with carefully structured plots, Egoyan's films are serious, at times solemn. More recently Egoyan has graduated to name actors and larger budgets, but shows no sign of attempting to ingratiate himself. *The Adjuster* (1991) concerns an insurance claims adjuster whose wife is a film censor. Like *Exotica* (1995), screened at the Sundance Film Festival and set in a strip club, it explores themes of voyeurism and sexual secrecy. *The Sweet Hereafter* (1997) takes place in a small Canadian town which has been devastated by the death of some schoolchildren in a bus crash. Precisely, in an intricate pattern of flashback and a visual style that preserves a distance from the characters, it explores the motives and emotions of those involved. Bob Hoskins stars in *Felicia's Journey* (1999) as a lonely caterer who befriends a young Irish girl arrived in London to search for her boyfriend. As usual in Egoyan's films, the true nature of the characters is only gradually revealed. Egoyan's *Ararat* (2002) is a complex and multi-layered work of historical recovery dealing with the massacre of Armenians by the Turks in 1915.

English-speaking mainstream cinema in Canada has had more difficulty differentiating itself from Hollywood. Its most successful tactic has been to give popular genres a distinctive Canadian inflection. Don Shebib's *Goin' Down the Road* (1970) is a road movie in which two labourers from Cape Breton, on the eastern edge of Canada, journey to Toronto in search of work. It is a film that lays bare class and regional differences. Phillip Borsos's *The Grey Fox* (1982) stars Richard Farnsworth in a Western about an ageing train robber. A film of great charm, it contrasts the relative civility of the Canadian West with the brutal lawlessness below the border.

More recently, the fissure between the French- and English-speaking parts of the nation has become overlaid by films from other quarters which offer their own challenge to any

easy assumption of national unity. Canada has a strong tradition of funding avant-garde work by women, though this is outside the scope of this book. Patricia Rozema's sprightly comedy *I've Heard the Mermaids Singing* (1987) is more mainstream, even if Polly, its heroine, is a lesbian who falls in love with the female curator of the gallery where she works. In Rozema's subsequent feature, *When Night Is Falling* (1995), a woman teacher at a divinity college falls for a circus girl, with ensuing soft-focus sex scenes and some wry comedy. Ethnic minorities, too, are making themselves heard. Bruce McDonald's *Dance Me Outside* (1995) is set on a Native reservation. Though McDonald is white, the film makes a determined attempt to get beyond regressive stereotypes. *Honey Moccasin* (1998), directed by a Mohawk, Shelley Niro, is the first Canadian feature written, directed by and starring people of the First Nations. *Masala* (1991), directed by and starring Srinivas Krishna, is a densely textured, freewheeling film tracking a young man as he cuts a swathe through Canada's Hindu community, though not all Canadians of Indian descent found the film an acceptable representation. *Atanarjuat: The Fast Runner* (Zacharias Kunuk, 2000) is an Inuit film set in the distant past, a powerful epic that to an outsider feels totally authentic. No longer homogenous, not even necessarily English-speaking, Canadian national identity as reflected in its cinema may still have a precarious economic foundation but it is in no danger of being confused with Hollywood.

A Film for the Nation
Atanarjuat: The Fast Runner (2000)
Dir: Zacharias Kunuk

This is the first film made in the Inuktitut language spoken by the native peoples of the Canadian Arctic. It tells a legend from two thousand years ago, about Atanarjuat, who incurs the jealous enmity of Oki when he marries Atuat. Oki kills Atanarjuat's brother, but Atanarjuat escapes in a stunning sequence, running naked across the ice floes, outstripping his pursuers until, his feet torn and bloody, he is taken in by a friendly shaman. Atuat is later raped by Oki. Years later, with the help of the shaman, Atanarjuat outwits Oki, beats him in a fight and expels him from the community.

Shot in digital Betacam, the film makes the most of the immense snowy landscapes. It is also acted with complete conviction by its mostly first-time cast. Director Zacharias Kunuk is the first of his family to live in a permanent settlement, to read, write and make films. Inevitably the film will be compared to *Nanook of the North*, the famous 'creative' documentary made in 1922 by Robert Flaherty. *Atanarjuat* concedes nothing in the way of authenticity, with sequences that show in realistic detail the training of sled-dogs, cutting up animal carcasses or making an igloo. But the convincing ethnographic elements only serve to enhance the compelling story and characters, which take on a truly epic dimension.

If the purpose of a national cinema is to represent the culture of the peoples it belongs to, then *Atanarjuat: The Fast Runner* achieves this triumphantly, both the content of the film and the manner of its telling being wholly specific to Canada, yet in the process achieving a universal appeal.

Country of Origin: Canada
Running Time: 168 mins

Production Company: Igloolik Isuma Productions Inc
Producers: Paul Apak Angilirq, Norman Cohn, Zacharias Kunuk, Germaine Ying Gee Wong
Writer: Paul Apak Angilirq
Photography: Norman Cohn
Editors: Zacharias Kunuk, Norman Cohn, Marie-Christine Sarda
Music: Chris Crilly

Atanarjuat: Natar Ungalaaq
Atuat: Sylvia Ivalu
Oki: Paul Henry Arnatsiaq
Puja: Lucy Tulugarjuk
Qulitalik: Pauloosie Qulitalik

Far left, top and centre: Atanarjuat is chased across the ice floes where he manages to outrun his pursuers.
Far left, below: Lucy Tulugarjuk (l) plays Puja, Atanarjuat's second wife.
Centre: Natar Ungalaaq as Atanarjuat, epic hero.
Top: How to build an igloo.
Above: Atanarjuat's wife Atuat, played by Sylvia Ivalu, with traditional face markings.

19.   Latin America

LUIS: **Was it him?**

EL CHIVO: **I don't know. You think so?**

LUIS: **How much ?**

EL CHIVO: **Five thousand pesos.**

LUIS: **Only 5,000 fucking pesos!**

EL CHIVO: **And ... tickets to the Rolling Stones.**

Luis (Jorge Salinas), El Chivo (Emilio Echevarría),
Amores perros (Alejandro González Iñárritu, 2000)

In the 1960s Latin America was at the forefront of attempts to define a new kind of cinema, one that could hold back the onward march of Hollywood. The growing confidence of the so-called 'third world' fed through into debates on the role of cinema within the wider project of political resistance. This new cinema had to make virtues of its limitations. It had to find new forms of production that did not rely on big budgets, find new ways of reaching an audience, but above all it insisted on the social function of cinema, its capacity to raise consciousness and force change.

Meetings at Mérida in Venezuela and at Viña del Mar, Chile, at the end of the 1960s, and later at the annual Havana festival of Latin American cinema, begun in 1979, provided opportunities for Latin American film-makers to discuss common goals and see each other's work. (The assumption that because, with the exception of Brazil, the countries shared a common language, films would move easily around the continent, was quite erroneous. A Mexican film-maker was far more likely to have seen recent Hollywood films than anything new from Argentina.) Yet despite the growth of an internationalist perspective, cinema in Latin America has remained heavily determined by national formations, by the economics, politics and cultural traditions of separate countries.

By the late 1930s, Mexico had established a highly successful film industry based on popular genres, producing large numbers of comedies, often starring Cantinflas, melodramas with Dolores del Río and Maria Félix, and the 'comedia ranchera', musicals in a rural setting. Such popular works gave Mexico a dominant position within Latin American cinema. But by the late 1960s the film industry, like much else in Mexico, had ossified, unable to take note of the simmering social unrest just starting to challenge the seemingly endless rule of the Partido Revolucionario Institucional (PRI), Mexico's governing party. Even the cheap horror films and masked wrestler films of the 1950s and early 1960s had begun to lose their appeal; Juan López Moctezuma's *Alucarda* (1975), a tale of demonic possession with copious nudity and buckets of blood, was a kind of last gasp. Alejandro Jodorowsky's *The Mole* (*El topo*, 1971) was a one-off which led nowhere, a demented cross between a spaghetti Western and Luis Buñuel on a bad day (Buñuel had worked in Mexico until the early 1960s), with a black-clad gunman and a naked child wandering the desert, encountering monks, cripples and sacrilegious bandits who tear out pages of the Bible to wipe their noses.

Mexican cinema began to change in 1970 with the election of Luis Echeverría Alvarez as the country's president. Following the installation of his brother, Rodolfo, as head of the Banco Nacional de Cinematografía, the state became closely involved in film-making, and a form of auteurist cinema developed as a counterbalance to the purely commercial industry. Among those who took their chance was Arturo Ripstein, the son of a film producer, who had been the assistant of Luis Buñuel on *The Exterminating Angel* (*El angel exterminador*, 1962), and directed his first film at the age of twenty-two in 1965. Ripstein's *El Santo Oficio* (1973) concerns a Jewish family that runs foul of the Inquisition in the sixteenth century. Felipe Cazals, trained in France at the Institut des Hautes Études Cinématographiques, employed a documentary style in *Canoa* (1975), about the murder of a group of university employees by a rural mob urged on by a priest. Cazals's *El apando* (1975) was an equally powerful work exposing the brutality of Mexico's prison system. Jaime Humberto Hermosillo was another director who began to make distinctive films in this period. His *El cumpleaños del perro* (1974) ushered in his characteristic satire of middle-class sexuality. Working outside the state sector, Paul Leduc made *Reed: México insurgente* (1970), shot in black and white and following the US reporter John Reed, later the subject of Warren Beatty's film *Reds* (1981), as he covered the Mexican Revolution in 1913.

All these directors would go on to successful careers. Others who began in this period include Jorge Fons and Alfonso Arau. But though the PRI remained in control, the six-year period of each presidency frequently produced abrupt changes of direction politically, with marked effects on the film industry. When José López Portillo became president in 1976, he appointed his sister, Margarita López Portillo, head of the film industry. It proved a disaster.

Previous pages: Emilio Echevarría is El Chivo, an ex-hitman who lives in squalor with his beloved dogs in *Amores perros* (2000). One of the highest-grossing Latin American films ever and shot entirely using a hand-held camera, this emotionally powerful film is extraordinary. Dir: Alejandro González Iñárritu Below: Brontis Jodorowsky as his son and Alejandro Jodorowsky as El Topo in *The Mole* (*El topo*, 1971). Dir: Alejandro Jodorowsky

LATIN AMERICA

The promising beginnings of the early 1970s were ignored. The state progressively withdrew from production, backing only five films in 1981. Though production nationally was up to over 100 films a year, auteur cinema was replaced by the 'family' films favoured by the president's sister, and by a glut of sex comedies (known as *ficheras*) and violent action films about drug trafficking. At the end of this period, in 1982, came a catastrophe full of symbolism – a fire at the Mexican film archive which incinerated a large part of Mexico's cinema heritage.

Despite the difficulties, some excellent films were made. Paul Leduc continued his innovative attempts to get away from the mainstream. His *Frida, naturaleza viva* (1984) is a biography of the painter Frida Kahlo, wife of the muralist Diego Rivera, constructed as a series of impressionistic sequences with little dialogue. Leduc's *Latino Bar* (1991), set in a squalid seaside bar, avoids dialogue altogether.

Ripstein reworked the melodrama genre with *The Place without Limits* (*El lugar sin límites*, 1977), set in a seedy provincial brothel run by the camp transvestite 'La Manuela'. When he attempts to distract Pancho, a macho customer who is molesting his daughter, he arouses first his lust and then his anger, with murderous results. Ripstein's *Cadena perpetua* (1978), about a small-time crook blackmailed by a policeman, is another compelling study of desperation among the dispossessed. Hermosillo also kept working, though his breakthrough film, *Doña Herlinda and Her Son* (*Doña Herlinda y su hijo*), did not come until 1985. When she realizes that her son Rodolfo is in a gay relationship with Ramón, Doña Herlinda invites Ramón to move in while at the same time encouraging Rodolfo's forthcoming marriage to Olga. The film's deftly handled sexual politics made it an international art-house success.

Under the presidency of Miguel de la Madrid from 1982, the state once more involved itself in the fate of the industry, leading to the creation of the Instituto Mexicano de la Cinematografía (IMCINE). Though the results were initially disappointing, the appointment of Ignacio Durán Loera as head of IMCINE under the presidency of Carlos Salinas de Gortari (1988–94) saw IMCINE find its feet. Though by this time the political tide, in Mexico as elsewhere, had turned in favour of the privatization of state assets, IMCINE made itself the facilitator of coproductions, and ushered in a lively period for Mexican production. Alfonso Arau's *Like Water for Chocolate* (*Como agua para chocolate*, 1991) is a love story, in which Tita, forced by her mother to abandon her sweetheart to her sister, finds solace in cooking for him. Though some critics found it overly sentimental, it became a huge hit in the United States. Guillermo Del Toro's *Cronos* (*La invención de Cronos*, 1993), another international success, was a stylish and artful horror film in which

Top left and right: Lumi Cavazos as Tita, finding solace in cooking in *Like Water for Chocolate* (*Como agua para chocolate*, 1991). Dir: Alfonso Arau
<u>Above</u>: Marco Antonio

Treviño as Rodolfo and Arturo Meza as Ramón, the lovers in *Doña Herlinda and Her Son* (*Doña Herlinda y su hijo*, 1985). Dir: Jaime Humberto Hermosillo

Popular Mexican Cinema
Deep Crimson
(*Profundo carmesí*, 1996)
Dir: Arturo Ripstein

Though it has its experimental side, the best Mexican cinema has its roots firmly planted in popular genres. *Deep Crimson* is a crime film, based on the real-life exploits of the so-called Lonely Hearts Club killers in the post-war United States. Nicolás and Coral are a grotesque version of Bonnie and Clyde, who rob not banks but vulnerable rich women. Nicolás is a dapper man of seedy charm with an unconvincing wig, who appeals to the snobbery of elderly widows by his ability to pose as a Spaniard, affecting the accent and mannerisms of the expatriate. Coral is an overweight single mother who ditches her children and takes off with Nicolás, pushing him from robbery to murder.

Though money is the ostensible motive, Coral is addicted to romance, as we see in the first shot of her bedroom, stuffed with cheap but gaudy clothes, Mills & Boon-type novels, and photographs of film stars. The killings the pair commit are dictated by Coral's passion for Nicolás. He seduces women in order to rob them, and this incurs Coral's murderous jealousy.

Arturo Ripstein is one of the few directors living and working in Mexico who has found international success with his films. *Deep Crimson* won awards at major film festivals both in South America and Europe when it was released in 1996. Essentially it is a study of thwarted passion turning nasty. Coral is vicious, even to the extent of killing a young girl who has witnessed her mother's murder. Yet her gesture of offering her own hair to make Nicolás a new wig is at once tender and ridiculous. When at the end the pair are callously shot in the back by the police whom Nicolás has confessed to, it does not feel like justice. It is a stylish film, with a camera that roams elegantly around the cluttered interiors of 1940s Mexico and occasionally out to the empty spaces of the plains.

Country of Origin: Mexico/France/Spain
Running Time: 114 mins

Production Companies: Ivania Films/IMCINE/MK2 Productions
Producers: Miguel Necoechea, Pablo Barbachano
Writer: Paz Alicia Garciadiego
Photography: Guillermo Granillo
Editor: Rafael Castanedo
Art Directors: Mónica Chirinos, Patricia Nava, Marisa Pecanins, Macarena Folache
Music: David Mansfield

Nicolás Estrella: Daniel Giménez Cache
Coral Fabre: Regina Orozco
Irene Gallardo: Marisa Paredes
Rebeca Sanpedro: Verónica Merchant
Juanita Norton: Julieta Egurrola
Mrs Ruelas: Patricia Reyes Spíndola

Above: Marisa Paredes as Irene (l) undergoes a form of marriage with Nicolás (Daniel Giménez Cache), watched by Coral (Regina Orozco).
Left: Director Arturo Ripstein.
Right: The romance of murder: Nicolás and Coral.

Above: María Rojo
and José Alonso
make home movies
in *La tarea* (1990).
Dir: Jaime Humberto
Hermosillo
Right: Tenoch (Diego
Luna) and Julio (Gael

García Bernal) make
a threesome with the
unhappily married
Luisa (Maribel Verdú)
in *And Your Mother
Too* (*Y tu mama
también*, 2000).
Dir: Alfonso Cuarón

a piece of antique jewellery turns its owner into a vampire. Del Toro followed this with a Mexican-Spanish coproduction, *The Devil's Backbone* (*El espinazo del diablo*, 2001), another well-crafted horror film, before going off to Hollywood to make *Blade II* (2002), a sequel to the smash-hit vampire film with Wesley Snipes. Women directors were also given their chance. Maria Novaro's *Danzón* (1991) is a charming story of middle-aged love, making the most of popular music. In Dana Rotberg's *Angel de fuego* (1992) a teenage circus performer, cast out by the troupe when she becomes pregnant, finds refuge with a group of wandering evangelicals.

Jorge Fons's *Red Dawn* (*Rojo amanecer*, 1989) – a film made outside the system of state support – about the massacre of student demonstrators in Tlatelolco, Mexico City, at the time of the Olympic Games in 1968, had to struggle against censors before being released. Fons's reworking of a popular format, *El callejón de los milagros* (1995), told interlocking stories in a single neighbourhood, with a tragic outcome for Abel, a young barber who goes to the United States to make money to marry Alma, only to find on his return that she has become a high-class callgirl. Attempting to rescue her, he is stabbed and dies in her arms.

Hermosillo had another success with *La tarea* (1990), a low-budget film shot in a series of ten-minute takes in which, as an exercise for a television production class, a woman films herself having sex with a former boyfriend. Before its ingenious ending the film entertainingly lays bare not only the persons of its performers but male sexual presumptions.

Arturo Ripstein has gone from strength to strength, mining a rich seam of low life. As he says of himself: 'I love the lecherous, I love the lonely and the lost.'[1] Perhaps his masterpiece is *Deep Crimson* (*Profundo carmesí*, 1996). Based on a true story about an ill-assorted couple who tour the Mexican countryside seeking out rich widows and murdering them for their money, it is a beautifully staged study of the banality of evil and the vulnerability of the lonely. In careful compositions and in intricately ordered long-takes Ripstein observes the emotional pain of his frequently disturbed characters. *Such Is Life* (*Asi es la vida*, 1999) is a tale of vengeance loosely based on Euripides' *Medea*, set in the Mexico City slums and shot on digital video.

Mexican cinema, recently increasing production to around forty films a year, has had further international success by staying close to its roots as a cinema of genre. *Amores perros* (2000), directed by the Spaniard, Alejandro González Iñárritu, is a cunningly constructed thriller which gives an insight into the brutality of contemporary criminal life in Mexico City and its interconnection with other strata of society. Alfonso Cuarón's *And Your Mother Too* (*Y tu mama también*, 2000) is a road movie with a satirical edge, in which an unhappily married woman takes a trip with a couple of spoiled teenage boys. There are laughs at the expense of the male ego, but compared to *Amores perros* its social commentary is just window-dressing, and the shock ending is a highly manipulative tug at the heartstrings.

Argentina's turbulent political history since World War II has profoundly marked its cinema. Oscillating between the populism of Peronism and military dictatorship, with

Above: Jarocho (Gustavo Sànchez Parra) and his dog Pancho in one of the brutal dog fighting scenes from *Amores perros* (2000).
Below: Vanessa Bauche and Gael García Bernal in *Amores perros* (2000). Dir: Alejandro González Iñárritu

JAROCHO: What gives, Octavio? Know what your dog did?

OCTAVIO: Yeah.

JAROCHO: So?

OCTAVIO: It's OK, huh? It's cool ...

JAROCHO: Cool? It's not cool at all. Bring Pancho. See what he did? That dog was worth at least 20,000 pesos.

OCTAVIO: Have him stuffed for your mantle.

Jarocho (Gustavo Sánchez Parra), Octavio (Gael García Bernal), *Amores perros* (Alejandro González Iñárritu, 2000)

uneasy intervals of civilian rule, what should be the richest country in Latin America has seen its economy slide inexorably downwards. In such a situation the cinema cannot avoid its share of pain.

At the end of the 1960s Fernando Solanas and Octavio Getino made *Hour of the Furnaces* (*La hora de los hornos*, 1968), a four-hour agit-prop montage of photographs, newsreels, advertising commercials and mock travelogues which poked fun at the bourgeoisie and laid stirring opera music over images of the poor. It attempted to destroy once and for all the passive spectator of commercial cinema, calling on the viewer to participate in its Peronist project. Quoting Franz Fanon, theorist of the third world struggle, it maintains that 'Every spectator is a coward or a traitor.'

Traditionally, serious Argentinian cinema had been less genre-based than in Mexico, looking more towards the model of the European art cinema in the 1950s and 1960s, when director Leopoldo Torre Nilsson was the darling of the international art-house circuit. Solanas and Getino published a manifesto in 1969, 'Towards a Third Cinema', which argued for films that were neither the commercial pap of Hollywood ('First Cinema') nor the personalized and 'nihilistic' individualism of the auteur cinema of Europe ('Second Cinema'). Instead, 'Third Cinema' was to be based on reality, a kind of rough and ready work in progress, always socially relevant.

The return of Peron in 1973 led to a brief flowering of film production in Argentina, cut short by the military coup of 1976, which initiated the so-called 'dirty war' in which at least 9,000 civilians 'disappeared', murdered by the armed services and their paramilitary henchmen. (Unofficial figures go as high as 30,000.) Those film-makers not victims of the brutal repression could either remain silent or seek exile. Solanas chose the latter. The early 1980s, when the military's power began to crumble, saw confidence trickle back. The debacle in the Falklands/Malvinas hastened the departure of the generals and a return to civilian rule under Alfonsín in 1983. The same year saw the release of *A Funny, Dirty Little War* (*No habrá más penas ni olvido*, Héctor Olivera, 1983), set in 1974, in which following Peron's return the administrator of a seedy little provincial town recruits an elderly park-keeper, a jailbird and a policeman in a fight against the local bigwig who is determined to root out 'Marxists'. The tone of the film is uneven, veering between black farce and scenes of beating and torture, but it brilliantly satirizes the national paranoia.

The mid-1980s was a productive period for Argentine cinema, despite rampant inflation and shrinking audiences. Though domestic production was unprotected by any exhibition quotas, some state money was available for production. Luis Puenzo's *The Official Version* (*La historia oficial*, 1986) had as its heroine a middle-class teacher of history who discovers that the child she has adopted is the daughter of parents who 'disappeared' under the military. Stylistically conventional if craftsman-like, the film effectively dramatizes the bad faith of those who pretend not to know what went on, even if the ending, in which the teacher is beaten by her husband, a prosperous businessman who knows the full dirty story, is overly melodramatic.

Another film about the years of military dictatorship is Miguel Pereira's *La deuda interna*, also known as *Verónico Cruz* (1987). In a bleak mountain province Verónico, an Indian boy, is brought up by his grandmother when his widowed father goes to the town to find work. The boy is befriended by a young school teacher. After the military coup of 1976 policemen arrive at the little backwater and the teacher's books are searched. 'Are they sending books to prison now?' asks an elderly villager. The teacher takes Verónico to the town to search for his father, but realizes the boy's father has 'disappeared'. Verónico grows up, joins the navy and drowns when the *General Belgrano* is sunk during the Falklands/Malvinas war.

In *Un lugar en el mundo*, directed by Adolfo Aristarain in 1992, a young boy watches his left-wing parents, victims of repression, trying to rebuild their lives in a country town by running a medical centre, teaching in a school and organizing an agricultural co-op. The arrival of a Spanish geologist working for the local landowner provokes spirited political discussions among the grown-ups. Meanwhile the boy is more interested in

Above: Not so funny: a trapped civilian faces torture in the farcical *A Funny, Dirty Little War* (*No habrá más penas ni olvido*, 1983). Dir: Héctor Olivera

teaching his girlfriend to read against the wishes of her father, who thinks it will give her ideas above her station.

One of Argentina's most accomplished film-makers, Maria Luisa Bemberg, had introduced a homosexual character into *Señora de nadie* (1982), something of a provocation when the military were still in charge. Her career blossomed in the more relaxed atmosphere of civilian government. *Camila* (1984) was a notable success, a story based on true events in 1847 set against a background of military rule. Camila is oppressed by her father, who offers her a choice of an arranged marriage or the convent. She chooses neither, instead falling in love with a priest. After a fleeting moment of passion the two are captured and shot, despite the fact that Camila is now pregnant.

In *I the Worst of All* (*Yo la peor de todas*, 1990) Bemberg again explored a woman entwined in the coils of religion, in a biography of the seventeenth-century Mexican nun Juana Inés de la Cruz. A poet and progressive thinker, Juana is forced to recant by the men who rule the church, once she loses the protection of the vicereine, with whom she has an intense emotional relationship. Bemberg's *We Don't Want to Talk about It* (*De eso no se habla*, 1993) is a brilliant fable with much deliciously acid humour, about a dwarf whose mother deals with the handicap by pretending her daughter is normal, but who eventually accepts herself for what she is and joins a circus. As John King has remarked, a story about wilful blindness to the truth has many contemporary resonances.[2]

After the establishment of civilian rule Solanas returned with *Tangos, el exilio de Gardel* (1985), a film about a troupe of tango dancers in Paris which explores the meaning of exile. The traditional dance of Argentina, tango represents the survival of national culture. With *South* (*Sur*, 1988) Solanas attempted a reworking of his Peronist politics in the light of all that had happened, telling the story of a prisoner incarcerated in the south who returns to pick up the threads of his political and emotional life. It is a complex film of multiple layers, perhaps fully understandable only by those familiar with the complexities of Argentine politics, in which Peronism can stand for a bewildering range of ideological positions from left to right.

Argentina met the end of the century with a spate of enterprising films, assisted by a government levy which diverts money from both cinema and video back to film producers. Five films were selected for the London Film Festival in 2000 and five more the following year, among them *Close to the Border* (*Cerca de la frontera*, Rodolfo Durán, 1999), another return to the period of military rule; *Fuckland* (José Luis Marquès, 2000), an eccentric but revealing tour around the Falklands/Malvinas by a mischievous Argentine; *The Swamp* (*La Ciénaga*, 2000), a satire directed by Lucrecia Martel on the country's listless middle classes, oblivious to the decay setting in around them; and *Nine Queens* (*Nueve reinas*, Fabián Bielinsky, 2000), a slickly-made tale about a couple of confidence tricksters which could be taken as an implied comment on the present state of the country, bankrupted by its rulers. Whether the quality or quantity of production (around forty titles a year) can be sustained as Argentina's economic situation lurches from one crisis to another is questionable.

Of Argentina's neighbours along the River Plate, Uruguay and Paraguay, little can be said here except to note that the Uruguayan Cinemateca in Montevideo is one of the most important film archives in the world. To the north, however, is the third major force in Latin American cinema, Brazil. By 1970 Brazilian cinema had an enviable international reputation for innovation and ambition, reflecting the country's rich racial and cultural mix. Starting in the early 1960s Cinema Novo, as its name implied, intended to be a new kind of cinema, one appropriate to Brazil's situation: a cinema of auteurs, certainly, but working with low budgets, small crews, shooting mostly on location with non-professional actors. One of its foremost practitioners, Glauber Rocha, described it as a 'cinema of hunger'. Yet by the end of the decade, Cinema Novo had moved a long way from its neo-realist origins, no longer content to tell unadorned tales of street life. Rocha's *Antonio das Mortes* (1969) is the colourful, often bizarre story of a bandit and a celebration of the mystical wisdom of the people. Joaquim Pedro de Andrade's *Macunaíma* (1969), an adaptation of a classic novel of the 1920s, turned into a fantastical comedy which played with racial stereotypes in a tale of country bumpkins at large in the city, where the local Mr Big feeds his victims to man-eating fish, a metaphor for modern Brazil consuming its citizens. Nelson Pereira dos Santos's *How Tasty Was My Little Frenchman* (*Como era gostoso o meu francês*, 1971) is another film about man-eaters, in which an early French explorer finds himself in the hands of Indians, who take him into the tribe but eventually consume him. Cannibalism is not condemned, merely observed as an element in a different culture.

The military had taken power in Brazil in 1964, and from 1968 repression became more severe. Several leading directors, including Glauber Rocha, Ruy Guerra and Carlos Diegues, went into exile. Yet there was increased state support for cinema in the 1970s, leading to the establishment of the government film organization, Embrafilme, in 1975, with funds for production, an active role in distribution and quotas for Brazilian films in theatres. Soon state funding accounted for between a quarter and a half of all production. By the end of the decade the number of cinema spectators in Brazil had doubled.

One way of avoiding censorship was to make literary adaptations. Bruno Barreto's *Dona Flor and Her Two Husbands* (*Doña Flor e seus dois maridos*, 1976) was a hugely popular version of a novel by Jorge Amado in which a widow, splendidly played by Sonia Braga, marries a respectable but dull doctor as her second husband, but regularly summons her sexy first husband's ghost to her bed. Only she can see him as, naked, he accompanies her and the new husband to church. Ruy Guerra, too, ventured into adaptation with *Eréndira* (1982), based on a book by Gabriel García Marquez.

Though Cinema Novo was over, its major directors continued to be the mainstays of serious Brazilian cinema through the 1970s. Carlos Diegues's *Xica da Silva* (1976) is a jovial tale about a black woman who rises to eminence in eighteenth-century Brazil by the flagrant use of her sexual power. Dos Santos in *O amuleto de Ogum* (1974) digs deep into the bedrock of Brazilian popular mysticism. Ruy Guerra's *A queda* (1977) is a kind of sequel to his 1963 black and white Cinema Novo film *Os fuzis*, in which a group of soldiers confront a village of starving peasants. In *A queda* the soldiers are now building workers in Rio, struggling against the corruption and cruelty of their employers.

The 1980s were difficult years for Brazilian cinema. Civilians came back to power, but the economy struggled. The audience contracted once again, halving during the decade. Large parts of the industry were converted to the production of sex films, the so-called *pornochanchadas*. Yet some vital films were made, such as Diegues's *Bye Bye Brasil* (1980), a colourful road movie in which a couple of itinerant musicians encounter the kaleidoscope of modern Brazil. Dos Santos produced another major film with *Memories of Prison* (*Memórias do cárcere*, 1984). Under the dictatorship of Getúlio Vargas during the Depression, a writer is imprisoned without trial under increasingly degrading conditions. Refusing to collaborate with the authorities, he gradually forges a bond with his fellow prisoners. When he is searched before being released, the prisoners hide the manuscript of the book he has written by distributing its pages among themselves. A grim picture of the

Top and above: Sonia Braga as Dona Flor, between her two husbands, the ghostly Vadinho (José Wilker) and Teodoro (Mauro Mendonça) in *Dona Flor and Her Two Husbands* (*Doña Flor e seus dois maridos*, 1976).
Dir: Bruno Barreto

Above: Maurício do Valle as the eccentric bandit in the title role of *Antonio das Mortes* (1969).
Dir: Glauber Rocha
Right: The colourful Caravana Rolidei rolls into town carrying a group of entertainers in *Bye Bye Brasil* (1980). But society is changing and threatens the future of their lifestyle.
Dir: Carlos Diegues

Opposite: Josue
(Vinicíus de Oliveira)
and Dora (Fernanda
Montenegro) embark
on a journey up country
in *Central Station*
(*Centro do Brasil*, 1998).
Dir: Walter Salles
Above: Being prepared
for execution in *The
Jackal of Nahueltoro*
(*El chacal de
Nahueltoro*, 1969).

Dir: Miguel Littín
Above right:
Contemplating his
future: Tonho (Rodrigo
Santoro) is torn
between duty to his
father by avenging
his brother's death or
rebelling against him
in *Behind the Sun* (*Abril
despedaçado*, 2001).
Dir: Walter Salles

contemporary national condition was furnished by Hector Babenco's film *Pixote* (1981), about street children caught in the brutalizing poverty of the urban jungle. Its faithfulness to its subject was chillingly underlined when its youthful protagonist, Fernando Ramos da Silva, was later killed by the police. *At Play in the Fields of the Lord* (1991) is an odd but interesting film, directed by Babenco with a largely Hollywood cast, about a group of ill-fated missionaries in the Amazon.

State control was out of fashion by the 1990s, and Embrafilme was shut down. Quotas were abandoned, and production slumped to a mere three films in 1993. Inflation and the rise of television, especially the TV Globo network, took their toll. Under the presidency of Cardoso there was a modest revival in the later 1990s, with tax breaks and some direct financial assistance enabling production to rise to forty films by 2000. Diegues's *Orfeu* (1999) was a celebration of music and carnival. Brazilian music is also at the centre of Bruno Barreto's *Bossa nova* (1999). Yet the social indignation behind Cinema Nova still burned in Walter Salles's *Central Station* (*Centro do Brasil*, 1998), a huge international hit in which a child of the streets not unlike the boy in *Pixote* forms an unlikely friendship with a cynical middle-aged woman, who against her better judgement takes him on a voyage of discovery into the hinterland in search of his father. Salles followed this with another venture into the wild: *Behind the Sun* (*Abril despedaçado*, 2001) is a beautifully shot portrait of rural desperation, again with a child at the centre, set in the arid north-east in 1910 and telling of a family that scratches a living from sugar cane while conducting a bitter feud with their neighbours. Fernando Meirelles's *City of God* (*Cidade de Deus*, 2002) is another exploration of the underbelly of Brazilian urban society, a compelling portrait of youthful gangs trading drugs and bullets in the favelas.

In Chile, under the cautious government of the Christian Democrats, five feature films were made at the end of the 1960s, among them the experimental and enigmatically titled *Tres tristes tigres* (1968), directed by Raúl Ruiz, and Miguel Littín's *The Jackal of Nahueltoro* (*El chacal de Nahueltoro*, 1969), a reconstruction of the life of a peasant imprisoned then executed for murders committed while drunk. Littín explores the social background to the crime in a variety of styles, exposing the miserable conditions which give rise to such horrors.

The advent of the Popular Unity government under Salvador Allende produced ambitious plans under the aegis of a state organization, Chile Films, but no actual feature films. When Allende's government was overthrown in 1973, Pinochet's military dictatorship embarked on a brutal suppression of left-wing culture. Film-workers were arrested and murdered, films were banned (including some Hollywood titles) and both Littín and Ruiz went abroad, the former to Mexico, the latter to Paris. Until the return of democracy at the end of 1989 Chilean cinema existed only in exile, and even since then its local production has hardly amounted to a dozen films.

Littín made a couple of literary adaptations in Mexico before moving on to Nicaragua to make *Alsino y el condor* (1982), a story about a young boy's dream of flying that allegorizes the revolutionary project of the Sandinistas. Ruiz stayed mainly in Europe, where he has

Top: Catherine Deneuve as Odette and Marcello Mazzarella as the writer Marcel Proust in *Time Regained* (*Le Temps retrouvé*, 1999). Dir: Raúl Ruiz
Above: Jorge Perugorria and Vladimir Cruz in *Strawberry and Chocolate* (*Fresa y chocolate*, 1994). Dir: Tomás Gutiérrez Alea
Above right: Slaves invited to dinner in *The Last Supper* (*La última cena*, 1976). Dir: Tomás Gutiérrez Alea

become more of a French film-maker than a Chilean. His *The Hypothesis of the Stolen Painting* (*L'Hypothèse du tableau volé*, 1978) is a teasing, elliptical investigation of a painter through the construction of living tableaux of his work. *Treasure Island* (*L'Île au trésor*, 1985) bears only a tenuous connection to Robert Louis Stevenson's classic story. Like *Three Crowns of the Sailor* (*Les Trois Couronnes du matelot*, 1982) and *Life Is a Dream* (*La mémoire des apparances*, 1986), it is a characteristically fractured narrative, densely textured with references to arcane cultural works (*Life Is a Dream* is based on a play by the Spanish dramatist Calderón de la Barca), the likeness to dreams underpinned by Ruiz's interest in psychoanalysis. However, with *Three Lives and Only One Death* (*Trois Vies et une seule mort*, 1996), a comedy with Marcello Mastroianni, *Time Regained* (*Le Temps retrouvé*, 1999), his sumptuous but subtle version of Proust, and *Comédie de l'innocence* (2000), in which the story of a child's two mothers explores the resonances of Freud's notion of the 'family romance', Ruiz seems to have taken a turn towards work less wilfully obscure.

Obscurantism and an overly personalized style were not encouraged in Cuba, where the film industry had been nationalized following the victory of Fidel Castro's forces in 1959. The Cuban Institute of Cinematographic Art and Industry (ICAIC) set about defining a policy for production while at the same time expanding exhibition with mobile cinemas in rural areas. As a result of these policies (or despite them, some might say), Cuba produced some notable films in the hundred or so fiction features made in the first quarter-century of the revolution.

One of the most celebrated was *Memories of Underdevelopment* (*Memorias del subdesarrollo*, 1968), directed by Tomás Gutiérrez Alea, in which a middle-class intellectual picks his way through the cultural and political conundrums of Marxist Cuba. While exposing the hero's opportunism, the film's subtle analysis of the current state of society is by no means lacking in critical distance. Alea proved to be one of Cuba's most accomplished directors, and *The Last Supper* (*La última cena*, 1976) is a sardonic analysis of the Christian piety of an eighteenth-century slave-owner who invites twelve slaves to be his guests at dinner and then has them brutally hunted down when they take the opportunity to revolt. Another film from the mid-1970s is *One Way or Another* (*De cierta manera*, 1974), directed by Sara Gómez, a witty and incisive look at issues of both race and gender among the marginal slum dwellers of Havana.

In the 1980s Cuban production was upped to around eight features a year and there were opportunities for new young directors. Several of them chose to work in comedy, such as Juan Carlos Tabío, whose *Plaff* (1988) has been described as a screwball soap opera, with lots of self-reflective moments where the presence of the camera is revealed. However,

LATIN AMERICA

the collapse of Communism in the Soviet Union, which took away most of the crutches supporting Cuba's tottering economy, together with the continuing US blockade, made the 1990s a difficult decade. Cuba's social achievements in the fields of health and education were undeniable; a huge increase in literacy rates and an equally dramatic drop in infant mortality, two key indicators of social welfare, speak for themselves. But film production has faltered; Cubans hope cheaper digital technology and coproduction will help .

Shortly before his death in 1996 Gutiérrez Alea directed *Strawberry and Chocolate* (*Fresa y chocolate*, 1994), which raised the vexed question of homosexuality in Cuba. Back in 1984 two Cuban exiles, Orlando Jiménez Leal and Néstor Almendros, the distinguished cinematographer, made *Improper Conduct* (*Mauvaise Conduite*), a documentary which sought to indict Cuba's treatment of homosexuals. The film aroused great controversy, being attacked by defenders of Cuba and defended by its enemies. Alea's film treads warily but is sympathetic to an openly – even outrageously – gay intellectual, Diego, who undertakes the cultural enlightenment of David, a young militant (sorely needed, since David thinks Truman Capote dropped the A-bomb on Japan!). It falls short of endorsing homosexuality, since David is finally 'saved' by being bedded by a female friend of Diego, but its discussions of the revolution's stance on the issue are frank and open.

In the Andean countries of Bolivia and Peru, cinema has faced some of the most difficult conditions of the continent. At the end of the 1960s, working with a Bolivian group known as Ukamau (taken from the name of an Indian tribe), Jorge Sanjinés made *Blood of the Condor* (*Yawar Mallku*, 1968), a complex and passionate work about Indian resistance to enforced sterilization. The film attracted audiences both at home and abroad. A military coup in 1971 forced Sanjinés into exile. His later film, *The Secret Nation* (*La nación clandestina*, 1989), like the earlier work, employs a fractured narrative and tells the story of Sebastián. Against the background of a military coup in La Paz, Sebastián is trying to get back to his village, carrying on his back a huge multi-coloured mask he will wear in a sacred dance. As he

Below: Sacred dances performed by villagers in the Andes in *The Secret Nation (La nación clandestina,* 1989).
Dir: Jorge Sanjinés

Above: One of four angry cadets who attempt to liven up the restrictive life in a military academy with tragic results in *La ciudad y los perros*

(1986).
Dir: Francisco Lombardi
Below: Stealing a motorbike relieves the boredom in *Rodrigo D: No futuro* (1989).
Dir: Victor Gaviria

journeys through an extraordinary mountain landscape, frequent flashbacks recount his time as a paramilitary, when he was disparagingly called 'the Indian' (he has the high cheekbones and oval eyes of the indigenous people), leading to his decline into a hopeless drunk and expulsion from his village. Sanjinés continued his career into the 1990s, directing *To Hear the Bird Song* (*Para recibir el canto de los pájaros*, 1996), another complexly structured story in which a crew making a film about the Spanish conquest meet with indifference from the local villagers.

In the 1970s the nationalist military government in Peru offered some assistance to the makers of short films and by the end of the decade some features had appeared. Francisco Lombardi made his first in 1977, and followed with *La ciudad y los perros* (1986), from the novel by Peru's most famous writer, Mario Vargas Llosa, about the indoctrination of military cadets. In Lombardi's film *The Mouth of the Wolf* (*La boca del lobo*, 1988) soldiers are besieged by the Peruvian guerrilla group Sendero Luminoso (Shining Path), though critics found the film stronger on action than political analysis. Lombardi returned to Vargas Llosa as a source with a film of *Captain Pantoja and the Special Service* (*Pantaleón y las visitadoras*, 1999), another study of military machismo.

In Colombia there was support for feature films from the state cinema organization FOCINE (Compañía de Fomento Cinematográfico) in the 1980s, with the imposition of quotas for the exhibition of domestic product and loans for financing, leading to the production of around ten films a year. One of them, *Rodrigo D: No futuro* (1989), illustrated all too starkly the background against which films in Colombia are made. A story about bored young men immersed in the drug and gun culture of the city of Medellín, it was made with largely non-professional actors, of whom a high proportion met their deaths before the film had completed its run. Its director, Victor Gaviria, later made *The Rose Seller* (*La vendedora de rosas*, 1998), revisiting the deadly streets of Medellín in a version of Hans Christian Andersen's 'The Little Match Girl'.

LATIN AMERICA

A more optimistic view of contemporary Colombia appears in *The Strategy of the Snail* (*La estrategia del caracol*, 1993), directed by Sergio Cabrera, in which the tenants of a Bogotá apartment block combine forces to defeat the wealthy owner who is trying to evict them. The film was a huge success in its home country, and Cabrera's later film *Golpe de estadio* (1998), a lively satire based around the national passion for football, was also a crowd-pleaser. The same year Cabrera was elected to the Colombian parliament. Unfortunately, *The Strategy of the Snail* proved to be the last film financed by FOCINE, which was wound up at the end of 1992. Colombian cinema is now largely reliant on coproduction finance from abroad, especially Spain.

Next door in Venezuela the government, enriched by oil revenues, was able to offer support for cinema from the mid-1970s, dictating a quota for home-produced films and dispensing funds based partly on a levy on the box office. As a result feature film production climbed to about a dozen a year. The vagaries of the international oil price, however, has meant that continuity has not always been possible. In 2001 the state cinema organization CNAC (Centro Nacional Autonomo de Cinematografía Venezolana), which had been part-financing half a dozen films a year, suffered a severe budget cut. Venezuela's most successful director, Román Chalbaud, has managed fifteen features since 1974, most recently *Pandemonium, la capital del infierno* (1997), an ambitious but sometimes obscure satire of Venezuelan society. Fina Torres, one of Venezuela's few women directors, has had considerable success at festivals, with *Oriana* (1985) winning a prize at the Cannes Film Festival. *Mecánicas celestes* (1995) was also successful, a comedy about a singer trying for fame which has fun satirizing the world of international opera. But her most recent film, *Woman on Top* (1999), a Hollywood comedy starring Penélope Cruz as a cook whose marriage breaks up because she always has to be on top during sex, was criticized as too reliant on Latin stereotypes.

When he met Mexican President Zedillo in 1994, Arturo Ripstein told him, 'A country without film is a sad country.' Mexico, Brazil and even Argentina, despite the severity of its economic crisis, are big enough to ensure that their populations do not go without film. In the rest of the continent, the smaller national cinemas have suffered even more than the larger from the usual disadvantages: massive competition from Hollywood, the ongoing erosion of their audiences by television, the retreat from funding by the state. Yet things are not as sad as this implies. Coproduction, both between Latin American countries and with Spain and other Europeans, offers a lifeline. Venezuela, Peru, Chile and Cuba – all had features in competition at the 2002 Havana Festival of New Latin American Cinema. The optimism of film-makers seems undiminished.

20. | Cinema Tomorrow

Cinema is largely a nineteenth-century technology, relying on the chemistry of photography, in itself now over 175 years old. In the last century, sound, colour and wider screen processes were added, but none of these made any significant difference to the nature of the feature-length narrative film, which has been the economically dominant form since about 1915, when D W Griffith made *The Birth of a Nation*. Now, however, the digital revolution threatens radical change, in that for the first time cinema will no longer be dependent on photography.

Digitization is already well advanced. Cinema sound has long benefited from advances in digital recording technology within the music industry. So far as the image is concerned, it is now over ten years since the first digitally animated characters were introduced into live-action films. In James Cameron's *Terminator 2* (1991) the cyborg can take human form but also morphs into other shapes, such as the blade of a knife, all of them created in the computer. In Steven Spielberg's *Jurassic Park* (1993) the computer-generated dinosaurs went a step further towards images that had the convincing reality of photography. *Toy Story* (John Lasseter, 1995) was the first film in which everything on screen was digitally originated.

For some time now, major feature films have been edited by converting the photographed images into digital information, then transferring the edited material back to film prints for distribution. But high-quality digital cameras are also now available to record live-action footage, which means that it can now be manipulated in exactly the same way as digitally originated signals. This has troubled some commentators, who see it as a break from cinema's roots. Cinema, in one view, is essentially a kind of realism. No matter that the image to be photographed may be artificial, constructed through the use of sets, costumes, make-up and so forth; cinema works by convincing the audience that what they see is real. Destroy that and you destroy cinema's power, reducing it to the childish fantasies of animated cartoons.

Yet those who object to digital manipulation on the principle that it goes against the nature of cinema are on shaky ground. Not only is photography itself a manipulative process employing techniques of framing, camera placement and lighting, but cinema has used special effects since the beginning, memorably in the 'trick' films of Georges Méliès in the early 1900s. Indeed, cinema can be seen as the marriage of photography with Victorian devices for the production of optical illusions. Digital technology is only an extension of this process.

Coming at the question another way, one can also argue that the way in which the images are created will not profoundly affect the nature of the cinema experience. It seems likely that people will still pay to watch a public performance of a narrative feature film which mimics the acts of recognizable human beings, because this kind of drama appeals to a deeply felt social and psychological need. And far from digital technology destroying the link to the real world, the whole tendency of the technology as presently evolving is towards ever-more realistic effects, designed to sustain the illusion that we are watching real people perform real acts.

For some people it is a disturbing thought that technology will soon advance to the point where it becomes possible to dispense with live actors. Future film stars could be entirely digital constructs. But just because something is technically feasible that does not mean it will happen. That depends on whether there is an economic imperative, and on whether the innovation satisfies the audience. 'Synthespians', as they have been dubbed, might allow savings on the astronomic salaries of film stars, but whether the audience will prefer electronically created personalities to Julia Roberts and Brad Pitt only time will tell.

One area where one can confidently predict a digital outcome within the next decade is in the means of distribution and exhibition. It costs around $1,000 to make a 35 mm print of a feature film, and usually several hundred copies are needed. Instead of cumbersome cans of film being shipped to each cinema, before too long films will no doubt be distributed in digital form, either on disk or by satellite. The threat of piracy will require ever-more sophisticated systems of encryption, but the savings will be considerable. Now that the technology is advancing, the only problem seems to be, who will pay for the installation of the new projection equipment? The distributors will make most of the savings, but the exhibitors will no doubt be expected to meet the cost of the hardware.

There is also the possibility of films being distributed directly into people's homes via the internet. Technically this is already feasible. Two things may count against it. In the first place, Hollywood is reluctant to go down that route because of the increased opportunity it gives for piracy. Second, Hollywood will be loath to abandon the 'event-status' afforded by the release of a new movie on a big screen in dedicated theatres, since the whole apparatus of publicity and promotion is organized around such 'premiere' events. There is also the fact that watching a film at home, on a desk-top computer or even on a TV set in the living room, is a different experience from watching it in a movie theatre. Clearly, movies are already consumed in vast quantities on video and DVD. But audiences' attachment to the big-screen experience shows little sign of waning. In the United States and the European Union – those countries with the highest standard of living, who may be assumed to have the most comfortable living rooms and the best audio-visual equipment – cinema attendance has been going up. Combined admissions have increased from 1,678 million in 1988 to 2,407 million in 2001.[1]

Although the two-hour feature film continues to be the privileged form of cinema, the kind of film we will see in the future depends not only on technological advance but is also profoundly affected by social and economic factors. A recurrent theme of this book is the struggle that many indigenous cinemas around the world have to endure in order to maintain even a precarious existence in the face of ever fiercer competition from Hollywood. US films are the most successful in the world in terms of box office receipts. In part this is because they provide audiences with the pleasure they seek, and, as we have seen, they also address many of our deepest concerns. But some in Hollywood are not satisfied with its overwhelmingly dominant position in the world film market; they wish to remove the remaining barriers to total hegemony. The determination of the United States to pursue its 'free trade' agenda directly threatens the measures of protection and public subsidy on which many national cinemas are dependent. Its defence of 'free speech' and 'consumer choice' in pursuing goals that may result in other voices being silenced and choice being restricted to one supplier is disingenuous indeed.

The concern must be that the new technologies now being introduced may only enhance Hollywood's position of strength. Efficiencies in distribution will make it even easier and cheaper to distribute Hollywood films around the world. And the huge investment in digital special effects will make it harder for the poorer cinemas of the world to compete. But the effects of digitization may cut both ways. Production could become simpler and cheaper. This would benefit not only indigenous cinemas, seeking to retain a distinctive national identity, but it could also empower the independent sector within the United States, which already offers a vibrant alternative to Hollywood fare. Moreover, despite cable and video, it is still difficult, even in metropolitan centres, to see more than a tiny proportion of world cinema output, since the cost of making prints is high in proportion to the potential revenue. Digitized distribution could make it much easier to find an audience for such films. There has probably never been as much film-making talent in world cinema as there is today. A digital revolution, making it easier for films to be not only made but also shown, may well inaugurate the Fourth Age of cinema.

Notes

INTRODUCTION
1 See Jon Lewis (ed.), *The End of the Cinema as we know it: American Film in the Nineties* (New York: New York University Press, 2001).
2 Toby Miller, Nitin Govil, John McMurria and Richard Maxwell, *Global Hollywood* (London: BFI Publishing, 2001), p.5.

1. HOLLYWOOD AND THE RISE OF THE BLOCKBUSTER
1 See Tino Balio (ed.), 'Introduction to Part II', *Hollywood in the Age of Television* (Cambridge, MA: Unwin Hyman, 1990), p.259.
2 Richard Maltby, '"Nobody Knows Everything": Post-classical historiographies and consolidated entertainment', in *Contemporary Hollywood Cinema*, edited by Steve Neale and Murray Smith (London and New York: Routledge, 1998), p.24.
3 Ibid., p.24.
4 Thomas Schatz, 'The New Hollywood', in *Film Theory Goes to the Movies*, edited by Jim Collins, Hilary Radner and Ava Preacher Collins (London and New York: Routledge, 1993), p.25.
5 Toby Miller, Nitin Govil, John McMurria and Richard Maxwell, *Global Hollywood*, op. cit., p.159.
6 Thomas Schatz, 'The New Hollywood', op. cit., p.33.
7 Thomas Elsaesser, 'Specularity and engulfment: Francis Ford Coppola and *Bram Stoker's "Dracula"*', in *Contemporary Hollywood Cinema*, op. cit., p.193.
8 Richard Maltby, '"Nobody Knows Everything": Post-classical historiographies and consolidated entertainment', op. cit., p.22.
9 Thomas Schatz, 'The New Hollywood', op. cit., p.35.

3. NEW SCIENCE FICTION
1 See the Internet Movie Database – www.imdb.org/Movies
2 The myth of the *vagina dentata*, or 'vagina with teeth', relates to a man's fear of castration or impotence during intercourse.
3 See J P Telotte, *Replications: A Robotic History of the Science Fiction Film* (Urbana and Chicago, IL: University of Illinois Press, 1995).
4 Fredric Jameson, *Postmodernism, or, The Cultural Logic of Late Capitalism* (Durham: Duke University Press, 1991), pp.15–16.
5 Sean French, *The Terminator* (London: BFI Publishing, 1996).
6 Michael Rogin, *Independence Day* (London: BFI Publishing, 1998).

4. HORROR
1 Andrew Britton (ed.), *American Nightmare: Essays on the Horror Film* (Toronto: Festival of Festivals, 1979).
2 See Carol Clover, *Men, Women and Chainsaws: Gender in the Modern Horror Film* (London: BFI Publishing, 1992).
3 Noël Carroll, *The Philosophy of Horror, or The Paradoxes of the Heart* (New York: Routledge, 1990), p.31.
4 Robin Wood, 'Burying the Undead: The Use and Obsolescence of Count Dracula', in *The Dread of Difference: Gender and the Horror Film*, edited by Barry Grant (Austin, TX: University of Texas Press, 1996).

5. COMEDY AND COMEDIANS
1 William Paul, *Laughing, Screaming: Modern Hollywood Horror and Comedy* (New York: Columbia University Press, 1994).
2 Frank Krutnik, 'Love Lies: Romantic Fabrication in Contemporary Romantic Comedy', in *Terms of Endearment: Hollywood Romantic Comedy of the 1980s and 1990s*, edited by Peter William Evans and Celestino Deleyto (Edinburgh: Edinburgh University Press, 1998).
3 Virginia Wright Wexman, *Creating the Couple: Love, Marriage, and Hollywood Performance* (Princeton, NJ: Princeton University Press, 1993).

6. CLASSIC GENRES REVIVED
1 See Rick Altman, *Film/Genre* (London: BFI Publishing, 1999).
2 Jane Feuer, *The Hollywood Musical* (London: Macmillan, 1993), p.129.

8. X-RATED
1 Michael Atkinson, *Blue Velvet* (London: BFI Publishing, 1997), p.44.
2 Laurence O'Toole, *Pornocopia: Porn, Sex, Technology and Desire* (London: Serpent's Tail, 1998), p.165.

9. WOMEN AND FILM
1 Yvonne Tasker, *Working Girls: Gender and Sexuality in Popular Cinema* (London and New York: Routledge, 1998).
2 According to a report by Martha Lauzen, only six per cent of the 250 top-grossing films in the United States in 2001 were directed by women (see www.5050summit.com).

11. HOLLYWOOD AND ETHNICITY
1 Ed Guerrero, 'Be Black and Buy', in *American Independent Cinema*, edited by Jim Hillier (London: BFI Publishing, 2001).

12. NATIONAL IDENTITIES IN WESTERN EUROPE
1 See Toby Miller, Nitin Govil, John McMurria and Richard Maxwell, 'Introduction', *Global Hollywood*, op. cit. *Variety* magazine, 24 December 2001, reported that Hollywood did less well in 2001, but the long-term trend is unmistakable.
2 Unless otherwise indicated, film statistics are usually taken from *Focus 2002: World Film Market Trends. A report by the European Audiovisual Observatory*, edited by André Lange and Susan Newman-Baudais (Cannes: MIF), and from *International Film Guide 2002*, edited by Peter Cowie (London: Faber and Faber, 2001). It should be noted that sources do not always agree on the figures: different criteria are often used for calculations (for example, some count co-productions or video productions; some do not).
3 See www.the-numbers.com

13. EASTERN EUROPE AND THE FORMER SOVIET UNION
1 Milada Hábrová and Jitka Vysekalová (eds.), *Czechoslovak Cinema* (Prague: Československý filmový Ústav, 1982), p.8.
2 *Time Out Film Guide 2002*, edited by John Pym (London: Penguin Books, 2001).
3 Vladimir Jovicic, quoted in Daniel J Goulding, *Liberated Cinema: The Yugoslav Experience* (Bloomington, IN: Indiana University Press, 1985), p.80.
4 Quoted in Dina Iordanova, *Cinema of Flames: Balkan Film, Culture and the Media* (London: BFI Publishing, 2001), pp.111–35.

14. THE MIDDLE EAST AND THE MUSLIM WORLD
1 Hamid Naficy, 'Iranian Cinema', in *Companion Encyclopedia of Middle Eastern and North African Film*, edited by Oliver Leaman (London: Routledge, 2001), p.188.
2 *The Guardian*, 20 November 2001.

15. BOLLYWOOD AND NEW INDIAN CINEMA
1 Ashish Rajadhyaksha and Paul Willemen, *Encyclopaedia of Indian Cinema* (London: BFI Publishing, 1994), p.461.
2 Mira Reym Binford, 'Innovation and Imitation in Indian Cinema', in *Cinema and Cultural Identity: Reflections on Films from Japan, India and China*, edited by Wimal Dissanayake (Lanha, MD: University Press of America, 1988), p.83.

16. AFRICAN VOICES
1 Manthia Diawara, 'Popular Culture and Oral Traditions in African Film', in *African Experiences of Cinema*, edited by Imruh Bakari and Mbye Cham (London: BFI Publishing, 1996), p.216.
2 Férid Boughedir, 'African Cinema and Ideology: Tendencies and Evolution', in *Symbolic Narratives in African Cinema: Audiences, Theory and the Moving Image*, edited by June Givanni (London: BFI Publishing, 2000), p.120.
3 Ibid., p.120.
4 Adewale Maja-Pearce in *London Review of Books*, 10 May 2001.

17. CINEMA IN THE FAR EAST
1 Note that in accordance with the usual practice, Chinese and Japanese names are given with the family name first.
2 Ian Buruma, *Behind the Mask: On sexual demons, sacred mothers, transvestites, gangsters and other Japanese cultural heroes* (New York: Meridian, 1984), p.55.
3 Tony Rayns, in *Time Out Film Guide 2002*, op. cit., pp.1183, 1199.
4 Annette Hamilton, 'Family dramas: film and modernity in Thailand', *Screen*, vol.33, no.3, Autumn 1992.

19. LATIN AMERICA
1 *Film Quarterly*, Summer 1999.
2 John King, *Magical Reels: A History of Cinema in Latin America* (London: Verso, 2000), p.266.

20. CINEMA TOMORROW
1 *Focus 2002: World Film Market Trends. A report by the European Audiovisual Observatory*, op. cit., p.8.

Chronology

1970
- Salvador Allende becomes President of Chile
- Polish leader Wladyslaw Gomułka resigns after riots in Gdańsk
- End of the civil war in Nigeria

- Raymond Chow founds the Golden Harvest film company in Hong Kong
- African film-makers form FEPACI (Fédération Pan-africaine des Cinéastes)
- Nationalization of the film industry in Sri Lanka

- *Five Easy Pieces* (Bob Rafelson); *MASH* (Robert Altman); *Tristana* (Luis Buñuel)

1971
- Bangladesh declares independence from Pakistan
- British Parliament votes to join the European Common Market

- Director Yilmaz Güney is imprisoned in Turkey
- Nikkatsu film studio in Japan goes over to production of soft-core sex films

- *A Clockwork Orange* (Stanley Kubrick); *WR: Mysteries of the Organism* (*WR: Misterije Organizma*, Dušan Makavejev); *The French Connection* (William Friedkin)

1972
- Attack on Israeli athletes at the Munich Olympics
- Break-in at the Watergate Building in Washington DC

- Alexei Romanov, Head of Goskino, the USSR's film organization, is replaced by the modernizing Filipp Yermash
- Danish Film Institute is founded in Copenhagen
- *Deep Throat* (Gerard Damiano) opens in New York, the first pornographic film to be shown to a mainstream audience

- *Tout va bien* (Jean-Luc Godard and Jean-Pierre Gorin); *The Bitter Tears of Petra von Kant* (*Die bitteren Tränen der Petra von Kant*, Rainer Werner Fassbinder); *The Godfather* (Francis Ford Coppola)

1973
- Coup against Salvador Allende in Chile
- Israel is at war with Egypt and Syria
- Juan Domingo Peron returns to Argentina from exile

- Deaths of actor Bruce Lee (b.1940)

and director John Ford (b.1894)
- Kim Jong II, son of North Korean leader, publishes *The Theory of Cinematic Art*
- Sacheen Littlefeather substitutes for Marlon Brando at the Oscars ceremony in protest against the treatment of Native Americans

- *The Spirit of the Beehive* (*El espíritu de la colmena*, Victor Erice); *Don't Look Now* (Nicolas Roeg); *American Graffiti* (George Lucas)

1974
- US President Nixon resigns from office
- Civilian rule re-established in Greece
- Revolution in Portugal introduces democracy

- Sensurround, the augmentation of violent action on screen by intense waves of high decibel sound, gives physical shocks to audiences of *Earthquake* (Mark Robson)
- Black Film-makers Hall of Fame inaugurated

- *Xala* (Ousmane Sembène); *The Mirror* (*Zerkalo*, Andrei Tarkovsky); *Chinatown* (Roman Polanski)

1975
- Fall of Saigon to North Vietnamese forces
- Death of General Francisco Franco y Bahamonde (General Franco, b.1892)
- Angola becomes independent from Portugal

- Murder of Pier Paolo Pasolini (b.1922)
- Founding of Embrafilme, the state film organization of Brazil
- Foreign films out-perform domestic productions for the first time in Japan

- *Picnic at Hanging Rock* (Peter Weir); *The Travelling Players* (*O Thiassos*, Theo Angelopoulos); *Jaws* (Steven Spielberg)

1976
- 100 demonstrators are killed by police in Soweto, South Africa
- Death of Mao Zedong (Chairman Mao), head of the Chinese Communist Party (b.1893)
- Military coup in Argentina leads to the 'dirty war'

- Women's Film Fund established in Australia
- Steadicam camera system first used in a feature film, *Rocky* (John G Avildsen)
- *In the Realm of the Senses* (*Ai No*

Corrida, Oshima Nagisa); *Taxi Driver* (Martin Scorsese); *Nine Months* (*Kilenc hónap*, Márta Mészáros)

1977
- Military coup by General Zia-ul-Haq in Pakistan
- Eritrea fights for independence from Ethiopia
- First flight of US Space Shuttle 'Enterprise' from Edwards Air Force Base, California

- Film Institute established in Angola
- *Star Wars* (George Lucas) makes extensive use of computer graphics and Dolby sound
- Matsushita introduce the VHS home video-recording system

- *Annie Hall* (Woody Allen); *Man of Marble* (*Cz lowiek z marmuru*, Andrzej Wajda); *Padre padrone* (Paolo and Vittorio Taviani)

1978
- Murder of Italian premier Aldo Moro by the Red Brigade
- Sandinistas fight a guerrilla war in Nicaragua

- Re-opening of Beijing Film Academy to receive 'Fifth Generation' students
- New Zealand Film Commission is established
- Columbia establishes FOCINE, a national film development body

- *The Deer Hunter* (Michael Cimino); *The Chant of Jimmie Blacksmith* (Fred Schepisi); *Violette Nozière* (Claude Chabrol)

1979
- Vietnamese defeat the Khmer Rouge in Cambodia
- Exile of the Shah and declaration of Islamic Republic in Iran
- Soviet forces invade Afghanistan

- Universal sue Sony to try to prevent home video-recording
- Rental of films on video takes off in the United States

- *Alexandria, Why?* (*Iskindiriyya, Lih?*, Youssef Chahine); *Alien* (Ridley Scott); *Apocalypse Now* (Francis Ford Coppola)

1980
- Birth of the Solidarity movement in Poland
- War between Iran and Iraq
- Ronald Reagan is elected President of the United States

- Robert Redford opens the Sundance Institute in Park City, Utah

- The Rank Organization withdraws from film production in the UK
- Sherry Lansing is the first woman to head a Hollywood studio at Twentieth Century Fox

- *The Elephant Man* (David Lynch); *The Contract* (*Kontrakt*, Krzysztof Zanussi); *Bye Bye Brasil* (Carlos Diegues)

1981
- The AIDS virus is identified in the United States by the Center for Disease Control, Atlanta
- Race riots in Brixton, London
- President Sadat of Egypt is assassinated (b.1918)

- United Artists and MGM merge
- Goldcrest begins production in the UK

- *The Way* (*Yol*, Yilmaz Güney); *Pixote* (Hector Babenco); *The German Sisters* (*Die bleierne Zeit*, Margarethe von Trotta)

1982
- Britain defeats Argentina in Falklands/Malvinas War
- Israel invades Lebanon
- Soviet President Brezhnev dies

- Death of Rainer Werner Fassbinder (b.1946)
- Channel Four begins film production in UK
- Columbia Pictures acquired by Coca-Cola Co.

- *Fitzcarraldo* (Werner Herzog); *Boat People* (*Touben Nü Hai*, Ann Hui); *Fanny and Alexander* (*Fanny och Alexander*, Ingmar Bergman)

1983
- Argentina returns to civilian rule
- South Korean airliner shot down by Soviets
- Opposition leader Benigno Aquino assassinated in Philippines

- Establishment of the Instituto Mexicano de la Cinematografía in Mexico (IMCINE)
- Production subsidies introduced by Pilar Miró, Spanish film minister

- *Money* (*L'Argent*, Robert Bresson); *The Ballad of Narayama* (*Narayama Bushi-ko*, Imamura Shohei); *The Wind* (*Finyé*, Souleymane Cissé)

1984
- Indira Gandhi is assassinated
- Miners' strike in UK
- 2,000 killed in gas leak at Union Carbide plant in Bhopal, India

- Disney forms Touchstone Films to make more adult films
- Deaths of François Truffaut (b.1932), Sam Peckinpah (b.1925) and Yilmaz Güney (b.1937)
- UK abandons the Eady Levy, a tax on box office receipts to aid production

- *Camila* (Maria Luisa Bemberg); *The Terminator* (James Cameron); *Yellow Earth* (*Huang Tudi*, Chen Kaige)

1985
- Gorbachev elected General Secretary of Soviet Communist Party
- Death of Enver Hoxha (b.1908), Communist leader of Albania since World War II

- Rupert Murdoch buys Twentieth Century Fox
- Inauguration of the Sundance Film Festival in Park City, Utah

- *The Time to Live and the Time to Die* (*Tong nian wang shi*, Hou Hsiao-Hsien); *Come and See* (*Idi i smotri*, Elem Klimov); *Vagabonde* (*Sans toit ni loi*, Agnès Varda)

1986
- US Space Shuttle 'Challenger' explodes soon after take-off from the NASA Kennedy Space Center, Florida
- President Marcos is ousted in Philippines
- Explosion at Chernobyl, a Soviet nuclear plant

- Elem Klimov is elected First Secretary of the Soviet Film-Makers' Union
- David Putnam becomes Chairman of Columbia Pictures

- *Betty Blue* (*37,2 le matin*, Jean-Jacques Beineix); *She's Gotta Have It* (Spike Lee); *Tampopo* (Itami Juzo)

1987
- Collapse of the US and European stock markets
- IRA bomb at Enniskillen, Ireland

- Three million people attend the funeral of Indian film star and politician Marudur Gopalamenon Ramachandran (b.1917)
- Dawn Steel becomes President of Columbia Pictures

- *Wedding in Galilee* ('*Urs al-Jalil*, Michel Khleifi); *Yeleen* (Souleymane Cissé); *Pelle the Conqueror* (*Pelle Erobreren*, Bille August)

1988

– Terrorist bomb on Pan Am flight kills 270 people at Lockerbie
– President Zia (b.1936) is killed by bomb on a plane in Pakistan
– Ceasefire in the war between Iran and Iraq

– Museum of the Moving Image opens in London, UK
– Religious protests against Martin Scorsese's *The Last Temptation of Christ*

– *Cinema paradiso* (Giuseppe Tornatore); *Women on the Verge of a Nervous Breakdown* (*Mujeres al borde de un ataque de nervios*, Pedro Almodóvar); *Damnation* (*Kárhozat*, Béla Tarr)

1989

– Thousands killed in demonstrations in Tiananmen Square in Beijing, China
– Revolution in Romania leads to execution of dictator Nicolae Ceauşescu (b.1918)
– Berlin Wall pulled down

– Hou Hsiao-Hsien's *City of Sadness* is the first Taiwanese film to win a Golden Lion Award at the Venice Film Festival
– Death of Italian director Sergio Leone (b.1929)

– *Leningrad Cowboys Go America* (Aki Kaurismäki); *sex, lies and videotape* (Steven Soderbergh); *Time of the Gypsies* (*Dom Za Vesanje*, Emir Kustúrica)

1990

– Nelson Mandela is freed in South Africa
– Iraq invades Kuwait
– Lech Walesa is elected President of Poland

– Deaths of actresses Barbara Stanwyck (b.1907), Greta Garbo (b.1905) and Ava Gardner (b.1922)
– Average marketing cost of a US film now equals nearly half its production cost

– *Halfaouine* (*Halfawin 'Usfur Stah*, Férid Boughedir; *Dances With Wolves* (Kevin Costner); *Finzan* (Cheik Oumar Sissoko)

1991

– Iraq is defeated in the Gulf War
– Soviet Union is dissolved
– Boris Yeltsin becomes President of Russia

– Philippine director Lino Brocka (b.1939), is killed in a car crash
– Crédit Lyonnais takes over MGM-Pathé

– *Raise the Red Lantern* (*Dahong Denglong Gaogao Gua*, Zhang Yimou); *Basic Instinct* (Paul Verhoeven); *My Own Private Idaho* (Gus Van Sant)

1992

– Break-up of the Yugoslav Federation
– Rodney King riots in Los Angeles, California
– United States and Russia declare the end of the Cold War

– Disney opens a theme park in Paris, France
– Annual British film production falls to forty-seven features
– Death of Indian director Satyajit Ray (b.1921)

– *Hyenas* (*Hyènes*, Djibril Diop Mambéty); *Hard-Boiled* (*Lashou shentan*, John Woo); *The Double Life of Véronique* (*Podwójne zycie Weroniki*, Krzysztof Kieślowski)

1993

– Czechoslovakia splits into the Czech Republic and Slovakia
– President Ranasinghe Premadasa of Sri Lanka is assassinated (b.1924)
– Boris Yeltsin orders the military to crush a revolt in the Russian Parliament

– Prince Norodom Sihanouk, politician and film-maker, is crowned King of Cambodia
– Europeans resist attempts to ban film subsidies in the General Agreement on Tariffs and Trade (GATT) negotiations
– Dinosaurs in *Jurassic Park* demonstrate a new level of realism for digitally created images

– *The Scent of Green Papaya* (*Mui du du Xanh*, Tran Anh Hung); *The Piano* (Jane Campion); *Abraham Valley* (*Vale Abraão*, Manoel de Oliveira)

1994

– Massacre of thousands of Tutsi people in Rwanda
– US troops restore Jean-Bertrand Aristide to presidency in Haiti
– IRA declare ceasefire in Northern Ireland

– Revenue of Hollywood films from overseas distribution exceeds that of the domestic market for the first time
– Ridley and Tony Scott buy Shepperton Studios, London
– Death of British director Derek Jarman (b.1942)

– *Chungking Express* (*Chongqing Senlin*, Wong Kar-wai); *Ed Wood*

(Tim Burton); *Burnt by the Sun* (*Utomlennye solntsem*, Nikita Mikhalkov)

1995

– Yitzhak Rabin is assassinated in Israel
– US Federal building is blown up in Oklahoma City
– Nerve gas attack in the Tokyo subway system

– Steven Spielberg, David Geffen and Jeffrey Katzenberg form Dreamworks studio
– *Toy Story* (John Lasseter) is the first mainstream movie in which all images are digitally originated

– *Exotica* (Atom Egoyan); *La Haine* (Mathieu Kassovitz); *Heat* (Michael Mann)

1996

– Taliban capture Kabul in Afghanistan
– US President Clinton re-elected

– Scenes of sex and death in David Cronenberg's *Crash* upset censors around the world
– Mike Leigh's *Secrets and Lies* wins Palme d'Or at the Cannes Film Festival
– United States has 29,690 cinema screens; the European Union has 19,407

– *Fargo* (Joel and Ethan Coen); *Deep Crimson* (*Profundo carmesí*, Arturo Ripstein); *Breaking the Waves* (Lars von Trier)

1997

– End of British rule in Hong Kong
– Islamic militants kill sixty-two tourists at Luxor, Egypt
– Death of Princess Diana (b.1961)

– Egyptian director Youssef Chahine receives Lifetime Achievement Award at Cannes Film Festival
– Film attendance in Russia falls to 36 million (was 489 million in 1993)

– *A Taste of Cherry* (*Ta'm-e Gilas*, Abbas Kiarostami); *Fireworks* (*Hana-bi*, Kitano Takeshi); *Funny Games* (Michael Haneke)

1998

– Hindu nationalists are elected to power in India
– Indonesian leader Kemusu Argamulja Suharto is ousted
– US President Clinton admits to affair with Monica Lewinsky

– 529 feature films are produced in the European Union
– Former film actor Joseph Estrada

is elected President of the Philippines
– The deficit in Europe's audio-visual trade with the US reaches $6.6 billion

– *Happiness* (Todd Solondz); *Central Station* (*Centro do Brasil*, Walter Salles); *The Thin Red Line* (Terrence Malick)

1999

– NATO attacks force Serbs to pull out of Kosovo
– East Timor votes for independence from Indonesia
– Military coup in Pakistan

– Average cost of a feature film by US major studios is $51.5 million
– Indian film production rises from 693 in 1998 to 764
– Disney announces that *Tarzan* (Kevin Lima and Chris Buck) will be the first film both produced and released digitally

– *Beau travail* (Claire Denis); *Season of Men* (*Mawsim al-Rijal*, Moufida Tlatli); *Eyes Wide Shut* (Stanley Kubrick)

2000

– Vladimir Putin becomes the President of Russia
– Slobodan Milosevic is overthrown as Yugoslav President
– George W Bush is controversially declared winner of the US presidential election

– South Korean films gain 49.5 per cent of the domestic box office
– The United States earns $6.4 billion from Hollywood film exports
– Global film production reaches 3,540

– *A One and a Two...* (*Yi yi*, Edward Yang); *Amores perros* (Alejandro González Iñárritu); *Chunhyang* (Im Kwon-taek)

2001

– Attack on World Trade Center, New York
– Phoolan Devi (b.1963), member of the Indian Congress and subject of the film *Bandit Queen* (Shekhar Kapur, 1994), is assassinated
– Kyoto agreement on world climate signed without US participation

– Cinema attendance in the United States and Canada rises to 1.487 billion, the highest since 1959
– *Harry Potter and the Philosopher's Stone* (Chris Columbus) is the world's most popular film for 2001

– Afghanistan resumes film production after ten years of war

– *The Son's Room* (*La stanza del figlio*, Nanni Moretti); *Kandahar* (*Safar e Ghandehar*, Mohsen Makhmalbaf); *Who Knows?* (*Va savoir*, Jacques Rivette)

2002

– Adoption of the Euro as currency of the European Union
– Attempted coup against President Hugo Chavez in Venezuela
– Bomb in nightclub in Bali kills nearly 200 people

– Halle Berry is the first black woman to receive an Oscar for best actress, in *Monster's Ball* (Marc Forster)
– Death of Billy Wilder (b. 1906)
– Fiftieth anniversary of the National Film Theatre in London

– *Lord of the Rings: The Fellowship of the Ring* (Peter Jackson); *City of God* (*Cidade de Deus*, Fernando Meirelles); *Gangs of New York* (Martin Scorsese)

Select Directors' Filmography

Note: in general, these filmographies omit films made for television, documentaries, shorts and contributions to multiple-episode films. For reasons of space, some notable directors whose careers peaked before 1970 have had to be omitted.

Akerman, Chantal
b.1950, Belgium. Independent film-maker, popular for her minimalist narratives and avant-garde films.
Hotel Monterey 1972; *Hanging Out Yonkers* 1973; *Jeanne Dielman, 23 Quai du Commerce, 1080 Bruxelles* 1975; *News from Home* 1977; *Les Rendez-vous d'Anna* 1978; *All Night Long/Toute une nuit* 1982; *The Eighties/Les Années 80* 1983; *Paris vu par vingt ans après* 1984; *Golden Eighties; Letters Home* 1986; *Seven Women, Seven Sins* 1987; *Histoires d'Amérique* 1988; *Night and Day/Nuit et jour* 1991; *From the East/D'Est* 1993; *A Couch in New York/Un divan à New York* 1996; *Chantal Ackerman by Chantal Ackerman* 1996; *South/Sud* 1999; *The Captive/La Captive* 2000; *The Other Side* 2002; *Demain on déménage* 2003

Alea, Tomás Gutiérrez
b.1928, Cuba, d.1996. Began with political documentaries in support of Cuban revolution before moving into features.
Stories of the Revolution/Historias de la revolución 1960; *The Twelve Chairs/Las doce sillas* 1962; *Cumbite* 1964; *Death of a Bureaucrat/La muerte de un burócrata* 1966; *Memories of Underdevelopment/Memorias del subdesarrollo* 1968; *A Cuban Fight Against Demons/Una peleas cubana contra los demonios* 1971; *The Last Supper/La última cena* 1976; *The Survivors/Los Sobrevivientes* 1979; *Up to a Point/Hasta cierto punto* 1984; *Letters from the Park/Cartas del parque* 1988; *Strawberry and Chocolate/Fresa y chocolate* 1993; *Guantanamera* 1994

Allen, Woody
b.1935, USA. Began his career as a comedian and playwright, then director, screenwriter and actor.
Take the Money and Run 1969; *Bananas* 1971; *Everything You Always Wanted to Know about Sex* 1972; *Sleeper* 1973; *Love and Death* 1975; *Annie Hall* 1977; *Interiors* 1978; *Manhattan* 1979; *Stardust Memories* 1980; *A Midsummer Night's Sex Comedy* 1982; *Zelig* 1983; *Broadway Danny Rose* 1984; *The Purple Rose of Cairo* 1985; *Hannah and Her Sisters* 1986; *Radio Days* 1987; *September* 1987; *Another Woman* 1988; *New York Stories* 1989; *Crimes and Misdemeanors* 1989; *Alice* 1990; *Shadows and Fog* 1992; *Husbands and Wives* 1992; *Manhattan Murder Mystery* 1993; *Bullets Over Broadway* 1994; *Mighty Aphrodite* 1995; *Everyone Says I Love You* 1996; *Deconstructing Harry* 1997; *Celebrity* 1998; *Sweet and Lowdown* 1999; *Small Time Crooks* 2000; *The Curse of the Jade Scorpion* 2001; *Hollywood Ending* 2002; *Anything Else* 2003

Almodóvar, Pedro
b.1951, Spain. Controversial film-maker, a leading figure in Spanish cinema.
Folle folle fólleme Tim! 1978; *Pepi, Luci, Bom y otras chicas del montón* 1980; *Labyrinth of Passion/Laberinto de pasiones* 1982; *Dark Habits/Entre tinieblas* 1983; *What Have I Done to Deserve This?/Qué he hecho yo para merecer esto?!!* 1984; *Matador* 1986; *The Law of Desire/La ley del deseo* 1987; *Women on the Verge of a Nervous Breakdown/Mujeres al borde de un ataque de nervios* 1988; *Tie Me Up! Tie Me Down!/Átame!* 1990; *High Heels/Tacones lejanos* 1991; *Kika* 1993; *The Flower of my Secret/La flor de mi secreto* 1995; *Live Flesh/Carne trémula* 1997; *All About My Mother/Todo sobre mi madre* 1999; *Talk to Her/Hable con ella* 2002; *La mala educación* 2002

Altman, Robert
b.1925, USA. Successful TV director in 1950s and 1960s; first movie success with *MASH*. Great observer of American culture.
The Delinquents 1957; *The James Dean Story* 1957; *Countdown* 1968; *That Cold Day in the Park* 1969; *MASH* 1970; *Brewster McCloud* 1970; *McCabe and Mrs. Miller* 1971; *Images* 1972; *The Long Goodbye* 1973; *Thieves Like Us* 1974; *California Split* 1974; *Nashville* 1975; *Buffalo Bill and the Indians, or Sitting Bull's History Lesson* 1976; *3 Women* 1977; *A Wedding* 1978; *Quintet* 1979; *A Perfect Couple* 1979; *H.E.A.L.T.H.* 1979; *Popeye* 1980; *Come Back to the Five and Dime, Jimmy Dean, Jimmy Dean* 1982; *Streamers* 1983; *Secret Honor* 1984; *O.C. & Stiggs* 1985; *Fool for Love* 1985; *Beyond Therapy* 1987; *Vincent & Theo* 1990; *The Player* 1992; *Short Cuts* 1993; *Prêt-à-Porter* 1994; *Kansas City* 1996; *The Gingerbread Man* 1998; *Cookie's Fortune* 1999; *Dr. T & the Women* 2000; *Gosford Park* 2001; *The Company* 2003

Anderson, Paul Thomas
b.1970, USA. Acclaimed young writer/director who shot to fame with his second feature.
Sydney/Hard Eight 1996; *Boogie Nights* 1997; *Magnolia* 1999; *Punch-Drunk Love* 2002

Angelopoulos, Theo
b.1935, Greece. Trained at IDHEC, the French film school, before becoming Greece's most prestigious director.
Reconstruction/Anaparastassi 1970; *Days of 36/Meres Tou 36* 1972; *The Travelling Players/O Thiassos* 1975; *The Hunters/Oi Kynighoi* 1977; *Alexander the Great/Megaleksandros* 1980; *Voyage to Cythera/Taxidi sta Kithira* 1984; *The Beekeeper/O Melissokomos* 1986; *Landscape in the Mist/Topio stin omichli* 1988; *The Suspended Step of the Stork/To meteoro vima tou pelargou* 1991; *Ulysses' Gaze/To vlemma tou Odyssea* 1995; *Eternity and a Day/Mia aiwniothta kai mia mera* 1998

Antonioni, Michelangelo
b.1912, Italy. Graduate of the Centro Sperimentale di Cinematografía, his films focus on his uneasy relationship with modern society.
Story of a Love Affair/Cronaca di un amore 1950; *The Vanquished/I Vinti* 1953; *Camille Without Camelias/La Signora senza camelie* 1953; *The Girlfriends/Le Amiche* 1955; *The Cry/Il Grido* 1957; *L'Avventura* 1960; *The Night/La Notte* 1961; *The Eclipse/L'Eclisse* 1962; *The Red Desert/Deserto Rosso* 1964; *Blow-Up* 1966; *Zabriskie Point* 1970; *Profession: Reporter/The Passenger* 1975; *The Oberwald Mystery/Il Mistero di Oberwald* 1980; *Identification of a Woman/Identificazione di una donna* 1982; *Beyond the Clouds/Al di là delle nuvole* 1995

Arcand, Denys
b.1941, Canada. Best known for his socio-political commentary and satirical humour.
Seul ou avec d'autres 1962; *La Maudite galette* 1972; *Réjeanne Padovani* 1973; *Gina* 1974; *Le Confort et l'indifférence* 1982; *Le Crime d'Ovide Plouffe* 1984; *The Decline of the American Empire/Déclin de l'empire américain* 1986; *Jesus of Montreal/Jésus de Montréal* 1989; *Love and Human Remains* 1993; *Poverty and Other Delights/Joyeux Calvaire* 1996; *Stardom* 2000; *Les invasions barbares* 2003

Argento, Dario
b.1940, Italy. Horror specialist, began as screenwriter on action films.
The Bird with the Crystal Plumage/L'Uccello dalle piume di cristallo 1970; *Cat o' Nine Tails/Il Gatto a nove code* 1971; *Four Flies in Grey Velvet/4 mosche di velluto grigio* 1972; *The Five Days/Le Cinque giornate* 1973; *Deep Red/Profondo rosso* 1975; *Suspiria* 1977; *Inferno* 1980; *Unsane/Tenebre* 1982; *Creepers/Phenomena* 1985; *Opera* 1987; *Two Evil Eyes/Due occhi diabolici* 1990; *Trauma* 1993; *The Stendhal Syndrome/La Sindrome di Stendhal* 1996; *Il Fantasma dell'opera* 1998; *I Can't Sleep/Non ho sonno* 2001

Armstrong, Gillian
b.1950, Australia. Graduate of Australian Film School, now working mainly in Hollywood.
The Singer and the Dancer 1977; *My Brilliant Career* 1979; *Starstruck* 1982; *Mrs. Soffel* 1984; *High Tide* 1987; *Fires Within* 1991; *The Last Days of Chez Nous* 1992; *Little Women* 1994; *Oscar and Lucinda* 1997; *Charlotte Gray* 2001

Babenco, Hector
b.1946, Argentina. Naturalized Brazilian citizen working mainly in Brazil, known for his scrupulous social films.
King of the Night/O Rei da Noite 1975; *Lúcio Flávio, o Passageiro da Agonia* 1977; *Pixote: A Lei do Mais Fraco* 1981; *A Terra é Redonda Como uma Laranja* 1984; *Kiss of the Spider Woman* 1985; *Ironweed* 1987; *At Play in the Fields of the Lord* 1991; *Foolish Heart/Corazón iluminado* 1998; *Carandiru* 2003

Balabanov, Alexei
b.1959, Russia. Film school graduate, sometimes dubbed the Russian Tarantino.
Happy Days/Schastlivye dni 1991; *The Castle/Zamok* 1994; *Brother/Brat* 1997; *Of Freaks and Men/Pro urodov i lyudei* 1998; *Brother 2/Brat 2* 1999; *Vojna* 2002

Beineix, Jean-Jacques
b.1946, France. Proponent of 'cinéma du look'.
Diva 1981; *The Moon in the Gutter/La Lune dans le caniveau* 1983; *Betty Blue/37,2 le matin* 1986; *Roselyne and the Lions/Roselyne et les lions* 1989; *IP5: The Island of Pachyderms/IP5: L'île aux pachydermes* 1992; *Mortal Transfer/Mortel transfert* 2000

Bemberg, Maria Luisa
b.1922, Argentina, d. 1995. Foremost Argentine woman director.
Momentos 1980; *Nobody's Wife/Señora de nadie* 1982; *Camila* 1984; *Miss Mary* 1986; *I, the Worst of All/Yo, la peor de todas* 1990; *We Don't Want to Talk about It/De eso no se habla* 1993

Benegal, Shyam
b.1934, India. Began as a documentary film-maker before becoming part of New Indian Cinema.
The Seedling/Ankur 1974; *Night's End/Nishant* 1975; *Charandas the Thief/Charandas Chor* 1975; *The Churning/Manthan* 1976; *The Role/Bhumika* 1976; *The Boon/Kondura* 1978; *Junoon* 1978; *Anugraham* 1978; *Pashu Palan* 1979; *The Machine Age/Kalyug* 1980; *The Ascent/Arohan* 1982; *Market Place/Mandi* 1983; *Past, Present and Future/Trikal* 1985; *The Essence/Susman* 1987; *The Inner Voice/Antarnaad* 1991; *Seventh Horse of the Sun/Suraj Ka Satvan Ghoda* 1993; *Mammo* 1994; *The Making of the Mahatma* 1995; *Sardari Begum* 1996; *Conflict/Samar* 1999; *Hari-Bhari* 2000; *Zubeidaa* 2001

Bertolucci, Bernardo
b.1940, Italy. Originally an intensely political film-maker who now shoots his art-house films mainly in English.
The Grim Reaper/La commare seca 1962; *Before the Revolution/Prima della rivoluzione* 1962; *Partner* 1968; *The Conformist/Il conformista* 1969; *The Spider's Stratagem/La strategia del ragno* 1970; *Last Tango in Paris/Ultimo tango a Parigi* 1972; *1900* 1976; *La luna* 1979; *The Tragedy of a Ridiculous Man/La tragedia di un uomo ridicolo* 1981; *The Last Emperor* 1987; *The Sheltering Sky* 1990; *Little Buddha* 1993; *Stealing Beauty* 1996; *Besieged* 1998; *The Dreamers* 2003

Besson, Luc
b.1959, France. Director and producer, much influenced by American popular culture.
The Last Combat/Le Dernier combat 1983; *Subway* 1985; *The Big Blue/Le Grand bleu* 1988; *Nikita* 1990; *Leon* 1994; *The Fifth Element* 1997; *Joan of Arc/Jeanne d'Arc* 1999

Bigas Luna, Juan José
b.1946, Spain. Dissector of contemporary Spanish middle-class mores.
Tatuaje 1976; *Bilbao* 1978; *Caniche* 1979; *Renacer* 1981; *Lola* 1985; *Anguish/Angustia* 1986; *The Ages of Lulu/Las Edades de Lulú* 1990; *Ham, Ham/Jamón, jamón* 1992; *Golden Balls/Huevos de oro* 1993; *The Tit and the Moon/La Teta y la luna* 1994; *Bámbola* 1996; *The Chambermaid on the Titanic/La Femme de chambre du Titanic* 1997; *Volavérunt* 1999; *Sound of the Sea/Son de mar* 2001

Bigelow, Kathryn
b.1951, USA. Originally a painter, now a specialist in action genres.
The Loveless 1982; *Near Dark* 1987; *Blue Steel* 1990; *Point Break* 1991; *Strange Days* 1995; *The Weight of Water* 2000; *K-19: The Widowmaker* 2002

Blier, Bertrand
b.1939, France. Son of famous actor; director and screenwriter of cynical comedies.
Hitler – Never Heard of Him/Hitler, connais pas 1963; *If I Were a Spy/Si j'étais un espion* 1967; *Going Places/Les Valseuses* 1974; *Femmes fatales/Calmos* 1976; *Get Out Your Handkerchiefs/Préparez vos mouchoirs* 1978; *Buffet froid* 1979; *Beau-père* 1981; *My Best Friend's Girl/La Femme*

de mon pote 1983; *Our Story/Notre histoire* 1984; *Ménage/Tenue de soirée* 1986; *Too Beautiful for You/Trop belle pour toi* 1989; '*Mercie la vie*' 1991; *Un, deux, trois, soleil* 1993; *My Man/Mon homme* 1996; *Les Acteurs* 2000; *Les Côtelettes* 2002

Borowczyk, Walerian
b.1923, Poland. Trained as a painter and lithographer, began work as a film animator before specializing in elegant erotica.
Goto, Island of Love/Goto, l'îsle d'amour 1968; *Blanche* 1971; *Immoral Tales/Contes immoraux* 1974; *Story of a Sin/Dzieje grzechu* 1975; *The Beast/La Bête* 1975; *The Streetwalker/La Marge* 1976; *Behind Convent Walls/Interno di un convento* 1977; *Heroines of Evil/Les Heroïnes du mal* 1979; *Lulu* 1980; *The Blood of Doctor Jekyll/Docteur Jekyll et les femmes* 1981; *The Art of Love/Ars amandi* 1983; *Emmanuelle 5* 1987; *Cérémonie d'amour* 1988

Boughedir, Férid
b.1944, Tunisia. Also critic and historian of African cinema.
Halfaouine/Halfawin 'Usfur Stah 1990; *Halk-el-wad/Un été à La Goulette* 1995

Breien, Anja
b.1940, Norway. Also an actress and writer, she is the best known of Norway's feminist film-makers.
Dager fra 1000 år 1970; *Voldtekt* 1971; *Wives/Hustruer* 1975; *Games of Love and Loneliness/Den Allvarsamma leken* 1977; *Next of Kin/Arven* 1979; *The Witch Hunt/Forfølgelsen* 1981; *Papirfuglen* 1985; *Wives: Ten Years After/ Hustruer ti år etter* 1985; *Smykketyven* 1990; *Wives III/Hustruer III* 1996; *To See a Boat at Sail/Å se en båt med seil* 2000

Breillat, Catherine
b.1948, France. Films are frequently shocking and not conventionally feminist.
Une vraie jeune fille 1976; *Nocturnal Uproar/Tapage nocturne* 1979; *Virgin/36 Fillette* 1988; *Dirty Like an Angel/Sale comme un ange* 1990; *Parfait amour!* 1996; *Romance* 1999; *À ma soeur* 2001; *Sex Is Comedy* 2002

Brocka, Lino
b.1940, Philippines, d. 1991. Talented, unorthodox director, known for raising public awareness of Filippino life.
Wanted: Perfect Mother 1970; *Santiago* 1970; *Tubog sa ginto* 1971; *Stardoom* 1971; *Tinimbang ka ngunit kulang* 1974; *Manila: In the Claws of Darkness/Maynila, sa mga kuko ng liwanag* 1975; *Insiang* 1976; *Lunes, martes, miyerkules, huwebes, biyernes, sabado, linggo* 1976; *Tahan na, Empoy, tahan* 1977; *Inay* 1977; *Hayop sa hayop* 1978; *Rubia servios* 1978; *Wake up, Maruja/Gumising ka, Maruja* 1978; *Ang tatay kong nanay* 1978; *Init* 1979; *Jaguar* 1979; *Mother, Sister, Daughter/Ina, kapatid, anak* 1979; *Ina ka ng anak mo* 1979; *Nakaw na pag-ibig* 1980; *Bona* 1981; *In Dis Korner* 1982; *Angela Markado* 1983; *Strangers in Paradise* 1984; *PX* 1984; *Hot Property* 1984; *Bayan ko: Kapit sa patalim* 1984; *Adultery Aida macaraeg* 1984; *Macho Dancer* 1988; *Fight for Us/Les insoumis* 1989; *Dirty Affair/Gumapang ka sa lusak* 1990; *Kislap sa dilim* 1991

Burnett, Charles
b.1944, USA. Multi-talented member of the LA school of independent black film-makers.
Killer of Sheep 1977; *My Brother's Wedding* 1983; *To Sleep with Anger* 1990; *America Becoming* 1991; *The Glass Shield* 1994; *The Annihilation of Fish* 1999

Burton, Tim
b.1958, USA. Former animator who is famous for his unique 'gothic' films.
Pee-wee's Big Adventure 1985; *Beetlejuice* 1988; *Batman* 1989; *Edward Scissorhands* 1990; *Batman Returns* 1992; *Ed Wood* 1994; *Mars Attacks!* 1996; *Sleepy Hollow* 1999; *Planet of the Apes* 2001

Cameron, James
b.1954, Canada. Specialist in mega-budget, special-effects driven blockbusters.
Piranha II: The Spawning 1981; *The Terminator* 1984; *Aliens* 1986; *The Abyss* 1989; *Terminator 2: Judgment Day* 1991; *True Lies* 1994; *Titanic* 1997

Campion, Jane
b.1954, New Zealand. Graduate of Australian Film, Television and Radio School, she rose to prominence in the 1990s.
Sweetie 1989; *An Angel at My Table* 1990; *The Piano* 1993; *The Portrait of a Lady* 1996; *Holy Smoke* 1999; *In the Cut* 2002

Carax, Léos
b.1960, France. Third member (with Beineix and Besson) of 'cinéma du look'.
Boy Meets Girl 1984; *Bad Blood/Mauvais sang* 1986; *Les Amants du Pont-Neuf* 1991; *Pola X* 1999

Chabrol, Claude
b.1930, France. Veteran of *Cahiers du cinéma* magazine and specialist in socially observant thrillers.
Le Beau Serge 1959; *Les Cousins* 1959; *A Double tour* 1959; *Les Bonnes femmes* 1960; *Les Godelureaux* 1960; *L'Oeil du malin* 1962; *Ophélia* 1962; *Landru* 1963; *The Tiger Likes Fresh Blood/Le Tigre aime la chair fraîche* 1964; *Marie-Chantal contre le Docteur Kha* 1965; *An Orchid for the Tiger/Le Tigre se parfume à la dynamite* 1966; *The Champagne Murders/Le Scandale* 1966; *La Ligne de démarcation* 1966; *The Road to Corinth/La Route de Corinth* 1968; *Les Biches* 1968; *The Unfaithful Wife/La Femme infidèle* 1969; *The Beast Must Die/Que la bête meure* 1969; *The Butcher/Le Boucher* 1970; *The Break Up/La Rupture* 1970; *Just Before Nightfall/Juste avant la nuit* 1971; *Ten Days Wonder/La Décade prodigieuse* 1972; *Docteur Popaul* 1972; *Wedding in Blood/Les Noces rouges* 1973; *Nada* 1974; *Une Partie de plaisir* 1974; *Innocents with Dirty Hands/Les Innocents aux mains sales* 1975; *Folies bourgeoises* 1975; *Les Magiciens* 1976; *Alice or the Last Escapade/Alice ou la dernière fugue* 1976; *Les Liens du sang* 1978; *Violette Nozière* 1978; *The Horse of Pride/Le Cheval d'orgueil* 1979; *The Hatter's Ghost/Les Fantômes du chapelier* 1982; *The Blood of Others/Le Sang des autres* 1984; *Cop au vin/Poulet au vinaigre* 1985; *Inspecteur Lavardin* 1986; *The Cry of the Owl/Le Cri du hibou* 1987; *Masques* 1987; *Story of Women/Une Affaire de femmes* 1988; *Docteur M* 1990; *Quiet Days in Clichy/Jours tranquilles à Clichy* 1990; *Madame Bovary* 1991; *Betty* 1992; *L'Enfer* 1994; *A Judgement in Stone/La Cérémonie* 1995; *The Swindle/Rien ne va plus* 1997; *The Colour of Lies/Au coeur du mensonge* 1999; *Nightcap/Merci pour le chocolat* 2000; *La fleur du mal* 2003

Chahine, Youssef
b.1926, Egypt. Director, writer and producer. Most successful independent film-maker in Egyptian cinema.
Father Amin/Baba Amin 1950; *Son of the Nile/Ibn el Nil* 1951; *The Great Clown/al-Muharrij al-Kabir* 1951; *The Blazing Sky/Siraa Fil-Wadi* 1953; *The Lady on the Train/Sayedat al-Qitar* 1953; *Women without Men/Nissae bila regal* 1953; *Devil of the Desert/Shaytan al-Sahra* 1954; *Dark Waters/Siraa Fil-Mina* 1956; *My One and Only Love/Inta habibi* 1957; *Farewell My Love/Wadda'tu hubbak* 1957; *Cairo Station/Bab al hadid* 1958; *Djamilah* 1958; *Forever Yours/Hubb lel-abad* 1959; *In Your Hands/Bein edeik* 1960; *Lovers' Complaint/Nida al'ushshaq* 1961; *A Man in My Life/Rajul fi hayati* 1961; *The Victorious Saladin/al-Nasir Salah al-Din* 1963; *Dawn of a New Day/Fagr Yom gedid* 1964; *The Ring Seller/Biya el-Khawatim* 1965; *Sands of Gold/Rimal min dhahab* 1966; *The Feast of Mairun/Id al-Mairun* 1967; *People of the Nile/al-Nass wal Nil* 1968; *The Earth/al-Ard* 1969; *The Choice/al-Ikhtiyar* 1970; *Salwa* 1972; *The Sparrow/Al-'Usfur* 1973; *Forward We Go/Intilak* 1974; *Return of the Prodigal Son/Awdat al ibn al dal* 1976; *Alexandria, Why?/Iskindiriyya, Lih?* 1978; *An Egyptian Fairy Tale/Haduta Misriyya* 1982; *Adieu Bonaparte/Weda'an Bonapart* 1985; *The Sixth Day/al-Yawm al-Sadis* 1986; *Alexandria Now and Forever/Iskindiriyya Kaman Wa Kaman* 1990; *The Emigré/al-Muhaji* 1994; *Destiny/al-Massir* 1997; *The Other/El Akhar* 1999; *Silence, We're Rolling/Sukut hansawwar* 2001

Chen Kaige
b.1952, China. Member of 'Fifth Generation' of film-makers.
Yellow Earth/Huang Tudi 1984; *The Big Parade/Da yue bing* 1986; *King of the Children/Hai zi wang* 1987; *Life on a String/Bian zou bian chang* 1991; *Farewell My Concubine/Ba Wang Bie Ji* 1993; *Temptress Moon/Feng yue* 1996; *The Emperor and the Assassin/Jing Ke Ci Qin Wang* 1999; *Killing Me Softly* 2002; *Together/He ni zai yi qu* 2002

Chytilová, Vera
b.1929, Czechoslovakia. Foremost female Czech director.
A Bag of Fleas/Pytel blech 1962; *Something Different/O necem jiném* 1963; *Daisies/Sedmikrásky* 1966; *Fruit of Paradise/Ovoce stromu rajských jíme* 1969; *Kamaradi* 1971; *The Apple Game/Hra o jablko* 1976; *Prefab Story/Panelstory* 1981; *Kalamita* 1981; *Very Late Afternoon of a Faun/Faunovo velmi pozdní odpoledne* 1983; *The Wolf's Lair/Vlcí bouda* 1986; *The Jester and the Queen/Sasek a královna* 1987; *Tainted Horseplay/Kopytem sem, kopytem tam* 1988; *Inheritance or Fuckoffguysgoodbye/Dedictví aneb Kurvahosigutntag* 1993; *Traps/Pasti, pasti, pasticky* 1998; *Expulsion From Paradise/Vyhnání z ráje* 2001

Cissé, Souleymane
b.1940, Mali. Studied in Russia and returned to Mali where he gained critical attention for the burgeoning African film movement.
Cinq jours d'une vie 1973; *The Young Girl/Den Muso* 1975; *Baara* 1978; *The Wind/Finyé* 1983; *Yeleen* 1987; *Waati* 1995

Coen, Joel b.1954 and Ethan
b.1957, USA. Brothers who write, produce and direct together. Their style draws on film noir and classic American movie genres.
Blood Simple 1983; *Raising Arizona* 1987; *Miller's Crossing* 1990; *Barton Fink* 1991; *The Hudsucker Proxy* 1994; *Fargo* 1996; *The Big Lebowski* 1998; *O Brother, Where Art Thou?* 2000; *The Man Who Wasn't There* 2001

Coppola, Francis Ford
b.1939, USA. Director, screenwriter, producer, entrepreneur. One of America's most successful and controversial film-makers.
Dementia 13 1962; *You're a Big Boy Now* 1967; *Finian's Rainbow* 1968; *The Rain People* 1969; *The Godfather* 1972; *The Conversation* 1974; *The Godfather Part II* 1974; *Apocalypse Now* 1979; *One from the Heart* 1982; *The Outsiders* 1983; *Rumble Fish* 1983; *The Cotton Club* 1984; *Peggy Sue Got Married* 1986; *Gardens of Stone* 1987; *Tucker: The Man and his Dream* 1988; *The Godfather Part III* 1990; *Bram Stoker's Dracula* 1992; *Jack* 1996; *The Rainmaker* 1997

Craven, Wes
b.1949, USA. Specialist in horror, largely credited with invention of 'slasher' cycle.
The Last House on the Left 1972; *The Hills Have Eyes* 1977; *Deadly Blessing* 1981; *Swamp Thing* 1982; *A Nightmare on Elm Street* 1984; *The Hills Have Eyes Part II* 1985; *Deadly Friend* 1986; *The Serpent and the Rainbow* 1988; *Shocker* 1989; *The People Under the Stairs* 1991; *Wes Craven's New Nightmare* 1994; *Vampire in Brooklyn* 1995; *Scream* 1996; *Scream 2* 1997; *Music of the Heart* 1999; *Scream 3* 2000

Cronenberg, David
b.1943, Canada. Specialist in horror films for the thinking spectator.
Crimes of the Future 1970; *Shivers* 1975; *Rabid* 1977; *Fast Company* 1979; *The Brood* 1979; *Scanners* 1981; *Videodrome* 1983; *The Dead Zone* 1983; *The Fly* 1986; *Dead Ringers* 1988; *The Naked Lunch* 1991; *M. Butterfly* 1993; *Crash* 1996; *eXistenZ* 1999; *Spider* 2002

De Palma, Brian
b.1940, USA. Director of elaborate pastiches of popular genres, especially thrillers.
Murder à la Mode 1968; *Greetings* 1968; *The Wedding Party* 1969; *Hi, Mom!* 1970; *Dionysus* 1970; *Get to Know Your Rabbit* 1972; *Sisters* 1973; *Phantom of the Paradise* 1974; *Obsession* 1976; *Carrie* 1976; *The Fury* 1978; *Home Movies* 1979; *Dressed to Kill* 1980; *Blow Out* 1981; *Scarface* 1983; *Body Double* 1984; *Wise Guys* 1986; *The Untouchables* 1987; *Casualties of War* 1989; *The Bonfire of the Vanities* 1990; *Raising Cain* 1992; *Carlito's Way* 1993; *Mission: Impossible* 1996; *Snake Eyes* 1998; *Mission to Mars* 2000; *Femme Fatale* 2002

Denis, Claire
b.1945, France. A provocative director who avoids the woman's picture pigeon-hole.
Chocolat 1988; *S'en fout la mort* 1990; *I Can't Sleep/J'ai pas sommeil* 1994; *Nénette et Boni* 1996; *Beau travail* 1999; *Trouble Every Day* 2001; *Vendredi soir* 2002

SELECT DIRECTORS' FILMOGRAPHY

Dos Santos, Nelson Pereira
b.1928, Brazil. Entered the industry as an assistant director and became a leading exponent of Cinema Novo.
Rio 40 Graus 1955; *Rio Zona Norte* 1957; *Mandacaru Vermelho* 1961; *Vidas Secas* 1963; *Boca de Ouro* 1963; *O Justiceiro* 1967; *Fome de Amor* 1968; *Um Asilo Muito Louco* 1970; *How Tasty Was My Little Frenchman/Como Era Gostoso o Meu Francês* 1971; *Quem é Beta?* 1972; *The Amulet of Ogum/Amuleto de Ogum* 1974; *Tenda dos Milagres* 1977; *Na Estrada da Vida* 1980; *Memories of Prison/Memórias do Cárcere* 1984; *Jubiabá* 1987; *A Terceira Margem do Rio* 1994; *Cinema de Lágrimas* 1995;

Eastwood, Clint
b.1930, USA. Both a major star and a major director, moving between popular and more personal work.
Play Misty for Me 1971; *High Plains Drifter* 1973; *Breezy* 1973; *The Eiger Sanction* 1975; *The Outlaw Josey Wales* 1976; *The Gauntlet* 1977; *Bronco Billy* 1980; *Firefox* 1982; *Honkytonk Man* 1982; *Sudden Impact* 1983; *Pale Rider* 1985; *Heartbreak Ridge* 1986; *Bird* 1988; *Pink Cadillac* 1989; *White Hunter, Black Heart* 1990; *The Rookie* 1990; *Unforgiven* 1992; *A Perfect World* 1993; *The Bridges of Madison County* 1995; *Absolute Power* 1997; *Midnight in the Garden of Good and Evil* 1997; *True Crime* 1999; *Space Cowboys* 2000; *Blood Work* 2002; *Mystic River* 2003

Egoyan, Atom
b.1960, Egypt. Foremost art-house director of Canadian cinema.
Next of Kin 1984; *Family Viewing* 1987; *Speaking Parts* 1989; *The Adjuster* 1991; *Calendar* 1993; *Exotica* 1994; *The Sweet Hereafter* 1997; *Felicia's Journey* 1999; *Ararat* 2002

Erice, Victor
b.1940, Spain. One of the most respected but least prolific of film directors, he has also worked extensively as a film critic.
The Spirit of the Beehive/El espíritu de la colmena 1973; *The South/El sur* 1982; *The Quince Tree of the Sun/El sol del membrillo* 1992

Fassbinder, Rainer Werner
b.1946, Germany, d.1982. *Enfant terrible* of New German Cinema. Masterpiece, *Berlin Alexanderplatz* (1980), made for television.
Der Stadtstreicher 1966; *Das Kleine Chaos* 1966; *Love Is Colder than Death/Liebe ist kälter als der Tod* 1969; *Katzelmacher* 1969; *Götter der Pest* 1970; *Why Does Herr R. Run Amok?/Warum läuft Herr R. Amok?* 1970; *The American Soldier/Der amerikanische Soldat* 1970; *Beware of the Holy Whore/Warnung vor einer heiligen Nutte* 1971; *Whity* 1971; *The Merchant of Four Seasons/Der Händler der vier Jahreszeiten* 1972; *The Bitter Tears of Petra von Kant/Die Bitteren Tränen der Petra von Kant* 1972; *Fear Eats the Soul/Angst essen Seele auf* 1974; *Effi Briest* 1974; *Fox and his Friends/Faustrecht der Freiheit* 1975; *Mother Kuster's Trip to Heaven/Mutter Küsters Fahrt zum Himmel* 1975; *Chinese Roulette/Chinesisches Roulette* 1976; *Satan's Brew/Satansbraten* 1976; *Despair* 1978; *In a Year of 13 Moons/In einem Jahr mit 13 Monden* 1978; *The Marriage of Maria Braun/Die Ehe der Maria Braun* 1979; *The Third Generation/Die Dritte Generation* 1979; *Lili Marleen* 1981; *Lola* 1981; *Veronika Voss* 1982; *Querelle* 1982

Fellini, Federico
b.1920, Italy, d.1993. His flamboyant films and personality made him Italy's best known director.
Luci del varietà 1950; *The White Sheik/Lo sceicco biano* 1952; *I vitelloni* 1953; *La strada* 1954; *Il bidone* 1955; *Nights of Cabiria/Le notti di Cabiria* 1957; *La dolce vita* 1960; *8½* 1963; *Juliet of the Spirits/Giulietta degli spiriti* 1965; *Satyricon* 1969; *Roma* 1972; *Amarcord* 1974; *Casanova di Federico Fellini* 1976; *Orchestra Rehearsal/Prova d'orchestra* 1979; *City of Women/Città delle donne* 1980; *And the Ship Sails On/E la nave va* 1983; *Ginger and Fred/Ginger e Fred* 1986; *Intervista* 1987; *The Voice of the Moon/La voce della luna* 1989

Forman, Miloš
b.1932, Czechoslovakia. Made the difficult leap from New Wave Czech to director of Americana.
Konkurs 1963; *Peter and Pavla/Černý Petr* 1963; *A Blonde in Love/Lásky jedné plavovlásky* 1965; *The Firemen's Ball/Hoří, má panenko* 1967; *Taking Off* 1971; *One Flew Over the Cuckoo's Nest* 1975; *Hair* 1979; *Ragtime* 1981; *Amadeus* 1984; *Valmont* 1989; *The People vs. Larry Flint* 1996; *Man on the Moon* 1999

Frears, Stephen
b.1941, UK. Known for making provocative films about people on society's fringes, Frears moves between British cinema, Hollywood and television.
Gumshoe 1972; *Bloody Kids* 1979; *The Hit* 1984; *My Beautiful Laundrette* 1985; *Walter and June* 1986; *Prick Up Your Ears* 1987; *Sammy and Rosie Get Laid* 1987; *Dangerous Liaisons* 1988; *The Grifters* 1990; *Hero* 1992; *Mary Reilly* 1996; *The Van* 1996; *The Hi-Lo Country* 1998; *High Fidelity* 2000; *Liam* 2000; *Dirty Pretty Things* 2002

German, Aleksei
b.1938, Russia. Frequently in trouble with the censors during the Soviet era.
The Seventh Companion/Sedmoj sputnik 1967; *Trial on the Road/Proverka na dorogakh* 1971; *Twenty Days without War/Dvadtsat dnej bez vojny* 1976; *My Friend Ivan Lapshin/Moj drug Ivan Lapshin* 1984; *Khrustalyou, My Car!/Khrustalyou, mashinu!* 1998

Gitai, Amos
b.1950, Israel. Documentary director who has recently moved into features.
Kadosh 1999; *Kippur* 2000; *Eden* 2001; *Kedma* 2002

Godard, Jean-Luc
b.1930, France. Critic on *Cahiers du cinéma* and New Wave director who has retained his radical edge.
Breathless/A bout de souffle 1959; *Le Petit soldat* 1960; *Une Femme est une femme* 1961; *Vivre sa vie* 1962; *Les Carabiniers* 1963; *Contempt/Le Mépris* 1963; *Bande à part* 1964; *A Married Woman/Une Femme mariée* 1964; *Alphaville* 1965; *Pierrot le fou* 1965; *Masculin-Féminin* 1966; *Made in USA* 1966; *Two or Three Things I Know About Her/Deux ou trois choses que je connais d'elle* 1966; *La Chinoise* 1967; *Weekend* 1967; *Le Gai savoir* 1968; *Sympathy for the Devil* 1968; *Un film commes les autres* 1968; *Wind from the East/Vent d'est* 1969; *Lotte in Italia* 1969; *Tout va bien* 1972; *Numéro deux* 1975; *Every Man for Himself/Sauve qui peut (la vie)* 1979; *Passion* 1982; *First Name: Carmen/Prénom Carmen* 1984; *Hail Mary/Je vous salue, Marie* 1985; *Détective* 1985; *Keep Up Your Right* 1987; *King Lear* 1987; *New Wave/Nouvelle vague* 1990; *Germany Year 90 Nine Zero/Allemagne année 90 neuf zéro* 1991; *Hélas pour moi* 1993; *Les Enfants jouent à la Russie* 1993; *For Ever Mozart* 1996; *In Praise of Love/Eloge de l'amour* 2001

Gorris, Marleen
b.1940, Holland. Began with radical feminist work, moved into the mainstream but retained a distinctive female voice.
A Question of Silence/De stilte Rond 1982; *Christine M* 1982; *Broken Mirrors/Gebroken Spiegels* 1984; *The Last Island* 1990; *Antonia* 1996; *Mrs Dalloway* 1997; *The Luzhin Defence* 2000; *Carolina* 2002

Güney, Yilmaz
b.1937, Turkey, d.1984. Militant who was frequently imprisoned while others filmed his scripts under his instructions.
Horse, Woman and Gun/At avrat silah 1966; *Benim adim Kerim* 1967; *Pire Nuri* 1968; *Seyyit Han* 1968; *Bir çirkin adam* 1969; *Aç Kurtlar* 1969; *Yedi belalilar* 1970; *Hope/Umut* 1970; *Piyade Osman* 1970; *Canli Hedef* 1970; *Vurguncular* 1971; *The Hopeless Ones/Umutsuzlar* 1971; *Kaçaklar* 1971; *Ibret* 1971; *The Father/Baba* 1971; *Ac?* 1971; *Pain/Agit* 1972; *Anxiety/Endise* 1974; *The Friend/Arkadas* 1974; *Zavallilar* 1975; *The Herd/Sürü* 1978; *The Enemy/Düsman* 1979; *The Way/Yol* 1982; *The Wall/Duvar* 1983

Haneke, Michael
b.1942, Germany. Initially active in Austria, now prominent director of European art-house cinema.
The Seventh Continent/Der Siebente Kontinent 1989; *Benny's Video* 1992; *71 Fragmente einer Chronologie des Zufalls* 1994; *Wolfzeit* 1995; *Funny Games* 1997; *The Castle/Das Schloss* 1997; *Code inconnu/Code Unknown* 2000; *La Pianiste/The Piano Teacher* 2001; *Le Temps du loup* 2003

Hartley, Hal
b.1959, USA. One of the pioneers of contemporary US independent cinema.
The Unbelievable Truth 1989; *Trust* 1990; *Ambition* 1991; *Simple Men* 1992; *Flirt* 1993; *Amateur* 1994; *Henry Fool* 1997; *The Book of Life* 1998; *No Such Thing* 2001

Haynes, Todd
b.1961, USA. Best-known US director to emerge from the Queer Cinema movement.
Poison 1991; *Safe* 1995; *Velvet Goldmine* 1998; *Far from Heaven* 2002

Hermosillo, Jaime Humberto
b.1942, Mexico. Has alternated commercial productions with more experimental work on video.
La verdadera vocación de Magdalena 1971; *El señor de Osanto* 1972; *El cumpleaños del perro* 1974; *La pasión según Berenice* 1976; *Matinée* 1977; *Naufragio* 1977; *Las apariencas engañan* 1978; *Amor libre* 1978; *María de mi corazón* 1979; *Confidencias* 1982; *El corazón de la noche* 1983; *Doña Herlinda and Her Son/Doña Herlinda y su hijo* 1985; *Clandestino destino* 1987; *Intimidades de un cuarto de baño* 1989; *Homework/La tarea* 1990; *La tarea prohibida* 1992; *Encuentro inesperado* 1993; *De noche vienes, Esmeralda* 1997; *Escrito en el cuerpo de la noche* 2000

Herzog, Werner
b.1942, Germany. Prominent director of New German Cinema.
Signs of Life/Lebenszeichen 1968; *Even Dwarfs Started Small/Auch Zwerge haben klein angefangen* 1971; *Aguirre: Wrath of God/Aguirre: der Zorn Gottes* 1972; *The Enigma of Kaspar Hauser/Jeder für sich und Gott gegen alle* 1974; *Heart of Glass/Herz aus Glas* 1976; *Stroszek* 1977; *Woyzeck* 1979; *Nosferatu the Vampire/Nosferatu:* 1970; *Vurguncular* 1971; *The Hopeless Ones/Umutsuzlar* 1971; *Phantom der Nacht* 1979; *Fitzcarraldo* 1982; *Where the Green Ants Dream/Wo die grünen Ameisen träumen* 1984; *Cobra verde* 1988; *Cerro Torre: Scream of Stone/Schrei aus Stein* 1991; *La donna del largo* 1992; *Invincible* 2001

Holland, Agnieszka
b.1948, Poland. Associated with the Polish 'cinema of moral concern' before emigrating first to Western Europe and then to Hollywood.
Aktorzy prowincjonalni 1980; *A Lonely Woman/Kobieta samotna* 1981; *Goraczka* 1981; *Angry Harvest/Bittere Ernte* 1986; *To Kill a Priest* 1988; *Hitlerjunge Salomon* 1990; *Olivier, Olivier* 1992; *The Secret Garden* 1993; *Total Eclipse* 1995; *Washington Square* 1997; *The Third Miracle* 1999; *Julie Walking Home* 2001

Hou Hsiao-Hsien
b.1947, China. Highly regarded director whose films reflect the social and political history of Taiwan.
Cute Girl/Jiushi liuliu de ta 1980; *Cheerful Wind/Feng er ti ta cai* 1981; *The Green, Green Grass of Home/Zai na hepan qingcao qing* 1983; *The Boys from Fengkuei/Fengkuei-Lai-te Ren* 1983; *The Sandwich Man/Erzi de Dawan'ou* 1983; *Summer at Grandpa's/Dongdong de jiaqi* 1984; *The Time to Live and the Time to Die/Tong nien wang shi* 1985; *Dust in the Wind/Lianlian fengchen* 1986; *Daughter of the Nile/Niluohe nuer* 1987; *City of Sadness/Beiqing chengshi* 1989; *The Puppetmaster/Ximeng Rensheng* 1993; *Good Men, Good Women/Haonan Haonü* 1995; *Goodbye South, Goodbye/Nanguo zaijan, nanguo* 1996; *Flowers of Shanghai/Hai shang hua* 1998; *Millennium Mambo/Qianxi manbo* 2001

Hřebejk, Jan
b.1967, Czechoslovakia. Talented member of the new post-Communist generation of Czech directors.
Big Beat/Sakali leta 1993; *Ceská soda* 1998; *Cosy Dens/Pelísky* 1999; *Divided We Fall/Musíme si pomáhat* 2000; *Obsluhoval jsem anglického krále* 2002; *Pupendo* 2003

Hui, Ann
b.1947, China. A Hong Kong director, her films have a powerful sense of history and feminism.
The Secret/Fung gip 1979; *The Spooky Bunch/Zhuang dao zheng* 1980; *The Story of Woo Viet/Hu Yue de Gushi* 1981; *God of Killers/Woo yuet dik goo si* 1981; *Boat People/Touben Nü Hai* 1982; *Love in a Fallen City/Qing cheng zhi lian* 1984; *The Romance of Book and Sword/Shu jian en chou lu* 1987; *Romance of Book and Sword Part 2/Xiang xiang gong zhu* 1987;

Starry Is the Night/Gam ye sing gwong chaan laan 1988; *Swordsman/ Xiaoao Jianghu* 1990; *Song of the Exile/Ketu qiuhen* 1990; *My American Grandson/Shanghai jiaqi* 1990; *Zodiac Killer/Jidao zhuizhong* 1991; *Boy and His Hero* 1993; *Summer Snow/Xiatian de xue* 1994; *The Stunt Woman/Ah Kam* 1996; *As Time Goes By* 1997; *Eighteen Springs/Boon sang yuen* 1997; *Ordinary Heroes/Qian yan wan yu* 1998; *Visible Secret/ Youling renjian* 2001; *July Rhapsody/ Laam yan sei sap* 2002

Itami Juzo
b.1933, Japan, d.1997. One of the few Japanese directors to specialize in satirical comedy.
Death, Japanese Style/Ososhiki 1985; *Tampopo* 1985; *A Taxing Woman/ Marusa no onna* 1987; *A Taxing Woman's Return/Marusa no onna II* 1988; *Tales of a Golden Geisha/A-ge-man* 1990; *The Anti-Extortion Woman/Minbo no onna* 1992; *The Last Dance/Daibyonin* 1993; *A Quiet Life/Shizukana seikatsu* 1995; *Supermarket Woman/Supama no onna* 1996; *Marutai no onna* 1997

Jaglom, Henry
b.1941, UK. US independent director working in the USA whose films often contain strong roles for women.
A Safe Place 1971; *Tracks* 1976; *Sitting Ducks* 1980; *National Lampoon Goes to the Movies* 1981; *Can She Bake a Cherry Pie?* 1983; *Always* 1985; *Someone to Love* 1987; *New Year's Day* 1989; *Venice/Venice* 1992; *Lucky Ducks* 1993; *Babyfever* 1994; *Last Summer in the Hamptons* 1995; *Déjà Vu* 1997; *Festival in Cannes* 2001; *Shopping* 2002

Jancsó, Miklós
b.1921, Hungary. Modernist director whose highly stylized works deal obliquely with political matters.
The Bells Have Gone to Rome/A harangok Rómába mentek 1958; *Three Stars/Három csillag* 1960; *Cantata/ Oldás és kötés* 1963; *My Way Home/Így jöttem* 1964; *The Round-Up/ Szegénylegények* 1965; *The Red and the White/Csillagosok, katonák* 1967; *Silence and Cry/Csend és kiáltás* 1968; *The Confrontation/Fényes szelek* 1968; *Winter Wind/Sirokkó* 1969; *Agnus Dei/Égy bárány* 1970; *The Pacifist/La pacifista* 1970; *Red Psalm/Még kér a nép* 1971; *The Technique and the Rite/ La tecnica e il rito* 1972; *Rome Wants Another Caesar/Roma rivuole Cesare* 1973; *Elektreia/Szerelmem Elektra* 1974; *Private Vices, Public Virtues/ Vizi privati, pubbliche virtù* 1975; *Hungarian Rhapsody/Életünket és vérünket: Magyar rapszódia I* 1978; *Allegro Barbaro/Allegro Barbaro: Magyar rapszódia II* 1979; *The Tyrant's Heart, or Boccaccio in*

Hungary/A zsarnok szíve, avagy Boccaccio Magyarországon 1981; *Dawn/Hajnal* 1986; *The Monsters' Season/Szörnyek évadja* 1987; *Jésus Christ's Horoscope/Jézus Krisztus horoszkója* 1988; *God Goes Backwards/ Isten hátrafelé megy* 1991; *Blue Danube Waltz/Kék Duna keringő* 1992; *Let's Love One Another/Szeressük egymást gyerekek!* 1996; *Lord's Lantern in Budapest/Nekem lámpást adott kezembe az Úr, Pesten* 1999; *Anyád! A szúnyogok* 1999; *Last Supper at the Arabian Gray Horse/Utolsó vacsora az Arabs Szürkénél* 2001; *Kelj fel, Komám, ne aludjá* 2002

Jarman, Derek
b.1942, UK, d.1994. A unique film-maker whose experimental films centred on homosexuality and social criticism.
Sebastiane 1976; *Jubilee* 1978; *The Tempest* 1979; *The Angelic Conversation* 1985; *Caravaggio* 1986; *The Last of England* 1987; *War Requiem* 1989; *The Garden* 1990; *Edward II* 1991; *Wittgenstein* 1993; *Blue* 1993

Jarmusch, Jim
b.1953, USA. One of the best-known directors and scriptwriters of US independent cinema.
Permanent Vacation 1982; *Stranger Than Paradise* 1984; *Down by Law* 1986; *Mystery Train* 1989; *Night on Earth* 1991; *Dead Man* 1995; *Ghost Dog: The Way of the Samurai* 1999

Jordan, Neil
b.1950, Ireland. Novelist, writer and director who has moved between British cinema and Hollywood.
Angel 1982; *The Company of Wolves* 1984; *Mona Lisa* 1986; *High Spirits* 1988; *We're No Angels* 1989; *The Miracle* 1991; *The Crying Game* 1992; *Interview with the Vampire: The Vampire Chronicles* 1994; *Michael Collins* 1996; *The Butcher Boy* 1997; *In Dreams* 1999; *The End of the Affair* 1999; *The Good Thief* 2002

Kaurismäki, Aki
b.1957, Finland. Anarchic, unpredictable *enfant terrible* of Finnish cinema whose brother Mika is also a successful director.
Crime and Punishment/Rikos ja rangaistus 1983; *Calamari Union* 1985; *Shadows in Paradise/Varjoja paratiisissa* 1986; *Hamlet Goes Business/Hamlet liikemaailmassa* 1987; *Ariel* 1988; *Leningrad Cowboys Go America* 1989; *The Match Factory Girl/Tulitikkutehtaan tyttö* 1989; *I Hired a Contract Killer* 1990; *La vie de bohème* 1992; *Take Care of Your Scarf, Tatiana/Pidä huivistakiinni, Tatjana* 1993; *Leningrad Cowboys Meet Moses* 1994; *Drifting Clouds/Kauas pilvet karkaavat* 1996; *Juha* 1999; *The*

Man Without a Past/Mies vailla menneisyyttä 2002

Kiarostami, Abbas
b.1940, Iran. Doyen of the new Iranian cinema who made many short films before embarking on features.
The Traveller/Mosafer 1974; *The Report/Gozaresh* 1977; *The Firsts/ Avvaliha* 1984; *Where Is my Friend's House?/Khaneh-ye Doust Kojast?* 1986; *Homework/Mashq-e Shab* 1988; *Close-Up/Kelosup, Nama-ye Nazdik* 1989; *And Life Goes On/Zendegi Va Digar Hich* 1991; *Through the Olive Trees/Zir-e Darakhtan-e Zaitun* 1994; *A Taste of Cherry/Ta'm-e Gilas* 1997; *The Wind Will Carry Us/Bad Ma Ra Khahad Bord* 1999; *10* 2002

Kieślowski, Krzysztof
b.1941, Poland, d.1996. Actor, director, writer who started his career as a documentary maker. He became a prominent figure in international film.
The Scar/Blizna 1976; *Camera Buff/Amator* 1979; *Blind Chance/ Przypadek* 1981; *A Short Film About Killing/Krótki Film o Zabijaniu* 1988; *A Short Film About Love/Krótki film o milosci* 1988; *The Double Life of Véronique/Podwójne Zycie Weroniki* 1992; *Three Colours Blue/Trois couleurs bleu* 1993; *Three Colours White/Trois couleurs blanc* 1993; *Three Colours Red/Trois couleurs rouge* 1994

Kitano Takeshi
b.1948, Japan. Actor, writer, and director of crime films. In Japan he is best known as 'Beat' – a stand-up comedian.
Violent Cop/Sono otoko, kyobo ni tsuki 1989; *Boiling Point/3-4x jugatsu* 1990; *A Scene at the Sea/Ano natsu, ichiban shizukana umi* 1992; *Sonatine* 1993; *Getting Any/Minna yatteruka* 1994; *Kids Return/Kidzu ritan* 1996; *Fireworks/Hana-bi* 1997; *Kikujiro no natsu* 1999; *Brother* 2000; *Dolls* 2002

Klimov, Elem
b.1933, Russia. After difficulties with the censors he was elected First Secretary of the Film-Makers' Union in 1986.
Welcome, or No Unauthorised Admittance/Dobro pozhalovat', ili postoronnim vkhod vospreshchen 1964; *Adventures of a Dentist/Pokhozhdeniya zubnogo vracha* 1965; *Sport, sport, sport* 1970; *Agony/Agoniya* 1975; *And Nonetheless I Believe/I vse-taki ya veryu* 1976; *Farewell/Proshchanie* 1981; *Come and See/Idi i smotri* 1985

Kluge, Alexander
b.1932, Germany. Director, cultural activist and leading spokesman of the New German Cinema.
Yesterday's Girl/Abschied von gestern 1966; *Artists at the Top of the Big Top:*

Disorientated/Die Artisten in der Zirkuskuppel: Ratlos 1968; *The Big Mess/Der Grosse Verhau* 1970; *Occasional Work of a Female Slave/ Gelegenheitsarbeit einer Sklavin* 1973; *The Middle of the Road is a Very Dead End/In Gefahr und grösster Not bringt der Mittelweg den Tod* 1974; *Strongman Ferdinand/Der Starke Ferdinand* 1976; *The Patriotic Woman/Die Patriotin* 1979; *The Power of Emotion/Die Macht der Gefühle* 1983; *Miscellaneous News/Vermischte Nachrichten* 1985; *The Blind Director/ Der Angriff der Gegenwart auf die übrige Zeit* 1985

Kubrick, Stanley
b.1928, USA, d.1999. Influential film-maker whose provocative films are often considered masterpieces.
Fear and Desire 1953; *Killer's Kiss* 1955; *The Killing* 1956; *Paths of Glory* 1957; *Spartacus* 1960; *Lolita* 1962; *Dr Strangelove or How I Learned to Stop Worrying and Love the Bomb* 1964; *2001: A Space Odyssey* 1968; *A Clockwork Orange* 1971; *Barry Lyndon* 1975; *The Shining* 1980; *Full Metal Jacket* 1987; *Eyes Wide Shut* 1999

Kusturica, Emir
b.1955, Bosnia. Controversial director who though born in Sarajevo, took a generally pro-Serb position during the war in Bosnia.
Do You Remember Dolly Bell?/Sjecas li se, Dolly Bell 1981; *When Father Was Away on Business/Otac na sluzbenom putu* 1985; *Time of the Gypsies/Dom za vešanje* 1989; *Arizona Dream* 1993; *Underground/Bila jednom jedna zemlja* 1995; *Black Cat, White Cat/ Crna macka, beli macor* 1998; *The Nose* 2002

LaBute, Neil
b.1963, USA. Director and playwright whose films centre on the dark side of American life.
In the Company of Men 1997; *Your Friends and Neighbors* 1998; *Nurse Betty* 2000; *Possession* 2002; *The Shape of Things* 2003

Lee, Ang
b.1954, Taiwan. Has had critical and commercial success both in his Taiwanese dramas of family life and in his mainstream Hollywood films.
Pushing Hands/Tui shov 1992; *The Wedding Banquet/His yen* 1993; *Eat Drink Man Woman/Yin shi nan nu* 1994; *Sense and Sensibility* 1995; *The Ice Storm* 1997; *Ride with the Devil* 1999; *Crouching Tiger, Hidden Dragon/Wo hu cang long* 2000; *Chosen* 2001

Lee, Spike
b.1957, USA. America's foremost African-American director who,

through his persistence and talent, opened avenues for future black directors.
She's Gotta Have It 1986; *School Daze* 1988; *Do the Right Thing* 1989; *Mo' Better Blues* 1990; *Jungle Fever* 1991; *Malcolm X* 1992; *Crooklyn* 1994; *Clockers* 1995; *Girl 6* 1996; *Get on the Bus* 1996; *He Got Game* 1998; *Summer of Sam* 1999; *Bamboozled* 2000; *The 25th Hour* 2002

Leigh, Mike
b.1943, UK. Contemporary director whose films are known for their striking reality and characterization.
Bleak Moments 1971; *High Hopes* 1988; *Life Is Sweet* 1990; *Naked* 1993; *Secrets and Lies* 1996; *Career Girls* 1997; *Topsy-Turvy* 1999; *All or Nothing* 2002

Loach, Ken
b.1936, UK. His films combine radical politics with naturalistic acting.
Poor Cow 1967; *Kes* 1969; *Family Life* 1972; *Black Jack* 1979; *The Gamekeeper* 1980; *Looks and Smiles* 1981; *Fatherland* 1986; *Hidden Agenda* 1990; *Riff-Raff* 1990; *Raining Stones* 1993; *Ladybird Ladybird* 1994; *Land and Freedom* 1995; *Carla's Song* 1996; *My Name Is Joe* 1998; *Bread and Roses* 2000; *The Navigators* 2001; *Sweet Sixteen* 2002

Lucas, George
b.1944, USA. The hugely lucrative *Star Wars* franchise, not all of which he directed, has overwhelmed Lucas's talent for more personal films.
THX 1138 1970; *American Graffiti* 1973; *Star Wars* 1977; *Star Wars: Episode I: The Phantom Menace* 1999; *Star Wars: Episode II: Attack of the Clones* 2002

Lynch, David
b.1946, USA. One of the most original, if erratic, talents of his generation, whose TV series *Twin Peaks* was as personal as his films.
Eraserhead 1977; *The Elephant Man* 1980; *Dune* 1984; *Blue Velvet* 1986; *Wild at Heart* 1990; *Twin Peaks: Fire Walk with Me* 1992; *Lost Highway* 1997; *The Straight Story* 1999; *Mulholland Dr.* 2001

Makavejev, Dušan
b.1932, Yugoslavia. A pioneering modernist whose sexual and political daring was too much for the Communist authorities.
Man Is Not a Bird/Covek nije tica 1965; *The Switchboard Operator/ Ljubavni slucaj ili tragedija sluzbenice P.T.T.* 1967; *Innocence Unprotected/ Nevinost bez zastite* 1968; *WR: Mysteries of the Organism/WR – Misterije organizma* 1971; *Sweet Movie* 1974; *Montenegro* 1981; *The*

Coca-Cola Kid 1985; *Manifesto* 1988; *Gorilla Bathes at Noon* 1993

Makhmalbaf, Mohsen
b.1951, Iran. Together with Kiarostami, Iran's most important film-maker whose early films are strictly Islamist but whose later work is more interrogatory.
Nasuh's Repentance/Towbeh-ye Nasuh 1982; *Taking Refuge/Este'azeh* 1983; *Two Sightless Eyes/Do Cheshm-e Bisu* 1984; *Boycott/Baikot* 1986; *Peddler/Dastforush* 1987; *The Cyclist/Bysikelran* 1988; *Marriage of the Blessed/Arusi-ye Khuban* 1988; *A Time to Love/Nowbat-e Aseqi* 1990; *Zayandehrud's Nights/Shabha-ye Zayandehrud* 1990; *Nassered-Din Shah, the Movie Actor/Nassered-Din Shah, Aktor-e Sinema* 1991; *The Actor/Honarpisheh* 1992; *Salam Sinema* 1994; *Gabbeh* 1995; *The Bread and the Vase/Nun Va Goldhun* 1995; *Silence/Sokut* 1997; *Kandahar/Safar e Ghandehar* 2001

Malick, Terrence
b.1943, USA. Given the critical reception of his work, Malick's twenty-year silence remains a mystery, but he has made a triumphant return.
Badlands 1973; *Days of Heaven* 1978; *The Thin Red Line* 1998

Medem, Julio
b.1958, Spain. Basque director whose films combine disjointed narratives with psychological complexity.
Cows/Vacas 1991; *The Red Squirrel/La ardilla roja* 1993; *Earth/Tierra* 1996; *Lovers of the Arctic Circle/Los Amantes del Círculo Polar* 1998; *Sex and Lucia/Lucía y el sexo* 2001

Mészáros, Márta
b.1931, Hungary. The best-known woman director in Eastern Europe during the Communist era.
The Girl/Eltávozott nap 1968; *Binding Sentiments/Holdudvar* 1968; *Don't Cry, Pretty Girls/Szép lányok, ne sírjatok* 1970; *Riddance* 1973; *Adoption/Örökbefogadás* 1975; *Nine Months/Kilenc hónap* 1976; *The Two of Them/Ök ketten* 1977; *Just Like at Home/Olyan mint otthon* 1978; *On the Way/Útközben* 1979; *The Heiress/Örökség* 1980; *Anna* 1981; *Silent Cry/Néma kiáltás* 1982; *Diary for My Children/Napló gyermekeimnek* 1982; *Diary for My Loves/Napló szerelmeimnek* 1987; *Bye Bye Red Riding Hood/Piroska és a farkas* 1989; *Diary for My Father and Mother/Napló apámnak, anyámnak* 1990; *Fetus/A Magzat* 1993; *The Seventh Room/Siódmy pokój* 1998; *Daughters of Luck/A szerencse lányai* 1998; *Little Vilna: The Last Diary/Kisvilma – Az utolsó napló* 2000; *The Miraculous Manderin/Csodálatos mandarin* 2001

Miike Takashi
b.1960, Japan. Prolific director in the action and horror genres.
Eyecatch Junction/Topuu! Minipato tai 1991; *Lady Hunter: Koroshi no prelude* 1991; *A Human Murder Weapon/Ningen kyôki* 1992; *Bodyguard Kiba* 1993; *Oretachi wa tenshi ja nai* 1993; *Oretachi wa tenshi ja nai 2* 1993; *Shinjuku Outlaw* 1994; *Bodyguard Kiba: Shura no mokushiroku* 1994; *Daisan no gokudô* 1995; *Bodyguard Kiba: Shura no mokushiroku 2* 1995; *Naniwa yuukyôden* 1995; *Shinjuku kuroshakai: Chinese Mafia sensô* 1995; *Shin daisan no gokudô-boppatsu Kansai gokudô sensô* 1996; *Shin daisan no gokudô II* 1996; *Jingi naki yabô* 1996; *Rakkasei: Peanuts* 1996; *Kenka no hanamichi: Oosaka saikyô densetsu* 1996; *Fudoh: The New Generation/Gokudô sengokushi: Fudô* 1996; *Kishiwada shônen gurentai: Chikemuri junjô-hen* 1997; *Jingi naki yabô 2* 1997; *Full Metal Yakuza/Full Metal gokudô* 1997; *Rainy Dog/Gokudô kuroshakai* 1997; *Andromedia* 1998; *Kishiwada shônen gurentai: Bôkyô* 1998; *The Bird People in China/Chuugoku no chôjin* 1998; *Blues Harp* 1998; *Ley Lines/Nihon kuroshakai* 1999; *Silver* 1999; *Dead or Alive: Hanzaisha* 1999; *Sarariiman Kintarô* 1999; *Audition/Odishon* 1999; *The City of Lost Souls/Hyôryuu-gai* 2000; *The Guys from Paradise/Tengoku kara kita otoko-tachi* 2000; *Dead or Alive 2: Tôbôsha* 2000; *Family* 2001; *Visitor Q* 2001; *Ichi the Killer/Koroshiya* 2001; *Araburu tamashii-tachi* 2001; *Katakuri-ke no kôfuku* 2001; *Zuidô gensô-Tonkararin yume denetsu* 2001; *Kikuchi-jô monogatari – sakimori-tachi no uta* 2001; *Dead or Alive: Final* 2002; *Shin jingi no hakaba* 2002; *Tôgenkyô no hito-bito* 2002; *Onna kunishu ikki* 2002; *Graveyard of Honor/Shin jingi no hakaba* 2002; *Shangri-La/Kin'yuu hametsu Nippon: Tôgenkyô no hito-bito* 2002; *Deadly Outlaw: Rekka/Jitsuroku Andô Noboru Kyôdô-den: Rekka* 2002; *Man in White/Yurusarezaru mono* 2003

Mikhalkov, Nikita
b.1945, Russia. An actor, screenwriter and director – a major influence within contemporary Russian cinema.
At Home Among Strangers/Svoi sredi chuzhikh, chuzhoi sredi svoikh 1974; *A Slave of Love/Raba liubvi* 1975; *Unfinished Piece for Mechanical Piano/Neokonchennaia p'esa dlia mekhanicheskogo pianino* 1977; *Five Evenings/Piat' vecherov* 1978; *Oblomov* 1979; *Kinfolk/Rodnia* 1981; *A Private Conversation/Bez svidetelei* 1983; *Dark Eyes/Ochi chernye* 1987; *Autostop* 1990; *Close to Eden/Urga* 1991; *Burnt by the Sun/Utomlennye solntsem* 1994; *The Barber of Siberia/Sibirskii tsiriul'nik* 1998

Moodysson, Lukas
b.1969, Sweden. His films provide a fresh, often witty insight into contemporary Swedish society.
Show Me Love/Fucking Åmål 1998; *Together/Tillsammans* 2000; *Lilja 4-ever* 2002

Moretti, Nanni
b.1953, Italy. A major figure on the Italian left and an innovative film-maker.
I Am Self-sufficient/Io sono un autarchico 1976; *Ecce Bombo* 1978; *Sweet Dreams/Sogni d'oro* 1981; *Bianca* 1983; *La messa è finita* 1985; *Red Wood Pigeon/Palombella rossa* 1989; *Dear Diary/Caro diario* 1994; *Aprile* 1998; *The Son's Room/La stanza del filio* 2001

Muratova, Kira
b.1934, Romania. Independent-minded and gifted Russian woman director.
Our Honest Bread/Nash chestnyi khleb 1963; *Short Meetings/Korotkie vstrechi* 1967; *Long Goodbyes/Dolgie provody* 1971; *Getting to Know the World/Poznavaya belyi svet* 1979; *Among the Grey Stones/Sredi serykh kamnei* 1983; *Change of Fate/Peremena uchasti* 1987; *The Asthenic Syndrome/Astenicheskij sindrom* 1989; *The Sentimental Policeman/Chuvstvitelnyi militsioner* 1992; *Enthusiasms/Uvlecheniya* 1994; *Three Stories/Tri istorii* 1997; *Second-class Citizens/Vtorostepennyye lyudi* 2001; *Chekhovskiye motivy* 2002

Nair, Mira
b.1957, India. One of the new breed of Indian women directors, whose work has found favour in the West.
Salaam Bombay! 1988; *Mississippi Masala* 1991; *The Perez Family* 1995; *Kama Sutra* 1996; *Monsoon Wedding* 2001; *Hysterical Blindness* 2002

Oliveira, Manoel de
b.1908, Portugal. The most innovative film-maker in Portuguese cinema, he is still active in his nineties.
Aniki Bóbó 1942; *Past and Present/O Passado e o Presente* 1972; *Benilde or the Virgin Mother/Benilde ou a Virgem Mãe* 1975; *Doomed Love/Amor de Perdição* 1978; *Francisca* 1981; *The Satin Slipper/O Sapato de Cetim* 1985; *O Meu Caso* 1987; *The Cannibals/Os Canibais* 1988; *No, or the Vail Glory of Command/Non, ou A Vã Glória de Mandar* 1990; *The Divine Comedy/A Divina Comédia* 1991; *The Day of Despair/O Dia do Desespero* 1992; *Abraham Valley/Vale Abraão* 1993; *Blind Man's Bluff/A Caixa* 1994; *The Convent/O Convento* 1995; *Party* 1996; *Journey to the Beginning of the World/Viagem ao Princípio do Mundo* 1997; *Inquietude* 1998; *The Letter/La Lettre* 1999; *Word and Utopia/Palavra e Utopia* 2000; *I'm Going Home/Je rentre à la maison* 2001; *The Principle of Uncertainty/O Princípio da Incerteza* 2002

Ouedraogo, Idrissa
b.1954, Burkina Faso. A major figure in African cinema, despite his slim output.
The Choice/Yam Daabo 1986; *Yaaba* 1989; *The Law/Tilai* 1990; *Samba Traoré* 1993; *The Heart's Cry/Le Cri du coeur* 1997; *Kini and Adams* 1997

Peries, Lester James
b.1919, Sri Lanka. The doyen of Sri Lankan cinema, still directing well into his eighties.
The Line of Destiny/Rekava 1956; *The Message/Sandesaya* 1960; *Changes in the Village/Gamperaliya* 1964; *Between Two Worlds/Devolak athara* 1966; *The Yellow Robes/Ran salu* 1967; *Silence of the Heart/Golu hadawatha* 1968; *Five Acres of Land/Akkaa paha* 1969; *The Treasure/Nidhanaya* 1970; *The Eyes/Desa nisa* 1972; *The God King* 1973; *Enchanted Island/Madol duwa* 1976; *White Flowers for the Dead/Ahasin polawatha* 1977; *Rebellion/Veera puran appu* 1979; *Village in the Jungle/Baddegama* 1980; *The Time of Kali/Kaliyugaya* 1982; *End of an Era/Yaganthaya* 1983; *Mansion by the Lake/Vekanda walawwa* 2001

Polanksi, Roman
b.1933, Poland. A highly acclaimed and insightful director; a resident in France since the 1970s.
Knife in the Water/Nóz w wodzie 1962; *Repulsion* 1965; *Cul-de-sac* 1966; *The Fearless Vampire Killers* 1967; *Rosemary's Baby* 1968; *Macbeth* 1971; *What?* 1973; *Chinatown* 1974; *The Tenant* 1976; *Tess* 1979; *Pirates* 1986; *Frantic* 1988; *Bitter Moon* 1992; *Death and the Maiden* 1994; *The Ninth Gate* 1999; *The Pianist* 2002

Rathnam, Mani
b.1956, India. Director of successful Bollywood blockbusters, often with a political theme.
Pallavi anu pallavi 1983; *Unuru* 1984; *Pagal nilavu* 1985; *Idaya kovil* 1985; *Mouna ragam* 1986; *Nayakan* 1987; *Agni Nakshatram* 1988; *Gitanjali* 1989; *Anjali* 1990; *Dalapathi* 1991; *Roja* 1992; *Thiruda Thiruda* 1993; *Bombay* 1995; *Velu nayakan* 1995; *Iruvar* 1997; *Dil Se* 1998; *Alai payuthey* 2000; *Kannathil muthamittal* 2002

Ray, Satyajit
b.1921, India, d.1992. The best-known internationally of Indian directors, known for his humanistic approach to cinema.
Pather Panchali 1955; *Aparajito* 1956; *The Philosopher's Stone/Parash pathar* 1958; *The Music Room/Jalsaghar* 1958; *The World of Apu/Apur sansar* 1959; *The Goddess/Devi* 1960; *Two Daughters/Teen kanya* 1961; *Kanchenjungha* 1962; *The Expedition/Abhijaan* 1962; *The Big City/Mahanagar* 1963; *The Lonely Wife/Charulata* 1964; *The Saint/Mahapurush* 1965; *The Coward/Kapurush* 1965; *The Hero/Nayak* 1966; *The Zoo/Chiriyakhana* 1967; *The Adventures of Goopy and Bagha/Goopy gyne Bagha byne* 1968; *Siddharta and the City/Pratidwandi* 1970; *Days and Nights in the Forest/Aranyer din ratri* 1970; *Company Limited/Seemabaddha* 1971; *Distant Thunder/Ashani sanket* 1973; *The Golden Fortress/Sonar kella* 1974; *The Middleman/Jana aranya* 1976; *The Chess Players/Shatranj ke khiladi* 1977; *The Elephant God/Joi baba felunath* 1978; *The Home and the World/Ghare-Baire* 1984; *An Enemy of the People/Ganashatru* 1989; *The Branches of the Tree/Shakha proshakha* 1990; *The Stranger/Agantuk* 1991

Ripstein, Arturo
b.1943, Mexico. Director whose stylish films frequently explore the underbelly of Mexican life.
Time to Die/Tiempo de morir 1965; *Memories of the Future/Los recuerdos del porvenir* 1968; *The Children's Hour/La hora de los niños* 1969; *The Castle of Purity/El castillo de la pureza* 1973; *The Holy Office/El Santo Oficio* 1975; *Foxtrot* 1975; *Lecumberri* 1976; *The Black Widow/La viuda negra* 1977; *The Place Without Limits/El lugar sin límites* 1978; *Cadena perpetua* 1978; *La tía Alejandra* 1979; *La ilegal* 1979; *Seduction/La seducción* 1980; *Rastro de muerte* 1981; *The Other/El otro* 1984; *The Realm of Fortune/El imperio de la fortuna* 1986; *Love Lies/Mentiras piadosas* 1987; *Woman of the Port/La mujer del puerto* 1991; *The Beginning and the End/Principio y fin* 1993; *The Queen of the Night/La reina de la noche* 1994; *Deep Crimson/Profundo carmesí* 1996; *Divine/El evangelio de las maravillas* 1998; *No One Writes to the Colonel/El coronel no tiene quien le escriba* 1999; *Such Is Life/Así es la vida* 1999; *The Ruination of Men/La perdición de los hombres* 2000; *La Virgen de la lujuria* 2002

Rivette, Jacques
b.1928, France. Teasingly intellectual film-maker whose lengthy productions have become more accessible.
Paris Belongs to Us/Paris nous appartient 1960; *The Nun/La Réligieuse* 1966; *L'Amour fou* 1968; *Out 1: Noli me tangere* 1970; *Out 1: Spectre* 1972; *Celine and Julie Go Boating/Céline et Julie vont en bateau* 1974; *Twilight/Duelle* 1976; *Northwest/Noroît* 1976; *Le Pont du Nord* 1981;

Paris s'en va 1981; *Merry-Go-Round* 1983; *Love on the Ground/L'Amour par terre* 1984; *Wuthering Heights/ Hurlevent* 1985; *Gang of Four/La Bande des quatre* 1988/*La Belle Noiseuse* 1991; *Jeanne la Pucelle* 1994; *Up, Down, Fragile/Haut bas fragile* 1995; *Secret Defense/Secret défense* 1998; *Who Knows?/Va savoir* 2001

Rohmer, Eric
b.1920, France. Veteran New Wave director who has also been an influential critic.
The Sign of Leo/Le Signe du lion 1959; *La Collectionneuse* 1967; *My Night at Maud's/Ma nuit chez Maud* 1969; *Claire's Knee/Le Genou de Claire* 1970; *Chloe in the Afternoon/L'Amour l'après-midi* 1972; *The Marquise of O/Die Marquise von O* 1976; *Perceval le Gallois* 1979; *The Aviator's Wife/La Femme de l'aviateur* 1980; *The Well-made Marriage/Le Beau marriage* 1982; *Pauline at the Beach/Pauline à la plage* 1983; *Full Moon in Paris/Nuits de la pleine lune* 1984; *The Green Ray/Le Rayon vert* 1986; *Four Adventures of Reinette and Mirabelle/ 4 aventures de Reinette et Mirabelle* 1987; *My Girlfriend's Boyfriend/ L'Ami de mon amie* 1987; *A Tale of Springtime/Conte de printemps* 1990; *A Tale of Winter/Conte d'hiver* 1992; *L'Arbre, the maire et la médiathèque* 1993; *Les Rendez-vous de Paris* 1995; *A Summer's Tale/Conte d'été* 1996; *Autumn Tale/Conte d'automne* 1998; *The Lady and the Duke/L'Anglaise et le duc* 2001

Romero, George
b.1940, USA. Low-budget horror director who started a trend.
Night of the Living Dead 1968; *There's Always Vanilla* 1971; *Season of the Witch* 1972; *The Crazies* 1973; *Martin* 1977; *Dawn of the Dead* 1978; *Knightriders* 1981; *Creepshow* 1982; *Day of the Dead* 1985; *Monkey Shines* 1988; *The Dark Half* 1993; *Bruiser* 2000

Rosi, Francesco
b.1922, Italy. Director of lucid commentaries on Italian political life.
Anita Garibaldi/Camicie rosse 1952; *Kean* 1956; *The Challenge/La sfida* 1958; *I magliari* 1959; *Salvatore Guiliano* 1961; *Hands Over the City/Le mani sulla città* 1963; *The Moment of Truth/Il momento della verità* 1965; *More Than a Miracle/ C'era una volta* 1967; *Uomini contro* 1970; *The Mattei Affair/Il caso Mattei* 1972; *Lucky Luciano* 1974; *Illustrious Corpses/Cadaveri eccellenti* 1976; *Christ Stopped at Eboli/Cristo si è fermato a Eboli* 1979; *Three Brothers/Tre fratelli* 1981; *Carmen* 1984; *Chronicle of a Death Foretold/Cronaca di una morte annunciata* 1987; *To Forget*

Palermo/Dimenticare Palermo 1990; *The Truce/La tregua* 1996

Rudolph, Alan
b.1943, USA. Long-time associate of Robert Altman, then director of individually tailored films.
Premonition 1972; *Nightmare Circus* 1973; *Welcome to L.A.* 1977; *Remember My Name* 1978; *Roadie* 1980; *Endangered Species* 1982; *Choose Me* 1984; *Songwriter* 1984; *Trouble in Mind* 1985; *Made in Heaven* 1987; *The Moderns* 1988; *Love at Large* 1990; *Mortal Thoughts* 1991; *Equinox* 1992; *Mrs Parker and the Vicious Circle* 1994; *Afterglow* 1997; *Breakfast of Champions* 1999; *Trixie* 2000; *Investigating Sex* 2001; *The Secret Lives of Dentists* 2002

Russell, David O
b.1958, USA. After a couple of independent features, he has moved into big budgets and big stars.
Spanking the Monkey 1994; *Flirting with Disaster* 1996; *Three Kings* 1999

Salles, Walter
b.1955, Brazil. Former documentary film-maker, then a director of visually stylish films based upon social themes.
Exposure/A Grande Arte 1991; *Foreign Land/Terra Estrangeira* 1995; *Central Station/Centro do Brasil* 1998; *O Primeiro Dia* 1998; *Behind the Sun/Abril Despedaçado* 2001

Sanjinés, Jorge
b.1936, Bolivia. Militant film-maker forced into exile during the 1970s.
Ukamau 1966; *Blood of the Condor/Yawar mallku* 1969; *The Courage of the People/El coraje del pueblo* 1971; *The Principal Enemy/ El enemigo principal* 1973; *Lluschi Caymanta, fuera de aquí* 1977; *Las banderas del amanecer* 1984; *The Secret Nation/La nación clandestina* 1989; *To Hear the Bird Song/Para recibir el canto de los pájaros* 1996

Sayles, John
b.1950, USA. Director whose commercial writing projects provide the opportunity for his more political, personal works.
Return of the Secaucus 7 1980; *Lianna* 1983; *Baby, It's You* 1983; *The Brother from Another Planet* 1984; *Matewan* 1987; *Eight Men Out* 1988; *City of Hope* 1991; *Passion Fish* 1992; *The Secret of Roan Inish* 1994; *Lone Star* 1996; *Men with Guns* 1997; *Limbo* 1999; *Sunshine State* 2001

Schlöndorff, Volker
b.1939, Germany. A master craftsman and prominent director of New German Cinema.
Young Törless/Der junge Törless 1966; *A Degree of Murder/Mord und*

Todschlag 1967; *Man on Horseback/Michael Kohlhaas – der Rebell* 1969; *The Sudden Wealth of the Poor People of Kombach/Der plötzliche Reichtum der armen Leute von Kombach* 1970; *The Morals of Ruth Halbfass/Die Moral der Ruth Halbfass* 1971; *Summer Lightning/Strohfeuer* 1972; *The Lost Honour of Katharina Blum/Der verlorene Ehre der Katharina Blum* 1975; *Coup de grace/Der Fangschuss* 1976; *The Tin Drum/Die Blechtrommel* 1979; *Circle of Deceit/Die Fälschung* 1981; *Swann in Love/Un Amour de Swann* 1984; *The Handmaid's Tale* 1990; *Voyager/Homo Faber* 1991; *The Ogre/Der Unhold* 1996; *Palmetto* 1998; *The Legend of Rita/Die Stille nach dem Schuss* 1999

Scorsese, Martin
b.1942, USA. Italian-American graduate of New York University, the most critically acclaimed of contemporary US directors.
Who's That Knocking at My Door? 1968; *Boxcar Bertha* 1972; *Mean Streets* 1973; *Alice Doesn't Live Here Any More* 1974; *Taxi Driver* 1976; *New York, New York* 1977; *The Last Waltz* 1978; *Raging Bull* 1980; *The King of Comedy* 1983; *After Hours* 1985; *The Color of Money* 1986; *The Last Temptation of Christ* 1988; *GoodFellas* 1990; *Cape Fear* 1991; *The Age of Innocence* 1993; *Casino* 1995; *Kundun* 1997; *Bringing Out the Dead* 1999; *Gangs of New York* 2002

Scott, Ridley
b.1937, UK. Former TV commercials director. His best films portray visual flair and a sense of narrative.
The Duellists 1977; *Alien* 1979; *Blade Runner* 1982; *Legend* 1985; *Someone to Watch Over Me* 1987; *Black Rain* 1989; *Thelma and Louise* 1991; *1492: Conquest of Paradise* 1992; *White Squall* 1996; *G.I. Jane* 1997; *Gladiator* 2000; *Hannibal* 2001; *Black Hawk Down* 2001

Sembène, Ousmane
b.1923, Senegal. The doyen of African film-makers.
Black Girl/La Noire de... 1966; *The Money Order/Mandabi* 1968; *Emitai* 1971; *Xala* 1975; *Ceddo* 1977; *Camp de Thiaroye* 1987; *Guelwaar* 1992; *Faat Kiné* 2000

Sen, Mrinal
b.1923, India. Leading light of the New Indian Cinema of the 1970s.
The Dawn/Raat Bhore 1956; *Under the Blue Sky/Neel Akasher Neechev* 1959; *The Wedding Day/Baishey Shravana* 1960; *Over Again/Punasha* 1961; *And at Last/Abasheshey* 1962; *The Representative/Protinidhi* 1964; *Up in the Clouds/Akash Kusum* 1965; *Two Brothers/Matira Manisha* 1966;

Mr Shome/Bhuvan Shome 1969; *The Wish-Fulfilment/Ichhapuran* 1970; *Interview* 1971; *Calcutta 71* 1971; *An Unfinished Story/Ek Adhuri Kahani* 1972; *The Guerrilla Fighter/Padatik* 1973; *Chorus* 1974; *The Royal Hunt/Mrigayaa* 1976; *The Outsiders/Oka Oori Katha* 1977; *The Man with the Axe/Parashuram* 1978; *And Quiet Rolls the Dawn/ Ekdin Pratidin* 1979; *In Search of Famine/Akaler Sandhane* 1980; *The Kaleidoscope/Chaalchitra* 1981; *The Case Is Closed/Kharij* 1982; *The Ruins/Khandar* 1983; *Genesis* 1986; *Suddenly One Day/Ek Din Achanak* 1989; *City Life* 1990; *World Within, World Without/Mahaprithivi* 1992; *The Confined/Antareen* 1994

Smith, Kevin
b.1970, USA. Director of independent, often scurrilous comedies.
Clerks 1994; *Mallrats* 1995; *Chasing Amy* 1997; *Dogma* 1999; *Jay and Silent Bob Strike Back* 2001

Soderbergh, Steven
b.1963, USA. His first film won a Cannes Palme d'Or. He then lost his way but came back in the 1990s.
sex, lies & videotape 1989; *Kafka* 1991; *King of the Hill* 1993; *Underneath* 1995; *Gray's Anatomy* 1996; *Schizopolis* 1996; *Out of Sight* 1998; *The Limey* 1999; *Erin Brockovich* 2000; *Traffic* 2000; *Ocean's Eleven* 2001; *Full Frontal* 2002; *Solaris* 2002

Sokurov, Alexander
b.1951, Russia. One of the most individual and uncompromising advocates of Russian cinema's distinctive vision.
The Solitary Voice of Man/Odinokii golos cheloveka 1978; *Mournful Indifference/Skorbnoe beschuvstvie* 1983; *And Nothing More/I nichego bolshe* 1987; *Days of Eclipse/Dni zatmeniya* 1988; *Save and Protect/ Spasi I sokhrani* 1989; *The Second Circle/Krug vtoroi* 1990; *Stone/Kamen'* 1992; *Whispering Pages/Tikhie stranitsy* 1993; *Mother and Son/Mat' I syn* 1997; *Molokh* 1999; *Taurus/Telets* 2001; *Russian Ark* 2002; *Father and Son* 2003

Solondz, Todd
b.1959, USA. Independent director, a great success at The Sundance Festival and Cannes International Film Festival.
Fear, Anxiety and Depression 1989; *Welcome to the Dollhouse* 1995; *Happiness* 1998; *Storytelling* 2001

Spielberg, Steven
b.1947, USA. Commercially successful director whose later films aspire to be more serious.
Duel 1971; *The Sugarland Express* 1974; *Jaws* 1975; *Close Encounters of*

the Third Kind 1977; *1941* 1979; *Raiders of the Lost Ark* 1981; *E.T. The Extra-Terrestrial* 1982; *Indiana Jones and the Temple of Doom* 1984; *The Color Purple* 1985; *Empire of the Sun* 1987; *Indiana Jones and the Last Crusade* 1989; *Always* 1989; *Hook* 1991; *Jurassic Park* 1993; *Schindler's List* 1993; *Amistad* 1997; *The Lost World* 1997; *Saving Private Ryan* 1998; *A.I. Artificial Intelligence* 2001; *Minority Report* 2002; *Catch Me If You Can* 2002

Stillman, Whit
b.1952, USA. Independent director whose films are stylish dissections of the affluent young.
Metropolitan 1990; *Barcelona* 1994; *The Last Days of Disco* 1998

Szabó, István
b.1938, Hungary. Director who has aimed at the international market since the 1980s.
Age of Illusions/Álmodozások kora 1964; *Father/Apa* 1967; *A Film about Love/Szerelmesfilm* 1970; *25 Fireman's Street/Tüzoltó utca 25.* 1973; *Tales of Budapest/Budapesti mesék* 1976; *Confidence/Bizalom* 1979; *Der grüne Vogel* 1980; *Mephisto* 1981; *Bali* 1984; *Colonel Redl/Redl Ezredes* 1985; *Hanussen* 1988; *Meeting Venus* 1991; *Dear Emma, Sweet Bobby/Édes Emma, drága Böbe* 1992; *Offenbach titkai* 1996; *Sunshine/A napfény ize* 1999; *Taking Sides* 2001

Tarantino, Quentin
b.1963, USA. *Enfant terrible* of 1990s Hollywood who has yet to show he can sustain his reputation.
Reservoir Dogs 1992; *Pulp Fiction* 1994; *Jackie Brown* 1997; *Kill Bill* 2003

Tarkovsky, Andrei
b.1932, Russia d.1986. Director of metaphysical films. These often caused him difficulties with the Soviet authorities.
My Name Is Ivan/Ivanovo detstvo 1963; *Andrei Rublev* 1969; *Solyaris* 1972; *The Mirror/Zerkalo* 1975; *Stalker* 1979; *Nostalgia/Nostalghia* 1984; *The Sacrifice/Offret* 1986

Tarr, Béla
b.1955, Hungary. Director of bleak but challenging visions.
Family Nest/Családi tüzfészek 1979; *The Outsider/Szabadgyalog* 1981; *The Prefab People/Panelkapcsolat* 1982; *Almanac of Fall/Öszi almanach* 1984; *Damnation/Kárhozat* 1988; *Satan's Tango/Sátántangó* 1994; *Werckmeister Harmonies/ Werckmeister harmóniák* 2000

Taviani, Paolo b.1931, Italy and
Vittorio b.1929, Italy. Brothers who have experimented with a variety

of styles in films about several epochs of Italian life.

A Man for Burning/Un uomo da bruciare 1962; *I fuorilegge del matrimonio* 1963; *The Subversives/I sovverivi* 1967; *Under the Sign of Scorpio/Sotto il segno dello scorpione* 1969; *St Michael Had a Rooster/San Michele aveva un gallo* 1972; *Allonsanfan* 1973; *Padre padrone* 1977; *The Meadow/Il prato* 1979; *Night of the Shooting Stars/La notte di San Lorenzo* 1982; *Kaos* 1984; *Good Morning, Babylon* 1987; *The Sun Also Shines at Night/Il sole anche di notte* 1990; *Wild Flower/Fiorile* 1993; *Elective Affinities/Le affinità elettive* 1996; *You're Laughing/Tu ridi* 1998

Tlatli, Moufida
b.1947, Tunisia. A distinguished editor before becoming one of the few Arab women directors.
The Silences of the Palace/Samt al-Quoousour 1994; *Season of Men/La Saison des hommes* 1999

Tran Anh Hung
b.1962, Vietnam. The best-known Vietnamese director, mainly working in France.
The Scent of Green Papaya/Mui du du Xanh 1993; *Cyclo/Xich lo* 1995; *At the Height of Summer/A la verticale de l'été* 2000; *Je viens après la pluie* 2001

Trier, Lars von
b.1956, Denmark. Pioneer of the Dogme school of film-making.
The Element of Crime/Forbrydelsens element 1984; *Epidemic* 1988; *Europa* 1991; *Breaking the Waves* 1996; *The Idiots/Idioterne* 1998; *Dancer in the Dark* 2000; *Dogville* 2002

Trotta, Margarethe von
b.1942, Germany. Former actress and leading member of German women's film-making movement.
The Lost Honour of Katharina Blum/Die verlorene Ehre der Katharina Blum 1975; *The Second Awakening of Christa Klages/Das zweite Erwachen der Christa Klages* 1978; *Sisters, or the Balance of Happiness/Schwestern oder die Balance des Glücks* 1979; *The German Sisters/Die bleierne Zeit* 1981; *Friends and Husbands/Heller Wahn* 1983; *Rosa Luxemburg* 1986; *Three Sisters/Paura e amore* 1988; *The African Woman/L'africana* 1990; *The Long Silence/Il lungo silenzio* 1993; *The Promise/Das Versprechen* 1994; *Rosenstrasse* 2001

Truffaut, François
b.1932, France, d.1984. Former critic, occasional actor and prominent New Wave director.
The 400 Blows/Les Quatres cents coups 1959; *Shoot the Piano Player/Tirez sur le pianiste* 1960; *Jules et Jim* 1961; *Silken Skin/La peau douce* 1964; *Fahrenheit 451* 1966; *The Bride Wore Black/La Mariée était en noir* 1968; *Stolen Kisses/Baisers volés* 1968; *The Mississippi Mermaid/La Sirène de Mississippi* 1969; *The Wild Child/L'Enfant sauvage* 1970; *Bed and Board/Domicile conjugal* 1970; *Anne and Marie/Les Deux anglaises et le continent* 1971; *A Gorgeous Bird Like Me/Une Belle fille comme moi* 1972; *Day for Night/La Nuit américaine* 1973; *The Story of Adèle H/L'Histoire d'Adèle H* 1975; *Small Change/L'Argent de poche* 1976; *The Man Who Loved Women/L'Homme qui aimait les femmes* 1977; *The Green Room/La Chambre verte* 1978; *Love on the Run/L'Amour en fuite* 1979; *The Last Metro/Le Dernier métro* 1980; *The Woman Next Door/La Femme d'à côté* 1981; *Finally Sunday/Vivement Dimanche!* 1982

Tsai Ming-Liang
b.1957, Malaysia. Part of the younger generation of Taiwanese film-makers.
Rebels of the Neon God/Qing Shaonian Nezha 1992; *Vive L'Amour/Aiqing wansui* 1994; *The River/He liu* 1997; *The Hole/Dong* 1998; *What Time Is It There?/Ni neibian jidian* 2001

Tsui Hark
b.1951, Vietnam. Key figure as both director and producer in Hong Kong cinema.
The Butterfly Murders/Die bian 1979; *We're Going to Eat You/Diyu wu men* 1980; *Dangerous Encounters: First Kind/Di yi lei xing wei xian* 1980; *All the Wrong Clues/Gui ma zhi duo xing* 1981; *Zu: Warriors from the Magic Mountain/Shu shan* 1983; *Search for the Gods* 1983; *Aces Go Places III: Our Man from Bond Street/Zuijia paidang zhi nuhuang miling* 1984; *Shanghai Blues/Shanghai zhi ye* 1984; *King Worker* 1985; *Working Class/Da gung wong dai* 1985; *Peking Opera Blues/Do ma daan* 1986; *The Big Heat/Cheng shi te jing* 1988; *A Better Tomorrow III: Love and Death in Saigon/Yinghung bunsik III* 1989; *The Master/Long xing tian xia* 1989; *Swordsman/Xiaoao jiang hu* 1990; *The King of Chess/Kei Wong* 1991; *A Chinese Ghost Story III/Sinnui yauman III: Do Do Do* 1991; *The Raid/Cai shu zhi huang sao qian jun* 1991; *Once Upon a Time in China/Wong Fei-hung* 1991; *The Banquet/Haomen yeyan* 1991; *Dragon Inn/Xin long men ke zhan* 1992; *Once Upon a Time in China 2/Wong fei-hung ji yi: naam yi dong ji keung* 1992; *Twin Dragons/Shuang long hui* 1992; *Once Upon a Time in China III/Wong fei-hung tsi sam: Siwong tsangba* 1993; *Green Snake/Ching se* 1993; *Butterfly Lovers/Leung juk* 1994; *Once Upon a Time in China V/Huang fei-hung zhi wu: Long cheng jian ba* 1994; *The Chinese Feast/Jin yu man tang* 1995; *Love in the Time of Twilight/Hua yue jia qi* 1995; *The Blade/Dao* 1995; *Tristar/Da san yuan* 1996; *Double Team* 1997; *Knock Off* 1998; *Time and Tide/Seunlau ngaklau* 2000; *The Legend of Zu/Shu shan zheng chuan* 2001; *Black Mask 2: City of Masks* 2001

Van Sant, Gus
b.1952, USA. Director whose occasional forays into 'queer cinema' have been mixed with more mainstream work.
Mala Noche 1985; *Drugstore Cowboy* 1989; *My Own Private Idaho* 1991; *Even Cowgirls Get the Blues* 1993; *To Die For* 1995; *Good Will Hunting* 1997; *Psycho* 1998; *Finding Forrester* 2000; *Gerry* 2002; *Elephant* 2003

Verhoeven, Paul
b.1938, Netherlands. A successful career in Holland has been followed by commercial success in Hollywood.
Business Is Business/Wat zien ik? 1971; *Turkish Delight/Turks fruit* 1973; *Cathy Tippel/Keetje Tippel* 1975; *Soldier of Orange/Soldaat van Oranje* 1977; *Spetters* 1980; *The Fourth Man/Die Vierde man* 1983; *Flesh and Blood* 1985; *Robocop* 1987; *Total Recall* 1990; *Basic Instinct* 1992; *Showgirls* 1995; *Starship Troopers* 1997; *Hollow Man* 2000

Visconti, Luchino
b.1906, Italy, d.1976. Initially a neo-realist, then a director of art-house cinema on the grand scale.
Ossessione 1942; *La terra trema* 1948; *Bellissima* 1951; *Senso* 1954; *White Nights/Le notti bianche* 1957; *Rocco and His Brothers/Rocco e i suoi fratelli* 1960; *The Leopard/Il gattopardo* 1963; *Sandra/Vaghe stelle dell'orsa* 1965; *The Stranger/Lo straniero* 1967; *The Damned/La caduta degli dei* 1969; *Death in Venice/Morte a Venezia* 1971; *Ludwig II* 1972; *Conversation Piece/Gruppo di famiglia in un interno* 1974; *The Innocent/L'innocente* 1976

Wajda, Andrzej
b.1926, Poland. Already a great film-maker before the demise of Communism, Wajda distinguished himself further in the Solidarity period.
A Generation/Pokolenie 1955; *Kanał* 1957; *Ashes and Diamonds/Popiół i Diament* 1958; *Lotna* 1959; *Innocent Sorcerers/Niewinni czarodzieje* 1960; *A Siberian Lady Macbeth/Sibirska Ledi Magbet; Samson* 1961; *Ashes/Popioly* 1966; *Gates to Paradise/Vrata raja* 1967; *Everything for Sale/Wszystko na sprzedaz* 1969; *Hunting Flies/Polowanie na muchy* 1969; *Landscape After Battle/Krajobraz po bitwie* 1970; *The Birch Wood/Brzezina* 1970; *The Wedding/Wesele* 1972; *The Promised Land/Ziemia obiecana* 1974; *The Shadow Line/Smuga cienia* 1976; *Man of Marble/Człowiek z marmuru* 1977; *The Young Ladies of Wilko/Panny z Wilka* 1979; *Orchestra Conductor/Dyrygent* 1979; *Without Anaesthesia/Bez znieczulenia* 1979; *Man of Iron/Człowiek z żelaza* 1981; *Danton* 1982; *A Love in Germany/Eine Liebe in Deutschland* 1983; *Chronicle of Love Affairs/Kronika wypadków milosnych* 1986; *The Possessed/Les Possédés* 1988; *Korczak* 1990; *The Ring with a Crowned Eagle/Pierscionek z orlem w koronie* 1993; *Nastasja* 1994; *Holy Week/Wielki tydzien* 1995; *Miss Nobody/Panna Nikt* 1996; *Pan Tadeusz* 1999; *The Revenge/Zemsta* 2002

Wang, Wayne
b.1949, Hong Kong. Working in the United States, has directed sensitive studies of Chinese-American life.
A Man, a Woman, and a Killer 1975; *Chan Is Missing* 1982; *Dim Sum: A Little Bit of Heart* 1984; *Slamdance* 1987; *Eat a Bowl of Tea* 1989; *Life Is Cheap... But Toilet Paper Is Expensive* 1989; *The Joy Luck Club* 1993; *Smoke* 1995; *Blue in the Face* 1995; *Chinese Box* 1997; *Anywhere But Here* 1999; *The Center of the World* 2001; *Maid in Manhattan* 2002

Waters, John
b.1946, USA. Determinedly outrageous director of camp entertainments.
Mondo Trasho 1969; *Multiple Maniacs* 1970; *Pink Flamingos* 1972; *Female Trouble* 1975; *Desperate Living* 1977; *Polyester* 1981; *Hairspray* 1988; *Cry-Baby* 1990; *Serial Mom* 1994; *Pecker* 1998; *Cecil B. DeMented* 2000

Weir, Peter
b.1944, Australia. Director of thoughtful films who has made the successful transition to Hollywood.
The Cars That Ate Paris 1974; *Picnic at Hanging Rock* 1975; *The Last Wave* 1977; *Gallipoli* 1981; *The Year of Living Dangerously* 1982; *Witness* 1985; *The Mosquito Coast* 1986; *Dead Poets Society* 1989; *Green Card* 1990; *Fearless* 1993; *The Truman Show* 1998

Wenders, Wim
b.1945, Germany. International-minded and earnest leading director of New German Cinema.
Summer in the City 1970; *The Goalkeeper's Fear of the Penalty Kick/Die Angst des Tormannes beim Elfmeter* 1971; *The Scarlet Letter/Der scharlachrote Buchstabe* 1972; *Alice in the Cities/Alice in den Städten* 1974; *The Wrong Move/Falsche Bewegung* 1974; *Kings of the Road/Im Lauf der Zeit* 1976; *The American Friend/Der amerikanische Freund* 1977; *Lightning Over Water* 1980; *The State of Things/Der Stand der Dinge* 1982; *Hammett* 1982; *Paris, Texas* 1984; *Wings of Desire/Der Himmel über Berlin* 1987; *Until the End of the World/Bis ans Ende der Welt* 1991; *Faraway, So Close!/In weiter Ferne, so nah!* 1993; *Lisbon Story* 1994; *The End of Violence* 1997; *The Buena Vista Social Club* 1999; *The Million Dollar Hotel* 2000

Winterbottom, Michael
b.1961, UK. Acclaimed British film-maker known for his passionate films.
Go Now 1995; *Butterfly Kiss* 1995; *Jude* 1996; *Welcome to Sarajevo* 1997; *I Want You* 1998; *Wonderland* 1999; *With or Without You* 1999; *The Claim* 2000; *24 Hour Party People* 2003; *In this World* 2003

Wong Kar-wai
b.1958, China. Hong Kong's nearest to an art-cinema director.
As Tears Go By/Wong gok ka moon 1988; *Days of Being Wild/A Fei jing juen* 1991; *Ashes of Time/Dung che sai duk* 1994; *Chungking Express/Chongqing Senlin* 1994; *Fallen Angels/Duoluo tianshi* 1995; *Happy Together/Cheun gwong tsa sit* 1997; *In the Mood for Love/Hua yang nian hua* 2000; *2046* 2001

Yang, Edward
b.1947, China. One of the most important directors of Taiwanese cinema, and an associate of Hou Hsiao-Hsien.
That Day, on the Beach/Haitan de yitian 1983; *Taipei Story/Qingmei Zhuma* 1985; *The Terroriser/Kongbu fenzi* 1986; *A Brighter Summer's Day/Guling die shaonian sha Ren Shijian* 1991; *A Confucian Confusion/Duli shidai* 1994; *Mahjong* 1996; *A One and a Two.../Yi yi* 2000

Zhang Yimou
b.1951, China. Talented member of the Fifth Generation of Chinese film-makers.
Red Sorghum/Hong Gaoliang 1987; *The Puma Action/Daihao meizhoubao* 1989; *Ju Dou* 1990; *Raise the Red Lantern/Dahong Denglong Gaogao Gua* 1991; *The Story of Qiu Ju/Qiu Ju Da Guan Si* 1992; *To Live/Huozhe* 1994; *Shanghai Triad/Yao a yao yao dao waipo qiao* 1995; *Keep Cool/You hua hao hao shup* 1997; *Not One Less/Yi Ge Dou Bu Neng Shao* 1999; *The Road Home/Wo De Fuqin Muqin* 1999; *Happy Times/Xingfu shiguang* 2000; *Hero/Ying xiong* 2002

Bibliography

Note: With certain exceptions, this bibliography contains only English-language books and does not include books on specific films or individual film-makers. In addition to these sources I have received valuable assistance from a number of specialist journals and other publications such as *Cinema Papers*, *East-West Film Journal*, *Ecrans d'Afrique*, *Film Comment*, *International Film Guide* and *Sight & Sound*.

1. HOLLYWOOD AND THE RISE OF THE BLOCKBUSTER
– Peter Biskind, *Easy Riders, Raging Bulls: How the Sex-Drugs-and-Rock 'n' Roll Generation Saved Hollywood* (New York: Simon and Schuster, 1998)
– Peter Krämer, *The Big Picture: Hollywood Cinema from 'Star Wars' to 'Titanic'* (London: BFI Publishing, 2002)
– Jon Lewis (ed.), *The New American Cinema* (Durham, NC: Duke University Press, 1998)
– Jon Lewis, *The End of Cinema as we know it: American Film in the Nineties* (New York: New York University Press, 2001)
– Toby Miller, Nitin Govil, John McMurria and Richard Maxwell, *Global Hollywood* (London: BFI Publishing, 2001)
– Steve Neale amd Murray Smith (eds.), *Contemporary Hollywood Cinema* (London and New York: Routledge, 1998)
– Stephen Prince, *Hollywood Under the Electronic Rainbow 1980–1989* (New York: Charles Scribner's Sons, 2000)

2. CRIME AND ACTION SPECTACULARS
– José Arroyo (ed.), *Action/Spectacle Cinema: A Sight & Sound Reader* (London: BFI Publishing, 2000)
– Steve Cohan and Ina Rae Hark (eds.), *Screening the Male: Exploring Masculinities in the Hollywood Cinema* (London and New York: Routledge, 1993)
– Chris Holmlund, *Impossible Bodies: Femininity and Masculinity at the Movies* (London and New York: Routledge, 2001)
– Susan Jeffords, *Hard Bodies: Hollywood Masculinity in the Reagan Era* (New Brunswick, NJ: Rutgers University Press, 1994)
– Geoff King, *Spectacular Narratives: Hollywood in the Age of the Blockbuster* (London: I B Tauris, 2000)
– Neal King, *Heroes in Hard Times: Cop Action Movies in the US* (Philadelphia, PA: Temple University Press, 1999)
– Pat Kirkham and Janet Thumim (eds.), *Me Jane: Masculinity, Movies and Women* (London: Lawrence & Wishart, 1995)

– Peter Lehman, *Running Scared: Masculinity and the Representation of the Male Body* (Philadelphia, PA: Temple University Press, 1993)
– Peter Lehman (ed.), *Masculinity: Bodies, Movies, Culture* (London and New York: Routledge, 2001)
– Constance Penley and Sharon Willis (eds.), *Male Trouble* (Minneapolis, MN: University of Minnesota Press, 1993)
– Andrew Perchuk and Helaine Posner (eds.), *The Masculine Masquerade: Masculinity and Representation* (Cambridge, MA: MIT List Visual Arts Center, 1995)
– Nicole Rafter, *Shots in the Mirror: Crime Films and Society* (New York: Oxford University Press, 2000)
– Yvonne Tasker, *Spectacular Bodies: Gender, Genre and the Action Cinema* (London and New York: Routledge, 1993)
– Robin Wood, *Sexual Politics and Narrative Film: Hollywood and Beyond* (New York: Columbia University Press, 1998)

3. NEW SCIENCE FICTION
– Scott Bukatman, *Terminal Identity: The Virtual Subject in Postmodern Science Fiction* (Durham, NC: Duke University Press, 1993)
– Deborah Cartnell, I Q Hunter, Heidi Kaye and Imelda Whelehan (eds.), *Alien Identities: Exploring Differences in Film and Fiction* (London: Pluto Press, 1999)
– Geoff King and Tanya Krzywinska, *Science Fiction Cinema: From Outerspace to Cyberspace* (London: Wallflower Press, 2000)
– Annette Kuhn (ed.), *Alien Zone II: The Spaces of Science Fiction Cinema* (London: Verso, 1999)
– Kim Newman, *Millennium Movies: End of the World Cinema* (London: Titan, 1999)
– Vivian Sobchack, *Screening Space: The American Science Fiction Film* (New York: Ungar, 1987)
– J P Telotte, *Replications: A Robotic History of the Science Fiction Film* (Urbana and Chicago, IL: University of Illinois Press, 1995)

4. HORROR
– Linda Badley, *Film, Horror and the Body Fantastic* (Westport, CT: Greenwood Press, 1995)
– Andrew Britton (ed.), *American Nightmares: Essays on the Horror Film* (Toronto: Festival of Festivals, 1979)
– Noël Carroll, *The Philosophy of Horror, or the Paradoxes of the Heart* (London and New York: Routledge, 1990)
– Carol Clover, *Men, Women and Chainsaws: Gender in the Modern Horror Film* (London: BFI Publishing, 1992)

– Vera Dika, *Games of Terror: Halloween, Friday the 13th and the Films of the Stalker Cycle* (Cranbury, NJ: Associated University Presses, 1990)
– Ken Gelder, *Reading the Vampire* (London and New York: Routledge, 1994)
– Ken Gelder (ed.), *The Horror Reader* (London and New York: Routledge, 2000)
– Barry Grant (ed.), *The Dread of Difference: Gender and the Horror Film* (Austin, TX: University of Texas Press, 1996)
– Mark Jancovich (ed.), *Horror, the Film Reader* (London: Routledge, 2001)
– Kim Newman (ed.), *Science Fiction/Horror: A Sight & Sound Reader* (London: BFI Publishing, 2001)
– Laurence Rickels, *The Vampire Lectures* (Minneapolis, MN: University of Minnesota Press, 1999)
– Steven Jay Schneider (ed.), *Fear Without Frontiers: Horror Cinema Across the Globe* (London: FAB Press, 2002)
– Philip L Simpson, *Psycho Paths: Tracing the Serial Killer through Contemporary American Film and Fiction* (Carbondale, IL: Southern Illinois University Press, 2000)
– Gregory Waller (ed.), *American Horrors: Essays on the Modern American Horror Film* (Urbana and Chicago, IL: University of Illinois Press, 1987)
– Paul Wells, *The Horror Genre: From Beelzebub to Blair Witch* (London: Wallflower Press, 2000)

5. COMEDY AND COMEDIANS
– Peter William Evans and Celestino Deleyto (eds.), *Terms of Endearment: Hollywood Romantic Comedy of the 1980s and 1990s* (Edinburgh: Edinburgh University Press, 1998)
– Dan Harries, *Film Parody* (London: BFI Publishing, 2000)
– Shannon Hengen (ed.), *Performing Gender and Comedy: Theories, Texts and Contexts* (London: Gordon and Breach, 1998)
– Andrew S. Horton, *Comedy/Cinema/Theory* (Berkeley, CA: University of California Press, 1991)
– William Paul, *Laughing, Screaming: Modern Hollywood Horror and Comedy* (New York: Columbia University Press, 1994)
– Kathleen Rowe, *The Unruly Woman: Gender and the Genres of Laughter* (Austin, TX: University of Texas Press, 1995)

6. CLASSIC GENRES REVIVED
– Gilbert Adair, *Hollywood's Vietnam: From The Green Beret to Full Metal Jacket* (London: William Heinemann, 1989)

– Jane Feuer, *The Hollywood Musical* (London: Macmillan/BFI Publishing, 1993)
– Steve Neale (ed.), *Genre and Contemporary Hollywood* (London: BFI Publishing, 2002)

7. AUTEURS AND INDEPENDENTS
– Yoram Allon, Del Cullen and Hannah Patterson (eds.), *The Wallflower Critical Guide to Contemporary North American Directors* (London: Wallflower Press, 2000)
– Geoff Andrew, *Stranger Than Paradise: Maverick Film-makers in Recent American Cinema* (London: Prion Books, 1998)
– Jim Hillier (ed.), *American Independent Cinema: A Sight & Sound Reader* (London: BFI Publishing, 2001)
– Xavier Mendik and Steven Jay Schneider (eds.), *Underground USA: Filmmaking Beyond the Hollywood Canon* (London: Wallflower Press, 2002)

8. X-RATED
– Jon Lewis, *Hollywood vs. Hardcore: How the Struggle over Censorship Saved the Modern Film Industry* (New York: New York University Press, 2000)
– Laurence O'Toole, *Pornocopia: Porn, Sex, Technology and Desire* (London: Serpent's Tail, 1998)
– Linda Williams, *Hard Core: Power, Pleasure and 'the Frenzy of the Visible'* (Berkeley, CA: University of California Press, 1999)

9. WOMEN AND FILM
– Alison Butler, *Women's Cinema: The Contested Screen* (London and New York: Wallflower Press, 2002)
– Diane Carson, Linda Dittmar and Janice Welsch, *Multiple Voices in Feminist Film Criticism* (Minneapolis, MN, and London: University of Minnesota Press, 1994)
– Gwendolyn A Foster, *Women Film Directors: An International Bio-critical Dictionary* (Westport, CT: Greenwood Press, 1995)
– Molly Haskell, *From Reverence to Rape: The Treatment of Women in the Movies* (New York: Holt, Rinehart and Winston, 1973)
– Maggie Humm, *Feminism and Film* (Edinburgh: Edinburgh University Press, 1997)
– E Ann Kaplan (ed.) *Feminism and Film* (Oxford: Oxford University Press, 2000)
– Julia Knight, *Women and the New German Cinema* (London: Verso, 1992)
– Annette Kuhn, *Women's Pictures: Feminism and Cinema*, 2nd ed. (London: Routledge and Kegan Paul, 1994)

– Annette Kuhn and Susannah Radstone (eds.), *The Women's Companion to International Film* (London: Virago, 1990)
– Christina Lane, *Feminist Hollywood: From Born in Flames to Point Break* (Detroit, MI: Wayne State University Press, 2000)
– Marsha McCreadie, *The Casting Couch and Other Front Row Seats: Women in Films of the 1970s and 1980s* (New York: Praeger, 1990)
– Patricia Mellencamp, *A Fine Romance: Five Ages of Feminism* (Philadelphia: Temple University Press, 1996)
– Murray Pomerance, *Ladies and Gentlemen, Boys and Girls: Gender in Film at the End of the Twentieth Century* (New York: SUNY Press, 2001)
– Jacinda Read, *The New Avengers: Feminism, Femininity and the Rape-revenge Cycle* (Manchester: Manchester University Press, 2000)
– Judith M Redding and Victoria A Brownworth, *Film Fatales: Independent Women Directors* (Seattle, WA: Seal Press, 1997)
– Ruby Rich, *Chick Flicks: Theories and Memories of the Feminist Film Movement* (Durham, NC: Duke University Press, 1998)
– Yvonne Tasker, *Working Girls: Gender and Sexuality in Popular Cinema* (London and New York: Routledge, 1998)
– Elizabeth G Traube, *Dreaming Identities: Class, Gender and Generation in 1980s Hollywood Movies* (Boulder, CO: Westview, 1992)
– Amy L Unterburger (ed.), *Women Filmmakers and their Films* (Detroit, MI: St James Press, 1998)

10. GAY AND LESBIAN CINEMA
– Corey K Creekmur and Alexander Doty (eds.), *Out in Culture: Gay, Lesbian and Queer Essays on Popular Culture* (London: Cassell, 1995)
– Alison Darren, *Lesbian Film Guide* (London: Cassell, 2000)
– Alexander Doty, *Flaming Classics: Queering the Film Canon* (London and New York: Routledge, 2000)
– Richard Dyer, *Now You See It: Studies in Lesbian and Gay Film* (London and New York: Routledge, 1990)
– Richard Dyer, *Culture of Queers* (London and New York: Routledge, 2001)
– Brett Farmer, *Spectacular Passions: Cinema, Fantasy, Gay Male Spectatorships* (Durham, NC: Duke University Press, 2000)
– Martha Gever, John Greyson and Pratibha Parmar (eds.), *Queer Looks: Perspectives on Lesbian and Gay Film and Video* (London and

New York: Routledge, 1993)
- Ellis Hanson (ed.), *Out Takes: Essays on Queer Theory and Film* (Durham, NC: Duke University Press, 1999)
- Judith Mayne, *Framed: Lesbians, Feminists and Media Culture* (Minneapolis, MN: University of Minnesota Press, 2000)
- Raymond Murray, *Images in the Dark: An Encyclopedia of Gay and Lesbian Film and Video* (London: Titan, 1998)
- Thomas Waugh, *The Fruit Machine: Twenty Years of Writings on Queer Cinema* (Durham, NC: Duke University Press, 2000)
- Andrea Weiss, *Vampires and Violets: Lesbians in the Cinema* (London: Cape, 1992)
- Clare Whatling, *Screen Dreams: Fantasising Lesbians in Film* (Manchester: Manchester University Press, 1997)
- Tamsin Wilton (ed.), *Immortal, Invisible: Lesbians and the Moving Image* (London and New York: Routledge, 1995)

11. HOLLYWOOD AND ETHNICITY
- Rosa Linda Fregoso, *The Bronze Screen: Chicana and Chicano Film Culture* (Minneapolis, MN: University of Minnesota Press, 1993)
- Diane Negra, *Off-White Hollywood: American Culture and Ethnic Female Stardom* (London and New York: Routledge, 2001)
- Chon A Noriega, *Chicanos and Film: Representation and Resistance* (Minneapolis: University of Minnesota Press, 1992)
- Chon A Noriega and Ana M López (eds.), *The Ethnic Eye: Latino Media Arts* (Minneapolis: University of Minnesota Press, 1996)
- Sharon Willis, *High Contrast: Race and Gender in Contemporary Hollywood Film* (Durham, NC: Duke University Press, 1997)

12. NATIONAL IDENTITIES IN WESTERN EUROPE
- Yoram Allon, Del Cullen and Hannah Patterson (eds.), *Contemporary British and Irish Film Directors* (London: Wallflower Press, 2001)
- Guy Austin, *Contemporary French Cinema: An Introduction* (Manchester: Manchester University Press, 1996)
- Francesco Bono and Maaret Koskinen (eds.), *Swedish Film Today* (Stockholm: Swedish Film Institute, 1996)
- Peter Cowie, *Scandinavian Cinema: A Survey of Films and Film-makers in Denmark, Finland, Iceland, Norway and Sweden* (London: Tantivy, 1992)
- Peter Cowie, Jan Erik Holst and

Astrid Dehli Blindheim, *Straight from the Heart: Modern Norwegian Cinema 1971–1999* (Kristiansund: Kom, 1999)
- Marvin D'Lugo, *Guide to the Cinema of Spain* (Westport, CT: Greenwood Press, 1997)
- Gwynne Edwards, *Indecent Exposures: Buñuel to Almdóvar* (London: Marion Boyars, 1995)
- Thomas Elsaesser, *New German Cinema* (London: Macmillan/BFI Publishing, 1989)
- Thomas Elsaesser and Michael Wedel (eds.), *The BFI Companion to German Cinema* (London: BFI Publishing, 1999)
- Peter William Evans (ed.), *Spanish Cinema: The Auteurist Tradition* (Oxford: Oxford University Press, 1999)
- Jill Forbes, *The Cinema in France: After the New Wave* (London: Macmillan/BFI Publishing, 1992)
- Manuela Gieri, *Contemporary Italian Filmmaking: Strategies of Subversion: Pirandello, Fellini, Scola and the Directors of the New Generation* (Toronto: University of Toronto Press, 1995)
- Terri Ginsberg and Kirsten Moana Thompson (eds.), *Perspectives on German Cinema* (London: G K Hall and Co, 1996)
- Susan Hayward, *French National Cinema* (London and New York: Routledge, 1993)
- Susan Hayward and Ginette Vincendeau (eds.), *French Films: Texts and Contexts* (London and New York: Routledge, 2000)
- John Hill, *British Cinema in the 1980s: Issues and Themes* (Oxford: Clarendon Press, 1999)
- Barry Jordan and Rikki Morgan-Tamosunas, *Contemporary Spanish Cinema* (Manchester: Manchester University Press, 1998)
- Marsha Kinder (ed.), *Refiguring Spain: Cinema/Media/ Representation* (Durham, NC: Duke University Press, 1997)
- Marcia Landy, *Italian Film* (Cambridge: Cambridge University Press, 2000)
- Martin McLoone, *Irish Film: The Emergence of a Contemporary Cinema* (London: BFI Publishing, 2000)
- Philip Mosley, *Split Screen: Belgian Cinema and Cultural Identity* (New York: SUNY Press, 2001)
- Robert Murphy (ed.), *British Cinema of the 90s* (London: BFI Publishing, 2000)
- Geoffrey Nowell-Smith, Gianni Volpi and James Hay (eds.), *The BFI Companion to Italian Cinema* (London: BFI Publishing 1996)
- Per Olov and Peter von Bagh, *Guide to the Cinema of Sweden and Finland* (Westport, CT: Greenwood Press, 2000)

- Phil Powrie, *French Cinema in the 1980s: Nostalgia and the Crisis of Masculinity* (Oxford: Clarendon Press, 1997)
- Phil Powrie (ed.), *French Cinema in the 1990s: Continuity and Difference* (Oxford: Oxford University Press, 1999)
- Paul Julian Smith, *The Moderns: Time, Space and Subjectivity in Contemporary Spanish Culture* (Oxford: Oxford University Press, 2000)
- Tytti Soila, Astrid Soderbergh Widding and Gunnar Iverson (eds.), *Nordic National Cinemas* (London and New York: Routledge, 1998)
- Matthew Stevens, *Directory of Contemporary Dutch Films and Filmmakers* (Trowbridge: Flicks Books, 1990)
- Rob Stone, *Spanish Cinema* (London: Pearson Education, 2002)
- Núria Triana Toribo, *Spanish National Cinema* (London and New York: Routledge, 2002)
- Ginette Vincendeau (ed.), *Encyclopedia of European Cinema* (London: Cassell/BFI Publishing, 1995)
- Mike Wayne, *The Politics of Contemporary European Cinema* (Bristol: Intellect, 2002)

13. EASTERN EUROPE AND THE FORMER SOVIET UNION
- Seán Allan and John Sandford, *DEFA: East German Cinema 1946-1992* (New York: Berghahn Books, 1999)
- Birgit Beumers, *Burnt by the Sun: The Film Companion* (London: I B Tauris, 2000)
- Frank Bren, *World Cinema 1: Poland* (Trowbridge: Flicks Books, 1990)
- Bryan Burns, *World Cinema 5: Hungary* (Trowbridge: Flicks Books, 1996)
- George Faraday, *Revolt of the Filmmakers: The Struggle for Artistic Autonomy and the Fall of the Russian Film Industry* (University Park, PA: Penn State University Press, 2000)
- Val S Golovskoy and John Rimberg, *Behind the Soviet Screen: The Motion-picture Industry in the USSR 1972–1982* (Ann Arbor, MI: Ardis, 1986)
- Daniel J Goulding, *Liberated Cinema: The Yugoslav Experience* (Bloomington, IN: Indiana University Press, 1985)
- Daniel J Goulding (ed.), *Post New Wave Cinema in the Soviet Union and Eastern Europe* (Bloomington, IN: Indiana University Press, 1989)
- Julian Graffy and Geoffrey Hosking, *Culture and the Media in the USSR Today* (London: Macmillan, 1989)

- Milada Hábová and Jitka Vysekalová (eds.), *Czechoslovak Cinema* (Prague: Československý Filmový Ústav, 1982)
- Ronald Holloway, *The Bulgarian Cinema* (Rutherford, NJ: Associated University Presses, 1986)
- Andrew Horton and Michael Brashinsky, *The Zero Hour: Glasnost and Soviet Cinema in Transition* (Princeton, NJ: Princeton University Press, 1992)
- Dina Iordanova, *Cinema of the 'Other Europe': The Industry and Artistry of East Central European Film* (London: Wallflower Press, 2003)
- Anna Lawton, *Kinoglasnost: Soviet Cinema in Our Time* (Cambridge: Cambridge University Press, 1992)
- Boleslaw Michalek and Frank Turaj, *The Modern Cinema of Poland* (Bloomington, IN: Indiana University Press, 1988)
- David W Paul, *Politics, Art and Commitment in the Eastern European Cinema* (New York: St Martin's Press, 1983)
- Thomas J Slater (ed.), *Handbook of Soviet and East European Films and Filmmakers* (New York: Greenwood Press, 1992)
- Michael J Stoil, *Balkan Cinema: Evolution after the Revolution* (Ann Arbor, MI: UMI Research Press, 1982)
- Richard Taylor, Nancy Wood, Julian Graffy and Dina Iordanova (eds.), *The BFI Companion to Eastern European and Russian Cinema* (London: BFI Publishing, 2000)

14. THE MIDDLE EAST AND THE MUSLIM WORLD
- Roy Armes, *Dictionary of North African Filmmakers/Dictionnaire des Cinéastes du Maghreb* (Paris: Editions ATM, 1996)
- Hind Rassam Culhane, *East/West, an Ambiguous State of Being: The Construction and Representation of Egyptian Cultural Identity in Egyptian Film* (New York: Peter Lang, 1995)
- Hamid Dabashi, *Close Up: Iranian Cinema Past Present and Future* (London: Verso Books, 2001)
- Mustafa Darwish, *Dream Makers on the Nile: A Portrait of Egyptian Cinema* (Cairo: American University in Cairo Press, 1998)
- Rose Issa and Sheila Whitaker (eds.), *Life and Art: The New Iranian Cinema* (London: BFI Publishing, 1999)
- W Kronish, *World Cinema 6: Israel* (Trowbridge: Flicks Books, 1996)
- Oliver Leaman (ed.), *Companion Encyclopedia of Middle Eastern and North African Film* (London and

New York: Routledge, 2001)
- Agah Ozguc, *A Chronological History of the Turkish Cinema 1914–1988* (Istanbul: Ministry of Culture and Tourism, 1988)
- Viola Shafik, *Arab Cinema: History and Cultural Identity* (Cairo: American University in Cairo Press, 1998)
- Ella Shohat, *Israeli Cinema: East/West and the Politics of Representation* (Austin, TX: University of Texas Press, 1989)
- Richard Tapper (ed.), *The New Iranian Cinema: Politics, Representation and Identity* (London: I B Tauris, 2002)

15. BOLLYWOOD AND NEW INDIAN CINEMA
- Sumitra S Chakravarty, *National Identity in Indian Popular Cinema* (Austin, TX: University of Texas Press, 1993)
- Wimal Dissanayake and Ashley Ratnavibhushana, *Profiling Sri Lankan Cinema* (Boralesgamuwa, Sri Lanka: Asian Film Centre, 2000)
- Rachel Dwyer and Divia Patel, *Cinema India: The Visual Culture of Hindi Film* (London: Reaktion Books, 2002)
- B D Garga, *So Many Cinemas: The Motion Picture in India* (Colaba, Bombay: Eminence Design, 1996)
- Mushtaq Gazdar, *Pakistan Cinema 1947–1997* (Karachi: Oxford University Press, 1997)
- K Moti Gokulsing and Wimal Dissanayake, *Indian Popular Cinema: A Narrative of Cultural Change* (Stoke-on-Trent: Trentham Books, 1998)
- Nasreen Munni Kabir, *Bollywood: The Indian Cinema Story* (London: Macmillan, 2001)
- Vijay Mishra, *Bollywood Cinema: Temples of Desire* (London and New York: Routledge, 2002)
- Ashis Nandy (ed.), *The Secret Politics of Our Desires: Innocence, Culpability and Indian Popular Cinema* (London: Zed Books, 1998)
- Ashish Rajadhyaksha and Paul Willemen (eds.), *Encyclopedia of Indian Cinema* (London: BFI Publishing, 1999)
- Yves Thoraval, *The Cinemas of India* (New Delhi: Macmillan, 2000)
- Aruna Vasudev, *Frames of Mind: Reflections on Indian Cinema* (New Delhi: UBSPD, 1995)
- Ravi S Vasudevan, *Making Meaning in Indian Cinema* (New Delhi: Oxford University Press, 2000)

16. AFRICAN VOICES
- Imruh Bakari and Mbye Cham (eds.), *African Experiences of Cinema* (London: BFI Publishing, 1996)

- Olivier Barlet, *African Cinemas: Decolonizing the Gaze* (London: Zed Books, 2000)
- J Blignaut and M Botha (eds.), *Movies, Moguls and Mavericks: South African Cinema 1979–91* (Cape Town: Showdata, 1992)
- Manthia Diawara, *African Cinema, Politics and Culture* (Bloomington, IN: Indiana University Press, 1992)
- June Givanni (ed.), *Symbolic Narratives/African Cinema: Audiences, Theory and the Moving Image* (London: BFI Publishing, 2000)
- Kenneth W Harrow (ed.), *African Cinema: Post-colonial and Feminist Readings* (Trenton, NJ: Africa World Press, 1999)
- Lizbeth Malkmus and Roy Armes, *Arab and African Film-making* (London: Zed Books, 1991)
- Françoise Pfaff, *Twenty-five Black African Filmmakers: A Critical Study* (Westport, CT: Greenwood Press, 1988)
- Sharon A Russell, *Guide to African Cinema* (Westport, CT: Greenwood Press, 1998)
- Keith Shiri (ed.), *Directory of African Film-makers and Films* (Trowbridge: Flicks Books, 1992)
- Keith Shiri, *Africa at the Pictures* (London: BFI Publishing, 1993)
- Frank Nwachukwu Ukadike, *Black African Cinema* (Berkeley, CA: University of California Press, 1994)

17. CINEMA IN THE FAR EAST
- Chris Berry (ed.), *Perspectives on Chinese Cinema* (London: BFI Publishing, 1991)
- David Bordwell, *Planet Hong Kong: Popular Cinema and the Art of Entertainment* (Cambridge, MA: Harvard University Press, 2000)
- Nick Browne, Paul G Pickowicz and Vivian Sobchack (eds.), *New Chinese Cinemas: Forms, Identities, Politics* (Cambridge: Cambridge University Press, 1994)
- Rey Chow, *Primitive Passions: Visuality, Sexuality, Ethnography and Contemporary Chinese Cinema* (New York: Columbia University Press, 1995)
- Sheila Cornelius, *New Chinese Cinema: Challenging Representations* (London: Wallflower Press, 2002)
- Joel David, *Fields of Vision: Critical Applications in Recent Philippine Cinema* (Quezon City: Ateneo de Manila University Press, 1995)
- Stephanie Hemelryk Donald, *Public Secrets, Public Spaces: Cinema and Civility in China* (Lanham, MD: Rowman and Littlefield, 2000)
- Linda C Ehrlich and David Desser (eds.), *Cinematic Landscapes: Observations on the Visual Arts and Cinema of China and Japan* (Austin,

TX: University of Texas Press, 1994)
- Poshek Fu and David Desser (eds.), *The Cinema of Hong Kong: History, Arts, Identity* (Cambridge: Cambridge University Press, 2000)
- Rafael Ma Guerrero (ed.), *Readings in Philippine Cinema* (Manila: Experimental Cinema of the Philippines, 1983)
- David Hanan (ed.), *Film in South East Asia: Views from the Region* (Hanoi: South East Asia-Pacific Audio Visual Archive Association, 2001)
- Sheldon Hsiao-peng Lu (ed.), *Transnational Chinese Cinemas: Identity, Nationhood, Gender* (Honolulu: University of Hawai'i Press, 1997)
- Jack Hunter, *Eros in Hell: Sex, Blood and Madness in Japanese Cinema* (London: Creation Books, 1998)
- Hyangjin Lee, *Contemporary Korean Cinema: Identity, Culture, Politics* (Manchester: Manchester University Press, 2000)
- Arthur Nolletti Jr and David Desser (eds.), *Reframing Japanese Cinema: Authorship, Genre, History* (Bloomington, IN: Indiana University Press, 1992)
- Tony Rayns and Simon Field, *Seoul Stirring: 5 Korean Directors* (London: ICA, 1995)
- Donald Richie, *A Hundred Years of Japanese Film* (Kodansha International, 2002)
- Emmanuel Ryes, *Notes on Philippine Cinema* (Manila: De La Salle University Press, 1989)
- Salim Said, *Shadows on the Silver Screen: A Social History of Indonesian Film* (Jakarta: Lontar, 1991)
- Mark Schilling, *Contemporary Japanese Film* (New York: Weatherhill, 1999)
- Krishna Sen, *Indonesian Cinema: Framing the New Order* (London: Zed Books, 1994)
- Jerome Silbergeld, *China into Film: Frames of Reference in Contemporary Chinese Cinema* (London: Reaktion Books, 1999)
- Lisa Odham Stokes and Michael Hoover, *City on Fire: Hong Kong Cinema* (London: Verso, 1999)
- Stephen Teo, *Hong Kong Cinema: The Extra Dimension* (London: BFI Publishing, 1997)
- Dennis Washburn and Carole Cavanaugh (eds.), *Word and Image in Japanese Cinema* (Cambridge: Cambridge University Press, 2001)
- Thomas Weisser and Yuko Mihara Weisser, *Japanese Cinema Encyclopedia: The Sex Films* (Miami, FL: Vital Books Inc, 1998)
- Ellen Widmer and David Der-wei Wang, *From May Fourth to June Fourth: Fiction and Film in Twentieth-Century China* (Cambridge, MA: Harvard University Press, 1993)

- Esther Yau (ed.), *At Full Speed: Hong Kong Cinema in a Borderless World* (Minneapolis, MN: University of Minnesota Press, 2001)
- Yingjin Zhang and Zhiwei Xiao, *Encyclopedia of Chinese Film* (London and New York: Routledge, 1998)
- Zudong Zhang, *Chinese Modernism in the Era of Reforms: Cultural Fever, Avant-garde Fiction and the New Chinese Cinema* (Durham, NC: Duke University Press, 1997)

18. CINEMA IN AUSTRALIA, CANADA, NEW ZEALAND
- Geoffrey B Churchman (ed.), *Celluloid Dreams: A Century of Film in New Zealand* (Wellington: IPL Books, 1997)
- David Clandfield, *Canadian Film* (Toronto: Oxford University Press, 1987)
- Ian Craven (ed.), *Australian Cinema in the 1990s* (London: Frank Cass, 2001)
- Jonathan Dennis and Jan Bieringa (eds.), *Film in Aotearoa, New Zealand* (Wellington: Victoria University Press, 1992)
- Susan Dermody and Elizabeth Jacka (eds.), *The Imaginary Industry: Australian Film in the Late 80s* (North Ryde, NSW: Australian Film, Television and Radio School, 1988)
- Michael Dorland, *So Close to the State/s: The Emergence of Canadian Feature Film Policy* (Toronto: University of Toronto Press, 1998)
- Christopher Gittings, *Canadian National Cinema* (London and New York: Routledge, 2001)
- Helen Martin and Sam Edwards, *New Zealand Film 1912–1996* (Auckland: Oxford University Press, 1997)
- Brian McFarlane, *Australian Cinema 1970–1985* (London: Secker & Warburg, 1987)
- Brian McFarlane, Geoff Mayer and Ina Betrand (eds.), *The Oxford Companion to Australian Film* (Melbourne: Oxford University Press, 1999)
- Scott Murray, Raffaele Caputo and Alissa Tanskaya (eds.), *Australian Film 1978–1994: A Survey of Theatrical Features* (Melbourne: Oxford University Press, 1995)
- Tom O'Regan, *Australian National Cinema* (London and New York: Routledge, 1996)
- Jonathan Rayner, *Contemporary Australian Cinema: An Introduction* (Manchester: Manchester University Press, 2000)
- Nicholas Reid, *A Decade of New Zealand Film: 'Sleeping Dogs' to 'Came a Hot Friday'* (Dunedin: John McIndoe, 1986)
- James Sabine (ed.), *A Century of

Australian Cinema* (Melbourne: William Heinemann, 1995)
- Graeme Turner, *National Fictions: Literature, Film and the Construction of Australian Narrative* (St Leonards, NSW: Allen & Unwin, 1993)

19. LATIN AMERICA
- Timothy Barnard and Peter Rist (eds.), *South American Cinema: A Critical Filmography 1915–1994* (New York: Garland, 1996)
- Charles Ramírez Berg, *Cinema of Solitude: A Critical Study of Mexican Film 1967–1983* (Austin, TX: University of Texas Press, 1992)
- Michael Chanan (ed.), *Chilean Cinema* (London: British Film Institute, 1976)
- Michael Chanan, *The Cuban Image* (London: BFI Publishing, 1985)
- David William Foster, *Contemporary Argentine Cinema* (Columbia, MO: University of Missouri Press, 1992)
- David William Foster, *Gender and Society in Contemporary Brazilian Cinema* (Austin, TX: University of Texas Press, 1999)
- Joanne Hershfield, *Mexico's Cinema: A Century of Film and Filmmakers* (Wilmington, DE: Scholarly Resources, 1999)
- Randal Johnson and Robert Stam, *Brazilian Cinema* (New York: Columbia University Press, 1995)
- John King, *Magical Reels: A History of Cinema in Latin America* 2nd ed. (London: Verso, 2000)
- John King, Ana M López and Manuel Alvarado (eds.), *Mediating Two Worlds: Cinematic Encounters in the Americas* (London: BFI Publishing, 1993)
- Michael T Martin (ed.), *New Latin American Cinema: Volume One: Theory, Practices, and Transcontinental Articulations* (Detroit, MI: Wayne State University Press, 1997)
- Michael T Martin (ed.), *New Latin American Cinema: Volume Two: Studies of National Cinemas* (Detroit, MI: Wayne State University Press, 1997)
- Carl J Mora, *Mexican Cinema: Reflections of a Society* (Berkeley: University of California Press, 1989)
- Ricardo Garcia Oliveri, *Argentine Cinema: A Chronicle of 100 Years* (Buenos Aires: Manrique Zago, 1997)
- Paulo Antonio Paranaguá (ed.), *Mexican Cinema* (London: BFI Publishing, 1995)
- Zuzana M Pick, *The New Latin American Cinema: A Continental Project* (Austin, TX: University of Texas Press, 1993)
- Robert Stam, *Tropical Multiculturalism: A Comparative

History of Race in Brazilian Cinema and Culture* (Durham, NC: Duke University Press, 1997)
- Ann Marie Stock (ed.), *Framing Latin American Cinema: Contemporary Critical Perspectives* (Minneapolis, MN: University of Minnesota Press, 1997)
- Ismail Xavier, *Allegories of Underdevelopment: Aesthetics and Politics in Modern Brazilian Cinema* (Minneapolis, MN: University of Minnesota Press, 1997)

20. CINEMA TOMORROW
- Ib Bondebjerg, *Moving Images, Culture and the Mind* (Luton: University of Luton Press, 2000)
- Wheeler Winston Dixon, *The Transparency of Spectacle: Meditations on the Moving Image* (Albany, NY: SUNY Press, 1998)
- Thomas Elsaesser and Kay Hoffman (eds.), *Cinema Futures: Cain, Abel or Cable? The Screen Arts in the Digital Age* (Amsterdam: Amsterdam University Press, 1998)
- Peter Lunenfeld, *The Digital Dialectic: New Essays on New Media* (Cambridge, MA: MIT Press, 2000)
- Lev Manovich, *The Language of New Media* (Cambridge, MA: MIT Press, 2001)
- Michael Rush, *New Media in Late 20th Century Art* (London: Thames and Hudson, 1999)
- Patrick von Sychowski, *Electronic Cinema: The Big Screen Goes Digital* (London: Screen Digest, 2000)

MISCELLANEOUS
- Roy Armes, *Third World Film-making and the West* (Berkeley, CA: University of California Press, 1987)
- Peter Cowie (ed.), *World Cinema: Diary of a Day* (London: Mitchell Beazley/BFI Publishing, 1994)
- Wimal Dissanayake (ed.), *Cinema and Cultural Identity: Reflections on Films from Japan, India and China* (Lanham, MD: University Press of America, 1988)
- Mette Hjort and Scott MacKenzie (eds.), *Cinema and Nation* (London and New York: Routledge, 2000)
- Fredric Jameson, *The Geopolitical Aesthetic: Cinema and Space in the World System* (London: BFI Publishing, 1992)
- Gorham Kindem (ed.), *The International Movie Industry* (Carbondale, IL: Southern Illinois University Press, 2000)
- John Pym (ed.), *Time Out Film Guide* (London: Penguin, 2001)
- *The Movie Book* (London: Phaidon Press, 1999)

Index

Acknowledgements

Author's Acknowledgements

I am fortunate in having received invaluable advice and the loan of materials from many whose knowledge is greater than mine. Such errors of fact and judgement as the book may contain are, of course, my own. I particularly wish to thank the following: Geoff Andrew, Birgit Beumers, Constanza Burucua, Roma Gibson, June Givanni, Peter Hames, David Hanan, Dina Iordanova, Clyde Jeavons, Nasreen Munni Kabir, John King, Oliver Leaman, Phil McDonald, Denise Miller, Toby Miller, Hamid Naficy, David Parkinson, Andrzej Pitrus, Catherine Portuges, Tony Rayns, Markku Salmi, Viola Shafik, Keith Shiri, Heather Stewart, Martin Stollery, Rosie Thomas and David Thompson. I have benefited greatly from the resources of the Library of the British Film Institute and the Internet Movie Database (www.imdb.com). Vivian Constantinopoulos commissioned this book and I hope she still feels she made the right decision. I could not have brought it to a conclusion without the tenacious and skilled editorial work of Victoria Clarke and Ann Simmonds, and Mari Knutsson must take much of the credit for the illustrations. I must also thank Stephen Coates whose design gives cohesion and vitality to the images and text. Finally, a special word of thanks to Sarah Boston, who sat through so many films with me – some wonderful, others only 'interesting'.

Illustration Acknowledgements

Aamir Khan Productions: 398B (Photo: Hardeep Singh Sachdev), 399ML; Amitabh Bachchan Corporation Limited (A.B.C.L): 395L; Arab Film Distribution: 371TR (Cinétéléfilms/Satpec); Arthur Cohn Productions: 483R (Photo: Walter Carvalho); ©Athanor, Courtesy Illuminations Films: 356BL (Photo: Boris Baromykin), 356R (Photo: Boris Baromykin); Aquarius Collection: 17BR (20th Century Fox/Aspen), 22T (Universal), 22BL (Universal), 24BL (20th Century Fox/LucasFilms), 29B (Paramount/Photo Stephen Vaughan), 41TR (Monarchy/Regency/Warner Bros/Photo: Merrick Morton), 41B (Polygram/Spelling), 56 (Eon Productions), 62–63 (Warner Bros/Ladd/Blade Runner Partnership), 78BR (Guild/Carolco/Pacific Western/Lightstorm), 89R (Warnes/Hoya), 92 (Lion's Gate/Photo: Kerry Hayes), 93R (Vortex/Tobe Hooper), 94BL (New Line/Media/Smart Egg/Elem Street Venture/Photo: Robert Shaye), 98TL (Paramount), 98LMR (Filmways), 111R (© Miramax Films), 125 (Paramount), 128BR (Castle Rock/Nelson Entertainment/Columbia), 135 (Warner Bros), 141TL (United Artists/Photo: Bruce McBroom), 142M (Paramount), 148B (Universal/Photo: David James), 149B (20th Century Fox/Photo: Merie W Wallace), 150–151 (© Disney Enterprises, Inc.), 152M (Dreamworks LLC), 152B (© Disney Enterprises Inc.), 153T (Dreamworks LLC/Allied Filmmakers/Aardmaan), 153B (Warner Bros/Photo: Peter Mountain), 163L (United Artists), 164T (Universal/ Photo: Philip V Caruso), 167TL (Paramount), 167B (Canal +/© Touchstone Pictures/ Photo: Melissa Moseley), 168B (© Touchstone Pictures/Photo: Suzanne Tanner), 173 (Paramount/Scott Rudin Productions/Photo: Melinda Sue Gordon), 176ML (Bedford Falls/Initial Entertainment/Photo: Bob Marshak), 186 (Vanguard Production), 188 (United Artists/PAA/PEA/Photo: Angelo Novi), 207T (Electric Pictures/Photo: Liam Longman), 221L (Merchant Ivory), 246B (© Buena Vista/Hollywood Pictures/Ixtlan Productions), 258–259 (CNC/France 2 Cinéma/Le Studio Canal +), 296T (El Deseo), 303T (Warner Bros/Goodtimes), 360–361 (Forum/Television of Sarajevo), 458B (Film Victoria/Momentum Films/AFFC/Photo: L Tomasetti), 460–461 (Working Title/Film Ariane/AFFC); BFI: 6–7 (Mirabai/Jane Balfour), 11 (MGM), 93L (Vortex/Tobe Hooper), 99L (© Touchstone Pictures/Photo: David Lee), 105TR (20th Century Fox-Brooksfilm/Photo: Attila Dory), 112–113 (Monty Python Films), 118B (Cinemarque – New World), 121B (Paramount), 171B (Perdido/Lexington Rd Prod/Photo: Shane Young), 176T (Outlaw), 190 (New Realm Pictures Ltd), 210T (MGM/Pathé Entertainment/Photo: Roland Neveu), 211B (MGM/Pathé Entertainment/Photo: Roland Neveu), 215 (Feature Film Company), 220B (Planet-Film/Albatross/Gaumont), 231 (Trial by Fire), 235 (Columbia), 237L (American Playhouse/WMG/Geechee), 253 British Film Institute, 261 (Cargo Films/Constellation/Photo: Marian Rosenstiehl), 264M (Paradise Films/Unite Trois), 266 (Action/Citel/Gaumont), 269 (Gaumont), 271BL (Road Movies Film Production/Argos Films/Channel Four), 274TL (TMS/Solaris/BBC/WDR), 275BL (Le Studio Canal +/MK2/Les Films Alain Sarde/CNC), 277BL (Orion), 278 (Alfa), 287BR (RAI/IC/GPC), 291L (Iberoamericana/Ellepi/TV Espanola), 291R (Lola Films/Ovideo TV), 292R (Sociedad General de Cine), 293 (El Desea-Lauren), 293 (El Desea-Lauren), 296M (El Deseo), 296B (El Deseo), 298B (Photo: Teresa Isasi), 299T (Madragoa/Gemini/Light Night), 299B (CNC/ICAM/Le Studio Canal +/Madragoa Filmes/RTP), 302 (Warner Bros/Russo), 306TR (Columbia), 308 (BFI/Channel Four Films), 309BR (Ciby 2000/Photo: Simon Mein), 310–311 (Thin Man/Alain Sarde/Studio Canal/Photo: Simon Mein), 312BR (Fox Searchlight), 313TR (Polygram), 314–315 (Polygram), 316 (Warner/Goldcrest/Enigma), 318–319 (Svenska Film Institutet/SVT Dama/Gaumont), 320TR (Svenska Film Institutet/SVT Drama/Gaumont), 320TL (Svenska Film Institutet/SVT Drama/Gaumont), 324BL (Zentropa Entertainment), 325 (Central Film/Kommunenes Film/Norsk Film AS), 326–327 (Guild/Zentropa/Trust/Liberator/Argus/Northern Lights), 338BL (Lenfilm), 341B (Gorky Film Studios), 342TR (CTB Film Company/Gorky Film Studios/Roskomkino), 342BL (CTB Film Company/ORT), 346 M (MK2/CAB/CED Productions/Artificial Eye/Photo: Piotr Jaxa), 346B (MK2/CAB/CED Productions/Artificial Eye/Photo: Piotr Jaxa), 348 (MK2/CAB/Le Studio Canal +), 349 (Siderel Productions/Canal + /Photo: Monika Jeziorowska), 351L (MAFILM Objektív Filmstúdió), 351BR (Hungarofilm), 354R (Filmove Studio Barrandov), 355T (Filmove Studio Barrandov), 356TL (Casa de filme 1), 357R (Boyana Film/Sofia Film Studios), 358 (DEFA - Studio für Spielfilme), 359 (Connoiseur Films Ltd), 362L (Forum/Television of Sarajevo), 362R (CIBY), 367BR (MISR International Films/La Sept/Paris Classics Productions), 368–369 (MISR International Films/La Sept/Paris Classics Productions), 370T (Films A2/MISR International Films), 370L (ONCIC/Arab Film Distribution), 373 (Les Films du Losange/Maghrebfilms Cartharge/Arte France Cinema), 374B (2M/Alexis Films/Canal +/Playtime), 375TL (Istinai Filmler Ve Reklamas Ltd), 376TL (Art Cam/Filma Cass), 376TR (8 Productions/ACCI/CNC/La Sept Arte), 377 (Noah Films), 383TR (Makhmalbaf Productions/Studio Canal), 384 (Jafar Panahi Film Productions/Mikado Lumière & Co), 385R (MK2/Makhmalbaf Productions), 401TL (Indus Films), 401ML (Mrinal Sen Productions), 401BR (Film Valas), 402–403 (Mirabai/Photo: Jane Balfour), 404TL (Mirabai Films/Delhi Dot Com), 404BR (Tropicfilm), 406BL (Government of West Bengal), 407 (The National Film Corporation of Sri Lanka), 408–409 (California Newsreel), 411 (Films Domireew/Ste. Me. Production du Senegal), 413 (California Newsreel), 414 (ADR Productions/Thelma Film AG), 415M (Grey Films/Shango Films), 416T (Les Films Cissé/Les Films du Carrosse/CNC), 416M (Les Films Cissé/Les Films du Carrosse/CNC), 417 (Les Films Cissé/Les Films du Carrosse/CNC), 418 (California Newsreel), 420–421 (MGM), 423T (© Miramax Films/BBC/Vanguard Films), 423B (Goi-Goi Productions/Ministry of Promotion and Development/Tele-Chad), 428R (Century Communication/China Film Co-production Corporation/ERA International/Salon Films), 431T (Artificial Eye/Thomson/China Film/Beijing Film), 432R (Beijing Film Studio/Asiatic Films/Eastern Television), 433R (Beijing Bastards Group), 434 (New Line/Roger Birnbaum/Photo: Bob Marshak), 436T (Bluebird Photoplays Inc), 436B (Block 2 Pictures/Jet Tone), 438M (3H Productions/Shochiku Co. Ltd), 438B (Atomfilms/Omega/Pony Canyon Inc.), 439T (3H Productions/Shochiku Co. Ltd), 439B (Cinemien/Stimkim), 440L (Hisa Ino/Kiss Films), 441 (Herald Ace/Nippon Herald/Greenwich), 445R (Kadokawa Shoten Publishing Co. Ltd/Omega Project), 447 (Cinema Service/Taewon Entertainment), 448–449 (Productions Lazemmec/La SFP/La Sept/Canal +), 450 (Productions Lazemmec/La SFP/La Sept/Canal +), 451B (Aichi Arts Center/Film Bangkok /Five Star Productions Inc), 457R (Mad Max), 463B (CNC/NFB/Le Studio Canal +/Telefilms Canada), 464TR (CNC/NFB/Telefilm Canada), 465 (NFB/The Ontario Arts Council/Telefilm Canada), 466B (Igloolik Isuma/CTV), 466–467M (Igloolik Isuma/CTV), 468–469 (Alta Vista), 470 (Productiones Panicas), 473 (IMCINE/Ivania Films/MK2 Productions), 474BR (Anhelo Producciones), 475B (Alta Vista), 476 (Aries Cinematográfica Argentina/ICA), 477TR (Aura Film/Mojame SA/Oscar Kramer SA), 477L (Naya Films), 478–479 (GEA Producciones/Impala Film), 481B (Carnaval Unifilm/Gaumont/Luiz Carlos Barreto Produções Cinematográficas), 482 (Le Studio Canal +/MACT Productions/Riofilmes), 483L (Cine Experimental de la Universidad de Chile/Cinematográfica Tercer Mondo), 484TR (ICAIC), 485 (Grupo Ukamau/TVE/Channel Four Films), 486T (Inca Films SA), 486B (Compañía de Fomento Cinematográfico/FOCINE/Producciones Tiempos Modernos Ltd), 487 (Arion Productions/Pandora Films); Bubonic Films: 406TL (Photo: Omar Ali Khan/Design: S Khan, Lahore); Cinéplus/Les Archives du Cinéma: 94BR (New Line/Media/Smart Egg/Elem Street Venture/Photo: Robert Shaye), 210B (UIP/Pathé Entertainment); Courtesy Cineteca Argentino: 474 TL (Jaime Humberto Hermosillo), 474ML (Jaime Humberto Hermosillo), 474BL (Jaime Humberto Hermosillo); COE photographic archives: 415T (Cinegrit/Studio Kankourama), 422T (Afrocult Foundation); Conaculta Cineteca Nacional Mexico: 471BL (Clasa Films Mundiales); Corbis UK Ltd: 255L (Filmel/Cinevideo), 389 (© Catherine Karnow/CORBIS), 410L (© Caroline Penn/CORBIS), 416BL (© Caroline Penn/CORBIS); Deutsches Filminstitut, Frankfurt: 108L (Gaumont), 207TL (Bioskop), 267L (Action/FR3/Citel/Janus), 340R (Goskino/Odessa Film Studio), 341T (Mosfilm), 346T (MK2/CAB/CED Productions/Artificial Eye/Photo: Piotr Jaxa); Courtesy Somaratne Dissanayake: 406B (Rupareka Productions); El Deseo: 297TR; Courtesy Jillali Ferhati: 374TL (Heracles Productions); Film Archiv Austria: 262TR (Films A2/Films Christian Fechner/Gaumont), 263T (Channel Four Films/Ciné Tamaris /Films A2), 265T (Iblis Film), 271TL (Waldleitner/Roxy/CIP), 275TL (© Cult Film/Progress Film), 328TL (Dis Film/Europa Film AS), 333B (101 Ltd/Filmhuset AS/Icelandic Film Fund/Liberator Productions), 340L (Kazakhfilm Studios); Joel Finler Collection: 12–13 (Paramount), 15 (20th Century Fox), 18–19 (20th Century Fox/Aspen), 46TL (Rank Film Distribution/Manifesto), 48TL (United Artists/Photo: Elliott Marks), 48ML (United Artists/Photo: Elliott Marks), 77 (Warner Bros/DC Comics), 88 (Paramount), 98TR (Filmways), 98UMR (Filmways), 105BL (20th Century Fox-Brooksfilm), 109 (Geffen Pictures/Photo: Francois Duhamel), 110 (Columbia Tristar/American Zoetrope/Osiris), 114BL (Orion/Warner Bros/Photo: Bruce McBroom), 134BL (Cinema Center), 147T (Omni Zoetrope), 181 (12 Gauge Productions/Pandora), 187 (Connoisseur Films Ltd), 189BR (United Artists/PAA/PEA), 194 TL (CaseyProds/Eldorado Films), 194ML (CaseyProds/Eldorado Films), 194BL (CaseyProds/Eldorado Films), 225BR (Columbia Tri-Star), 236T (Universal/Photo: David Lee), 240 (Paramount), 254TL (Joel Finler Collection), 284–285 (Cristaldifilm/Films Ariane), 307 (Indo-British/International Film Investors), 323BL (Det Danske Filminstitut/Panorama), 364–365 (Güney Film/Cactus Film), 375R (Güney Film/Cactus Film), 400, 440B (Herald Ace/Nippon Herald/Greenwich), 453L (Cine Manila Artist); Hyphen Films Collection: 386–387 (Madras Talkies), 388 (Madras Talkies), 390T (Madras Talkies), 390B (Madras Talkies), 391T (Yashraj Films), 391M (Yashraj Films), 391B (Yashraj Films), 392T (Bhansali Productions), 393T (Sippy Films/United Producers), 397 (Arclightz and Films Pvt. Ltd/Dreamz Unlimited), 399T (Aamir Khan Productions/Photo: Hardeep Singh Sachdev); Image.net: 376B (Vision Pictures); Kavithalayaa Productions: 395R; Kipa: 94T (Cat's), 282BR (Mars/Marianne/Maran), 250–251 (Werner Herzog Filmproduktion), 481T (Glauber Rocha Comunicações Artísticas/Producoes Cinematograficas Mapa); The Kobal Collection: 4–5 (Warner Bros/Polestar/Hobby/Photo: Manuel Harlan), 14 (Photo: Neil Setchfield), 17BL (20th Century Fox/Aspen), 20L (Paramount), 20R (Paramount), 21 (Warner Bros/Photo: Josh Weiner), 22BR (Universal/Louis Goldman), 23L (Universal/Louis Goldman), 23R (Universal), 24R (20th Century Fox/LucasFilms), 25 (20th Century Fox/LucasFilms), 26–27 (20th Century Fox/LucasFilms/Photo: John Jay), 27T (20th Century Fox/LucasFilms/Photo: John Jay), 27M (20th Century Fox/LucasFilms/Photo: John Jay), 27B (20th Century Fox/LucasFilms/Photo: John Jay), 28T (20th Century Fox/LucasFilms),28B (20th Century Fox/LucasFilms), 30–31 (20th Century Fox/Paramount/Photo: Merie W Wallace), 32 (20th Century Fox/Paramount/Photo: Merie W Wallace), 32 (PBS), 34–35 (© Miramax Films and Buena Vista/Photo: Linda R Chen), 38–39 (20th Century Fox), 40B (Paramount), 41TL (Monarchy/Regency/Warner Bros/Photo: Merrick Morton), 42T (Paramount/Photo: Andrew Schwartz), 42B (Paramount/Photo: Andrew Schwartz), 43T (Navaron Films), 43L (River Road Prods), 44 (Columbia/Photo: Josh Weiner), 45L (Columbia/Photo: Josh Weiner), 45MR (Columbia/Photo: Josh Weiner), 46B (© Miramax Films and Buena Vista/Photo: Linda R Chen), 47 (© Miramax Films and Buena Vista), 48TR (Columbia/Tri-Star/Photo: Bruce McBroom), 49T (20th Century Fox/Photo: Zade Rosenthal), 51 (Carolco/Indieprod/Photo: Juergen Vollmer), 52TL (Warner Bros/Photo: John Shannon), 52BR (Warner Bros/Photo: John Shannon), 52–53 (Warner Bros/Photo: John Shannon), 53T (Warner Bros/Photo: John Shannon), 53M (Warner Bros/Photo: John Shannon), 53B (Warner Bros/Photo: John Shannon), 54 (20th Century Fox/Sorel, Peter), 55 (20th Century Fox/Photo: Peter Sorel), 57 (Eon Productions/Photo: George Whitear), 58–59 (Paramount/Photo: Murray Close), 60 (20th Century Fox/Warners), 61TL (Milestone), 61TR (20th Century Fox/Photo: Richard Foreman), 61B (Paramount/© Touchstone Pictures/Photo: Stephen Vaughan), 64T (MGM/Stanley Kubrick), 67TR (Universal), 67B (Universal), 68–69 (Dreamworks LLC/Warner Bros/Photo: David James), 70TL (Jack H Harris Enterprises), 70BL (20th Century Fox/Brandywine), 71 (20th Century Fox/Brandywine/Photo: Bob Penn), 74–75 (Ladd Company/Warner Bros), 76 (Ladd Company/Warner Bros/Photo: Stephen Vaughan), 78BL (Guild/Carolco/Pacific Western/Lightstorm/Photo: Zade Rosenthal), 79T (Guild/Carolco/Pacific Western/Lightstorm/Photo: Zade Rosenthal), 79B (Guild/Carolco/Pacific Western/Lightstorm/Photo: Zade Rosenthal), 80–81 (Warner Bros/Village Roadshow), 84–85 (20th Century Fox), 86–87 (Orion/Photo: Ken Regan), 90–91 (Warnes/Hoya/Photo: Josh Weiner), 95 (Maljack Prods), 96–97 (Orion/Photo: Ken Regan), 99 (New Line Cinema/Photo: Peter Sorel), 100–101 (New Line Cinema/Photo: Peter Sorel), 102 (United Artists/Redbank/Photo: Dave Friedman), 103TL (Universal/Photo: Rick Porter), 103BR (Mantle Clinic II/Photo: Attila Dory), 104 (20th Century Fox-Brooksfilm/Photo: Attila Dory), 105TL (20th Century Fox-Brooksfilm/Photo: Attila Dory), 106T (Monarchia), 106BL (ADC Films), 108T (Kaiju Theatre Productions), 115 (MGM/United Artists/Photo: David Appleby), 116TL (Columbia/Photo: Peter Sorel), 116R (Monty Python Films/Photo: David Appleby), 116BL (20th Century Fox/Photo: Jack Rowand), 117 (Universal), 118T (20th Century Fox/Photo: Don

Smetzer), 119TL (Universal/Photo: Vivian Zink), 119B (20th Century Fox/Photo: Glenn Watson), 120T (Morgan Creek International/Photo: J Farmer), 120B (Paramount/Photo: Philip V Caruso), 121T (Paramount/Photo: Bob Akester), 121M (Paramount/Photo: Bob Akester), 122 (© Touchstone Pictures), 123 (20th Century Fox/Photo: Phil Bray), 124R (Columbia/Photo: Joseph Lederer), 126L (MGM/United Artists/Photo: David James), 127 (New Line/Tribeca/Photo: Philip V Caruso), 128T (Warner Bros), 130–131 (Guild Films Distributors/Photo: Ben Glass), 132–133 (Dreamworks LLC/Universal/Photo: Jaap Buitendijk), 133R (United Artists), 134T (Warner 7 Arts), 134BR (Warner Bros/Photo: Marcia Reed), 136T (United Artists/Photo: Ernst Haas), 138–139 (20th Century Fox/Morgan Creek/Photo: Frank Connor), 140 (Paramount), 141BL (20th Century Fox/Photo: Sue Adler), 141BR (MGM), 142T (Warner Bros/Photo: Howard Bingham), 142B (Warner Bros/Photo: Ben Glass), 143T (Working Title/Havoc/Photo: Demmie Todd), 143B (Columbia/Photo: Holly Bower), 144 (Orion/Photo Ricky Francisco), 145T (Universal/EMI), 145B (United Artists), 146–147 (Omni Zoetrope), 147MR (Omni Zoetrope), 147BR (Omni Zoetrope), 148T (Universal/Photo: David James), 149T (Universal/Photo: Roland Neveu), 149BL (Warner Bros/Amblin/Photo: Murray Close), 154–155 (Warner Bros/Polaris/Hawk Films), 156B (Paramount), 161L (Warner Bros/Polaris/Hawk Films), 164UM (Universal/Photo: Philip V Caruso), 165 (Universal/Philip V Caruso), 166TL (Taplin-Perry-Scorsese/Warner Bros), 166TR (Warner Bros/Photo: Barry Wetcher), 166BR (Paramount/Pierre Associates/Photo: John Shannon), 167R (AFI/Libra), 169 (Geffen/Warner Bros), 170 (Working Title/Polygram/Photo: Michael Tackett), 171TR (© Touchstone Pictures/Universal/Photo: Melinda Sue Gordon), 171TL (Working Title/Photo: Melinda Sue Gordon), 172T (Warner Bros/Photo: Merrick Morton), 172B (New Line/Photo: Peter Sorel), 174–175 (New Line Cinema), 176B (Bedford Falls/Initial Entertainment/Photo: Bob Marshak), 177 (Abstrakt/Gramercy/IMF/Photo: Bruce Birmelin), 178 (Zenith/Killer Films/Channel 4/Photo: Peter Mountain), 180B (Zenith/UGC/True Fiction/Photo: Richard Ludwig), 183 (Warner Bros/Photo: Murray Close), 184–185 (De Laurentiis/Photo: Umberto Montiroli), 189T (United Artists/PAA/PEA/Photo: Angelo Novi), 189M (United Artists/PAA/PEA/Photo: Angelo Novi), 189BL (United Artists/PAA/PEA/Photo: Angelo Novi), 191T (Artistes Associes/PEA), 192–193 (Argos/Oshima/Shiba Daiei/Nippon Herald), 195 (MGM/United Artists/Photo: Barry Wetcher), 196L (Saul Zaentz Company/Photo: Phil Bray), 198 (Warner Bros/Polestar/Hobby/Photo: Manuel Harlan), 199T (New Line/Photo: G Lefkowitz), 199B (CTB Film/Soyuzkino), 202L (Warner Bros), 202B (Warner Bros), 203L (20th Century Fox), 203R (20th Century Fox), 205L (Lightstorm Entertainment/Photo: Merie W Wallace), 205B (Lightning Pictures/Photo: Joel Warren), 206 (Carolco/Rambling Rose/Midnight Sun/Photo: Merie W Wallace), 206R (Sigma Films), 207B (Westdeutcher Rundfunk), 211T (MGM/Pathé Entertainment/Photo: Roland Neveu), 213 (Fried Green Tomatoes Productions), 214

(Universal/Photo: Bob Marshak), 216–217 (New Line), 218 (Warner Bros/Photo: Muky), 221T (Dreamland Productions), 221BR (HB Filmes/Sugarloaf Films), 222–223 (BFI/Channel 4), 224T (New Line), 224B (Working Title/Channel 4/Photo: Mike Laye), 226T (Fox Searchlight/Photo: Bill Matlock), 226B (Fox Searchlight/Photo: Bill Matlock), 227T (Alliance Releasing/Dansk F/Memphis/SVT/SVI), 228–229 (Polygram/Australian Film Finance/Photo: Elise Lockwood), 230L (Brad Zions Films/Photo: Hope Wurmfeld), 232–233 (MGM), 234L (Melvin van Peebles), 234R (MGM), 236B (Warner Bros/Photo: David Lee), 237R (SVS Films), 238–239 (40 Acres and a Mule/New Line/Photo: David Lee), 241 (Tri-Star/Photo: Forooz Zahedi), 242–243 (Columbia/Photo: Frank Connor), 244L (20th Century Fox/Photo: Nicola Goodge), 245 (Lions Gate/Photo: Jeanne Louise Bulliard), 247 (Central Motion Pictures/Samuel Goldwyn Productions), 248T (Columbia/Sony/United China Vision/Photo: Chan Kam Chuen), 249 (Columbia/Sony/United China Vision/Photo: Chan Kam Chuen), 265BL (Les Artistes Anonymes/Photo: Jean-Claude Moschetti), 265BR (Les Artistes Anonymes/Photo: Jean-Claude Moschetti), 268TR (Filmverlag der Autoren/Herzog/Zweite Deutsches Fernsehen), 270 (Tango/Film Verlag der Autorem), 272–273 (Seitz/Bioskop/Hallelujah), 274TR (Bavaria/Radiant/Twin Brothers/Photo: Karl Heinz Stempel), 274B (X Filme Creative Pool/Photo: Bernd Spauke), 277BR (De Verenigde Nederlandsche Film Compagnie), 280–281 (MGM), 282T (Artistes Associes/PEA), 283B (Stella/Bibo TV/Anthea/PEA), 286 (Italoneglio/Lotar Film), 288–289 (© Miramax Films/Dimension Film), 294–295 (El Desea-Lauren), 300T, 300BL (Centre du Cinema Grec), 304–305 (20th Century Fox/Allied Stars/Enigma/Photo: Graham Attwood), 306TL (Columbia/Photo: Murray Close), 309T (Parallax/Photo: Paul Chedlow), 309BL (Ciby 2000/Photo: Simon Mein), 312TR (Polygram/Photo: Clive Coote), 313BR (Channel 4 Film Consortium/UA/Revolution/Photo: John Shard), 313L (Polygram/Ska Films/Photo: Sebastian Pearson), 317L (Palace Pictures/Photo: Tom Hilton), 317R (Geffen/Warner Bros/Photo: Tom Collins), 320B (Per Holst/Egmont/SF1/SVT/Photo: Rolf Konow), 321 (Svensk Filmindustri/AB Film-Teknik/Photo: Denise Grunstein), 328BL (Moviemakers), 329 (Norsk Film AS), 334–335 (Film Polski), 336 (Mosfilm), 343 (Studio Trite/Camera One), 344TL (Severny Fond/O-Film), 345TL, 350T (Jadran Film), 350B (Film Polski), 352–353 (MA Film/Studio Objectiv), 354L (MA Film/Studio Objectiv), 355M (Czech TV/THA/Photo: Martin Spelda), 355B (Czech TV/THA/Photo: Martin Spelda), 363 (Vardar), 371B (Cinétéléfilms/Scarabee/Photo: Anouar Ben Aissa), 378–379 (Agav Hafakot/MP Productions/Canal +), 381B (MK2/Kiarostami Productions), 385L (MK2/Makhmalbaf Productions), 398T (Aamir Khan Productions/Photo: Hardeep Singh Sachdev), 399MR (Aamir Khan Productions/Photo: Hardeep Singh Sachdev), 399BR (Aamir Khan Productions/Photo: Hardeep Singh Sachdev), 405 (Bend it/Road Movies/Roc Media/The Film Council), 412–413 (Films de L'Avenir/Waka/Rhea), 426L (© Miramax Films/Photo: Lawrence Ng), 432L (Columbia-Tristar), 433L (Concord Productions Inc/Golden Harvest Company Ltd), 435R (Film

Workshop), 442BR (Altamura), 443 (Right Vision/Bandai), 446 (CJ Entertainment/Taehung Pictures), 453B (Strand Release), 456 (Picnic/BEF/Australian Film Commission/Photo: David Kynosh), 457T (Paramount/Photo: Barry Wetcher), 458T (Chapman Productions/AFFC), 459B (New Zealand Film Commission/Photo: Kerry Brown), 462BL (Jan Chapman Prods/Ciby 2000/Photo: Polly Walker), 463T (New Line/Saul Zaentz/Wing Nut/Photo: Pierre Vinet), 464R (Speaking Parts/Alliance Commission/Photo: Johnnie Eisen), 466M (Igloolik Isuma/CTV), 467BL (Igloolik Isuma/CTV), 472T (IMCINE/Ivania Films/MK2 Productions), 472B (Ivania/IMCINE), 475T (Alta Vista); Movie Boy: 37 1L (Cinétéléfilms/Satpec); The Moviestore Collection: 2–3 (Warner Bros/Malpasc), 37 (Warner Bros/Malpasc); Photos 12/Collection Cinema: 49B (Universal), 78TR (Guild/Carolco/Pacific Western/Lightstorm), 106BR (Seda Spettacolli/International Classics – 20th Century Fox); 220BL (Planet-Film/Albatross/Gaumont), 225TL (Bronze Eye), 230T (Central Motion Picture Corp./Good Machine), 248B (Columbia/Sony/Photo: Chan Kam Chuen), 252 (Anouchka Films/Empire Films/Vicco Films), 254TR (Les Films du Losange/Renn Productions), 256L (Les Films du Losange), 262L (CAPAC/Société Nouvelle Prodis/UPF), 264T (Mathonet/Cinevog/Taurus), 267R (Pandora Filmproduktion/Prisma Film/T&C Film), 279L (F.C. Rome/P.E.C.F.PARIS), 279R (F.C. Rome/P.E.C.F.PARIS), 297L (El Deseo/Photo: Miguel Bracho), 297BR (El Deseo/Photo: Miguel Bracho), 298T (Las Producciones del Escorpión SL/Les Films Alain Sarde/Sociedad General de Televisión SA), 301(ETI), 308B (Merchant Ivory/Goldcrest), 312L (Beacon Communications/20th Century Fox), 333T (Sputnik OY), 338BR (Mosfilm), 344TR (Artificial Eye Film Company Ltd), 344BR (Artificial Eye Film Company Ltd), 366T (General Egyptian Cinema Organisation), 366B (MISR International Films/AISR International Films), 367TL (MISR International Films), 367BL (MISR International Films), 372T (Cinétéléfilms/Mat Films), 372BR (Amilcar Films/Mandala Productions), 372BL (Amilcar Films/Mandala Productions), 380 (LPA/Marisa Films), 381T (Institute for the Development of Children and Young Adults/ICA), 382–383 (Makhmalbaf Productions/Studio Canal), 383BR (Makhmalbaf Productions/Studio Canal), 410B (Films Domireew/Ste. Me. Production du Senegal), 415B (Les Films Cissé/Les Films du Carrosse/CNC), 435L (International Film Company/Lian Bang/Union Film Company), 438TL (Central Motion Pictures Corporation), 451L (Brink Creative/Springroll Entertainment/Zhao Wei Films), 452 (Christine Hakim Film), 454–455 (Jan Chapman Prods/Ciby 2000/Photo: Polly Walker), 466T (Igloolik Isuma/CTV), 467T (Igloolik Isuma/CTV), 484TL (Le Studio Canal+/CNC/France 2 Cinema/Genemi Films); Pictorial Press: 182L (View Askew), 194R (Blue Light), 246T (American Playhouse); Prakash Mehra Productions: 392L; Elias Querejeta PCSL: 290; The Ronald Grant Archive: 16 (Columbia/Photo: Peter Sorel), 17 (Columbia/Photo: Bernie Abramson), 24TL (Universal), 29L (© 1979 20th Century Fox), 36L (Monarchy/Regency/Photo: Frank Connor), 36R (Monarchy/Regency/Photo: Frank Connor), 40T

(Paramount/Long Road), 45T (Columbia/Photo: Josh Weiner), 45B (Columbia/Photo: Josh Weiner), 46TR (Live Entertainment), 48B (United Artists/Photo: Elliott Marks), 50 (Tri-Star), 64TL (© Disney Enterprises, Inc.), 64BL (© Disney Enterprises, Inc.), 65 (MGM), 66 (Columbia/Photo: Pete Turner), 67L (20th Century Fox/LucasFilms/Photo: John Jay), 70TR (UIP/Universal/Amblin Entertainment/Photo: Murray Close), 72L (20th Century Fox/Brandywine/Photo: Bob Penn), 72R (20th Century Fox/Photo: Bob Penn), 73L (20th Century Fox/Photo: Bob Penn), 73TR (20th Century Fox/Photo: Suzanne Stenner), 73BR (20th Century Fox/Photo: Suzanne Stenner), 82T (Orion/Photo: S Karin Epstein), 82B (Columbia Tri-Star/Photo: Stephen Vaughan), 83 (Columbia/Photo: Melinda Sue Gordon), 89L (Image Ten), 98B (Filmways), 103BL (Mantle Clinic II/Photo: Attila Dory), 107 (K2 Spirit/Kaijyu Theater/SEN), 111B (Universal/ILM (Industrial Light & Magic/Photo: Keith Hamshire), 114T (Universal), 119TR (Columbia/Photo: Melissa Moseley), 124L (Universal/Photo: Philip V Caruso), 126T (Polygram/Channel 4/Working Title/Photo: Stephen Morley), 129 (New Line), 136B (Alliance/Goldwyn/Photo: Takashi Seida), 137 (Guild Films Distributors/Photo: Ben Glass), 146B (Omni Zoetrope/Photo: Chas Gerretsen), 152TL (© Touchstone Pictures and Amblin Entertainment Inc./Photo: Bob Penn), 156TL (Tri-Star/Photo: Brian Hammill), 156TL (Tri-Star/Photo: Brian Hammill), 157 (United Artists/Photo: Brian Hammill), 158–159 (Paramount), 160T (Spelling/Fine Line/Photo: Joyce Rudolph), 160B (Warner Bros/Polaris), 161T (Warner Bros/Polaris/Hawk Films), 161MR (Warner Bros/Polaris/Hawk Films), 161B (Warner Bros/Polaris/Hawk Films), 162 (Warner Bros), 163TR (United Artists/Fantasy Films/Photo: Peter Sorel), 163B (Saul Zaentz Company/Photo: Phil Bray), 164LM (Universal/Photo: Philip V Caruso), 164B (Universal/Photo: Philip V Caruso), 168TR (Paramount/Photo: Edie Baskin), 168TL (Paramount/Photo: Edie Baskin), 180T (October Films/Photo: Henny Garunkel), 180M (American Playhouse/Channel 4/Photo: Gabòr Szitanyl), 182T (Westerley Films), 191B (Trinacra/Orphee/Photo: Dave Freidman), 196BR (Columbia/Tri-Star/Photo: Sidney Baldwin), 197 (Carolco), 200–201 (Electric Pictures/Photo: Liam Longman), 204 (Orion/Photo: Andrew Schwartz), 208–209 (Paramount/Photo: Rob McEwan), 212 (Tri-Star/Photo: Zade Rosenthal), 218T (Spike Prod/BBC/Photo: Anne Fishbein), 219 (BFI/Channel 4/Photo: Mike Laye), 220T (United Artists/PAA/DA MA/Photo: Mario Tursei), 225TR (Artificial Eye Film Co. Ltd), 227L (Guild Film Distribution Ltd/Photo: Bernard Prim), 244B (Independent Productions/American Playhouse), 254B (CNC/George Reinhart Productions/Le Studio Canal +), 256BR (Les Films du Carrosse/STP/Sédif Productions/TF1), 257 (DD Productions/Films A2/Renn Productions/Photo: George Pierre), 260T (Cargo Films/Constellation/Photo: Marian Rosenstiehl), 260M (Le Studio Canal +/Kasso Inc. Productions/Les Productions Lazennec/Photo: Guy Ferrandos), 260B (Gaumont), 262B (Caroline Productions/La Sept Cinéma/MK2/Wim Wenders Productions), 263B (Le Studio Canal +/MMC/Tapioca Films/UGC/Victoires Productions/Photo: Bruno Calvo), 264B (Maya Films/PC Mediterranea/Roxy Films/

Showking Films), 268TL (W Herzog/Project Filmproduktion/Zweite Deutsches Fernsehen/Wildlife Films, Peru/Photo: Beat Presser), 268M (W Herzog/Project Filmproduktion/Zweite Deutsches Fernsehen/Wildlife Films, Peru/Photo Beat Presser), 268B (W Herzog/Project Filmproduktion/Zweite Deutsches Fernsehen/Wildlife Films, Peru/Photo: Beat Presser), 271BR (Road Movies Film Production/Argos Films/Channel Four/Photo: Robin Holland), 275TR (Le Studio Canal +/MK2/Les Films Alain Sarde), 276 (Orion), 277T (First Floor Features), 282BL (Artistes Associes S.r.l/Radiotelevisione Italiana (RAI), 287BL (Melampo Cinematográfica/Photo: Sergio Strizzi), 292L (Sociedad General de Cine/Photo: Teresa Isasi-Isamindi), 300BR (Centre du Cinema Grec/Photo: Josef Koudelka), 303B (Warner Bros/Russo), 330–331 (Villealfa Productions), 332B, 338T (Mosfilm/Photo: Vadim Murashko), 339, 342TL (Karavan/BG Productions), 345CR (Film Polski), 347 (MK2/CAB/CED Productions/Artificial Eye/Photo: Piotr Jaxa), 375BL, 394 (Kaleidoscope/Arrow), 396 (Arclightz and Films Pvt. Ltd/Dreamz Unlimited), 404BL (Umbi Films/Channel Four/Photo: Christine Parry), 419 (Oasis/Les Films de l'Avenir/Thelma Finch/Arcadia Films), 422B (David Hannay Productions/Electric/Haverbeam), 424–425 (Herald Ace/Nippon Herald/Greenwich/Photo: Yoshio Sato), 426B (Xi'an Film Studio/Hal Roach Films), 427 (Guangxi Film Studio), 428L (ICA/Tokuma Shoten/Cina Film/X'ian Film Studio), 429T (Century Communications/China Film Co-production Corporation/ERA International/Salon Films), 429B (Century Communications/China Film Co-production Corporation/ERA International/Salon Films), 430 (Artificial Eye/Thomson/China Film/Beijing Film), 431B (Artificial Eye/Thomson/China Film/Beijing Film), 437 (Jet Tone Productions), 442T (Itami Films), 442BL (Engine Film Inc/Sputnik Productions/TV Man Union), 444 (Bandai Visual), 459T (M & A Film Corp/Photo: Philip Lee Masurier.), 462TL (Hibiscus Films/Sharmill Films), 462BR (Jan Chapman Prods/Ciby 2000/Photo: Polly Walker), 471TL (Arau/Cinevista/Aviacsa), 471TR (Arau/Cinevista/Aviacsa), 480T (Embrafilme/Luiz Carlos Barreto Produções Cinematográficas/Regina Filmes), 480B (Embrafilme/Luiz Carlos Barreto Produções Cinematográficas/Regina Filmes), 484BL (ICAIC/IMCINE/© Miramax Films);
Sight & Sound: 287TL (Melampo Cinematográfica); Studio 24: 322 (Photo: Istvan Borbas); Svenska Film Institutet: 323T (SVT Drama/Film I Väst/TV1000 AB/Zentropa/Photo: Per-Anders Jörgensen), 323BR (Svensk Filmindustri/Danish Film Institute/Photo: Rolf von Konow), 324TL (Zentropa Entertainments/Photo: Jan Schut), 324TR (Zentropa Entertainments/Photo: Jan Shut), 328BR (Finnish Film Foundation), 332T (Finnkino OY); Les Films des Tournelles: 357L; Trimurti Films Pvt. Ltd: 393B.

Jacket front cover: Joel Finler Collection (Monarchy/Regency/Warner Bros)
Back cover from top: BFI (Trial by Fire);
The Ronald Grant Archive (Paramount/Long Road); The Ronald Grant Archive (MK2/CAB/CED Productions/Artificial Eye Film Company Ltd/Photo: Piotr Jaxa); The Kobal Collection (Right Vision/Bandai).